Slavery's Capitalism

EARLY AMERICAN STUDIES

Series editors:
Daniel K. Richter, Kathleen M. Brown,
Max Cavitch, and David Waldstreicher

Exploring neglected aspects of our colonial, revolutionary, and early national
history and culture, Early American Studies reinterprets familiar themes and
events in fresh ways. Interdisciplinary in character, and with a special emphasis
on the period from about 1600 to 1850, the series is published in partnership
with the McNeil Center for Early American Studies.

A complete list of books in the series is available from the publisher.

SLAVERY'S CAPITALISM

A New History of American Economic Development

Edited by

Sven Beckert

and

Seth Rockman

PENN

UNIVERSITY OF PENNSYLVANIA PRESS

PHILADELPHIA

Published by
University of Pennsylvania Press
Philadelphia, Pennsylvania 19104-4112
www.upenn.edu/pennpress

Printed in the United States of America on acid-free paper
10 9 8 7 6 5 4 3 2 1

A catalogue record for this book is available from the
Library of Congress.
ISBN 978-0-8122-4841-8

To Ruth J. Simmons, President of Brown University, 2001–2012

CONTENTS

Introduction

Slavery's Capitalism

SVEN BECKERT AND SETH ROCKMAN

During the eighty years between the American Revolution and the Civil War, slavery was indispensable to the economic development of the United States. Such a claim is at once self-evidently true and empirically obscure. A scholarly revolution over the past two decades, which brought mainstream historical accounts into line with long-standing positions in Africana and Black Studies, has recognized slavery as the foundational American institution, organizing the nation's politics, legal structures, and cultural practices with remarkable power to determine the life chances of those moving through society as black or white. An outpouring of scholarship on nineteenth-century public health, criminal justice, foreign policy, popular culture, and patterns of everyday life leaves little doubt that the new United States was a "slaveholding republic."[1] In comparison, only a small segment of recent scholarship has grappled with the economic impact of slavery. Only in the past several years has scholarship on finance, accounting, management, and technology allowed us to understand American economic development as "slavery's capitalism." And only now is there enough momentum to leverage some basic facts—that slave-grown cotton was the most valuable export made in America, that the capital stored in slaves exceeded the combined value of all the nation's railroads and factories, that foreign investment underwrote the expansion of plantation lands in Louisiana and Mississippi, that the highest concentration of steam power in the United States was to be found along the Mississippi rather than on the Merrimack—into a fundamental rethinking of American history itself.[2]

Nineteenth-century Americans had little difficulty grasping slavery's capitalism. Advocates of national economic development presumed the reciprocal relationship of the slaveholding and nonslaveholding states, as well as the mutual interests of the slaveholder, manufacturer, and merchant. "On the White mountains of New Hampshire we find the sugar of Louisiana, and in the plains beyond the Mississippi the cotton cloths of Rhode Island are domesticated," explained the famed editor Hezekiah Niles in 1827. Abolitionists such as William Lloyd Garrison recognized the North as a "partner in iniquity" and credited the Panic of 1837 with delivering a deserved ruin to those New York City mercantile firms engaged in commerce with the South. In turn, southern nationalists lambasted northern sanctimoniousness. "Many of the abolitionists of the present day affect to have such tender consciences, and to feel such abhorrence of slavery, that they declare they will not wear the cotton of the South, because it has been cultivated by slaves," observed the Baltimore minister Alexander McCaine, "yet, these extremely sensitive, and pre-eminently holy characters, feel no qualms of conscience, to sell Southern planters their boots and shoes, their negro cloth, and all the *et cetera* that make up a cargo of *Yankee notions*, and put the money, arising from the labour of slaves, in their pockets." Indeed, an 1845 manufacturing census found that nearly half the woolens manufacturers in Rhode Island produced textiles for plantation markets. A South Carolina industrialist such as William Gregg might rightfully lament that such thriving northern cities as Bridgeport, Connecticut, had "been built by the capital of Charleston," while a compatriot writing in *De Bow's Review* could declare slavery the "nursing mother of the prosperity of the North."[3]

The escalation of political tensions in the 1850s generated ever more vivid renderings of the economic relationship between the sections. The New England minister Orpheus Lanphear described slavery as "a huge serpent" menacing "Northern Capital, Trade, and Manufactures": its "hiss was heard in the Stock-market, and in the Counting-house, making the very Ledgers tremble in their cases. It was audible in the whirl of every spindle, and the vibration of every loom, in the muttering of every waterwheel, and in the whistle of every engine; and rang its menace along the edge of the ship-carpenter's adze." Those attempting to stave off disunion tabulated "Southern Wealth and Northern Profits" and championed a national economy that emanated from the cotton fields of Mississippi and Louisiana and flowed into every corner of prosperity in New England. "Every man at the North, who makes a plough, a hoe, a shovel, or a cotton-gin, to aid the production of cotton, should be counted as a hand engaged in that crop," argued one advocate of reconciliation. It was a familiar refrain that the North was poised to "kill the goose that has laid their golden egg."[4]

That the plantation and the factory composed a coherent national economy was less controversial 175 years ago than it is today. Although such a claim may now appear straightforward to academic historians, we nonetheless remain in the early stages of scholarly discovery; the argument is more easily asserted than substantiated. Like Abraham Lincoln in his second inaugural address, we know that slavery was "somehow" tied to the particular instantiation of capitalism in the United States, but the actual "how" remains elusive. The long-held presumption of slavery's prima facie irrelevance to capitalism has left us without many of the crucial details necessary to grasp slavery's influence on American economic development. The perception of slavery as an inefficient way of organizing labor and a hindrance to economic development stretches back to the eighteenth century and still appears commonsensical in the wake of the industrializing North's victory over the slaveholding South in the Civil War. Historians have until recently excluded the slaveholding regions of the United States from the so-called "transition to capitalism" and have looked elsewhere for the "market revolution" that channeled larger and larger segments of American life toward the cash nexus. Slaveholders declared themselves the antagonists of capitalism, making South Carolina's John C. Calhoun, in Richard Hofstadter's memorable phrase, the "Marx of the Master Class." In turn, the North's familiar forms of entrepreneurship, innovation, and market competition beg the counterfactual claim that the American economic takeoff could have happened without slavery. Perhaps it might have, but the fact remains that it didn't. Nor does it matter that we can locate other capitalist societies that developed without slavery, or other slave societies that possessed few traits of capitalism.[5] As capitalism expanded from within the world market it had created, slavery came to play a central, even decisive, role—first in the Caribbean and Latin America, and then in North America—tightly connected to the world-altering Industrial Revolution and the so-called Great Divergence. By virtue of our nation's history, American slavery is necessarily imprinted on the DNA of American capitalism. However, we are only now cataloguing the dominant and recessive traits passed down since the first enslaved Africans arrived in the British colonies that would become the United States. It is plainly obvious that the history of American capitalism is a history with slavery, yet it remains to be shown how exactly slavery is embedded within that larger story of capitalism.

Other capitalist nations have a substantial head start searching for the place of slavery in their specific developmental paths. More than seventy years ago, the Afro-Caribbean intellectual Eric Williams advanced one of the most powerful—though often ignored—arguments in modern historiography, namely, that the story of British economic development was inextricably linked to West Indian slavery. First, profits derived from slave-grown sugar and the transatlantic slave trade underwrote the Industrial Revolution that gave England the world's first modern economy. Only once this new manufacturing regime had taken hold and profits from slavery appeared less certain in comparison did British abolition of the slave trade become economically viable and ideologically useful. Williams's *Capitalism and Slavery* has structured an ongoing and contentious debate over the relationship of slavery's profits to the rise of industrial capitalism and the timing of abolition.[6] Williams's British story is often universalized to assert that nothing new remains to be discovered about slavery's centrality to American capitalism, a perception perhaps enhanced by the enduring richness of scholarship on slavery and the British Empire, as exemplified by Sidney Mintz's *Sweetness and Power,* Joseph E. Inikori's *Africans and the Industrial Revolution in England,* Nicholas Draper's *The Price of Emancipation,* and most recently Catherine Hall's *Legacies of British Slave-ownership: Colonial Slavery and the Formation of Victorian Britain.*[7]

While the relationship of slavery to British economic development has generated a robust scholarship, research on slavery's importance to American capitalism has been episodic: Philip Foner's 1941 account of New York merchants' deep ties to the cotton trade, a brief mention of the value of North-South trade in Douglass C. North's 1961 volume of economic history, Barrington Moore's reference of the importance of slave-grown cotton to American capitalism, James Oakes's 1982 argument for slaveholders as robust devotees of liberal conceptions of private property, John Ashworth's 1995 effort to link slave resistance in the South to middle-class sensibility in the North, Adrienne Davis's powerful naming of slavery's "sexual political economy" of coerced reproduction, and Robin Einhorn's 2006 study of slavery as foundational to the American love of low taxes offer select examples of empirical work that embeds slavery in U.S. economic development. Only over the last twenty years could one assemble a convincing bibliography, running from Ronald Bailey's survey of the "slave(ry) trade" to David Waldstreicher's account of Benjamin Franklin's extensive entanglements with bound labor.[8]

Yet many of the most basic facts about the role of slavery in American economic development remain unknown. To explain the relative inattentiveness of American history as told over much of the last century would take a volume unto itself, grappling with the legacies of a Jim Crow regime of white supremacy that excluded black Americans from the national story and access to the institutional means of changing it and of a Cold War that required touting the superiority of America's "free enterprise" system and its indivisible link to democracy, and with a neoliberal economic ideology in the present that presumes markets will inevitably maximize human freedom rather than constrain (and commodify) it. The persistent erasure of slavery from American history and memory is precisely why new research on slavery's importance for American capitalism is worthy of media coverage, as evidenced by the publicity given to recent books, such as Greg Grandin's *Empire of Necessity*, Sven Beckert's *Empire of Cotton*, and Edward Baptist's *The Half Has Never Been Told.*

This flourish of attention seemed purely aspirational when scholars gathered in 2011 for the "Slavery's Capitalism" conference, sponsored jointly by Brown University and Harvard University. The conveners recognized that many historians—graduate students and senior scholars alike—were conducting the archival research necessary to sustain a slavery-centered account of American economic development. A critical mass of dissertations and monographs would provide an empirical basis for challenging slavery's presumptive remoteness to the main story of innovation, entrepreneurship, and finance at the heart of American capitalism. Although terms like "complicity" had already become shorthand for slavery's lengthy economic reach, capitalism's specific connection to slavery was coming into focus only thanks to the collective efforts of scholars working on different pieces of the puzzle. An outgrowth of that original conference, this volume is intended to provide the most multidimensional account to date of slavery as a constitutive element of American capitalism. The story begins with the exploitative labor regime of the plantation itself but quickly expands outward along the nation's financial and mercantile networks to infuse the broader cultures and practices of American business: for that labor regime sustained a political economy that predicated liberal capitalism's unrivaled opportunities on the unforgiving oppression of chattel slavery. And the story does not end at the nation's borders. As the primary supplier of cotton, the commodity at the heart of the first Industrial Revolution, the United States occupied a distinctive position in the global economy. American reliance on world markets to vend cotton and supply capital shaped the nation's political economy in ways that would ultimately limit the life expectancy of slavery's capitalism and make way for the more recognizable iterations of industrial and financial capitalism of the late nineteenth and twentieth centuries.

The Rediscovery of Slavery

To recognize slavery's national reach and to argue for its national economic importance is to challenge one of the most persistent myths in American history, namely, that slavery was merely a regional institution, surely indispensable for understanding the South, but a geographically confined system of negligible importance to the nation as a whole. As one scholar has recently put it, "U.S. historians traditionally have treated slavery rather like an extended cul-de-sac, an interesting road full of twists, turns, and unexpected consequences, but ultimately a dead end in the path towards the nation's 'modern' political and economic institutions."[10] If a new consensus is emerging, one that instead treats slavery as the interstate highway system of the American past, its origins can be traced to several distinctive conversations in the scholarship, as well as to a swell of public interest and social activism.

The growing awareness of slavery's national reach, for example, owes less to the accomplishments of academic historians than to the dogged work of legal activists, investigative journalists, and museum curators. A political movement for reparations gained traction in the 1990s, marked by Randall Robinson's compelling *The Debt: What America Owes to Blacks*, Representative John Conyers's proposed legislation to study slavery's legacies, and Deadria Farmer-Paellmann's federal lawsuit against Aetna for its issuance of slave life insurance policies. Although reparations claims yielded no success in the courtroom, the threat of lawsuits initiated by Harvard Law School professor Charles J. Ogletree, Jr., and the Reparations Coordinating Committee pressured banks, insurance firms, and universities to delve into their records and publicize historical ties to slavery. One outcome was Brown University's multi-year study of the Atlantic slavery origins of the wealth of their first benefactors and namesake (and, in turn, subsequent self-studies at Emory University, the College of William and Mary, the University of Virginia, and Harvard University, among others). Additional pressure came from state and municipal disclosure ordinances that required firms like J.P. Morgan and Wachovia to reveal slave mortgages held by predecessor banks; such revelations made front-page news in the *Wall Street Journal* and the *Washington Post*.[11] Calls for reparations dissipated after 2008 and the election of President Barack Obama but are now gaining a new hearing as the administration of America's first black president comes to a close. A more global discussion of reparations has also accompanied the recent efforts of Caribbean nations to press claims against European nations such as Britain and France in the diplomatic realm. A lightning-rod political issue, "reparations talk" has created a heated but ultimately productive exploration of slavery as the material basis of present-day economic inequalities, enabling both American wealth and American poverty. Other contemporary social movements, such as the global fight against human trafficking, have also served to show that modern capitalist economies harbor no inherent antipathy to coerced labor.[12]

The American public has also confronted slavery with greater frequency in popular media, museum exhibitions, and political controversies. In the midst of the Civil War sesquicentennial, commentator Charles Blow observed, "America has slavery on the brain these days." The first three months of 2014 witnessed the comedian Larry Wilmore denouncing slavery as economic theft on the *Daily Show*, a slave rebellion serving as the setting for a highly popular video game, and *Twelve Years a Slave* garnering an Academy Award; a wider (and younger) segment of the American population than ever before has been asked to surrender misleading perceptions of slavery as tangential to the national past. Slavery often bubbles to the surface of the national political and cultural discourse in response to tragedy, such as the 2015 massacre at Charleston's Emanuel A.M.E. Church; the subsequent removal of the Confederate battle flag from the grounds of several southern statehouses provided opportunity for a public discussion of the Confederacy's investment in slavery. Sustained attention to police violence against black bodies, political mobilization against mass incarceration, and student protest against racial exclusion on college campuses have created new space to consider slavery and its legacies in American society.[13]

Over the past fifteen years, journalists and museum interpreters in New England and the Mid-Atlantic states have taken an unsparing look at their regions' relationship to slavery. The mythology of a "free" North has withered under the impressive investigative reporting of the *Hartford Courant* and *Providence Journal* and the efforts of numerous public history sites to highlight the region's material investment in slavery. The New-York Historical Society's blockbuster 2005 exhibit, *Slavery in New York*, poignantly featured an installation of a television monitor mimicking the screen design of a present-day financial news network, but with the prices of slaves, cotton, sugar, and rum flying along the so-called crawl, as runaway slave advertisements scrolled down the side of the screen. The slave-labor origins of cotton now figure more prominently in National Park Service exhibitions in Pawtucket, Rhode Island, and Lowell, Massachusetts, while local historical societies, libraries, and house museums have rethought exhibitions and devoted substantial programming to the North's ties to slavery. *Traces of the Trade: A Story from the Deep North*, a 2008 documentary about the descendants of the leading slave-trading family of Bristol, Rhode Island, has been screened hundreds of times on college campuses, at film festivals, and for community groups. The new understanding of slavery's importance to the national story is scarcely universal among the American public—just wait a week for another politician or celebrity to make an ill-informed statement about the causes of the Civil War or the romance of the plantation—but the present moment seems particularly auspicious for rethinking American economic history through the lens of slavery.[14]

Likewise, several new directions in historical scholarship support a reconsideration of the economic past of the United States. Global and imperial frameworks, for example, situate the United States in longer developmental trajectories, including those that foreground Atlantic slavery in early modern global integration, interrogate the so-called rise of the West, or posit the inseparability of racism and capitalism as social formations. Such perspectives, while currently much in vogue, have a distinguished lineage. More than a century ago, W. E. B. Dubois recognized American slavery as an outgrowth of European colonialism, and scholars such as Stuart Hall, Eric Wolf, Cedric J. Robinson, and Robin Blackburn have long situated the plantation-driven economies of British North America and the subsequent United States within an international history of capitalism and empire.[15] Economic history has more recently explored comparative questions, puzzling over the late emergence of England as a rival to China for global economic dominance. Slave-mined silver in the Americas first provided European empires the opportunity to gain access to Chinese markets and consumer goods, and slave-grown agricultural commodities gave England specifically the possibility of supplanting China by escaping the environmental constraints on its population growth. As Kenneth Pomeranz has argued, one factor in England's ability to break the "Malthusian trap" was that nation's access to calories and fibers in the form of sugar and cotton harvested on American plantations. Such research has recognized slavery's material contributions to the process of global integration and the "takeoff" that gave modern capitalism its fundamental structures of production and consumption and enabled the emergence of the great inequalities that have characterized our world during the past 300 years.[16] In its attentiveness to extractive environmental regimes, transoceanic flows of coerced labor, and the racial ideology undergirding "settler colonialism," this early modern history has an analogue in recent work on empire in the late nineteenth and twentieth centuries. Bringing together insights from critical geography, subaltern studies, and other fields, scholars of modern empire have stressed the enduring importance of plantation agriculture on the periphery to culture and capital in the metropole.[17] Collectively, the new scholarship on early modern economic history and the history of modern empires beckon historians of the early republic and antebellum United States to recognize American history as resolutely swept up in—and certainly not an exception to—the broader currents of world history.

Equally encouraging has been a "new" history of capitalism, one that brings business history, labor history, and political economy together under a single umbrella to challenge the perception of capitalism as an inevitable or natural system of organizing markets. One finds a growing number of undergraduate courses and doctoral seminars devoted to the history of capitalism, and an outpouring of recent scholarship has eclectically deployed the methods of cultural, legal, social, and political history to explore regulatory regimes, business practices, commodity flows, and concepts such as risk, profit, and failure. One distinguishing characteristic of the field has been its departure from Marxist theorizations that separate slavery and capitalism into antithetical modes of production; but neither does the field embrace neoclassical and neoliberal certainties regarding the tendencies of markets to maximize freedom.[18] In formulating a more contingent narrative of capitalist development, scholars have looked outside England and beyond factory wage labor to create an origins story that assimilates the Atlantic plantation complex. The historian John Tutino, for example, has claimed a foundational role for the Bajío region of Spanish North America where ambitious entrepreneurs and workers of diverse legal statuses and racial identities created a vibrant capitalist economy in the seventeenth and eighteenth centuries. Such flexible labor regimes positioned enslaved Africans alongside other unfree or marginal workers to make capitalism's defining characteristic the general commodification of labor, begetting the "motley" Atlantic proletariat of Peter Linebaugh and Marcus Rediker. From the perspective of global labor history, Marcel van der Linden has argued that the most fully capitalist society of the Atlantic world might have been the island of Barbados, circa 1650.[19] Historians of capitalism

have also made slavery foundational to the history of finance. Capitalist understandings of risk and financial liability gained their clearest articulation
in the maritime insurance cases resulting from disastrous slaving voyages,
while slave life insurance policies transformed death into a site of speculation.
Global financial crises such as the South Sea Bubble and the Panic of 1837
emerged from ruptures in the credit networks that financed slave sales, plantation purchases, and speculation in cotton and sugar.[20] Whereas an older
scholarship saw capitalism and abolitionism as concurrent and mutually reinforcing, newer work highlights the material and ideological convergence of
capitalism and slavery in the dynamic emergence of long-distance markets
for financial securities, agricultural commodities, and labor power.[21] While
the essays in this volume do not provide an explicit theorization of the relationship between capitalism and slavery, they show how slavery became central to and perhaps even constitutive of a particular moment in the history
of capitalism, and how slavery helped constitute capitalist modernity in the
workplace, the counting house, the countryside, and the factory.

In a reciprocal set of scholarly developments, historians of slavery are increasingly attentive to the institution's economic dimensions, recognizing the
entrepreneurial innovation, "rational" calculation, and sophisticated coordination mechanisms that made human bondage a big business. The economic
history of slavery has labored in the shadows of the interpretive controversies
surrounding the 1974 publication of Robert Fogel and Stanley Engerman's
Time on the Cross, criticized for its cold quantification of human suffering and,
in the context of contemporary debates, its important conclusion that the
South's violent regime of plantation labor was economically efficient. Fogel's
subsequent *Without Consent or Contract* (1989) strove to distinguish between
the system's productivity and its inherent status as a moral abomination.[22]
More recently, economic and business historians have focused on the transatlantic slave trade, drawing on the remarkable database of 35,000 voyages
(spanning 1514–1866) compiled by David Eltis and numerous international
collaborators. Since first published in CD-ROM format in 1999 and enlarged
a decade later as an open-access website, *Voyages: The Trans-Atlantic Slave Trade
Database* has allowed researchers to grasp the systematic dimensions of the
Middle Passage. Stephen Berhrendt, for example, discovered the trade's seasonal rhythms, as Liverpool merchants carefully coordinated markets for
sailing vessels, maritime labor, trade goods, food provisions, and capital in
Europe with comparable markets for provisions and slaves in West Africa and
the seasonality of demand for slaves in the Americas. Having mastered these

"transaction cycles," British traders transformed the Atlantic slave trade from a set of high-risk speculative enterprises into a routinized and predictable source of profit. The perspective of business history has informed recent studies of investor tolerance for risk in slaving voyages, mechanisms of mercantile trust in West African ports, ship captains' decision making at sea, and the remittance procedures for slave purchases in the Americas.[23] To come at slavery as *only* a set of economic practices remains fraught, and scholars generally strive not to confuse human captives struggling for survival with the passive widgets of an introductory microeconomics textbook; a crime against humanity is never reducible to a "negative externality." Nonetheless, approaching slavery in transactional terms reveals the institution's fundamental consistency with the emerging business practices and market logic of capitalism, and even its constitutive role.

Scholars of slavery have gone further to recognize the technologies of capitalism as indispensable to transforming human beings into commodities. For a Yoruba man or an Ibo woman to become a slave required more than the violent extraction of individuals from their natal communities. It involved practices of quantification and abstraction to render people into units of exchange, an epistemological shift made manifest, as Stephanie Smallwood has argued, in the account books of Atlantic slaving vessels and other mundane commercial paperwork. Marcus Rediker has urged attention to the slave ship as something more than a means of conveyance: as a technology of race-making that transformed Wolof Muslims, Biafran farmers, and Akan soldiers into "Negroes" for sale in the Americas. Before the word "factory" invoked sites of industrial production in Europe, it referred to, among other places, the slave-trading depots on the West African coast, whence oceangoing ships and merchants' account books created racialized subjects and transformed them into commodities. Scholars of Atlantic slavery, such as Jennifer Morgan, have recognized women's reproductive labor as the fundamental mechanism of wealth creation for American slaveholders, who appropriated generations of black children for the perpetuation of generations of white wealth. The focus on women's reproductive labor remains strong in new scholarship on the nineteenth-century United States as well.[24]

One of the most promising new paradigms in the scholarship is that of "Second Slavery," first suggested by Dale Tomich and weaving together transnational and imperial frameworks, the history of capitalism, and the study of slavery as a profit-seeking enterprise. In the wake of the Haitian Revolution and the Anglo-American withdrawal from the transatlantic slave trade in 1808, it might have seemed reasonable to doubt slavery's longevity in the Americas. But instead of getting weaker in the ensuing decades, slavery found a second life in Cuba, in Brazil, and on the southwestern lands acquired by the United States through the Louisiana Purchase and the dispossession of the Creeks and other Indian nations. Instead of being ruled by a distant colonial power, slaveholders in these places now ruled themselves and steered the state apparatus toward the specific protection of their interests and the consolidation of their authority. They pursued ever more regimented systems of plantation labor in the production of sugar, cotton, and coffee, and they applied steam engine technology to the processing and transportation of agricultural commodities for market. They aggressively imported slaves, whether through a domestic trade that carried more than a million African Americans from the eastern seaboard of the United States to the cotton frontier of the Gulf Coast or through an African slave trade that brought workers to Cuba and Brazil in numbers that mocked English efforts to police Atlantic sea-lanes. With particular attention to the slave plantation as a site of modernity, the Second Slavery paradigm urges scholars to rethink the fundamental processes of nineteenth-century history—industrialization, bureaucratization, mass migration, nationalism, and imperialism, for example—"through the prism of slavery."[25]

From the vantage of the current political and cultural moment in the United States, the time appears right to construct a new narrative of American economic development. Writing the history of the United States, and writing the history of slavery into the center of the national narrative and not, as previously, relegating it to its margins, does not signify that global perspectives do not matter. Quite the contrary: both capitalism and slavery can be properly understood only from a global perspective. Yet their histories also unfolded within particular national spaces and were shaped by specific distributions of social power and politics therein. As the advent and expansion of capitalism went hand in hand with the formation of states, the one enabling the other, slavery, just as much, was facilitated, regulated, and policed by states, which in turn grew some of their strength from the wages of slavery.[26] States forged national political economies and provided the stage on which political conflicts unfolded. Slavery's history, and thus slavery's capitalism, rested on institutional arrangements, the outcome of political struggles and bureaucratic, administrative, legal, and infrastructural capacities that were defined, negotiated, and constructed within national political spaces.

The American nation-state matters, furthermore, as a set of institutions, shared cultures, and political possibilities. Policymakers, planners, and politicians are invested in national economies, but so are radicals and reformers who seek to direct state power toward the more equitable distribution of resources. National histories inform civic culture and either enable or impede claims to social justice. This function is especially clear for the United States, a self-proclaimed "land of opportunity" in which the legal enslavement of a substantial segment of its population has rarely figured in accounts of its rise to economic dominance. To that end, this book concerns itself with the national economy of the United States during its first decades not as a self-contained space but as an important political arena in which strands of the story of slavery's capitalism unfolded and in which answers to its legacy need to be found. Moreover, so long as the United States grapples with the legacies of its slaveholding past, it remains useful to understand those legacies in the precise terms of American national history.

Plantation Technologies

The relationship of slavery to American capitalism rightfully begins on the plantation, where enslaved workers grew the cotton that made the United States into the nineteenth-century version of what Saudi Arabia would become with respect to oil in the twentieth: a place that became vastly wealthy as the largest producer of the commodity most desired by the world's industrial regimes. Eli Whitney's 1793 "invention" of the cotton gin is where this story typically begins, and, although hackneyed, the truth remains that American cotton production took off almost immediately. Annual production rose from 8 million pounds in 1795 to 48 million pounds in 1801 and 80 million pounds in 1806, at which point U.S. production exceeded that of the British West Indies and accounted for the bulk of the cotton imported by English manufacturers. Already cotton was the most valuable thing made in America, and propelled the conquest and development of the Lower South in the aftermath of the Louisiana Purchase and the Creek Wars of the 1810s. The Virginian Benjamin Parker put it most bluntly when he arrived in Alabama in 1835: "This is one of the finest Countries for making money I ever saw."[27]

Enslaved African Americans were the pioneers who felled trees, leveled fields, and transformed conquered Indian lands into the fertile plantations of

Alabama and Mississippi. The ever-expanding demand for forced labor on this cotton frontier launched an internal slave trade that would ultimately relocate a million black men, women, and children from their birthplaces on the eastern seaboard to the new states of what was then considered the American southwest. Slave-trading firms in cities like Baltimore and Richmond used new technologies like steamboats to move captives to New Orleans, where slaves were repackaged as consumer goods and sold on terms of credit that linked aspiring planters to banks and bondholders thousands of miles away. The domestic slave trade witnessed some of the crassest entrepreneurship anywhere in the nineteenth century and helped transform slavery into something more than a labor system: a property regime in which wealth could be stored, transferred, leveraged, collateralized, and bequeathed through black men, women, and children held under legal title.[28]

To start in the South might seem counterintuitive in the face of the long-standing scholarly tendency to cast the region as premodern and its richest men as something other than capitalists. The work of Eugene Genovese and Elizabeth Fox-Genovese fashioned a distinctive southern civilization that repudiated any notion that market forces should govern human relations; slavery in this regard was not human commodification taken to its extreme but rather a system of "organic" social relations that nurtured a preternaturally "Old" South. Only in recent years has the history of the antebellum South been rewritten as a quest for modernity and an embrace of progress.[29] Prominent slaveholders rallied behind "scientific" agriculture and transformed plantations into sites of business innovation. Literally the nation's first "big" businesses, plantations managed large labor forces—how many northern enterprises had more than twenty workers?—through factory-like modes of regimentation, careful accounting practices, and the active pursuit of industrial machinery. By 1860, for example, nearly 80 percent of Louisiana's sugar mills relied on steam engines, creating what Richard Follett has called "the most heavily capitalized and investment-rich agricultural region in the country." Pretenses of paternalism went hand in hand with practices of profit maximization and an unrivaled investment in the sanctity of private property rights, making it increasingly fruitless now to saddle slaveholders with labels like *pre-*, *proto-*, or *quasi-*capitalist.[30]

One of the most astounding productivity improvements during the nineteenth century had nothing to do with machinery but rather with the human capacity to perform agricultural labor with one's hands. According to Edward Baptist, the daily amount of cotton that enslaved men or women picked increased 400 percent between the 1810s and the 1850s, owing to advances in the disciplinary technologies brought to bear on plantation management. Baptist proposes "torture" as the most apt explanation for the new efficiencies of field labor. The violence of the lash, in the field and at the weighing house, pushed workers to ever-greater feats of picking. Most notably, daily quotas were not determined by customary measurements ("the task") but were set individually, written on slate boards where they could be adjusted upward based on the previous day's intake. Baptist considers the bodily alienation besetting a novice picker attempting to make his two hands work independently of one another as he moved down a row, and then turns to the largest macroeconomic questions of the West's economic takeoff. Access to slave-grown cotton, not simply coal reserves, provided the basis for the so-called Great Divergence, thereby making the violence of the plantation central to economic modernity itself. And in this story, no technology was more important than the whip.

Caitlin Rosenthal traces the innovations of modern management to the slave plantation, where regimentation and violence allowed for experiments in accounting that predated the factory and the railroad. Rosenthal is among several scholars who have urged the centrality of slavery in the histories of management and accounting.[31] Slavery encouraged the development of ever more sophisticated accounting techniques, especially as Thomas Affleck's standardized and preprinted plantation record books made it possible to calculate depreciation on (slave) assets and to combine multiple tabulations into a simple bottom-line total. These findings challenge the primacy that Alfred Chandler awarded the railroad as the testing ground for modern management. Like the railroads, the plantations also relied on hierarchical reporting structures (from overseers to owners and trustees) and long-lived assets (human beings). Of particular importance was the creation of a metric of equivalence—the hand—that allowed for better comparisons, planning, and measures of efficiency and productivity (akin to the ton per mile equivalence for railroads). Such equivalences figured in the South's robust agricultural improvement literature, where annual production targets were pegged to the number of quarter, half, and full "hands" put into labor. Innovations in plantation accounting did not necessarily cause the intensification of management by measurement in the North, but they do suggest that historians of business and accounting need to tell a new origins story, one dating to the first half of the nineteenth century and located far from the factory floor.

Other crucial capitalist technologies also emerged from plantation contexts, which are becoming increasingly important sites of study for historians of science and technology.[32] As Daniel Rood argues in his chapter, the amber waves of grain emblematic of American agricultural abundance have their origins not in the Midwest but on the slave plantations of the Upper South, where innovators like Cyrus McCormick struggled to break the grain-harvesting bottleneck that limited the exportation of Virginia flour to Brazilian consumers. Richmond flour found its number one market among Brazilians desiring whiter white bread, and Rio de Janeiro imported more flour from Virginia than from anywhere else. This commerce differed from the Chesapeake export economy of an earlier era insofar as Richmond capitalists sought vertical integration of processing, packing, shipping, and sales. Watching the Brazilian market closely, Richmond firms sought new means of quality control, brand recognition, and automated production. The weakest link in the supply chain was the plantation harvesting of the wheat, and this provided the context for the 1830s and 1840s experiments with a new reaper. The goal of both McCormick and his rival inventor, Obed Hussey, was not a labor-saving technology but rather a time-saving one, to expedite the speed of the harvest in order to get wheat milled and exported more quickly; this speed was crucial to the brand quality of Richmond wheat. Far from saving labor, plantation trials demonstrated that the reaper required even more enslaved toil to reap, tie, and move grain once it had been cut by the machine. Only after McCormick took the reaper to Chicago in the late 1840s did further improvements transform it into the labor-saving device that launched the midwestern—and free—family farm. But it remained the crucial time-saving technology of the thriving Upper South plantation economy of the same period. The reaper emerged as a "creole technology" produced with inputs from enslaved workers as well as educated inventors.

Slavery and Finance

An enormous river of credit flowed from plantation headwaters. Slaves were purchased on credit and then further collateralized in pursuit of additional financing. At the same time, the agricultural commodities that slaves produced—or were anticipated to produce in a coming season—underwrote local, regional, and international networks of credit, fostered unprecedented speculative schemes, and undergirded Anglo-American investment banking in the nineteenth century. Since William Cronon's *Nature's Metropolis*, historians of capitalism have been attentive to the commodification of nature and to the technologies that transform crops into abstract financial instruments. The story of plantation finance adds to that story, not only by restoring cotton to the forefront of tradable nineteenth-century agricultural commodities but also by adding a second layer of commodities—enslaved human beings—to the nation's financial history.[33]

Vast amounts of capital were stored in the bodies of slaves, but was it possible to access that capital without selling one's slaves outright? Bonnie Martin reconstructs a vibrant mortgage market that allowed small farmers and planters to do just that. By taking a loan with a slave as collateral, small farmers and planters could purchase additional land and slaves. Many slaves were initially purchased using mortgages, in the same way that homes are financed today with a modest down payment and an extended period for repayment. And akin to drawing on a home equity line of credit today, slaveholders could take money out of a slave through a second mortgage. Mortgages proved especially useful for gaining the anticipated value of an enslaved child before his or her value appreciated with the onset of physical maturity. "Slave owners worked their slaves financially, as well as physically," argues Martin. The consequences for local economies were substantial. In some counties in Louisiana, South Carolina, and Virginia, slave mortgages generated more circulating capital in a given year than did the revenues from crops produced by slave labor. The key issuers of loans on collateralized slaves were neighbors rather than distant merchants and banks; these credit relationships served as engines of local development, especially in frontier areas such as St. Landry Parish, Louisiana. This chapter raises comparative questions about lending practices in localities undergoing rapid market expansion. Whereas only land could secure credit in upstate New York or Ohio, southern credit networks made use of land, cotton, and slaves in ways that animated the anonymous operations of the marketplace and local networks of neighborly exchange.

Joshua Rothman explores the interplay of the free market and the slave market, especially as lengthening chains of credit served to fasten the chains of bondage on Mississippi's slave population. A "culture of speculation unique in its abandon" propelled the state's rapid rise in the 1820s: banks multiplied on "a series of bookkeeping fictions," and vast amounts of credit facilitated the purchase of public lands as well as of the slaves who would hack frontier plantations from tracts only recently belonging to the Choctaw and Chickasaw Nations. Of the 130,000 slaves brought into Mississippi during the 1830s, perhaps half arrived in the hands of professional slave traders, who sold them on credit to aspiring cotton planters. Land and labor alike were wholly leveraged on anticipated cotton production, and, should cotton prices drop, the entire house of cards would collapse. Indeed, Mississippi leaders worried about the perception of the state as an unstable climate for outside investment and actually barred the importation of additional slaves in the 1832 state constitution. This prohibition was observed in the breach, but it raises the question of the reliance of states such as Mississippi on northern and European investors to purchase shares in the banks underwriting the market in land and slaves, or to purchase the bonds to fund internal improvements facilitating cotton exports. Governor Charles Lynch supported the slave trade ban as necessary to the state's economic security, but worried (unironically) about the conflict with "our free institutions." The Panic of 1837 brought that tension into sharp relief, for the collapse of the cotton market encouraged speculative planters to default on the debts they owed to slave traders; indeed, some claimed that those contracts were invalid because the 1832 constitution had banned slave importation. The U.S. Supreme Court ultimately ruled against these scheming debtors and the Mississippi lawmakers in *Groves v. Slaughter* (1841), a decision protecting unfettered interstate commerce in the abstract, and sustaining the speculative slave trade in particular. The state's slave population would nearly double during the 1840s, exposing the deep connection between supposedly "free" financial markets and the violence of slavery.

"It is fearful to think that the capital of a nation, and its almost sole means of support, and worth, as it is rated, $4,000,000,000, is on *legs*, and may some morning turn up *missing*," observed one northerner on the eve of the Civil War.[34] But running away was not the only way that enslaved people contested their commodification. As Daina Ramey Berry reveals, when enslaved men and women took their own lives, the slaveholding regime worked diligently to reconstitute the value of the dead. Slaveholders sought to insure themselves against slaves' untimely deaths (whether by suicide, murder, or accident) and could rely on the state's legal apparatus to establish valuations and adjudicate suits. Most troubling were slave suicides at the moment of sale, as buyer and seller alike hoped to deflect liability and recoup the value of the now deceased man or woman. Courts could take years to resolve these questions, meaning that a slave's commodification lingered long after he or she had been buried and mourned. Thus, enslaved people were understood as human capital long before they were born and well after they were dead. As slaves continued to be commodities even after their death, they created ghost values that confounded the standard temporality of slavery and forced a rethinking of a given slave's "life cycle." But as Berry makes clear, enslaved people maintained competing understandings of time that resisted slaveholders' belief in eternal commodification.

Barings. Browns. Rothschilds. The most famous banking houses of the nineteenth century used cotton consignments as a crucial stepping-stone to more specialized operations later in the century, explains Kathryn Boodry. The key moment occurred in the wake of the Panic of 1837, when these large firms were among the only remaining entities capable of offering advances on cotton. Relative to the speculative mania surrounding cotton earlier in the decade, the large Anglo-American firms had acted cautiously; they missed huge profits in 1836, but were only minimally exposed when the bubble collapsed the following year. Yet they still at times ended up in legal possession of plantations and slaves when their southern customers failed. However, the barren post-panic credit landscape offered bankers such as August Belmont, the Rothschilds' agent in New York, a tremendous opportunity to move cotton eastward across the Atlantic and to arbitrage the foreign currencies thereby generated in Liverpool, Le Havre, and Bremen. As rising cotton prices encouraged speculation in the 1840s, the large firms began to withdraw from cotton (even as some of their American agents, like Belmont, went in deeper) and turned their expertise toward new—and recognizably modern—facets of commercial banking. Alexander Brown & Sons, once among the largest cotton consigners for the Liverpool market, reoriented itself to currency exchange in U.S. cities. Barings turned its attention to marketing American loans in Europe. The Rothschilds seized on the California gold rush to specialize in bullion and specie. But even in these capacities, financial firms that discounted paper, invested in regional banks, and brokered state bonds were never far removed from the slave-grown cotton that animated Atlantic commerce up to the Civil War. And in this light, any history of the origins of modern finance needs to foreground cotton as the preeminent global commodity of the nineteenth century.

Networks of Interest and the North

The legal boundaries of slavery did not contain the institution of slavery or limit its importance to the social, cultural, and economic lives of Americans living far removed from plantation regions. As Steven Hahn has recently argued, a preoccupation with the "sections" that would come to animate the politics of the 1840s and 1850s has blinded scholars to the reality of slavery as an engine of the nation's history. Perhaps more accurate was the assessment of the 1850s polemicist David Christy, who observed, "slavery is not an isolated system, but is so mingled with the business of the world that it derives facilities from the most innocent transactions." Geographic distance from human bondage by no means diminished the benefits accruing to northern colonies and states from American slavery, and indeed, the modernizing economy of the nineteenth century offered new ways of profiting from the labor of slaves in remote locations. For example, several principals of the New York Life Insurance and Trust Company helped fund similar enterprises in Florida and Alabama, continuing a longer tradition of northern investment in plantation regions that stretched back to Georgia's notorious Yazoo land sales of the 1790s and flourished in the 1830s with such enterprises as the New York and Mississippi Land Company and the Boston and Mississippi Cotton Land Company. A remapping of the nineteenth-century United States is necessary, one that conceptualizes places such as Haddam, Connecticut, or North Brookfield, Massachusetts, as important nodes in an expansive slave economy, along with the merchants and bankers of New York and Boston. Interregional commerce not only offered New England localities the opportunity to profit from slavery, but also provided plantation regimes with access to low-cost provisions and new technologies to boost the returns from coerced labor. Such analysis makes it difficult to determine where the slave economy ended and the so-called free economy began.[35]

In Eric Kimball's account, New England's maritime commerce with the West Indies reveals the economic indispensability of slavery to a region that seemingly lay on a remote periphery of the Atlantic plantation complex. That eighteenth-century New England was merely a "society with slaves" rather than a "slave society" in no way diminishes the region's role in reproducing the institution of slavery elsewhere by vending and transporting the commodities produced by slaves and by provisioning plantations with food and other supplies. Long before the advent of a New England textile industry that converted slave-grown cotton into wealth, the carrying trade between the ports of Providence, Boston, or Portsmouth and the West Indian sugar islands created economic ties essential to both regions. From the seventeenth century on, New Englanders recognized a global division of labor that allowed them to obtain European manufactures with West Indian commodities that they had purchased with provisions of their own making, such as fish, horses, lumber, and candles. Barbadian and Jamaican planters grasped this commercial circuit with equal acuity and were able to devote ever-growing resources to sugar production precisely because New Englanders made the ships and barrels to transport their commodities and caught the fish and raised the cattle to provision their plantations. Such linkages become clear in the striking example of Caribbean slaves processing sugar on an overnight shift made possible by lamps burning New England whale oil. These intracolonial circuits of exchange did not diminish with American independence. John Adams had noted the mutual dependence of the U.S. and Caribbean economies in 1783, and trading patterns over the next forty years would bear this out (despite—or perhaps because of—the interruptions attending European warfare). The famed "reexport" trade that turned American neutrality (or irrelevance) into a commercial asset was almost entirely devoted to transporting slave-grown commodities or conveying provisions to plantation regions. During the first decade of the 1800s, the participation of New Englanders in the European slave economies of the Caribbean increased. If economic historians have long debated the importance of the carrying trade to New England's fortunes in the early national period (and the generating of capital that could be directed into manufacturing soon thereafter), virtually no scholarship mentions Caribbean slaves as the key agents in this commerce. New England's economic fortunes depended on slaves, though ones who lived and labored for owners in other locations. Data from the crucial period between American independence and the War of 1812 show that New England's entanglements with slavery were neither limited to the colonial period nor dependent on the rise of the textile industry.

Continuing the theme of the "offshoring" of New England's slave economy, Stephen Chambers focuses on American investment in the Spanish colony of Cuba. Evidence for Cuba's value to New England merchants can be found in a surprising locale: St. Petersburg, Russia, which received 10 percent of U.S. exports (by value) in 1810, primarily in the form of Cuban sugar and coffee rather than American-grown cotton. Only a year earlier, John Quincy Adams had arrived as U.S. minister in St. Petersburg, and his primary concern was to protect New England ships carrying Caribbean goods to the Baltic. At a moment when men like Adams could serve as both diplomats and commercial agents, it was striking how many of those stationed in Russia had familial connections to or investments in Cuban plantations. A similar cohort of merchant-diplomats occupied Spanish Cuba and played a key role in developing Matanzas as a key port. Their goal was not to acquire Cuba as a state but rather to maintain the status quo of lax regulation regarding slave importations and to prevent British intervention in their commerce. Largely successful in both Russia and Cuba, these American diplomat-merchants translated their experiences abroad into elective office at the end of the 1810s. As congressmen, they pursued legislation to protect U.S. trade routes to Cuba, in particular by enlarging the U.S. Navy to interdict pirates (especially those who might surpass British patrols in jeopardizing New England ships involved in the illegal Atlantic slave trade). Perhaps most notorious was the Rhode Island senator James D'Wolf, who owned Cuban plantations and sought naval appropriations to protect the viability of that property. By the 1820s, with the U.S. Navy functioning as "an instrument for the protection of private commerce," Cuba had become the nation's second largest trading partner. Through this overlapping cohort of merchants, diplomats, and elected officials, the apparatus of the American state was deployed in the service of New England's slave economy.

The so-called Second Middle Passage involved the relocation of more than one million slaves from the Upper South to the plantation frontiers of Mississippi, Louisiana, Arkansas, and Texas. Many of those slaves traveled by boat from Baltimore or Richmond to New Orleans, and perhaps again from New Orleans to Galveston. By reconstructing the network of merchants, shipbuilders, captains, and investors, Calvin Schermerhorn expands the cast of characters associated with the domestic slave trade and shows the wide distribution of the profits derived from the buying and selling of human beings. Initially, the story highlights opportunistic cooperation between slave traders and shippers with space to fill in their vessels. A transatlantic merchant ship whose holds were filled with linens, quills, and iron on routes between Baltimore and Bremen could readily become a "sometime slave ship" as it traveled with a dozen slaves from Baltimore to New Orleans. This transformation required no legal reclassification, no loss in the ability to transport paying passengers in comfortable accommodations, and no major retooling of the hold. Aggressive slave traders, such as Baltimore's Austin Woolfolk, gained significant advantages over their competitors in the 1820s by packing slaves aboard ships destined for New Orleans and loaded with other manufactured goods or intending to pick up cotton bound for Europe; merchants, shipowners, captains, and crew made little complaint, as each stood to profit from Woolfolk's transactions in human property. Franklin & Armfield, the firm that supplanted Woolfolk in the 1830s, rationalized coastal slave trading through vertical integration. The firm purchased its own dedicated ships—primarily manufactured in places like Haddam, Connecticut—and sailed on a regularized schedule. In addition to moving people, these ships moved currency, transporting bank notes back to their point of origin on the eastern seaboard and cycling funds generated in the New Orleans slave market back to Maryland and Virginia to purchase yet more slaves. By the 1850s the largest coastal slaving vessels were the steamships plying the Gulf of Mexico owned by Charles Morgan, Henry R. Morgan, and Israel C. Harris of New York. These massive ships carried first-class passengers, the U.S. mail, and slaves between New Orleans and Texas, generating revenue for an international transportation conglomerate.

National Institutions and Natural Boundaries

The institutional supports of economic development were planted in the nation's universities, legal culture, and political parties. A "new institutional history" now highlights the importance of the state in nineteenth-century American history. Questions of national policy and regulation were inevitably assessed for their bearing on the legitimacy of slave property, a fact not lost on the Whig politicians, whose American System was predicated on national economic integration. As the sons of the South pursued their education in New Haven, and as institutions like Brown University furnished southern universities with their first faculties and presidents, the development of human capital through higher education marks a further component to national integration. Likewise, core educational, religious, and charity organizations in the American North rested on the generosity of wealthy donors, many of whom had accumulated much of their wealth through their involvement in the slave economies of the South and the Caribbean. If American capitalism depended on specific policies and the emergence of cultural norms to legitimate market engagement, then the relationship of slavery to national institutions is essential to the larger history of capitalism. The final essays in this volume explore these connections.[36]

Craig Steven Wilder reveals that the eighteenth- and nineteenth-century version of *human capital*—property rights in enslaved human beings—helped facilitate the more salutary sense of human capital as a society's commitment to the education of its population in the name of economic growth. Embedding American higher education in the wealth and white supremacy that Atlantic slavery produced, Wilder narrates the founding of Georgetown College, an institution intended to educate prosperous Catholics whose wealth could not initially overcome sectarian hostility to provide full integration into

American society. As other denominations developed campuses in British North America, colonial Catholics relied on wealth drawn from slave ownership to travel abroad for education. The War of Independence raised the status of American Catholics and allowed for the 1789 creation of the first American diocese in Baltimore and the establishment of a new college at Georgetown and a seminary at St. Mary's. Attaining legal incorporation in Maryland in 1792, the Corporation of the Roman Catholic Clergy supported the campuses with the enslaved workers and plantation lands it owned; slave labor helped keep Georgetown tuition-free for its first forty years. The students who passed through its gates were, unlike many of their fathers and grandfathers, in possession of civic equality and deeply integrated into the social and economic elite of the nation. It is in this respect that one form of human capital begat another.

Andrew Shankman offers a political biography to convey the importance of slavery to the high politics of the early republic. If a transition from republicanism to liberalism characterized early national political economy, it was Mathew Carey who best articulated the possibilities and perils of this reorientation. Carey's Jeffersonian predilections could scarcely survive the 1810s, challenged as it was by the disunionism of New England Federalists, the political tensions of Missouri statehood, and the economic dislocations of the nation's first financial panic in 1819. Eager to preserve national unity while protecting the rough equality of white men and avoiding the kinds of political and economic inequalities of European society, Carey stressed the importance of a domestic market. Rather than a neomercantilist orientation toward Atlantic commerce, Carey envisioned the economic integration of North, South, and West into something that would eventually come to be known as the American System. Slavery was taken as a given in this national economy: for Carey, the "empire of liberty" called for integrating plantation and manufacturing economies, drawing on slave-grown agricultural commodities and a market created by slave masters. There was an unintended consequence: Carey's political economy required the stewardship of the national government, a deployment of implied powers that caused alarm among slaveholders fearing that a federal government capable of imposing tariffs or chartering corporations could ultimately claim the power to emancipate slaves. Carey devoted increasing energy to convincing northern allies that slavery was essential to their financial futures, while assuring planters that they were better off within a strong developmental regime. Ultimately these arguments required defenses of slavery and black inferiority—both being for Carey the necessary, if regrettable, costs of promoting American nationalism and white equality. Most explicitly, Carey sought to quell unrest over Missouri statehood by contending that "the peace and prosperity of eight millions of freemen and Christians, may [not] rightfully be sacrificed to promote the welfare of a million and a half slaves." For the United States to avoid the fate of a proletarianizing Europe, it would have to deny freedom to its black inhabitants.

One result of the decades of historiography focused on the relationship of capitalism to antislavery and on the anticapitalist arguments of proslavery ideologues is that we have missed the reinforcing tendencies of slavery and capitalism in the national legal culture. In that culture, argues Alfred L. Brophy, there was far more consensus than conflict. Antebellum America privileged the "rule of law," an ideological support for the status quo, property rights, and the legitimacy of federal and state legislation upholding slavery. Literary addresses delivered at northern colleges, for example, frequently espoused hostility to "reform" as a worthwhile pursuit. Meanwhile, the "dominant ideas in the United States were of classical liberalism," with a particular emphasis on economic progress. Southern jurisprudence was anything but hostile to market competition, as appellate courts favored the protection of the market and its utility instead of the fate of slaves. Jurists like Thomas Ruffin and Joseph Henry Lumpkin privileged utility over abstract morality and sentiment, sometimes acknowledging such a conflict in their decisions but ultimately choosing a "proslavery instrumentalism." Most important, this jurisprudence embraced the rights of corporations. For all the scorn that proslavery ideologues heaped on northern capitalism for treating workers as disposable, southern jurists just as quickly upheld a "fellow-servant rule" to protect corporations from liability in the event of workplace accidents. Ultimately, the law supported slavery, as it went hand in hand with judges' desire to stabilize property. The consideration of law as a technology—as a vehicle for achieving mastery over nature and other human beings—reinforces the themes of earlier chapters on accounting practices, plantation management, and agricultural machinery.

Antebellum politicians and political economists argued vigorously over the "natural" boundaries of slavery. Presumably human bondage required environmental, social, and political preconditions in order to flourish, and the absence or presence of these demarcated the "free" North from the "slave" South. How, then, asks John Majewski, are we to make sense of a thriving slaveholding region whose environmental, social, and political endowments were virtually indistinguishable from those of neighboring "free" regions? The

Limestone South (defined by its soil type) extended from northern Virginia to Kentucky's Bluegrass Region and Tennessee's Nashville Basin. By any number of measures, this zone had rates of urbanization and population density that rivaled those of Ohio and Illinois, as well as a comparable development of civic culture (as measured by public libraries) and nationalism (as measured by such leaders as Henry Clay and Andrew Jackson). As slavery flourished in the diversified economy of the Limestone South, its further expansion north was not unimaginable. With no inherent differences between the Limestone South and the American Midwest, it proves difficult to declare slavery inherently incompatible with economic progress. Put differently, "If slaveholders in the Bluegrass Region could expropriate the labor of tens of thousands of slaves, there was no climatic, geographic, or environmental reason why Ohioans could not." Only political choices could police the boundary between slavery and freedom, and were it not for the Northwest Ordinance, there is no reason to expect that an Ohio, an Indiana, or an Illinois would not have developed into a thriving slave state. Ultimately, it was a particular iteration of capitalism, as conceptualized by the emergent Republican Party of the 1850s, that saw slavery as a problem. Gesturing to the Civil War, Majewski proposes an "answer to the paradox of why a political party representing the interests of capitalism so ardently opposed slavery, even though slavery was in many ways foundational to the nineteenth-century economy."

Recognizing Slavery's Capitalism

In the decades between the American Revolution and the Civil War, slavery—as a source of the cotton that fed Rhode Island's mills, as a source of the wealth that filled New York's banks, as a source of the markets that inspired Massachusetts manufacturers—proved indispensable to national economic development. Slave-grown cotton was the most valuable export of the United States and one of the few American-made goods that attracted specie into the nation's financial system. Cotton also offered a reason for entrepreneurs and inventors to build manufactories in such places as Lowell, Pawtucket, and Paterson, thereby connecting New England's Industrial Revolution to the advancing plantation frontier of the Deep South. And financing cotton growing, as well as marketing and transporting the crop, was a source of great wealth for the nation's merchants and bankers. When Charles Sumner decried the alliance of the "lords of the lash and the lords of the loom," he highlighted only one of the interregional dependencies that powered the nation's economic takeoff in the decades between the American Revolution and the Civil War. New York shippers, insurers, bankers, and dry goods wholesalers had as great an investment in the price of cotton as did any Mississippi planter, while Massachusetts entrepreneurs found prosperity in making brogans, shirts, and shovels for southern slaves to wear and use. Institutions such as universities, churches, and hospitals benefited from donations that originated in profits from slavery. The importance of slavery to the national economy was not only an abolitionist talking point or exclusively a retort offered by aggrieved proto-Confederates; it was also a reflection of the nation's political economy as it had unfolded in the seven decades before the Civil War.

By juxtaposing the stories of New York financiers, Virginia slaves, Connecticut shipbuilders, and Mississippi land speculators, the chapters that follow make a claim for slavery's national economic importance. In an "age of industry" predicated on the transformation of slave-grown cotton into textiles, the plantation and the factory must necessarily be discussed together rather than separately. In the blur of commodities and capital that flowed between regions, the sectional categories that organize so much nineteenth-century American scholarship begin to crumble, rendering an unclear line of demarcation between a capitalist North and a slave South, with consequences for how we understand North and South as discrete economies—and whether we should do so in the first place. The issue is not whether slavery itself was or was not capitalist (an older debate) but rather the impossibility of understanding the nation's spectacular pattern of economic development without situating slavery front and center. To foreground slavery in the story of the American economic takeoff offers a radical reconsideration of not merely the national past but also the history of capitalism more generally, intertwining the North's industrialization and the concurrent expansion of plantation slavery across the landscape of the South. Yet because the economic integration of North and South flowed in so many different directions, the research of multiple scholars is necessary to tell this story in its entirety. This book marks a beginning.

PART I

Plantation Technologies

CHAPTER I

Toward a Political Economy
of Slave Labor

Hands, Whipping-Machines, and Modern Power

EDWARD E. BAPTIST

Charles Ball had been a family man, a skilled worker. From his cabin on Maryland's Eastern Shore, he had seen a brighter future. True, he was enslaved, like his wife and children. Yet in 1805, men with his intelligence and drive were finding ways to buy their freedom from enslavers in Maryland's tobacco districts. But on this morning, when a blaring horn jerked him out of sleep before dawn, he sat up in a loft bed at the top of a cabin 500 miles to the southwest, and he was no longer who he had been. In fact, he was not even—by some reckonings—a whole body any more.

A few weeks earlier, Ball had been bought by a slave trader who purchased men, women, and children in the Upper South, so that he could march them south and west and sell them to the cotton planters who were pushing the frontier of that commodity south and west into the Carolina and Georgia backcountry. Ball had carried iron chains on his wrists and neck for 500 miles to a new owner's slave labor camp on the Congaree River in South Carolina.[1] Now more than ever the appendage to another man's dreams, Ball looked down from his loft bed, remade at modernity's dawn not into an insect like Gregor Samsa but into something just as strange as a fly on a Prague ceiling. He was a hand.

Though historians have written tens of thousands of pages on the enslavement of people like Charles Ball, relatively few of those pages have considered the specific labor he was about to do in Wade Hampton's cotton fields. That is odd, for within a few short years from 1805, cotton made by enslaved African Americans not only accounted for the majority of U.S. exports, but also helped to generate a transformation unprecedented in human history. In the years between the late eighteenth century and the early twentieth century, Western societies achieved rates of sustained economic growth and transformation that had never been seen before. These gave the West extraordinary power over other societies and their peoples. Industrial transformation, virtually all accounts agree, emerged in northwestern Europe. More specifically, almost all agree that it proceeded from England, and most concede that it proceeded specifically from northwest England's cotton textile industry, from the late eighteenth century on. All human societies today ride on a trajectory of growth and innovation, of creation and destruction, launched from Manchester.[2]

Since this initial acceleration out of the Malthusian world's gravity well shapes us all, a little more every day, I will use the first person plural in the next paragraph or two. We historians have been trying to explain the causes of this transformation ever since. In many ways, explaining it has been (along with hymning the nation) our main alibi for existence. And we've collectively offered a great many explanations for this set of changes. We've said that industrialization was written in the book of fate long before, because of a specific market orientation encoded in the genes of Western culture. We've argued that an existing technological lead was transformed by a burst of innovation in machine and other technologies in eighteenth-century Britain. We've argued that legal and other fundamental rules were changed to open up the British market for land and labor, making wage-labor manufacturing employment and a true credit market possible. We've read that the Puritan sensibility pushed Western capitalists to accumulate well beyond their needs, rather than wasting their profits in display. We've even heard, though this idea has often been flatly dismissed by those who see capitalism as a purely Western creation, that "primitive accumulation" in the course of early imperial conquest, the Atlantic slave trade, and the sugar plantations of the British and French West Indies provided the basis for the Industrial Revolution.

For all that arguing, we historians have spent relatively few pages on the connection between the South's cotton fields and the cotton textile industry, an oversight especially noteworthy in light of how direct that connection was. And we certainly haven't argued that all that came from modernization and modernity was impossible without the cotton-field work of "hands," to use the body part by which enslavers described whole people like Charles Ball. Above all, we haven't argued that the character of that labor was quintessentially modern, and particularly important for creating the modern world economy.[3] Indeed, we have done the opposite. True, the history of cotton slavery is usually told as that of a pivot on a machine, the cotton gin, for which Eli Whitney claimed credit. Every high school history student hears that the gin broke the processing bottleneck. But there the story is dropped. After all, the remainder of the labor that began with clearing a densely forested South Carolina or Alabama acre and ended at the steamboat landing with the delivery of a cotton bale—400-odd pounds of clean fiber ready for the spinning machines on the far side of the Atlantic—was hand labor. Enslaved African Americans did it, and they did it unaided by machine.

Yet the invention of the cotton gin still left two significant choke points in the production of raw cotton. This meant, therefore, two bottlenecks for the nascent textile industry as well, and here they were: growing the plants and harvesting their fiber. Over a relatively short period of time, enslavers in the United States managed to break them. Within two decades of Charles Ball's first morning in the cotton fields, American planter-entrepreneurs would deliver for sale enough cotton to dominate the world market in this, the Industrial Revolution's most essential commodity. To do so they began by using political, military, and financial power to get more cotton land and labor: taking land from the Indians, developing a set of new slave trades to transport captives to the frontiers. After that, they forced transported captives to work, and to work in new ways. So when the overseer's horn blew a second time, propelling Charles Ball out into the predawn humidity of a July morning, he was about to learn what we historians have not known: how enslavers were going to break that remaining bottleneck.[4]

Ball's bare feet hit the dirt floor. He stumbled out of his hut and soon was marching behind the overseer, along with 170 other workers, into the fields.[5] When they came to the vast field in which they were to labor that day, cultivating the soil around the waist-high cotton plants to drive back the competing growth of weeds that migrated southwest with the monocrop system, the overseer portioned the laborers in dozens, each under a "captain." And so Charles began to learn about a dynamic system of labor extraction designed by white people whom the enslaved identified as "pushing men."[6]

Pushing men like Ball's owner, whose right hand wrote out the instructions for the equally pushing overseer, deployed several innovative techniques of labor control to fill new fields with ever-greater quantities of cotton. One such technique was that of forcing fast workers like Ball's captain, a man named Simon, to "carry the fore row"—to work at top speed, and thus set a pace that the others had to match. "By this means," Ball decided, "the overseer had nothing to do but to keep Simon hard at work, and he was certain that all the others must work equally hard."[7] If not, their slowness would be visible as a break in the line of workers. In the vast fields in which cotton was being grown, such a technique allowed an overseer to surveil scores of workers simultaneously, alerting him to anyone who lagged behind the leaders, whom he was consciously pushing at higher and higher speed. Enslavers also eliminated customary breaks and meals, forcing slaves to eat huge breakfasts, passing out cold meals in the fields, and detailing one older slave to make suppers so that field workers could toil until full dark.[8]

This "system," implemented by pushing men, was new for those who had learned to labor in the "task" system of the rice swamps or cotton fields of the Carolina Lowcountry where enslaved people had to furnish a fixed quantity of labor, set by custom, after which they might have some free time. (In the Lowcountry, enslaved workers cultivated and harvested a specialized variant of cotton on the task system, Sea Island cotton, which generally grew only in coastal regions.) These developments were also new for those who, like Ball, had grown up in the gang labor system of Chesapeake tobacco and wheat fields. In Virginia, Maryland, and much of North Carolina—as well as Kentucky, settled by enslavers and enslaved from the Chesapeake—enslaved people usually toiled in small groups that worked at somewhat individualized paces, often supervised by enslaved "drivers" out of whites' vision.[9]

"A good part of our rows are five hundred and fifty yards long," wrote one Tennessee cotton planter in the 1820s. Not only had he created a kind of space where he could easily identify stragglers, he could also use it as a stage on which to inflict immediate and exemplary punishment in front of a large audience. In Mississippi, Allen Sidney saw a man who had fallen behind the fore row fight back against a black driver who tried to "whip him up" to pace. The white overseer spurred up, pulled out his pistol, and shot the prone man dead. "None of the other slaves," Sidney claimed, "said a word or turned their heads. They kept on hoeing as if nothing had happened."[10] Enslaved migrants in new cotton fields quickly discovered that they had to adapt to what pushing men demanded, or face ruthless violence. And like many other forced migrants, Charles Ball insisted that the violence used on slavery's commodity frontier was of a greater order of magnitude. Even the whip was different. Here it was a lead-loaded handle from which snaked a ten-foot lash of heavy plaited cowskin, whose tip ripped open the air with a sonic boom. Many other mi-grants, including some white ones, reported Ball's feeling of shocked discov-ery at their first witness of the new lash in use. The shock of the whip *made bales of cotton*, to borrow words from a Mississippi overseer.[11]

Enslavers used whatever violence was necessary to make forced migrants accept the elimination of both the Lowcountry task system and other customs of slavery developed in the early modern southeast. Part of this violence was the forcible disruption of people's lives by forced migration and separation from community and family. Like Ball, other survivors in their accounts repeatedly tell us that in their minds and memories they constructed the passage into the southwest of the expanding United States as a moment of transformation of the self, though not self-transformation. The experience of that forced migration was a huge one, in time or space or on any other scale. Over seventy years, from the signing of the Constitution, in 1787, to the start of the Civil War, enslavers turned a vast area of 800,000 square miles, as big as Saudi Arabia and inhabited almost exclusively by about 50,000 Native Americans, into a subcontinent of slavery. Enslavers and their allies dispos-sessed two European empires, two postcolonial states, and six Native American nations. They moved one million forced migrants to the new territory. Within a single lifetime the entrepreneurs who masterminded this process had created a complex that produced 80 percent of the cotton sold in Britain, the world's central market. Cotton made by people enslaved on the United States' south-western frontier was both the world's most widely traded commodity and its most crucial industrial raw material.[12]

Indeed, each year the cotton country cycled through its channels and pipes a good part of the English-speaking world's most high-velocity money, the commercial credit backed by quasi-national banks in Britain and the United States and deployed by the world's most innovative merchant firms. And why not? The cotton region was a massive sink of collateral in the form of commodified human beings who generated massive revenues. Creditors around the Western world liked to lend money with slaves as collateral. An active domestic slave trade meant that in normal times, one could always re-coup one's losses on a mortgage that went bad by foreclosing and selling the man, woman, or child treated as property.

Enslaved people could be sold so readily that in almost any year they con-stituted in their bodies almost one-fifth of all national accounting wealth, and a far higher proportion of its liquid wealth. In enslaved people, the world's money worked, usually generating high returns at low risks. Of course, the essential interweaving of enslaved people and their labor product into the financial patterns of the United States and of the Atlantic nations in general meant that any credit crisis for southern cotton planters would automatically lead to a worldwide credit crunch. Dynamic, creative-destructive cycles of boom and bust followed the succession of international financial relationships linking the cotton frontier to world markets for cotton, credit, textiles, and textile labor. Still, by 1860, five of the six states in the Union with the highest average white income were in the belt that cotton entrepreneurs wrapped across the South. The region would have been among the world's ten largest economies, and by one accounting its fourth most prosperous one. The three million white people in the cotton states were per capita the richest people in the United States, and probably the richest group of people of that size in the world.[13]

That was the macroscale. But Charles Ball lived his life at the microlevel. In this experience—which would be repeated a million times over—the unwilling migrant would inevitably be forced down a thermocline of brutal learning. In their narratives, formerly enslaved people repeatedly allegorized this process in this fashion: it happened on the first day in the new fields. Or they realized the nature of the new labor the first moment they stepped across the first cotton row. Such a pattern, imposed on experience, can surely play a major role in any construction-of-self analysis if cultural historians and others who analyze the texts of ex-slaves focus closely on the gigantic forced migration that made the South. The scale and significance of this process are force multipliers for the weight of any analysis that can explain it.

Understanding how enslaved people constructed and reconstructed their own analyses of their internal worlds, under conditions of extreme stress, is an important task. But the same trope in the sources also tells us that on slavery's cotton frontier, enslaved migrants recognized in the world around them a new system of power emerging, being imposed on them through new modes of labor extraction. Charles Ball was now going to have to contend with that power.

There are several ways to talk about the history and nature of power, but over the last four decades of historical study, one of the most influential has been the set of ideas about power associated with poststructuralism. This genealogy of modern power was inspired, directly or indirectly, by Marx, Freud, and Nietzsche—those whom Paul Ricoeur famously identified as masters of suspicion for their efforts to demystify emergent modernity's pieties. Yet their late twentieth-century successors associated the acolytes of the first two thinkers in particular with other kinds of systematization and coercion that were reproduced in the master narratives of those who attacked the triumphant bourgeois. Poststructuralists writing between the sixties and the nineties carried the flag of the assault on the *logos*, the Western idea (gifted from neoplatonism and other deep sources) that a unified system of universal knowledge was possible. In Foucault, its most cogent and systematizing exemplar, this poststructuralist approach leads to a map of history in which the way to obtain and hold power is to construct epistemes or grids of power-justifying knowledge. Power-knowledge is a will that aims to convince every object-of-rule that it is exactly what the grids map it as being. These epistemes emerged in the ways that the state categorized and counted people, in the way that sex became a problem to be regulated and that psychological and other discourses named the abnormal. The real work of modernity and modernization was the project of convincing modern citizens to see disciplining the self as a crucial project—one in which they should participate.[14]

At the same time, in Foucault's scholarship, in his own personal activism, and in the performativity of his life, he insisted that every power creates a resistant counterpower. Every decree creates an opportunity; every attempt at normalization creates an opportunity for resistant transgression. Modernity made and was made by discourses of power, but everywhere that the state and society tried to enact those discourses, people pushed back against the disciplining grid.[15] Those who have written histories of culture and the self in the years since Foucault have sometimes seen their project as championing people who fashion alternative identities. Such histories are in turn obviously linked to the liberatory projects for which millions of people have struggled, individually and collectively, in the decades since the watershed of 1968.

But this history of power cannot fully address the kinds of power that wrecked Charles Ball's life. Nor, as should now be all too painfully clear, does the project of universal demystification and deconstruction by itself do much to reshape the devastations that are the obverse face of globalizing modernization and commodified modernity. We shall see those devastations all too clearly as we follow Ball's story and that of a million others, and shall see how they were not accidental but constitutive. Instead, before Charles Ball entered the cotton fields of Congaree, we could map the relationships between the rulers and the ruled in the world along two axes of power. James Scott calls these axes "domination" and "resistance," the power of the powerful versus the weapons of the weak. Here's an illumination: the theologian Robert Farrar Capon, revising Martin Luther, calls the first of these "right-handed power," the strength to intervene directly to force an outcome. Capon writes about right-handed power when he critiques the idea of God held by many believers of many religions: a deity working in straight-line ways, exerting crushing force, throwing the wicked into the flames, drowning the sinful Earth. Right-handed power is the power of domination, kings, weapons, the letter of the law; it is the power of God (and gods) the Father, of Just Because and In the Beginning.[16]

On the other hand, according to Capon, are the parabolic arts of resistance that have been deployed ever since the first peasant slowed down her work when out of sight of the first mud-pyramid god-king. Her knowledge, her craft is "left-handed" power: the strength of the poor and the weak, of secret ways of seemingly passive resistance to evil. For Capon, this is the power of life-through-death, the seed in the dark earth and the stone the builder rejected. Long before Paul or Isaiah, even before Moses fled Pharaoh's house as a fugitive from a cop-murder charge, those compelled to knuckle under to right-handed power in traditional societies—serfs, peasants, women, and slaves—had been using the arts of secret resistance to undermine the sway of the dominant. They slowed down the pace of work when out of sight of overseers. They broke employers' tools, lied, played dumb to lords, escaped from masters. They learned the path of the trickster. They left signals at its every crossing to guide those who came after them, secret signs in stories for children and older people, too—folktales that around the world follow the same 10,000 plot types.[17]

Over the 10,000 years since agricultural civilization emerged and quickly developed significant internal distinctions of wealth and power, the left hand had developed vast resources with which to resist, with which to claim terrains of independent thought, critique, creativity. One concrete example of what left-handed power could force right-handed power to yield was the task system that had developed in the South Carolina Lowcountry. The bargains that limited the amount of labor in rice or Sea Island cotton that could be extracted in a day were the product of a history of negotiations between the power of the masters and the cunning of the enslaved. They allowed many enslaved people to finish their task before dark, which in turn meant that they could tend their own gardens and take care of their family and fellows. At the same time, enslavers also benefited: the bargains lessened the cost of supervision, damped down resistance, cut the cost of rations to the bone, and allowed the wealthiest whites to spend much of their time away from the malarial swamplands where enslaved people toiled.[18]

One could identify similar bargains in the narrow opportunities for advancement built into the job structures of the Caribbean sugar complex's boiling houses, or the layers of skill and administration that allowed a strong Maryland worker like Charles Ball to think that he could become an enslaved overseer or even a free man. But by 1805, the nature of right-handed power was already changing in the West. In the early nineteenth century, those societies and individuals who were winning in the sorting out of power and status progressed to higher stages of right-handed power. As economic systems expanded in complexity and reach in the era of merchant capital leading up to 1800, this meant some men and women could move goods and profits and peoples at rates and distances of time and space that had once been reserved for pharaohs and the like. These beneficiaries got more guns and bullets, more soldiers, the ability to knock down other peoples' defenses and force them to trade on the terms most favorable to the West. They got more political rights as citizens—bourgeois ones, anyway—and claimed the right to rule themselves, as sovereigns equal to each other.

In the first half of the nineteenth century, the societies that most dramatically increased their quotient of right-handed power came to dominate other peoples to a degree unprecedented in human history. And within those victorious new modernized nations, right-handed power was increasingly distributed in a lopsided fashion. Apparatuses and systems of power that could be extended and multiplied much higher than in previous eras meant that more people could get what they wanted by direct, or direct-seeming, action. Even though the effects of entrepreneurs' decisions sometimes played out a long way from the places where the decisions were made, they were still straight-line, right-handed effects. The letter is written in New Orleans and sent by ship bound out through the mouth of the Mississippi; the Maryland trading partner receives it, reads it, deposits the enclosed bill of exchange in a Baltimore bank. He rides across the worn-out soil of Eastern Shore tobacco country to the probate auction at a county seat. He buys a woman advertised as a house servant and takes her to the next Louisiana-bound vessel. The turning circles of the cotton economy, wrote one white man (to whom Louisiana success, he said, had given a new "sense of independence"), "put it in *your* power"—into your hands, he told his Virginia relative—"to enrich yourself."[19] And when eager participants talked about using the new possibilities of the global economy that had begun to emerge by the time Charles Ball was dragged to Congaree, it was hard to tell whether they understood that the networks and tools that gave them unprecedented economic leverage were not part of their own bodies—and a specific part, in fact. They wrote notes and letters that informed their correspondents that they held slaves "on hand" and money "in hand." Important letters "came to hand." They got cotton "off [their] hands" and into the market. Waiting for prices to rise, John Richards offered the Bank of the State of Mississippi a note to ensure he would not yet have to sell "the cotton that I now have in hand." Individual bills of exchange that drew on credit with other merchants were "notes of hand."[20]

So press a button (with the index finger of your *right* hand) on the machine of the trading world, and things happen to benefit the man with sterling bills, a huge pile of cotton, a long roster of slaves, abundant credit that allows him to extend his reach across time and space. The emerging modern world offered those people whose right hand it strengthened the opportunity to make everything new and different, to shape it along the lines of their desires. Like the domestic slave trade, which sold *hands* as commodified extensions of purchasers' power into the market for which hands would produce, the system that "pushing men" used to increase the number of cotton plants that enslaved people planted and cultivated was a direct application of right-handed power as a technique for organizing and controlling human behaviors. In fact, it was probably a spin-off of one of the techniques Western states developed to help them exert power over other societies, by first exerting it over the bodies of its own soldiers. Over the preceding century, Western European armies had implemented a new kind of battlefield organization. In this military drill, soldiers advanced across the battlefield in even line, matching their steady pace and keeping in file with sergeants and junior officers. The lockstep march exposed soldiers to a lengthy time of vulnerability as they marched against their enemies, but the payoff came in their disciplined ability to cow and ultimately crush the other side.[21]

Between 1790 and 1860, more land, a vast and highly capitalized slave trade, punishment, increased surveillance, decreased breaks, and lockstep labor—all the innovative violence and right-handed power of the pushing men's system—let's call it the *pushing system*—made possible a vast increase in the number of cotton plants being tended in the United States. The amount of cotton produced in the United States grew from 20 million pounds around 1805, when Charles Ball reached South Carolina, to over two billion pounds of cotton in 1860, an increase of 10,000 percent (in the same time, the number of slaves in cotton-specializing areas grew from about 50,000 to two million, or by 4,000 percent.) By the 1820s, the United States had achieved dominance over a rapidly expanding international market, controlling about

80 percent of the world's most widely traded commodity in its most important markets. It rose from irrelevance in the world cotton market to a dominant position.[22]

The flood of cleaned cotton fiber reshaped the economy of the Atlantic and then of the globe. Indeed, slave-made cotton may have been the sine qua non of the greatest revolution in human material circumstances since the domestication of food crops ten millennia before.[23] Kenneth Pomeranz argues that in the late eighteenth century, the developing Western European economy faced a Malthusian resource cul-de-sac that limited the scope of development and raised the price of key inputs. But Europe escaped. The millions of acres taken from Native Americans and planted by enslaved migrants like Ball were that many acres that Britain would not have to devote to the production of raw fiber. Indeed, it could not have afforded to do so.[24] To replace the fiber it imported from American slave labor camps with the same amount of wool, Britain would in 1830 have had to devote 23 million acres to sheep pasture—more than all the island's agricultural land.[25] The rise of the Lancashire textile industry, which in turn drove a chain of other changes in the Western world, could not have occurred without an escape from these Malthusian constraints. What Pomeranz calls the "ghost acres" of the expanding cotton South were the way out of the cul-de-sac.[26]

Yet it was not foreordained that the United States would be able to produce the ever-increasing quantities of cotton that the world's growing textile industry—and textile consumers—demanded. Or that the United States would harvest those quantities more cheaply than competitors like India, Brazil, or China. The cotton gin and the pushing system opened two choke points in the production flow. But the most difficult clog remained in place.

On an early morning at the beginning of September, the overseer ordered the enslaved people at Congaree back into fields, where the cotton was now open in a blaze of white fiber. He gave each man, woman, and child a long bag and ordered them to take a row and start picking. Bending to his new task, Ball quickly found that picking required sharp eyes and good coordination. Slip up, and the hand clutched a leaf, or fingers were pricked by the hard points of the drying "square" at the base of the boll. Grab too much, and a mess of fiber and stem sprang loose in one's hand. Grab too little and the fingers twisted only a few strands. Finally at the end of his first row, Ball saw women and even children speeding past him in the neighboring rows, their hands blurs, and not just their right hands but, in the fastest cases, their left as well. Some demon seemed to pursue them, but Ball didn't yet know where the secret of their fear was hidden. All day, as the sun crawled in a slow parabola, the sound of click, click, click rose from the almost silent fields as nails tapped on hard pods. The only other sound was the occasional hoarse cry of "Water, water!" as children ran back and forth. Buckets rested on their heads, where within a few weeks a circle of hair would wear off and stay bald until February. There was no singing.[27]

"A man who has arrived at the age of twenty-five, before he sees a cotton field," Ball decided, "will never, in the language of the overseers, become a *crack picker*."[28] Yet many millions of enslaved people did become crack pickers. The amount of cotton enslaved people harvested increased dramatically over time. In 1801, 28 pounds per day per picker was the average in the South Carolina labor camps for which we have records. In 1846, the hands on a Mississippi labor camp averaged 341 pounds each on a good day, and in the next decade averages climbed higher still.[29] A study of planter account books that recorded daily picking totals for individual enslaved people on labor camps across the South finds a growth in daily picking averages of some 400 percent between 1800 and 1860, or a 2.1 percent growth in productivity each year.[30]

The increase in the efficiency of cotton picking was extremely high, comparable in magnitude to key measures of growing efficiency in the British textile factory, the breeding ground of the factory system's technological innovations. From 1819 to 1860, the productivity of workers in Manchester spinning mills increased by a little less than 400 percent, while those in weaving mills improved by over 600 percent.[31]

Yet until very recently, most historians missed the increase in cotton-picking efficiency. And this means they missed a secret at the heart of the modern world's emergence.[32] Recently, however, two economists who noticed the increase and confirmed it by creating a massive database from the thousands of daily cotton weigh-ins recorded in enslavers' cotton-picking ledgers tried to offer an explanation. They rejected the idea that enslavers implemented a new labor system to extract continual gains in cotton picking, or that enslaved people worked faster and with greater efficiency. Instead, they postulated that a crucial shift in planter-directed "biotechnology"—new varieties of short-staple cotton seeds, especially, from the 1820s on, a breed called Petit Gulf, adapted for heavy growth and "pickability"—was responsible for transforming the efficiency of cotton harvesting.[33] But their argument cannot explain all the available facts.

The inadequacies of the economists' explanation emerge as soon as one begins to look at the very cotton record books on which the claim for pickability is based. These records measure nothing about seeds and everything about the performance of individual laborers. Yet to explain the performance thus recorded, the economists uncritically reproduce the seeds-did-it assertion from the claims of planters who dabbled in seed dealing.[34] Self- advertisement usually does not make the most objective of sources about products, as other cotton planters who were skeptical about such claims often pointed out.[35] The economists also make a series of logical errors in their attempt to draw the conclusion that seeds, and not an increased intensity of labor or new systems of labor, led to the rise in cotton picking rates.[36]

In the absence of the kind of slavery into which Ball had been sold, seeds seem to have been incapable of driving picking-efficiency increases. From the 1830s on, British officials and entrepreneurs repeatedly tried to resuscitate the Indian export cotton sector, which had been crushed by its peasant produc- ers' inability to compete with the continually falling real price of cotton produced by enslaved African Americans. They imported North American planters' seeds, North American cotton planters' gins, and even North Amer- ican planters themselves, all to help them to learn how to produce cotton of the high quality and low price that, shipped from New Orleans to Liverpool, dominated the world market. But the British didn't import North American slavery, and without it, these attempts to compete with the U.S. South's enslaved cotton pickers always failed.[37] Meanwhile, back in the United States, after slavery ended in 1865, picking rates appear to have stopped increasing, and may have even declined.[38] Perhaps some change in the nature of cotton DNA meant that seeds, by a remarkable coincidence, stopped driving increases in picking rates right at the time when slavery ended. But this would be strange, because the late nineteenth and early twentieth centuries were exactly when the United States saw the emergence of a new scientific research complex in higher education, industry, and government, much of it devoted to agricul- tural innovation. Yet with the end of slavery's systems of labor extraction, the cotton South experienced a systemic decline in productivity from which it never fully recovered.[39]

Any persuasive explanation for the rise in picking efficiency must take seriously something that the economists in question admit they never consid- ered. Those who survived this incredible increase in labor efficiency knew that something well, however, and focus on it in the testimony they left for history. Using their testimony, I will explain why picking totals actually rose, and what that meant. First, however, I want to consider why the astonishing dynamic increase in the efficiency of slave labor has remained largely unknown to history.

Historians' model for economic modernization, the constant process of seeking greater efficiencies, is the industrial transition from hand labor to machine technology, from human or animal power to water and then steam power. This archetype comes, in other words, from the textile mills of Manchester in Britain, and Lowell in Massachusetts, which wove the cotton picked by Ball and his successors into cloth in ever more mechanized and efficient ways.[40] In contrast, the attempts of Adam Smith and virtually all his successor political economists to classify slave labor have usually proceeded from two points of dogma. The first point of departure is the belief that slave labor was a premodern excrescence, a baroquely grown cul-de-sac off the road to modernity. Such accounts are typically written in the mode of *telos*. Generation after generation have found new reasons why slavery in the United States, for instance, could not have persisted for long after 1865, even if there had been no Civil War. This belief in predestination is the Calvinism, the Puritan ethic underlying the historiography of capitalism. In such accounts, slave labor is antithetical to modernity, industrialization, and capitalism in every sense, and so would have inevitably faded. It denies the rights of free contract that are the alibi for a society whose wage-labor relations produce unequal outcomes while also founding political stability on representative politics structured by republican or natural rights claims. Slave labor is antithetical to the sense of progress that is meant to justify the destruction of tradition and the disruption of human relationships that comes with rapid economic transformation. And slave labor is thus depicted as something that will be or would have been inevitably destroyed by some action of advancing modernity. Sometimes the nature and mechanism of that action are spelled out and sometimes they are not. But usually, we assume that we truly modern people would have chosen the more efficient and productive path.

For the second axiom is this: ever since Adam Smith, it has been assumed that slave labor is inherently inefficient because the laborer has no incentive. "The work done by free men comes cheaper in the end than the work performed by slaves. Whatever work he does, beyond what is sufficient to purchase his own maintenance, can be squeezed out of him by violence only, and not by any interest of his own."[41] Not only does the slave laborer's lack of incentives imply shoddy work in this view, it also implies unchanging productivity—doing things the same way, over and over again, for centuries. The laborer has no incentive to increase his or her industriousness. She or he has no incentive to create innovations of time-and-motion use or of tool invention. The enslaver has no incentive to introduce mechanical inventions that will create more output for a given set of inputs of time, labor, or raw materials. Why? Well, for one thing, the enslaver already has one massive capital investment, and supposedly has no incentive to render it less significant on the scale of social power. Let us also bracket, but hang on to, another assumption: that increases in the efficiency of hand labor are always limited by hard physical barriers or limitations, compared to the supposedly unending possibilities of productivity increase available with machine technology and inorganic sources of power.[42]

There is also an assumption that enslavers are or become *different*—that they are not like moderns, that they do not seek efficiencies because they do not have to do. But above all, slave labor does not become more efficient, we are also told, because one cannot introduce machines. Slaves break machines— they have no incentive not to do otherwise, and besides, they unsurprisingly resent those who steal from them. Without machine technology, we are told, natural limits to already disincentivized hand labor render slave labor un- competitive in an industrializing, free-labor-focused modern world. And certainly the Whitehall reformers who helped end slavery in the British Em- pire in the 1830s promised sugar cultivated by free labor would be cheaper than that cultivated by the enslaved. Likewise, the Liberty Party critics—who in the early 1840s launched the political economic critique of U.S. slavery that would eventually find a home in the Republican platform—believed that the post-1837 financial crisis in the United States revealed that slave labor in cot- ton was inefficient. Most white abolitionists already shared this point of view. Their critique was taken up in the 1850s by Frederick Law Olmsted. It was re- tailed as gospel by many of the contractors who leased conquered plantations from the federal government in 1861 and after. Free laborers would work harder and more efficiently than the enslaved.[43]

Hidden within the second axiom is a further assumption that is used to explain why slavery sometimes *appeared* to be more successful than free labor as a system of production. The costs of direct supervision in slavery societies would eventually be too high to justify slavery as a labor system in a world where markets were steadily becoming more competitive and interlinked. However, at certain places and in certain times, slavery—or its cousin, serfdom—could, in early capitalist economies, be profitable. The Manchurian economist Evsey Domar, translating older Russian scholarship, argued that where and when land was abundant there would be no opportunity to per- suade free laborers to work at unpleasant resource extraction processes for someone else. Thus forced labor would become relatively profitable despite the cost of supervision, and thus we see the expansion of slavery in the New World after 1492, and of serfdom at the same time in Europe's eastern regions.[44]

Yet the Domar thesis is a variation on the teleology—or so it has been read. Typically appended to it are variations on one of these two further theses. The first is the "Prussian Road" argument, identified with Barrington Moore and mid-career Eugene Genovese. This holds that the political-economic formations that build development on forced labor sacrifice social and cultural freedom. Prohibitions against internal criticism make them unpleasant places for many creative personalities, and the resistance to external criticism leads them into fights they cannot win. Hence the Civil War and World War I, both of which the thesis attributes to "Prussian" decision making. Such political-economic formations also suffer from constraints imposed by path dependence on the economic sectors controlled by slave masters or serf lords. And because they depend on slave labor, these economic sectors are not susceptible to technological innovations or sustained productivity increases.[45]

If you do not swallow the Prussian Road argument—if, for instance, you doubt its assumptions of cultural uniformity and centralized decision making—you could also turn to the second thesis, the "energy poverty" argument. This thesis accounts for the persistent inability of some oil-rich nations—Venezuela and Nigeria are favored examples—to deliver sustained economic growth to a majority of their citizens by arguing that the early profitability of extracting a single natural resource produces lasting patterns of bad governance and nonexistent transparency. Because of the profitability of political control of the key resource, the stakes of political power are very high. Unscrupulous strongmen and their cliques set aside rules to gain and retain power. Competitive economics, contract enforcement, transparency in allocating business—all of these things become irrelevant. The society becomes both structurally and culturally incapable of carrying out the modern business practices needed to develop a complex, diversified economy. The prescription is simple: eliminate corrupt government, impose consistent legal processes and enforcement of contracts, allocate capital based on efficiency, and so on. While contemporary oil-rich nations are one group of proof-texts, accounts such as that of Daron Acemoglu and James Robinson cite slavery as a classic case of the long-term negative effects of resource-extraction economies. Slavery, of course, institutionalized violence and the unequal enforcement of contracts, and created hypertrophied single sectors that dominated entire political-economic formations.[46]

Yet all of these accounts return to their foundational assumption that production by the enslaved was essentially inefficient and less productive than what could be achieved over the long run by the more iconic techniques of modernity: machine technology, free wage labor, incentives internalized by choice or by Foucauldian structures of power that impose on us a way of knowing that permits only participation in the ebb and flow of market society.

Certainly, Charles Ball would have agreed with Adam Smith and others that slavery *was* wasteful. Slavery's captives knew that slavery wasted the days and years extorted from them. The first day Ball spent in the cotton fields was of no use to him as a human being whose life mattered. He made nothing of it for himself except, as we will see, to begin to develop a new power in his hands that he would be forced to turn against himself. But the manual cotton labor of hands in the field was anything but resistant to increases in productivity, as the numbers reveal, and when his first day of picking closed, Ball was about to learn where the secret resided. When the sun finally settled on the white glow of the cotton field, the exhausted people in it hefted their cotton baskets and carried them to the shed where the owner kept his cotton gin. In a semicircle, they put down their load and waited while the drivers hung each basket, one by one, by its handles on a "steelyard," a balance-beam scale. The overseer took down each number in chalk by the picker's name on the slate held in his hand. When Ball's turn came, he had "only thirty-eight pounds." Most of the other men in his field had picked fifty to sixty pounds. Ball would soon learn that even some of the faster pickers would be beaten for not picking enough.[47]

Twenty years after Ball's first day of picking, Israel Campbell went through his own first season of this kind of work at a Mississippi slave labor camp. The planter and his Irish overseer had told the young man that his daily minimum would be 100 pounds. Both owner and overseer had told him that he would "have as many lashes as there were pounds short." The overseer had his slate and list of names ready, on which he recorded each "draft of cotton." (A draft was a check that paid off a debt, in the commercial lingo of the time.) At the end of the day, Campbell knew that he had been able to pick no more than ninety pounds between first light and full dark. When he brought his basket up to the cotton yard, Campbell—desperate to avoid the reconciliation of his negative balance—silently set his basket down and slipped away. He hid in a hut, but then the door opened. Looming on the threshold was the planter Belfer, a lantern in one hand, and a bullwhip and four stakes in the other: " 'Well, Israel, is that you?' " The Irishman had weighed the basket. The account was short. " 'I will settle with you now,' " Belfer said, "adding an oath for emphasis."[48]

A system of measurement, accounting, and torture was used to coerce enslaved people to pick large amounts of cotton. People who were enslaved reported it again and again.[49] Of course, some readers may wonder whether or not people who had once been enslaved told the truth about this. And a few critics will inevitably suggest that survivors of slavery were charlatans, or too illiterate to speak for themselves, or that they catered to the whims of white abolitionist editors who were dogmatically intent on depicting slavery as a parade of cruelties. Such critiques have been made since at least the late 1830s, when the first African American autobiographies began to appear in significant number as part of the emergent North American abolitionist antislavery movement. Enslavers launched every one of those critiques against Charles Ball, Frederick Douglass, and many others. Today, criticisms—sometimes identical ones—still appear. When they do, they usually take no account of the tremendous amount of work done by scholars of slavery's history and survivors' culture to authenticate, assess, and understand the testimony that has survived.[50]

Whether we are talking about autobiographies and memoirs created by nineteenth-century escapees from enslavement or interviews done in the 1930s with elderly formerly enslaved people, these ex-slave narratives are, in the end, sources like other sources.[51] They have their flaws, as do all sources. They need to be interpreted, as must other sources. They need to be weighed and tested. One must understand when the interests of the people involved in creating these sources were served and when they were not. All that is exactly what we must do with all sources. (Of course, all too often scholars have been willing to let enslavers' accounts of slavery—including their claims about cotton seeds—escape such scrutiny.)

When we do serious interpretive work with the narratives and interviews left behind by slavery's survivors, we find that what people who picked cotton said about picking cotton was probably derived from their own experience. The white abolitionists who were involved in the editing and publication of many of the nineteenth-century narratives did not ask for it. They were not interested in hearing about slave labor as an efficient system of production. Most were ideologically committed to the position that slave labor was inefficient. We can document the fact that white abolitionist audiences took slave labor's inefficiency as a given and often didn't even ask about it.[52] The fact that survivors of cotton-frontier slavery depicted that system as one that compelled intensively measured labor that (we now know) grew more efficient over time thus appears likely to have been included in texts by the choice of the survivors.

Nor were such depictions of cotton labor exceptional or isolated. In fact, virtually every nineteenth-century narrator who had spent time in a cotton field—about twenty individuals in all—depicted a similar system of pushing, quotas, and whipping for those whose end-of-day accounting came up short. Did these survivors lie? If so, they must have all agreed to tell the same lies, and to tell them for a century, and to do so without thereby gaining any apparent benefits for themselves. The fact that their testimony so often agrees with the testimony of 1930s interviewees, whose interlocutors were often southern whites deeply embedded in the system of segregation, further verifies this evidence.[53] Indeed, when those interviewed in the 1930s spoke about the process of cotton picking or about cotton weighing, they too appear to have done so by their own choice. Lists of questions generated by the national and state bureaucrats who directed the 1930s interviews usually do not mention these aspects of slavery. Certainly those survivors interviewed by southern whites deeply embedded in Jim Crow power structures—which is to say, most of the 1930s interviewees—do not appear to have been prodded by their interlocutors to speak of whippings and theft of labor, or to have been encouraged to speak of enslavers as exploiters.[54] And yet approximately thirty of them chose to talk about quotas and whipping.[55]

Together, then, fifty-odd survivors testified directly to the existence and characteristics of the dynamic system of labor extraction with whose 1805 version Charles Ball was trying to grapple on that late-summer evening in South Carolina.[56] These sources cannot be dismissed or disregarded, despite the many inconvenient truths they tell about how the modern world emerged. Last-ditch attempts to dismiss these sources still occur, of course. And the language and character of attempts to dismiss these sources often reveal an issue that is deeply embedded in U.S. and Western public and private culture, but which also has not been rooted out from the world and words of scholars. That is the persistent unwillingness of many white readers and listeners to accept black testimony about black life—or death—as legitimate.[57]

It would be hard to think of more legitimate sources for helping one understand how cotton picking worked than those who picked cotton. Then again, those who prefer sources from southern whites will be interested to learn that they too testify to the existence of this incentive system structured by whip, scale, and ledger—and not only by the existence of thousands of pages of daily cotton-picking records. "You are mistaken when you say your negroes are ignorant of the proper way of working," wrote Robert Beverley, handling a new crew transported from Virginia to Alabama. "They only require to be made to do it . . . by flogging and that quite often." Meanwhile, here's a Natchez doctor, in 1835: "The overseer meets all hands at the scales, with lamp, scales, and whip. Each basket is carefully weighed, and the nett weight of cotton set down upon the slate, opposite the name of the picker." "The countenance of an idler may be seen to fall," for the penalty for failure to meet his or her quota was coming out of their back. Or, as travelers less friendly to the enslavers report hearing: "So many pounds short, cries the overseer, and takes up his whip, exclaiming, 'Step this way, you damn lazy scoundrel' . . . 'Short pounds, you bitch.'"[58]

Charles Ball understood that his first-day total on the slate would be his new individual minimum. He also understood that if he failed the next day to pick at least thirty-eight pounds, "it would go hard with me. . . . I knew that the lash of the overseer would become familiar with my back." This was not a task system like that of the South Carolina rice swamps and Sea Island cotton plantations.[59] Here, on the cotton frontier, enslaved people picked from first light till dark. They did not get to stop, even if they had made their quota. Here, each person was given an individual quota rather than a limit of work fixed by custom. Those who picked more found themselves saddled with a higher quota. They were also subject to whippings, just like the slower ones—perhaps, in some cases, they were in even greater danger. Finally, once enslaved people learned how to meet the quota consistently, the enslaver erased his chalk and wrote a higher quota on the slate for the next day.[60]

Over time, quotas climbed, and so, in general, did the quantity picked by each enslaved person on each day. We know from enslavers' cotton-picking books that the average amount picked per day by enslaved picker rose by 400 percent from 1800 to 1860, in a steady curve. When we map the quotas reported by survivors of the enslaved, we find they report that daily requirements rose in the same pattern.[61] Survivors report that enslavers raised enslaved people's personal quotas (or "stints," as they were sometimes called). Sometimes this was done by simply measuring the amount that enslaved people, desperate to avoid the whip, had picked over their stint, and adding that to the old quota to make a new, higher one.[62]

In other cases, enslavers used positive incentives to get people to pick faster, setting up races between individuals with prizes like a cup of sugar, a hat, or a small amount of money.[63] But such speed-ups shouldn't be seen simply as attempts to import positive incentives into a system dominated by negative ones. They were also tricks, designed to get enslaved people to reveal capacities they were hiding. In Georgia, John Brown's enslaver Thomas Stevens would "pick out two or more of the strongest and sturdiest, and excite them to a race at hoeing or picking, for an old hat, or something of the sort. He would stand with his watch in his hand, observing their movements, whilst they hoed or picked across a certain space he had marked out. The man who won the prize set the standard for the rest. Whatever he did, within a given time, would be multiplied by a certain rule, for the day's work."[64]

But enslavers also whipped greater picking speed out of enslaved people in the field itself, forcing their targets to devote sustained attention and unrelenting effort to their speed and accuracy (less leaves, dirt, "trash," etc. in the picked fibers). This kind of invigilation reveals yet again the major differences between the labor system used on the cotton frontier and that used in the Lowcountry. It also reveals the essence of the enslavers' plan: to force enslaved people to show their left hands. Here, on the cotton frontier, enslavers "whipped up" enslaved people to force them to reveal capacities they were hiding, or that had not yet been created. "As I picked so well at first," remembered John Brown, "more was exacted of me, and if I flagged a minute the whip was applied liberally to keep me up to my mark. By being driven in this way, I at last got to pick a hundred and sixty pounds a day," after starting at a minimum requirement of 100.[65] "Old man Jonas watched us children and kept us divin' for that cotton all day long," remembered Irella Battle Walker, and "us wish him dead many a time."[66]

At the end of the day came the weighing, and then, for those "not up to the task," the whipping. Sometimes they locked people in metal boxes overnight instead, or beat them with handsaws, or locked them in stocks. But the whip was the most typical. The master had a "'black snake,'—some called it a 'bull whip'," remembered Austin Grant. "He cut the blood outta the grown ones . . . right on your naked back. They said your clothes wouldn't grow but your hide would."[67] Some tried to run as the dusk fell, but, as Williamson Pease remembered: "They caught him . . . beat him in the head with the handle of the strap. They stripped him naked. . . . I saw it done—I was looking through the palings. Then they whipped him with a piece of white oak made limber. I saw his back and it was all raw. The man was sent to work next day, but he gave out, and was laid up . . . until the cotton had been picked over. Three times." That wasn't what mattered, what mattered was "they caught him, and showed no mercy," and above all, that "I saw it done."[68]

Whether the next day or a month later, when the victims of these brutal assaults went back into the field with their shirts stuck to bloody cuts, they'd be an example as well. Quotas rose. Planters and overseers consulted the cotton-picking books to see who was falling off from previous days' and previous years' quotas. (What else are the hundreds of cotton-picking books kept by enslavers but guides to whipping?) Whips rose and fell. And cotton-picking rates rose inexorably, sometimes picker after picker; but always the average across the expanding South's expanding slave labor camps rose: year after year after year.

The whip made cotton. And whip-made increases in the efficiency of picking had global significance. They pushed down the real price of cotton, which by 1860 had fallen to one quarter of its 1800 price, even as demand had increased many times over. U.S. cotton producers effectively set the world price for this all-important commodity. So efficiency gains in picking created a pie from which many could take a slice. Lower raw material costs meant more capital could be invested in creating better machines, higher wages for mill workers, revenue for enslavers, and of course benefits passed on to the consumers of cloth, as most of the world eventually acquired clothes made in the industrial sectors of the West from cotton grown and picked in the U.S. South. Consumers were among those who benefited most from the ever more efficient production of the enslaved. In Western countries, and soon around the world, people had access to a much greater variety of light, adaptable, printable textiles. An astonishing variety of clothes became accessible to a much higher percentage over the world population. Bourgeois and, eventually, proletarian houses would acquire a new kind of room, the closet, to store the sudden variety. One of the greatest problems for the entire chain of those actors who profited financially from the labor of slaves in U.S. cotton fields became that of convincing consumers that they needed even more clothes, to soak up the endless flood of fiber spilling out of the sacks and baskets of enslaved people. Fashion magazines with illustrations, research on what cloth was desired in markets as distant as East Africa: so was born modern marketing as a process of simultaneously responding to consumers' wants and endlessly stimulating new ones with new forms of media. And so, in lurches and starts, consumption broadened and deepened across class and geography, staving off the beast of overproduction more often than not.[69]

The fluctuations in cotton supply and demand drove many of the ups and downs of the wider global economy. In part this was because cotton was an essential input of the global supply chain for the first and most important factory-made good, cotton textiles, and in part because so much of the world's financial capital was invested in making this crop. Of course, the interlinking of daily picking totals with the dynamic ongoing transformation and modernization of world commodity and capital markets ran both ways: world demand for cotton shaped the demands of enslavers and the responses of the enslaved.[70]

This particular new constellation of power was not confined to the United States. Even as slavery-made cotton from the southern United States became the most widely traded commodity in the world, the radical, dynamic, and continuous transformations that began with slave labor were shaping two other major societies in the New World, Cuba and southeastern Brazil. Each region produced a commodity that also became a key component of industrial transformation. And just as with cotton, the processes in these two societies not only drove economic modernization but also partook of the creative destruction of economic modernity. Finally, just as in the U.S. cotton states, the nineteenth century saw a massive increase in the number of enslaved people who lived and toiled and died in the Cuban and Brazilian zones where new commodities were being made.

After 1807, the United States and Britain banned their citizens from participating in the Atlantic slave trade. Over the next fifty years, most Western nation-states also signed treaties banning the international slave trade. But despite the optimistic hopes of some reformers, the reality that followed these slave trade "abolitions" was quite different. Between 1808 and the start of the U.S. Civil War, more than 2.7 million people were moved by force from Africa to the New World, most of them to Cuba and Brazil. This was more than during any other half century of the Atlantic slave trade, save the 3.4 million toll of the 1750–1800 period. This was also more than the total number of free immigrants who moved to the United States between the time of the Revolution and 1850.[71]

Thus, slave trades continued after 1807, especially to rapidly growing commodity-producing zones. U.S. citizens were deeply involved in both the Brazilian and Cuban slave trades, as well as in the sugar plantation zone of Cuba, as owners, technicians, and investors. And while the post-1807 illegal slave trade to the United States itself was miniscule, the internal slave trade was not. In this same time period, more than one million enslaved African Americans were moved from the older states of the South to the newer ones in the Mississippi Valley. Their experience was also one of absolute displacement and an introduction to new levels of violence, and so was not so different from those who went through the Middle Passage. When we add those one million people to the 2.7 million of the post-1807 Atlantic slave trade, we find that the fifty years that preceded Lincoln's election were actually the highest point so far of the long-distance slave trade to the commodity-producing regions of the Americas. More than four million enslaved people had been moved by brutal processes of forced migration into New World slavery's most profitable zones. And despite the emancipations of all slaves in the British empire, and of most of the enslaved people in the newly independent states of Spanish-speaking Latin America, the total number of enslaved people in the New World had increased dramatically, from about five million to about seven million.

The millions of acres taken from Native Americans and cleared, planted, and harvested by enslaved migrants from the Chesapeake and the Carolinas were an ecological windfall for the industrializing West, absolutely crucial for escaping older economies' Malthusian constraints. So too were the new, modernized sugar plantations of Cuba and the coffee estates of the Brazilian frontier. By 1850, as British working-class factory towns swelled with millions of factory workers, that island's changing agricultural sector struggled to keep up with all the new mouths to feed. Much as with cotton, by the 1830s and 1840s, innovations in Cuban sugar production processes permitted individual Cuban slave labor camps to produce four times as much sugar as eighteenth-century predecessors. From 16,000 metric tons in 1800, just 5 percent of world production, Cuba rapidly scaled up its production to half a million metric tons by the 1850s—50 percent of all the sugar made in the world. As the price of sugar fell, British and North American cuisines came up with more and more ways to deliver its cheap calories to the urban masses. By 1860, British workers consumed 10 to 20 percent of their daily calories in the form of sugar inserted in jam, as sweetener for tea and other drinks, and in baked goods. Eventually sugar became a key component of far more processed foods than we even now realize. This was crucial to industrialization. Western societies experienced a measurable average adult height decline in the nineteenth century. This was probably attributable to the new dietary restrictions imposed by the new increase in geographic and social distance from sources of food supply. Without the cheap calories provided by sugar, the general health deficit this decline signals could have been significantly worse.[72]

Meanwhile, in Brazil, where the sugar industry had grown decrepit, enslavers opened a vast new hinterland in the interior of Rio de Janeiro state and São Paulo state. In the 1700s this region had been a backwater; by the early twenty-first century, it was the core of one of the most rapidly growing economies in the world. And it started with coffee. In 1800 Brazil exported only 580 tons of coffee; by 1860 that number was 800,000 tons. By the late nineteenth century, 80 percent of world coffee exports came from Brazil. While to say coffee was a major factor of industrialized, capitalist production might sound like a joke, it really isn't. The shift from old ways to a world of constant innovation, from an agricultural and religious calendar to one of the clock and nonstop work and business, was as much a cultural shift as it was a shift from wood to iron. Coffee replaced alcohol as the beverage of the work break, especially in the United States. Around 1800, U.S. workers drank immense quantities of alcohol, especially during the workday. One can imagine the effects this had on labor discipline and efficiency. In contrast, coffee stimulated, delivered sugar, gave energy for work, and did all this without intoxication and alcohol's other effects. Along with a massive campaign of religious revival and reform, the availability of coffee is the major reason why the average consumption of alcohol dropped dramatically from a peak of 7.1 annual gallons of absolute alcohol per capita early in the nineteenth century to well under three gallons by the Civil War decades.[73]

In both these other two new regimes, sugar and coffee, labor productivity grew continuously throughout the nineteenth century. In Cuba, a series of innovations in the chemistry, machine technology, and production process organization was what made the Cuban sugar planters so efficient. They broke the bottleneck in sugar production, which was (as of 1800) not in planting or cutting but in grinding and refining sugar cane into juice and juice into sugar and molasses. Of course, these improvements—steam-driven mills, vacuum pans, centrifuges, continuous-flow processing, careful organization of the space and sequence of harvesting—stole the last remaining secrets and skills from the left hands and right brains of enslaved African and Creole Cubans. The sons of enslaved sugar refiners went out into the fields as cane cutters. The secrets now rested inside the machines, in the control of the white technicians, who increasingly were the ones who ran them. The technology, and the more rapid pace of production overall, led to a machine-geared speedup for the slaves who cut cane by hand.[74]

Machine technology was a big part of the dominance of Cuban sugar. The success of Brazilian coffee, on the other hand, was built to a large extent on pure hand labor, sped up by a process much like that occurring in the cotton fields. The bottleneck in production here was picking. Coffee planters in the Paraíba Valley created new processes of driving enslaved pickers across hillsides of bushes, and then of measuring their output. Just like cotton planters, coffee barons and their minions weighed daily picking totals and balanced accounts, whipping those who defaulted on the debts imposed by their quotas. And just like coffee planters, the coffee entrepreneurs increased their prices over time, extracting by the late nineteen century daily picking totals that were 200 to 300 percent of those gathered early in the century.[75]

The disruption of enslaved people's lives and the measurement, surveillance, and violent coercion of enslaved people's labor were key components in the massive efficiency increases that made the Industrial Revolution possible. This history, once we know it, demands that we give up truisms of choice and incentive, premodern versus modern, or hand versus machine. But how, then, are we to understand and explain the kinds of labor that transformed the world during the nineteenth century, and the kinds of power that emerged? Maybe we could start by looking at how the gains of nineteenth-century slave labor were extracted. Cotton productivity grew because pickers themselves were forced to pick faster, better, more efficiently. Clever entrepreneurs extorted the benefit of new gains they themselves could not imagine. To do so, they did not have to be scientists of motion or choreographers of efficiency. But they did have to press the most skillful hands ever harder. Seeds were surely part of this story. But every time seeds got better, enslaved people did not find their work got easier. Instead, they were pressed to their new maximum, and beyond: forced to become better, faster pickers.[76] Ultimately, it was calibrated torture, not the seed selecting of science-minded planters, that became the technology that kept the Industrial Revolution fed with cheap, high-quality cotton, that broke through the resource constraints that had imprisoned previous civilizations in a Malthusian cul-de-sac.

Torture is not a word we use often in the study of slavery's history, much less that of capitalism. We see torture as inherently inefficient, not something that a professor could put on the chalkboard as a variable in an equation or a graph (T stands for torture, one component of S, or supply.) But understanding torture as a technology, a means of accomplishing what the philosopher Martin Heidegger called the "challenging-forth" of nature, putting nature (the nature of human beings and the second nature they have developed in their embodied culture) to the test and making it yield all that it can—this helps incorporate the astonishing increases in productivity in both field and factory into the story of the rise of the modern world. Here's an illuminating metaphor for the process, one offered by a man named Henry Clay. Born into slavery in the Carolinas, he was moved west as a boy, and seventy years after slavery ended he recalled that his Louisiana owner had once possessed a machine that by his account made cotton cultivation and harvesting mechanical, rapid, and efficient. This contraption was "a big wooden wheel with a treadle to it, and when you tromp the treadle the big wheel go round. On that wheel was four or five leather straps with holes cut in them to make blisters, and you lay the negro down on his face on a bench and tie him to it." When the operator pumped the treadle to turn the wheel, the straps thrashed the back of the man or woman tied to the bench into blistered, bloody jelly. According to Clay, the mere threat of the whipping-machine was enough to speed his own hands and hoe.[77]

The contraption may have actually existed. I think, however, that it was not a material thing of wood and leather but instead, Clay's telling tale. It tells us that we could see the scientific principle of every cotton labor camp ever carved out of the southwestern woods as a metaphorical whipping-machine: a technology for controlling and exploiting human beings, calibrating increments of torture to extract both efficient production of pounds of cotton and endless, dynamic improvements to that efficiency. They measured the increments with steelyard scales, and by then checking totals against the cotton-picking accounts they kept on slates and then copied into ledgers. These books had no purpose besides that of measuring cotton pickers and holding them responsible for exceeding their previous gains. Hundreds of these cotton-picking ledgers survive. They are the most numerous artifacts and—once we understand why they existed—they are also the most overwhelming evidence of both the function and the functionality of enslavers' whipping-machines.

In fact, the whole vast archipelago of slave labor camps that eventually stretched from western South Carolina into Texas, extracting from the hands of the enslaved an unprecedented level and quality of field labor, was a dynamically evolving technology of measurement, torture, and forced innovation, a whipping-machine writ large and built full scale. This whipping-machine challenged enslaved people every day to exceed yesterday's gains in production and profit. The whipping-machine also challenges historians' willingness to adopt, from the powers that be and have been, definitions that implicitly distinguish "torture" from "discipline." Historians of torture have defined the term as extreme torment that is part of a judicial or inquisitorial procedure. Torture, in this view, might give psychological rewards to sadistic torturers, but the key feature that distinguishes it from mere brutal torment is that it aims to extract "truth." Instead, we see the whipping of slaves as either psychopathy or as part of an archaic structure of power and labor "discipline" that is in nature no more efficient at creating true work efficiency than the beating of children and domestic servants is at creating true love.[78]

The whipping-machine did, in fact, continually extract a truth: the maximum poundage that a man, woman, or child could pick. Once the victim surrendered to that fact, the torturer then challenged the enslaved person's reason again, to force the creation of and then extract from his hands a new truth, an even greater capacity to pick. (As we know, torture can create new truths.) How did enslaved people create a truth that answered the ever-higher demands? Some tried to fool the weight and cheat the whip, hiding rocks, dirt, or melons in their baskets to make them heavier. George Womble remembered that cotton pickers tried to sprinkle white sand on the dew-wet cotton as they put it in their bags in the first hours of the long day.[79]

But overseers were selected for "hardness." They inflicted severe punishment on enslaved people caught trying to cheat the scales on daily cotton debts. The steady upward curve of efficiency proves that overseers and enslavers usually won that struggle. And every forced adaptation made to survive defeat added more revenue for enslavers. Thomas Cole recalled that small children who picked were allowed to add the cotton to their parents' baskets—another way to use family ties and parental authority to support planter profits. In general, enslavers opposed cooperation, preferring the leverage that individual measurement gave them. (In the opposite of cooperation, remembered Austin Grant, some enslaved people stole cotton from each other's baskets to add it to their own.) Instead, most enslaved people had to train their forces of individual innovation. Fearing punishment or even death, minds scrambled to come up with ways to speed their own hands as minimums increased. Parents and elders taught children to pick faster: Grant's grandfather "would tell us things, to keep the whip off our backs. He would say, 'Chillen, work, work and work hard. You know how you hate to be whipped, so work hard!'" They taught individual adaptation in a world of perpetual vulnerability to violence, and sometimes themselves used violence to prepare their own children for the picking season. Berry Smith's mother beat him, "took a pole to me if I didn't do it [pick cotton] right."[80]

Looking at the dramatic increase over time in the quantity picked, one must concede that above all, enslaved people succeeded in picking more cotton. But it is interesting that enslavers' language, with its assumption that some human beings could be reduced to the hands, the appendages of others, was in its way the mirror of the words enslaved people used to describe the experience of picking cotton. To pick it well, the way that cotton entrepreneurs needed it to be done so that they could make calculations about a harvest's profit into reality, one had to disembody oneself, to separate the mind from the hand—to become for a time, in fact, little more than a hand. Or two hands. While novice Solomon Northup, for instance, lurched down his row, his neighbor Patsey worked both sides of her row in perpetual motion, picking with both hands, moving like a dancer in an unconscious rhythm—though one of dissociation rather than of pleasure. Like a pianist her hands—both her hands, right and left—did their own separate thinking.[81]

Symmetry can be beautiful to witness. In laboratory tests, people are consistently attracted to more symmetrical faces and bodies. But human beings are in crucial ways asymmetrical. For most people, however, the left hand did not want to do its own thinking. And they did not want to make it (or make the right hand, if they were left-handed.) Most of us prefer to use the right hand for most tasks. Virtually all of us are "handed," preferring one hand over another. Consciousness and handedness are intertwined. So are handedness and selfhood. Many of us are aware that the left side of the brain generally controls the right hand, and vice versa. In fact, in both language and work with one's hands, each side of the brain plays a different role, and thus so does each hand. We write, we touch, we gesture, we take more with one hand than another. We work with one hand more than another. Our strong hand, whether we are right- or left-handed, is the dextrous partner of our conscious, planning mind. In the skilled tasks that Charles Ball could perform, or those of any enslaved person coming from older regions of the South and older systems of labor, one hand was always the leader. And such tasks in which one hand was the leader, the mind at work, could be an expression of the self—even if it was forced, even if the product was stolen.[82]

People could move faster and faster. They could get up early and sneak out to the fields and pick by moonlight to meet their unusually high quotas, like a Georgia woman named Nancy.[83] But as time went on, more and more enslaved people had to figure out how to use each hand equally. As "stints" increased, many were only able to meet their picking quotas by learning how to unhook their nondominant hand from the tethers of bodily asymmetry and brain architecture founded in human anatomy and genetics and built on over the course of a lifetime. The whipping-machine continually demanded that they come up with ways to pick more cotton: by watching or talking to others and learning from their speed, by creating new efficiencies that would shorten the path of hand from plant to sack and back again in both space and time. And above all, by shutting down some pathways in the brain so that the body could pick with the left hand as well as the right, and thus dance like a Patsey—becoming, for a time, the disembodied "hands" of enslavers' fantastic language.

"Some hands can't get the sleight of it," said a white man who had tried to whip a young woman to "make her a hand at cotton-picking." "Sleight" means "left," but also craft, cunning, a special knack or trick. There is something left-handed about the word, something distinct from right-handed force. We think of sleight of hand as something employed by pickpockets, magicians, three-card monte dealers. Sleight is an art of resistance, play against right-handed power. This sleight of hands was different: it was required, extracted by power that compelled, exposed, and commodified hidden, individual capacities. Torture—the whipping-machine as a whole, in fact—was cunning. In its design was embedded a secret as consequential as the secrets of capital that Marx believed he exposed when he peered beneath the veil of the working day. The technology of torture required the use of a creativity that would generate new tricks and knacks, but not for the service of the trickster him- or herself. It then measured left-handed power, the safeguard for millennia of the poor and the less powerful against the domination of the great. And then it turned the sleight and creativity of left-handed power against the self, forcing from enslaved hands skillful but endless and depersonalizing labor.[84]

For those who succeeded in developing the sleight of hands did so by achieving a kind of detachment from their own consciousness. Patsey was impressive as she moved, even beautiful—that sense drips out of Northup's description of her performance between the rows—but her achievement was also a thing of horror. She had become not just a person forced to toil in a hot field but one of the "hands" sketched in words written down on paper by men sitting in cool dark offices. Sometimes, especially once they achieved freedom, the formerly enslaved talked about how this process felt. The repetitiveness, and above all the demand that one become a different person—or not even a whole person, but a hand—or be tortured—these things made cotton picking horrible. It was "irksome," "fatiguing"; "I was never thoroughly reconciled to it." It never felt like one's own work or one's own body, because it wasn't: not in the same way that felling trees or threshing wheat or topping tobacco was one's work, however stolen. The psychological torment of alienating one's own hands from the old integuments that tied them to one part of the mind or another and rewiring them in different ways for someone else took a tremendous and painful effort. This effort, and the torture that drove it, left their mark on the body, but perhaps even more indelibly on the mind. As late as the 1930s an elderly woman named Adeline Hodges, who had learned to pick cotton in Alabama in the 1850s, couldn't stand to watch clerks weighing her food at the grocery store "cause I remembers so well that each day that the slaves was given a certain number of pounds to pick. When weighing up time come and you didn't have the number of pounds set aside, you may be sure that you was going to be whipped."[85] Only something more violent than the forced self-rewiring of the body could have carried hands through the deepest, thickest layers of the cotton bottleneck, and she was still traumatized from that torture a lifetime later.

Thus, another way to tell the story of how the modern world came to pass is to tell it as one in which left-handed power was exposed, commandeered, turned against its possessors and built into something much different. At the heart of that process are the experiences, day after day, of one million people like Charles Ball. The work of hands and enslaved people's creative, exploited minds, a work driven by the measured creaking of the whipping-machine, seems the opposite of what is modern, industrial, technological. Yet the data reveal that those in the cotton fields were not only absolutely necessary to the developments on the factory floor but in dynamic efficiency were their equals. And it will not take us long to draw links between the whipping-machine— and the entrepreneurial history of slavery's expansion in the nineteenth-century United States in general—and our own world.[86] These are links of resonance, and even of direct causation. This isn't just Charles Ball's story. We are part of it as well.

CHAPTER 2

Slavery's Scientific Management

Masters and Managers

CAITLIN ROSENTHAL

On Monday, October 10, 1842—"A beautiful day" on Pleasant Hill Plantation in Amite County, Mississippi—Eli J. Capell noted the precise amount
of cotton picked by each of his fifteen slaves. Every hand, including the enslaved overseer, Tone, picked at least 100 pounds, and Capell's top pickers,
Terry, Isaac, and Peter, exceeded 200 pounds apiece. All told, they had brought
in 2,545 pounds, "the best ever done here in one day."[1] Capell knew that the
day was remarkable because he was in the habit of keeping diligent records.
He kept a yearly plantation journal that tracked his output, and his records
show that over the coming decades, he would repeat the achievement of that
October day many times. As he increased the size of his workforce and improved his management methods, he pushed the daily picking totals ever
higher.

Capell and other "book farmers" of the American South paid close attention to how efficiently enslaved men and women picked cotton, frequently
experimenting with new methods for maximizing output. They recorded and
analyzed data diligently and precisely, keeping accounts and comparing them
year after year. Their efforts—as well as those of planters growing sugar,
rice, wheat, and other staples—were remarkably sophisticated for their time.
Planters paid more attention to labor productivity than many northern manufacturers, foreshadowing the rise of scientific management in the 1880s and
beyond. They excelled in determining the most labor their slaves could do,
and in pushing them to attain that maximum.

Most historians of management have overlooked these skilled calculations, beginning their research instead in the factories of England and New England. In his classic study of American business, Alfred Chandler described plantations as a fundamentally ancient form of production. Acknowledging that the plantation overseer was the "first salaried manager in the country," he nonetheless concluded that slave plantations were more like feudal estates than modern factories.[2] The meticulously kept ledgers and careful calculations of the most sophisticated planters complicate this view, which Bill Cooke has called the "denial" of slavery in management studies.[3] Historians are currently working to integrate the South more fully into the story of American capitalism. New research describes a vigorous, violent system where innovation and brutality went hand in hand.[4]

Understanding the connection between slavery and business innovation is the subject of this chapter. Sophisticated accounting techniques were not incidental to plantation slavery: the power of masters gave them power as managers. Instead of attracting and retaining labor, planters acquired it and accelerated it, aided by the threat of violence. They subjected enslaved men and women to experiments, allocating and reallocating labor from task to task, planning meals and lodging, and measuring and monitoring productivity and reproductivity. To be sure, slaves resisted planters' efforts, but a combination of calculation and control constrained their attempts. Slavery became a laboratory for the use of accounting because neat columns of numbers more closely matched the reality of life on plantations than in many other early American enterprises.

Put differently, the commoditization and capitalization of lives made it easier to put numbers to work. Innovation was, in a sense, a by-product of bondage. I begin by describing accounting practices, particularly Thomas Affleck's popular plantation record books. From here I explore the ways planters used accounting to increase their profits, first by pushing up the pace of work, next by standardizing labor using units such as the "prime hand," and finally by optimizing their investments in human capital.

Plantation Accounts

Eli Capell took over the management of Pleasant Hill Plantation after the death of his father, Littleton Capell, in the 1830s. Under his direction the plantation thrived, expanding from a small farm of six quarter-sections into a plantation of 2,500 acres worked by a force of eighty slaves.[5] Capell recorded his progress in a series of detailed journals stretching from 1842 to 1867. In the earliest of these records, he experimented with a variety of differently for-matted diaries and blank books, but none suited his needs. On days when he attempted to record every slave's individual picking, his calculations spilled into the margins.[6] In 1850, he remedied the problem by adopting Affleck's pre-printed *Plantation Record and Account Book*. Affleck's journal was an all-in-one account book designed to facilitate plantation management, and among an array of different forms it included specially lined forms for recording cot-ton picking.[7]

Thomas Affleck worked as a planter and gardener in the small town of Washington, Mississippi, about fifty miles west of Capell's plantation in Amite County. Born and educated in Scotland, he had migrated to the United States in 1832, moving from the East Coast to Ohio before relocating to Mississippi, where he began to plant cotton. His background combined experience in fi-nance, scientific agriculture, and publishing. In Edinburgh, he had worked as a bookkeeper for the Bank of Scotland, and he boasted in his correspondence that the experience had accustomed him "to the strictest business habits."[8]

When he arrived in Mississippi, Affleck found that although some of his neighbors "had kept regular plantation books for many years," their records varied dramatically, lacking the uniformity and regularity that would enable comparisons across plantations. In response, Affleck "prepared 2 books with the pen," giving one to each of his overseers.[9] After testing the journal and revising it, he published his first plantation account book.[10] Affleck's *Planta-tion Record and Account Book* provided a preprinted, all-in-one system for planters wishing to improve their accounting practices. As his advertisements boasted, his journal combined "Day Book, Journal, Stock Book, Ledger and Daily Record" all in "one large folio volume."[11] In all, the cotton journals in-cluded fifteen different forms, labeled A through O (Table 2.1), and the sugar journals included twenty-one forms, labeled A through U. Each form ad-dressed a different aspect of plantation production. Affleck instructed plant-ers to fill in some of the forms every day, including the record of activities and the record of cotton picked. Other pages in the journal, including the inventories of tools, supplies, and the slaves themselves, were completed only quarterly or annually.[12]

The many forms in Affleck's journal composed an interlocking system that enabled planters to make sophisticated comparisons and calculations.

Table 2.1. Forms in Thomas Affleck's *Plantation Record and Account Book*

Form	Title	Frequency completed
A	Daily Record of Passing Events	Daily
B	Inventory of Stock and Implements	Quarterly (monthly in 1st ed.)
C	Record of Cotton Picked	Daily from late July, weekly totals
D	List of Articles Given Out to the Negroes	As distributed
E	Overseer's Record of Supplies Delivered to Him	As received
F	List of Births and Deaths	As needed
G	Check on the Physician's Account	As needed
H	Weights of Cotton by Bale	At weighing and sale
I	Inventory of Negroes	Beginning and end of the year
J	Planter's Annual Record of Stock	Beginning and end of the year
K	Planter's Annual Record of Tools	Beginning and end of the year
L	Statement of the Several Products of the Plantation	Yearly
M	Statement of the Sale of Cotton	As sold
N	Condensed Account of the Expenses of the Plantation	Yearly
O	Planter's Annual Balance Sheet	Yearly

Several forms offered different ways to calculate the same total, providing opportunities to cross-check information. For example, on form H, the overseer recorded the weight of every bale of cotton, the total of which should match the total on form M, where the owner weighed the bales as they were sold. These checks helped planters monitor the honesty of the overseer and of the slaves. The journal culminated in form O, an end-of-year balance sheet on which planters could calculate their yearly profits. This balance sheet ensured that every cost and revenue was tallied up, drawing inputs from five different forms elsewhere in the book. Capital costs, including those for land, slaves, tools, and stock, were charged at a recommended interest rate of 6 percent, and any change in the value of capital was methodically recorded. By consulting the balance sheet and comparing it with prior years, planters could assess their overall profitability and identify the cause of their success or failure: improvements made to their property, sales of cotton, or changes in the value of slaves. Planters and overseers very rarely completed all of these forms; more often they selected what they found most useful and ignored the rest.[13]

Despite their complexity, the journals required very little specialized knowledge of bookkeeping. As Affleck explained in an 1860 advertisement, "The plan of the book is so simple, and yet complete, that any man who can write at all legibly, whether or not he has any knowledge of the principles and practice of book-keeping, is capable of making his entries correctly." The detailed instructions and fill-in-the-blanks balance sheet meant that only basic addition and subtraction were required to strike a "true balance" and to determine "whether the year's labors have resulted in profit or loss."[14] This relative simplicity made Affleck's journals ideal for monitoring overseers, who rarely had any skill in bookkeeping. When James Henry Hammond complained to Affleck that he had "no hope of ever getting an overseer who will or can keep such a book" in South Carolina, Affleck wrote that in Mississippi there were many such men. He recommended making the completion of the books a stipulation of their contracts, giving newly hired overseers little choice in the matter.[15] Affleck hoped that his forms would spare the "non-resident Planter" "much vexation and loss" and the overseer "undeserved blame."[16]

Affleck published his journal in six different versions, specialized by crop and plantation size (Figure 2.1).[17] Eli Capell originally used Affleck's smallest book, designed for cotton plantations with forty or fewer slaves, but by the late 1850s his operations had outgrown this volume, and he purchased the *Cotton Plantation Record and Account Book No. 2*, for plantations with up to eighty hands.[18] Affleck offered an even larger edition, with space to record the work of as many as 120 working hands, and by 1860 he had published a fourth edition, for up to 160 working hands. He also offered two volumes for sugar plantations with 80 and 120 working hands. Because many enslaved men and women were too young or infirm to labor in the fields, these largest books targeted elite planters whose holdings could reach as high as 200 or even 300 total slaves. The smallest journal sold for $2.00, and the prices of the larger editions increased in increments of $0.50. These prices were higher than those for other blank books but were nonetheless affordable, relative to the total investment involved in operating a large plantation.[19]

Affleck's journals appear to have sold well, remaining in print until the Civil War and running to eight editions.[20] Although it is difficult to verify their circulation, Affleck claimed annual sales of 2,000 and believed that he could reach 5,000 if production were managed efficiently.[21] He applied the same entrepreneurial calculations to his publishing business that he instructed planters to use with their crops. In a letter to a potential partner, he described his business plan in great detail:

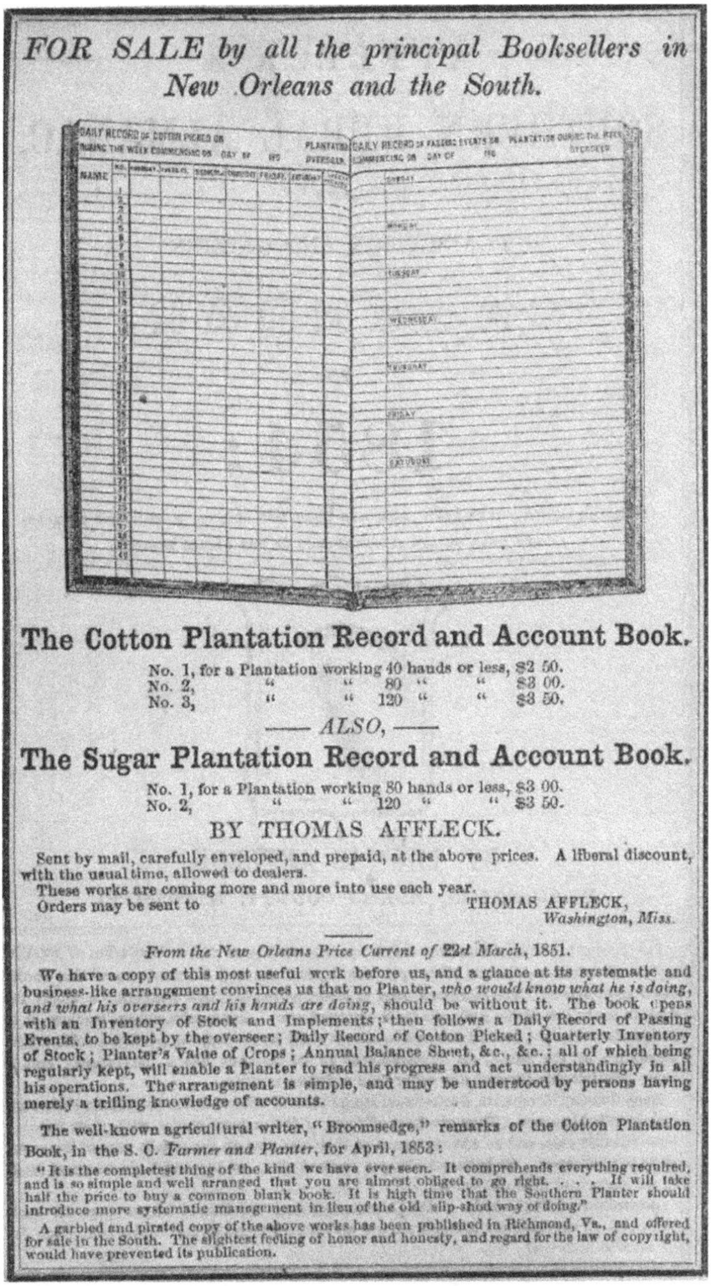

FOR SALE by all the principal Booksellers in New Orleans and the South.

The Cotton Plantation Record and Account Book.

No. 1, for a Plantation working 40 hands or less, $2 50.
No. 2, " " 80 " " $3 00.
No. 3, " " 120 " " $3 50.

— *ALSO,* —

The Sugar Plantation Record and Account Book.

No. 1, for a Plantation working 80 hands or less, $3 00.
No. 2, " " 120 " " $3 50.

BY THOMAS AFFLECK.

Sent by mail, carefully enveloped, and prepaid, at the above prices. A liberal discount, with the usual time, allowed to dealers.

These works are coming more and more into use each year.

Orders may be sent to THOMAS AFFLECK, *Washington, Miss.*

From the New Orleans Price Current of 22d March, 1851.

We have a copy of this most useful work before us, and a glance at its systematic and business-like arrangement convinces us that no Planter, *who would know what he is doing, and what his overseers and his hands are doing*, should be without it. The book opens with an Inventory of Stock and Implements; then follows a Daily Record of Passing Events, to be kept by the overseer; Daily Record of Cotton Picked; Quarterly Inventory of Stock; Planter's Value of Crops; Annual Balance Sheet, &c., &c.; all of which being regularly kept, will enable a Planter to read his progress and act understandingly in all his operations. The arrangement is simple, and may be understood by persons having merely a trifling knowledge of accounts.

The well-known agricultural writer, "Broomsedge," remarks of the Cotton Plantation Book, in the S. C. *Farmer and Planter*, for April, 1853:

"It is the completest thing of the kind we have ever seen. It comprehends everything required, and is so simple and well arranged that you are almost obliged to go right. . . . It will take half the price to buy a common blank book. It is high time that the Southern Planter should introduce more systematic management in lieu of the old slip-shod way of doing."

A garbled and pirated copy of the above works has been published in Richmond, Va., and offered for sale in the South. The slightest feeling of honor and honesty, and regard for the law of copyright, would have prevented its publication.

Figure 2.1. Advertisement for Thomas Affleck's account books. Thomas Affleck Papers, MSS 3, 1263, Louisiana and Lower Mississippi Valley Collections, Louisiana State University Libraries, Baton Rouge. Courtesy of Special Collections, LSU Libraries, Louisiana State University.

The Acct. books can be got out at 60c to 70c p copy—say an average of 75c. Weld writes me he has got over $650 of advertisements for this coming edition. I feel confident that 5,000 copies of all the editions, Sugar & Cotton can be sold per annum, at an average retail price of $3.00, Netting $2.00, counting freight &c. &c. & losses. $500 can be had for adverts., reducing the cost of the books 10c. p copy. I am keeping a long way within bounds. Say 5,000 copies net $1.35 each = $6,750.[22]

In practice, Affleck appears to have had difficulty realizing his projections, not because of lack of demand but because of difficulty finding and maintaining a dependable printer. Over the run of the journal, Affleck employed several printers, at least one of whom "absquatulated," leaving Affleck with neither the funds nor the volumes for several months.[23]

Competitors peddled systems similar to Affleck's, taking advantage of the popularity of his accounting system. Affleck railed against these texts, considering them inferior substitutes for his own. In 1854 he requested a copy of one "bastard acct. book" from bookseller B. M. Norman.[24] A year later, when a friend alerted him to a copycat book being sold by a "Mr. Bland," he exclaimed in reply that "such plagiarism" was "quite common," complaining of "an almost literal reprint of my books—but with the part of Hamlet omitted! Most shabbily gotten up & some of the most important records left out."[25]

Still, improving planters were a minority among slaveholders. In 1860, more than 20,000 cotton planters owned more than thirty slaves. Even if Affleck's most hyperbolic sales figures were correct, he would not have reached more than a quarter of all larger planters. Still, they were a vocal, highly articulate minority that evangelized their practices through fairs, newspapers, and the southern agricultural press.[26] Large planters had disproportionate influence and produced disproportionate amounts of cotton. Only a small proportion of planters had holdings sufficient to warrant using one of Affleck's books. However, these large plantations produced the vast majority of all cotton.[27]

Though Thomas Affleck's were the most popular plantation blanks, they were not the first. A number of preprinted books preceded Affleck's, and the variety of these texts suggests that the formatted ledger was a well-developed genre of job printing in the South. By the time he corresponded with Affleck, James Henry Hammond had already experimented with several different books on his Sugar Bluff Plantation.[28] One of the books used by Hammond appears to have circulated widely. By 1840, Andrew Flynn of Mississippi was using an identical or nearly identical book. These ledgers contained two varieties of printed pages: first, an up-front inventory of animals and equipment, and second, a series of pages listing activity by day of the month.[29] In 1835 a Florida planter named Farquhar Macrae wrote to Edmund Ruffin's *Farmer's Register* to recommend that planters adopt a new system of bookkeeping. Macrae sent Ruffin an essay on accounting, along with a diagram of his proposed system. The forms began with a section for documenting the daily activities of the workforce and also provided space for recording any increase or decrease in the number of slaves and cattle, the planting of fields, the harvest of various crops, and a number of other metrics. Macrae proposed to sell bound volumes of these forms, but he may or may not have attempted the venture.[30]

Most surviving formatted ledgers for North American plantations date from after 1830, but scattered documents survive from significantly earlier. Earlier plantation texts circulated in the British West Indies, particularly in Jamaica, Barbados, and British Guiana, where preformatted ledgers were distributed and completed as early as the 1780s.[31] In contrast to the North, where most accounts were kept in custom-lined ledgers with little formatting, prelined plantation books enabled a remarkable level of complexity and standardization. Some prelined books were available for northern factories; however, they differed in both complexity and focus from manuals like Affleck's. For example, a pocket-sized *Workman's Account Book*, copyrighted in the late 1820s, was designed to help employers keep track of wages. It consisted of a single table reprinted on each of the book's twenty-four pages, and appears to have been used primarily for recording incidental labor in quarter- or half-day increments.[32] Unlike picking records, books like this did not venture into the terrain of productivity. A few preprinted ledgers, like Scotsman David Young's *Farmer's Account-Book* of 1788, provided space for tracking farm produce, sales, and the weather, but ignored labor.[33] Northern entrepreneurs wanting to keep more detailed payroll and wage records would have needed to have them custom-lined by a stationer. Among books available at the time, only plantation journals contained complete systems designed to help capitalists manage labor and monitor their profits.[34]

Putting Numbers to Work

Tracking information was only the first step for planters. They also put their data to work, analyzing it to increase the productivity of their operations.

Relentlessly efficient overseers distinguished themselves by determining the maximum sustainable pace of labor and driving slaves to achieve that maximum. Virginia wheat planter Pleasant Suit urged his overseers to use "every means" in their power to understand "what is a day's work for a hand in every variety of plantation business." Suit recommended an array of strategies, including "calculation, trials, and inquiries of experienced persons."[35]

Among the details meticulously recorded and analyzed by planters, the most important tracked slaves' daily cotton picking. In Affleck's books, form C, the record of cotton picked, tracked the pounds of cotton each slave picked every day (Figure 2.2).[36] The first column on form C noted the names of each slave, and to the right of this list were columns for each day of the week, Monday through Saturday. These columns could be tallied to determine the daily picking, which could be summed for a weekly total. In 1854, Affleck added a space for a running total, so that the sum from the prior page could be brought forward to find the total picking thus far in the year.[37] Completing form C required the overseer or planter to weigh and record hundreds of data points over the course of a week, and many thousands over the course of a season.

After emancipation, the minister and former slave Charles Thompson recollected the basic process of picking, weighing, and accounting for cotton. As he wrote, "each picker had a 'stint' or daily task to perform; that is, each of them was required to pick so many pounds of cotton." Thompson, high up in the internal hierarchy of the plantation's enslaved workforce, was "placed over the hands as 'boss' and cotton-weigher." To monitor the picking of the slaves under him, Thompson weighed their picking "three times each day." In this way, throughout the day, the slaves, armed with knowledge of their progress, could be induced to strive toward their assigned task. Ironically, Thompson, who could add and write, was forced to conceal his numerical abilities because of laws against educating slaves. But this did not stop his owner from benefiting from his numeracy: he kept "the weights of each hand separate and correctly in my mind" and reported them to the overseer each night.[38]

Some planters used incentives to accelerate picking, relying on the use of precise calculation. After his escape from slavery, Henry Bibb described the use of contests to speed up the pace of labor. As he explained, instead of extorting picking from their slaves "by the lash," some planters would "deceive them by giving small prizes." An overseer began by "dividing the hands off in three classes" by skill, and "offering a prize to the one who will pick out the most cotton in each of the classes." By this means, the slaves of every level increased their pace in pursuit of the prizes. After repeating such challenges

DAILY RECORD OF COTTON PICKED on *71* Plantation,
during the week commencing on the *15* day of *October* ~~185~~ *1860*

Overseer.

NAME.	No.	Monday. 15	Tuesday. 16	Wednesday. 17	Thursday. 18	Friday. 19	Saturday. 20 Bro't Forward.	Week's Picking.
Leah	41	45	40	30	50	35	40	240
Old Maria	42	60	65	75	55	70	65	340
Maria Anderson	43	95	Sick	Sick	Sick	Sick		95
Big Amanda	44	175	215	220	215	235	235	1295
Celeste	45	75	100	50	Sick	Sick	Sick	225
Big Sarah	46	135	150	160	160	160	180	945
Lit Amanda	47	180	190	195	200	185	185	1130
Eliza Ann	48	140	160	155	155	140	155	925
Patsy Ann	49	135	155	165	150	Sun	Sun	605
Betty Nelson	50	100	Child	Born		Born		100
C Caroline	51	120	150	150	140	140	145	845
Sarah	52	105	115	145	135	140	155	795
Susan	53	35	45	50	70	85	85	400
Lit Clarissa	54	155	170	175	165	190	180	1035
Lit Patsy	55	135	145	155	150	170	170	925
Lit Sarah	56	145	145	135	140	155	155	875
	57	3470	3755	3840	3450	3550	3155	
	58	2580	3050	3335	2530	2505	2855	
	59	6450	6875	7225	6510	6485	6050	
	60	6875						
	61	225						
		6510						
		6485						
		6050						
	62	39595						
	63				246310 lbs up to Oct 21			
	64				39595			
					280,905			
	65							
	66							
	67							
	68							
	69							
	70							
	71							
	72							
	73							
	74							
	75							
	76							
	77							
	78							
	79							
	80							

C2–D

Amount previously picked,

Figure 2.2. Form C, "Record of Cotton Picked." Eustatia Plantation Account Book (1861). Ohio Historical Society, Columbus. Courtesy of the Ohio History Connection (vol. 649).

several times and "weighing what cotton they pick every night," the overseer could tell "just how much every hand can pick." After giving the small reward to the winners, he then required them to "pick just as much afterward" or be "flogged."[39]

The most complex incentive systems stretched over the course of the year. In 1851, a Mississippi planter who owned forty-nine slaves explained his scheme. As he wrote, "I pay them money at the end of the year. . . . The amount given to all depends on the crop and the price; the amount to each one upon his good behavior, his activity, obedience and efficiency during the year." He allocated the payment by class: "The negro who has discharged all his duties through the year most faithfully is put in the first class. As many as deserve it are put there and all get the largest and same amount of Money. The amount paid them is lessened as they fall into lower classes." Slaves could draw on their accounts throughout the year, and the planter furnished "any extra clothing that any of them may want," charging their accounts, and "at pay day, as they call it, it is brought up against them."[40]

Recordkeeping could make punishment just as calculating as payment. Although some book farmers advocated more humane treatment, others translated data into violence. They meted out lashes in precise relation to picking, whipping slaves as many strokes as the number of pounds they fell short of their daily or weekly tasks. In the 1840s, Henry Watson described a state of almost constant terror on the plantation where he labored. As Watson wrote, "each individual having a stated number of pounds of cotton to pick, the deficit of which was made up by as many lashes being applied to the poor slave's back."[41] John Brown described the same cruel system: "For every pound that is found short of the task, the punishment is one stroke of the bull-whip." Though Brown himself "never got flogged for short weight," many others did, "and dreadful was the punishment they received."[42]

Even when slaves avoided punishment, the weighing of cotton could be harrowing. Solomon Northup's 1855 slave narrative described the fear that motivated him to accelerate his work. As Northup wrote, "a slave never approaches the gin-house with his basket of cotton but with fear. If it falls short in weight—if he has not performed the full task appointed him, he knows that he must suffer." But the cost of success was high. As Northup reflected, if "he has exceeded it by ten or twenty pounds, in all probability his master will measure the next day's task accordingly. So, whether he has too little or too much, his approach to the gin-house is always with fear and trembling."[43] John Brown also described how his task was pushed progressively upward from

100 pounds per week to 160 pounds. On the plantation where he labored, the rule for a new picker was "a hundred pounds for each hand," but on the first day, he "picked five pounds over this quantity." Much to his "sorrow," Brown found that because he had "picked so well at first, more was exacted of me, and if I flagged a minute, the whip was liberally applied to keep me up to the mark." By constant driving, the overseer gradually pushed Brown's task higher until he "at last got to pick a hundred and sixty pounds a day."[44]

Enslaved men and women recognized the high stakes of tactics designed to reveal their maximum picking rates. Many saw prizes and payments for what they often were—a temporary ruse that masters could discontinue once they knew what work could be performed. And they responded with subtle modes of resistance. Frederick Law Olmsted described enslaved men's and women's attempts to slow down plantation speedups in *The Cotton Kingdom*. As he explained, slaves "very frequently cannot be made to do their master's will." They did not "directly refuse" to obey orders but rebelled more subtly, undertaking their tasks "in such a way that the desired result is sure not to be accomplished." Olmsted labeled this behavior "sogering," a term he had defined approximately a decade earlier when describing the slow pace of work on a packet ship in England. Sogering, he wrote, is "pretending to work, and accomplishing as little as possible." The management scholar Bill Cooke has traced sogering to the same root as Frederick Winslow Taylor's "soldiering," also meaning to shirk, or to pretend to work in order to obscure one's true ability.[45]

Planters used accounting and measurement to uncover slaves' resistance. Israel Campbell, a slave who struggled repeatedly to meet his task, described hiding "a good sized melon" in his basket before it was weighed. The possibility of discovery terrified him, but he knew that otherwise "a whipping was sure." At first, Campbell thought himself "pretty smart to play such a trick . . . but a day of reckoning was to come." Before the cotton was sold, "it had to be ginned. . . . As they always put down the amount picked, allowing so much for waste, they could calculate very nearly the amount it ought to make." Comparing these weights revealed a shortfall, and though the overseer never implicated Campbell, he could not repeat the trick.[46]

Planters used incentive schemes to hold all accountable for such deceptions. In 1842, a planter and minister from Virginia described a particularly complex scheme that he used to enforce slaves' honesty. Every year, he gave "each laboring hand a barrel of corn, or its equivalent in money," to be settled at Christmas. If any theft or "depredation is committed, *no matter by whom,* my negroes are responsible for it, and double its value is deducted from the Christmas present." However, if "the thief is given up . . . the whole responsibility rests on him." Thus, he explained, "a few barrels of corn are made the means of saving my property to perhaps ten times the amount the whole year."[47] This scheme resembled the fidelity funds that companies like the Singer sewing machine corporation would adopt to prevent embezzlement in the coming decades.[48]

The many surviving account books from southern plantations suggest that by the early to mid-nineteenth century, sophisticated accounting practices were relatively widespread. Amid the destruction of the Civil War, it is remarkable how many volumes were preserved. And these records—typically the most formal elements of plantation accounting—only scratch the surface of the ways in which numbers were used on plantations. Beyond bound books, there would have been loose paper notations, and still more impermanent slates that were filled and erased daily. Only traces of these more informal technologies are visible in account books. In September 1852, the column for Monday, September 13, has no data, reading instead "To days picking was Rubbed off the Slate."[49] In several narratives, enslaved authors recall overseers setting down the weights of cotton on slates. Like progress reports tacked to the walls of modern corporations, these constant notations made the data of plantation operations daily visible.[50]

Sophisticated management practices paid large dividends for planters. In recent work, the economists Alan Olmstead and Paul Rhode have analyzed cotton-picking records—many of them Affleck's—to show the tremendous increase in productivity during the sixty years preceding the Civil War. Between 1801 and 1860, the average amount of cotton picked per slave per day increased about fourfold, or 2.3 percent per year. Olmstead and Rhode show that much of this gain results from the adoption of new strains of cotton. The historian Edward Baptist rejects this explanation, placing violence at the center of the picture. And Walter Johnson's recent *River of Dark Dreams* emphasizes both new varieties of cotton and violence.[51] Plantation account books show how these multiple causes operated in connection with each other. In a sense, accounting practices knit innovation and violence together. New strains of cotton resulted in higher yields in part because planters could calculate and enforce new picking targets.[52]

Accounting became a broader language that helped planters reap productivity gains from all kinds of other sources. Thomas Affleck himself was not just an accountant, he was also a nurseryman, and he would have recognized that keeping detailed accounts helped him learn from his agricultural experiments. Profit calculations helped planters quantify and compare the benefits of new types of soil, manure, and seed. Balance sheets enabled them to sift through the boosterism of seed peddlers and decide when to purchase new products and adopt new practices. Similarly, accounting helped planters recalibrate their benchmarks after adopting new innovations. When planters adopted easier-to-pick strains of Mexican cotton, daily picking records would have enabled them to set new targets, thereby extracting higher output from their slaves. The language of accounts facilitated the implementation and dissemination of other innovations.[53]

When he first published his account book, Affleck touted both its benefits for individual planters and the salutary influences he expected them to have on agriculture across the South. As he exclaimed to Hammond in a letter recommending the books, "Think of the advantage to both planters & overseers, of even 1,000 books written from day-to-day experience, scattered over the country!"[54] Such books, kept in a standardized format, would enable precise comparisons, turning the full community of southern book farmers into a vast laboratory for agricultural improvement.

Prime Hands

Sharing and comparing data required the adoption of standardized metrics. In the 1850s, railroads across the nation would begin to develop comparable measures of productivity, such as the cost per ton-mile. Their innovations have been heralded as important milestones in the coming of modern management.[55] Like railroad superintendents, early nineteenth-century planters devised a unit of analysis that enabled comparisons across the infinite diversity of the men and women they enslaved.

A "prime field hand" was an enslaved man or woman whose productivity was among the maximum that could be expected from a single individual. All other slaves were measured against this ideal, their value denominated in fractions of a hand. When he prepared an 1841 slave list for planters Edward Frost and Thomas Horry, overseer N. Thomas first listed the plantation's forty full hands. Then he went on to name fifty-eight "hands that were not full," labeling their value in quarter hand increments. He rated Affa at three quarters of a hand, Sam the carpenter at half of a hand, and "Cripple Susey" at zero.[56] In his various accounts of southern life, Frederick Law Olmsted described similar practices on several plantations. On one, "there were 135 slaves, big and little, of which 67 went to field regularly—equal, the overseer thought, to fully 60 prime hands." There were also a number of highly skilled hands, including a blacksmith, a carpenter, a wheelwright, and a nurse, who "would be worth more, if they were for sale, the overseer said, than the best field-hands."[57] A contributor to the *Southern Cultivator* wrote in with a comparison of profits from 1844 and 1845. The author, Alexander McDonald of Alabama, owned "13 hands, mostly boys and women," but for the purpose of analysis, these could be "counted at" only "10 good hands." He calculated that the value of these hands was $5,800 and added it to his other capital costs, charging the total sum at 8 percent interest.[58]

Planters' calculations rendered slaves not as individuals but as abstract, commoditized units of labor, many of which could be combined to make a whole. The number of hand-equivalents on a large plantation rarely exceeded half the number of enslaved men and women. On a rice plantation in North Carolina "the whole number of negroes" was "two hundred," reckoned "to be equal to about one hundred prime hands." By the overseer's assessment, this was "an unusual strength for that number of all classes."[59] However, a lower ratio of prime hands to total hands might not necessarily be a sign of weakness. Another planter, who described his "whole force" as having a "proportion . . . somewhat smaller than usual," explained that it was not the result of infirmity or weakness among his workers. Rather, "his women were uncommonly good breeders." He had "never heard of babies coming so fast as they did on his plantation."[60]

The "hand" was the basis for an array of calculations. In Issaquena County—north of Affleck and Capell, along the Mississippi River—overseer George R. Clark of Eustatia Plantation diligently completed one of Affleck's account books. Each week he wrote the names of each hand who went into the fields, and every day he recorded the cotton they brought back. He tallied up the daily picking, adding the days to find the weekly picking, and combining that total with the prior weeks' amounts to derive the running total for the season. After calculating this total, either Clark or the planter who employed him set aside his pen and picked up a pencil to analyze his data. Each week he divided the running total by the total number of pounds he believed a prime field hand could pick during a week. Over time, he tried 1,400 pounds, 1,300 pounds, and 1,350 pounds. The resulting quantity was the number of prime hand-weeks expended thus far in the picking of cotton.[61]

Planters shared their calculations in the southern agricultural press, using hand-equivalents to facilitate comparisons. Alexander McDonald, an Alabama planter, sent the *Southern Cultivator* an account of his profits from
1844 and 1845. He owned "13 hands, mostly boys and women," and for the
purposes of his analysis, these were "counted at" only "10 good hands." Mc-
Donald valued these hands at $5,800 and added it to his capital costs, charg-
ing the total sum at 8 percent interest.[62] A few years later, another contributor
tabulated the results of his efforts at growing cotton between 1830 and 1847.
He reported his results in three columns: yield of cotton per acre, average
price per pound, and net proceeds per hand.[63] From the "hand," planters also
developed other comparative metrics. For example, the "task-acre" was a unit of
land measure that varied according to what a prime hand could accomplish.[64]

Agricultural journals printed and reprinted data and essays from southern planters, circulating information throughout the South. At various times,
Eli Capell subscribed to the *American Agriculturist*, the *American Cotton
Planter*, the *Cultivator*, the *Soil of the South*, the *Southern Agriculturist*, the
Southern Cultivator, the *Horticulturist*, and the *Horticultural Review and Bo-
tanical Magazine*. He also took the *New Orleans Picayune*.[65] Affleck's alma-
nacs and account books sometimes advertised for these journals. One of the
cotton books listed an array of magazines, including eighteen agricultural jour-
nals, seven of which were published in the South.[66] In August 1857, *De Bow's
Review*, whose motto was "Commerce is King," published a description of
Texas based on Frederick Law Olmsted's travel writing. Though the essay argued at length against elements of Olmsted's abolition-inflected depiction, it
nonetheless found much worth repeating. Among the details reproduced from
Olmsted's account was a comparison of profits between "Cotton on a Large
Scale" and "Sheep on a Large Scale." In the pro forma calculations for the
cotton plantation, Olmsted listed all the investments necessary to run a plantation. Among these were fifty prime field hands, fifty half hands, and fifty
quarter hands.[67]

The language planters used to describe their efforts to improve labor productivity bears a striking resemblance to the late nineteenth-century language
of scientific management. In his 1911 classic, *The Principles of Scientific Management*, Frederick Winslow Taylor described the goals of his experiments in
labor productivity. As he wrote, "our endeavor was to learn what really constituted a full day's work for a first class man; the best day's work that a man
could properly do year in and year out and still thrive under."[68] More than

half a century earlier, the South Carolina planter Plowden C. J. Weston had described the fundamental maxim of good management in almost identical terms. As he instructed his overseers, *In nothing does a good manager so much excel a bad, as in being able to discern what a hand is capable of doing and in never attempting to make him do more.*[69]

The fundamental aim of scientific management was to discern and extract the maximum amount of labor from workers. This required managers and owners to think about men and women as inputs of production that could be adjusted and improved in the same manner as machines and trained and rewarded like animals learning new tricks. When Taylor described the ideal profile of a pig iron handler, he revealed this mind-set. Those who were "fit to handle pig iron as a regular occupation" should be "so stupid and so phlegmatic" that their mental capacity "more nearly resembles . . . the ox than any other type."[70] The circumstances of slavery lent themselves to a similar mode of thinking. Taylor's "first class men" were very much like the "prime hands" who labored in the cotton fields. Taylor and the "college men" whom he hired to follow them and study their motions thought of them as "first class" only in their ability to perform physical work.[71]

In exceptional cases, the level of observation planters applied to their slaves approached the time-and-motion studies of scientific management. One particularly striking contribution to the southern agricultural press came from a planter writing under the proto-Taylorist pseudonym "One Who Follows His Hands." In 1848, this unnamed planter wrote two essays titled "A Day's Work." The articles enumerated exactly how much work a prime field hand could complete across an array of tasks. He could plow twenty to twenty-four miles (with allowances for turning the plow and team), open furrows for sowing twelve acres of cotton, drop cotton seed across seven to ten acres, and haul out 600 to 800 yards, and three "good fellows" could "make a ditch 3 feet wide at top, 2 feet deep, and 2 wide at bottom, 220 yards long." The author continued in this vein, specifying what constituted "a day's work" across dozens of tasks. Throughout his experiments he claimed literally to follow his hands, requiring that every hand be closely observed, for "unless he is watched he will not do it."[72]

The essayist appears at first to be prone to exaggeration, and perhaps he was. Still, readers took him seriously enough to respond in detail and on his terms. One skeptical reply contributed by "A Voice from the Seaboard" responded by precisely analyzing his calculations. "Really, Mr. Editor," he wrote, "Let us take his example in ditching, under the most favorable circumstances.

He says—'Three good fellows, somewhat versed in spade &c. can make a ditch three feet wide at top, two feet deep, and two feet wide at bottom, 220 yards long in a day in old land.' Or 3,300 cubic feet, (being 1,100 cubic feet apiece.). . . . What sort of hands has he?"[73]

Planters' most sophisticated experiments extended beyond setting daily tasks to smoothing labor over the long term. Because planters controlled the activities of their slaves year-round, they developed methods for staggering labor requirements seasonally. The best-known example of seasonal management involved the planting of cotton and corn, the labor requirements of which were anticyclical, allowing planters to allocate time in the off-season to grow corn to feed their slaves (and their hogs, which in turn provided meat for the plantation).[74] George Washington proposed growing wheat of different varieties in order to stagger the harvest. This would have obviated hiring additional labor to assist his slaves. As he wrote in his diary, "if Wheat of different kinds are sowed so as to prevent the Harvest coming on at once, it is my opinion that hirelings of any kinds may be dispensed with."[75]

Planters also considered the impact of nutrition and medicine on productivity. On sugar plantations, centralized kitchens spared prime hands the need to cook during periods of peak labor. Cooking facilities also enabled overseers and planters to monitor slaves' diets during times when maximum effort was required.[76] They debated slaves' consumption in much the same way they considered the addition of marl or guano to southern soils, hypothesizing about what foods and beverages might expedite their slaves' labor. One writer to an agricultural periodical proposed serving coffee with lots of sugar during the winter months,[77] while another recommended refreshing slaves with a blend of water, ginger, and molasses as they toiled in the fields.[78] Thomas Affleck, posing as the expert in nutrition and reproduction as well as plantation accounting, even offered recommendations on how long mothers should be allowed to suckle their children.[79] Scientific agriculture shaped even the most intimate aspects of slaves' lives.

Human Capital

Perhaps the most remarkable element of plantation accounting can be found in planters' analysis of depreciation. Widely regarded by accounting historians as a landmark in the advancement of management practices, depreciation involves allocating capital costs over the useful lifetime of an asset. Thomas

Affleck included instructions for calculating depreciation from the first edition of his plantation journal. In his directions to overseers, Affleck specified that a balance sheet "is charge-able . . . with any depreciation in the value of the negroes, occasioned by overwork and improper management." He also explained that the balance sheet could be improved by appreciation of the slaves. For example, "should the number of children have greatly increased . . . the strength and usefulness of the old been sustained by kind treatment and care; the youngsters taught to be useful, and perhaps some of the men instructed in trades, and the women in house manufactures, the increased value of the entire force will form a handsome addition to the side of profits."[80]

To help planters assess the appreciation and depreciation of the men and women they owned, Thomas Affleck provided form I, which fed into the final balance sheet for the year. On form I, planters listed each slave by name, occupation, age, and current price (Figure 2.3). They could then tally up the price of every slave to determine the total value of their human capital. For example, in 1861 John H. Gibson used this form to value the slaves on Malvern Hill plantation. He priced the foreman, Hercules, age forty-eight, at $500; he valued Middleton, a prime field hand of twenty-six, at $1,500; and he rated young George Washington, a nine-month-old infant, at $150. Planters could repeat this process at the end of the year, adjusting the values of slaves to reflect any changes in their health, skills, or temperament, as well as variations in market prices. The increase or decrease in price over the course of the year became appreciation or depreciation on the final balance sheet.[81]

Despite Affleck's simple process for calculating depreciation, the management implications of appreciation and depreciation were far from simple. In 1850 Eli Capell completed every form in Affleck's journal, including the balance sheet. At the end of the year, his calculations showed a profit of approximately $10,000. But much of this profit reflected appreciation in the value of slaves and stock, not the sale of cotton. And with no intention to sell his slaves or tools, this surplus was deceptive. Perhaps Capell could have used it to secure a loan, but otherwise the profits he realized on paper did not match his cash in hand. As a result, the next year he used the book more selectively. Capell still recorded the value of the men and women he enslaved on form I, and he always completed form C, the record of cotton picked. But at the end of the year he did not return to form I to calculate the change in price of his human chattel (Figure 2.4). He cared about value of his human capital, but he focused more attention on what he could profit from in the shorter term: day-to-day productivity.[82]

THE PLANTER'S ANNUAL RECORD *of his Negroes upon* Pleasant Hill

Plantation, during the year 1850   E. J. Capell   Overseer.

MALES.				FEMALES.			
NAME.	Age.	Value at commencement of the year.	Value at end of the year.	NAME.	Age	Value at commencement of the year.	Value at end of the year.
John	70	$50 00	75 00	Hannah	60	100 00	125
Fone	49	1000 00	1250 00	Mary	34	800 00	900
Sandy	38	600 00	800 00	Fanny	23	800 00	900
Edmund	45	1000 00	1300 00	Rachel Sen	32	675 00	750
Dicy	40	700 00	950 00	Martha	27	675 00	700
Solomon	38	700 00	950 00	Celia	25	675 00	750
Peter		700 00	950 00	Rachel Jun	24	675 00	750
Isaac	30	700 00	950 00	Diana	31	600 00	700
Anthony	25	800 00	950 00	Chany	32	600 00	675
Scott	25	800 00	950 00	Lucy	28	600 00	750
George	20	750 00	1000 00	Let	28	550 00	650
Tim	37	800 00	950	Azalene	13	600 00	700
Dotson	20	700 00	900	Amanda	13	400 00	600
Bill	18	700 00	900	Sarah	9	350 00	450
William	24	1000 00	1200	Harriet	8	300 00	400
Charles	10	500 00	650	Bet	7	350 00	400
Henry	9	375 00	400	Hannah	7	350 00	450
Henderson	8	300 00	350	Maryan	7	275 00	300
Johnson	6	250 00	275	Ellen	6	200 00	250
Stephen	4	250 00	225	Louisa	5	175 00	200
Tom	5	250 00	275	Susan	4	200 00	250
Monroe	4	200 00	225	Melissa	3	100 00	125
Daniel	2	150 00	175	Matilda	5	200 00	225
Sim	2	150 00	175	Jinny	3	150 00	150
Aaron	3	175 00	200	Caroline	3	150 00	150
Jerry	1	75 00	100	Frances	2	100 00	125
		$9625 00	$9675 00	Laura	1	100 00	125
				Amarintha	1	75 00	100
				Saraan	6m	75 00	100
				Rose	6m	75 00	100
						$10975 00	$12850
				Ann			100
				Delia			100
							$13050

Figure 2.3. Form I, "Inventory of Negroes," 1850. Capell Family Papers, MSS 56, 257, 1751, et al., Louisiana and Lower Mississippi Valley Collections, Louisiana State University Libraries, Baton Rouge. Courtesy of Special Collections, LSU Libraries, Louisiana State University.

THE PLANTER'S ANNUAL RECORD *of his Negroes upon* Pleasant Hill
Plantation, *during the year* 185_1_   Jone   Overseer.

MALES				FEMALES			
NAME	Age	Value at commencement of the year.	Value at end of the year.	NAME	Age	Value at commencement of the year.	Value at end of the year.
John	71	50 00		Hannah	61	100 00	
Jone	50	1200 00		Mary	35	800 00	
Sandy	39	800 00		Rachel	33	750 00	
Edmund	34	1300 00		Diannah	32	750 00	
Jerry	41	900 00		Chany	33	675 00	
Solomon	39	900 00		Celia	26	800 00	
Peter		900 00		Lucy	29	800 00	
Isaac	31	900 00		Litt	29	650 00	
Anthony	26	950 00		Rach Junr	25	800 00	
Scott	26	950 00		Martha	28	750 00	
George	21	1000 00		Fanny	24	950 00	
Jim	28	950 00		Catharine	19	850 00	
Dotson	21	900 00		Azaline	14	750 00	
Bill	19	900 00		Amanda	14	600 00	
William	25	1100 00		Sarah	10	500 00	
Charles	11	700 00		Hannah	8	450 00	
Henry	10	450 00		Bett	8	450 00	
Henderson	9	350 00		Harriet	9	400 00	
Johnson	7	300 00		Maryan	8	300 00	
Stephen	5	250 00		Ellen	7	250 00	
Tom	6	300 00		Louisa	6	200 00	
Monroe	5	250 00		Susan	5	250 00	
Daniel	3	200 00		Melissa	4	125 00	
Jim	3	200 00		Matilda	6	225 00	
Aaron	4	200 00		Jinny	4	150 00	
Jerry	2	100 00		Caroline	4	150 00	
				Frances	3	125 00	
Hetty				Laura	2	125 00	
Joe				Amarintha	2	100 00	
				Sarahan	1	100 00	
				Rose	1	100 00	
				Ann	1	100 00	
				Delia	6mo	100 00	
				Priscilla	20	700 00	

Figure 2.4. Form I, "Inventory of Negroes," 1851. Capell Family Papers, MSS 56, 257, 1751, et al., Louisiana and Lower Mississippi Valley Collections, Louisiana State University Libraries, Baton Rouge. Courtesy of Special Collections, LSU Libraries, Louisiana State University.

Plantation accounting practices shaped slaveholders' practices on multiple time scales. Picking records influenced day-to-day activities, and outside of basic daybooks and ledgers these were the most common type of account kept by planters. By contrast, calculations of appreciation or depreciation of the enslaved (and the balance sheets these numbers fed into) influenced longer-term choices about capital investment. Thomas Jefferson described the appreciation of slaves as a "silent profit" of between 5 and 10 percent annually, and he advised friends to invest accordingly. He estimated that the enslaved population would increase at approximately 4 percent per year and that this increase, combined with rising prices, would result in a large profit beyond what was earned in the sale of commodities.[83] Likewise, Capell appears to have found it valuable to record the evolving value of his property intermittently, but not to use it in calculations of profit on an annual basis.[84]

Historians of accounting have given a number of explanations for the emergence of depreciation as an accounting technique. Though an earlier generation of scholars dated the practice to the late nineteenth century, most now hold that the concept was understood in America by the early 1830s, when the State of Massachusetts required corporations to provide estimates of the value of real and personal corporate property. On issuing stock, corporations had to revalue this property. Thus, those with large investments in machinery (primarily textile mills) occasionally estimated depreciation. However, these calculations were not performed annually, nor did they regularly appear on balance sheets when proprietors bothered to compile them. Similarly, accounting textbooks did not usually mention depreciation until the late nineteenth century.[85] Affleck's instructions and the ways in which they were used by a wide array of planters reflect a remarkably high level of standardization and sophistication for the period.[86]

The search for precedents aside, what is most striking is the parallel logic that animated the adoption of depreciation on slave plantations and in northern industries. Historians most often connect the emergence of depreciation to investment in complex, long-lived assets, such as railroad cars and tracks. The high capital costs of these investments required managers to allocate costs over time in order to accurately calculate profits and set prices. Planters assessing the profitability of their operations saw slaves in similar terms. As human capital, slaves' value evolved over the course of their lifetimes, making them as important a source of profit or loss as the commodities they grew. Children's value increased as they approached adulthood, and the value of the elderly diminished with sickness and frailty. Most striking, women of childbearing age had not only productive potential but reproductive as well. Ownership over the entirety of slaves' productive potential—from day to day, season to season, year to year, and mother to child—made depreciation useful. That is, encountering slaves as expensive, complex, long-lived assets made owners aware of the complexity of measuring their value. Like railroad managers, planters began to speak in the language of depreciation.[87]

The valuation of slaves vividly displays their dual status as humans and as salable commodities that could be reduced to a price. On annual inventories like the one recommended by Affleck, planters and overseers only rarely valued their slaves at less than $50 or $100. Even infants and the very elderly were assigned some value. Occasionally, however, in preparation for sale, slaves were valued at $0 or below. A slave list prepared by Duncan Clinch in 1859 gives the prices of slaves sorted into "lots" of between two slaves and ten slaves—presumably from family groups. In lot no. 27, Katy is valued at −$100, her cost deducted from the value of Cato, Hagaar, Frank, Saturn, James, Margaret, and Will. In lot no. 44, Old Betty and Phillip are valued at −$50 each, their cost offset by the value of Betsy, Bella, and an unnamed infant.[88] In the language of the market, these slaves became less than worthless, the cost of their upkeep exceeding their value.

Losing Control

After emancipation, Eli Capell contracted with his former slaves to continue their work. At first, most remained on the plantation, laboring in freedom much as they had under slavery. But the regularity of Capell's precise operations soon gave way to disorder. In July 1865, Capell signed contracts with his slaves, and work proceeded as usual until almost the end of the year. After Christmas, however, the freedmen refused to resume work. Only at the end of January did he manage to sign contracts for 1866, and at the end of 1866, confusion erupted anew. On Christmas Day, the plantation remained "very quiet," but less than a week later there was "a great confusion in the country among the whites and blacks as regarding for next year." Capell, accustomed to almost complete control over the details of labor, felt "perfectly disgusted with free negroes." He described them as "roving all over the country . . . showing very little sense." After another week, there was still "nothing doing on my place, negroes very unsettled and won't say what they are going to do. I never saw such a state of things."[89]

Emancipation broke down the systematic processes that had enabled disciplined agricultural experimentation. Freedpeople might offer their labor for wages, but they did it on their own terms. Planters like Capell could no longer allocate and reallocate freedpeople's time from task to task, experimenting freely with their diet and lodging to maximize output and minimize expense. Even running experiments with new fertilizers and crop varieties could be stymied in an environment of labor uncertainty. Why devote resources to experimentation when hands might not be available to harvest the results? The relative simplicity of organizing labor under slavery had enabled planters to think complexly about an array of problems, sharing and comparing their results with others in near-identical circumstances. Experimentation became far more difficult when the design of experiments and the collection of data were complicated by the uncertainty of hiring and retaining suitable labor.

Account books provided planters with an opportunity to imagine, commodify, and organize the world around them. Thomas Affleck's accounts, for all their complexity, were also extraordinarily simple in many ways. Aside from the purchase of slaves and the final sale of cotton, almost none of the important decisions in running a plantation involved markets or contracts. Under the threat of violence, slaves allowed masters to direct and redirect their activities at will. To be sure, enslaved men and women had resisted discipline in myriad ways, but their inability to quit constrained the scope of their resistance. After emancipation, they could exercise their freedom, and planters like Affleck had to find new ways to organize labor. On the eve of the war, Affleck had relocated to Brenham, Texas, where he opened a nursery and established Glenblythe Plantation. In 1865 and 1866, frustrated by his loss of control, he joined in a scheme for "securing industrious laborers for Texas" from Scotland. In order to entice migration, Affleck and a group of other planters established an agency that offered loans for purchasing land and aid in finding work.[90]

Accounting for Control

By the standards of modern management accounting, typical plantation account books exceeded many northern ledgers in both precision and sophistication. Although the North advanced ahead of the South in general business education, its textbooks merely popularized techniques that had existed for hundreds of years. In contrast, southern blanks spread innovative, comprehensive accounting systems. Thomas Affleck's texts and others like them were remarkably precise and specialized, and they appear to have been effective in both ensuring the honesty of overseers and extracting maximum effort from slaves.

There are a number of plausible explanations for the sophistication of southern techniques. Most basically, a large number of cotton plantations conducted similar business and thus could benefit from similar kinds of records—what worked for one planter might also meet the needs of another. However, something more specific to slavery also spurred the development of plantation accounting. Slavery became a laboratory for the development of new types of accounting in part because the control drawn on paper more closely matched the reality of the plantation than that of other early American business enterprises. The power of planters over their slaves also gave them power as managers. The "control" of slavery contributed to the development of the metrics that would later be called "management controls."

The soft power of quantification complemented the driving force of the whip. Systematic accounting practices thrived on slave plantations not despite the chattel principle but because of it. Planters used their control to drive up the pace of labor, conduct experiments, distribute incentives, and mete out punishment. The incredible power of masters over their slaves transformed slaves into interchangeable inputs of production. This transformation was never complete: the complexity and humanity of individual lives constantly subverted full commodification. But slaves' tenacious resistance and subtle soldiering could only partially constrain their masters' control. Through accounting, human figures became figures on paper, and human beings appeared as no more than hands.

CHAPTER 3

An International Harvest

The Second Slavery, the Virginia-Brazil Connection, and the Development of the McCormick Reaper

DANIEL B. ROOD

A memorable image from one of America's most frequently rendered patriotic songs, "amber waves of grain" holds a special place in the nation's understanding of itself. The planting of the prairies after 1850, the story goes, benefited American citizens as well as the people of the world, ushering in modernity and providing a livelihood for countless impoverished European immigrants. As the labor-saving device that enabled the settlement and cultivation of millions of acres, the McCormick reaper plays a starring role in the story of freedom's dominion spreading west. Yet this most successful of automatic harvesters was invented on a slave plantation in Virginia. In the following pages, I suggest that we reimagine the McCormick reaper, this quintessentially American machine, as a Creole artifact, a tropical technology, and, more than anything, a product of Atlantic slavery. For the reaper is the product of counterintuitive connections between faraway places that shared a dedication to bondage: Richmond, Virginia, and Rio de Janeiro, Brazil.

In the thirty years before the Civil War, Brazil became the number one export market for the wheat flour of the United States. And no city in the nation sold as many barrels of flour to Brazil as Richmond. Of a total of about 2.6 million barrels of wheat flour exported by the United States annually in the mid-1850s, approximately 400,000 barrels went to South America from Richmond and Baltimore combined. This means that more than 15 percent of total U.S. flour exports went from the slave-exploiting zones of the Upper South to the slave society of southeastern Brazil. This single destination in turn dominated the balance sheets of Richmond milling firms. For the three-year period of 1858, 1859, and 1860, Richmond sent 87 percent of its total flour exports to South America.[1]

The sudden rise of the midwestern wheat-growing states in the antebellum decades encouraged this binodal trade pattern. While other traditional wheat producers, such as New York, Pennsylvania, and Ohio, saw their yields fall when canals and railroads began bringing millions of bushels of cheap western grain to eastern cities, Virginia was able to continue expanding its own wheat flour industry by intensifying already existing ties to its counterpart slave society in Brazil. Virginia traders were largely successful in this venture as a result of new patterns of Brazilian bread consumption and the type of product Virginians were able to supply.[2]

Rio's bakers preferred Virginia flour for a variety of reasons. The soft red winter wheat grown in Virginia, containing more gluten and less water than northern wheat varieties, was widely thought to be less vulnerable to rotting on the lengthy and humid trip over the equator. Moreover, being easier to grind than hard wheats, the bran of each grain did not fracture and speck the flour; southern flour came out of the mill looking especially white.[3] However, the bakers of southeastern Brazil went a step further than demanding flour made from southern wheat. Finding the flour of particular industrial mills such as Haxall-Crenshaw or Gallego to be finer, whiter, and more resistant to rot than the products of other southern U.S. cities or even of less well-known milling firms within Virginia itself, the urban bread-baking industry in southeastern Brazil showed clear brand preferences, consistently paying top dollar for the most expensive barrels of imported flour held in Rio's warehouses.

As vertically integrated firms, Richmond's well-known companies had the capital to maintain their own clipper ships for the Brazil voyages, to hire the most skilled millers, and to invest in the best automated drying machines, barrel-packing apparatus, and smut machines, which scraped the grains clean of mold or fungus before grinding. The city's millers were recognized throughout the Atlantic world as standard setters, their product the high-water mark of fine, consistent, and durable flour, especially fit for tropical climes.[4] The brand recognition these firms enjoyed in Brazil is one major reason for the atypical concentration of Richmond's milling industry. The selectivity of southeastern Brazilian bread makers, then, was one of the foundations for large-scale, centralized flour milling in Richmond, an industry whose firms were national leaders in the vertical integration and automation of grain processing. While their milling technologies and shipping facilities were surely important, sourcing well-cleaned, promptly delivered wheat from nearby farms was probably the pivotal factor ensuring their capture of the high end of Brazil's flour market. For this supply, millers turned to inland Virginia planters who had formerly ground their grains locally and shipped them coastward as flour.

The new Atlantic political economy linking slavery, mechanization, and middle-class consumption habits involved the transformation of daily production on the plantations of Virginia. The rise of a geographically centralized flour-milling industry in Richmond spelled doom for the thousands of small-time country gristmills scattered across the state while encouraging the intensification of wheat production in those same neighborhoods. An uneven geographic development in the state as a whole ensued. Wheat-growing zones tended toward a concentration of landholdings and slaveholding and away from diversified agricultural production for local consumption—in other words, large portions of Piedmont and Shenandoah Valley of Virginia shifted toward plantation societies as the industrial phases of production shifted to urban areas such as Richmond.[5]

Planters responding to the demand of Richmond's export mills led efforts to revitalize Atlantic seaboard agriculture through frequent experimentation with new techniques, new crop varieties, and new machines, as well as new ways of organizing and coercing laborers.[6] With five new railroad lines acting as commodity highways to the state capital, growing export markets for Virginia flour would encourage the widespread employment of home-grown agricultural technologies such as steam-driven threshing machines in parts of the state tributary to Richmond. More general improvements included the limitation of acreage, five-field rotation systems, marling, and the use of imported guano from South America. Such efforts paid off in increased yields of wheat per acre, from an average of four bushels in 1840 to twenty-five bushels per acre by 1860.[7] Giving further impetus to the reform of market-oriented plantation production was Edmund Ruffin, one of the nation's best-known advocates of agricultural improvement. Dubbed by later observers the father of soil chemistry, Ruffin was a planter who lived in Petersburg, Virginia, and marketed upward of 5,000 bushels of wheat annually.[8]

The Shenandoah Valley, and in particular McCormick's home counties of Augusta and Rockbridge, also boasted dynamic iron industries.[9] The geographic intersection of agricultural improvement, wheat boom, and ironworking skills cross-fertilized in the Piedmont and Shenandoah Valley regions of Virginia, creating an experimental milieu whose residents at once understood the major challenges of extensive wheat planting and had the requisite machinist know-how to develop a workable solution to the problem of harvesting large fields of wheat faster and more thoroughly. Many of the residents who possessed this sort of knowledge, of course, were enslaved. Captive blacksmiths, cradlers, and field workers appear to have played important if hard to detect roles in the experimental development of the automatic harvester.[10]

The conjunction of wheat boom, ironmaking skill, and a deindustrializing hinterland reshaped in accord with Brazilian demand drove the simultaneous investment in farm mechanization and slaves we see in McCormick's Virginia. This conjunction made Richmond's hinterland a nexus for "real-time" experiments taking place within the intensified labor and management experience of the brief wheat harvest. Scores of experiments, it turned out, were necessary: a decade of improvements, alterations, and an embarrassing failure or two stood between McCormick's original model and the wide sales it would achieve by the mid-1840s.[11]

From today's perspective, it is clear that the "invention" of the reaper was an extended stop-and-start, trial-and-error, piecemeal, collaborative process that took place over several years. Even though the *time* required for this piecemeal evolution was extended, the *space* of invention was compressed. While Obed Hussey, McCormick's main competitor, traveled from Ohio to New York and beyond to develop a reputation for his machine, McCormick stayed right at home in the Valley.[12] Between the first trial run in 1831 and the beginning of large-scale marketing in 1843, all of the experiments, all of the sales, and most of the publicity occurred within a seventy-mile radius of the McCormicks' Walnut Grove plantation.[13] It is not without reason that when his machine achieved national and international fame and was being mass-produced with interchangeable parts in a factory in Chicago during the Civil War, McCormick made sure it was known as the Virginia Reaper. The brand name of the product suggests that its point of origin was not incidental but integral to its success.[14]

This chapter does not make any claims regarding the comparative "inventiveness" or "modernity" of the Old South as a whole. Instead it zooms in, to underscore that particular places and particular times in the history of capitalism have given rise to a sort of routinized innovation. The wheat-growing, flour-milling region of Virginia, surprisingly, appears to have been such a place.[15] Plantation neighborhoods in this locale became crucial sites in the development of a key technology of capitalism. As such, the wheat flour industry between Virginia and Brazil in the antebellum period should be treated as an important piece of the nineteenth-century world economy, particularly in its technological facets.

Most important for our purposes, Second Slavery scholars have shown that dynamically expanding zones of slave-based production incorporated novel economies of scale and technologies of speed, such as steam-powered sugar mills, railroads, and telegraphs, which were adopted to keep apace in a highly competitive global regime of free trade.[16] Since innovation and experiment arguably became a routine aspect of business during the Second Slavery, knowledge embedded in technologies, as well as the emergence of certain new forms of plantation expertise, must be seen as central to the story of slavery's capitalism in the nineteenth century. Yet the knowledge history of the Second Slavery remains to be written. This chapter represents an initial effort.[17]

Commodity Intersections: Wheat, Iron, and Slaves

Perhaps no one quite embodied the synergy of wheat cultivation and ironworking in Virginia as fully as Cyrus McCormick. The son of a wheat farmer and avid tinkerer, McCormick was raised in an area known both for its wealthy ironmasters and for its large wheat planters. On the McCormicks' estate, the flour mill and the blacksmith shop, both powered by water diverted from a nearby stream, stood side by side, an architectural reflection of the intertwined character of ironworking, wheat planting, and flour milling.[18] In the autumns of his youth, moreover, when Valley of Virginia resident Cyrus McCormick loaded a wagon with farm produce and took the seven-day trip to Richmond, he would certainly have seen the multistory flour mills rising along the banks of the lower James River in the early 1830s, which augured connections between improved wheat culture in the Valley and the global milling industry of antebellum Richmond (Figure 3.1).[19]

The McCormicks counted as friends nearby wheat planters, among them William Massie. Practicing what Lynn Nelson calls "capitalist intensification," Massie imported new crop varieties and improved livestock breeds from abroad, while augmenting his soil fertility with high-powered fertilizers and using mechanized farm equipment to prepare and clear his fields. In general, Massie and other wealthy planters like him willingly sacrificed a locally grown,

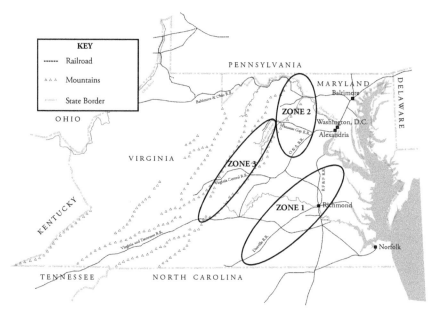

Figure 3.1. The wheat heartlands of antebellum Virginia. Zone 1 is the Central Piedmont, zone 2 is the Northern Piedmont, and zone 3 is the part of the Shenandoah Valley embracing Augusta, Rockbridge, Rockingham, Botetourt, Shenandoah, and Roanoke Counties. McCormick hailed from zone 3, the only one of the three wheat heartlands to have significant overlap with iron mines and blast furnaces. For the data on which the map is based, see Daniel Rood, "Bogs of Death: Slavery, the Brazilian Flour Trade, and the Mystery of the Vanishing Millpond in Antebellum Virginia," *Journal of American History* 101 (2014): 19–43. Map created by Nic Champagne.

Jeffersonian ideal of independence to pursue larger fortunes on the global market. Massie also abandoned his flour and gristmills, exemplifying a new level of plantation specialization.[20] Countervailing forces therefore marked the Virginia countryside: on the one hand, there occurred a dediversification of rural production as country folk depended increasingly on urban products brought in by out-of-town merchants, while planters focused insistently on wheat and tobacco farming. On the other hand, there also existed a large minority of improving, book-reading, scientific agriculturists in the Valley who continued to engage in iron production and flour milling.[21]

Because of the money to be made in supplying Richmond's voracious mills with clean, dry grains, the logistical complexities of the wheat harvest captured the attention of this group of cultivators. The wheat crop had to be felled at just the right moment if it were not to become overripe; once it was downed, either by scythe or by cradle, laborers had to work quickly. First they gathered and bound the crop into bundles of stalks known as sheaves; the sheaves were then propped against one another in groups of three or four, with one sheaf laid over the top. This operation, called shocking, helped keep grains dry. Next, slaves took the sheaves to a horse- or steam-powered threshing machine, which separated the grain from the rest of the plant; then a wheat fan separated the wheat from the chaff. While the norm in the South was to use livestock to thresh grain by walking over it on a threshing floor, this tended to soil the grain. Cleanliness was very important to the high-end Richmond millers, whose business depended largely on the pleasure of quality-conscious Brazilian bakers. Therefore, planters trying to win the patronage of these mills increasingly invested in the mechanization of threshing.[22] With the grain threshed, fanned, and packed in barrels, it was finally ready to be carted to the nearest railroad depot and sent on to Richmond. Because the entire process had to be completed within a week or so, mostly to avoid the blight, rust, or other pests that often ruined grain harvests, the pulse of daily life on the plantation picked up considerably at reaping time.[23]

The accelerated pace of work during the wheat harvest was given further impetus in the antebellum period by new agricultural and marketing factors associated with this export-oriented enterprise. First of all, planters began harvesting the crop earlier in the summer. The pushing forward of reaping to a moment when the crop was not yet ripe, apparently widespread among Virginia planters, represented a subtle but significant change, linked to the market advantage for those who could get wheat to Richmond soonest.[24] The Piedmont planter and nationally known agricultural improver Edmund Ruffin had long advocated early reaping. He was thus pleased to note that, since 1821, "a very general change has taken place, by somewhat advancing the time of reaping." He nevertheless urged farmers to gather their crops even earlier, observing that "there are but few farmers who will venture to reap as soon as the time we advocated." Furthermore, new varieties of wheat, adopted in the Mid-Atlantic region during the nineteenth century, added urgency. Some Upper South farmers chose a particular variety because it ripened early, even though the price it brought might be lower, showing how important timely delivery had become for the success of market-oriented wheat farmers in the relatively distant markets of Baltimore and Richmond.[25]

An 1837 letter to the editor of the *Richmond Enquirer* helps explain the harrying pace of harvesttime, and why planters were adopting various means to speed up the delivery of their goods. The writer, identified only as "Agricola," was a self-professed advocate of the small farmer. He accused the Richmond millers of forming a "combination" that conspired to push prices down as the harvest season progressed, favoring those suppliers who could deliver early in the summer, when markets were bereft of fresh flour (in the days before preservatives, wheat flour had a shelf life of around three months). Meanwhile, the wheat "which is sent in by *that class of farmers* who are obliged to carry their crops to market at a particular period, to wit, in August and September, is bought at a reduced price."[26] The earlier one got one's crop to market and the bigger the crop, Agricola claimed, the better the price one could expect. Big wheat suppliers to the Richmond mills held an advantage over smaller farmers, who had formerly had to compete only with other farms in the neighborhood of a local country mill. Railroads in particular fomented this broader integration of producers into a unified field, giving rise to a new dynamic within which large, concentrated, single- or double-crop farms from throughout Richmond's expanding wheatshed struggled over the patronage of a shrinking number of milling firms. The consolidation of wheat farming into larger, specialized units mirrored the concentration of Richmond's giant mills preparing flour for Brazil's baking industry.

Wheat is a particularly land-costly crop. Since only a tiny portion of each stalk of wheat actually went into white flour, it had to be planted in large fields to be worthwhile. While tobacco, with its delicate handling and high dollar value per plant, encouraged close supervision and limited acreage, wheat acreage, uneconomic in small batches, was restrained only by how much could be reaped in a week or two. Those who could afford extra laborers or time-saving machinery to expand acreage thus had a double advantage over their smaller competitors, and many local planters sought to press this advantage by investing in the development of new farm machines.[27]

Pools of Expertise and the Plantation Laboratory in Virginia

In the summer of 1831, on a wheat farm in Virginia's Shenandoah Valley, Cyrus H. McCormick carried out the first experimental run of his mechanized reaper. The moment was famously memorialized in an 1891 painting, after McCormick was renowned the world over for his mass-produced, labor-saving machine. In the image, a slave from a nearby farm operates the reaper as a mixed-race crowd looks on. There were many scenes like this one in the wheat-growing areas of Virginia in the 1830s and 1840s, the same areas that supplied Richmond's millers with so much of their wheat. These experiments show that the Second Slavery's plantation was an abode of knowledge production (not simply the application of existing knowledge of an agronomic or managerial sort): what I have elsewhere called the plantation laboratory.[28]

As McCormick and his two or three competitors ran dozens of field tests on plantations through the 1830s and 1840s, they took their place in an existing Upper South tradition of plantation experiments. George Washington, Thomas Jefferson, the Randolph family, and other members of the Virginia gentry were all agricultural improvers and experimenters of note in the early republic. John Taylor, author of an important 1813 farming manual and the dean of scientific planters until Edmund Ruffin successfully challenged some of his theories, continued their tradition. However, the antebellum period witnessed a shift in the class makeup of implement vendors and users. A colonial-era elite with what Peter McClelland calls "idle time and abundant funds to investigate elaborate contrivances with questionable economic payoffs" was joined in the antebellum period by pragmatic, improving agriculturalists desirous of spending a little money to increase profits with easy-to-use, dependable machines.[29]

Planters looking for an advantage in the race to deliver clean wheat to Richmond at the earliest possible date took an interest in new machinery that might help them. Skeptical about the reaper at first, and unconvinced by the boosterism of farming journals and implement salesmen, Upper South wheat growers turned out in large numbers to watch "practical field tests."[30] At "a Public Exhibition" of Hussey's reaper in Maryland, for example, "several hundred persons principally farmers, assembled to witness it, and express[ed] themselves highly satisfied with the result."[31] Such well-attended performances demonstrated new technologies to a broad spectrum of the population, enslaved as well as free, rich as well as poor.[32] Once planters became convinced of the potential of the invention, they often collaborated in its refinement by running field experiments and suggesting particular improvements. But they were not the only collaborators in the picture.

In the Jim Crow–era depiction of the reaper's first run, the slaves appear overjoyed, slack-jawed. The painting tells a story of brute Uncle Toms liberated by the strange genius of white invention. The truth, however, was quite different. Enslaved workers played various parts in the development of the new harvesting machinery. Local historians in Augusta County even claim that "much of the credit [for the invention of the reaper] may belong to a farm slave" named Joe. A blacksmith on the plantation, Joe fashioned the first reciprocal cutting bars, which would in the end distinguish McCormick's reaper from those of his competitors by allowing damp and thick stands of wheat to be felled cleanly.[33] Joe's contribution should come as no surprise, since skilled slaves in the Valley possessed a potent combination of ironworking expertise and a familiarity with the challenges of wheat farming. Slaves in Virginia built and operated gristmills, worked as plantation blacksmiths, fashioned shoes, and otherwise took charge of rural manufacturing and handicraft responsibilities.[34] When harvesttime came around, moreover, many of these men laid down their blacksmith aprons and picked up wheat cradles, eager to make some cash during the hectic weeks of the harvest. In their roles as blacksmiths, mechanics, cradlers, teamsters, plowmen, and drivers, slaves were the indispensable technological brokers of the plantation system. For a new technology like the reaper to be incorporated into the flow of production on the plantation, and for the machine to be kept in working order, planters and overseers would submit to the skills and the hard-won practical knowledge of enslaved men.[35] As rival reaper entrepreneur Obed Hussey noted on his plantation visits, "the farmer, as is often the case, depends entirely on his laborers to manage the machine."[36]

Joe Anderson, for example, a slave of McCormick's who was interviewed in the 1880s, often worked as a raker in the early experiments, even assisting during the original 1831 trial at Steele's Tavern.[37] When it came to explaining the operation of the machine he had just delivered to William C. Peyton's Roanoke Plantation in 1843, McCormick chose not to discuss technical matters with the machine's new owner. Instead, he sat down with "the negro mechanic, Edmund," to explain how the reaper worked, as well as, presumably, how best to repair it. Edmund must have been a quick study, for Peyton was soon boasting of the harvester's efficient clearing of his wheat fields.[38] In the same year, still unknown among the Tidewater elite, McCormick asked the wealthy planter Corbin Braxton to help him break into the eastern Virginia sales market. Braxton "assured him that his plantation carpenter would add the raker's seat improvement [the machine's newest feature] to those reapers if their owners requested it."[39]

While slaves like Joe, Edmund, or Braxton's unnamed "plantation carpenter" often helped promote, disseminate, and refine new farm technologies, sometimes field workers saw their interests threatened by mechanization.

Hazard Knowles, chief machinist of the U.S. Patent Office, made a reaper in 1837 that attracted the eye of a Shenandoah Valley farmer, who purchased the patent rights but abandoned the project in 1841, "when laborers in his neighborhood threatened its destruction."[40] Another reaper inventor frustrated with a failed experiment complained darkly of "the *designed* awkwardness of a class of cradlers, whose interest it is that the machine should fail."[41] These episodes of skilled workers (who could well have been enslaved or free, white or black) warily defending the limited prerogatives they gained during harvest season present a starkly different picture from the 1891 painting. Whether active participants in the reaper's improvement or its determined foes, both enslaved and free agricultural laborers shaped the trajectories of farm mechanization.[42]

Even when sales of his new reaper topped 100 per year in Virginia after 1842, McCormick's family and his enslaved workers continued to pound out the machines one by one at small smithies on the family farm. They found themselves overwhelmed, and agreed to farm out some of the manufacturing to nearby machinists. These individuals continued to tweak the design. J. M. Hite, a contractor in Clarke County, for example, added a wheeled platform on which the raker could stand while he gently swept the felled stalks from the platform, instead of walking alongside it all day.[43]

McCormick's corner of the South was a reservoir of experienced manufacturers and adroit ironmongers.[44] Local metals industry competition in the Valley was magnified by the rise of larger urban firms such as Richmond Plow Manufacturing, which built and marketed seed drills, harrows, and other farm machinery, in addition to the latest plow designs.[45] Increased demand for metal implements from improving wheat planters spurred growth in the agricultural tool manufacturing industry and the further multiplication of machine-shop skill. Thus, when developing his reaper, McCormick could enlist the help of local artisans such as the well-known blacksmith John McCown, who used a water-powered tilt hammer to make important improvements to the cutting blade on McCormick's reaper during the 1830s.[46]

The McCormick reaper, then, was not the product of an isolated genius whose only shortcoming was corrected when he relocated to Chicago in 1846. Rather, it was the product of a particular southern milieu characterized by the intersection of wheat cultivation, iron manufacture, and export-oriented, large-scale flour milling—all of which was molded along the finicky contours of mass consumer demand in southeastern Brazil. Plantation experiments— the ongoing, real-time field tests that gradually transformed the machine from the clunky beginnings of a hopeful idea to a useful harvesting aid—helped bring wheat harvesting up to speed with the accelerated pace of wheat and wheat flour marketing necessitated by the seasonal calendar of Atlantic trade.

Lords of Lash, Loom, and Landscape

The new reaper technology matured in step with the seasonal rhythms governing life on the farm: hurried experiments in the fields during harvesttime were followed by a long winter of improvements based on observations gleaned from those tests. Much as in the case of plantation experiments taking place at the same time on Cuban sugar estates, the short harvesttime of winter wheat imparted a sense of urgency to data-gathering activities: "on-the-job" experiments had to be conducted on actual wheat crops, from which farmers desperately needed to make money.[47]

McCormick's rival inventor, Obed Hussey, noted the difficulty that the short harvests presented for the cycle of experimentation and improvement. That the question of his machine's usefulness "is not so settled in many sections of the country," Hussey remarked, "may be accounted for by the very short time it can be used in each year, and from the fact that, like all other machines, it must be tried, improved, and tried again. Hence the reaping machine requires more time to perfect it than those improvements which can be experimented with every day in the year."[48] To have more opportunities to test the reapers, experimenters sometimes ran them through rusted wheat or less valuable grains such as oats, but the knowledge gained was of limited use, since the physical properties of a harvest-ready wheat crop were unique.[49] As the planter William B. Harrison explained in 1841, "so much depends on the locality, the length of the rows and the heaviness of the crop . . . that the time saved is constantly varying; and to approximate the truth, therefore, is as much as can be expected."[50] With the reaper experiments, therefore, there was no such thing as a rehearsal: untested machines were tossed into the fray of an ongoing harvest and expected to stem the tide of inexorably ripening grain.

Because of the irreducible singularity of a field of wheat, McCormick and his contemporaries were forced to fish data out of the uninterrupted flow of commodity production (itself happening within the compressed time frame of the harvest).[51] Men such as the wheat estate manager A. Nicol, an early adapter of the Hussey reaper who published an account of the 1841 harvest,

could ill afford to assess the machine in the abstract, isolated from its sur-
roundings, as one might ponder a blueprint. Instead, Nicol sought to mesh a
hybrid labor force of slaves, hirelings, machinery, and environment, as well as
the production of reliable data about how they all fit together. As a plantation
administrator in the early phase of American farm mechanization, Nicol was
neither simply a lord of the lash nor of the loom: he was a technocrat charged
with managing the relationship between and among lash, loom, and landscape. In the midst of an unpredictable and ever-shifting set of conditions, he
constantly tweaked the ratios in search of a golden mean that would yield an
uninterrupted flow of grain.[52]

On the first day of the 1841 harvest, concerns of overripening were exacerbated by rainfall, moving Nicol to transfer his "ploughing force of 15 hands"
(who had been tilling other parts of the farm) to cradling. Just as quickly, he
instructed them to drop their cradles and help arrange the binds of wheat into
shocks to avoid "passing showers." After three more days of frustrating rain
delays, the weather finally turned favorable for reaping, but then it became so
hot that "Laborers suffered considerable inconvenience in consequence; four
reapers became unwell and unable to work."[53] Under these harrying circumstances (conditions were unfavorable whether skies were overcast or clear!), one
can understand the pressure to adopt the automatic reaper. Nicol's employer,
Robert Bolling, decided to give it a shot.

On the morning of the fifth day of the harvest, an odd-looking contraption appeared at the end of the field, together with a stranger in a suit fiddling
nervously with its undercarriage. Obed Hussey and his reaper had arrived,
"and after some little delay [it] was got into operation." "After a short trial and
some experience on the part of the laborers and teams employed," Nicol exclaimed, the reaper "performed its work beautifully." For the estate manager,
incorporating the machine into a preexisting work routine was the paramount
challenge. He emphasized how the time savings achievable with the machine
were a matter of training. "The awkwardness of the hands employed," Nicol
noted, caused "several delays." Once the proper dexterity was achieved and
the machine operation was brought up to speed, however, "all the operations
connected with reaping it performed infinitely better than that done by the
cradles."[54]

Yet July's urgency was barely mitigated by the arrival of the reaper. "Our
harvest operations are now *hastily drawing to a close*," Nicol reported on the
first of the month. "Hussey's reaping machine was again started this morning
so soon as the dew had dried off, and after some little delay, caused by a bolt

becoming loose and dropping out, performed admireably." In a business in which delays were not acceptable, this day's challenges suggest, Hussey's clunky reaper could add to the difficulties. On July 2, Nicol increased the number of cradlers to thirty-eight. And luckily so, as the reaper's "large propelling wheel became loose and shifted its position, and before it could be again put to rights, caused the loss of a half day's work." Nicol, his enthusiasm now somewhat tempered, opined that Hussey's machine performed well when not in need of repair.[55] Then, on July 3, came the harvesttime's crescendo at Sandy Point. An expanded workforce of forty-two cradlers swept the remainder of the standing wheat into sheaves, while one acre seems to have been politely "left for reaping with Hussey's reaper."[56]

Finally exhaling that evening, Nicol sat down to write in his journal. "Our harvest operations may now be considered as nearly completed. The laborers, including hirelings, have wrought well and cheerfully." In Nicol's experiment-derived estimation, the reaper required three horses, one driver, one raker, and eight binders to harvest one acre per hour. Focusing again on the importance of labor discipline to the success of the machine, he thought that the reaper would be "capable of performing from one-third to one-half more, as the laborers become more efficient"—that is, if they were willing to do so. Nicol added an unsettling afterthought about the laborers who had made up for the reaper's shortcomings: "As was to be expected, amongst so many negroes, frequent reproofs and admonitions were necessary; it is, however, a gratifying retrospect that in no instance was corporeal punishment deemed necessary, or inflicted." Nicol's language makes clear that the withholding of the lash was exceptional enough to merit a mention, which means the *threat* of physical violence operated silently, hovering over the fields of wheat like a menacing fog. The invisible hand of the implied lash pushed the workers onward, as important an element of the harvest operations as the tallow greasing the wheels of Hussey's machine.[57]

On the large-scale plantations of the Upper South wheat belt, the automatic reaper had to be incorporated into a complex, shifting, and highly organized mode of production during the short harvest. The hardware of gears, wheels, belts, cradles, and twine was to be meshed with the software of incentive and threat more traditionally utilized on antebellum plantations. So, while enslaved blacksmiths like Joe or Edmund may have maintained and even improved the machines, experts in the technologies of coercion like Nicol would be in charge of incorporating it efficiently into the hierarchical organization of harvest labor. The whip, the watch, and the automatic reaper were all parts of his calculus, and the harvesttime plantation experiments were the context in which the equations were worked out. Fractures in the tyranny of routine, the experiments heralded the rise of a flexible regime of coercion reigning on the large-scale antebellum wheat plantation, a context in which the production of knowledge could be blended into the ongoing production of commodities. The many field tests of the automatic reaper reveal a critical attribute of the capitalist plantation during the Second Slavery. Plantation technocrats like Nicol folded into and concealed within the uninterrupted flow of farmwork a complicated process of knowledge production, temporarily transforming the plantation into a laboratory for technical innovation as well as a source of empirical data.

Contexts of Mechanization

The extensive, specialized character of wheat farming in antebellum Virginia gave rise to an especially significant and almost entirely overlooked chapter in the technological history of the reaper. Not designed for frequent turnarounds or changes in direction, McCormick's contraption was an economy-of-scale technology ineffective in small batches. The reaper was first designed for use in uninterrupted fields of grain amid a *surplus* of workers.

The traditional view is that the abundance of captive labor under a slave regime obviated the pursuit of labor-saving innovations.[58] But this machine was developed not to save labor but to save time. When later operated on the western prairies, it is true, the reaper became a labor-saving device—a different technology, in a way. The raker attachment and McCormick's reaper-binder were invented after McCormick departed for Chicago in 1846 and marketed his products to labor-poor midwestern farmers. These inventions were clearly driven by the need to save on labor, allowing the farmer, and perhaps one assistant, to handle the harvest operations singlehandedly. On the Virginia slave plantation, however, the reaper was aimed at accelerating the pace of production, both so that more acreage could be harvested before overripening and because of the marketing advantages associated with early delivery. In fact, early experimenters noted that the incorporation of the automatic reaper into the flow of the harvest, far from saving labor, brought increased drudgery upon the heads of enslaved field workers. The laborers working as binders and pickers-up found it nearly impossible to keep up with the accelerated pace, and often had to be increased in number.

As opposed to simply reducing the need for manual labor, the planter William B. Harrison discovered, early models of the automatic reaper transformed the ratios of different harvesttime tasks. Like A. Nicol of neighboring Sandy Point Estate, Harrison found that using the automatic reaper did in fact save laborers engaged directly in reaping, but at the same time created the need for more binders to keep up with the reaper. These workers had to be drawn from the cradling force, giving the observer the false impression that the number of total workers had been reduced. Harrison worried not only about the number of cradlers he might lose but also about having to give up his best cradlers to tend the reaper. While "good policy . . . would always suggest the propriety of stopping the worst" of the workers, he also wanted his most trusted slaves to handle the expensive machine. The simple addition and subtraction of commensurable units of labor power would not do in Harrison's case. On the contrary, the skill of individual workers had to be included in any accurate cost-benefit analysis. Still other variables had to be factored into the equation "in order to determine precisely the time saved." Wringing dependable measurements out of an actual harvest, he was forced to acknowledge, represented a daunting transformation of plantation norms of management and recordkeeping.[59]

He also learned by hard experience that when the weather did not cooperate and the wheat got damp, Hussey's reaper became ineffective. In such an unfortunate situation, Harrison informed readers, "the hands that tend the machine have to be employed in some other way; and moving from one kind of work to another is always attended with more or less loss of time."[60] One can almost see the labor-supply curves dancing in Harrison's head. His technocratic prose evoked both the imperious caprices of nature and procedural concerns with the judicious expenditure of labor power across time and space, seemingly distinct preoccupations that nevertheless combined for many antebellum planters.

Much like his technocratic descendant Frederick Winslow Taylor, Harrison was particularly vexed by the loss of time occasioned by workers' transition between tasks.[61] Since Harrison always used "the same horses and hands" to run the machine in order to avoid investing time in training different shifts of workers, the unavoidable refueling of his one and only machine-tending workforce was a source of frustrating delay. Eventually, however, "When [the horses and hands] can be conveniently changed, so as to lose no time in feeding, the amount of work will no doubt be much greater," because a relief team could take over the reaper while the first team ate.[62]

Meals of the enslaved members of Harrison's "plantation family" were thus folded unthinkingly into a survey of management logistics. Indeed, he wrote of the enslaved as loads on a circuit, sources of friction that had to be smoothed over to achieve continuous operation of the automatic reaper. Such bloodless administrative challenges dragged to the surface of Harrison's prose the realities of slavery lurking just below the sun-dappled surfaces of antebellum paternalism. Neither the fulminations of the proslavery fire-eater nor the smug diagnoses of the northern abolitionist laid bare the functional equivalence of slave, animal, and machine under capitalist slavery as clearly as the measured estimations of the plantation technocrat confronted with a harvest timetable.

These remarkable plantation experiments, an early form of Taylorist time-motion studies (Harrison had been "timing these machines repeatedly" during the harvest), were aimed at figuring out how to insert the machine into the flow of production on the plantation.[63] The finer points of this insertion required concentric circles of management vis-à-vis the machine—management at different scales of removal from actual work. Harrison the planter was out in the fields, watching over the whole man-animal-machine-landscape system, while his overseer dealt with the machine up close ("My overseer, Mr. Adams, who superintended the machines").[64] So slaves tended the machine, the overseer super-intended, and the planter managed the system.

If we zoom out from the plantation level, the concentric circles of management continue to replicate. During the wheat harvest, for example, large planters in a given neighborhood would gather local slaves, tenants, and hirelings and allocate the group estate by estate, depending on whose crop ripened first.[65] Wheat planters thus integrated management across properties, cobbling together a sequential geography of labor exchange. This complex of labor-machine-landscape management was then linked by a growing system of railroads and canals to the big Richmond flour mills, which shipped the product to Rio, where it was baked into crusty white loaves by large baking firms.

Conclusion

Of course, some of this is the stuff of fantasy. The writings these planters and managers left behind provide reliable pictures only of their ambitions, and we can merely speculate on the degree to which the architectures of power and efficiency they sketched out in their prose fairly reflected reality on the plantation. Taking into account the actions of slaves like Joe and Edmund, as well as those workers who uttered admonitions of their own to the erstwhile Shenandoah Valley planter-entrepreneur, we can treat with skepticism Nicol's picture of an enslaved workforce eminently relocatable, reticent, and ready.

Nevertheless, it was this fantasy of a scientific, collectivist, and technocratic approach to labor management that McCormick took with him to Chicago, where he became a pioneer of assembly-line techniques in the 1860s, renaming his company International Harvester. Once the technology had been considerably refined, it is true, McCormick saw greater potential in the rising "Nature's Metropolis" of Chicago. For the early phases of the reaper's technical development, however, no other region of the country combined the requisite characteristics of accelerated grain harvesting, ironworking skill, and mass labor control as well as the Piedmont and Valley regions of Virginia. The automatic reaper gradually and painstakingly emerged from an agricultural milieu in which the close accounting of labor expenditure on a mass scale was customary, in which experimentation had become a routine part of plantation business, in which expertise in iron and wheat industries coexisted, and finally, in which the harried exigencies of Virginia's export economy spurred innovation. The lone prairie farmer in the western territories, bereft of labor, could not share McCormick's proto-Taylorist approach to farm management.

Without this nurturing environment, it is hard to imagine McCormick's Virginia Reaper having developed in the way that it did, at the time that it did, and playing as important a role for the post-1850 midwestern grain economy as Whitney's cotton gin had half a century earlier for the Cotton Kingdom of the southwest. It was both the automated, industrial-scale Richmond mills and the demand issuing from the slave society of Brazil that pushed this technology regime forward. Thus, some of the technologies crucial to the rise of the U.S. Midwest as the world's leading exporter of grain were already in place by the 1850s, developed in Virginia slave country. The southern, slavery-centered history of wheat flour that I have exhumed in this chapter has been long been hidden in the shadow of King Cotton, as well as the monumental growth of the "world's breadbasket" on the North American plains, but deserves recognition as the indispensable preamble to Middle America and its amber waves of grain. That Atlantic slavery was at one time a centerpiece of this vision of American exceptionalism might be quite unsettling to such a narrative. All the more reason to tell the story.

PART II

Slavery and Finance

CHAPTER 4

Neighbor-to-Neighbor Capitalism

Local Credit Networks and
the Mortgaging of Slaves

BONNIE MARTIN

On July 11, 1803, Armand Duplantier sold three enslaved women to Juan Bautista Massi, a free mulatto, in Baton Rouge, Louisiana. They were Helena and her daughter, Marieta, and Clara, an unrelated thirteen-year-old girl. The price quoted was 1,800 hard pesos—the silver coins minted in Mexico and a premier form of currency—but no cash changed hands. It was a credit sale, 100 percent leveraged. Massi did provide collateral. He gave Duplantier two mortgages, one on the three slaves being purchased and a second on five slaves he already owned, two men, Pedro and Francisco, one woman, Mary, and Mary's unnamed daughter and son. Another clause in the contract further assured Duplantier that he would receive full payment. Massi expressed his intention to free two of the females, Helena and Marieta. He did not identify them as his wife and child, but most likely there was some family relationship. From Duplantier's point of view, Massi's personal interest in Helena and Marieta was an additional guarantee that the 1,800 pesos would be paid on time because if they were not, Helena and Marieta could be repossessed and sold.[1]

Research into agreements like that between Massi and Duplantier provides many fresh insights into slavery's capitalism. We are quite familiar with the capitalistic exploitation of slave laborers producing staple crops but only recently have turned our attention to slavery as a system of finance.[2] European colonists had used slaves to secure loans in their earliest settlements—those in the Caribbean, South America, and South Africa—and later in North America. Whether to establish the sixteenth-century sugar centers in the Caribbean and Brazil or to finance the nineteenth-century cotton boom in Louisiana, slaves were used to support the loans necessary to raise development capital for colonial expansion. Slaves were excellent collateral on agricultural frontiers because they were in great demand and reasonably fungible. If a borrower failed to repay, the slaves could be seized and sold. In financial terms, slave property was valuable and highly liquid, that is, easily turned into cash. The data compiled and described below indicate that there were thousands of transactions similar to the one between Armand Duplantier and Juan Bautista Massi and suggest the importance of slave mortgaging to the economic development of the eighteenth- and nineteenth-century North American South.[3]

This chapter draws on data collected from more than 10,000 Virginia, South Carolina, and Louisiana loans in which slaves served as collateral.[4] Slave owners worked their slaves financially as well as physically from colonial days until emancipation. While the recent research of Edward Baptist has highlighted human collateral in transatlantic financial networks, it was ordinary southerners, not international bankers, who made the most of this fiscal strategy.[5] Local planters, small farmers, and ordinary craftsmen mortgaged their slaves and other property to each other, and they raised a large amount of capital locally. As neighbors borrowed from neighbors, they spun nets of local credit that helped to circulate resources and encourage economic development in their communities. The matrix of overlapping local credit networks they created across the South provided pools of community credit that proved resilient in times when national and international credit contracted severely. Although the use of slaves as collateral varied over time and region, the data presented below show that the amount of capital raised was impressive, ranging from 20 percent of the value of the staples produced by slave economies to over 175 percent in a given year. We therefore need to see the financial history of slavery as an integral part of the social history of ordinary people: the neighbors who lent to their neighbors, along with the enslaved men, women, and children who were trapped in the credit web of slavery's capitalism.

Turning Slaves into Collateral

How were slaves worked as collateral in regional networks? Like Duplantier and Massi, thousands of southerners sold and bought slaves on installment plans secured by mortgages.[6] It was a tradition of credit financing that included slaveholders of every economic rank. The parties to these contracts publicly recorded them with notaries, clerks of court, and even military commanders. They did so thousands of times during the eighteenth and nineteenth centuries and across the southern regions sampled for this chapter. The earliest slave mortgages in Louisiana date from the French period, at least as early as 1738. On March 4 of that year in New Orleans, Antoine Patin bought Yama, a "high quality" male slave, from Jean Robinet and his wife, Perine Zeide Genovy LaCostet, for 1,500 livres. In a contract similar to the 1803 bargain between Duplantier and Massi, Patin gave the sellers a mortgage on Yama and on another slave that he already owned to guarantee payment.[7] Virginia colonists also were mortgaging slaves in the 1730s. For example, William Chamberlayne's 1734 loan of £18 13s to his neighbor, William Maynard, was secured by mortgage on "a Negro man slave named Cesar" and a 200-acre plantation in Goochland County.[8] Farther south, Carolina settlers continued the Barbadian tradition of mortgaging enslaved people to help finance their agricultural expansion.[9]

Enormous reservoirs of county-level data documenting such transactions remain unexamined in courthouses and public archives. Exploring these sources can help us better understand the ways credit was extended on slaves, land, and other property; how this credit accelerated the growth of slave societies; how it shaped the ways slaveholders and enslaved people saw one another; and how all these factors affected enslaved families. The Duplantier-Massi contract exemplifies each of these uses of human collateral. Massi was using the credit system of slavery's capitalism to free two women and possibly reunite his family, but he also used it to buy the labor, profit, and appreciation potential of another young girl. What promised a brighter future for Helena and Marieta increased the risks of displacement for Clara and the other five slaves who served as human collateral in the transaction. Pedro, Francisco, Mary, and Mary's children joined Clara as property that Massi could use in whatever way he deemed to be in his economic or emotional interest. Children, whose value was likely to increase over time, found themselves particularly susceptible to multiple mortgages. In St. Landry Parish, Louisiana, the planter Etienne Fusilier purchased an eight-year-old boy named Jacques in 1833 with 100 percent financing secured by a mortgage. Jacques was mortgaged three more times in the next four years: twice for quick cash, and finally when Fusilier sold Jacques to a neighbor.[10] Similarly, in September 1838, despite the tight credit climate following the Panic of 1837, Julie Marianne, a free woman of color living in New Orleans, mortgaged Sally, her sixteen-year-old slave, in order to borrow $200 from the widow Louise Marin.[11]

When slave sellers like Duplantier accepted a purchase money mortgage on slaves like Helena, Marieta, and Clara from purchasers like Massi, they enlarged the field of potential slave buyers. The pool now stretched beyond those who could manage cash sales. Those who had slaves could sell them more quickly, and they could charge higher prices for their human property since the overall demand was not limited to those with ready money. On the other hand, slave buyers also benefited. Purchasers like Massi could offer slaves they already owned as collateral using an equity mortgage. These equity mortgages allowed them to stretch their cash and credit resources even further by reducing the size of down payments when they purchased new land and the additional slaves needed to work that land. Thus, slave seller Duplantier accessed the capital he had invested in his slaves by selling those he no longer needed or could afford to keep. Slave purchaser Massi also reached the capital stored in his slaves simply by mortgaging them. When slave owners mortgaged slaves instead of selling them, they retained the slaves' labor, appreciation, and reproductive potential. Massi and owners like him could continue to work slaves physically, while also working them financially to obtain credit and quick cash.

Courthouse records show that free people of color like Massi participated in the local credit networks that spread across Louisiana and the South and helped provide the capital needed to buy the slaves necessary for investment and development. For example, Pablo Reuben, also a free Negro, signed as guarantor of Massi's slave purchase. Now, in addition to the slaves that Massi mortgaged, Duplantier could look to another member of the local economic community for repayment. Reuben and Massi were members of a subsidiary system within the general credit market, one in which free people of color supported each other as they tried to work slavery's capitalistic opportunities. Sometimes this inner circle used mortgages on human property. At other times, as in the case of Pablo Reuben, a free person of color made a personal pledge to guarantee another's loan.[12]

By using mortgages, all borrowers and lenders increased the circulation of cash, credit, and slaves in their communities. These resources were redistributed more rapidly, spurring the development of local agriculture and the slave trade itself in region upon region. To be sure, borrowers mortgaged land and other personal property such as equipment, livestock, and household furnishings, as well as slaves. Sometimes slaves were the only property offered as security; sometimes only land or personal property was used. At other times, however, lenders constructed packages of slaves, land, and other personal property. Reliance on slave collateral varied from region to region and over time, and the credit patterns in frontier settlements could look quite different from those in well-established districts.

How much capital was raised by these thousands of small loans in overlapping, neighbor-to-neighbor credit networks? We can begin to estimate this by looking at the data on equity mortgages created in Virginia and Louisiana, that is, the mortgages that borrowers gave on property they already owned to encourage lenders to provide cash or credit—such as the mortgage Massi gave Duplantier on five other slaves to support his purchase of Helena, Marieta, and Clara. Of the total amount of capital raised by equity mortgages, the percentage of capital raised by those using human collateral was the same in both Virginia and Louisiana during their early frontier eras: in each colony more than two-thirds of the capital lent was backed by a borrower pledging slaves as all or part of the security for the loan. There are, however, significant differences in the absolute amounts of capital raised and in the number of equity mortgage transactions recorded in colonial Virginia and Louisiana. In contracts using human collateral, Virginians raised just over $50 million (unless noted, all figures in this chapter are in 2015-U.S. dollar equivalents), as compared to $3.3 million in Louisiana. That is not a surprising result if we consider Virginia's larger and more densely settled population. The most striking contrast in the Virginia and Louisiana patterns of collateral use in equity mortgages emerged in the early national period. On the Louisiana cotton frontier in the nineteenth century, the colonial pattern of the high use of slaves as collateral in equity mortgages continued and even intensified, from 68 percent to 80 percent—involving more than $150 million. In the state of Virginia, however, there was a dramatic shift to other forms of collateral, mostly land. Loan contracts that included slaves as collateral dropped from 68 percent in the colonial era to only 33 percent during the fifteen years sampled in the national era. While these contracts generated $60 million, compared to approximately $50 million in the colonial era, those using land and nonslave chattel raised just over $120 million. Why did slaves become less prevalent as collateral in equity loans compared to other kinds of property in early national Virginia? Slaves were clearly still viewed as attractive collateral since mortgages involving them raised even more absolute dollars than in the colonial era. However, the Virginia population of free nonslaveholders had continued to grow in the cities and the countryside. When in need of an equity-based loan, therefore, these Virginians had no choice but to mortgage other kinds of property as collateral. In addition, the change may simply also reflect the fact that land had appreciated, and resales of land had become more frequent (thus improving its liquidity).[13]

We can analyze this latter point further by taking a closer look at the credit dynamics on frontiers versus those in established regions by comparing the equity mortgage activity in individual counties. For example, in the colonial period, Goochland County, located in the Piedmont region of Virginia, relied on slave collateral to generate the bulk of local capital, 73 percent, a rate only slightly higher than that for the colony as a whole. By the early national period, Goochland County had witnessed a strong rise in the percentage of capital raised by equity mortgages that did not use slaves as collateral; slave-secured capital fell to only 18 percent. Well settled by the national period, it is quite likely that Goochland's land values had appreciated with population growth and that, as competition for land increased, land became a more robust form of collateral. To contrast this, we can look at what happened in a more remote Virginia district, Lunenburg County, an agricultural frontier on the Virginia–North Carolina border. Here the use of slave collateral in equity mortgages actually *increased* by nine percentage points, to 74 percent, in the early national period. The colonial pattern of reliance on slaves as collateral did not disappear. Indeed, collateral use in the backcountry regions of Virginia such as Lunenberg County mirrored patterns in other more remote locales such as St. Landry Parish, Louisiana, a frontier district west of Baton Rouge. As in Lunenburg, the percentage of capital raised in St. Landry by equity mortgages involving slaves increased in the national era (from 69 percent to 76 percent). Farmers in these more remote places, where land was lightly settled and relatively undeveloped, had to depend on other collateral to raise the investment capital they needed.

Data from St. Landry Parish also provide an opportunity to compare the use of a different type of mortgage. In an equity mortgage, a buyer or borrower gave a seller or lender a loan secured by property he or she already owned (slaves, land, livestock, etc.). Purchase money mortgages, on the other hand, were created when a buyer did not pay the full price for property in cash but rather in installments over time. The seller kept a mortgage on the property in case the buyer did not pay according to the contract. We recall here that Juan Bautista Massi gave Armand Duplantier both types of mortgage, a purchase money mortgage on Helena, Marieta, and Clara and an equity mortgage on the five slaves he already owned (Pablo, Francisco, Mary, and Mary's two children). Comparing the use of equity and purchase money mortgages in St. Landry Parish over time, we find that during the eighteenth century residents generated much more cash and credit using equity mortgages. More than two-thirds of the capital raised by these equity loans used slaves as all or part of the security. These contracts supplied $1.8 million (again, in 2015-U.S. dollar equivalents). In contrast, the purchase money mortgages raised only $165 thousand, with 64 percent ($105,000) coming from slave purchases. Local residents who used slaves as collateral were raising more than seventeen times the capital with equity than with purchase money mortgages. Similarly, the equity mortgages secured by property other than slaves produced fourteen times as much capital as the non-slave-related purchase money mortgages ($832,000 versus $60,000). By the national era, however, mortgage patterns had shifted somewhat. The total amount of capital delivered by equity mortgages rose to $27 million, increasing by seven percentage points, from 69 percent to 76 percent, of the combined equity plus purchase money mortgage totals. However, the percentage of purchase money mortgages involving slaves did the opposite, dropping ten percentage points to 54 percent. Nevertheless, these purchase contracts produced a value of over $50 million—double that raised by equity mortgages. The explosion of purchase money mortgages on slaves among St. Landry neighbors both in the number of contracts and in the amount of credit raised was a natural result of the dramatic increase in the number of enslaved people trafficked into the region. Residents were eager to participate in the cotton boom, and the demand for slave labor was high. Louisiana's climate of easy credit facilitated mortgages on purchase of slaves.

One characteristic of the local mortgage pattern remained consistent, however. Data from St. Landry Parish reinforce the activity pattern of the region's creditors, the evidence that lenders were much more likely to be fellow residents than institutions. Credit flowed from neighbor to neighbor in overlapping local and regional webs of borrowing and lending. The data show that the parties to the contracts were individuals acting in a private capacity, not as agents for institutions. In a fifteen-year sample of St. Landry credit relations, banks appeared as parties to purchase money and equity mortgages in only 2 percent of the total transactions, and these mortgages raised only slightly more than 5 percent of the total capital and accounted for only 10 percent of all the slaves used as collateral. There are similar results for merchants. Merchants were parties in another 6 percent of the mortgage transactions, which generated 4 percent of the total capital, exploiting only 7 percent of the slaves actually used as collateral in the parish.

The corresponding data for South Carolina and Virginia, based on the sample of equity mortgages only, reveal that there were more institutional loans in the longer-established East than on the cotton frontier. In South Carolina, equity mortgages with banks or merchants listed as contracting parties accounted for approximately 19 percent of the capital raised (with bank mortgages raising 14 percent and merchant contracts raising 5 percent). In Virginia, equity mortgages with banks or merchants as contracting parties represented approximately 18 percent of the capital raised (only 3 percent from banks and 15 percent from merchants). Unlike Louisiana settlers, Virginians and South Carolinians had regional economies with long-standing ties to national and foreign institutional financiers.[14] It is natural that the commercial lenders would represent a higher percentage of total lenders. Even in these regions, however, the vast majority of the sampled contracts did not involve banks or merchants. The ratio of capital raised through merchants or lending institutions in Louisiana, South Carolina, and Virginia shifted by region, but neighbor-to-neighbor transactions continued to make up more than 80 percent of the capital generated in each state. Moreover, the South Carolina and Virginia data show that the significance of human collateral was not limited to colonial and national frontiers. Mortgages on slaves were part of the financial fabric across the South in the nineteenth century.

Neighbors lending to neighbors kept the flow of credit from completely drying up during the panics of the nineteenth century. Table 4.1 shows the total capital raised in 2015-U.S. dollar equivalents by local equity mortgages in South Carolina and Virginia in years sampled before, during, and after the onset of the Panics of 1819, 1837, and 1857.[15] Louisiana, owing to data limitations, is discussed separately below. Beginning with the Panic of 1819, the capital amassed by lending networks in South Carolina continued to edge slowly upward despite the crisis. The Virginia total dipped in the year of the panic but had rebounded strongly by 1821. In contrast, the reactions of the South Carolina networks to the 1837 panic showed a steady decline, but loan activity was still substantially strong, while Virginia capital rose out of a serious trough to almost recover to its 1821 peak by 1839. The years surrounding the 1857 panic contained large differences. In South Carolina, amounts dropped precipitously in 1857 and had not recovered by 1859, while in Virginia, amounts actually rose in 1857 and then dropped off thereafter. Nevertheless, given that, as we have seen, 80–90 percent of the amounts raised were local private loans from neighbor to neighbor, credit conditions would have been even more restricted if neighbor had not continued to lend to neighbor.

Table 4.1. Capital Raised by All Mortgages Sampled in South Carolina and Virginia

Year	South Carolina	Virginia
1818	$8,003,000	$14,180,000
1819	8,216,000	10,289,000
1821	9,434,000	22,977,000
1835	20,534,000	5,574,000
1837	16,660,000	7,209,000
1839	12,980,000	21,297,000
1855	20,820,000	12,332,000
1857	2,881,000	17,414,000
1859	2,836,000	9,044,000

Note: Values in 2015 U.S. dollar equivalents.

While the Louisiana data are not yet complete for all three parishes in each of the sample years, it appears that the impacts of the panics were mixed. For example, the capital raised in Orleans Parish on both equity and purchase money mortgages from the notaries sampled dropped from the 1818 level of $17.3 million (in 2015-U.S. dollar equivalents) to $6.9 million in 1821. In St. Landry, however, the total rose from $2.8 to $3.6 million. Comparing 1835 and 1838, we see that mortgage-secured cash and credit in Orleans Parish dropped from $38 million to $29.4 million, while again St. Landry swelled from $2.3 million to $8.5 million. Finally, comparing 1855 to 1859, we find that Orleans and St. Landry both had tremendous increases, with Orleans rising from $11.3 million to $44.8 million and St. Landry from $14.4 million to $31.2 million.

Neighbor-to-neighbor lending was especially vital in the backcountry of Virginia, South Carolina, and Louisiana during the national panics. Table 4.2 gives us a closer look at data from an agrarian district in each state. Louisiana's St. Landry Parish had the most robust rebound in the post-panic years, whereas in Virginia and South Carolina the reverse was true in all but one period, Virginia around the 1837 panic. Nevertheless, local networks continued to operate at some level in Goochland and Fairfield as well. Thus, the documentary record shows that community networks remained active throughout the crises of the Panics of 1819, 1837, and 1857, helping to fill voids left by bank closings and tighter lending restrictions. For example, while the Bank of the State of South Carolina approved equity loans totaling just

Table 4.2. Capital Raised by All Mortgages Sampled in Selected Counties

Year	Fairfield County, S.C.	Goochland County, Va.	St. Landry Parish, La.
1817	$1,049,000	$2,845,000	$912,000
1819	1,742,000	2,687,000	4,029,000
1821	829,000	993,000	3,615,000
1835	2,937,000	1,890,000	2,299,000
1837	3,388,000	1,130,000	9,209,000
1839	250,000	3,059,000	4,887,000
1855	2,269,000	2,620,000	14,381,000
1857	1,341,000	3,870,000	12,089,000
1859	945,000	1,935,000	31,188,000

Note: Values in 2015 U.S. dollar equivalents.

over $9 million during the fifteen years sampled in the nineteenth century, accepting 1,120 slaves as collateral, this represented only 9 percent of the slaves that appeared in the sampled South Carolina mortgages and only 7 percent of the capital raised by loans secured by human property.[16]

These numbers reflect the power of informal regional credit networks. What they do not easily convey, however, is the frenzied activity of the boom-and-bust times of the 1830s. Banks multiplied their risky loans, fed by eager speculators in the North as well as the South, all hoping to get their share of soaring profits on the cotton frontier. Also absent from the local mortgage data is the activity of the international financiers. In the 1830s, firms like Alexander Brown & Sons, the Barings, and the Rothschilds enabled cotton shipments to move from the piers of New Orleans, New York, Charleston, and Savannah to Liverpool and beyond. Yet the links between these local credit networks and the national and international systems are clear. For example, the credit market in Mississippi in the boom days before the Panic of 1837 was grossly inflated with bank loans as "funds streamed into the state from around the country and around the world."[17] No doubt capital did pour in from the North and beyond, but the public mortgage records show that neighbor-to-neighbor lending operated concurrently with loans channeled through banks. Then, during the depression and the severe contraction of bank credit, neighbors continued to lend to neighbors. Local loans offered second chances to many individuals and their communities.[18]

The role of international finance also looks different when seen in the light of neighbor-to-neighbor lending. The impact of global capital is undeniable, but again, we should remember that foreign credit augmented powerful local lending pools already established—pools still available when the financial giants tried to shift from local purchasing relationships to the carrying trade and as providers of short-term credit for buyers and sellers of staples produced by slave labor. International powerbrokers like Brown & Sons and the Rothschilds actively tried to minimize their reliance on land and slave collateral and had begun to back away from slave-backed mortgages even before the 1837 collapse. Brown & Sons and the Rothschilds were made fiscally uncomfortable, and in the latter case perhaps were ethically repulsed, by collateral packages offering land and slaves in the South. After this shift in international fiscal policy, not many of the small planters or the holders of a few slaves would have been connected to this group for the operating credit they needed. The number of institutional lenders was decreasing before and after the panic, yet the data show that the neighbors in local credit networks continued to supply substantial amounts of capital.[19]

The data on local lending networks reveal that perhaps the most consistent credit that allowed the slave economy of the United States to grow efficiently and rapidly was the amalgamation of the tens of thousands of quiet transactions between neighbors like Armand Duplantier and Juan Bautista Massi. The continuities in these practices over time are striking. The boom-and-bust decade of the 1830s was transformative both for regional and national banking and for international finance. In contrast, local credit networks in the South functioned in highly consistent ways to use slaves to finance their own purchase and that of additional enslaved workers, land, and personal property.

We have seen that local networks used slave collateral to create streams of cash and credit, but what were the economic consequences of neighbor-to-neighbor lending? Although more research is needed, we still have reasonable options for evaluating whether mortgages using human collateral had a powerful impact on local, regional, and national economies. Projections from the data support the conclusion that the capital raised using human collateral was likely a major driver of economic development. One approach is to compare the amounts of capital generated by loans on slaves with the values of commodities produced by slaves in the same locales. Table 4.3 shows the average annual capital raised by equity mortgages on slaves as a percentage of the value of the three most valuable commodities harvested in various locations in 1860. But purchase money mortgages generally accounted for twice the capital generated by equity mortgages, and thus Table 4.3 also shows the projected amounts of capital raised on slaves by both types of mortgages.[20]

Table 4.3. Average Annual Capital Raised by Mortgages Using Human Collateral
Compared to Values of Commodities (Selected Counties, 1860)

Mortgage capital values/ Commodity values	Goochland County, Va.	Fairfield County, S.C.	St. Landry Parish, La.
Wheat (in 1860 $)	230,000	63,000	N/A
AA value EMs/Wheat value	13%	45%	
AA est. all SMs/Wheat value	40%	134%	
Corn (in 1860 $)	199,000	418,000	393,000
AA value EMs/Corn value	16%	7%	25%
AA est. all SMs/Corn value	47%	20%	102%
			Actual values
Sugar (in 1860 $)	N/A	N/A	227,000
AA value EM/Sugar value			43%
AA est. all SMs/Sugar value			176%
			Actual values
Cotton (in 1860 $)	N/A	949,000	820,000
AA value EM/Cotton value		3%	12%
AA est. all SMs/Cotton value		9%	49%
			Actual values
Tobacco (in 1860 $)	174,000	N/A	N/A
AA value EM/Tobacco value	18%		
AA est. all SMs/Tobacco value	53%		

Note: AA, average annual value; EMs, equity mortgages; est., estimated value; N/A, not
applicable; SMs, all slave mortgages. Dollar values rounded to nearest thousands.

The three most profitable commodities harvested in Goochland County,
Virginia, according to the 1860 census, were wheat, corn, and tobacco. Table 4.3
shows that the average value of capital raised by equity mortgages alone in
Goochland County for 1860 was approximately 13 percent of the value of the
wheat harvested. If we add the purchase money mortgage estimates to the equity mortgage amounts, we would project that the total value of mortgages
(equity plus purchase money) using human collateral in 1860 equaled approximately 40 percent of the value of the wheat harvested, 47 percent of the corn
crop, or 53 percent of the tobacco in this Piedmont county.

The projected values for all mortgages using slaves as collateral in Fairfield County, South Carolina, and St. Landry Parish, Louisiana, reveal that
human collateral also mattered significantly in cotton regions. In Fairfield
County, due north of the state capital of Columbia, slave mortgages ex-

ceeded the total value of the 1860 wheat crop by more than 33 percent and reached 20 percent of the corn crop or 9 percent of the cotton baled. In St. Landry Parish, where a higher percentage of the slave population (more than 25 percent) was mortgaged, the amount of capital raised by both purchase money and equity mortgages in 1860 equaled 102 percent of the corn crop, 176 percent of the sugar crop, or 49 percent of the cotton crop. While the mortgage capital is significant in Goochland and Fairfield Counties, the importance of slave collateral on the St. Landry cotton frontier is particularly impressive. Surprisingly, if we look at the data for a less agricultural parish, East Baton Rouge, Louisiana, the pattern holds and, in fact, intensifies.[21] In East Baton Rouge, where there was virtually no manufacturing, planters produced about half the cotton baled in St. Landry. Nevertheless, in 1860 Baton Rouge residents raised more than four times the capital with mortgages using human collateral than was raised by St. Landry planters. What the East Baton Rouge and St. Landry data confirm is that slaves were crucial for attracting capital on economic frontiers in the nineteenth century, whether those frontier zones remained heavily reliant on cash crops or had become more diversified. All of the counties and parishes sampled show that local capital was raised in economically significant amounts relative to the most valuable commodities produced locally. Whether on the southwestern frontier or in the more established Atlantic states, both the capital generated by mortgaging enslaved people and the crops produced through their labor expanded local economies and contributed to the growing prosperity of the nation.

Conclusion

There is still much to discover about slavery's capitalism, yet all the chapters in this volume share an image of capitalistic sophistication that runs counter to the traditional assumptions about the economy of the South.[22] This frees us to reconceptualize the former, more rigid, North/South historiographical dichotomy. Rather than putting the South and North on a sliding scale that is preset to rank the North as the model of complex nineteenth-century capitalism and the South as an inferior replica, it may be more useful to think of northerners and southerners as performing various social and economic experiments in capitalism. Looking beyond the Americas for comparisons—contemporaneous developments in Russia, for example—may help, too. When facing the challenges of financing their economy during industrialization in the nineteenth century, Russian financiers adapted the fiscal tool of mortgaging serfs as part of the modernization of banking in Russia—this at the same time that slaves were being mortgaged in the United States.[23] Another fresh interpretation comes from David Hancock, who has posited an unexpected relationship between local and international trade. Hancock found that small merchants in colonial North America developed direct relationships with clients across the Atlantic. The resulting networks resembled "a spider's web" more than "the traditional 'hub and spoke' model, with European merchant houses as the 'hubs.'"[24] This is another indication that we should be looking at the power of the local to create strong spurs to economic development.[25]

With emancipation in the mid-nineteenth century, the southern economy collapsed. Among the many social and financial repercussions was that an enslaved labor force was no longer available as collateral. Over time, the northern and southern systems of capitalism began to look more similar. Memories of the days when slaves were mortgaged faded. Within a decade or so after the Civil War, the lawsuits tied to local credit webs were resolved. The threads attached to human collateral were reeled in and tightly wound, stored out of sight in the files of county courthouses. Historians have begun to unwind those long-forgotten contract strands and to use them to trace fresh connections between slavery and economic development. We have begun to plot the data points that we retrieve as on some vast pointillistic canvas. As we gather and examine more and more mortgages like that between Armand Duplantier and Juan Bautista Massi, the design will begin to emerge, and our view of slavery as a capitalist system will refocus to appreciate the large amount of capital raised through loans from neighbor to neighbor and supported by slave property. It will become as customary to envision slaves being worked in the financial arenas as collateral as it is now to picture them laboring in fields and foundries. We will learn more about how the use of slaves as collateral varied over time and region and how much capital was raised. We will have a clearer idea of the impacts of these loans on the growth of local, regional, and national economies. The scale of local mortgaging of slaves will adjust our traditional assumptions about the interplay between foreign financiers, northern institutional lenders, and the ordinary southerners who made the most of this fiscal strategy. We will learn more about where and when the matrix of local credit networks spanning the South preserved the pools of community credit, which became even more important when national and international credit nearly evaporated. We will learn more about where and when slave collateral produced capital that rivaled the sales of rice, wheat, and cotton. Finally, we will learn more about how many of these mortgages were repaid. With that we will know more about how many families of enslaved people were shattered when borrowers defaulted and "the collateral" of fathers and mothers, daughters and sons—like Helena, Marieta, Clara, Pedro, Francisco, Mary, and Mary's two children—were seized by local sheriffs. We are recovering our national memory of mortgaging slaves, and with that knowledge we are beginning to paint a more complete picture of slavery's capitalism.

CHAPTER 5

The Contours of Cotton Capitalism

Speculation, Slavery, and Economic Panic in Mississippi, 1832–1841

JOSHUA D. ROTHMAN

As a young man, Jesse Mabry showed an enterprising spirit but little tendency toward extravagance. Born in South Carolina in 1791 or 1792, by 1810 Mabry had married a woman named Nancy and the couple had established an independent household in Union County, situated in the northwestern Piedmont section of the state. They did not own much and likely brought in some income by selling cloth that Nancy wove herself, but they amassed wealth slowly and steadily over time. Sometime around 1820, they left South Carolina to pursue new economic opportunities in Mississippi, and by 1830 Jesse Mabry had become a moderately prosperous man. Living in Wilkinson County below Natchez in the extreme southwestern corner of the state, Mabry was the father of three children, the owner of eleven slaves, and a partner in the newly founded mercantile firm of Ware and Mabry.[1]

Being a merchant was a decent way to make a living in Mississippi, but serious money came from cotton planting, and in the spring of 1832 Jesse Mabry showed his aspirations when he made his first foray into that world. He used seven slaves as collateral for a $1,500 loan from the Bank of Mississippi, took around $5,000 already in his possession, and pooled it all with the funds of a partner named Mason Saunders. Together, Mabry and Saunders bought 225 acres of land near the town of Pinckneyville, close to Mississippi's border with Louisiana along the Mississippi River, along with four slaves and all the livestock and farming utensils belonging to the land's previous owner. Mabry and Saunders then went to Natchez, where they purchased sixteen more slaves from Isaac Franklin, partner in the largest slave-trading firm in the South. By the end of April 1832, Mabry and Saunders owned a fully stocked cotton plantation with more than twenty-five bound laborers at their disposal.[2]

But Mabry aborted this initial attempt to launch himself into the planter class. Perhaps he and Saunders reaped less of a profit than they had anticipated. Perhaps they fought or never intended their arrangement would be a lasting one. Whatever the case, in January 1833 the two sold their land and the slaves they had purchased from Franklin, and they went their separate ways. Mabry returned to the mercantile business in the Wilkinson County town of Woodville, partnering this time with a man named Austin, and the firm did quite well, selling $30,000 worth of merchandise in 1834. Mabry owned no land, but he still owned a number of slaves and was a trusted enough businessman that several individuals in nearby Louisiana parishes asked him to serve as their Mississippi agent on some economic dealings.[3]

By the middle of the 1830s, then, Jesse Mabry was almost forty-five years old and over the course of nearly fifteen years in Mississippi had followed a relatively careful path to modest economic success. But in 1835 he finally saw the big chance to realize his ambitions beyond the retail world, and he was going all in. In January, the mercantile firm of Mabry and Austin dissolved. A few months later, Mabry went to Madison County, a booming center of cotton production around 150 miles northeast of his Woodville home. If the $30,000 he brought with him was not all the money he had in the world, it must have been nearly so. When he got to Madison, he put down that $30,000, took out a mortgage for another $180,000 from a planter named Mark Cockrill, and bought Cockrill's entire plantation—more than 1,700 acres of land near the Big Black River—along with 127 slaves and every horse, mule, cow, farming utensil, and piece of furniture Cockrill owned.[4]

This was an exorbitant price for a cotton plantation, and assuming so much debt to pay it was seemingly out of character for someone like Mabry, who owed what financial standing he had achieved largely to sensible prudence rather than excessive risk. But the economic environment of the 1830s had a way of tempting even cautious and patient men to adventurism. Historians have long observed the speculative bubble that characterized the U.S. economy during this era. As accelerated market development, infrastructural improvements, and the public sale of large swaths of expropriated Indian land converged with a dramatically increased money supply and federal policies that enabled growing numbers of state and local banks to unleash a deluge of cheap paper notes and liberal loans, Americans understood themselves to be living in an expansive moment when anything was possible for those willing to hustle. Easy credit could be leveraged into a staggering fortune, and a clever man acting quickly could borrow his way right to the top, transforming himself almost magically into a giant among his fellows. Indeed, Jesse Mabry had become the second largest slaveholder in Madison County with just one economic transaction.[5]

Being in Mississippi in particular perfectly placed Mabry to find such an opportunity. During the 1830s cotton was America's most important export, market prices for it kept rising, and the federal government made millions of acres of land where it might be profitably grown available for sale in the state. Capital accordingly poured into Mississippi, and the same scholars who describe the rage for speculation that swept the country during these "flush times" almost universally note that it was most furious in the nation's southwestern Cotton Belt. But only recently have scholars begun appreciating how extensively slaves and slavery inflated the bubble of the flush times, and how cotton capitalism rested on the capacity of the enslaved as both laborers and assets to underwrite what men like Jesse Mabry imagined for their futures. By 1835, Mabry had already used the enslaved to guarantee a loan with at least part of which he bought more slaves, who were then to produce the cotton that would let him repay that same loan. His purchase of Mark Cockrill's plantation, meanwhile, entailed assuming nearly $200,000 in debt, the largest portion of which paid for the coerced workforce that simultaneously became Mabry's most valuable property and the people through whose sweat he projected his dreams of being a planter.[6]

Because there would be no cotton without slaves, the prospective success of the cotton economy in Mississippi was predicated ultimately on countless intertwined and multilayered loops of speculation in commoditized human beings like those into which Jesse Mabry inserted himself. Planters like Mabry knew that making this alchemy work required a property regime where their investments were secure and a labor regime effective enough to yield the cotton that paid their debts. But neither was assured, which exacerbated slavery's cruelty and created anxiety that could turn extraordinarily violent at the slightest provocation. And in the end, no amount of violence could deter the logic of economic contraction. When the Panic of 1837 came to the United States, it began in Mississippi, and as the shaky foundations of the state's economy collapsed, with reverberations felt across the country and around the world, the imbrication of slavery and capitalism was thrown into stark relief. Jesse Mabry would discover the consequences of that firsthand. So would the slaves who had made possible his illusory rise.

Many observers noted that Americans in the 1830s enthusiastically engaged in moneymaking ventures of nearly any sort, no matter how questionable. With the number of banks in the United States and their cumulative capital more than doubling between 1830 and 1836, and with Andrew Jackson's withdrawal of federal deposits from the Second Bank of the United States effectively destroying whatever regulatory influence that institution had exercised over the broader economy, Americans loaded with cash and credit leapt at chances for putting their money into motion wherever they could find them.[7] Real estate schemes seemed particularly widespread. Newspapers across the country reported skyrocketing land prices that bore no plausible relation to their actual worth—Maine timberland purchased in the 1820s for $620 that sold for $180,000, town property in Louisville bought for $675 in 1815 that brought its owner an offer of $275,000, a remote river island in northwestern Ohio that cost $1,000 and sold less than two months later for $3,000, village lots along the Erie Canal whose buyers paid ten times what the land had sold for six months earlier. One editor, astonished that "men risk their thousands, and tens of thousands in the purchase of property, with less care and examination, than they would bestow on the purchase of a vest pattern of a dollar's value," concluded that "the speculating fever" in land amounted to a national "mania."[8]

In the southwestern Cotton Belt, however, Americans built a culture of speculation unique in its abandon. Joseph Baldwin, a young Virginia lawyer who headed to the region in 1836, recalled literally sensing a shift in the economic environment as he rode into it. Contrasting the "picayune standard" of the East with "the wild spendthriftism, the impetuous rush and the magnificent scale of operations" of the southwestern Cotton Belt, Baldwin noted that "the new country seemed to be a reservoir, and every road leading to it a vagrant stream of enterprise and adventure." None of the usual rules of business and finance appeared to apply. "Money, or what passed for money," Baldwin remembered, was the "only cheap thing to be had," and real estate costs "rose like smoke. Lots in obscure villages were held at city prices; lands, bought at the minimum cost of government, were sold from thirty to forty dollars per acre, and considered dirt cheap at that." It all mystified Baldwin, who worried that fantasy had supplanted reason. Men accumulated "paper fortunes" and imagined instant riches at "every cross-road and every avocation," but to Baldwin the southwest was a "hell-carnival" where "avarice and hope joined partnership" and everything stood "on its head with its heels in the air."[9]

Baldwin's accounts of the flush times in the southwest were not published until years later, and in some measure he intended them as caricature. Contemporary evidence, however, suggests he exaggerated little. Baldwin's fellow Virginia lawyer Thomas Gray, for example, got thoroughly taken in by the region's infectious economic environment in 1835. Gray had only planned on passing through the southwestern Cotton Belt en route to Texas, where he was to act as land agent for some men from Washington, D.C. But on hearing of "great speculations in lands," Gray stopped to do some business for himself. He spent days in the southwest poring over maps and examining settlements where every parcel had been bought and sold as many as four times in five years at prices that spiraled higher and higher. Speed was critical: Gray met men who dropped tens of thousands of dollars on plantations without ever seeing the property and others who came away disappointed because land they had been scouting got snatched out from under them before they could get back to a government land office to purchase it. But Gray was not dissuaded. The energy of the "*new world*" he had stumbled into was intoxicating. "I cannot help feeling the contagion," Gray wrote in his diary, "and want to be dealing in tens and hundreds of thousands."[10]

Joseph Baldwin may have been dubious, but the frenzy he and Thomas Gray described was not hard to understand. The southwest possessed the continent's most fertile soil for growing cotton, for which the demand from the domestic and British textile industries was insatiable. Though cotton was already vital to the American economy by the start of the 1830s, average New Orleans market prices for the crop increased by 80 percent in the first half of the decade, and by its end southwestern growers had cemented cotton's place as the most significant commodity in the world.[11]

Any number of figures might be mustered to demonstrate cotton's economic might and the southwest's central role in its accretion. In 1831, the United States produced around 350 million pounds of cotton, just under half the planet's raw cotton crop. The bulk of that crop was shipped abroad, and cotton exports, worth a shade under $30 million, accounted for 35 percent of the value of all goods exported from the United States. By 1835 the cotton crop had increased to more than 500 million pounds, roughly 70 percent of it grown in Alabama, Mississippi, Louisiana, and Georgia. Cotton exports, now worth nearly $65 million, amounted to more than half the value of all goods America sent overseas, a majority cotton maintained every year until 1841 and for most years prior to the Civil War. In 1834, thanks almost entirely to southwestern cotton production, New Orleans bypassed New York as the country's most important export city and would hold that position for almost a decade. In 1839 the United States produced more than 800 million pounds of cotton. Its share of global production had become nearly two-thirds, and 80 percent of American cotton now came from the southwest. Of the 86 percent of the crop shipped overseas, two-thirds of it went to England, which relied on the United States for 81 percent of the cotton its mills turned into yarn and cloth.[12]

Amid the prospective bonanza to be extracted from cotton in the 1830s, the richest vein lay in Mississippi, which, in the words of one historian, was "the best example of a state totally absorbed in the boom psychology."[13] The removal of the Choctaw and Chickasaw Indians early in the decade opened the northern half of the state to white settlement, and hopeful purchasers swarmed federal land offices for months on end when they commenced business. The national government sold more than one million acres of public land in Mississippi in 1833 alone, twice as much as in any other state. In 1835 the government sold nearly three million acres, which was more public land than had been sold in the entire country just a few years prior.[14]

Facilitating Mississippi land sales was a proliferating banking sector. The number of banks incorporated in the state grew from one in 1829 to thirteen in 1837. Most had multiple branches, and their collective volume of loans bulged from just over $1 million to more than $15 million, seemingly with good reason. The nearly 75,000 white people who moved to Mississippi and doubled the state's white population between 1830 and 1836 provided an eager market for that money. Moreover, their ability to pay back what they borrowed appeared beyond question. In 1834 Mississippians produced 85 million pounds of cotton, a more than eightfold increase over the amount they had produced less than fifteen years earlier. In 1836 they brought more than 125 million pounds to market, and by 1839 the Mississippi cotton crop amounted to nearly 200 million pounds, at which point Mississippians grew almost a quarter of America's cotton, more than the residents of any other state in the nation.[15]

Because cotton had the potential to yield returns very quickly and the efflorescence of banks made Mississippi a place where, as one man observed in 1836, "credit is plenty, and he who has no money can do as much business as he who has," nearly anyone able to procure even a small piece of land could believe he was on the road to success. Casual assessments of Mississippi's circumstances made it hard to argue with the results. To Natchez lawyer William Henry Sparks, the 1830s were years when it appeared a "new El Dorado had been discovered . . . and unexampled prosperity seemed to cover the land as with a golden canopy . . . where yesterday the wilderness darkened over the land with her wild forests, to-day the cotton plantation whitened the earth." Author Joseph Holt Ingraham, who toured Mississippi in 1834, similarly considered cotton growing a craze that would not pass "till every acre is purchased and cultivated" and the state became "one vast cotton field." Ingraham concluded that "if the satirical maxim, 'man was made to make money,' is true . . . [then] the mint of his operations lies most temptingly" in Mississippi. Burrell Fox, a farmer who migrated to Mississippi in the early 1830s, was not as lettered as Sparks or Ingraham, but refinement was unnecessary for seeing what cotton made possible. "I like this cuntry," he wrote to relatives in North Carolina, "better then any cuntry I have evry yet seen for making money."[16]

To be sure, there was a lot of money in Mississippi. The residents of the state's Natchez District in particular were among the wealthiest in the United States, and they funneled resources into land, banks, internal improvements, and other promising investment opportunities. The selection of the Planters' Bank of Mississippi as a depository for federal funds withdrawn from the Second Bank of the United States kept government monies flooding in, and funds streamed into the state from around the country and around the world as nonresident investors from New York, Boston, Philadelphia, and other financial centers pumped millions into land companies, state bonds, and bank stocks. By way of example, just one land company comprising investors mostly from New York mustered hundreds of thousands of dollars to speculate on public lands in Mississippi, and a company agent reported in 1835 from the site of an impending land sale that "capital has been constantly flowing into the country." He remarked that "every house within several miles" of the land office was packed with "wealthy planters from all parts of the southern states, with ready money, eager to purchase" land, and that Mississippi merchants told of being pestered in northern cities by people wondering "who might be recommended to invest" on their behalf. All told, the agent guessed there was "probably at present upwards of two millions of Dollars ready for investment" just at the sale he was awaiting.[17]

But the extent of Mississippi's affluence rested on a series of bookkeeping fictions. Ostensibly, Mississippi's banking capital increased roughly by a factor of ten between 1830 and the beginning of 1837. But banks often had only a small fraction of their capital actually in hand. They counted money stock-holders committed as if they had already paid it in, printed notes and issued credit on promised rather than actual holdings, and provided sweetheart loans to institution officers and political cronies, who used property purchased with that financing as collateral for additional credit at other banks. Public land sales further distorted bank operations, as purchasers used paper money bor-rowed from banks to buy cheap land from the federal government, which re-deposited the funds back into those same banks, which then loaned that same money out over and over again, creating ever-greater speculative momen-tum.[18]

The combination of increasingly high cotton prices and increasingly large cotton crops necessary to sustain this pyramid of debt-fueled delirium was an unlikely one. Nonetheless, it continued to manifest itself through the first half of the 1830s, with the production side of the equation made possible only by the massive importation of slave labor to the state. The white population of Mississippi grew fast in the 1830s, but the black population grew even faster. Just over 65,000 in 1830, by 1836 the number of enslaved people had jumped to more than 164,000, an increase of roughly 250 percent and substantial enough that blacks had come to outnumber whites in the state. Whites brought still another 30,000 slaves into Mississippi before the end of the decade. By 1840 the enslaved population sat at nearly 200,000, approximately 52 percent of the state's population and triple what it had been ten years earlier.[19]

Every white man intending to become a cotton planter in Mississippi aimed to own slaves, and those who already owned some aimed to own more. As the French engineer Michel Chevalier noted while visiting the United States between 1833 and 1835, a cotton plantation was essentially "a sort of agricul-tural manufactory," and assembling a productive workforce was the key to maximizing output and profits. The more slaves a man owned, the more land he could cultivate and the more cotton he could bring to market. It was no secret that slave labor made everything about the flush times possible. Joseph Ingraham remarked that the heads of young white men coming to Mississippi were filled with cotton plantation dreams, but that there was only one proven path to making those dreams come true. "To sell cotton in order to buy negroes—to make more cotton to buy more negroes, 'ad infinitum,' is the aim and direct tendency of all the operations of the thorough-going cotton planter; his whole soul is wrapped up in the pursuit. . . . [W]ithout slaves there could be no planters. . . . Without planters there could be no cotton; without cot-ton no wealth. Without [slaves] Mississippi would be a wilderness, and revert to the aboriginal possessors. Annihilate them to-morrow, and this state and every southern state might be bought for a song."[20]

It might seem that white Mississippians actually insulated themselves against financial failure by so unreservedly expanding slavery. Enslaved people grew cotton that would make slaveholders wealthy, and as relatively liquid assets slaves could also be converted into cash should an indebted slaveholder find himself in a tight spot. So long as regional market prices for field hands rose alongside cotton prices, as they did in the early 1830s, owning slaves in Mississippi would appear to be both vital to making cotton and fairly sturdy protection against unpredicted and catastrophic changes in circumstances.[21]

But in truth, the explosive growth of slavery in Mississippi aggravated the financial risk underpinning the state's development, because white Mississippians' engagement with the slave trade intensified the leveraging of their operations and introduced greater insecurity into their enterprise. Many white settlers who moved to Mississippi from other states were already slaveholders, and dragged their slaves with them on their southwestern migration. But professional slave traders did booming business throughout the region and provided a substantial minority if not an outright majority of the 130,000 slaves forcibly imported into Mississippi during the 1830s. It was true that traders engaged in a deeply speculative business as they capitalized on the labor demands of southwestern cotton farmers, and white southerners expressing disdain for traders' line of work commonly referred to them as "negro speculators." Yet when white Mississippians purchased bondmen from slave traders they were speculating too, and arguably they were more reckless.[22]

In some degree that was true because whites financed slave purchases as they did anything of great value—by borrowing against anticipated cotton production. Southwestern banks existed fundamentally to provide capital to develop the plantation economy, and their loans underwrote slaves as they did land, draft animals, and farm equipment. Moreover, with credit flowing so freely, whites did not necessarily need a loan directly from a bank to finance buying enslaved laborers. Joseph Baldwin remembered that during the flush times, "negroes were brought into the country in large numbers and sold mostly upon credit, and bills of exchange taken for the price." Michel Chevalier similarly remarked that "the internal slave trade furnishes hands in abundance which are easily procured on credit when one has friends, but no patrimony."[23]

In fact, as the 1830s progressed, slave traders became increasingly lavish with the credit they offered themselves. One man, summarizing the escalation for a Philadelphia newspaper, noted that through 1833, slave traders in Mississippi "required cash in hand" when they made sales, and the trade proved so lucrative that growing numbers of traders flocked to the state. Many began selling slaves on credit so they might better compete with their fellows, yet the demand for slave labor drove prices higher despite the increased supply and generous terms of sale. In 1834, the man reported, slave traders began offering slaves that could be paid for up to four months after sale. They "sold out, at fine profits." In 1835, even more traders appeared in Mississippi. Many extended credit up to fifteen months and started charging purchasers 10 percent interest, but average prices rose nonetheless, from $700 to $1,200. In 1836, "all the public highways to Mississippi became lined . . . with slaves," which severely glutted the market and led to lagging sales. But by early 1837 traders were selling slaves on terms as long as two years, enticing many planters "to purchase a second, and even a third supply at from 12 to $1800 each. All the slaves were soon sold."[24]

The extent of white Mississippians' obligations to pay for slaves cannot be reckoned precisely, but no one doubted it was staggeringly large. The man describing matters in the newspaper surely exaggerated when he figured that white Mississippians collectively borrowed $90 million to buy slaves in only three years, while another estimate from 1841 that Mississippians still owed more than $3 million to slave traders for their purchases between 1832 and 1837 was probably too low. The *Natchez Courier,* publishing from the site of the state's largest slave mart, offered a snapshot that may provide a relatively accurate feel for the whole. It reported that white residents of Mississippi bought as many as 10,000 slaves on credit between the fall of 1835 and the fall of 1836. At an average cost of at least $1,000, the *Courier* concluded that cotton planters thus "created a debt for slaves alone, to be paid out of the crop of 1836, equal to ten millions of dollars."[25]

It might have been sensible and even shrewd for white Mississippians to pile debt upon debt in this fashion had the enslaved been as sound an investment in practice as they were in theory. Compounding the speculative nature of cotton capitalism was that they were not. Mississippians who bought bondpersons from slave traders had to assess the value of their most crucial assets on the basis of limited information. Purchasing unfamiliar people from unknown distances, prospective slaveholders relied mostly on traders' assurances that the enslaved people offered as merchandise were healthy and submissive, possessed of solid work habits, and legally acquired. Yet none of those things was necessarily true. An insalubrious climate and harsh work regime yielded high death rates and considerable resistance among brutalized slaves. Title fraud was widespread, traders sometimes lied about the fitness of people they sold or concealed histories of rebelliousness, and filing suit against deceptive traders could prove protracted, expensive, or fruitless. Rather than stabilizing economic conditions by serving as a hedge against uncertainty, borrowing to buy slaves drew attention to the contingencies of building a property regime grounded in human chattel.[26]

Political leaders in Mississippi recognized that the slave trade was problematic and repeatedly tried to control it. In 1808 the territorial legislature enacted a law mandating certificates of good character for all adult slaves imported into Mississippi for sale. That law was reenacted in 1822, five years after Mississippi attained statehood, and in 1825 the state began taxing slave auction proceeds and slave sales conducted by itinerant traders. Most dramatically, the revised Mississippi constitution of 1832 outlawed the interstate slave trade altogether, banning "the introduction of slaves into this state as merchandize, or for sale" as of May 1, 1833.[27]

On its surface, the constitutional ban on the interstate trade reflected concerns about public safety and scorn for traders' supposedly shady and brutish business practices. Several years after the ban was enacted, James Trotter, who had been a delegate to the constitutional convention in 1832 and member of a committee created by the convention to consider the slave trade, recalled the logic behind it. Those who crafted the ban, he remembered, had been motivated by a desire "to prevent a too rapid increase of slave population in our state" and by the sense that it was particularly "dangerous to the moral and orderly condition of our own slaves" to allow "the introduction of slaves from abroad of depraved character, which were imposed upon our unsuspecting citizens by the artful and too often unscrupulous negro trader." Moreover, Trotter asserted that white Mississippians had had their fill of "the barbarities, the frauds, [and] the scenes so shocking in many instances to our feelings of humanity and the sensibilities of our nature" that accompanied the importation and exhibition of slaves for sale. All in all, Trotter concluded, it was widely believed that "the time had arrived, when the traffic in this species of property, as 'merchandize,' should cease."[28]

Mississippi was not the only southwestern state that tried prohibiting the activities of interstate traders. Louisiana, Alabama, and Georgia implemented interdictions in the early 1830s too, and all were moved to act at least partially in response to the Southampton insurrection that broke out in Virginia during the summer of 1831. As whites in the southwest grappled with the implications of the slave trade, however, considerations of safety were never far from economic considerations. Really, there was little substantive distinction between the two. By banning the interstate trade on the pretense that devious and unsavory traders brought too many slaves from too many places infected with the contagion of rebellion, white Mississippians signaled to investors and potential immigrants alike that the state remained a secure place to put their money. Slave unrest was bad for business, but as of 1833 safeguards existed in Mississippi such that it would neither threaten white lives nor interfere with cotton production.[29]

Had Mississippi authorities earnestly upheld the interstate slave trade ban, it might also have contained the level of debt Mississippians owed non-residents and kept capital from leaving the state in the pockets of slave traders. But white Mississippians never took paper prohibitions seriously. The same constitutional clause outlawing the interstate trade explicitly protected the right of Mississippi residents to purchase slaves anywhere in the country and bring them into the state for their personal use, a guarantee that spurred the practice of men buying slaves from traders just across the Mississippi River in Louisiana. Most did not even bother with the technical adherence to the law such a ruse allowed. The ban on the interstate trade was deeply unpopular, and rather than pass enabling legislation clarifying the penalty for violating it, during its 1833 session the state legislature revived the tax on slave sales, thereby sanctioning a form of commerce that violated the state constitution. Little wonder that traders sold more slaves in Mississippi in the years after 1833 than they ever had before.[30]

Thus, while white Mississippians outwardly had clamped down on the potential influx of rebellious slaves and established a method for managed expansion of the enslaved population, the facts of the situation were nearly the opposite. Consequently, the flush times proceeded apace, but an underlying sense of their precariousness lingered. Able to satisfy their financial obligations and emerge as genuinely wealthy men only if the project of turning the forests into money went absolutely smoothly, Mississippi's cotton farmers were an edgy bunch who did not take perceived threats to their investments and their futures lightly. Already balancing their economic dependence on enslaved laborers with a readiness to inflict tremendous suffering on them, slaveholders in Mississippi were prepared to act ruthlessly should anything endanger such a delicate equilibrium.

That reality was never clearer than during the summer of 1835, when slaveholders in the west-central portion of the state became convinced that a conspiracy of white men, led by a purported master criminal named John Murrell, had imminent plans for inciting an insurrection among the slaves of Mississippi, designed ultimately to engulf all southern states in a storm of racial unrest and opportunistic pillage. Hysteria ensued. Over the course of several weeks between late June and the middle of July, patrols imprisoned scores of people, and hastily formed vigilance committees held makeshift trials at which witnesses were intimidated, beaten, and tortured to extract confessions of guilt and information about other supposed conspirators. By the time the frenzy subsided, five white men had been hanged, one committed suicide in jail, numerous others had been exiled from the state, and roughly two dozen slaves had been executed.[31]

In truth, there probably was no conspiracy, and there decidedly was not one on the scale imagined by Mississippi's slaveholders. It was rather their own racial and financial insecurities that left them vulnerable to the warnings offered in a lurid if almost self-evidently ludicrous pamphlet circulating in the state that told tales of Murrell as a preternaturally expert slave stealer who presided over a syndicate of bandits one thousand strong. With enslaved people increasingly outnumbering them and often not yet even paid for in full, Mississippi slaveholders were terrified by the notion that white men lurked among them undermining their property rights and encouraging rebellion. Real or chimera, these were chances not worth taking, and a man like Jesse Mabry was not about to let any of it happen. He had gone deep into debt just months before the Murrell scare broke, and everything he had was riding on making the slaves who embodied much of that debt pay off. It might seem that he overreacted by personally torturing suspected slaves while interrogating them about their roles in the alleged plot, or that he lost his sense of perspective while assuming a leadership role on the primary vigilance committee in the state, whose members took it upon themselves to adjudicate and administer the fates of accused conspirators. But Mabry probably considered those things to be matters of risk management.[32]

George Fall, editor of the *Jackson Mississippian,* saw precisely how disastrous a threat like that posed by Murrell could be for the southwest's economic future, whether or not it was as genuine as his state's planters seemed to think. In an editorial published as the insurrection scare subsided, Fall wrote that other newspapers had exaggerated the danger of an uprising. Tellingly, though, even as he downplayed the scare, Fall stressed that white control over the most important form of capital in the region was absolute. Professing to be worried less about Murrell's plot than that "a stranger would suppose that the whole white population of the State had narrowly escaped massacre and death by the rising of the savage and infuriated blacks," Fall sought to put at ease anyone considering moving to or spending money in the state. "We can assure those who are disposed to emigrate hither," Fall concluded, "that they have nothing to fear in Mississippi from insurrectionary movements among the blacks. Property and life are as safe here as in any of the States where slavery exists, and recent occurrences should not prevent emigration to our State, or deter capitalists from investing their funds in our Stocks. They can do so with as much security and profit as ever; and our negroes, uninfluenced by base and designing white men, are as orderly and obedient as the negroes of any State in the Union."[33]

Fall's assurances aside, not all was well in Mississippi's economy. Some people saw it coming. James Davidson, a lawyer traveling through the state in 1836, considered the speculative enthusiasms of Mississippians totally absurd. Confiding to his diary that there would "be a tremendous failure here some day, and that not far hence," Davidson was sure that the state would "be a fine field for Lawyers in two or three years." Others, like a correspondent of the *Jackson Mississippian* calling himself "Curtius," could make no sense of what was happening at all. Within a matter of weeks, as winter became spring in 1837, the excess of cash that had fueled the flush times dried up, property values plummeted, and farmers and planters throughout the state faced bankruptcy and destitution. Convinced that Mississippi remained "in the highest state of prosperity" and that "the intrinsic value of property" had "in nowise diminished," Curtius insisted that "the present pressure" was "purely artificial." A believer in most circumstances in "letting trade regulate itself," Curtius now called on the state government to take remedial action for those who, "when all the productive industry was in the full tide of success," failed to "anticipate that an unseen hand would hurl back the flood, and leave them stranded on the naked shore." Without relief, he argued, "Mississippi will stand a MONUMENT OF DEVASTATION."[34]

Curtius was not entirely wrong to blame an "unseen hand" for the economic crisis he saw unfolding in Mississippi in 1837, at least to the extent that people and forces outside the state played important roles in precipitating it. He certainly could not have chosen a more apt metaphor than the shifting tides for what transpired, as the dynamics that had inundated Mississippi with the appearance of boundless wealth early in the 1830s reversed themselves almost completely in the second half of the decade. Where land sales had filled the vaults of Mississippi banks with federal monies, congressional legislation passed in June 1836 provided for redistribution of federal surpluses among the states based on their numerical representation in Congress, presaging a currency drain from the southwest and leading bankers to begin calling in loans and restricting credit terms. President Jackson's executive order requiring that federal land purchases be made in gold or silver, issued just weeks later, might have helped stem the prospective outflow of money from Mississippi. But it also threatened an abrupt curtailment of speculation in the state and raised the specter of undercapitalized banks unable to pay hard money to note holders demanding redemption. These conflicting congressional and presidential policies created uncertainty about the government's management of its precious metal supply and enhanced doubts foreign investors and creditors had already begun to have about the overall strength of the American economy. Late in the summer of 1836, the Bank of England raised interest rates, and that fall it tightened credit available to British firms engaged in business and trade with the United States. Monetary pressure on the American side of the Atlantic intensified accordingly, and when cotton prices then fell by 25 percent between November 1836 and April 1837, collapse was inevitable.[35]

The suffering experienced in the United States during the depression that followed the Panic of 1837 was severe, widespread, and long-lasting, and signs of its impact could be seen and felt first in Mississippi. On May 4, both the Planters' Bank and the Agricultural Bank in Natchez suspended specie payments, touching off a cascade of suspensions by nearly every bank in the country before the month ended. Cotton's indispensability to the American economy made Mississippi a logical bellwether of a broader downturn when market prospects for the crop declined. Nonetheless, Curtius's position that Mississippians themselves bore no responsibility for their predicament was hard to square, as the enticements offered by the southwest were matched only by the carelessness the region's residents displayed as they gave in to them. Behaving as if the flush times would last forever and as though they could extend themselves indefinitely without repercussions, Mississippians were left hopelessly exposed to changing conditions.[36]

The underlying weaknesses of Mississippi's economy were reflected in the extent of its desolation in the years after 1837. Speculators and other purchasers of public land who had yet to make payment defaulted and forfeited title to tens of thousands of acres when they could not muster the necessary specie, and new federal land sales in the state plummeted from more than three million acres in 1836 to fewer than half a million in 1837. Farmers and planters who had borrowed against future cotton crops scrambled to keep their enterprises afloat as prices fell, but court dockets still became crammed with so many debt lawsuits "that some of the lawyers had their declarations in *assump-sit* printed by the quire, leaving blanks only for the names of the debtors, creditor and the amounts." Announcements of sheriff's sales would fill Mississippi newspapers for years.[37]

William Wills, a merchant, cotton planter, and minister from North Carolina, was shocked by what he observed in Mississippi when he traveled there in 1840. "The actual condition of affairs," he wrote in his diary, "is much worse than the report." Mississippi had recently been so wealthy and its land some of the most coveted in the nation, but now Wills saw real estate that had been valued at $50 an acre available for just $5 and that which had been worth $10 an acre purchasable for as little as fifty cents. All told, he estimated that in the counties he passed through "it may probably be said that *not one man in fifty*, are solvent and probably less a number than this." Wills tried to withhold judgment, but he could not help thinking that Mississippians had failed to note when "limits have been passed, lost sight of & forgotten as things having no existence." As a result, Mississippi was "ruined, her rich men poor and her poor men beggars. . . . We have hard times in No. Ca.; hard times in the east, hard times everywhere, but Miss: exceeds them all." Wills would have gotten no argument from Mississippi plantation owner Martin Phillips, who recorded in his own 1840 diary that the state was "now paying penance for her past extravagance." To him it seemed that all of Mississippi was "*bankrupt;* never was there a time when insolvency was more general."[38]

Just as slaves and slavery had sat at the core of Mississippi's economy before the crash, many white Mississippians now turn to their enslaved property to stave off financial disaster. Bearing the brunt of their owners' failures, thousands of slaves who had already lost families and communities through forced migration to the southwest disappeared back into the cash nexus as planters tried stanching losses by selling off their most valuable remaining assets, along with their land and their livestock. In other cases, whites had put themselves so far in a hole that they forsook any expectation of getting out of it and abandoned their land altogether, sometimes in the middle of the night and one step ahead of their creditors. But even as they left fires burning, cows in their pens, and wagons in their places, they never left behind their slaves. If they could just make it out of the United States and into Texas, land and food could be replaced, but no property could help a farmer start over faster than enslaved laborers. Martin Phillips was not the only planter who noticed his formerly rich neighbors "running off with their negroes."[39]

Creditors sometimes chased down debtors attempting to abscond to Texas, but flight remained arguably the most effective salvaging strategy, as the dramatic drop in slave prices during the depression limited the utility of other approaches that relied on the enslaved to bail white men out of debt. Driven unreasonably high during the flush times, prices bottomed out in the early 1840s at less than half what they had been at their peak a few years earlier, but stories emerged from Mississippi in the earliest stages of the panic about farmers whose needs for cash were so pressing that they sold slaves for a quarter of what they might have been worth months before. Most problematic, of course, was that many white Mississippians had purchased the slaves in their possession with borrowed money that they had yet to pay back. Selling those slaves at depreciated prices might mean some small return for banks, slave traders, and other creditors, but it could not forestall overgrown plantations and humiliating auctions, every one of which reminded the white farmers and planters of Mississippi how foolish they had been to gamble their livelihoods on someone else's misery.[40]

As Mississippi's governing officials confronted the state's dire situation, meanwhile, their first priority was shoring up the banking system. Although banks played a principal role in creating Mississippi's plight through mismanagement and irresponsible lending practices, legislators considered the presence of more specie and a renewed expansion of loans as the best way for the state to regain fiscal soundness and for its citizens to avoid ruin. Thus, rather than undertake major banking reform, the legislature responded to the grievously distressed condition of the banking sector, already evident by late 1836, with the creation of even more banks, the largest and most important of which was the Union Bank of Mississippi. Chartered in January 1837, the Union Bank was authorized to raise the substantial sum of $15.5 million, mostly through the sale of bonds backed by the credit of the state and secured by mortgages on the property of bank stockholders, who were required by law to be residents of Mississippi. A state-supported institution in its origin, the Union Bank's reliance on the state escalated in 1838, when a supplemental law allowed the governor to use proceeds from the initial bond sales to purchase $5 million of bank stock directly.[41]

Even as they directed some of their energies to reviving capital flows, however, state officeholders well understood the significance of investments in slave property to their woes. The enslaved, for instance, buttressed the bonds issued in support of the Union Bank of Mississippi, as they made up a substantial portion of the estates stockholders mortgaged to secure them. Moreover, just months after the legislature chartered the Union Bank, Governor Charles Lynch called legislators back to the statehouse for a special session to consider additional steps to address "the existing embarrassment" and put Mississippi's "confidence and credit . . . upon a better and more stable basis." Speaking to the immediate problem, Lynch argued for banking policies designed to give debtors additional time to pay what they owed. But Lynch also urged legislators to look "beyond the moment" and "investigate the propriety of adopting certain measures that may tend to *arrest* and guard against similar occurrences." Among those measures, first and foremost of value in Lynch's mind was a law that actually penalized violations of the constitutional interdiction on "the introduction of slaves into this State as merchandize."[42]

Lynch admitted that he had voted against the ban at the 1832 constitutional convention, thinking that a law putting the ban into operation "would be at variance with the broad principles of our free institutions" and that enforcing it would be challenging. Given the economic situation, though, Lynch thought the "principle" of white Mississippians' right to unconstrained dealings in slaves should yield to the "practical benefit" that would be achieved by "checking the immense drain of capital annually made upon us by the sale of this description of property." The legislature conceded the point, perhaps aided in doing so by the onset of bank suspensions in the state. Just a week after those suspensions began, legislators formally proscribed the importation of slaves for sale in Mississippi. Imposing a fine of up to $500 and as much as six months in jail for each slave a violator brought into the state, the law also voided all contracts signed and debts incurred for illegal slave purchases after its passage.[43]

If the chartering of the Union Bank of Mississippi potentially saved some of the state's planters through loans exchanged for mortgages on their property, putting the force of law behind the constitutional ban on slave imports potentially saved those planters from themselves. Where indebted planters might have deluded themselves into thinking that the labor and possible future appreciation of even more slaves purchased on even more credit could push their accounts into the black, the new law finally removed that temptation altogether. Neither the creation of the Union Bank nor the prohibition on the slave trade fixed the problems white Mississippians had created for themselves, but at least the policies nudged them away from assuming additional bad debts and toward paying down those they had already incurred.

But some slaveholders saw the new law banning the slave trade as a chance to evade paying some of those debts altogether. They simply denied they owed them. If the state constitution had banned the importation of slaves for sale since 1832, and if the law annulled sales made in violation of that ban, then perhaps every sale made after the ban went into effect had been illegal all along and slaveholders had no liability to fulfill their terms. This was a radical reading of the legal situation. When calling the legislature into session, Governor Lynch had explicitly warned members not to pass relief legislation that might "be construed as impairing the obligation of contracts," and the law itself clearly voided only sales made "after the passage of this act," suggesting that legislators knew that the constitutional ban had never been in force before. Nonetheless, a legal interpretation retroactively nullifying slave sales could collectively save Mississippi property owners millions of dollars and significantly ease the debt burden of the state as a whole. Such considerations surely entered the minds of Mississippi judges, including those on the state supreme court, who began ruling that deals made for imported slaves any time after May 1, 1833, were not legally binding.[44]

The weighty implications of those rulings became clear in 1841, when the Supreme Court of the United States took up the case of *Groves v. Slaughter.* The facts of the case were relatively straightforward. In 1835 and again in 1836, Robert Slaughter, a resident of Louisiana, brought slaves into Mississippi. There he sold them on credit for nearly $15,000 to one John Brown, only to have Brown and three men who cosigned promissory notes on his behalf refuse either to pay what they owed when the notes came due late in 1837 or to return the slaves they had purchased. Slaughter sued in federal court and won his case, whereupon the losing parties appealed to the U.S. Supreme Court, claiming that the 1832 Mississippi constitution banned the importation of slaves for sale and invalidated the promissory notes.[45]

Delivering the 5-2 decision on behalf of the majority, Justice Smith Thompson upheld the ruling of the lower court, asserting that Mississippi's constitutional prohibition on importing slaves as merchandise "required legislative action to bring it into complete operation" and that all contracts for slave sales entered into prior to the state legislature's taking that action in 1837 were legitimate and enforceable. By his own admission, Thompson's ruling was a narrow one that avoided the question of "whether this article in the constitution of Mississippi is repugnant to the constitution of the United States" because it appeared to assume for a state the power to regulate interstate commerce. The considerable importance of that larger question, though, had been evident throughout. Oral arguments before the court had lasted for seven days, and elite women of Washington society had crowded available seats to listen. So had a number of senators and congressmen, drawn not only by the constitutional matters at stake but also by the prospect of hearing plaintiffs' lawyer Robert Walker, then a sitting senator from Mississippi, square off against Henry Clay and Daniel Webster, both of whom served as attorneys for the defendant.[46]

In a way, the broad issue engaged by *Groves v. Slaughter* projected the fears that had animated the insurrection scare of 1835 nationally and into the political arena, as a decision explicitly concluding the interstate slave trade fell solely within the regulatory purview of Congress opened the possibility of federal interference that could destabilize the value of enslaved property generally. Justice Thompson was willing to skirt that question, but several of his fellows were not, even among those who concurred with the court's decision. Both Justice John McLean and Chief Justice Roger Taney, for example, felt obliged to comment on what McLean considered the "momentous and most delicate subject" of who had control over the interstate trade. Both concluded that such authority rested entirely with the individual states and that with the proper enabling legislation in place, Mississippi was within its commercial rights to limit the scope of slave imports if it chose to do so.[47]

Justice Henry Baldwin, however, maintained that his colleagues failed to grasp how property rights had to function if they were to work efficiently in a modern economy. Baldwin argued that it might be constitutionally permissible for individual states to limit or prohibit slave imports as "a regulation of police, for purposes of internal safety to the state, or the health and morals of its citizens, or to effectuate its system of policy in the abolition of slavery." But allowing states to regulate imports as a matter of commerce suggested that states might legitimately determine that items recognized as property elsewhere in the country were not property once within their boundaries, which Baldwin thought unacceptable. Such circumstances would make it impossible, he pointed out, for slaveholders to transport their slaves through a free state without risking confiscation, even though such transit, "whether of slaves or bales of goods, is lawful commerce among the several states. . . . Any reasoning or principle which would authorize any state to interfere with such transit of a slave, would equally apply to a bale of cotton, or cotton goods; and thus leave the whole commercial intercourse between the states liable to interruption or extinction by state laws, or constitutions."[48]

Unlike McLean and Taney, Baldwin reasoned that by discriminating against the commercial rights of nonresidents, Mississippi's effort to prohibit the importation of slaves for sale could never be sustained constitutionally.

By his reckoning, no state could make itself entirely off-limits to human trafficking so long as any state recognized property in slaves, and the authority
over interstate commerce that lay exclusively with Congress trumped the attempt of any state to do so, just as it did for attempts to limit interstate trade
in anything salable. Indeed, as Baldwin saw things, even Congress could not
constitutionally impede interstate dealings in slaves, because the Fifth Amendment guaranteed citizens the right to dispose of property as they saw fit. Regardless of whether the particular contracts in *Groves* were "invalid by the
constitution of Mississippi," in other words, they "would be valid by the constitution of the United States."[49]

Although speaking directly to legal and constitutional issues that would
remain controversial long after 1841, in pointing toward what he saw as both
the impracticability and the danger of separating out enslaved property from
other categories of property Baldwin also gestured implicitly to specific challenges facing Mississippi and the country as a whole during the Panic of 1837
and its aftermath. Rarely had it been clearer that the extent to which slavery
was interwoven in the fabric of American commercial life necessitated contending with it as a national concern, and whereas Baldwin worked from the
proslavery premise that commercial exchanges in enslaved people required
congressional protection, abolitionists used the economic crisis of the 1830s
instead as evidence that slavery fundamentally compromised the fiscal health
of the entire United States. They argued, in fact, that blame for the collapsing
American economy could be placed squarely on foolish and hasty speculation
in human bondage and its products.

In the spring of 1837, for example, the Executive Committee of the American Anti-Slavery Society observed that "the commercial world is now passing into one of those collapses which never fail to succeed an overblown system
of credit" and that responsibility for this particular collapse lay with slaveholders and their financial enablers. No people in the United States had more
avidly sought credit during the flush times than slaveholders, and their inability to cover their debts was now bringing "the whole system to its ruin."
Northern merchants were no less reproachable. "Anxious to partake the rich
plunder," they had "furnished the capital for the extension of slave labor" and
"reap[ed] great profit from the carrying trade," even as "the enormous extravagance and mad speculation that have grown out of the slave system" made "a
re-action upon the system itself" inevitable. That northern capitalists were paying a steep price for their greed, the committee concluded, was their own
doing. "Madly hastening to be richer, they have outbid each other in long cred-

its, to secure Southern custom, till the South, like all well-trusted and prodigal customers, has squandered her own means and theirs, and they are left in the lurch."[50]

As the depression deepened, abolitionists continued harping on the notion that the nation's economic misery owed itself to the intertwining of northern capital and southern slavery. The argument probably climaxed in 1840 with the publication of Joshua Leavitt's "The Financial Power of Slavery," one of the most widely circulated and influential antislavery tracts of the era. Contending that slavery was "the chief source of the commercial and financial evils under which the country is now groaning," Leavitt called on readers to recognize how slavery systematically sucked capital out of the economy and how every American suffered for the lost millions northern investors had sunk into the South. "Ask any man of business in our cities," Leavitt suggested, "where his capital is gone, and where his *hopelessly irrecoverable* debts are, and he will point to the South. . . . And behind every one of these stands another class, who have sold goods, or lent money, or given their endorsement to others that have trusted their all at the South, and now cannot pay. And behind these another class, and another, and another, until there is hardly a remote hamlet in the free States that has not been directly or indirectly drained of its available capital by the Southern Debt."[51]

Leavitt and his fellow abolitionists oversimplified the extent to which slavery and slavery alone could be blamed for the Panic of 1837. Like any economic crisis, it resulted from a concatenation of factors, and even leading antislavery activists conceded there was propaganda value in focusing on slavery's role in the downturn. That there was something to their critique was undeniable nonetheless. Whatever profligacy might be attributed to white southerners gorging themselves on cheap loans for land and slaves, financially facilitating the binge were men outside the region who were no less able to resist the lure of what looked like easy money. Complicity in the flush times was general, and what the Panic of 1837 revealed in especially painful fashion was the entanglement of supposedly free financial markets with the dark violence of slavery that was normally invisible and that many outside the South preferred to pretend did not exist.[52]

As the Executive Committee of the American Anti-Slavery Society observed, one could "count the men who have direct intercourse with the South, and then take into account the circles of their northern friends—each intersecting or touching other circles," and one would find "that there was not an individual in the whole country whose opinion is not in a greater or less degree acted upon by an influence which was set in motion by a southern bribe." When economic times were good, the committee continued, the wealth produced by slavery was "the common plunder of the country. . . . Northern merchants, northern mechanics, and manufacturers, northern editors, publishers, and printers, northern hotels, stages, steamboats, rail-roads, canal boats, northern banks, northern schoolmasters, northern artists, northern colleges, and northern ministers of the Gospel, all get their share of emolument from this general robbery" of the enslaved. When the South suffered the kind of financial failure seen in the late 1830s, however, there was no way to maintain that pecuniary ties to slavery might coexist with moral and political opposition to the institution, because interregional credit networks meant "the natural result of this extraordinary bankruptcy" was "to throw the ownership of large numbers of slaves upon Northern capitalists."[53]

No place better demonstrated such things than Mississippi, as both the Executive Committee and Joshua Leavitt were well aware. More than any other state, the Executive Committee pointed out, Mississippi had resorted to the "necromancy of banking" to keep itself solvent, only to see rampant inflation and extensive mortgaging of property "to Northern merchants." Nowhere served as a better example of how the slave trade enhanced demands for investments that had vanished in the panic, Leavitt argued, than Mississippi, where the "trade was carried on by the aid of Northern capital . . . until the bubble burst, and all that capital is gone, sunk, irrecoverable." And the Executive Committee's assertion that the credit extended by northerners in flush times would make them slaveholders in a depression was exactly so. By the middle of the 1840s, for example, just one trust created by the United States Bank of Pennsylvania to recover its substantial debts in Mississippi owned four plantations. In the estimate of economic historian Richard Kilbourne, the trust "probably ranked among the largest slaveholders in Mississippi."[54]

In the end, no amount of debt negotiation or forfeiture could save the state of Mississippi, and it seems unlikely that a U.S. Supreme Court decision allowing its residents to shirk their contractual obligations would have either. Cotton prices, which rebounded for a few months in 1838, nosedived in 1839, and would not return to what they had been in the middle of the 1830s for decades. The Union Bank scheme, meanwhile, proved a failure. By the time the Supreme Court issued its decision in *Groves v. Slaughter,* in fact, Mississippi had already defaulted on interest payments for Union Bank bonds, and in 1842 the legislature repudiated the bonds altogether. By the end of the 1840s only two banks operated in the state, and Mississippi would neither charter another one nor receive foreign credit again until after the Civil War.[55]

For his part, Jesse Mabry's fortunes were resolved even before his state's economic prostration became quite so epic. In November 1839, he sold everything he owned—all the land he had bought from Mark Cockrill, 800 additional acres he had acquired since that purchase, scores of animals, the 800 bales of cotton and 10,000 bushels of corn raised on his plantation the previous season, his household furniture, his farm equipment, and 150 slaves—for $58,500 to a buyer from a neighboring county. That was roughly a quarter of what Mabry had paid for Cockrill's plantation alone just four and a half years earlier, and he would never again attain the elevated standing he had held so fleetingly during the flush times.[56]

Still, whatever humiliations Mabry experienced as a consequence of his fall paled in comparison to the distress and suffering experienced by the slaves who became pawns in his attempts to scratch his way back to respectability. Moreover, neither Mabry nor most other whites in Mississippi seemed to learn anything from their experience. Jesse Mabry's credit might have been ruined, but his wife Nancy's was not. In 1841 she borrowed more than $8,000 to buy land, and by 1850 the Mabrys once again owned a Mississippi cotton farm, worked by sixteen slaves. Those sixteen, in turn, represented just a tiny fraction of the more than 300,000 in the state, roughly twice the number that had lived there when cotton capitalism came crashing down in 1837.[57]

CHAPTER 6

"Broad is de Road dat Leads ter Death"

Human Capital and Enslaved Mortality

DAINA RAMEY BERRY

In December 1800, Jacob, "a valuable Waterman" and "an honest inoffensive negro," committed suicide by "stab[bing] himself." Because he was considered valuable, his enslaver, William Wilson, submitted a petition to the Virginia governor's office seeking compensation for the loss of Jacob, whom he referred to as his "chief support."[1] It might seem unusual to contemporary readers that a slaveholder would file for compensation on the death of his bondman, but this was common in the late eighteenth- and nineteenth-century United States. Today we think of compensation for the enslaved as reparations, but rarely do we think about payments being made to those who profited from owning slaves. Historical records in British and U.S. archives confirm that enslavers received compensation on the death of their human chattel under specific circumstances. Enslaved bodies, valued for their labor while alive, also had value in death. Such practices indicate that the life cycle of the enslaved extended beyond human years and into postmortem spaces that few scholars have explored.[2]

Enslaved people represented a movable form of property known as chattel. They had monetary values reflecting their net worth and were itemized the same way as other forms of property. From Jacob's story we learn that enslaved bodies had value even after they died.[3] In the same vein, some colonial legislation valued enslaved people before they were born. Seventeenth-century Virginia laws confirmed enslavement through the bodies of enslaved women according to the legal doctrine of *partus sequitur ventrem*, which held that the offspring followed the condition of the mother.[4] This evidence compels us to rethink notions of the life cycle of the enslaved. The biological, spiritual, and economic bodies of enslaved people preceded birth and extended after death. This chapter explores how enslaved persons died, what role they had in their death, and the economic value attributed to their death. It also addresses the link between the cause of death and the price tag put on it.

How are we to make sense of the value of black life in a historical context? How are we to make sense of the value of black life in a contemporary moment? These are important questions in current conversations about slavery, social justice, and reparations. This interest in how black lives are valued appears in protest language and news coverage associated with the black lives matter movement. One way to understand the historical antecedent is to examine the life cycle of the enslaved, looking beyond the embodied presence and the humanity to explore enslaved bodies as commodities in both the physical and the nonphysical worlds. Doing so acknowledges that the thought of a person's life marked the beginning of valuation, and interment or legal proceedings after death represented the end of his or her capital value. With this in mind, there are two concurrent and contrasting perspectives on human property: one, the commodity logic of slaveholding, which viewed the enslaved as an economic body that could be commodified from before conception to after death, thereby exceeding the normal temporal frame set by these two endpoints, and the other representing the humanity logic of the enslaved that worked against their commodification during and after their natural lives.

Scholars have been involved in these conversations for some time. Contemporary political discourse questions the temporal meaning of slavery, the value of life, and the legacy of the peculiar institution. Legal scholars have advanced this discussion by looking at specific cases relating to the arguments for and against reparations.[5] Historians of slavery are also trying to make sense of the ways in which slavery and capitalism are interrelated. Activists such as Randall Robinson, Senator John Conyers, and Deadria Farmer-Paellmann, among others, started this conversation in the 1980s by arguing that the U.S. government had a debt to pay the descendants of African Americans who toiled in fields, factories, and homes as enslaved laborers for nearly 300 years. I enter this conversation with others who have recently addressed capitalism and slavery and are interested in seeking historical explanations for the commodification of enslaved laborers who shaped the American economy. Wilson,

Jacob's enslaver, certainly made this connection, as the petition he filed after Jacob's death illustrates.

By Virginia law, slaveholders like Wilson could receive $500 for the death of an enslaved worker under court-specified circumstances. Wilson had a large family, and he hoped that the state would provide him with enough compensation to replace Jacob, his once trusted servant. However, the court rejected his claim, and it is with this decision that the historical record of Jacob ends.[6] We know that this was the end of his natural life, and it appears that it was the end of his life as a commodity. What happened to Jacob's body? Was he laid to rest, or was his body desecrated and discarded? Did he have a funeral during which family and friends paid their final respects? The answers to these questions remain a mystery because the institution of slavery in the United States defined Jacob as a marketable commodity, not a human being. However, his insurrectionary actions, and the fact that he literally chose death, represent the point at which the commodification and the humanity of the enslaved converge. This convergence marks a point in our understanding of human chattel that warrants further attention. Enslaved people had economic values that extended beyond their natural and spiritual lives.

How does one identify the moment a human captive becomes a measurable commodity? At what point or stage of development does "humanness" disappear, transforming the person into a tradable good, primed and ready for the market? Unlike ginning equipment, plows, whips, or other plantation tools, enslaved people embodied a unique form of commodity. Often described as "human hoeing machines," bondpeople represented the instrument used by planters to cultivate crops for the market.[7] They also served as valuable goods that were traded at the market. Enslaved people could never escape commodification, but they found clever ways to assert their humanity. They cried and moaned when being separated from loved ones at auction, often leaving a deep impression on bystanders and potential buyers. Their very public and terrible grief made it difficult for some to ignore their humanity. Scholars interested in the value of human chattel identify the complexities of appraisals and sales based on a variety of factors, including age, sex, skill, health, and region.[8] However, a slave's value at death has scarcely been addressed.[9] The enslaved could not even escape commodification at the moment of death and beyond.

This chapter tells the story of the enslaved body in life *and* in death. It is a story of the history of exploitation, marketability, and adaptation. It is also a story about the financial decisions people make to end their lives, knowing that their lives have already been taken. In the case of enslaved mortality, one cannot overlook slaves' dual status as property and person. They were "a person with a price," and this led to several responses to their passing, from sophisticated capital transactions to respectful burials to callous disregard of black life in the moment of death.[10] This chapter moves through the arenas of homicide and suicide, life insurance, and state violence to see where the temporal boundaries of life diverged, before devoting some final thoughts to how enslaved people understood and responded to death.

Jacob's death gives us insight into enslaved people's actions within the larger history of capitalism and slavery, one that included a reign of terror that sometimes resulted in rebellions, conspiracies, and widespread death. He took his own life in 1800 after being "implicated in the late conspiracy of the Slaves," along with well-known martyrs such as Gabriel Prosser, the leader of this group of "rebels." Several scholars interested in the aftermath of slave rebellions and conspiracies have discussed deceased rebels such as Charles Deslondes (1811), Denmark Vesey (1822), and Nat Turner (1831) in the context of trials, confessions, executions, or acquittals. However, few historians have explored the literal and figurative expressions of death anchored in capitalism. In short, what happened when the enslaved died? Were the "rebels" buried? How did the slave community respond? Did their slaveholding families receive compensation? Even though we know very little about Jacob, his demise and afterlife cast into sharp relief the relationship between and among capitalism, slavery, and death.

Suicide and Homicide

Recent scholarship on death among the enslaved, including deaths by suicide and homicide, supports my thesis of the commodification of bodies beyond death.[11] Suicide, or, as I prefer to call it, the "act of self-destruction," was a bold decision for an enslaved person. It served as the final act of their commodification and should not carry the contemporary negative stigma often attached to such events. Court records show that enslavers took one another to court seeking compensation when their human property died through homicide. Yet exploring the cause of death in both cases allows conversations about the enslaved as active participants in controlling their own destiny to take place. Viewed as an assertion of their humanity, suicide and homicide meant that they could escape the commodification of their lives; they had no idea the commodification would continue post-mortem.

In November 1848, the lives of a South Carolina enslaved family were about to be turned upside down. Bob, Binah, and two children worked for Andrew Bunch, and it is likely that they were well adjusted to their routine on the Bunch plantation. However, William Smith purchased them from Bunch, agreeing to pay $1,100 for the lot. When he arrived with the notes in hand, he asked Bob if he would like him to be his new master. Bob said he "would not suit." Smith explained to Bob, "I have not come to consult you . . . you are mine." The new owner instructed his human property to "reconcile to the change" and give him no trouble. Bob finished his task and got up and walked toward his cabin. Anticipating flight, Smith offered a word of caution: "it is no use for you to run, for I have my dogs, and can catch you." Bob said that he "would run from no man," and he proceeded to his cabin. After some time passed, Smith and the other people present went to the cabin. "Bob came out of the door with his throat cut, and bleeding; he made a few turns in the yard, fell on his knees, sank to the ground, and there bled to death."[12] Before his body had stiffened, the two gentlemen started arguing over the sale because Bob died on the scene and had not been delivered to Smith.

Even though Bob was responsible for his own death, his "life" continued in court for three years more. Immediately after the harrowing scene, Smith amended the note to create "A new trade . . . for $650" instead of $1,100, since Bob had killed himself. But agitated by "the shocking spectacle of Bob's death," Bunch spent the next three years pursuing the $450 value of his deceased bondman. Bunch believed Smith should bear the financial burden of Bob's death, and sued to recover the original terms of sale. The court agreed, and "the jury found a verdict for the plaintiff for $456, with interest, from the 14th November 1848," requiring Smith to cover Bob's value with interest for three years post-mortem even though he had never reaped the benefits of Bob's labor.[13] The jury's willingness to charge Smith interest clearly confirms the expanded life cycle of enslaved people's economic value beyond death. Even though Bob's physical body was gone, his financial value lived on in the courts for three years, while state funds were used to hear the case and appeals. Bob's deceased body continued to make money for Bunch at a rate of 0.5 percent per year: interest on dead slaves was another way their fiscal impact continued in post-mortem spaces.

Slaveholding whites sought compensation for enslaved laborers' deaths, especially when others were responsible. Southern magistrates recognized that communities contained dishonest slaveholders as well as slaves, yet their charge was to render decisions based on the material presented. In the case of an Alabama bondman murdered for stealing "a piece of old carpet," a local inn-keeper and his son took the law into their own hands and beat him. First, the innkeeper "struck him with a stake . . . [and] punched him in the face and mouth," knocking out some of his teeth. The remaining details come from Theodore Dwight Weld, an abolitionist who wrote about the horrors of slav-ery. The following quotation provides insight into abolitionist discourse on the value of enslaved bodies:

> They whipped him by turns, with heavy cowskins, and made the dogs shake him. A Mr. Phillips, who lodged at the house, heard the cruelty during the night. On getting up he found the negro in the bar-room, terribly mangled with the whip, and his flesh so torn by the dogs, that the cords were bare. He remarked to the landlord that he was dangerously hurt, and needed care. The landlord replied that he deserved none. Mr. Phillips went to a neighboring magistrate, who took the slave home with him, where he soon died. The father and son were both tried, and acquitted!! A suit was brought, however, for damages in behalf of the owner of the slave, a young lady by the name of Agnes Jones. I was on the jury when these facts were stated on oath. Two men testified, one that he would have given $1000 for him, the other $900 or $950. The jury found the latter sum.[14]

In this case, a magistrate tried to care for the badly beaten bondman, but a jury trial acquitted the father-and-son duo of the crime. When the alleged owner, Agnes Jones, sued for damages, she received $950 for the death of her bondman. One cannot determine how long it took for Jones to receive com-pensation for her deceased slave. However, his postmortem financial value in-cluded at least two hearings, confirming that the court contested his worth beyond his death.

In some cases neighbors took legal action against slaveholders for using excessive force on their own human chattel. Such was the case of Major Har-ney, who went to court for a coroner's inquest on the death of his bondwoman Hannah and the suicide of her unnamed husband. Witnesses claimed that Harney excessively beat her for "three successive days" because he believed she stole his keys. Apparently "Her flesh was so lacerated and torn, that it was im-possible for the jury to say whether it had been done with a whip or hot iron; some think both." In the end, Hannah "was tortured to death." Did members of the jury see sketches of the deceased bondwoman's body, or was her lacerated frame brought to court and displayed? It is likely that the jury visited the coroner's office to gaze at the "evidence," or that they read an autopsy detailing Hannah's badly maimed body. In either case, this postmortem analysis extended Hannah's physical existence in court after an unusually violent death. But the story did not end there. When Major Harney failed to locate his keys, he turned to Hannah's "husband" and "commenced [to] torturing him." In response, Hannah's husband "ran into the Mississippi [River] and drowned himself." Although his motive is unclear, it seems probable that he desired to join his wife in death rather than suffer similar consequences. During the coroner's inquest, community members testified about the "pious" and "industrious" nature of the deceased bondman.[15] The value of Hannah and her husband lived beyond their deaths through state-administered funds used to investigate Harney's behavior and his financial loss.[16]

The actions of Samuel Williams, a slaveholder from Bourbon County, Kentucky, represent another side to the story of human capital and enslaved mortality. This case illustrates the distance people traveled to collect human property and their responses when enslaved persons, as Bob did, destroyed themselves at the moment of sale or transfer. Just before the Panic of 1837 plunged the nation into financial turmoil, Williams experienced a different sort of crash when a recently purchased slave took his own life. Williams had sent his agent, "Frank," to purchase and deliver this "Negro fellow" to his son, who lived nearly 500 miles away. Frank paid "nine hundred dollars and put [the bondman] in jail for safe keeping" in preparation for the long journey ahead. But when the jailer went to retrieve the bondman, "he found him dead hanging by the neck." Apparently Williams lost other human capital that year, for he noted, "This is about the 10th we have lost and like to lose." He wrestled with the ramifications of such loss, conceding that "the hand of providence is sorely against us." Even though the death of this bondman saved Williams transportation expenses, it left him with no one to "do jobs" for him. It also forced him to reevaluate his assets as he sought to recover the $900 paid for the now deceased bondman.[17] We do not have records indicating whether or not Williams took legal action to record the loss of the bondman, but we do know he felt burned by the "Negro fellow's" action.

Like most nineteenth-century investors, Williams faced financial losses in human and agricultural property. The loss in 1837 was profound. Investors rushed to collect on debts and tried to find ways to circumvent an inevitable decline. Williams was not alone; like many others, he persevered through this difficult financial time by pursuing payment for outstanding loans. For example, Williams asked his son to collect monies owed to him by a man named George Redman, but the debtor failed to cooperate. Surveying the situation, Williams instructed his son to warn Redman that "he had better mortgage his land and negroes" to raise the money owed because he was no longer paying "for dead negroes," perhaps reflecting on the $900 loss from the undelivered bondman.[18] When an enslaved person took his or her own life, some members of the planter class questioned the meaning of their investments in human chattel. Even if they did not abandon slaveholding altogether, slave suicide may have encouraged some enslavers to recognize the enslaved as human beings.

For some captives, self-destruction marked an active rejection of their commodification and served as a final, tragic attempt to claim their personhood. Sales and transfers from one slaveholder to another marked moments in which a human being was treated as a commensurable commodity. Aside from livestock and other animals, no other products have personalities, express feelings, or display opinions. There is something unique about enslaved people because they represented and produced marketable goods. Those who terminated their lives just before a sale saved themselves from witnessing the capital side of their existence. They hastened their transition into the spiritual realm, allowing their humanity to have the last word. Like Jacob's decision to evade trial by stabbing himself in the aftermath of the Gabriel Prosser uprising, Bob's suicide protected him from the physical transfer to a new slaveholder. Yet the sale still took place, three years after his death. In both cases, the postmortem financial value of these bondmen appeared in legal records that documented the commodification of their bodies beyond their physical existence.

Bondpeople knew their labor held value; some defied slaveholders through self-destruction or death by suicide.[19] Their objective was to prevent traders, agents, and slaveholding whites from capitalizing on their value, and they chose to do so through self-destruction. No other marketable product had the ability to destroy or botch a sale. For some it was a hasty response to separation from a loved one; for others it was an overt rejection of their captivity and commodification. Annie Tate of North Carolina, for example, vividly remembered her grandmother's death following the severe beating and sale of her grandfather. The moment her grandmother learned that her husband had been sold, she was "'bout crazy so she walks off en de plantation." The North Carolina plantation on which she lived bordered the Neuse River, and "gran maw gits dar, and jumps in."[20] Similarly, Michael, a bondman from Missouri, could not tolerate being separated from his wife when shipped to the Deep South. During his transport, "at the mouth of the Ohio River," he filed off his irons and attempted to flee to her residence. Michael "refused to be sent to the South, unless his wife should also accompany him." He resisted separation at every stage, but when he failed to "surrender himself," he was placed in jail. The moment he learned he was "about to be sent away without his wife, and that he would in all probability, never again see her, he resolved to end both his life and his servitude." Michael hanged himself in the jail cell, alone on a Tuesday evening in the summer of 1835.[21] Like Tate's grandmother, he chose death over separation through one final act, asserting his humanity through suicide. Francis Black, on the other hand, lost the desire to live after being kidnapped as a young girl, yet she did not choose self-destruction. During her abduction from a Mississippi plantation, she yelled and screamed, but the kidnapper told her to "shet up . . . or I'll kill you." Her response was simple, "kill me if you wants to—you stole me from my folks."[22] In her eyes, the kidnapper literally took her life. Black, like many enslaved people, could not imagine life without her parents. Although she lived to experience freedom, marry, and give birth to six children, she never reunited with her birth family. Years later, when she shared her testimony with Works Progress Administration workers in the 1930s, she was blind and approximately eighty-seven years old.

No matter how often their humanity was ignored, enslaved people yearned to be treated as respectable individuals. Former bondman Charles Ball noted that owners tried to cover up an enslaved person's suicide because of the negative social stigma it brought to their homestead. "When a negro kills himself," he explained, "the master is unwilling to let it be known, least the deed should be attributed to his own cruelty." Evidently, "A certain degree of disgrace falls upon the master whose slave has committed suicide."[23]

Life Insurance and Compensation

Life insurance policies provided a measure of security for those uncertain about investing in human chattel. As a relatively new area of slavery scholarship, historians argue that insurance policies were designed to protect slaveholders' fiscal investment in the enslaved, but legal proceedings sometimes did not rule in favor of administering funds.[24] Evidence of this appears in ship records of the transatlantic slave trade, particularly in the case of the *Zong* massacre. This famous case involved the murder of approximately 132 African captives who were thrown overboard a slave ship in 1781. They were alive and sacrificed so that the crew could focus their efforts on saving the remaining cargo, given limited supplies. Upon the ship's arrival in Jamaica, the ship owners filed an insurance claim for their loss. The court ruled in favor of the owners, identifying the African captives as goods, not people. However, the insurers appealed and won their case with a ruling that overturned the original decision.[25] The debates surrounding this case created a public discourse on the value of captives' lives.

Similar conversations occurred in the United States in 1841 when captives rebelled on the *Creole*.[26] However, in this case the enslaved people mutinied on board the slave ship and won the case because they had been illegally enslaved. Both cases led to questions about whether or not shippers were indemnified against loss. More important is the idea that enslaved captives were insured in anticipation of a loss, and that their lives held value at death. Slaveholders lost value in enslaved people without slaves having died; and indeed, slaves had the ability to lower their market values significantly through various actions of self-destruction and self-liberation, such as damaging their bodies or running away.[27] Yet slaveholders maximized the value of their enslaved laborers in life and in death. They tried to recover the financial loss of deceased bondpeople in private and public settings through legislative petitions, coroner's inquests, and other legal actions. They also tried to make wise financial decisions about speculation in human capital, seeking healthy and obedient laborers who they believed would not give them trouble.

Insurance protected their investments in a slave workforce, particularly when their laborers toiled in risky work environments, traveled to markets, or worked in urban settings. The insurance industry wavered over slave policies in the 1830s, then developed them in the 1840s, and by the mid- to late 1850s planters in the South had several options for slave policies.[28] In February 1854, the Alabama Senate and House of Representatives submitted "an act to incorporate the Planters' Insurance Company." Section 5 included security "upon the Lives and Health, both of white persons and slaves" in the event of "loss in any manner, by Fire, Dangers of the Seas, Rivers, or otherwise."[29] Slaveholders who purchased a policy through this company could rest assured that death during transportation guaranteed compensation. Because of the vague language, it is also likely that slaveholders could collect the financial value of deceased slaves who committed suicide as some—but not all—policies covered "loss in any manner."

The Petersburg Marine Insurance Company specialized in insuring slaves transported from Virginia to Louisiana. On April 18, 1853, William Haxall purchased a $1,850 policy to insure five slaves: Cairo and Jepe, valued at $300 each; Beverly, valued at $350; Charlotte, valued at $400; and Sydney, valued at $500. In addition to this protection, Haxall listed the brig and captain as responsible parties, holding the latter accountable for payment with "no deduction to be made from the sum insured, except two per cent." The policy also contained protection against "fire, enemies, pirates, rovers, thieves, jettisons."[30] It is difficult to determine whether Haxall ever had to cash in on this policy, yet we know that slaveholders throughout the United States protected the transportation costs of their newly purchased bondpeople as part of the domestic slave trade.[31]

Mary Moncure, also a Virginia resident, insured two enslaved laborers under much different circumstances. Rather than insuring bondpeople prior to travel, Moncure secured four-year policies from the Virginia Life Insurance Company for her valuable house servants.[32] In June 1860, Moncure insured Austin for $1,000 and Mary Jane for $800. The policy, however, contained a unique clause that protected the insurance company, not the policyholder, in the event of self-destruction. Virginia Life stipulated that "in case the said slave shall commit suicide, or shall die by any means of any invasion, insurrection, riot, or civil commotion . . . the policy shall be void, null, and of no effect."[33] In other words, the company refused to indemnify enslavers for enslaved people who participated in insurrections, perhaps because Virginia Life's directors recalled compensation provided to slaveholders whose bondpeople fled to the British during the American Revolution and the War of 1812. They also may have denied insurance for "rebels," given the recompense enslavers received in the aftermath of the Southampton rebellion.[34]

Slaveholders such as H. C. Cox, J. R. Cates, and W. H. Wilson agreed to one-year policies for their bondmen, Alfred, Charles, and Stephen, despite Virginia Life's suicide exemption. They insured these bondmen because of the risky nature of their work.[35] Enslaved men faced death on a daily basis as they labored in Virginia coal mines. The records of the Chesterfield County mines are replete with accounts of individual bondmen losing their lives in explosions, fires, floods, and other mining accidents. Enslaved men such as Bob Burton, David Depp, John Goode, and Richard Handcock, among countless others, died as a result of "pit explosions."[36] Their deaths were reported in local newspapers such as the *Daily Dispatch*, the *South-Side Democrat*, and the *Richmond Enquirer*, and some of their owners cashed in insurance policies. Ninety-seven enslaved workers in the Virginia coal mines had life insurance policies from companies such as Baltimore Life, Nautilus Insurance Company of New York, and Virginia Life. The sort of one-year policies taken out on Alfred, Charles, and Stephen usually cost $10 or less annually, and several mandated medical examinations.[37] Such examinations represent another space—beyond the auction block—where enslaved people were subjected to degrading inspection to assess their monetary value. Slaveholders were willing to pay extra money to insure their slaves in order to avoid, in the words of the aggrieved Kentucky slaveholder Samuel Williams, "paying for dead negroes."[38]

State Violence and Redemption

Enslaved people had values that their enslavers capitalized on, but, owing to their chattel status, the state also had rights over their bodies. In addition to being able to take enslaved people away, the state also provided monetary redemption for them. Despite their status as private property, it is clear that their dual identity as human beings led to tenuous rights and ownership issues among slaveholders, who went to the state for protection and compensation.

Slaveholders who sent their bondpeople to work on public projects also turned to the state when their laborers died by accident or homicide. Some of these projects included building roads, canals, and bridges, as well as service on fire brigades and in repairing levees.[39] In July 1848, William B. Williamson, William Maxey, and John D. Turner of Polk County, Texas, lost three bondmen in the Trinity River. They believed that Thomas (age twenty-five), Charles (age twenty-one), and Goodwin (age twenty-one) had "accidently" died for lack of "proper care and attention" while conducting roadwork on the bank of the river. Three years after their deaths, these slaveholders submitted a petition to the Senate and House of Representatives of Texas seeking compensation for the $800–$900 value of these enslaved men. It is not clear why there was a delay in submitting the petition, but a local newspaper confirmed that the Texas legislature "indefinitely postponed" any discussion of this request.[40] It is likely that Wilson, Moxey, and Turner filed for compensation prior to the1851 legislative session, but we do not have records to confirm such actions. We do know, however, that the men felt that "private property under the Constitution of our state cannot be taken for public use without just compensation."[41] Since their slaves were "taken" unjustly and used to benefit the state rather than individual owners, Williamson, Maxey, and Turner sought "reasonable compensation" for their losses. In November 1851 the postmortem values of Thomas, Charles, and Goodwin were still being contested, and the case was referred to "the committee on state affairs."[42] The historical record of these bondmen ends at this point, but it appears that the state continued its investigation. Once again, valuation of deceased slaves continued beyond the immediate time of death. We may never know whether Williamson, Maxey, or Turner received compensation for their enslaved workers, but it is clear that the enslaved men were still "alive" financially, three years post-mortem.

Sometimes former slaveholders profited from the death of their slaves, often their most rebellious ones. Evidence of compensation for murdered slaves can be found in scholarship on slave resistance and rebellion.[43] The Virginia court of Oyer and Terminer set a precedent for compensation of executed enslaved "felons" as early as 1705. According to a legal historian, Philips J. Schwarz, "the intention of that compensation was to enable slave owners to regain the financial value of the executed person." This practice also sought to "encourage owners not to cover up felonies in order to retain—or to sell away privately—a particularly valuable laborer."[44] In South Carolina, an enslaved man named Prince participated in a similar hearing, though for a lesser crime. He received the death penalty after being accused and convicted of burglary. Prior to the day of execution, Prince was valued at $500 and his owner, John Davidson, received compensation.[45]

Some enslavers, such as Samuel Davis, also from South Carolina, took advantage of the law. He "procured the conviction and execution of his own slave for stealing" a gingerbread cake from a local baker in order to capitalize on the man's monetary value.[46] Even when the shopkeeper forgave the accused bondman, Davis insisted on the conviction because the slave's "assessed value, brought him more money than he could have obtained for the slave in market."[47] The idea that a dead slave could be worth more than a living one presented a problem that the courts had to resolve, and had been trying to rectify since the 1781 *Zong* case. As a result, court investigations involved detailed depositions, thorough medical examinations, reviews of diverse evidence, and sometimes a trial by jury.

Burial Rituals and Enslaved Humanity

Enslaved people's funerary rituals and concepts of death have long been the subject of scholarly inquiry. From the 1970s scholarship of Albert Raboteau and Eugene D. Genovese to the recent work of Vincent Brown, Walter Rucker, and Stephanie Smallwood, we have a deeper understanding of how the enslaved responded to death.[48] Some of this work comes from the field of historical archeology, where sites of study reveal the rituals and experiences of enslaved people.[49] This scholarship has allowed us to enter a sacred space where the human side of chattel slaves celebrated life and death. It is a rich and well-documented literature that is too long to recap here. Instead, I will close with a reading of the first few stanzas of "I'se Born to Die," the 1763 hymn composed by Charles Wesley, an itinerant Methodist clergyman who visited colonial Georgia and South Carolina during the peak years of the first Great Awakening. Enslaved people sang this hymn and others at their loved ones' funerals.

The use of this hymn reflects the temporal understanding of life and death that this chapter highlights. Just as the economic body lived on in postmortem spaces, this song does so as well. Many who sang this hymn believed life continued on in some fashion beyond the expiration of the body. Scholars of African and African American religious philosophies describe the importance of the African afterlife, noting that ancestor spirits played a role in the everyday lives of Africans and their descendants. Family tradition and lore gave Africans and African Americans familiarity with departed extended family members whom they had never met. Likewise, African conceptions of time allowed people to think about the afterlife as a place that was active in the present.[50]

In response to their commodification, the enslaved cleaved to their humanity in a variety of ways. Knowing that the slaveholding class viewed them as goods used to produce marketable items, some enslaved people embraced death as a tangible escape from commodification. Here I recall the story of Jacob, the bondman who took his life in Gabriel's rebellion rather than face execution. But the acceptance of death as an exit strategy did not satisfy all. Some shrugged their shoulders and kept on working when an enslaved comrade passed away; others were sad and mourned for weeks.[51] "If a slave died on our place," a bondman named Robert recalled, "nobody went to de fields 'til atter de buryin.' "[52] His slaveholder required strict burying practices, for he "never let nobody be buried 'til dey had been dead 24 hours."[53] According to Robert, his owner implemented this rule because "it warn't right to hurry 'em off into de ground too quick atter dey died."[54] Since there were no "undertakers dem days," bondpeople helped prepare the body. Robert's slaveholder provided "cooling boards" and coffins to his enslaved property. Robert's Uncle Squire served as the coffin maker, and the community pitched in and "painted [them] to make 'em look nice."[55] It seems as though his slaveholder made an effort to balance the duality between humanity and property.

During slave funeral services, a preacher shared words of encouragement and sang songs. Staking claim to their humanity in the face of commodification, enslaved mourners grappled with the meaning of death. The first three stanzas of Wesley's hymn are as follows:

AND am I born to die?
To lay this body down?
And must my trembling spirit fly
Into a world unknown -
A land of deepest shade,
Unpierced by human thought,
The dreary regions of the dead,
Where all things are forgot?

Soon as from earth I go,
What will become of me?
Eternal happiness or woe
Must then my portion be;
Waked by the trumpet's sound,
I from my grave shall rise,
And see the Judge with glory crowned,
And see the flaming skies.

How shall I leave my tomb?
With triumph or regret?
A fearful or a joyful doom,
A curse or blessing meet?
Will angel-bands convey

Their brother to the bar?
Or devils drag my soul away,
To meet its sentence there?[56]

Identifying with the hymn, enslaved people tried to understand the meaning of the afterlife. These words reflected their hope for redemption, resurrection, and likeness with Jesus, but they also questioned and gave some comfort during difficult times. Slaves embraced a spiritual Judge whom they hoped to see "with glory crowned." But, with humility, they also saw tension between good and evil, "a curse or blessing," and perhaps recognized God's final judgment. After the song and a prayer at the grave, the body was laid to rest, and the mourners shoveled dirt to cover the coffin.

The burial practices on Robert's estate may have been the exception, not the rule. Kate of Texas remembered that her owner made the coffin and instructed them not to take too long with the burial. Maintaining a tight rein on burial rituals may have been a strategy Kate's slaveholder utilized to quash the humanity of those enslaved and emphasize their role as human machines. They were not allowed to sing or pray; instead, he reprimanded them to "jus' put them in the ground and cover 'em up and hurry back to that field."[57] John, also from Texas, recalled that "dey didn't have no funerals for de slaves, but jes' bury dem like a cow or a hoss, jes' dig a hole and roll 'em in it and cover 'em up."[58] Regardless of funerary rituals, slaves remembered scriptures and songs, often resulting in formal or informal funerals. They used these moments to grapple with the cycles of life and found ways to make peace with the departed.

"Broad is de Road dat Leads ter Death / An' there an' here we travel": this remark captures one bondwoman's reflection on her experience with slavery.[59] It is taken, a bit out of context, from Matthew 7:13–14, which reads: "Enter through the narrow gate. For wide is the gate and broad is the road that leads to destruction, and many enter through it. But small is the gate and narrow the road that leads to life, and only a few find it."[60] This bondwoman understood that enslaved people faced more occasions to die than to live; she also recognized that they traveled on the road to death and destruction on a daily basis. Whether they found solace in life or in taking their own lives, slaves understood the circumstances of their enslavement, even if their opinions differed from those of their enslavers.

Despite the denial of their humanity, enslaved people strived to be viewed as people, not products.[61] In the eyes of slaveholders, the enslaved were human capital, not only during their lifetime but also before birth and after death. Unpredictable loss from suicide and murder carried significant consequences in the southern marketplace. The outcomes of these events were capricious, but some planters found security through insurance policies. From the first appraisal of the enslaved to their valuation at death, southern slaveholders used extreme measures to protect their investment. They appraised, hired, insured, transferred, mortgaged, and used slaves as collateral for debt. By contrast, bondpeople embraced their humanity in public and private settings. They struggled with the balance between being both person and product on a daily basis because their existence did not start or end with commodification. Their lives as people began when they entered the physical world and ended when they departed, whereas their lives as products began prior to conception and lasted years into postmortem. Funerary rituals challenged their enslavers to recognize them as human beings. As a result, enslaved men, women and children entered their graves hoping for a seat in God's Kingdom, clinging to their humanity until their very last breath.

CHAPTER 7

August Belmont and the World the Slaves Made

KATHRYN BOODRY

Recent work on the financial history of slavery has focused on the creation of slave-backed securities and the entangled relationship of state-chartered banks, government-issued bonds, and remote investors in Europe and the northern United States. Such scholars as Edward Baptist and Richard Kilbourne have recovered the precarious schemes of the Consolidated Association of the Planters of Louisiana (a bank that took slaves as collateral for loans issued to purchase additional slaves) and the United States Bank of Philadelphia (Nicholas Biddle's post–Bank War enterprise that invested heavily in upstart southern banks). It is crucial, however, to remember that the most important transactions in the financial history of slavery involved the transatlantic marketing of agricultural commodities produced by enslaved people under violent coercion. Indeed, the place where American slavery most significantly intersected with the global financial system was in the credit-driven method of marketing the cotton of the American South to brokers in Liverpool and merchant bankers in London and Lancashire.[1]

In the nineteenth century, cotton was the primary export item produced by the United States for a global market. As early as 1815 the United States was the largest producer and Great Britain the largest consumer of cotton. As Friedrich Engels noted, "England and the United States are bound together by a single thread of cotton, which, weak and fragile as it may appear, is, nevertheless, stronger than an iron cable." But this common thread was woven not only from a raw fiber but also from increasingly sophisticated ways of providing credit. In everything from the purchasing of slaves and supplies to the sending of harvested crops to market, plantation agriculture depended on frequent infusions of money to keep things running. Though they constituted the wealthiest cohort of antebellum Americans, slaveholders held little cash on hand. Instead, they borrowed against cotton that in some cases had not yet been planted, let alone picked, baled, or sold. An entire financial infrastructure sustained this system of advances and consignments, with mercantile "factors" usually responsible for transforming a planter's cotton (harvested or anticipated) into the cash necessary to meet the previous year's debts and the credit to secure the coming year's need for capital.[2]

The credit that allowed slaveholders "to sell cotton in order to buy negros—to make more cotton to buy more negros 'ad infinitum'" (as one insightful observer described the economic logic of the plantation South in 1835) ultimately is traceable back to London, the global financial capital of the nineteenth century. Loans that ran through a New Orleans factor or a New York bank often originated in England, both because the bulk of American cotton was sold there and because the largest financial houses saw promising investment opportunities in the United States. Alexander Brown & Sons, Baring Brothers, and the Rothschilds devoted a great deal of energy in the 1820s, 1830s, and 1840s to investing in the American economy and analyzing American markets. They purchased government securities, underwrote upstart banks, and brokered cotton. These firms' involvement in the cotton trade was important to their long-term development, for it was here they gained expertise and tested business models that would eventually prove even more lucrative in other sectors of the economy.[3]

The Rothschilds perhaps best illustrate the volatile and productive relationship of international finance and American slavery. When the Rothschild houses initially entered American markets in the 1820s, they focused on the purchase of state and municipal bonds. From 1834 to 1843 they served as the bankers of the United States in Europe, a position they happily wrested away from Baring Brothers. They relished the political capital that accompanied the position but derived little profit from the processing of payments for diplomatic figures across the continent. For a short period between 1837 and 1849, the Rothschilds invested in cotton, but in 1849 the firm began to aggressively purchase gold in San Francisco. The firm's primacy in that market resulted in no small measure from earlier lessons learned in the cotton trade. Wealth and knowledge generated from what was a brief and intensive engagement with slave-grown cotton facilitated later specializations in American markets by firms that have come to define modern capitalism.

The Rothschild presence in American plantation agriculture owed largely to a single man, August Belmont. As the New York agent for the Rothschild houses in Paris and London, Belmont arrived in the United States just as the cotton-driven system of Atlantic finance collapsed in the spring of 1837. Seeing opportunities among the wreckage, Belmont is an ideal guide through the logic of the large Anglo-American merchant bankers who had financed the rapid extension of the cotton frontier and the accompanying markets in land, slaves, and staple agricultural commodities. Since Belmont was initially learning the ways of American markets himself and was eager to lead both the London and Paris Rothschild houses into diverse areas of investment, his letters provide a great deal of insight into the changing economic and political landscape of the antebellum United States. Belmont wrote to the Rothschilds daily from 1837 on, commenting on American and global affairs, investment markets, and finance. The irony is that his initial misapprehensions and mistakes are often more instructive than his successes. Belmont and the Rothschilds learned how to navigate American markets together, stumbling through early operations in cotton and tobacco, learning the rhythms and methods vital to success, and then applied that knowledge to good effect when moving decisively into gold in 1849.

How Finance Wove Together an Atlantic Cotton Kingdom

To understand the world Belmont found in May 1837, it is necessary to consider briefly how the world of finance and cotton worked before his arrival. Trade in cotton in the early nineteenth century was characterized by the direct purchase of cotton by mill owners in Lancashire from agents in the southern United States and sales from brokers in Liverpool. A few early cotton merchants based in Liverpool also supplied some cotton to mills further inland, in the Manchester region and Scotland.[4] As trade in cotton grew, more agents were attracted to transactions in the article, and business was increasingly conducted through agents located in Liverpool, New York, and southern port cities such as New Orleans. As more cotton was planted and sold, speculation in the article increased as well, with frenzied buying from 1824 to 1826 driving prices of the commodity to excessive heights and resulting in a corresponding crash in price later in 1826. This crash, unlike the Panic of 1837, had far greater effects in England than in the United States, and resulted in a bullion drain and 20 percent drop in specie. With this panic, many English merchant manufacturers who had previously been active in cotton operations pulled out of American markets, leaving the field open for larger merchant bankers eager to invest their capital in ventures that offered more potential for profit than was available in England or Europe. Given the conditions in Europe, many Anglo-American houses were eager to invest in the United States despite the risks, especially in cotton.

British merchant bankers had abundant motivation to expand their operations in American markets in the 1820s: between 1820 and 1830 over a third of American exports went to Britain, and more than 40 percent of American imports were British. A remarkable 80 percent of the cotton in Lancashire came from the southern United States.[5] Further, because of a marked expansion in trade across the Americas, a relative dearth of investment opportunities in England, and the use of British sterling as a global currency, British capital became an export item in the 1820s. London had become "the money meter of the world," and savvy banking houses such as the Rothschilds and the Browns sought to turn profit abroad. The houses that failed to invest in the Americas stagnated. For the House of Baring, for example, this was a period of negligible growth. It was still regarded as a stable, prosperous and well-capitalized firm, but comparatively speaking it had lost ground. The firm returned to U.S. markets with renewed energy in the late 1820s, appointing Thomas Wren Ward its American agent in 1828. Yet in 1830, still seeking a firmer foothold, the firm was losing ground to its main competitors: the combined resources of the five Rothschild houses dwarfed the once preeminent British financial house. Barings held a relatively modest £492,803 ($2,500,000 in American dollars) to the Rothschilds' more than £4,330,433. The combined capital of the Brown houses in Baltimore, New York, Philadelphia, and Liverpool stood at $3,230,000.[6]

All three of these firms looked to the United States as fertile ground for investment. More people speculating in cotton increased volatility, so timing was often crucial. Many merchant banking houses in this era became entangled in cotton's various threads. For the most part, these ensnarements proved profitable if occasionally disconcerting, insofar as involvement with cotton entailed involvement with slavery as well. Although the contradictions and conflicts that came of this blending of disparate systems would not be made explicit until much later, trade in cotton often meant not only financial exposure but also an uncomfortable association with an institution that many of these firms found troubling. N. M. Rothschild provided the funds necessary to carry forward the Abolition Act of 1833, and both the Paris and London houses refused reimbursement in land and slaves in later years.[7] Likewise, Barings also steadfastly refused compensation on bad debts with land and slaves.[8] The Browns voiced antislavery sentiments yet found themselves the reluctant owners of operating plantations in the American South, acquired when consignments went sour.[9] Nevertheless, all of these firms actively traded in commodities produced with slave labor. The fact of the matter is that, in the nineteenth century, involvement in the American trade, whether in goods produced for commercial sale or in financial instruments such as bonds, meant involvement in some fashion with slave labor.

The price of cotton increased steadily over the early 1830s as the U.S. economy expanded, bolstered in part by access to easier credit in the southern states. This growth in finance is demonstrated by the proliferation of banks: by 1835 there were close to 700 banks operating in the American South, and over the course of the decade another 200 would open their doors for business, with a total capital that exceeded $358 million.[10] However they were ultimately financed, whether privately or capitalized by states, property banks sold bonds to planters, who paid with mortgages on their estates for up to two-thirds of their market value. The banks, or in some cases states, then issued bonds backed by this mortgage pool and typically sold them for working capital in the money markets of the northeastern United States or in London. Subscribing planters could then borrow from the fund thus created, pledging their crops as security. So long as commodity prices held reasonably steady—and this was the key—the land bank system in the South provided capital and credit to a region chronically short of both. Cotton planters needed it, and the banks provided one way in which they could convert cotton into cash, often employing British and northern U.S. capital to do so.[11]

Large advances on crops became common, a credit mechanism developed in accordance with the dictates of commercial production and marketing of the commodity. Cotton not only served as security for advances; when specie was scarce, it also served as a reserve for the issue of notes, and as collateral for the issuing of stock by property or plantation banks. Simply put, an advance on cotton meant that the firm to which the article was consigned would provide the consignor with a portion of the anticipated sale price in advance. The consignor, whether he was a planter, factor, merchant, or broker, did not have to wait until sale of the commodity for money—partial payment was made immediately. On the eventual sale of the article, fees and commissions would be deducted before the final remittance on sold goods was made to the consignor, or the planter's outstanding debt was carried forward to the following year. Generally, advances on cotton ranged between two-thirds to three quarters of the value of the crop on the local market. Planters would generally ship their cotton to a factor and the factor would then sell the cotton for a commission of 2.5 percent. The factor also typically performed other services for the planter, including the purchase of cloth, groceries, wine, and plantation supplies; the transport, warehousing, and shipping of cotton; and the weighing and sampling of bales of cotton and repair of broken bales. All of these purchases included a 2.5 percent commission on funds expended, and often a markup on prices above market rates. Thus the factor acted as banker, agent, broker, and reference for southern planters.[12]

Factors, and merchant bankers in some cases, also provided advances on cotton in the fields. These advances were often in the form of drafts on New York banks or in the form of sixty-day sterling bills. Planters or factors could redeem these bills and drafts for immediate cash through a process known as discounting, which involved the planter selling the bill at a discount of the face value of the bill or draft instead of waiting for the bill to mature. The bank would hold the bill until maturity and either redeem it or use it to pay debts with other houses at full value. The entire operation of the plantation system in the South depended on the factorage system and these provisions of credit. Since planters focused on producing cotton, they were deeply dependent on goods produced away from the plantation. Likewise, the long interval from planting to harvesting, sale, and payment also contributed to the speculative nature of the system as a whole.[13] As more acres came into cotton cultivation, requiring more slaves to work the land and more credit to purchase both land and slaves, instability followed, especially when transactions were collateralized with cotton still in the field and prices far from certain.[14]

With such parameters in place, advances on cotton of 75 or 80 percent of anticipated market value would be risky—unless one believed that cotton prices could only move unidirectionally higher. To consider offering an advance over that amount with prices already running inordinately high would be foolish, yet planters found creditors willing to indulge them again and again. "It seems as if the cotton trade was never to be governed by the same commonsense rules that prevail in other commercial transactions," observed William Bowen, the Brown's trusted agent in the South, adding, "there seems to be a charm in the great southern staple that leads people out of their sober senses."[15] Reckless speculation characterized the business throughout the antebellum period. Investment in cotton, and in American operations generally, was widely understood to be risky. As N. M. Rothschild & Sons noted in a letter to Alphonse de Rothschild, the son of James, head of the Paris house, during his American travels: "you will find while living among the Americans, that they are too fast in many more ways than with their horses. We have noticed . . . that upon getting our orders + credits in America they had a notion they were 'great guns' + that they could not do things on too large a scale or draw too largely on our capital."[16]

By 1835, some actors in American markets, notably Thomas Ward Wren and Joshua Bates, respectively the American agent for Barings and a partner in the London house, had noted irregularity in cotton markets and anticipated a decline in prices. Ward in particular spotted trouble, and in a letter to Joshua Bates voiced agreement with his dour assessment: "If your views of cotton are correct, business must be lessened considerably. . . . [W]e are now on top of a wave. It requires care in descending." Ward also noted that the competition was fierce and that this created chaos in the markets because "there is very little calculation to be made on what others are willing to do."[17] The frantic activity and abundance of easy credit in southern markets contributed to rising cotton prices, while generous advances pumped money into local economies and increased speculative activity. An earlier example of this type of rampant speculative activity fueled by credit and easy access to funds would be the initially wild success of John Law's Mississippi Company in the 1710s.[18] The point is, easy access to credit makes speculation easier because more people are able to put their hands on funds that allow them to enter the market and try their luck. This increases volatility. For wizened investors eager to earn a modest yet consistent return, this spells trouble. It is thus understandable why, following Barings, Alexander Brown & Sons stepped back quickly. Although both firms missed claiming a share of the profits in 1836, they also avoided the catastrophic losses of the following year. The Browns held their ground going into the 1836–1837 season, stating, "as regards cotton we have made up our minds to do nothing in it this season except to put a few hundred bales in our ships to give them a start in freight."[19] They further made clear they were not willing to advance over three quarters or four-fifths of the present value of cotton, despite the higher advances offered elsewhere. Yet money continued to course through the American markets, and because of the amount of credit already extended and sundry bills moving through the system, the money supply effectively expanded.

In January 1837 the price of cotton began to decline, right at the height of the season. The timing of the fall in prices was particularly troubling insofar as the tumble commenced as cotton was coming to market, with consignments and advances often already made. From January to May the price of cotton declined by 18.5 percent in New Orleans. By April, cotton prices were 30 percent lower than they had been a year previously, a catastrophic decline following a boom period from 1832 to 1837 during which cotton prices had consistently risen between January and April. Shippers from New Orleans lost 18 percent on cargoes to New York and 15 percent on those destined for Liverpool. For many firms involved in the speculative frenzy and already overextended from bloated advances, the losses were unsustainable. Financial houses, agents, and factors began to fall like dominoes as all actors began calling in debts, creating a shortage of money.[20]

The Cotton Kingdom of Manhattan

This was the setting for August Belmont's arrival in New York. Amschel von Rothschild, the head of the Rothschild Frankfurt house, had first sent him to Cuba to investigate the repercussions of the first Carlist War for Rothschild interests in the region. Belmont disembarked in Manhattan in the aftermath of the panic, one of the largest financial contractions ever to seize the United States and one that some historians have attributed in part to overspeculation in southern cotton.[21] As he walked the strangely subdued streets in May 1837 observing this malaise, he saw only untarnished opportunity. What was obvious to the young man eager for something more than what he had known in Europe was that he had skills that could be put to good use in a city bereft of commercial activity. There was in fact business to be done by those with cash to hand. He was instructed by the London house to remain in New York "for the present time" since he would "have more opportunity for protecting our interests in New York in receiving our property from Mssrs Josephs & Sons," who had suspended payments two months earlier.[22]

Belmont was perceptive enough to recognize the chance of a lifetime, and, contrary to the wishes of his employers, he immediately set to work establishing his own agency. He rented a small office at 78 Wall Street and wrote to the London and Paris houses within days requesting their business for his new firm, August Belmont & Company. James de Rothschild could only conclude, "he is a stupid young man. . . . Such an ass needs to be kept on a short leash."[23]

Yet within three years of his arrival, Belmont was reputed to be one of the wealthiest men in New York, as well as one of the most important bankers in the country, known as "the king of the money changers" because of his mastery of arbitrage.[24] Belmont's initial impressions of the potential in American business after the panic were sound, and his view of cotton was shared by many other observers of the market. Belmont, and by extension his employers, engaged in what became increasingly common speculative activity in agricultural commodities produced with slave labor.

In the aftermath of the panic, prices for cotton fell even further, and the few houses left standing began to operate in cotton markets again. The Rothschild houses, along with the Browns and Barings, both of which reentered the market in spring of 1837, made money through the consignment, sale, and outright purchase of these goods. It was, after all, most advantageous to enter the market after panics, when money was scarce, prices were low, and competition was minimal. It is at this juncture, with the Browns handling all the business they could and Barings taking a good deal of the rest, that Belmont began to press the issue of cotton consignments with renewed zeal in his letters to the Paris and London Rothschild houses. He wrote to London that the Paris house was considering accepting consignments of cotton during the coming season. "I think that no more precipitous time could be selected. The low prices of cotton and the want of competition will allow those who come early in the market to make their own conditions."[25] Belmont saw the money to be made in the article, but his employers had a different view of cotton, one that considered the interplay between profit and risk. Baron James de Rothschild advised his nephews in London that "all the people are speculating on cotton which will now be sold at any price and we will have to consider very carefully whether we do in fact want to get so deeply involved in the American business."[26] The Rothschild houses were also not inclined toward the consignment business. In October 1837 the firm had been approached by factors in New Orleans and Liverpool seeking advances on cotton, and it had replied that advances and consignments were presently outside the purview of its operations.[27] Despite Belmont's repeated efforts to explain the process and assuage their fears of risk, the Rothschild houses most often preferred to purchase cotton outright.

In retrospect, it is clear that the advice Belmont proffered on cotton investments was not always prescient. Nevertheless, his letters display a thorough consideration of the complex influences at play in determining supply, demand, and pricing, and an astute grasp of the interplay of larger regional and global interests. Belmont often considered commodity sales, the abundance or scarcity of money, and political events when determining what investments were most likely to yield "handsome profits," and was quick to scold when his advice was not followed and profit was forfeited as a result.[28] He also anticipated the effects that sales, or lack thereof, would have in other markets. "The effect of the heavy transactions in cotton at the southern markets is beginning to be felt upon exchanges & I think that henceforth the export of specie to Europe will be on a small scale until next spring."[29] He went on to note that exchange had already dropped in New Orleans and that in this instance, the London house had lost out on a handsome profit by not giving him permission to act. Eventually, Betty de Rothschild begrudgingly acknowledged Belmont's detailed understanding of the American markets, stating that "he knows inside-out all the country's resources; he holds the key to all the wheeling and dealing in the commercial world and he knows which sources to tap, which are the means of success, which are also the pitfalls that must be avoided."[30] Much of this knowledge was hard-earned, the result of years of work and time invested in the cultivation of business relationships in the North and South.

Belmont was compelled to master quickly many of the difficulties attendant on trade in cotton and, by extension, in stocks, bonds, and discount paper. Planters were often cash-hungry and capable of all types of crafty tricks to increase their profits, resulting in the need to evaluate critically all reports from the South. Since southern planters were often deeply in debt, they sought opportunities to bolster prices when the fruits of their slaves' labor were sent to market. Their chronic indebtedness, like their machinations to increase the price per pound paid on cotton, was connected to the rhythms of the plantings and harvests. The cotton year began in March, with the sowing of the fields; the harvest started in July and ran through to the end of December, when cotton began to arrive in the markets. The rhythm of the year made advances helpful, but credit also played a vital role; thus the wisest of agents and cotton merchants learned when a healthy dose of skepticism was warranted, developing an intimate sense of weather, borrowing, and sale patterns throughout the Cotton Belt. Additionally, like Belmont, they cultivated information networks across the region, often receiving daily reports from correspondents. In years when there was an expectation of a large crop, knowledge of which pushed prices downward, planters would sometimes spread rumors of frost striking the plants, or of worms or bolls reducing yields. Often they would hold back the cotton in hopes of diminishing expectations of the yield and driving up the price, despite the advice of factors to send cotton to market as quickly as possible. Invariably Belmont would pass on the reports of these erratic and spontaneous outbreaks of frigid weather, infestations, and early frosts, noting when he had "not much belief" in the veracity of the accounts.[31]

Although Belmont was an astute on-the-ground observer, he did not see what other brokers and larger houses had ascertained from abroad: buying cotton outright in the wake of the panic was more prudent than issuing advances on future sales. Theoretically, extending credit to the planter and letting him carry the risk of fluctuation in market prices in different ports made the most sense, but with planters demanding exorbitant advances in a downward market, the outright purchase of cotton gave these firms more latitude for action in exchange for a negligible increase in risk. Yet, Belmont insisted, "it would be perfectly safe & you might do some very good & profitable business. I recommend these suggestions . . . as by the general distrust a good many houses in that line are altogether thrown out & your house would have a beautiful chance."[32] Belmont stated that as long as the cotton was sold before the drafts were due, there was no risk, but that was not true. There was no risk *unless* the amount of the advance exceeded the value of the cotton, which was exactly what had happened in the winter of 1837. Belmont went further and suggested he could pull in many profitable consignments for his employers if only they would ease their objections and fall in with what he presented as standard practice. As late as 1848, Belmont continued to insist that "consignments of cotton are also very safe with the present cheap rates, but . . . you must, as I had the honor to observe to you on former occasions, give me more latitude for the amount you authorize me to advance. With an advance of ¾ of the invoice I cannot compete with Brown, Tilden & others . . . who advance ⅞."[33] Belmont was obviously eager to enter into this trade, so eager that he misrepresented the policies of these long-established houses and presented risky activity as sound. Belmont saw that money could be made on consignments, and overplayed his hand. Like many of the Americans he criticized as being overly confident and reckless, he minimized the risk of large advances and the speculative nature of the cotton trade generally, apparently sharing that same "speculative & impressionable character of the Americans . . . they always push under the apprehension of a short cotton crop prices much beyond what the facts warrant & on the other hand depress them more than necessary in anticipation of a large yield."[34]

In 1848 Belmont again raised the issue of consignments, claiming that the Browns had gained the upper hand because of the reluctance of both houses to offer higher advances. Yet by this point the Browns had already moved decisively away from consignments, opting instead to focus on letters of credit, currency exchange, and the operation of the Collins packet lines. In 1845 the Liverpool branch's commission revenues on cotton consignments totaled $53,000. By 1852 these revenues had dropped to around $5,000, a reduction of more than 90 percent.[35] Other firms in the industry adopted the Browns' system of making consignments during the 1840s and took up a good deal of the consignment business they left behind. Through their operations in cotton, both purchasing and making consignments, they developed an expertise in the handling of letters of credit and bills of exchange, a business they came to dominate after 1845, as they had the consignment business earlier. With the Browns, their involvement in a commodity produced for a commercial market with slave labor in the antebellum South enabled their transition into a business focused exclusively on banking and finance.

Belmont was keen to follow their lead and work with bills of exchange as well, but when he attempted to do so in the 1840s, he found himself unable to effectively intervene in the market. He was never able to compete effectively for southern paper. As early as 1843 he complained that "the agents of Brown & some others buy all what they can lay hands on."[36] In 1845 the London house authorized Belmont to operate in bills of exchange, but he found the market unattractive. "As regards direct arbitrages between London + here I have always a watchful eye upon them . . . unfortunately the high rates of all continental exchanges here & the sudden decline of £ precludes . . . every chance of doing anything in that line to advantage."[37] The fact that the Browns undercut and undersold him at every turn did not help matters. Even though one of Belmont's strengths was arbitrage, he was able to do little business in bills of exchange around cotton. By 1859 he was lamenting, "Brown bros who buy up all the cotton + produce bills all over the south having their agents in every shipping port . . . monopolize the market as they can sell ⅛–⅜ % below me."[38] Insofar as Belmont and, by extension, the Rothschild houses were unable to effectively control operations in various areas tangential to the cotton trade, and more often than not felt frustrated by what trade they could get, it is not surprising that they moved away from these markets after 1849, especially in light of all the perils of activity in the commodity.

From the beginning, the Rothschilds never shared Belmont's fascination with cotton and had other views on investment in such a volatile commodity, their thoughts colored by different assessments of risk. They found the erratic nature of the cotton market in some seasons simply not worth the bother, noting that the inherent capriciousness in pricing was exacerbated by the fact that entry into the world of cotton speculation was relatively simple. This made it very difficult for anyone to control or dominate trade in the article, and no firm ever managed to gain much more than 15 percent of the market in the antebellum period.[39] It has been suggested by some historians that the Rothschilds failed to take advantage of opportunities in America. However, a more considered view of their involvement in financial ventures in the nineteenth-century United States reveals a thoughtful and cautious approach that, although it did not yield extravagant profit (at least in cotton), also avoided catastrophic losses.[40] This careful approach to trade in cotton in particular was one also shared by other Anglo-American firms in this era.

All that said, the Rothschild congeries of houses did profit from its involvement with cotton. From 1839 to 1848 the Rothschild houses purchased, on average, in excess of 3,000 bales per year. Although they preferred to purchase cotton outright, they also made consignments within well-prescribed limits. They never dominated the trade, but Belmont and both houses also engaged in lucrative arbitrage transactions. Most vitally, they made good use of the knowledge and skills they had gained in the American South to decisively enter into the trade in gold in California. From their experience in southern markets and years spent chasing the Browns, Belmont and the Rothschilds realized there was a distinct advantage to establishing a strong and decisive presence in regional markets early, running both shipping and much of their bill discounting through New York and then on to London and Paris. The firm found that having trusted and exclusive agents in both locations was advantageous. Because of the volatility of southern markets and the shift in political winds, avoiding involvement with plantation slavery looked increasingly attractive as well. The firm also aggressively employed a policy of vertical integration, controlling as many factors in the gold business as was feasible.

From Bales of Cotton to Bars of Gold

The Rothschilds established an agency in San Francisco in August 1849 under the direction of their cousin, Benjamin Davidson. In one of his initial letters, Davidson described the great profits to be made both in the purchase of gold and gold dust and in the discounting of bills.[41] Although much of this was new to Davidson, the Rothschild houses recognized a familiar tune. Against their wishes, Davidson purchased a building and a lot of property in the city

shortly after his arrival (the discordant notes were familiar as well). Nevertheless, he was given a line of credit by the London house and was also authorized to draw on Belmont when necessary. He worked with Belmont to
coordinate the shipping of gold and the discounting of bills. Davidson's agency
was one of the few well-capitalized firms, leaving him well positioned to operate decisively. Additionally, his coordination with Belmont gave him access
to news and information from New York and Washington, D.C. This system
worked well for both houses and allowed them to import more gold than
any other European house in this period. As Belmont noted, "ever since the
Calif gold has been discovered I have myself alone from year to year shipped
more than one half the gold exported to Europe, that is to say my shipments amounted to little more every year than those of all the other houses
combined. . . . [A]s a mere matter of arbitrage there is not a house in England
connected with the American trade who here for the last eight years received one fifth of the gold which I shipped to you, not including my shipments to your Paris house."[42]

In 1849 Alphonse de Rothschild, the son of James, visited the United
States, traveling to New York and Louisiana. It is abundantly clear from Betty
de Rothschild's letters to her son during his sojourn in America that the establishment of an American house in New York was a topic of discussion
among Alphonse, his parents, and the London house. She mentions various
schemes, claiming, at one point, "I would not want to abandon the plan to
see one of you established in America for anything in the world, and deliver
this great future from the stupidity and greed of an agent."[43] Betty proved herself particularly aware of Belmont's status in American society and his value
to the firm, even though she considered him untrustworthy and incorrigible.[44]
During his sojourn in the South, the younger Rothschild sacked J. N. Hanau,
their New Orleans broker, before heading to New York. There Belmont narrowly averted a similar fate, although he himself feared he would lose all
that he had built for himself in the United States.[45] Belmont was fortunate
that his social status and political capital made him difficult to remove, a point
begrudgingly noted by Betty de Rothschild at the time: "B. has created for
himself a strong and independent position," she noted, concluding, "all that
makes him an important man these days."[46] The gold rush in California offered the potential of immediate profit for those positioned to act. After years
of running behind the Browns, chasing bits of cotton and trying to wrest away
part of the trade in discount bills, they opted instead to gain the upper hand

in an emerging market in California and to forgo the establishment of a Rothschild house in New York for the time being.

Davidson's operations in San Francisco expanded, and in 1850 Johannes May was dispatched from the Frankfurt house to assist Davidson in running the firm, and, perhaps, to keep him in line as well. May was made a partner in 1851, and the shipments of gold increased. This proved to be of particular benefit to the London house, which acquired the lease on the Royal Mint Refinery in 1852, allowing it to refine gold independently and mint bars in London. This movement into refining and processing was one that the firm did not consider with either tobacco or cotton but that proved immensely profitable with gold. The lease on the refinery allowed the firm to ride the wave of heightened levels of gold production through the nineteenth century, capitalizing on discoveries in both California and Australia, and, later, South Africa.[47]

As the case of the Rothschilds demonstrates, for many Anglo-American firms, their operations in cotton gave them knowledge of markets, connections, and capital that provided the base for their further development and expansion. The Browns transferred the knowledge and capital they gained through sales and consignments of cotton into Atlantic exchange and credit operations after 1845. Barings left the trade later than the others, moving out in the 1850s. Barings remained involved in large measure because of a pronounced desire to avoid the increasing specialization the firm saw occurring with other houses. Nevertheless, it seemed to focus on certain activities at the expense of others. From the 1840s forward, the firm became increasingly involved in the marketing of American loans on European markets. The firm's experience in cotton and property banks allowed it to determine the relative strength of banks throughout the country. Each firm chose a different area of specialization. This was determined by the presence of other firms in the market, the unique expertise they gained in their American operations, and the cities in which they had placed agents or opened offices.

By the end of the Civil War in the United States, the Atlantic financial world had changed irrevocably, no longer governed by King Cotton. Merchants and bankers had decisively moved on to other, more profitable, as well as characteristically modern, avenues of activity. As we have seen, the Rothschilds, like the Barings and Browns, diversified and moved away from cotton. All three firms entered into the more lucrative markets, selling specie, making arbitrage trades, operating in gold, and behaving much more like modern investment bankers. This shift in activities was not a conscious choice, nor was it immediately apparent. It was governed by the availability of opportunity and can be seen in retrospect in changing patterns of investment and specialization. At its root lay changes in the American economy and the incorporation of the American West into larger global markets and institutions.[48]

In a letter to the London Rothschild house in 1863, August Belmont commented acerbically, "It will always remain a mystery to the future historian to explain the sympathy which a large portion of civilized Europe gave in the nineteenth century to a rebellion the principal aspect of which was the extension & perpetuation of the odious system of slavery."[49] Belmont's disingenuous claim belies the fact that he, like most agents of Anglo-American financial houses, was well aware that the American Civil War, at least in part, was about the revenue generated from agricultural goods produced in the American South. Tobacco, sugar, cotton, and rice, all commodities produced in the southern United States with slave labor, were vital exports for the emergent nation. The income from the sale of these goods became less important with the opening of the West and shifts in the American economic landscape, diminishing southern political influence. This earlier trade in people and goods facilitated the development of financial instruments that in turn eased the completion of these transactions, transactions that, not coincidentally, were also reliant on forms of credit. The evolution of many of these Anglo-American firms from merchant banking into financial operations more characteristic of modern investment houses is attributable to involvement with this earlier trade in goods produced with slave labor and lessons learned from the trade in cotton.

PART III

Networks of Interest and the North

CHAPTER 8

"What have we to do with slavery?"

New Englanders and the Slave Economies
of the West Indies

ERIC KIMBALL

Frederick Douglass wrote that before the American Civil War, "The people of the North had been accustomed to ask, in a tone of cruel indifference, 'What have we to do with slavery?' "[1] This remains an important question today. Recent scholarly attention has refocused on the direct, nineteenth-century linkages between the American North and South—what Senator Charles Sumner of Massachusetts decried as the "unhallowed alliance between the lords of the lash and the lords of the loom."[2] However, an earlier economic relationship had tied New England's commercial fortunes to the very epicenter of the Atlantic slave economy. The first "Deep South" for New Englanders was really in the West Indies.

For more than a century, colonial New Englanders sustained the Caribbean plantation infrastructure: New England ships, crewed by New England men, carried fish, livestock, timber, and slaves to the sugar colonies located in the West Indies. On return voyages they brought back slave-produced commodities such as sugar, molasses, and rum, which were reexported through a coastal trade throughout British North America. Trade with the West Indies provided the means for New Englanders to make payments on their debts to English creditors for their growing and seemingly insatiable appetite for European and English imports. Following independence, the British West Indian markets were "officially" closed to New Englanders, but the colonial pattern of smuggling continued, as did trade with the Danish, Dutch, and French West Indies. The chaos of the French Revolutionary wars in the 1790s created new opportunities for New Englanders to forge a new link with the Atlantic slave economies: they became "neutral carriers" of goods between European imperial powers and the Caribbean. We must recognize that New Englanders were just as invested in slavery, and slave labor, prior to the Boston Associates building the famous Waltham Mills in Massachusetts in 1813, or even before 1793, when Samuel Slater established his cotton mill in Pawtucket, Rhode Island.

Based on population data alone, slavery might appear unimportant to the economic development of colonial New England. The number of slaves living and working there was relatively small—about 2 percent of the total population.[3] There were fewer slaves in New England than in any of the colonies that declared independence from Great Britain in 1776. Such facts have led some to conclude that colonial New England was a "society with slaves" and that slavery was "marginal to commerce and agriculture."[4] By comparison, the substantial slave populations living and working in the West Indies have allowed historians to characterize the Dutch, Spanish, French, Danish, and English island colonies as "slave societies" in which "slavery stood at the center of economic production."[5] David Brion Davis has argued that a "slave society" was one "totally dependent upon slave labor, as distinct from the many societies that simply possessed slaves."[6] However, when the demography of the labor force is the primary measure of slavery's importance, we run the risk of risk of missing the ways in which slavery structured the politics, economy, and culture of places thousands of miles removed from plantations. Moreover, the "societies with slaves/slave societies" framework leaves some important analytical questions unanswered. What about the linkages between these two areas, those "societies with slaves" and "slave societies"?[7] What about those who profit not from directly owning the slaves but either from the product of their labor or by supplying the infrastructure for their labor? How should we conceptualize those individuals or groups or classes that did not own slaves directly but helped to reproduce slavery as an institution? To put it another way, how should we frame our understanding of those who did not directly own slaves but profited from those who did?

This chapter provides some answers to these questions by investigating New Englanders and their integration with the slave labor regimes of the West Indies.[8] An alternative to the slave societies/societies with slaves paradigm measures the importance of slavery based on the circulation of commodities produced by and for the Atlantic slave economy.[9] This moves us away from a "terracentric" focus on local demography and broadens our vision to what Ronald Bailey has categorized as "the slave(ry) trade" and Philip Curtin has called "the plantation complex."[10] For Curtin, the plantation complex refers to the full range of people, tasks, and products involved in the production of commodities on plantations in the West Indies. This approach takes us away from the fixed, landed boundaries of the plantation and into the extended reaches of all that sustain and promote it.[11] As Curtin observes, understanding the linkages that made the success of the plantation complex possible requires an Atlantic approach, one that eschews the nation-state paradigm: "the North American segment of the plantation complex is hard to understand if it is merely seen in the context of U.S. history."[12] This comment is especially apt when contemplating the economic history of New England from the colonial era through the early years of the republic, and its deep connections to slavery.

The story really begins with the first generations of English settlements in the early seventeenth century. When the struggling Massachusetts economy plunged into a depression in the late 1630s, John Winthrop chronicled how "these straits set our people on work to provide fish, clapboards, plank, etc. and to sow hemp and flax (which prospered very well) and to look out to the West Indies for a trade."[13] The economic situation had become quite serious: "as our means for English commodities were grown very short, it pleased the Lord to open to us a trade with Barbados and other Islands in the West Indies."[14] Winthrop described the pattern of exchange between the two regions: "the commodities we had in exchange for our cattle and provisions, sugar, cotton, tobacco, and indigo, were a good help to discharge our engagements [debts] in England."[15] The trade expanded significantly and became equally important for the plantations, as evidenced by the 1667 governor of Barbados noting that "His Majesty's Colonies in these parts cannot in tyme of peace prosper, nor in tyme of war subsist, without a correspondence with the people of New England."[16] Thus, in the seventeenth century the essential links between New England and the plantation complex in the West Indies were forged; they would continue and intensify through the eighteenth century.

One vital aspect of this trade with the West Indies was that it generated a trade surplus that allowed New Englanders to make payments toward their trade imbalance with England. From 1697, the first year for which such data are available, through 1773, New Englanders never once achieved either parity or a surplus.[17] New Englanders imported a vast array of commodities, visible in customs records, probate accounts, and newspaper ads.[18] In general, clothing and other manufactured goods dominated arriving cargoes, alongside such East Indian commodities as tea.[19] Moreover, the need to pay for imports was not an isolated development found only among the occupants of New England's major port cities, as several studies have demonstrated that "the flow of new consumer goods in the eighteenth century was reaching relatively isolated towns" in New England.[20] The surplus they ran with buyers in the West Indies—by providing them with key elements to sustain the plantation complex—allowed them to make payments against their debts to England.[21]

West Indian planters needed New Englanders to supply them with the vital components for the plantation infrastructure. This originated because, as Barbadian planter George Walker explained, "To the sugar cane every thing is sacrificed."[22] This process began in the mid-seventeenth century following the "sugar revolution" in Barbados, and established a pattern that was replicated across the islands throughout the colonial era.[23] As "*the planters of His Majesty's Sugar Colonies*" declared in 1776, "the Sugar Plantations in the West Indies are subject to a greater variety of contingencies than many other species of property from their necessary dependence upon external support."[24] Those contingencies included "dry weather, or excess of wet weather, hurricanes, blasts, vermin," to which must be added imperial wars, earthquakes, fires, and slave revolts.[25] Alongside these challenges were others: "the certain charges of a sugar-work are so great, and the casualties so many; that it were no easy manner to bear up against them," principally because "the wear of our mills is also a continual charge."[26] As the planters focused on plantation development, they utilized the New Englanders to supply them with everything essential to production, including, as Rhode Island governor Richard Ward concluded, "our African trade," which "often furnishes them with slaves for their plantations."[27]

Participation by New Englanders in the "African trade" began in 1645 and, despite the disruption caused by the American Revolution, legally continued until 1808.[28] Rhode Islanders dominated the Atlantic slave trade operating from New England during this time. Of the roughly 139,000 enslaved Africans aboard New England ships, more than 110,000, or 79 percent, found themselves aboard a vessel launched from Rhode Island. These ships were locally owned and crewed, and direct investment in successful voyages spread far beyond just a few merchants.[29] Enslaved Africans who survived the Middle Passage were most often sold to West Indian buyers in Barbados and Jamaica, though after the American Revolution the primary destination in the region shifted to Cuba. Slaves were also sold in mainland markets, and between 1701 and 1770 more than 3,100 enslaved Africans were brought north from the West Indies as "additional cargo" and sold to mainland buyers in North America. In addition, between the 1730s and 1760s, Rhode Islanders directly imported slaves from Africa into the colony, bringing nearly 5,000 for sale.[30] During the 1784–1808 era, South Carolina and Georgia became the largest mainland markets as buyers sought more enslaved Africans for the newly developing cotton plantations.[31]

New Englanders in general—and Rhode Islanders in particular—used rum as the primary article of trade to acquire slaves from Africa.[32] Between 1709 and 1807, Rhode Islanders exported nearly 11 million gallons to Africa, and "locally distilleries supplied most of that rum."[33] By 1772 at least twenty distilleries were manufacturing rum, while additional molasses imports from the West Indies were reexported along the coastal trade, with some kept for domestic consumption within the colony.[34] To the north, Massachusetts imported even more molasses, accounting for nearly half of all molasses imports into British North America from the West Indies between 1768 and 1772.[35] If imports into New Hampshire and Connecticut are added, New Englanders accounted for almost three quarters of all molasses imports from the West Indies into British North America. They also led in rum production, with fifty-one distilleries in Massachusetts, twenty in Rhode Island, five in Connecticut, and three in New Hampshire by 1770.[36] Thus, New Englanders were converting slave-produced raw materials into valuable export commodities long before the construction of cotton textile mills during the antebellum era.

Even larger than the slave trade was the direct export trade between New England and the West Indies for commodities to sustain the plantations. Among those items were oil and spermaceti candles, both of which came from whales, whose brains were used to bring the sugar plantations to light. As the Barbadian sugar planter George Walker stated, "whale oil was necessary . . . for the many lamps in the sugar works."[37] New Englanders supplied nearly all the oil burning in the sugar works, courtesy of the whaling fleets built and operated from Massachusetts.[38] Seth Jenkins, a Nantucket resident and an expert on the whaling industry, estimated that by 1775, "the whole number of the whale fishery ships" was more than 300, and more than 80 percent sailed from Massachusetts ports.[39] In addition to oil, beginning in the 1750s chandlers began transforming the head matter of whales into spermaceti candles. Nantucket whalers shipped head matter to Rhode Island, which quickly became the dominant center of spermaceti candle manufacture.[40] Between 1768 and 1772 almost two-thirds of all the spermaceti candles exported to the West Indies from British North America arrived from Rhode Island. When exports from ports in Massachusetts, New Hampshire, and Connecticut are added the collective market share of New Englanders rises to over 90 percent.[41] In a very literal way, New Englanders helped to illuminate the labor processes of West Indian sugar plantations. While spermaceti candles helped to illuminate the plantation house, they were critical during one of the key moments in the sugar harvesting cycle. The months between January and May were the best time to harvest the sugar stalks and bring them to the grinding mills to extract the juice.[42] Here, at the "engine," the mill rollers, powered by water, wind, or animals, crushed the stalks, and the juice ran down troughs and into cisterns which were then moved into the boiling house.[43] Sugar was boiled to evaporate the water, skim off any impurities, and drain away the molasses. This three-step process of harvesting, milling, and boiling constituted the main sugar cycle. Since "a sugar works often operated around the clock at harvest time,"[44] spermaceti candles provided the best illumination possible for night work.

However, the sea was harvested for more than sources of artificial lighting: the dried, salted cod fished from it became "the meat of all the slaves in all the West Indies."[45] Despite the plethora of fish surrounding the West India islands, planters emphasized sugar production for export over obtaining domestic plantation supplies, and so they imported vast amounts of fish.[46] In the Atlantic fishing port towns north of Boston, entire communities specialized in fishing and became directly interlinked with the center of the plantation complex. Customs records reveal that the vast majority of fish from British North America arrived in ships from Salem and Marblehead, two ports renowned for their fishing fleets. Higher-grade fish, known as "merchantable," fetched better prices and was exported across the Atlantic for consumers in southern Europe. Lower-grade fish, called "refuse" and deemed unacceptable by European standards, was sold throughout the West Indies. In addition to catching their own fish, New Englanders also traded "a considerable quantity of rum" for fish caught by Newfoundland fishermen.[47]

Before 1776, fish imports into the British West Indies arrived from either North American colonies, which principally carried salted cod or pickled mackerel, or ships from English or Irish ports, which carried herring.[48] Jamaica exemplifies this import pattern. In 1709, for example, 2,794 quintals (312,928 pounds) of fish were imported into Jamaica; 53 percent came from New

England and 47 percent from English or Irish ports.[49] Over the next sixty-five years, Jamaican demand for imported fish grew by nearly twenty times; New England provided 54 percent of the nearly 11 million pounds arriving in the island in 1774.[50] Alongside the pickled mackerel sent to Jamaica, New England fisheries provided a staggering amount of cod to the Caribbean plantations. In just the five years between 1768 and 1772, Massachusetts ports, primarily Salem and Marblehead, exported more than 70 million pounds of dried salted cod to West Indian markets. As a whole, New England colonies were responsible for 90 percent of the fish exported from British North America to the British Caribbean.[51]

Along with lighting materials and food supplies like fish, New Englanders sustained the plantation infrastructure by providing livestock—a critical transportation resource—especially cattle and horses. In 1774, Connecticut's governor, Jonathan Trumbull, concluded: "The Principle Trade of this Colony is to the West India Islands," including "the French, and Dutch West Indies."[52] In addition, he explained, "Those vessels that go from hence to the French and Dutch Plantations . . . carry horses, cattle, sheep, hogs, provisions, and lumber."[53] These ships brought back in exchange "molasses, cocoa, cotton, and some sugar," with one exception—"from the Dutch plantations, Bills of Exchange."[54] Trumbull explained these were used to pay off merchants' debts in England, accrued through the importation of merchandise, "the sorts are almost all that are useful or ornamental in common life," which were acquired directly through the coastal trade with Boston, New York, and Rhode Island rather than from bilateral trade with English ports.[55] Yet even this coastal trade ultimately depended on the core export function of Connecticut: supplying livestock to the West Indies.[56]

West Indian planters also had their slave workers harness cattle to crush cane, transport goods, and manure the soil. Cattle were especially in demand among the Leeward Islands of Kitts, Nevis, and Montserrat, where planters had slaves erect cattle mills in large numbers over wind or water mills. Collectively, New Englanders were the largest exporters of cattle and Connecticut farmers were the leading suppliers. Between 1768 and 1772, three out of every four head of cattle sent to the West Indies from North America came from Connecticut. When combined with cattle shipments from the other New England colonies, exports exceeded 90 percent. Similarly, Connecticut suppliers dominated horse exports to the West Indies, exporting three out of every four horses to the region.[57] Rhode Islanders were the next largest exporters, though they focused on shipments to the Dutch West Indies, and Surinam in particular.[58] Collectively, New Englanders controlled more than 90 percent of horse exports to the greater Caribbean.[59] Horses were used in a variety of tasks, but the most important was that they provided an essential nonhuman energy power. They pulled the carts carrying goods from the ships to the plantations, and vice versa. After all, the main goods produced on the plantation—sugar, molasses, and rum—were all heavy when loaded into hogshead containers for export. Every commodity, whether large or small, entering or leaving the West Indian ports had to be transported inland somehow, and that required animal power, lots of it. Other horses were used in mills to drive the rollers to crush the sugar stalks. Finally, the white planter elite rode on horseback or in horse-drawn carriages, symbolizing their wealth, power, and status. Some islands, Jamaica in particular, had enough space to raise horses locally, but even these sources were insufficient for all their needs.[60] The smaller islands, such as Barbados, and the Leeward Islands were so dedicated to sugar production that they overwhelmingly imported horses rather than raise them domestically.[61]

In addition to horses, cattle, fish, and lighting products, the plantation economies across the wider West Indies required endless lumber products for carts, buildings, wharfs, and other structures. Between 1768 and 1772 more than 161 million feet of pine board were exported from British North America to the West Indies, and New Englanders were the largest suppliers, exporting more than 112 million feet, or 70 percent of all pine board exported; half this quantity came from New Hampshire alone.[62] Trees were logged, hauled, milled, and transformed into finished products through a complex labor chain linking loggers, sawyers, riverboat operators, dockhands, sailors, shipbuilders, and merchants to the Caribbean slave economies.[63] Almost the entire physical infrastructure of the plantation system was dependent on wood. New Hampshire's forests provided vital commodities for the West Indian plantations, especially toward the maintenance of the physical infrastructure, which was under constant assault from a variety of environmental factors. Hurricanes constantly pounded the islands; seventy-five hit the area between 1700 and 1775, often leveling houses, mills, wharves, and any other structures, in addition to the damage inflicted on crops and people.[64] Even in those few years when hurricanes spared the islands, the strong gusts, heavy winds, and rainstorms might still cause extensive damage. If trouble borne on water was one concern, that from fire was yet another—whether the fire was caused by accident, lightning strikes, or slave rebellions. Fires were also started during periods of warfare, especially as the English and French battled across the region for half the time between 1694 and 1775.[65] The climate itself also took its toll against wooden buildings and structures, as high humidity led to wood rot. Thus, from the planter's house overlooking the fields, to the wharves where ships lay anchor, to the slaves' huts, one of the primary building materials was under constant siege and required perennial replacement.[66]

Equally important in sustaining the infrastructure were the wooden containers that held all the sugar, molasses, and rum that left the West Indies. Barrels or casks were "the universal container" for shipping commodities.[67] The work of making suitable barrels required skilled woodworkers and a fair amount of time. One estimate is that "only a good workman could produce two barrels in a day's work," and the West Indian trade had an insatiable appetite for containers.[68] In a single year, 1770, the British West Indies alone produced roughly 3.2 million pounds of sugar, 200,000 gallons of molasses, and almost 11 million gallons of rum.[69] New Englanders supplied nearly one-third of the imports of staves and heading essential for barrel making into the West Indies between 1768 and 1772, but nearly all of this originated from reexporting slave-produced staves from the southern colonies of Virginia, North Carolina, South Carolina, and Georgia.[70]

Other areas in New England were also wood exporters, particularly Falmouth, Maine, and Boston, Massachusetts.[71] A prodigious amount of wood left on ships from Maine's only official customs port, Falmouth. Between 1768 and 1772, ships carried 17,212,144 feet of pine board and plank.[72] This amount represented nearly 10 percent of the total amount exported from all of British North America to the West Indies and made the Falmouth region the fourth largest supplier overall to the plantations in the Caribbean. Farther south, almost 19 million board feet were loaded on vessels clearing Boston, and a nearly equal amount cleared from Salem and Marblehead. However, wood loaded on ships clearing from these other two ports originated elsewhere in the colony, where shipbuilders had established a strong milling infrastructure, such as Newbury, Salisbury, Amesbury, Wells, and York.[73]

Carrying all the exports from New England to the West Indies required a significant maritime fleet. These ships represent yet another critical component to consider when assessing the linkages between the West Indies and New England. Shipbuilding was considered by many contemporaries to be "one of the greatest articles of trade and manufacture," employing more than "thirty different denominations of tradesmen and artificers."[74] New Englanders were building boats from almost the moment of first colonization, and they continued to do so through the entire era.[75] An analysis of customs records reveals that from the early 1760s through 1775, the vast majority of the ships entering and clearing New England ports were built in New England—and were crewed by New Englanders as well. Thus, whether they were on fishing fleets, whaling ships, coastal boats, slavers, or vessels bound directly for the West Indies, sailors left from harbors across New England in locally built ships.

*   *   *

Though their journeying was disrupted during the American War of Independence, and they were barred from direct trade with the British West Indies in 1783, New Englanders evaded the laws, just as they had during the colonial era, and continued to set sail for the islands anyway; they recognized the importance of the plantation complex for their own economic livelihoods.[76] As John Adams remarked in 1783, "the commerce of the West India islands is a part of the American system of commerce. They can neither do without us, nor we without them."[77] He further noted that "The commerce of the West India islands falls necessarily into the natural system of the commerce of the United States. We are necessary to them, and they to us; and there will be a commerce between us. If the governments forbid it, it will be carried on clandestinely."[78] Still, the British officially closed the islands to other countries' shipping from 1783 until 1793, when war with France convinced the English leaders that they could not rely on their own shipping to sustain the plantations.[79] In the interim, smuggling persisted, as John Adams had predicted it would, often through the use of false papers and entrances via French and Dutch West Indian ports.[80] Of course, direct exports to the French West Indies in particular continued to command New Englanders' attention, as they had in the colonial era.[81]

There was one significant change to the historical trading patterns between New Englanders and their Caribbean partners that emerged during the Napoleonic Wars. In addition to continuing a direct trade between the two regions, New Englanders became prodigious carriers of material for the European powers to and from their Caribbean colonies.[82] The "reexported" products were all, in effect, either products directly produced by slave labor or products produced in support of that labor. Joseph Inikori's recent work especially has amassed data in support of this view.[83] In the case of the British West Indies, as Seymour Drescher has noted, plantation economies "were generally the most important sector to Britain for the entire century between 1722 and 1822," and were even more valuable during part of the years under discussion here, those prior to the embargo of 1807.[84] Some indication of the importance of the Caribbean-based plantation complex emerges from Drescher's work, which also stresses the importance of the reexport trade from the United States.[85] The larger, macrolevel importance of the Atlantic slave economy has become quite clear recently; the fact that "black slave labor provided the foundation for the wealthiest and most dynamic New World economies from 1580 to 1800" has, in David Brion Davis's estimation, become "the now conventional view." As Davis elaborates, "the economic importance of slavery increased in the nineteenth century along with the soaring global demand for such consumer goods as sugar, coffee, tobacco, and cotton textiles."[86]

New Englanders were direct beneficiaries of their historical integration with the Atlantic slave economies. Indeed, it is difficult to overstate the importance of the Caribbean plantation complex, and the labor power of the enslaved Africans working on them, to the economic fortunes of New Englanders in the years *before* the massive expansion of cotton textile manufacturing following the creation of the mills in Lowell in 1812. From approximately 1793 through 1812, individuals from the United States built, crewed, insured, and supplied ships that carried out "the vast colonial trade of Europe."[87] And New Englanders were significant participants in this process, which is typically referred to as the "carrying trade." Slave-produced commodities were first imported into the United States, a duty was paid on them, and then they were reexported to European ports. A similar process worked in the opposite direction as "manufactures from Europe found their way to colonial ports via the United States."[88]

Indeed, contemporaries were well aware of the importance of this trade, and in 1818 Adam Seybert, a Pennsylvania congressman, provided an extremely useful description of it.[89] In 1818, Seybert concluded that "we not only supplied the demand in our markets, but also furnished a considerable portion of Europe with the valuable productions of the Colonies of France, Spain, and Holland. The surplus re-exported produced a general activity in the sea ports of the United States."[90] He further noted that "without the intercourse with the colonies and the countries above enumerated, we should not have been able to extend our trade in the Europeans markets; in consequence of it we carried rich cargoes to the ports of France, Holland, Spain, Germany, and Italy." This element, Seybert concluded, was critical: "it was from the profits of that trade, that we discharged our enormous debts in England."[91] Seybert estimated that a profit rate of $50 per ton in this branch of trade between 1795 to 1801 was "a moderate allowance" and that "intelligent merchants calculated it as high as 70 dollars per ton, on voyages of every description."[92]

Despite Seybert's estimates, precise comparisons by port and state for the colonial and postcolonial years will be extremely challenging, if not impossible, owing to the absence of key customs records for New Hampshire and for Boston after 1790.[93] Despite these absences, some existing data indicate the level of activity regarding the reexport trade (Table 8.1). From 1802 through 1807, existing data provide the value of domestic exports (that is, products produced within the United States, though not necessarily within the state in which the exported commodity was recorded in cargo) and the value of reexports (commodities produced outside the United States).[94] Quantifying this information shows the dramatic rise in exports in both categories, but it is the value of reexports that most clearly demonstrates the importance of the plantation complex. Table 8.1 provides the value of this trade, measured as a percentage of the total value of all exports, in every New England state, including landlocked Vermont. Between 1802 and 1807, the percentage rose in New Hampshire from 10 percent to 46 percent; in Vermont, from 24 percent to 53 percent; in Massachusetts, from 38 percent to 69 percent; in Rhode Island, from over 48 percent to over 55 percent; and in Connecticut, from less than 1 percent to over 11 percent. Regionally, the value of the reexport trade for New Englanders rose from 34 percent in 1803 to 63 percent in 1807.[95] In essence, New Englanders were increasing their participation in the plantation complex of the European slave empires.

To briefly summarize: until the American Revolution, New Englanders depended on the slave labor plantation regimes of the West Indies to purchase their exports. The profits from these transactions, in turn, provided payments against their debts for English goods. New Englanders were led by the Rhode Islanders in importing slave-produced molasses from the West Indies and manufacturing it into rum to purchase slaves from Africa for future sale in the Caribbean. In addition, New Englanders supported the plantation regimes in the Caribbean by supplying critical infrastructure elements like oil, candles, fish, livestock, and wood. To carry these commodities, New Englanders built a vast maritime fleet and employed locals to crew their ships. Even the American Revolution failed to rupture the links forged with the West Indies as New Englanders continued to trade, sometime legally, though often not, in the 1780s and early 1790s across the greater Caribbean, but they added a new economic component. During the era of the French Revolutionary wars, between 1790 and 1812, they acted as the principal maritime carriers of goods

Table 8.1. Total Value of All Exports (including Reexports) from New England States, 1802–1807

State	Domestic exports, 1802–1803 (D)	Foreign exports (reexports), 1802–1803 (R)	Total exports (T)	Reexports (%)
New Hampshire	443,527	51,093	494,620	10
Vermont	89,510	27,940	117,450	24
Massachusetts	5,399,020	3,369,546	8,768,566	38
Rhode Island	664,230	611,366	1,275,596	48
Connecticut	1,238,388	10,183	1,248,571	>1
New England total	7,834,675	4,070,128	11,904,803	34
	1803–1804 (D)	1803–1804 (R)	(T)	Reexports (%)
New Hampshire	453,394	262,697	716,091	36
Vermont	135,930	55,795	191,725	29
Massachusetts	6,303,122	10,591,256	16,894,378	62
Rhode Island	917,736	817,935	1,735,671	47
Connecticut	1,486,822	29,228	1,516,050	2
New England total	9,297,004	11,756,911	21,053,915	56
	1804–1805 (D)	1804–1805 (R)	(T)	Reexports (%)
New Hampshire	389,595	218,813	608,408	36
Vermont	101,997	67,405	169,402	40
Massachusetts	5,697,051	13,738,606	19,435,657	70
Rhode Island	1,065,579	1,506,470	2,572,049	58
Connecticut	1,353,537	90,190	1,443,727	6
New England total	8,607,759	15,621,484	24,229,243	64
	1805–1806 (D)	1805–1806 (R)	(T)	Reexports (%)
New Hampshire	411,379	383,884	795,263	48
Vermont	91,732	102,043	193,775	53
Massachusetts	6,621,696	14,577,547	21,199,243	69
Rhode Island	949,336	1,142,499	2,091,835	55
Connecticut	1,522,750	193,078	1,715,828	11
New England total	9,596,893	16,399,051	25,995,944	63
	1806–1807 (D)	1806–1807 (R)	(T)	Reexports (%)
New Hampshire	365,950	314,072	680,022	46
Vermont	148,469	55,816	204,285	27
Massachusetts	6,185,748	13,926,377	20,112,125	69
Rhode Island	741,988	915,576	1,657,564	55
Connecticut	1,519,083	105,644	1,624,727	>1
New England total	8,961,238	15,317,485	24,278,723	63

Note: D, all domestic exports; R, all "foreign" exports; T indicates the total of both. U.S. Customs officers and Treasury officials used these categories in their reports.
Source: *American State Papers*, vol. 7 (Washington, D.C.: Gales and Seaton, 1832), 544, 591, 672, 697, 722.

between the islands and European ports. So, while new connections were made with the rising Cotton South, old links to the plantation complex in the Caribbean continued, and remained vibrant. The standard narrative of New Englanders' involvement in slavery begins too late, by emphasizing cotton textile mills, and this framework hides the earlier and persistent involvement with the plantation complex based in the Caribbean. A new history remains to be written, and Frederick Douglass needs our answer. What have we to do with slavery? New Englanders knew the answer: everything.

CHAPTER 9

"No country but their counting-houses"

The U.S.-Cuba-Baltic Circuit, 1809–1812

STEPHEN CHAMBERS

> The Count was perfectly good-humored, and avowed his prejudices
> against the class of merchants without reserve. He says they are
> the cause of all these wars, without ever taking part in them or
> suffering from them. They fatten and grow rich upon the misery,
> and blood of nations. That they have no country but their
> counting-houses. No God but gain.
> —John Quincy Adams, St. Petersburg, Russia, May 15, 1812

Cuban slavery impacted early American capitalism through Russia. In the
early nineteenth century, as the U.S.–West Indies trade increasingly centered
on the Spanish colony of Cuba, a small nexus of elite Americans—particularly
New Englanders—became owners of Cuban plantations.[1] Intensive American participation in the Cuban slave regime both reinforces and complicates
scholars' recognition of slavery as a national rather than sectional bedrock
of U.S. state formation. When convenient or profitable, the character of U.S.
slavery was also transnational.[2] At the very moment of the continued expansion of the North American plantation frontier and the formation of the
U.S. South, northern and Atlantic merchants became planters and investors
in another, offshore plantation frontier owned by Spain. Many more U.S.
citizens also invested in the reexport trade of Spanish sugar, coffee, and specie

from the island. Placing the vast papers of American statesmen, public figures, and diplomats alongside merchants' bills of lading, insurance policies,
and account ledgers reveals the striking degree to which American investment in the Cuban slave regime shaped U.S. economic development in the
early Republic. Remarkably, however, the full significance of these Cuban
investments is first apparent not in Boston or Havana but in St. Petersburg,
Russia.

Although scholars have typically linked the early United States with Cuba
only through the vagaries of the "West Indies trade," beginning in the 1790s
the Cuba trade became essential to the rise of U.S. capitalism.[3] The massive
amounts of specie that flowed from Spanish mines in the Americas through
Havana and into the United States helped buttress the nascent U.S. financial
infrastructure and offset U.S. trade deficits with England.[4] The Spanish economist Javier Cuenca Esteban has calculated that U.S. trade surpluses from
1790 to 1811 with Spanish colonies, primarily Cuba, offset 90 percent of U.S.
trade deficits with the rest of the world, which, Linda Salvucci has suggested,
"went a long way toward reducing the international indebtedness of the young
United States."[5] Meanwhile, elite U.S. merchants leveraged investments in foreign and coastal trade with banking and insurance investments to grow
larger fortunes. As James Fichter suggests, the majority of this wealth "was
denominated in coffee and sugar shipped back from the Caribbean and sent
on to Europe."[6] During the Napoleonic Wars, increasingly larger amounts of
these commodities came from Cuba.

Cuban sugar and coffee did not develop coincidentally with the North
American cotton frontier and U.S. finance but as a direct result and driver of
both. The expansion of the Cuban slave regime worked in tandem with the
expansion of the cotton South to ensure that American merchants—and the
banks and insurance companies they managed—could secure credit and bank
notes from the financial centers of England. Dale Tomich has succinctly characterized this process of transatlantic market integration, suggesting that
"merchants and bankers in New York, Boston, and Philadelphia could use the
trade surplus from cotton exports to draw bills on London banks in order to
finance," in part, the expansion of the Cuban slave frontier.[7] Financial intermediaries developed in the United States in the 1790s because the Cuba trade
provided greater access to credit and capital. In these decades, waves of turnpike, canal and manufacturing companies received corporate charters alongside new banks and marine insurance companies, which replaced private
underwriters.[8] This leveraged insurance investors' savings—including that of

many smaller investors—into an even wider variety of credit. Capital could also be reinvested in other financial structures (primarily banks), many of which contained overlapping and familial directors.[9]

It is no coincidence that the same small cohort of elite American merchants who had made their fortunes at sea now founded the nation's banks, insurance companies, and factories, even as they rose to public office. As ship captains became merchants became bankers became statesmen, the personal nature of credit and the outsized wealth of individual merchants meant that lending and investment was typically a family affair.[10] And they kept their ships. Most elite merchant bankers did *not* follow the traditional narrative of industrialization and leave the carrying trade for finance and manufacturing.[11] During the turmoil of the Napoleonic Wars, a number of elite merchants diversified their domestic holdings not as a reaction against but often *because* of the staggering profits they accumulated in the foreign carrying trade, as it became more dangerous. This was possible only through the careful leveraging of information and kinship in the public diplomatic offices of the United States.

Early American capitalism depended on reliable reexport markets for Cuban sugar and coffee. Because of the uncertainties of wartime trade, investors looked to well-placed U.S. diplomats for assistance in liberating seized vessels and as fonts of pricing information. In this, the U.S. super-elite was at a decided advantage. As public officials, these merchants wielded the powers of the state to profit from the expanding Cuban sugar and coffee frontier and to protect the outlawed slave trade, on which this nascent agro-industry depended. Preoccupied by American fantasies of Cuban statehood, historians have consistently neglected the reality of American-owned Cuban estates.[12] Although scholars have highlighted Secretary of State John Quincy Adams's 1823 comparison of Cuba to an apple that would naturally "gravitate only towards the North American Union," the early nineteenth-century expansion of U.S.-Cuba trade was the calculated result of the incorporation of the U.S. state into elite trade networks, not gravity.[13] American capitalism depended on it. More immediate than Adams's dreams of future Cuban incorporation were his actions on behalf of Americans already invested in the island. In fact, Adams's support of these U.S.-Cuban networks began more than a decade earlier, when he defended a major expansion of American trade with Cuba more than four thousand miles to the northeast, in St. Petersburg, Russia.

*   *   *

In 1809, John Quincy Adams had a problem. As newly arrived U.S. minister to Russia, he faced suspicions from officials in the Baltic that the vast amounts of sugar and coffee arriving in American vessels had come from British colonies, in violation of Napoleon's "Continental System." On December 26, 1809, Adams assured the Russians "that, with the exception perhaps of coffee, all the articles of colonial trade were produced within the United States." The sugar, according to Adams, came from Louisiana and Georgia or "the Spanish islands."[14] This was a lie, and Adams knew it. Not only was very little sugar produced domestically in the United States in this period but earlier that month Adams's secretary, Alexander Everett, had detailed exactly how merchants smuggled British colonial goods into Russia.[15] When he was later confronted by the French, Adams was drawn into an extended discussion of the nature of "the Havanna sugars arrived in American vessels," which he attributed to "the great increase of our trade with the island of Cuba."[16]

In 1809–1811, a solid majority of U.S. vessels arriving in the Baltic hailed from New England.[17] Determining the origin of the sugar and coffee onboard these vessels depends on tracing the trade circuits of their home ports, the busiest of which was Boston. Although scholars have tended to claim ignorance of specific shipping information in this period for Boston, because most records have been lost, a careful study of shipping information published in Boston newspapers is highly suggestive. A survey of 210 issues of the *Boston Gazette* from January 1, 1810, to January 2, 1812, reveals that 13 percent of all foreign entrances (of 4,428 total entrances) and 12 percent of all foreign port clearances (of 3,771 total clearances) originated at or were bound to Cuba.[18] In Boston, Havana consistently—and often dramatically—outranked all other foreign ports, such as Liverpool and Lisbon, in its share of shipping. And Boston was not alone: along the New England coast, other port records tell a similar tale about the outsized importance of the Cuba trade. Of 724 ships registered as entering Salem, Bristol and Warren, Portsmouth, and Newport from foreign ports in 1810–1811, 35 percent entered from Cuban ports. Whereas in Portsmouth just 4 percent arrived from Cuba, in the busier ports of Bristol and Warren (75 percent from Cuba), Newport (41 percent), and Salem (20 percent) the extensive influence of elite American merchants created a lopsided Cuba trade.[19] Throughout much of the region the New England "West Indies trade" was, more accurately, a Cuba trade. Adams was right: the sugar and coffee arriving in St. Petersburg overwhelmingly came from Havana.

Adams had arrived in the Baltic aboard a ship loaded with this same merchandise: in the fall of 1809, he sailed from Boston to St. Petersburg aboard the *Horace*, a "merchant-ship laden with sugar and coffee," which was owned by the wealthy New England merchant and future lieutenant governor of Massachusetts, William Gray.[20] Like the *Horace*, other American merchant ships arriving in the Baltic principally carried three staples of enslaved labor: sugar, coffee, and cotton. Although cotton has typically been central in this narrative, Caribbean sugar and coffee accounted for almost three times the volume of domestic cotton in this U.S.-Russia trade.[21] In an effort to profit from the disruptions of European warfare, the American merchant marine created a regular U.S.-Cuba-Russia circuit.[22]

American merchants' success in Cuba since the opening of trade in 1797 was not wholly a matter of long-standing commercial ties and fiscal ingenuity; it depended on the impact of European warfare on the British and French merchant marine. The Napoleonic Wars were a positive boon for U.S. merchants invested in Cuba in the decade before Jefferson's 1807 embargo: U.S. reexports of sugar and coffee had risen from respectively 1.1 million and 2.1 million pounds in 1792 to 143 million and 42 million pounds by 1807.[23] In an incisive study of tariffs and revenue, Douglas Irwin has demonstrated, based on the gap between gross customs revenue and net customs revenue, that the period from 1797 to 1811 (notwithstanding a period from 1804 to 1806) were consumed with the reexport trade, much of which increasingly centered on Cuban sugar and coffee.[24]

In 1809, faced with the overlapping trade restrictions of the Napoleonic Wars, which effectively barred American ships from continental European ports, U.S. merchants in Cuba sailed for the more remote markets of the Baltic. This trade was nothing new: American trade with St. Petersburg dated to at least the early 1780s, when New England merchants such as the Derby and Cabot families dispatched shipments of sugar, rum, and fish to the port, returning with cargoes of iron, hemp, and Ravensduck.[25] In the 1790s, the U.S.-Russia trade became more commonplace, and in 1808, the Rhode Islander John D'Wolf II—sailing, in part, for his better-known uncle, James—was reportedly the first American to link New England investment in the Pacific fur trade with St. Petersburg by traveling overland through Siberia.[26] Although the U.S.-Russia trade could produce considerable profits if traders timed their arrivals to match market demand, it was also notoriously unpredictable. As a result of the risks and vagaries of the carrying trade, elite merchants depended on the assistance of commercial agents, including salaried members of the U.S. diplomatic corps and well-placed family members, at each point in their trade networks. These agents not only worked with local commercial houses to secure sales and consignments, they also regularly reported on fluctuations in prices, tariffs, and bribes. Predictably, these merchant-diplomats expected to make a profit.

This was the reality of capitalism and U.S. foreign policy in the early republic: as Peter T. Dalleo suggests, "Many of those who did join the foreign service, especially the consular branch, were merchants already living abroad" who "sought consulships to enhance personal business ventures rather than to build diplomatic careers."[27] Perhaps no merchant was as active in exploiting the overlap between state power and the U.S.-Cuba-Baltic trade as Massachusetts native William Gray. By the mid-1790s, Americans in Havana were documenting numerous "American & Spanish vessels" entering Cuba "with Russia goods,"[28] and in the turbulence of an undeclared naval war with France, William Gray's ships provided an armed convoy for trade between Cuba and New England.[29] At least some portion of this trade reached the Baltic. On December 7, 1797, for example, Gray's ship, *American Hero*, left Salem for Havana, arriving in February 1798 to unload a cargo of "Russia sheeting."[30]

Soon, U.S. merchants faced a series of sustained, shifting trade restrictions, beginning with Jefferson's 1807 embargo. While U.S. trade with Cuba may have slumped slightly during the embargo years, U.S. merchants readily exploited loopholes in trade regulations—such as licensing foreign trade vessels for the domestic coastal trade or arriving in foreign ports in feigned distress—to ignore national law. Moreover, while opposition to Jefferson's embargo may have generally characterized Federalist New England, a number of elite American merchants actually backed the embargo.[31] This support of a public policy that would appear to directly challenge merchants' commercial success is indicative of the counterintuitive ways in which these circuits of elite trade operated. Laws were sometimes made to be broken.

At first glance, William Gray's 1808 support of Thomas Jefferson's trade embargo appears counterintuitive. Gray was reportedly the richest man in the United States; his fortune—estimated to have risen from $900,000 in 1799 to more than $2.5 million in 1808—was greater "than [that of] any other *five* men of all the New-England states" combined.[32] Once called "the first merchant of the United States" by Adams,[33] Gray operated an extensive, worldwide shipping network that employed at least 300 "hands" annually.[34] This network would have been threatened by a restriction of U.S. trade. Yet the reality of the U.S. diplomatic corps' relationship with American merchants meant that trade prohibitions benefited the super-elite. When William Gray supported the embargo, he also defected to the Republican Party and moved from the Federalist stronghold of Salem to Boston, where he found a ready ally in John Quincy Adams, who had just been ousted from the U.S. Senate for his support of the embargo.[35] Both men needed each other, Adams for the revival of his public career and Gray for the protection of trade profits. This was no secret at the time. In December 1809, for example, immediately after Adams's arrival in St. Petersburg, the Federalist *Salem Gazette* charged Adams with desertion and commercial dependency on Gray:

> They sacrifice without a struggle an old friend as they adopt a new
> one, like John Q. Adams, or, if I may be allowed to name him in
> the same line, William Gray—Democratic leaders must follow, not
> dictate, the measures of their dependents.[36]

While Adams has been applauded by historians for his diplomatic accomplishments in St. Petersburg, in Russia he acted as a de facto private commercial agent.[37] In 1810, William Gray forwarded Adams a letter of credit worth $30,000,[38] and in 1810–1811, Adams not only secured the release of all of Gray's ships that had been seized in the Baltic, he regularly wrote to Gray with commercial advice related to the manipulation of prices by Russian merchants and customs house bribes.[39] While the French continued to hold more than $2 million worth of American property seized in the Baltic, with Adams's help, Gray made a profit on every ship sent to Russia in 1810.[40] These profits were not incidental: in December 1810, U.S. consul Levett Harris estimated that shipments "from the U.S. to Russia" had on "average yielded a profit of at least 40 pcent."[41] The risks that made such profits possible were very real, as evidenced by fluctuating marine insurance premiums.[42]

U.S. agents such as Harris were themselves adept at turning a profit from their access to such information. While the wealthy Russian merchant Glukoff—"the agent of Mr. Gray"—made "a considerable profit" on the consignment of the goods onboard the *Horace*, Levett Harris made even more. As Harris bragged in February 1810, Russian merchants were at a disadvantage precisely because of the limitations of their information networks: "they are generally possessed of very limited correspondences abroad. This makes it easy for foreigners, who are possessed of that advantage, and who have a capital to trade on, to make large fortunes very easily." When Glukoff sold Gray's cotton, for example, Harris "knew from his correspondence that it was about to rise" and used his public office to manipulate Glukoff into selling him the cotton "as an act of friendship" and "without paying the money." Within "about fifteen days," Harris sold the cotton "at an advance of thirteen or four-teen thousand rubles."[43] In this case, Harris had no actual part in the shipment: he was not involved in the purchasing, shipping, or disbursement of the goods, and he was not acting as an agent for William Gray. Instead, he simply coordi-nated the information networks that flowed through the consular office to pur-chase and immediately sell these goods at a profit and no cost. Because of his public appointment as consul, Harris had not even had to front the purchas-ing money; information and public power allowed him to pluck profits out of thin air. And while Adams occasionally grumbled about Harris's transnational profiteering, he consistently defended Harris or looked the other way.[44]

And Adams had not arrived alone. Foreign secretaryships were well-known stepping stones in the networks of commercial patronage that defined the diplomatic corps, and it is unsurprising that three of Adams's legation secretaries were members of elite families invested in the Cuba-Russia circuit. They included Francis Calley Gray, William Gray's son; Alexander Everett, future U.S. agent to Spain and Cuba; and John Spear Smith of Baltimore, the son of West Indies merchant and U.S. senator Samuel Smith.[45] Reflecting on the danger to his father's commercial house from a Baltic market glutted with an "immense quantity of colonial produce," for example, John Spear Smith wrote from St. Petersburg, "May the Lord have mercy on S.S. & B. [Samuel Smith and Buchanan]."[46] And the same Russian commercial house, the Brothers Cramer, which had provided John Quincy Adams with infor-mation about Havana sugars, also worked as commission agents for elite American merchants such as Samuel Smith and the Rhode Islander and Cu-ban plantation owner James D'Wolf.[47] Unlike Samuel Smith and William Gray, however, James D'Wolf did not send his son with Adams to St. Peters-burg. Instead, in 1811, his nephew-in-law, Samuel Hazard, arrived as U.S. consul to Archangel, a position that Hazard's father hoped would lead to an "increase of lucrative business."[48] And a lucrative business it was. At its height in 1811, U.S. exports to Russia amounted to $6 million worth of goods, a sum equivalent, as Alfred Crosby writes, "in value to one-tenth of the entire ex-ports of the United States for 1811."[49] This proportion would not be reached again until World War II.

At the other end of this Atlantic network, elite American merchants, who were not as fortunate as Senator Samuel Smith to have a brother as secretary of state, relied on similar agents in Cuba. In the Spanish colony, authorities openly acknowledged the overlap of American political and commercial in-terests. The Spanish administration, fearful of anything that might encourage tendencies toward Cuban Creole independence, did not recognize foreign colonial diplomats and typically referred to American officials in Cuba as "commercial agents," a term significantly more apt than "consul" or "minister." By 1809, a number of these public American "commercial agents" had resided in Cuba as private traders for years.

Although North American trade with Cuba can be traced to long-standing networks of West Indies traders, the 1762 British occupation, and the American Revolution, the true rise of the Cuban agro-industry began with the Haitian Revolution, when the single largest Caribbean producer of sugar and coffee virtually vanished. Unlike Saint-Domingue or Jamaica, in 1790 Cuba was virtually undeveloped, but in the decades that followed, investors encouraged the expansion of the sugar and coffee frontier on an unprecedented scale.[50] After 1796, Spain's irregular trade restrictions also became more predictable for American traders, eager to exploit European warfare to expand existing trade networks and increase their presence in Cuba.[51] In the first decade of the nineteenth century, the expansion of the U.S.–Cuba trade was not wholly linear, but by 1809, Americans were poised to profit from the recent increase in *cafetales* (coffee plantations) and *ingenios* (sugar plantations).[52] As in Russia, elite Americans who invested in Cuba depended on merchant-diplomats. In the dense capital of Havana, their number included Vincent Gray and, briefly, William Shaler. Sixty miles east of Havana, Americans had also begun to invest in the port of Matanzas, as a more cost-effective depot. Here, American agents such as John Latting routinely aided U.S. merchants, while also ostensibly serving as "vice consul."

In 1800, the New England merchant George Cushing had described Latting as an unscrupulous "bankrupt from Long Island in the state of New York" who routinely boarded every slave ship that entered Havana in an attempt to procure the consignment.[53] Latting moved from Havana to Matanzas around 1805, and by 1808, according to James Anderson, the unrecognized U.S. consul in Havana, Latting had developed "a very good reputation" and was serving as a vice consul in Matanzas.[54] In 1810, Latting began construction of a dock in Matanzas for the benefit of his commercial house, and in the 1810s and 1820s he continued to hold the public position of vice consul as he worked to secure consignments of sugar, coffee, and slaves for American merchants and plantation owners.[55] The Matanzas-directed correspondence to James D'Wolf's agent, Edward Spalding, for example, arrived care of John Latting's commercial house, "Latting, Adams, and Stewart," which would eventually default in 1825.[56]

Whereas in Matanzas, American merchant-diplomats sometimes operated independent commercial houses, in the central hub of Havana, Americans more often worked in partnerships with Cuban merchants. This arrangement not only established credit and simplified the flow of information with U.S. commercial houses, it was also essential to gain the confidence of European merchants, who were concerned about the risks of the West Indies trade.[57] Although it is unclear whether the Massachusetts native and Havana merchant Vincent Gray was related to John Quincy Adams's benefactor, William Gray, it is certain that Vincent Gray, like Adams, was a staunch ally of elite Americans invested in the Cuba trade.[58] Vincent Gray had arrived in Cuba in the early 1800s to collect debts for American merchants, using his position as U.S. vice consul and merchant–slave trader in the Havana commercial house of Antonio de Frias.[59] In the coming years, he would operate in the slave trading/consignment house of Gray, Fernandez & Hermano.[60]

Gray would soon become one of the best-connected American commercial agents in the region and a regular participant in the slave trade. Although U.S. law banned the outfitting or building of slave ships in U.S. ports in 1794 and 1800, Cuban ports remained major supply points and depots for Americans involved in the slave trade.[61] In fact, the Spanish administrators of Cuba provided explicit incentives to encourage U.S. merchants, who might be transporting other goods, to supplement their cargoes with slaves. In 1802, for example, specie could be legally exported from Cuba only in slave sales, which led many U.S. vessels, even those not bound for Africa, to supplement their cargoes with small numbers of slaves from other Caribbean islands.[62]

In Havana, Vincent Gray's public position and Spanish connections in these early years allowed him to attract extensive American business and remain a key player in the U.S. establishment in Cuba for decades. By 1803 he was handling over $300,000 in lawsuits related to claims by U.S. merchants for American merchandise that had been seized in Havana.[63] That year, Gray solicited Alexander Hamilton to ask "if I can serve you or any of your friends in this quarter," and enclosed "a small turtle" as "a small memento" of goodwill.[64] The turtle paid off: by 1805 he was acting as an attorney in "suits pending upwards of 280,000 Dollars on account of citizens of the United States" and another $150,000 in claims for which "no suits [had] been commenced."[65] The elite circles Gray moved in are evident from his reception of the German nobleman, Alexander Von Humboldt, on Humboldt's second visit to the island for a month and a half in 1804, whom he "recommended to [the] attention and protection" of James Madison.[66]

Yet whereas John Quincy Adams successfully won the support of the Russian czar for his commercial-diplomatic mission, American agents in Cuba often found their tasks to be more arduous. In the revolutionary atmosphere of the early 1800s, Spanish authorities remained paranoid about the potential of foreign espionage, under the guise of commerce, to incite instability in Cuba. When Vincent Gray was briefly arrested in Havana in 1805, for example, sixty U.S. merchants protested, including investors from Massachusetts, Rhode Island, and Pennsylvania.[67] Because the Spanish refused to acknowledge the U.S. consulate in Havana, in 1805 Vincent Gray issued public consular "documents under a private seal," essentially acknowledging the fiction of a separation between private commerce and public service or diplomacy.[68] The private commercial seal of a slave trader, Vincent Gray, therefore became the de facto public seal of the U.S. foreign service in Havana. Soon the stakes in this illegal trade rose higher, after the British and U.S. outlaw of the transatlantic slave trade in 1807 and 1808.

The U.S. commercial agent James Anderson, for example, arrived in Havana in 1807 primarily on behalf of the Baltimore merchant William Patterson, expecting "to gross $10,000 a year."[69] But he sound found circumstances to be unexpectedly difficult. Anderson had also been instructed to monitor the slave trade into Cuba; this, he wrote to Secretary of State James Madison, would be impossible. The Spanish authorities remained determined to protect the expansion of the slave trade into Cuba, and many U.S. merchants were eager to profit from it. If Anderson got involved, he was likely to be arrested and expelled—or worse. Illegal trade was so essential to U.S. trade with Cuba that Anderson was convinced that any American or Spanish merchant "who thought that I stood in the way of his making a fortune" would "find an assassin" to "plunge a dagger into me at any moment of the day." "It does not require darkness," Anderson wrote, to commit murder in Havana.[70] In May 1807, for example, an American carpenter named Taylor, who had lived in Havana "for more than five years," was murdered and "tied to a tree, stark naked, and covered with wounds and blood."[71] U.S. "vice consul" Vincent Gray—who openly worked in the Cuban slave trade into the 1820s— had also been at the center of an assassination plot one month earlier, when rumors spread that Gray had received "a large sum of money." A cabal of "twelve Spaniards conspired" to kill Gray and rob his offices, but after word of the plot leaked, the Spanish captain-general agreed to provide Gray with soldiers. When one of the assassins attacked Gray's clerk with a stiletto, the clerk shot him, and Spanish soldiers cut the man down. Five others were soon arrested.[72] Not everyone, it seems, was eager to welcome Americans to Cuba.

William Shaler encountered similar obstacles when he arrived as the unrecognized U.S. consul to Havana in August 1810. Much more familiar to historians than Gray or Latting, William Shaler received an annual salary of $2,000—compared to John Quincy Adams's $9,000 salary in Russia—and would eventually bill $7,026 to the U.S. Treasury.[73] Like Adams, Shaler was bound to elite Americans invested in the island, including Nathaniel Ingraham of New York, who forwarded Shaler $1,000 in gold and a letter of credit prior to Shaler's departure. Shaler had worked as a commercial agent for Ingraham's firm of Ingraham, Phoenix and Nixsen for years.[74] During his time in Cuba, William Shaler forwarded many of his letters not to Washington but to Nathaniel Ingraham's New York commercial house, which he provided with regular updates.[75]

While historians have emphasized Shaler's interest in Cuban independence or potential annexation, when Shaler was expelled from Cuba in December 1811 it had less to do with revolution than with networks of American investment.[76] Immediately after Shaler's arrival, he was welcomed by Antonio de Valle Hernández, a secretary to the Spanish consulado, who had been born to Spanish parents in Russia and who worked for Shaler as an "expeditious translator."[77] Since 1791, Cuba's elite had seen their wealth grow exponentially with the expansion of the slave regime, and now—as the Spanish Empire began to fracture and disintegrate around them—they quietly considered alternatives to Spanish rule. Now the real push for U.S. annexation came not from Shaler but from the Creole elite, who resented Spanish trade regulations, sought greater access to foreign markets, and were terrified of abolitionism.

In June 1811, Shaler was approached by a member of the Creole elite, Joseph de Arango, cousin of the influential Francisco de Arango, who saw only "one course for us" (the "wealthy landed proprietors" in Cuba) should Spain attempt to abolish Cuban slavery and the slave trade: "to solicit a union with you [the United States], and become one of your confederate states." Arango's proposal provided an ideal opening for Shaler to advise the secretary of state to annex the island. Yet Shaler told Arango only that the United States would always be interested in what happened in the Spanish colony.[78] This was classic understatement. Shaler knew that the U.S.-Cuba trade depended on the illegal slave trade, which relied on lax Spanish administration.

As war between Britain and the United States loomed at the end of 1811, Shaler's translator, Antonio de Valle Hernández, suggested that if hostilities broke out, "a preliminary measure on the part of England would be, the occupation of Havana [and] its dependencies." Where, Hernández asked, would the United States stand? Shaler promised that if the planters resisted a British occupation, they could "rely with confidence on the American people."[79] The Creole elite were unconvinced. They worried that "Great Britain previous to a formal declaration of war against the United States will take measures to assure herself of the Port of Havana & others of the Island of Cuba under the pretext of defending them from foreign invasion." Worse, beset by French armies, Spain might even be forced to go along.[80] By late 1811, American influence in Cuba was under real threat. Rumors spread that the Spanish Cortes was negotiating a loan with the British government that might involve a much greater British intervention into the dissolving Spanish American Empire,[81] and as Spain and Great Britain both outfitted expeditions ostensibly to quell rebellions in Central and South America, the Creole elite worried that the forces might actually be intended for Cuba.[82] "The government of the American Union," they wrote, "is too feeble" to prevent it.[83] There was little Shaler could do to reassure them, and his approach to annexation was more reactionary than proactive. The survival of the Cuban slave trade—and the expansion of the slave regime—depended on maintaining the status quo.

Yet amid this geopolitical turmoil, as the Cuban Creole elite plotted revolution and the Spanish and British prepared expeditionary forces across the Atlantic, the immediate cause of William Shaler's expulsion in 1811–1812 was not his discussion of Arango's annexationist proposal. Instead, he was punished for placing commerce above diplomacy: in October and November of 1811, Shaler took an unauthorized leave from Havana to visit the Fundador coffee plantation owned by Massachusetts native Nathaniel Fellowes.[84] Fellowes had arrived in Cuba in the late 1790s with his uncle of the same name. Following his uncle's death in 1802, a legal dispute with the powerful Amory family led him to become one of the first true expatriate U.S. citizens in the island of Cuba in 1807.[85] By the time of Shaler's visit, Nathaniel Fellowes owned at least two Cuban slave camps and 170 enslaved African workers, worth more than $300,000.[86]

As was the case for most U.S. consuls to Cuba, Shaler had been dispatched based on his commercial contacts rather than his diplomatic abilities. This was most obvious in linguistics: unlike Vincent Gray, William Shaler was not even fluent in Spanish. In November 1811, Shaler returned to Havana to defend his absence for "three quarters of an hour" entirely "in French," which the captain-general could understand but had difficulty speaking.[87] Predictably, in the wake of the recent French occupation of Spain and the 1809 expulsion of French immigrants from Cuba, William Shaler soon found himself on a boat to New Orleans.

*   *   *

After Shaler's departure, the Creole elite's aspirations for independence were cut short by the outbreak of the Aponte Slave Rebellion of 1812.[88] Soon the entire U.S.-Cuba-Baltic circuit would be thrown into turmoil as French armies advanced into Russia and the United States declared war on Great Britain. The threads of trade that public officials and commercial agents had laid from Boston to Havana to St. Petersburg frayed and snapped. Because diplomacy had served private profit at every corner of the U.S.-Cuba-Baltic trade, these same circuits had routinely undermined international law, making the outbreak of war on both fronts much more likely. On the eve of Napoleon's invasion, for example, John Quincy Adams defended elite American merchants in Russia to the German nobleman, Count St. Julien. The count accused "the class of merchants" as having "no country but their counting-houses. No God but gain." He argued that merchants incited warfare without caring "who was victorious or who vanquished. They made their profit," he said, "with equal indifference out of all." A sensible merchant, Adams wrote, could have "turned the tables." But Adams did not argue. It would not have been appropriate, he reflected, precisely because Adams himself was—in his own words—"the champion of the merchants."[89]

In Cuba, "champions of the merchants" encouraged and profited from the outlawed slave trade, violating the U.S. ban and angering rival Creole and Spanish merchants and the British government. In the Baltic, American shipments of Cuban sugar and coffee became a major pretext for the French invasion of Russia in June 1812.[90] Operating at key points in the U.S.-Cuba-Baltic circuit, commercial agents such as John Quincy Adams and William Shaler consistently championed the interests of their elite American allies, even when this stance conflicted with U.S. national security. From St. Petersburg to Havana, the foreign policy apparatus of the early U.S. state was deployed for the sake of private profit. American capitalism depended on the expansion of U.S.-backed Cuban slavery, which in turn depended on the circuits of commercial information passing through elite U.S. diplomatic offices, "with equal indifference out of all."

CHAPTER 10

The Coastwise Slave Trade and a Mercantile Community of Interest

CALVIN SCHERMERHORN

What is a slave ship? Such vessels are among the most emblematic features of slavery's Atlantic history. Transatlantic slaving vessels were floating dungeons whose names evoke a "way of death," illustrated by the iconic *Brooks*, the *Zong* massacre, and the *Amistad* uprising. That "vast machine" was a race-making technology, a site of demonic cruelty, and an instrument of violence. Yet the slave ship looks different when viewed in its coastal U.S. configuration. Like their transatlantic and riverine counterparts, U.S. coastal slave ships were "floating engines of capitalism," but in the 1810s and 1820s most ships plying the domestic saltwater slave trade carried the miseries of captives alongside a cornucopia of consumer goods. They were floating jails whose owners and operators scooped up revenues from the commercial transport of slaves as part of competitive strategies.[1]

This chapter offers a new perspective on the question, "What is a slave ship?," by investigating the financial stakeholders in the slave system itself. It details the slaving passages of several wooden sailing ships in terms of the enterprises that owned and operated them and the supply chains they served. The underlying process of enslaving was no less morally repugnant in American ports than it was in Liverpool, England, or Whydah, on the West Coast of Africa. As in the transatlantic trade, African-descended captives were investments.

But the customs of American capitalism clothed the violence of the domestic slave trade in the banalities of ephemeral commerce, which blunted the edges of captives' defiance, blurred the focus of abolitionists' protests, and beckoned shipping merchants with a low bar to entry into the trade. This chapter follows three ships in three registers or acts in the drama of the domestic slave trade of the 1810s and 1820s. The *Unicorn*, the *Almy*, and the *Lapwing* were representative of the Mid-Atlantic merchant marine of the period. All were links in supply chains and distribution channels that crisscrossed an Atlantic commercial complex. Each delivered bound workers and much more, including agricultural commodities, consumer goods, and information.

All promised returns for investments for the firms that owned and operated them, but before 1825 the coastal slave trade was an incidental traffic. Aboard the *Unicorn*, enslavers tossed captives into a capacious cargo area crammed with consumer goods. The ship plied the cotton triangle, and the captives were an incidental cargo on a voyage touching New Orleans, delivering bulk commodities to Britain, and returning to North America with manufactured goods. Over time, the *Unicorn* was incorporated into an international interlocking partnership of merchant bankers as a high-technology instrument of slavery's capitalism. On the bottom rungs of the American merchant marine, the *Almy*'s Rhode Island owner and master scavenged for revenues and found them in a slaving port. New England furnished many such slavers to the domestic trade. Baltimore's *Lapwing*'s voyages illustrate the seamless integration of the Chesapeake–New Orleans slaving route with a West Indies trade in slave-produced products. It was also part of an intensification of the coastal commerce in captives into an essential trade or one in which human cargo was central. The transition from incidental to essential trade occurred at roughly the same time that cotton replaced foodstuffs as the United States' chief export. Jean Baptiste Moussier's firm illustrates the change in miniature. That New Orleans–based slave trader used both the *Almy* and the *Lapwing* as part of an ambitious strategy, and Moussier responded to the challenges of buying captives with cash and selling on credit by coming up with a way to expand the credit that his slaveholding clients consumed voraciously and demanded vocally.

Coastal slaving commenced as ventures of opportunity among enslavers, bankers, commission, and shipping merchants with excess capacity. Saltwater transport was costly for enslavers, but it was efficient. It also diverted some of the revenues of slave sales into the pockets of shippers, merchants, and mariners who had no direct relationship to a growing commerce in the hands, limbs, and bodies of African-descended Americans. Beginning in 1808, federal prohibitions on the landing of foreign captives gave U.S. shippers a legal monopoly on slaves' coastwise transport. After the United States took control of New Orleans and annexed Louisiana, a long-distance domestic slave trade to the lower Mississippi Valley developed incrementally, accounting for between a fifth and sixth of the forced migration from the Chesapeake to the Lower South by the peak decade of the 1830s.[2]

On nearly all American coastal voyages on which slaves were transported in the 1810s and early 1820s, the accent fell on shipping nonhuman cargoes. That incidental trade had deep roots. In the sixteenth and seventeenth centuries, oceangoing vessels carried captives across the Pacific from the Philippines to New Spain. Colonial Dutch and English shipmasters took on enslaved people as incidental cargoes on passages between strategic Atlantic and Caribbean ports. Following the War of 1812 and the ending of embargoes, the business of buying, selling, and transporting enslaved or captive Americans intensified, and as the fabric of a national economy took shape in the intricately laced configurations of domestic trade, the interstate slave trade became interwoven into those patterns.[3]

The *Unicorn*: An Atlas of Its World

The *Unicorn* of Baltimore carried a miniature version of the commercial world through which it sailed. It plied the "cotton triangle," which cemented reciprocal interests among United States, British, and European merchants, slave traders, industrialists, financiers, and slaveholders in the southern interior. Cotton was the engine of transatlantic capitalism in the nineteenth century. Knowledge and credit provided its locomotion. In the 1820s cotton replaced foodstuffs as the principal U.S. export commodity, and Baltimore was fast becoming a principal slaving port of the East Coast.[4]

Captives were a nearly invisible part of that mighty process. In late October 1820, a Baltimore customs inspector arrived at Ramsay's Wharf in Baltimore's Fell's Point district with an order to inspect the enslaved cargo aboard the *Unicorn*. Walking from the Custom House near the Basin to Fell's Point, the inspector glimpsed the makings of a national economy deeply implicated in slavery. Ramsay's Wharf was among many other long parking stalls for ships facing warehouses and backing up to the Patapsco River. (Today the wharf is gone, but the site contains the Frederick Douglass–Isaac Myers Maritime Park and heritage center.) Not all was well in the commercial district of the nation's third largest city. Hard times resulting from the Panic of 1819 compounded the adversities of recent bad harvests and London's closing the British West Indies to American grain, which was the lifeblood of northern Chesapeake trade. In good economic times and bad, few merchant shippers would turn away a consignment of enslaved cargo, and by 1820 concerned citizens suspected that too many of their African-descended neighbors were being kidnapped or transported illegally. Slaveholders often liquidated enslaved property even after promising manumission, and Quaker abolitionists asked the customs inspector to search the *Unicorn* for kidnap victims.[5]

Inside the *Unicorn* the inspector found twelve African Americans, surrounded by barrels, trunks, sacks, and other containers of cargo. Anguish had spread among those already cut off from loved ones and now subject to maritime discipline. Most of the enslaved people aboard were in their teens, but among them were a two-year-old baby and a four-year-old child, property of an aspiring planter. The people were confined in a dim space with little heat or accommodations. Twenty-four-year-old Thomas, twenty-six-year-old Jane, and Jane's six-year-old daughter, Anne, were destined for the cotton fields of Rapides Parish, Louisiana. Their twenty-year-old owner had plans to take them up the Red River. A New Orleans banker embarked seven enslaved people aged four to twenty-six. In response to the inspector's questions, some of the captives "acknowledge[d] themselves to be slaves for life."[6]

That response points to a narrative of ownership captives were forced to endorse. Lifetime servitude was nothing new in the Chesapeake, but more and more it was becoming a pretext for sale and removal. Slave ships were potent enforcers of owners' rights to disappear loved ones. By the 1820s some 20 percent of the enslaved population of the Virginia Tidewater would vanish, most through enforced migration. Others were manumitted, but a family of five could expect one member to disappear each decade. That social disruption was punctuated by personal and sexual violence, and as the decades rolled on, enforced migration became a demographic catastrophe among African-descended kinships. Violence was enslavers' great economizer, but its peculiar American form sheathed the blade or blunt instrument in a storyline of legitimacy.[7]

By the time most captives boarded the *Unicorn*, the brutality of enslavement had been honed to a commercial grammar of ownership that they were required to repeat. Some internalized it, but most spat out the required responses and crafted a counternarrative in the spaces owners could not sell or colonize. Most captives took their worldviews, their theologies, and their poetries with them through the ordeals of slavery, submerging violent responses in the recesses of their consciousness and the human connections they forged in an odyssey of loss and social wreckage. But for a miraculous reprieve, most of the African Americans put aboard the *Unicorn* had spent their last season in Maryland and by spring would find themselves tending sugarcane or weeding long furrows of cotton plants.[8] Despite the deeply personal ways in which the captives experienced their forced transport, they were incidental cargo.

The *Unicorn* held the material makings of the southern slave country. On its fall 1820 passage, the *Unicorn* was freighted with large metal kettles used to boil sugarcane juice, bellows to stoke the fires, and scales, chains, and weights to lend precision to the operation. Any enslaved person aboard would have cause to dread such items. Construction materials included hoops for barrels, bales of canvas, coils of cordage, wheels, axels, iron plates, and kegs of rivets. A cart and gears were aboard, too. The *Unicorn* carried refined and loaf sugar, along with several empty molasses casks. Much of the sugar was returning to the lower Mississippi Valley after being shipped to Baltimore for processing. The two dozen or so refiners centering on Baltimore's Sugar Alley and Sugar House Alley provided processing that was not yet available in areas where sugarcane was grown.[9]

The captives held belowdecks beheld a panorama of consumer goods. The ship carried coffee from the Caribbean, wine from Europe, tea from India or China, and local cider royal, a whiskey-cider blend that lent itself to storage. Most of the imported cargo, such as beverages and manufactured items, was subject to an import duty or tariff. That included $3,600 worth of consumer goods imported from the German state of Bremen and transshipped on the *Unicorn*, including mirrors, window glass, phials, demijohns, and other fine items such as violins and coffee mills. English linens complemented hats and other fashions, destined for the backs and heads of ladies and gentlemen.[10] Unlike on transatlantic slave ships, American captives were often plunked down in unimaginable material abundance, and the enslaved Marylanders must have had some sense that their robbed labors paid for a portion of the finery they were forbidden to enjoy. The *Unicorn* soon set sail, and besides winds and currents, a mighty political force shaped the contours of the trade it carried.

A federal legal framework that protected some industries through tariffs and others through a closed market helped to make a national economy out of a confederation of regional ones, and among all the cargo, bondspersons

were an exclusively national commodity. Flour was beginning to link Chesapeake producers to Mississippi Valley consumers, but the interstate slave trade
was responsible for a massive transfer of wealth from the Lower South to the
Upper South. Besides the flows of slave-produced goods and the capital accumulation they led to, voyages like that of the *Unicorn* diffused revenue from
the slave trade among a network of interests. Besides a protected market for
domestic enslavers, the national government incentivized slavery's commercial agriculture. In 1816 the United States levied a three cents per pound tax
on imported sugar, which was designed to protect domestic sugar producers
from foreign competition. That tariff, amounting to as much as a third of the
price of imported Caribbean sugars, helped to ensure that Louisianans had a
viable market.[11]

The *Unicorn*'s 1820–1821 voyages illustrate contours of economic nationalism in the context of Atlantic commercialization. After disembarking the
captives and nonhuman consignments, the *Unicorn* was freighted with cotton. In December 1820, the *Unicorn* sailed from New Orleans to Liverpool
carrying 782 bales of cotton shipped by the New Orleans merchants McLanahan and Bogart. At then current prices in New York, the cotton's market
value was over $42,000, or the equivalent of forty-two enslaved adult male
"prime field hands." James McLanahan and Wilhelmus Bogart traded in sugar
and cotton, and plied a direct trade with Britain and Europe. They sold slaves
as well. In Liverpool, the *Unicorn*'s skipper delivered its payload of cotton to
three leading merchant houses, including 592 bales to William and James
Brown & Co., the Liverpool arm of Alexander Brown & Sons of Baltimore.
They were Irish-American merchant bankers who by 1825 had branches in Baltimore, Philadelphia, Liverpool, and New York, along with correspondents
in several cotton ports, including New Orleans.[12]

On its passages, the *Unicorn* mediated much more than a trade in tangible goods. Merchant ships plied a knowledge economy. The House of Brown
had graduated from brokering individual shipments of goods and commodities to merchant banking. It issued letters of credit and traded in foreign and
domestic bills of exchange. By the time of Alexander Brown's death in 1834
his firm was the second largest exchange merchant in the United States, behind
the Second Bank of the United States. Like Brown's competitor, Baring
Brothers & Co., the House of Brown depended on timely and accurate delivery of business knowledge. Success in the credit and exchange business meant
mastering a staggering catalogue of merchants' financial standings and the
health of markets, firms, and individuals. In an age before mercantile agen-

cies collected and sold credit reports, the Browns and Barings did that business in-house, which required an information system that spanned oceans. In the age of sail, packet lines were also information technology. Packets sailed on schedule, ideally providing speedy conduits and initial exclusivity for their owners. The rise of New York City as North America's premier financial center had much to do with the flow and control of Atlantic business knowledge. Rival cities, such as Baltimore and Philadelphia, failed to launch viable competing lines.[13]

Baltimore and Philadelphia merchants had not lost that contest by the time the *Unicorn* sailed with slaves, and the House of Brown was organizing clients' merchant vessels into its own packet line. In part because the *Unicorn* was a fast and capacious ship, the House of Brown enrolled it into its line in 1822. On its winter 1820–1821 voyage, the *Unicorn* arrived in Liverpool in February and sailed back to New Orleans with an assortment of manufactured textiles. Since it arrived during the cotton shipping season, it sailed to Liverpool again in May, delivering more than 850 bales of cotton, including more than 300 to William and James Brown & Co. The *Unicorn* sailed for Baltimore in late July. The Browns were impressed by the *Unicorn*'s shipmaster and his dependability, even though the vessel was smaller than the typical transatlantic packet sailing from New York City. But by the time the *Unicorn*'s owners enrolled it into packet service between Philadelphia and Liverpool, there was stiff competition from several New York–based packet lines with weekly service to Liverpool and less frequent service to London and Le Havre. In the spring of 1822 the *Unicorn* made a swift passage from Liverpool to Philadelphia, "from land to land," in less than twenty-six days at a time when the average crossing from Liverpool to New York was forty days (and twenty-three eastbound). In subsequent years the erstwhile slave ship sailed between Liverpool and New Orleans regularly carrying goods, passengers, and market news before being lost at sea in 1825.[14]

Ships like the *Unicorn* were on the leading edge of capitalist information technology and vital links in chains of which bound workers were a part. But for the occasional inspection, carrying captives was a largely invisible part of that process and the strategies they supported. Wooden ships' holds were the voids in which a demographic catastrophe unfolded. The slave market was a province of the knowledge economy mediated by merchant sailing ships, and the bondpersons whose intensely personal ordeals verged on the hellish were part of a sophisticated commercial web. The continuous delivery of bondpersons buoyed confidence, which supported credit, and the effectiveness of the narrative imposed on captives as legitimate items of commerce was a test of the tensile strength of the fabric of nineteenth-century capitalism.

The *Almy*: Chains and Links

Docked at Newport, Rhode Island, the ninety-one-ton *Almy* was an unlikely slave ship. The two-mast brigantine was a transient or tramp ship on the lower rungs of the American merchant marine, on the opposite end of the ladder from the *Unicorn*. Yet revenues from the commercial transport of slaves filled the commercial sails of New England owner Gilbert Corey (Cory) and shipmaster Peter Corey of Tiverton. In late February 1819, the Coreys were in search of cargo to keep their small shipping firm afloat when they accepted a consignment of lime, lumber, oil, rum, and other goods on a passage to Richmond, Virginia. The *Almy*, named after an allied family, was small but new, finished in Massachusetts the previous year. En route from Newport at three o'clock one morning, the watchman discovered a fire in the hold, apparently caused by ignited lime. The blaze threatened to engulf the ship. Corey attempted to scuttle it but limped to New London, Connecticut, instead. The cargo was "principally destroyed, and the vessel greatly damaged," but the crew managed to save the sails and ropes, and avoided serious injury. After a monthlong repair, Corey sailed the *Almy* to New York City and three weeks later accepted another cargo bound for Richmond.[15]

Virginia's capital city saved an unfortunate shipping firm from immediate failure. The *Almy* was tied at the city dock on the James River when Corey met the slave trader Jean Baptiste Moussier in June 1819. Moussier sought passage for some thirty captives to New Orleans. The slaving season had all but ended, and it was risky to ship human beings to the Crescent City in summer. "The yellow fever rages with considerable violence amongst the shipping and lower parts of the city," cautioned a report of what would be the worst epidemic for thirty years. "This is certainly one of the filthiest, and in many respects the most wretched hole in the universe," the correspondent scorched. But Moussier was at the margins of the trade and had few alternatives, relying as he did on his own financing, judgment, and good fortune.[16]

Moussier was genial, enterprising, and ambitious but initially hesitated to form such alliances. He recognized an opportunity in the saltwater domestic slave trade, which promised high returns on investments in moveable human property. Moussier had been a cotton and sugar merchant in New Orleans. The commission business was highly competitive, and on that rough road to wealth he spied a shortcut through the interstate slave market, which remained robust despite the 1819 financial panic. Moussier's investments in bondpersons was an avenue to real estate investment and banking entrepreneurship. By the time of his death in 1831, Moussier would be known in the city as the inventor of Louisiana property banking. At its apex his real property included a Louisiana sugar plantation on Grande Terre. In the summer of 1819, however, Moussier was struggling to build his enterprise and needed to transport his coffle to New Orleans. He booked passage aboard the *Almy*, which was also freighted with coal and bricks.[17]

Moussier may have been a marginal figure who hired a miserable ship, but he held advantages. Moussier was a Creole businessman with an extensive knowledge of the labor demands of Francophone sugar planters and connections with several New Orleans notaries, who kept an informal index of the credit health of merchants, planters, and professionals. Without interregional allies or much capital, Moussier economized by taking upon himself the business of buying, selling, and financing his trade, arriving in Richmond and avoiding better-established traders' territories. To the captives, however, there was little distinction between an established trader and an upstart like Moussier.

Bondpersons like Norbonne carried the burden of Moussier's ambition aboard the *Almy*. In the summer of 1819, Moussier bought him from the Richmond auctioneer and director of the Bank of Virginia Robert Gamble. Norbonne bore an old Virginia name. Twenty-four years old, five feet eight inches tall and described as "Black," he fit the description of just the kind of worker Louisiana sugar masters wanted. Norbonne was likely jailed until Moussier exhausted his resources assembling a coffle including twenty-nine others, infants to adults as old as forty-six. Moussier embarked his coffle aboard the *Almy*, and the Corey kinsmen captured between $425 and $510 for the captives' passage if they charged the going rate of between $17 and $20 per adult and half that for children under thirteen. That was a generous return compared to freights of $4 per hogshead of tobacco or one cent per pound on cotton between New Orleans and New York City. Moussier was responsible for the costs of water, food, and incidentals, besides his cabin passage. The *Almy*'s sea passage was slow. Sailing to New Orleans should have taken four weeks. It took longer than six. However frustrating to those aboard, the extended passage meant less risk from yellow fever. Meanwhile, Norbonne and his fellow captives had plenty of time to inspect the ship's Yankee craftsmanship and size up their Creole captor.[18]

The *Almy* captives stepped onto dry land in a city more than twice the size of Richmond with one of the largest slave markets in North America. It did not take Moussier long to sell Norbonne. Four days after the *Almy* disembarked its human cargo, Moussier called on a New Orleans neighbor, the lawyer and notary Hugues Lavergne, to record his sale to a city exchange merchant, who was likely acting as a purchasing agent for a planter. Norbonne sold for $784. Meanwhile, the *Almy* sailed to Haiti's Cape Henry, the Turks Islands, Bahamas, and from there to Wilmington, North Carolina, and home to Rhode Island, delivering salt from Turks Island and cotton from New Orleans. After its initial voyage the *Almy* was refitted for whaling and sailed under a new shipmaster.[19] Moussier's fortunes meanwhile rose.

Self-finance and itinerancy gave way to credit and alliances. As Moussier built his slaving firm, he enrolled the firm of John and Philip E. Tabb of Norfolk, Virginia. That strategic alliance gave Moussier an entrée into a Chesapeake market for Louisiana sugar and the Tabbs a sales agent in New Orleans. Instead of Moussier sailing to Virginia and assembling captives, he would accept consignments and concentrate on selling them in New Orleans. The Tabbs were part of a larger network that joined slaving to trade in slave-grown commodities. Their main business was a direct trade in cotton and tobacco with William and James Brown of Liverpool. The Tabbs shipped Moussier a cargo of captives in the fall of 1820.[20]

Moussier's business grew. He bought a ship, the 240-ton brigantine *Brazillian*, which transported hundreds of captives from the Chesapeake to New Orleans and commodities in the other direction.[21] In October 1822, shipmaster Samuel Morton sailed the *Brazillian* from Norfolk with 107 captives aboard. Among them were twenty-five-year-old Phillis and her two children, John and Elizabeth. Passage was just under a month, and seven weeks after arriving in New Orleans, Moussier sold the trio to Raymond Lacoul of Royal Street. Moussier's firm was well capitalized enough to buy more than 100 captives and take mortgages from buyers like Lacoul.[22]

To build credit and expand his enterprise, Moussier formed another strategic alliance with Rogers and Harrison, a Richmond merchant house, acting as their agent in the maritime domestic slave trade. Rogers and Harrison was an interlocking international partnership with branches in Le Havre, London, New Orleans, and New York, dealing in tobacco and other commodities. Moussier may have been more ambitious than shrewd or fortunate, for in August 1823 the *Brazillian* became the property of William Kenner & Co., a merchant firm with ties to New York City merchants. In 1824 Moussier shipped a cargo of captives from Norfolk to New Orleans as an "agent for the planters of Louisiana." That self-designation hints that he viewed his work as mediating the interests of Upper South sellers and Creole buyers.[23] Moussier soon graduated from slave trading to real estate investment. Ships like the *Almy* continued to serve enslavers, and as Moussier's business grew along with the market for sugar and cotton workers, the commercial transport of slaves ramified.

The *Lapwing*: Taxi of the Seas

The *Lapwing* of Baltimore illustrates the seamless transport of captives within regular trade between Baltimore and the West Indies. Built in Baltimore, the 107-ton *Lapwing* was owned by Henry Thompson, a prominent shipping merchant and one-time president of the Baltimore Exchange. It was a regular trader, midway between packet and transient. Between 1818 and 1822, Thompson regularly sponsored voyages to the West Indies, delivering to Baltimore Cuban, Haitian, and Puerto Rican commodities and dyestuffs from Mexico. The *Lapwing* touched Philadelphia and New Orleans as well.[24]

By 1822 the saltwater domestic trade was intensifying as cotton exports soared. Seeking efficient and cheap transport, Moussier and his counterparts in the Chesapeake-to-New Orleans slave trade came to rely on merchant ships. The *Lapwing* was a sea taxi for hire. In March, Thompson was loading the Lapwing for Haiti when he took a consignment of sixty-one captives, including twenty-five belonging to the prominent slave trader David Anderson. Shipmaster Thomas Kennedy sailed for Louisiana with instructions to disembark the comparably more perishable human cargo before sailing to Haiti. Kennedy must have known that one of the female captives was in the final stages of pregnancy, and somewhere on the seas she gave birth to a baby, whom the New Orleans customs collector termed an "infant slave." The authorities did not record the parents' names or the child's. The mother survived. The *Lapwing* exhaled its human cargo and sailed back down the Mississippi River, returning to Baltimore in June carrying a cargo of coffee. It soon returned to the Caribbean trade.[25]

By the time the *Lapwing*'s owners accepted another cargo of enslaved Marylanders, a young Frederick Douglass had arrived in Baltimore. In February 1827, as Kennedy made his way from his Aliceanna Street residence to the docks to sail the *Lapwing* to New Orleans, he could have passed the nine-year-old Douglass, who lived on the same street with the Thomas Auld family. Then known as Frederick Bailey, Douglass was the same age as fellow enslaved Marylander Dick Hammond. But Hammond was the property of the Baltimore slave trader Austin Woolfolk. In mid-February, Woolfolk embarked Hammond and twenty-three others aboard the *Lapwing*. Austin's brother, Samuel M. Woolfolk, who had driven Anderson out of business on Eastern Shore, took on board nineteen captives. All of the human cargo was consigned to Reynolds, Byrne, & Co., New Orleans merchants in the cotton and slave business.

Shipboard conditions were woefully unpleasant. As Kennedy prepared to sail, social events in Baltimore were rescheduled on account of inclement weather, including Durocher's Ball and the meeting of the Friends of General Jackson. The hold of the *Lapwing* must have felt stone-cold as those assembled huddled hour upon hour, day after day. After the ship sailed out of the Chesapeake it was several more days before the *Lapwing* entered the Gulf Stream and the captives thawed. The forty-three Marylanders who arrived in New Orleans in late March were transferred to a steamboat and deposited at Natchez, Mississippi, for sale. After disgorging its enslaved cargo, the *Lapwing* took on passengers, cotton, and foodstuffs for the return trip to Baltimore by way of Charleston.[26]

Slaving was lucrative, and by the fall of 1827, the *Lapwing*'s shipmaster was acting as Moussier's agent. Thompson brokered the shipment, and Kennedy embarked fifty-nine bondpeople at Norfolk, Virginia, consigned to Moussier. The *Lapwing* sailed during the second week of December and was off the Double Headed Shot Keys north of Cuba when the British warship HMS *Nimble* approached and royal troops boarded the *Lapwing*. Like nearly all coastal vessels navigating around the Florida Peninsula, the *Lapwing* had sailed through the Bahamas rather than hazard the dangerous currents, reefs, and tides off the peninsula itself. The *Nimble* was patrolling for illegal slaving vessels, and the American vessel was in international waters. Yet the legal fiction of a domestic passage protected Kennedy from British authorities' seizing captives aboard the *Lapwing*. Instead, the *Nimble*'s captain pursued a transatlantic slaver, the *Guerrero*, a Spanish vessel that had sailed from Havana, Cuba, with a crew of ninety, embarking 573 African captives. In the chase, the *Nimble* and the *Guerrero* struck Carrysfort Reef off Key Largo. The slaver ran aground, and the *Nimble*'s officers and crew captured a portion of the surviving captives. The rest were taken to Santa Cruz, Cuba. Moussier's enslaved cargo was delivered safely.[27]

As the tide of the domestic saltwater trade rose, enslavers showed little hesitation in packing bondpersons aboard like cordwood and intensifying violence, a practice that inched toward conditions redolent of the transatlantic trade. Yet rebellions were haphazard and largely unsuccessful. Most saltwater passages from the Chesapeake to New Orleans went without incident, and remarkably, all U.S. shipboard rebellions or incidents involving captives' self-liberation ended up in court. Some captives did not go quietly. William Bowser aboard the *Decatur* (1826) and Madison Washington on the *Creole* (1841) led uprisings that killed shipboard whites and seized control of the vessels. Washington and most of the *Creole* captives reached freedom in the Bahamas, but Bowser's uprising led to his conviction and execution in New York.[28]

The *Lafayette* case suggests a change from an incidental trade of the 1810s and 1820s to an essential trade of the 1830s, one in which enslavers ratcheted up brutality and carried nonhuman cargoes to supplement captives. The *Lafayette* sailed from Norfolk, Virginia, in 1829 with 197 captives aboard the 120-ton schooner. A maritime ton at the time was forty cubic feet, which gave each captive a dedicated cargo area equivalent to 0.61 tons, or just over twenty-four cubic feet, the size of a casket. By comparison, abolitionists claimed that the notorious transatlantic slave ship *Brooks* designated 0.65 tons per slave in the late 1780s. As was common in the coastwise slave trade, the officers of the *Lafayette* were lightly armed, and the captives were evidently permitted on deck without restraints.

But the *Lafayette* captives did not go quietly to market. A group of male captives attacked the captain before being put down. After the captives were submitted to a shipboard tribunal, suspected leaders were ring-bolted to the deck for over two weeks as the ship sailed to its destination. In New Orleans, a handful of rebels were arrested and tried, and eventually four were given ten-year sentences and three five-year sentences, including hard labor (which presumably differed from the hard labor most captives performed as a matter of course). Following the uprising, the *Lafayette*'s owners put it back into the slave trade with the same shipmaster. In October 1830, the *Lafayette* sailed from Norfolk, again tightly packed with 168 captives (0.71 tons per slave). Following that voyage the slave-trading firm of Franklin & Armfield operated the *Lafayette* for two more years on at least three voyages and advertised it as a well-known packet. That firm built a dedicated fleet, first by enrolling regular slavers like the *Lafayette* and then by buying ships it assembled into a human conveyor from the Chesapeake to the lower Mississippi Valley.[29] Yet vessels like the *Lapwing* were not eclipsed, and both regular traders and transients continued to capture revenues in the commercial transport of captives.

Sailing on an Ocean of Credit

The coastal slave trade took shape in the early decades of the nineteenth century when seekers of commercial transport turned to merchants and shipping enterprises. The voyages of the *Unicorn*, the *Almy*, and the *Lapwing* show in small and episodic ways the configuration of a larger mercantile network of which slaving composed a small but important part. Maritime traffic was the vital conduit that permitted slave traders to enroll agents who acted as financiers, which reflects the importance of transatlantic financial integration in American economic development.[30]

The coastwise slave trade from the Chesapeake to New Orleans took shape within the cotton triangle and variants such as the West Indies trade in sugar, coffee, dyestuffs, and other commodities. It became an essential trade. To shipping merchants, slavery smelled not of perspiration and humiliation but of ink and paper. Enslavers' maritime and financial technologies complemented the advances in management and machinery that rendered slavery ever more profitable and divided it from its colonial predecessors. American merchants in such cities as Baltimore, New Orleans, and New York accumulated capital from trades in slave-produced products and from the proceeds of the commercial transport of slaves.[31]

A slave trader invented the key to sugar expansion in the 1830s. Jean Baptiste Moussier was behind Louisiana's credit expansion. Perhaps on the long passages from the Chesapeake to New Orleans Moussier hit on a banking scheme that permitted borrowers to bypass factors and access bank money that allowed them to leverage the equity in their bondpersons. He and the notary Hugues Lavergne masterminded the Consolidated Association of the Planters of Louisiana, a state-chartered bank that securitized land and slaves, then sold its Louisiana-backed bonds to British and European merchant bankers, including Baring Brothers & Co. and F. de Lizardi & Co. of London. The Consolidated Association and other property banks lent a portion of that equity back to the stockholders who had mortgaged their real and personal property, including slaves.[32]

Banking expansion launched a flotilla of slave ships. Property banks were part of an astonishing expansion of credit that helped to buy thousands of enslaved people, hundreds of plantations, and improvements in technology that eventually made Louisiana sugar competitive, even though the protective tariff was reduced in the 1830s. The volume of the interstate slave trade closely followed expansions and contractions of credit. In the late 1820s and early to mid-1830s, credit expansion and the financial integration of Britain and the United States helped to rationalize the interstate slave trade, and banks like the Consolidated Association gave the sugar industry the means to develop more efficient processing. Credit expansion tipped the state's agriculture toward sugar and away from cotton. Louisiana's 1820 sugarcane crop was valued at $2 million and its cotton crop at $7 million. By 1829 the sugar crop was worth more than $6 million, while cotton crops had sunk to $2 million. Sugar estates more than tripled between 1824 and 1830, and the number of enslaved people in sugar-producing southern Louisiana rose 86 percent during the decade of the 1820s. The toll taken on bondpersons like Norbonne was monstrous. Punishing sugar work and the harsh disease environment wracked the bodies of young workers, which sent owners scuttling to banks and factors for more credit and to slave traders like Moussier or the Woolfolks for replacement workers. Shipping merchants like the Coreys of Rhode Island were happy to capture the resulting revenues of transport.[33] Their activities did not go unnoticed.

The business network converging on slaving vessels drew criticism from abolitionists. In 1829, twenty-four year-old William Lloyd Garrison was investigating the interstate slave trade in Baltimore. "So much for New England principle!," the young activist yelped to readers of the *Genius of Universal Emancipation* as he exposed a New Englander taking on a consignment of captives bound for New Orleans. "Scarcely a vessel, perhaps, leaves this port for New Orleans," Garrison argued, "without carrying off in chains large numbers of the unfortunate blacks." Like the *Almy*, the *Francis* was a tramp ship whose owner, Francis Todd, was from Newburyport, Massachusetts. Garrison was a Newburyport native too. When Todd's ship needed cargo, the Baltimore merchant shipper Henry Thompson gave him a lucrative payload. By then Thompson had a long history of brokering slave cargoes. The *Lapwing*'s owner was also the principal broker of goods on the *Unicorn*'s 1820 voyage to New Orleans. Unfortunately for Garrison, the public tolerated the slave trade more easily than authorities tolerated his attacks on a merchant shipper. Maryland charged Garrison with criminal libel. At Garrison's trial in 1830, Thompson testified that shipowner Todd had no advance knowledge that his ship was being used to transport slaves from Maryland to Louisiana. Other shipowners were likely ignorant of their vessels' human cargo as well, finding out only later that a portion of their revenues came from slave traders. Garrison was convicted, jailed, and radicalized, and while the trade in human beings surged, so did his career as a professional agitator.[34]

What is a slave ship? In the 1810s and 1820s it was a vessel that mediated commercial ties with striking banality and extraordinary reach. The U.S. salt-water slave trade was firmly embedded within a developing North Atlantic capitalist system, and even abolitionists failed to grasp the commercial con-nections that made the plantation complex of the Lower South a vast economic suburb of London and New York City. Shippers knew those linkages and the commercial geography they traversed perhaps better than anyone. Had Gar-rison catalogued the flotilla of ships built, owned, financed, or operated by New York or New England and embarking slaves in the Chesapeake, he would have set himself a task similar to Thomas Clarkson's investigation of Liver-pool's ties to slaving in the 1780s. As the voyage of the *Almy* or *Francis* case suggests, the distinctions between merchants, slave traders, and shippers were blurred when city merchants and shippers bought and sold slaves. Chains of credit and supply linked interests in slavery among a vast network of market actors, whose interests were united in the human beings held captive in the holds of merchant vessels.[35]

PART IV

National Institutions
and Natural Boundaries

CHAPTER 11

War and Priests

Catholic Colleges and Slavery in the Age of Revolution

CRAIG STEVEN WILDER

I have been a faithful servant to the Society [of Jesus] going on
38 years, & my wife Molly has been born & raised in the Society,
she is now about 53 years of age[.] Now we have not a place to lay
our heads in our old age after all our service. We live at present in
[a] rotten logg house so old & decayed that at every blast of wind
we are afraid of our lives and such as it is it belongs to one of the
neighbours—all the rest of the slaves are pretty well fixed and
Father [Peter] Verhaegen wants me and my wife to live on the loft
of one of the outhouses where there is no fire place nor any way to
warm us during the winter, and your Reverence know it is cold
enough here—I have not a doubt but cold will kill both me and my
wife here—To prevent the evil, I am will[ing] to Buy myself & wife
free if you accept of 100 dollars[,] 50 dollars I can pay down in cash,
the rest as soon as I possibly can.
                    —Thomas Brown, enslaved, St. Louis University, 1833

In August 1797, shortly after the end of his final term in office, President
George Washington rode horseback to the Catholic college in Georgetown, a
settlement that the state of Maryland had ceded six years earlier to the federal

district. In 1789 John Carroll had founded the college. Carroll was the nation's first Catholic bishop and a former Jesuit—Pope Clement XIV had suppressed the Society of Jesus in 1773, a proscription that lasted forty-one years. Georgetown president Louis Guillaume Valentin DuBourg and a small faculty of French and Creole Sulpicians (Order of St. Sulpice) and ex-Jesuits from the United States, the West Indies, Ireland, and continental Europe greeted the general. Washington spoke to the faculty and a larger body of students from the porch of Old North, the second academic hall on campus. Enslaved people completed the scene. Slaves belonging to the faculty and officers and slaves owned by or leased from local craftsmen and merchants labored at Georgetown during its first four decades. The Catholic clergy owned several Maryland slave plantations that funded their missions, including the college and St. Mary's Seminary (founded in 1791) in Baltimore. In fact, the college had an account with the local tobacco merchant Brooke Beall—who owned Yarrow Mamout—before it had a single student. The vice president governed the campus servants, and the records offer glimpses into the routineness of that business: In 1793 the merchant Thomas Corcoran received "Cash [for] 1 p[ai]r shoes for Negroe Nat." Two years later the officers paid "Cash for Negro[es] Jos[eph] & Watt for 3 days work." In December 1798 they agreed to board "4 Negro Children @ $20. Each" with Margaret Medley in town.[1]

If George Washington's visit to Georgetown confirmed the incorporation of Catholics into the United States, then the enslaved people on campus captured the economic forces binding the new nation. Georgetown was a product of the American, French, and Haitian Revolutions—exiles of the Atlantic uprisings dominated the college—and it was a beneficiary of the slave economies that excited this age of political transformation. Higher education in the United States rose with the slave trade and evolved with the westward expansion of plantation slavery and the dependent rise of the manufacturing and banking economies of the northeastern cities. Colleges had advanced the commercial development of the American colonies. Europeans had used colleges to supply colonial administrations, impose religious orthodoxy, facilitate trade, and wage cultural warfare against aboriginal nations. Americans founded at least seventeen new colleges—an average of one per year—between the end of the Revolution and the turn of the century to secure their economic and political interests. The commodification of black bodies also underwrote those developments.

Washington had financial links to the town and personal ties to the college. He was a founder of the Potomac Company, a commercial partnership that sought to develop Georgetown—"the gateway to the West"—a Potomac River port situated at the narrowest land passage from the Atlantic seaboard across the Appalachian Range and into the rich territories of the Ohio and Mississippi River Valleys. Bishop Carroll, a slave owner, located his college at the center of this region, on a cliff overlooking an active tobacco port. Father Du-Bourg and the faculty had corresponded with George and Martha Washington, and the professors and students had visited the Washingtons at Mount Vernon. A small group of Protestants studied at the college during its first decade, among them the president's nephews, Bushrod and Augustine Washington.[2]

Of the possible years that Georgetown's governors could have chosen as their founding moment, they eventually selected 1789, a relatively late date but one concurrent with the ratification of the constitution and the inauguration of George Washington. "It gives me Pleasure to hear G[eorge]. Washington is chosen President," the Reverend John Fenwick wrote from the Catholic college in Flanders to his cousin, the prominent tobacco merchant Captain Ignatius Fenwick of Carrollsburg, Maryland, for "he deserves that Post to be sure if merit has any Weight."[3]

The crisis of the American Revolution had allowed Catholics to escape their status as a persecuted and despised minority, and Washington was the symbolic guarantor of the fragile compacts unifying a diverse nation. Early in his presidency, he sent assurances of religious liberty to Quakers, the Reformed Dutch, Episcopalians, and Presbyterians. He replied to a plea from the nation's Roman Catholics—signed by John Carroll and several lay leaders, including the wealthy planter Charles Carroll of Carrollton, Maryland—with an affirmation of freedom of conscience and faith. (John Carroll and Charles Carroll were maternal cousins through the Darnall family.) A few months later, the president promised the Jews of Newport, Rhode Island, a government that "gives to bigotry no sanction, to persecution no assistance." His response to John Carroll acknowledged the sacrifices of Catholics, domestic and foreign, during the Revolution.[4] The inclusion of Catholics in the citizenry rewarded their wartime contributions, but commerce opened this era of interdenominational concord and undergirded this political confederation.

*   *   *

In late 1633, three English Jesuits—Fathers Andrew White and John Gravener and Brother Thomas Gervase—set sail for Maryland aboard the *Ark* and the

Dove. The ships landed first in Barbados, which had a population of English and Irish Catholics. The captains piloted the vessels through the Caribbean before venturing up the mainland coast to Virginia. On Lady Day 1634 the Jesuits officiated the first Catholic mass in Maryland, and then turned their efforts to evangelizing Native Americans. Four other Jesuits arrived that decade. Reverend White opened an Indian academy near the Anacostia River. Father Roger Rigbie ministered to the Piscataway and translated the catechism into their language. By 1640 the Jesuits had plans for a college at the St. Mary's settlement to facilitate missionizing the Lenape, Anacostia, Nanticoke, Susquehannock, and other indigenous peoples.[5] At that time there was only one Protestant college in the Americas, Harvard (founded 1636), and it was constitutionally anti-Catholic.

Although Maryland was the most heavily Catholic of the English mainland colonies and the only Catholic proprietorship, Catholics were less than a tenth of the population. In 1649 the General Assembly and Cecil Calvert, Lord Baltimore, instituted religious tolerance in the colony, a modest protection that survived only a few decades. Following the outbreak of England's Civil War in 1642, Protestants arrested Fathers White and Copley and deported them in chains. They hunted the Reverends Roger Rigbie, Bernard Hartwell, and John Cooper and carried them to Virginia. Anti-Catholics gained strength after the Glorious Revolution of 1688—the overthrow of the Catholic James II, formerly the Duke of York, and the restoration of the Protestant monarchy—forcing the revocation of Baltimore's proprietorship. In 1692 the General Assembly established the Church of England. In 1704 it restricted the exercise of Catholic sacraments, prohibited Catholics from operating schools, limited the corporate ownership of property to hamper religious orders, and encouraged the conversion of Catholic children.[6]

Established churches in the English colonies were vigilant against Catholic infiltration, and colleges helped address these religious and political threats. During the English Civil War, Massachusetts banished Catholic clergy and assigned the death penalty for repeat trespassers. New England's proximity to New France fueled tensions. The colonists had a half dozen wars with New France, beginning with King William's War, the American theater of the Nine Years' War (1688–1697), and ending with the French and Indian War, the colonial arm of the Seven Years' War (1756–1763). Virginia established Anglicanism and forbade Catholics from voting, bearing arms, serving on juries, and testifying in court. In 1693, during King William's War, planters and ministers in Virginia organized the College of William and Mary under Anglican governance. Anti-Catholic literature filled the libraries at Harvard, William and Mary, and Yale (founded in 1701 by Connecticut's Congregationalists).[7]

The Glorious Revolution also swept New York, bringing the removal of Governor Thomas Dongan, a Catholic appointed by King James. As early as 1685 Governor Dongan had encouraged English Jesuits to establish a Latin school in New York City with hopes of raising a college. Many Protestants feared the Jesuit incursion. Jacob Leisler's 1698 rebellion sought to erase the vestiges of Catholic rule. After November 1, 1700, authorities could imprison for life any Catholic priest found in the colony, execute priests who were recaptured, and drag any persons who aided a Catholic cleric to the pillory.[8]

The colonial government's bloody response to the April 1712 slave revolt in Manhattan—during Queen Anne's War, the colonial arm of the War of the Spanish Succession (1702–1713)—fed in part on anti-Catholic rage. Following the revolt, the New York legislature assigned the death penalty for any slave who attempted or conspired to harm or kill any free Christian, and in 1730 it expressly broadened the law to punish slaves who assaulted "any Christian or Jew." By that time, Jewish merchants such as Rodrigo Pacheco, Jacob Franks, Moses and Samuel Levy, Nathan Simpson, Isaac Levy, and Mordecai and David Gomez were trading enslaved people and goods between the Dutch and British Caribbean, the North American mainland colonies, Africa, and Europe. They often partnered with leading Christian merchants, including Adolph Philipse, Robert Livingston, William Walton, Anthony Rutgers, Arnot Schuyler, Jacob Van Cortlandt, David and Matthew Clarkson, and Henry Cuyler.[9]

The 1741 slave conspiracy revealed how commerce was reshaping social relations. In April, as the investigations began, several Jewish merchants distanced themselves from the threats, domestic and foreign, by swearing loyalty to George II and acknowledging his absolute political and spiritual authority over the colonies. They then condemned as "impious & heretical" the "damnable Doctrine & position" of the Catholic Church that monarchs could be excommunicated, deposed, and "murthered by their Subjects." The authorities hanged John Ury, a suspected Catholic priest, and three other white people, and tortured, exiled, or executed scores of black people. Mordecai Gomez served as interpreter in the trial of several "Spanish Negroes," black captives from the Spanish colonies who claimed to be free men. The justices ordered death for a "Spanish Indian," a Native American prisoner from a nation allied to Spain.[10]

It was the violent expansion and integration of the Atlantic slave economies that created the financial and social conditions for the growth of higher education in the British colonies. In less than a quarter century, slave traders and other merchants in New England and the upper Mid-Atlantic and planters in the lower Mid-Atlantic, the South, and the West Indies funded six new colleges. In 1745 Anglicans in Barbados organized Codrington College, the only seminary in the British Caribbean. The following year, Presbyterians chartered the College of New Jersey (now Princeton University). About 1749, Anglicans, Presbyterians, and Quakers began the College of Philadelphia (the University of Pennsylvania). In 1754 the governing Anglican minority in New York City established King's College (Columbia University). A decade later, in 1764, Baptists founded the College of Rhode Island (Brown University). In 1766 the Dutch Reformed leadership in New Jersey opened Queen's College (Rutgers University). In 1769 New Hampshire granted a charter to the Congregationalist minister Eleazar Wheelock for Dartmouth College.[11]

Jewish families had used tutors and small private academies to educate their children, but they gained some access to the new colleges. Donations from the slave traders Jacob Rodriguez de Rivera and Aaron Lopez of Newport, Rhode Island, and the planter and merchant Moses Lindo of Charleston, South Carolina, led the trustees of the College of Rhode Island to admit Jewish students. The colleges in New York City and Philadelphia also opened admissions.[12]

Catholics had no colleges in the British colonies. Ordered priests ran small academies and sent privileged youth abroad to complete their education. A number of colleges in continental Europe specialized in training English and colonial Catholics. The cousins John and Charles Carroll studied at the somewhat clandestine preparatory school at the Jesuits' Bohemia Manor plantation in Maryland. Eleanor and Daniel Carroll then sent John to the Jesuit College of St. Omer in northern France. Elizabeth and Charles Carroll of Doughoregan, Maryland, enrolled "Charley" at the College of Rheims. Robert Plunkett and Robert Molyneux—later the first two presidents of Georgetown College—journeyed from England to the seminaries at Watten and Douai, respectively. The young Louis Guillaume Valentin DuBourg—Georgetown's third president—left Cap François, Saint-Domingue (now Cap-Haïtien, Haiti), to attend St. Omer. Another future president of the college, Stephen Larigaudelle Dubuisson, sailed as a boy from Saint-Marc, Saint-Domingue, to study in France. "I shall never be able to repay the care & pains you [have] taken of my education," Charley Carroll wrote to his "Dear Papa" while studying law at the Inner Temple in London.[13]

African slavery afforded these Catholics significant personal freedom. Charley Carroll served as his father's business liaison while studying in Europe. "I shall keep my Estate in and nigh Annapolis, two large seats of Land containing each about 13[,]000 Acres, my Slaves and [the Baltimore] Iron Works to ye last, so that you may chuse," Carroll of Doughoregan promised his son. The family estate neighbored those of a number of wealthy plantation and merchant families, including the final generation of Quaker slave owners, such as the elder Johns Hopkins.[14]

African slavery enabled colonial Catholics to survive, and even prosper, in the British Atlantic. "I shall always have a great Regard for any of our Countrymen; so that if you know of any Gentlemen, who chuse to send their children to the College, I shall be glad to have them here at Bornhem," the Reverend John Fenwick appealed from the Dominican (Order of Preachers) college in Flanders. Individual priests, including Father Henry Pelham, and lay leaders held the Jesuits' Maryland farms as personal property and bequeathed this real estate to other clerics and lay people to evade the legal restrictions on religious corporations. The Jesuits were also among the first slave owners in the colony, and they used similar legal maneuvers to secure their titles to hundreds of enslaved people.[15]

By the eighteenth century, the order owned plantations that reached from the northeast border with Pennsylvania and Delaware to the southwest boundary with Virginia. In 1637 the Calverts gave the Jesuits the St. Inigoes (Ignatius) plantation, which comprised 2,000 mainland acres and a thousand acres on St. George's Island in the St. Mary's River. In the summer of 1640 William Britton acquired the Newtown plantation. In February 1670 Father Pelham received 4,000 acres, along the Potomac near Port Tobacco, where the Jesuits built St. Thomas Manor. By the eighteenth century the Jesuit estates comprised more than 14,000 acres in Maryland—including St. Inigoes and Newtown in St. Mary's County, St. Thomas in Charles County, White Marsh in Prince George's County, and Bohemia in Cecil County—approximately 2,000 acres in Pennsylvania, and small parcels in other colonies.[16]

Visitors routinely documented the Catholic clergy's reliance on slavery. "Ten thousand acres of the best ground in Maryland forms at this hour, part of the property of the Jesuits," protested Patrick Smyth, an Irish priest who spent several months in Maryland and then published a treatise that accused the clergy of abusing enslaved people to support profligacy. He had ample evidence. Granny Sucky, a ninety-six-year-old enslaved woman, recalled that

Father John Bolton of St. Inigoes beat her when she was a child, in the mid-eighteenth century, for interrupting his self-flagellation. Violence was not the only form of abuse. Child mortality was high at St. Inigoes and the other Jesuit plantations. During the twenty-five year period ending in 1780, when Jesuit superior George Hunter resided at St. Thomas Manor, only twenty-six of the forty-eight black children born on the plantation survived to maturity. The Jesuits "have a prodigious number of negroes, and these sooty rogues will not work, unless they be goaded, and whipped, and almost slayed alive," Smyth charged.[17]

Lay Catholics were no less dependent on bondage. Carroll of Doughoregan taught his son the businesses of plantation management and manufacturing, which involved lessons in the application of violence. The Carrolls used enslaved black laborers on their estates and at the ironworks, for which they also purchased European indentured servants. On his return to America, the younger Carroll took ownership of a share of the lands and more than 300 human beings. "Two of them have been well whipped," he assured his father after hiring a new overseer, "& Will shall have a severe whipping tomorrow—they are now quite quelled."[18]

*   *   *

At the outbreak of the American Revolution, Charles Carroll could not vote, hold public office, or serve in the militia. His coreligionists from Georgia to New Hampshire also faced restrictions on their civil liberties. When he journeyed to the Continental Congress, he came not as a member but as a mere adviser to the Maryland delegation. Carroll was a strident defender of political freedom who had described the tendencies of tyranny in the pages of the same colonial paper that had carried advertisements for the family's runaway slaves. In July 1776, Carroll of Carrollton became the only Catholic signer of the Declaration of Independence. That August, Marylanders affirmed the right to the free exercise of religion for professing Christians. Another fifty years passed before the legislature approved a constitutional amendment to enfranchise Jews.[19]

The American Revolution required a radical transformation in the status of Catholics. Although Protestants in Ireland displayed broad sympathy and support for the American rebellion, David Doyle concludes, they ultimately rejected models of independence that required "sharing political power with Catholics." In contrast, "Long Live the King of France" ranks among the more noteworthy chants of a colonial army that had acquired its military experience in wars against the Catholic empires. The United States accepted a peculiar dependence on the Catholic powers of the Atlantic world. Benjamin Franklin sailed for Paris to lobby the court of Louis XVI. Congress sent James Jay of New York and Arthur Lee of Virginia to plead its cause before the Spanish crown. In September 1777 it authorized Ralph Izard of South Carolina to appeal for funds and support in Italy, where there was significant interest in the American conflict.[20]

For a war between the Protestant king of Great Britain and his Protestant colonists, the American Revolution was a decidedly Catholic affair. Several French Catholic general officers advised George Washington and the new United States government, devised military strategies, and even commanded colonial troops, including: Jean-Baptiste Donatien-Joseph de Vimeur, Comte de Rochambeau; the young Marie Joseph Paul Yves Roch Gilbert du Motier, Marquis de Lafayette; François Jean de Beauvoir, Marquis de Chastellux; and Claude-Gabriel, Duc de Choisy. Casimir Pulaski, a Polish Catholic, raised the cavalry for the colonial army, and Thaddeus Kosciuszko, also a Polish Catholic, served as the American army's chief engineer.[21]

The Americans embraced their Catholic allies. Yale granted an honorary degree to Conrad Alexander Gerard, French minister to the United States, and the College of William and Mary paid the same tribute to Chastellux. The Reverend John Carroll preached patriotism, and three of his nephews fought under Lafayette. Washington made camp at White Marsh, where General Thomas Conway, headquartered at the Jesuits' manor, sought Charles Carroll's advice on organizing Irish troops. The Catholic clergy set up a military hospital at Newtown. The United States commissioned a Catholic chaplain, and Abbé Claude Robin, a priest under Rochambeau's command, boasted of the enthusiastic crowds and extravagant official reception that greeted French forces in Philadelphia in early September 1781. The celebrants became even more raucous when they learned that French troops had also arrived in the Chesapeake.[22]

The French and Spanish crowns had given covert support to the American rebellion from its earliest stages. The colonists negotiated with Spain through the embassy in Paris, and Lafayette returned to France to appeal for direct military intervention in the American war. Spain attacked Britain's interests in South America, and smuggled supplies to the colonists across the Alleghenies. In 1778, France officially recognized the United States, and the following year Spain declared war on Great Britain. In the summer of 1780, forty-six French vessels carrying more than 12,000 soldiers and sailors landed in New England. Jacques-Melchior Saint-Laurent, Comte de Barras, brought his fleet south from Rhode Island, and François Joseph Paul, Marquis de Grasse, sailed north from Saint-Domingue and Martinique to force the British general Charles Cornwallis's surrender at Yorktown. The Spanish naval officer Francisco de Saaverda de Sangronis served under the Marquis de Grasse, raised money in Cuba and Santo Domingo for the offensive, and helped design the campaign. General Washington and three French officers—Rochambeau, Barras, and Grasse—signed the October 19, 1781, capitulation on behalf of the victorious United States.[23]

In 1783, as the British evacuation continued, John Carroll called the clergy to White Marsh to draft a governing structure for the church. The Corporation of Roman Catholic Clergy—which the Maryland General Assembly incorporated in 1792—also administered its financial affairs and took ownership of its estates. Carroll's vision took shape as the slave economies recovered, and it focused on a region of the new nation with a long history of commercial and social interaction between Protestants and Catholics. The English invasion had disrupted slavery, and enemy troops had ransacked Newtown Manor. The British navy had blockaded and occupied the Chesapeake Bay and the lower Potomac, empowering thousands of black people to escape the plantations in St. Mary's County and Port Tobacco. In December 1784 Father James Walton ordered the slaves at St. Inigoes to begin raising a new church. The following year, Father Carroll laid the cornerstone. Francis Neale, a future president of Georgetown College, presided at the dedication.[24]

*   *   *

The American victory and the subsequent unraveling of the French empire set the conditions for the institutionalization of the Catholic Church in the United States. In April 1789, George Washington was inaugurated in New York City. That same month riots broke out in Paris, and within weeks, France was in the throes of revolution. After mobs stormed the Bastille on July 14, 1789, the Marquis de Lafayette sent the key to the breached prison as a souvenir to his friend and ally, George Washington. That year Pope Pius VI established a United States diocese that became a refuge for French clerics. Urged by Benjamin Franklin, the Vatican also elevated John Carroll to bishop.[25]

The ripples of the French Revolution quickly reached the United States. The tobacco merchant Joseph Fenwick had left for France after the American

Revolution, a moment of great economic optimism. He soon encountered an Irish smuggler and Thomas Jefferson, and he received excellent advice from both. The smuggler convinced Fenwick to situate his business in Bordeaux, and Jefferson promised that French markets would be eager for American goods. After he became secretary of state, Jefferson appointed Fenwick consul in Paris. Fenwick's letters to his cousin and sponsor, Ignatius Fenwick of Carrollsburg, detailed the course of events. During the first year of the Revolution, the National Assembly abolished aristocratic titles and curtailed the authority of the church. The Sulpician John Dubois escaped from Paris in disguise. In August 1791 Dubois landed in Virginia with letters of introduction from Lafayette. The Lees, Randolphs, Monroes, and Beverlys assisted the young priest, and Patrick Henry tutored him in English. By that time, enslaved people on the island of Saint-Domingue, France's most valuable colony, were in full rebellion, after months of isolated uprisings. White families fled the island. Hundreds of French and Creole families relocated to Maryland, with assistance from the state, to wait out their respective revolutions.[26]

The Atlantic revolutions allowed Bishop Carroll to create a network of colleges and seminaries that threaded Catholicism into the social fabric of the United States. After opening Georgetown in 1789, the bishop turned his attention to helping the Sulpicians establish a seminary. The antichurch and anticlerical thrusts in France threatened the order's Parisian academy, and the Sulpicians began fundraising and recruiting European students for a Maryland seminary. In 1791, as the first class was entering Georgetown, the French priests opened St. Mary's. "All our hopes are founded on the seminary of Baltimore," Carroll confessed. In 1792 Bishop Carroll dispatched a group of Dominicans, who had come to Maryland as refugees, to the rapidly growing territory of Kentucky. Catholics were not the only Americans to recognize the opportunities in Europe's instability. In 1795 George Washington and Thomas Jefferson briefly plotted to resettle the whole faculty of the College of Geneva, thrown into turmoil by the European revolutions, in the United States.[27]

Georgetown was the child of the Atlantic rebellions. Émigrés of the revolutions in France and Saint-Domingue filled the faculty and the student body. The first class included François and Antoine Cassé, and students from France, Madeira, Martinique, St. Lucia, Guadeloupe, Cuba, St. John, and Saint-Domingue and Santo Domingo arrived in the following years. By 1798 the governors were publishing the college prospectus in English, French, and Spanish. Among the earliest presidents were Fathers Louis DuBourg and Stephen Dubuisson, born to slaveholding Creole families in Cap François and

Saint-Marc, respectively—key sites of the slave unrest that matured into the
Haitian Revolution. Reverend DuBourg traveled to Havana, Cuba, to open
a college, and, when that effort failed, he recruited the children of the planters to St. Mary's Seminary and St. Mary's College (chartered in 1805), which
the Sulpicians began under the presidency of John Dubois.[28]

"To American Commerce—May it ever derive greater pride from the dis-
tress it has relieved, than from the wealth it has accumulated," the guests
toasted during a feast on the evening of January 9, 1809. "The concourse of
French and American ladies and gentlemen was numerous and brilliant," the
Maryland Gazette boasted. Creoles from Aux Cayes came to honor the West
Indies trader Duncan M'Intosh and other merchants and captains who had
risked their vessels and money running rescue missions to Saint-Domingue.
Father DuBourg presented M'Intosh with an award for his humanitarianism.
M'Intosh was credited with saving more than 2,000 people. In an address to
the Free School Society that same year, New York City mayor DeWitt Clinton praised "the Refugees from the [French] West Indies" who had established
one of the city's early charity schools, an academy that was "patronized and
cherished by French and American gentlemen, of great worth and respectability."[29]

Slavery accelerated the absorption of these refugees into the American
church. The Corporation of Roman Catholic Clergy assigned Bohemia to the
Sulpicians, who used the profits from the plantation to fund St. Mary's Seminary. "That the managers of St. Thomas [plantation] be allowed the sum of
£75 for a Negro boy called Alexis in the service of the Bishop," read the
March 1797 minutes. The clergy also voted to sell a parcel of land to raise
$4,000 to complete the construction of Georgetown College. In the late sum-
mer of 1799, the Sulpicians protested that they had made major improvements
to Bohemia farm, and asked to be compensated with "the young negro girl,
called Peg, and the small boy, called Jack, both now in the Service of the
Seminary, and another boy also called Jack, now in the Service of Revd.
Mr. Marechal, at Bohemia." (Ambrose Marechal was the philosophy professor at Georgetown and the seminary.) A few months later the clergy voted to
allow the Sulpicians to keep Jack and Peg, "as long as they retain said negroes
in the Seminary."[30]

The bodies and the labor of enslaved people paid the Catholic Church's
debts, including the liabilities of Georgetown College, which was tuition-free
during its first forty years. In October 1799 the Roman Catholic Clergy approved the sale of "Kate & her two Children now belonging to Bohemia es-

tate." In April 1804 the corporation resolved to satisfy its obligations by selling expendable slaves from their Deer Creek property "to humane and Christian masters." A couple of years later, John Ashton demanded that the clergy give him "ye boy Davy . . . (Simon's son & now motherless)" from White Marsh to meet a debt. "Whereas, permission . . . was heretofore granted for two slaves of the estate of Bohemia to be sold for the benefit of Geo-town College," began a March 1808 inquiry from the trustees. Money and people flowed fluidly between the campuses, the churches, and the plantations. As late as 1820, nearly two dozen Georgetown undergraduates vacationed at the horse farm on Newtown plantation. The corporation typically held its meetings at St. Thomas, Newtown, and White Marsh. Robert Plunkett, Georgetown's founding president, began his ministry at White Marsh, and at least two early presidents had managed Jesuit plantations—Leonard Neale, St. Inigoes; and Francis Neale, St. Thomas—a duty that involved disciplining, acquiring, and disposing of people.[31]

The treatment of enslaved people on the Jesuit farms was alarming. After 1805 the Jesuit brothers began supervising the plantations. "Some years ago Blacks were more easily kept in due subordination and were more patient under the rod of correction than they are now, because then discipline flourished, but now it is going to decay," complained Brother Joseph Mobberly, manager of St. Inigoes. "The present white generation seems to lose sight of the old ob-servation, 'the better a negro is treated, the worse he becomes.'" Mobberly hired five overseers in the four-year period beginning 1816. He also served as the plantation doctor and only hired trained physicians for emergencies.[32]

The declining profitability and deteriorating management of the Mary-land farms created other crises. In 1820 the Irish priest Peter Kenney, official visitor to the Maryland province, documented awful conditions. The super-visors were providing insufficient rations to slaves, overworking servants, and inflicting *excessive* violence on enslaved men and women. Father Kenney es-pecially condemned the practices of whipping pregnant women and beating women "in the priests own parlor, which is very indecorous." The clergy paid little attention to the spiritual lives of the servants, and Kenney suggested that the order begin looking toward a moment when it could "get rid of the slaves, either by employing whites or letting out their lands to *reputable* tenants."[33]

Rather than retreating from slaveholding, the bishops built their church by tracking the westward expansion of plantation slavery. The 1803 Louisiana Purchase had opened a vast and heavily Catholic missionary field. After being named bishop of Louisiana in 1812, Louis DuBourg recruited veteran

Maryland priests—particularly a dozen Belgian Jesuits under Father Charles Van Quickenborne—to establish the Missouri province, manage its plantations, and elevate St. Louis Academy (founded 1818) into a university, the first west of the Mississippi River. Bishop DuBourg gave his Florissant farm and slaves to the Missouri Jesuits, and empowered the future St. Louis University president Van Quickenborne "to sell any or all of them to humane and Christian masters" if they proved recalcitrant or immoral.[34]

"The Indian Mission was the chief object of the establishment of the Society [of Jesus] in Missouri," Father Van Quickenborne admitted in January 1830, just months before Congress passed the Indian Removal Act, which initiated the relocation of the eastern Native American nations west of the Mississippi River. Bishop DuBourg had donated Florrisant on the condition that the Missouri Jesuits begin an Indian mission. The Belgians had also raised more than $3,000 in Europe for Christianizing Native Americans, and they staffed missions to the St. Johns and Kickapoo. "On the loftiest hill of the renowned Charbonniere (I do not recall whether you saw it) there is an Indian mound," Father Peter Verhaegen, another of the Belgian presidents of St. Louis University, wrote to Georgetown president William McSherry in 1838, "& this mound we undertook to explore . . . & found human bones, but no indian curiosities." Even weak religious missions could be used to legitimate expansion. "Our Belgians . . . have arrived safe," Verhaegen told McSherry of a new group of recruits in 1839, and "they wish to be remembered to their brethren at Georgetown."[35]

The enslavement of Africans and the dispossession of Native Americans had been tied together from the early years of European colonization, and assertions of the urgency of evangelizing Indians were routinely followed by declarations of the necessity of human bondage. In 1832, when Father Kenney had inspected the Missouri province, he complimented "the good conduct, industry, & christian piety of all the coloured servants of both sexes." Despite the broad use of enslaved labor, Missouri was the only province in which Kenney registered no serious concerns. However, a year later, Thomas Brown, enslaved to President Verhaegen, strongly disagreed. Brown begged the Jesuit superior for permission to buy his and his wife Molly's freedom. He had served the society for nearly thirty-eight years, and Molly Brown, fifty-three years old, had been born enslaved to the Jesuits. He accused Verhaegen of confining them to an outhouse with neither heat nor insulation as winter approached. "Now we have not a place to lay our heads in our old age after all our service," he continued. Father Kenney's visit had exposed troubling issues.

Kenney had to remind his brethren that it was beneath the dignity of priests to beat or threaten enslaved women. He recommended that they employ lay people to punish women, and assigned the Jesuit brothers the duty of whipping enslaved men, while cautioning that they should all avoid "severe punishments."[36]

*   *   *

In 1832 Georgetown's governors conceded that the college had to impose tuition, a business decision that intensified the Corporation of Roman Catholic Clergy's discussion of dissolving the Maryland slaveholdings. Financial concerns rather than moral considerations brought an end to slavery in the Maryland province. The order had been violating commitments to maintain families and find suitable Christian masters. It was now seeking bids on hundreds of human beings, and apparently even attempted to sell the whole group to the Missouri Jesuits. In June 1838 the former Georgetown president Thomas Mulledy contracted the sale of 272 men, women, and children to Henry Johnson, a Catholic and the former governor of Louisiana, for $115,000. Beginning that fall, the Jesuits shipped their slaves to Louisiana in three cargoes. About 15 percent of the revenues went to pay down Georgetown College's construction debts.[37]

Clergy trained in Maryland spread across the nation. Belgian and French priests governed expansion into the regions opened by the Louisiana Purchase and Indian Removal. John Dubois left St. Mary's to become bishop of New York, and was succeeded in that seat by one of his most famous students, the Irish immigrant, John Hughes, who had paid his tuition at St. Mary's by supervising servants in the college gardens. In 1841 Bishop Hughes founded the college that became Fordham University, the first Catholic college in New York. In 1843 Thomas Mulledy became the charter president of Holy Cross, the first Catholic college in New England. John McElroy, who also departed from Maryland, founded Boston College.[38]

Neither the Jesuits nor the antebellum Catholic Church disengaged from human bondage with the Maryland sale; rather, both followed the westward movement of plantation slavery in search of influence and affluence. African slavery had repeatedly rescued the Catholic community through a century and a half of oppression in the Protestant colonies. Catholics had used the slave economies to evade anti-Catholic laws and survive anti-Catholic violence. They embraced human bondage to secure their own liberty. The proslavery and anti-abolitionist tradition in the Catholic hierarchy began at the birth of the church in the Revolutionary era, when human slavery straightened and leveled the road to Catholic assimilation. The Atlantic slave economies laid the foundations of the Catholic Church in the United States, and underwrote the creation of a national church that helped to integrate future waves of Catholic immigrants.

CHAPTER 12

Capitalism, Slavery, and the New Epoch

Mathew Carey's 1819

ANDREW SHANKMAN

Looking back at the collapse of Napoleon's dream to forge a "universal empire," the Philadelphia printer, political economist, and staunch Jeffersonian Mathew Carey had no doubt that the end of Bonaparte had ushered in "a new epoch."[1] In this new epoch a British-dominated peace would end ready access to foreign markets, produce disastrous quantities of unmarketable agricultural surpluses, and place enormous, possibly unendurable, strains on republican institutions. Beginning during the frightening period of 1814–1815, between Napoleon's first and second exiles, Carey began to pull together his concerns regarding potential national disintegration and the limitations of republican institutions and political economy. Carey's efforts culminated in 1819, the eventful year that produced the divisive conflict over Missouri statehood and the worst economic slump the nation had yet experienced. The twin crises focused Carey's efforts. His response to the troubled half decade after 1814 propelled him into a leading role in articulating the ideas and policies that encouraged capitalist economic and social relations and the most extensive slave-based economy the world had ever seen.

In 1814 Carey concluded that a new direction for American political economy, one that created a much larger and more diverse domestic market, needed the labor of slaves. He also came to believe that a national polity could not be forged unless there was a genuine national embrace of slavery. Carey's thinking between 1814 and 1819–1820 had a tremendous impact on the formative years of nineteenth-century economic development. Carey was a prolific writer and an influential publisher. He did a great deal to conceive the arguments for and to promote the protective tariff, the Second Bank of the United States, and the mania for internal improvements. He was a staunch supporter of Henry Clay's "American System," and Clay believed his efforts were essential.[2] Carey's career allows us to assess the central role slavery played for those theorizing the American System, the political economy that became the core commitment of the Whig Party. Carey reminds us that Whig political economy was embedded in the national embrace of slavery. Despite the genuine commitment of many Whigs to moral reform, in its intellectual formation the political economy of the party most committed to rapid, diverse economic development could not be disentangled from slavery. For in Carey's thinking, a commitment to domestic commerce and manufacturing and the expansion of credit and banking, the world we know to call American capitalism, was inseparable from—indeed, could not be imagined or developed without—a dynamic and expanding American slavery.[3]

Slavery and National Harmony

For Mathew Carey, the War of 1812 was a terrifying experience. He believed that the nation should have been able to fund the war more efficiently and produce what it needed more effectively, and should never have descended into the shameful, internal conflict that made New England secession seem a real possibility in 1814. As the war drew to a close, and it became clear the United States would survive it, Carey sought to turn crisis into opportunity. In 1814 and 1815 Carey published the first two editions of *The Olive Branch*, his effort to unify the nation. Carey argued that national harmony could come from policies that allowed an active national government to promote a diverse domestic economy of agriculture, commerce, and manufacturing.[4] Yet Carey estimated that in New England, two-thirds opposed President Madison's government, and a sizable minority followed dangerous extremists. Some of the fault lay with New England Federalists, who "For eighteen years" had made "the most unceasing endeavors . . . to poison the minds of the people of New England towards, and to alienate them from, their fellow citizens of the southern states."[5]

Extreme Federalists, said Carey, had portrayed southerners "as demons incarnate, and destitute of all the good qualities that dignify and adorn human nature."[6] They grossly caricatured slavery and pretended to a concern unwarranted by southern practice. Federalists claimed that "the negroes are, in all respects, except to regard to life and death, the cattle of the citizens of the southern states." Further slander accused southerners of treating slaves "like brutes," and allowing them to be "bought and sold . . . beaten, turned out to the fury of the elements, and torn from their dearest connections, with as little remorse as if they were beasts of the field." Carey did not so much refute (for how could he?) as dismiss these charges as "infamous [and] unfounded caricature." Rather than argue that slaves were not bought and sold, forcibly separated from their loved ones, and regularly beaten, Carey instead insisted that such practices should not cause New Englanders to believe they were distinct from the South. Slavery was in fact a source of connection and unity for the nation. After all, Carey argued, most slaves "had been purchased, and sent from their homes and families by New Englanders, who were actually . . . engaged in the slave trade."[7] Indeed, New England had "literally lived upon the industry of the southern states."[8]

Carey made the case for interregional interdependence built on slavery even more explicitly in an 1814 pamphlet meant to supplement *The Olive Branch*. In *A Calm Address To The Eastern States*, Carey insisted that the economic needs of New England fit seamlessly with those of the rest of the nation, particularly the slave states.[9] If the people of New England ignored their own best interests and seceded, they alone would suffer. Southern states such as the Carolinas and Georgia enjoyed "delightful and luxuriant climate and fertile soil." If necessary, these states could diversify and develop manufacturing, but not without effort and not without expending resources on projects and practices best suited for New England. New Englanders needed to realize that southerners were in no way hostile to commerce, and that their increasing and expanding slave populations and staple crops depended on extensive manufacturing that every precept of political economy showed belonged in New England.

The relationship between New England and the South was the basis for a vital republic. "The eastern states," Carey explained, "have established manufactures on a large and extensive scale." In addition, manufacturing would only increase over time for the "extreme sterility of a large portion of the soil, and the comparative density of their population, render manufacturing establishments indispensably necessary to them." Yet at present, "the manufactures of the southern states [were] principally in private families." And so they would and should remain, Carey insisted, as long as the union endured and all regions realized how southern slavery gave each region the opportunity to specialize. Insofar as southerners free and slave would continue to "find full employment in agriculture," slave states had "little or no interest in the promotion of manufactures." A decline in commerce, manufacturing, or agriculture hurt each sector of the economy and section of the nation. Union met the needs of all, concluded Carey, and slavery, by benefiting all regions, was a truly national institution.[10]

A New Political Economy for a New Epoch

Arguing for slavery's national importance was part of Carey's effort to protect the Republic from the dangers of the new epoch. New conditions required new directions for the United States, most critically a shift in emphasis from overseas markets and oceanic commerce to production for a growing domestic market. Carey's efforts between the War of 1812 and the Panic of 1819 and the Missouri crisis were informed by a conviction he shared with many leading Jeffersonian Republicans, among them James Madison and Henry Clay, that peace in 1815 had transformed global circumstances and the place the United States occupied in the world. In this new epoch there would be a steady decline in the demand for American agriculture, for

> Europe could not be expected to allow us to continue the commerce that naturally belonged to them . . . when a cessation of the destruction caused by war and the return of so many of the soldiery to the labors of the field not only increased the capacity of supply but diminished the consumption of Europe.

Indeed, concluded Carey, "we enjoyed for twenty years a very great proportion of the trade of the world, far beyond our due share." With the abrupt end of this accidental condition, "sound policy" alone could find "other employment for our superfluous commercial capital," "a domestic market for our cotton," and the same for "our woolens and various other manufactures to an extent commensurate to our wants." Americans had "to secure themselves a grand domestic market, independent of the caprice of foreign nations."[11]

Those who cared about agriculture had to promote manufacturing, banks, internal improvements, an expanding, sound, and stable paper currency, and this grand domestic market. Those who thought farmers were best served by free trade and revenue tariffs below protective levels, tariffs that hindered the encouragement of domestic manufactures, were tricked by

> the narrow illiberal, and selfish maxim "to buy where goods could be had cheapest," . . . [which] has produced a system whereby the wealth of the nation was converted into a means of fostering and encouraging the industry of a distant hemisphere, and supporting foreign governments, while our own citizens were . . . reduced to mendicity, and our country impoverished.[12]

With the war's end, Carey explained, Americans indulged in foreign manufactures and failed to support domestic manufacturing and a home market. As the unfavorable balance of trade drained specie away, banks sprang up nevertheless, fueled by demands of rising consumption. Yet, since specie grew scarce, the banks issued dubious paper, and "the inordinate spirit of banking, carried in many cases to a most culpable excess, has done great mischief."

But banks were not inherently pernicious. Rather, the "great paramount evil is the immoderate extent of our importations." Failure to foster a home market by promoting manufacturing meant "the loss of our industry, the drain of our specie, and the consequent impoverishment of our country [which] affect[ed] all classes of citizens: the economical and the extravagant—the laborer, the artisan, the cultivator of the soil, as well as the landholder, the manufacturer, the trader and the merchant." Under these conditions "debts [could not] in general be collected . . . property [could not] be sold but at enormous sacrifices . . . [and] capitalists ha[d] thus an opportunity of aggrandizing themselves at the expense of the middle class of society to an incalculable extent." As a result, "citizens possessed of great wealth . . . increase it immoderately by purchasing the property of the distressed, sold at ruinous sacrifices by sheriffs, marshals, and otherwise—thus destroying the equality of our citizens, and aggrandizing the rich at the expense of the middle class of society." The "radical remedy for those evils" was "to limit the importation of such articles as we can manufacture ourselves and thus foster our domestic industry."[13]

Carey was deeply sensitive to traditional Jeffersonian Republican concerns about industrial development and the dependency of laborers. He readily acknowledged that the "overgrown manufacturing establishments in England" merited unreserved censure. But British economic and social conditions had nothing to do with republican America. In the United States, liberty, land, and the absence of the "aristocratic provisions of the English Constitution,

and operation of the vast funding system . . . [that] disturb[ed] the equable
and regular diffusion of labor" allowed a republican version of economic
development that would strengthen the nation and preserve the independence and autonomy of its citizens.[14]

Republican citizens understood that "the true art of government, and the
duty of governors, was to produce the greatest happiness of the greatest number of the governed." Republican institutions and geographic and demographic
conditions would prevent "overgrown manufacturing establishments." In republican America,

> The facility of acquiring landed property . . . has been uniformly so
> great, and the inducement to take an independent grade in society is
> so powerful . . . that the laborers and hired people of all descrip-
> tions, (having universally had such liberal wages, that by economy
> they might in a few years save enough to buy farms) have been
> at all times, with hardly an exception, scarce and in demand.
> Employers, therefore, have held their hired people in a very
> precarious tenure. The latter knew their own value, and would not
> submit to harsh treatment. The former, aware of the consequences
> of oppression or ill usage, found the necessity of courteous behavior.
> The steady operation of both the causes . . . has produced the
> delightful state of society, as regards the wealthy and those in
> humble life, in which the one would not dare to oppress, and the
> other would not submit to oppression.[15]

Just as manufacturing in a republic produced welcome outcomes, so too
would banks. Carey knew that many Jeffersonian Republicans were suspicious
of banks and, despite his objections, had dissolved the first Bank of the United
States in 1811.[16] Yet Americans needed to realize that banks in a republic would
not function as they did in Europe. There were republican maxims for republican banks. Chief among them, Carey wrote in 1817, was that banks existed first
to promote the public interest and only second "to hold out adequate advantages
to subscribers." In a republic, banks should not solely seek profit and so "pursue
it to the disregard of public accommodation." Republican banks were invaluable, for they "foster industry—extend trade and commerce—and enable men
of moderate fortune and good credit to compete with wealthy capitalists."[17]

Committed as he was to the expansion of republican banking, Carey
rejoiced at the rechartering of the Bank of the United States in 1816. He

reasoned that Americans would pay taxes and purchase public lands with local paper, which would flow to the Bank of the United States. Through judicious demands for specie repayment, it could force local banks to issue notes responsibly, and so keep paper sound and reliable. As manufacturing output increased and specie drain diminished, more specie would allow an increase in the supply of sound, reliable paper, an expansion of credit, and greater access to the domestic market for a greater number of "men of moderate fortune." Finally, this political economy would be guided by public figures devoted to the republican principles of the public good and the social conditions of equality and autonomy that made republican citizenship possible. Should they ever waver, their very accountability would correct for their lack of virtue. The new political economy, then, would sustain Jefferson's empire of liberty and a nation of farmers and planters precisely because it also nurtured merchants, bankers, manufacturers, craftsmen, and mechanics.

The Problem with Slaveholders in a Period of Transition

Yet this glorious national prospect was impossible to conceive without slavery. Carey could imagine the shift from the foreign to domestic market because he expected slavery to grow in size and importance. Properly understanding slavery seemed to solve all of the political problems that came from mistakenly thinking the sections had divergent interests. And even more obviously, slavery was a significant part of the solution to the problem of agricultural overproduction, the decline of foreign markets, and the ensuing vulnerability of republican households. Carey had no doubt that the political and economic problems produced by the post-1815 world would be resolved if the nation pursued proper economic policies. But doing so depended on "the transportation of raw materials from the southern to the middle and eastern states and of manufactured articles from the latter to the former."[18]

In light of how attractive he believed his political economy would be to people in New England, Carey must have thought in the first few years after the war that sectional harmony, union, and national unity would be relatively easy to achieve. His political economy had so much to offer New England, the one fearful region of secession; the rest of the union, led by southern statesmen, was properly republican and already devoted to preserving the conditions of liberty. And yet by the eventful year of 1819, Carey had begun to understand that slaveholders were the real source of hostility to his political economy, despite the central place of slavery in his economic thinking.

From the start, Carey's plans for the nation required a much more vigorous national government than most Republicans had ever been comfortable supporting. Here we may take as an example the rechartering of the Bank of the United States. Leading Republican statesmen such as President Madison tried to avoid the delicate issue of implied powers by arguing that the sovereign people had made the bank constitutional through their long acceptance of it. Yet this method of defending the bank could not protect federally sponsored internal improvements, since there was no corresponding record of long, popular endorsement. In one of his last public acts, in March 1817 Madison vetoed a federal internal improvements bill and urged a constitutional amendment to allow the nation to pursue policies that he, like Carey, had come to view as essential for the Republic's survival.[19]

Yet achieving a constitutional amendment was exceedingly difficult. Carey (and like-minded Republicans such as Henry Clay) understood that they could achieve their goals much more easily if the national government was bound by a constitutional order in which its powers were broad, expansive, and sometimes implied. Yet Carey's ally Clay also articulated as clearly as any statesman ever had the fear that this view of the Constitution and national governance could provoke: "that the chain of cause and effect is without end, that if we argue from a power expressly granted to all others, which might be convenient or necessary to its execution, there are no bounds to the power of this government."[20]

Clay expressed the concerns of many Republicans, and between 1815 and 1820 many whom Carey expected to be trusted allies reacted in fear and anger to the seeming rise of an "aggressive nationalism."[21] By no means were fears of national power and a rising insistence on states' rights confined to the South or to slaveholders. Between 1816 and 1820, rechartering the bank, the series of Marshall court decisions, and passage of the nation's first protective tariffs provoked fears in all regions. In the uncertain and rapidly changing years after the war, it took time for people to think through and decide what they believed and where they stood. Between 1816 and 1820 Carey had no stronger ally than John C. Calhoun. At the same time, the future staunch National Republican, the Ohioan Charles Hammond, denounced the majority decision in *McCulloch v. Maryland* and, prior to the early 1820s, Hezekiah Niles made his *Weekly Register* one of the severest critics of the new Bank of the United States.[22]

Yet between 1816 and 1820 Carey began to realize that southerners, especially slaveholders, seemed to have the gravest fears about the course of policy he advocated. Ideas such as Carey's were spreading fear and suspicion, and indeed were contributing to a process that was causing the South to begin to think like a region.[23] Ironically, in light of how devoted he was to the American System, which brought together the Second Bank of the United States, protective tariffs, internal improvements, and a defense of implied powers, no figure in the early Republic explained more clearly than Henry Clay slaveholders' particular fear of the policies Carey championed. Unlike Carey, in 1811 Clay had supported dissolution of the first Bank of the United States. When explaining why, Clay demonstrated why Carey would come to see that slaveholders, not New Englanders, were the people he would have to work the hardest to persuade.

In 1811 Clay argued that the creation of any corporation by the national government could not be separated from the doctrine of implied powers because "The power to charter companies [was] not specified in this grant." Clay insisted that the Constitution showed "How extremely cautious the convention was to leave as little as possible to implication."[24] The problem was not simply the bank but also the claim of the power to incorporate, "one of the most exalted attributes of sovereignty," that the bank represented. Cogently and relentlessly, Clay explained where that claim led. A corporation was "a splendid association of favored individuals taken from the mass of society, and invested with exemptions and surrounded by immunities and privileges." If the awesome power to create a corporation existed in the national government, which acted from a great distance on states and localities, then the power to grant corporate charters would extend directly from the distant national government to privileged entities within the states, entities that were free to bargain and make contracts. Corporations' rights to freely contract could bypass and be insulated from the municipal powers of regulation, enforcement, and local policing possessed by the localities and states in which they acted.

Once the national government established a corporate body enjoying many of the rights of citizens, a corporate body that potentially existed beyond the regulation of the locality in which it conducted its affairs, that corporation might undermine purely local and state laws and institutions that were not explicitly sanctioned by the Constitution or federal statute. Therefore, Clay insisted "that the states have the exclusive power to regulate contracts, to declare the capacities and incapacities to contract, and to provide as to the extent of responsibility of debtors and creditors." In case any missed the subtlety of his logic or the nature of his fears, Clay made his point explicit. If the national government could charter a corporation, "If Congress have the power to erect an artificial body and say it shall be endowed with the attributes of an individual—if you can bestow on this object of your own creation the ability to contract, may you not, in contravention of states' rights, confer upon slaves, infants, and femmes covert the ability to contract?"[25] Clay's remarks showed how quickly the effort by the national government to charter a corporation led to questions of constitutional governance, questions that could not be separated from issues of local authority, a matter that was virtually impossible to disentangle from the regulation of slavery. As long as slaveholders insisted that they alone could make decisions about an enormous group of people residing within the United States, policies that depended on more open-ended and expansive views of the power of the national government sooner or later would become arguments about slave law and the regulation of slavery.[26]

Clay was far less anxious and extreme than most slaveholders on these matters. Connections that he could make so easily were made even more stridently by others. Some opposed the Second Bank of the United States as a matter of banking policy. But increasingly after 1816, as writers like Carey popularized an all-encompassing and interconnected approach to the nation's political economy, an approach that depended in part on the growth of federal power, the connections Clay probably regretted having made so forcefully and so well became the basis for opposing the policies that he and Carey championed.[27] Between 1815 and 1820 many southerners began to make connections as easily as North Carolina congressman Nathanial Macon did in 1818 when he exclaimed, "examine the Constitution of the U.S. . . . and then tell me if Congress can establish banks, make roads and canals, whether they cannot free all the slaves in the U.S." For Macon, it was pointless to deny that "If Congress can make canals, they can with more propriety emancipate."[28] By 1819 such connections were becoming the basis for an emerging regional political philosophy.

Panic and Crisis

For Carey, the Panic of 1819 underscored that the Republic needed a high protective tariff, a systematic national policy of internal improvements, and the Second Bank of the United States. Carey argued that the conditions of 1819 resulted from overproduction in agriculture and a weak paper currency vulnerable to depreciation, conditions caused by an insufficiently protective tariff, the paucity of domestic manufacturing, and a home market too small to meet the nation's needs.[29] The destruction of the panic frustrated Carey, who did not doubt that "sound policy would have averted three-fourths of our sufferings."[30] Yet as he looked back on the previous five years, Carey could not ignore that the efforts to prevent protection, to cripple the Bank of the United States, and to thwart nationally sponsored internal improvements came predominantly from southern states and were led by slaveholding statesmen. Carey's ideas for how to sustain the Republic required a home market that relied on the labor of slaves and that promoted manufactures purchased in substantial quantities by slave owners. Yet slave owners led the efforts that caused destructive conditions for so many of their fellow citizens, and they did so, Carey believed, in contravention of their own interests.

In the midst of his efforts to convince the nation that the Panic of 1819 proved the necessity of his economic policies, Carey also had to confront how far the nation was from the harmony he had hoped for in *The Olive Branch*. Yet when the Missouri crisis struck, it made two things clear to Carey. First, the region that had to be convinced of his economic ideas was not New England but the South. But second, with Missouri he had a chance to pull all of his concerns together and show slaveholders and nonslaveholders that what they all needed was a national economy that would develop a diverse home market, in part by making use of a growing and robust region of slavery. As the Missouri crisis raged in 1819 and 1820, the nation confronted the dangers of regional disharmony. With so many people paying attention to issues of slavery and sectional conflict, Carey had an opportunity to explain how new thinking about slavery and political economy could promote sectional peace and improve the desperate conditions brought on by the Panic of 1819.

It was easy for Carey to see the connections between the southern defense of slavery and southern hostility to the sort of national government that he believed the nation needed. And by 1819 and 1820 it was just as easy for Carey to see that southern behavior was causing the rest of the nation to think in the ways he had associated in *The Olive Branch* with extreme New England Federalists. Even had he chosen to ignore the increasingly acrimonious congressional debate over Missouri, the letters Carey received during the months of panic and crisis constantly reminded him that the two events were connected.

By 1819 Carey had gained national stature, and his correspondence reflected his achievements. During the months of panic and crisis he received
letters from defenders of South Carolina slaveholders, as well as from New
York and New England protectionists. Taken together, these letters could only
have terrified someone who understood the problems of the Republic as Carey
did. One correspondent, Stephen Elliot of Charleston, explained to Carey why
South Carolina opposed the tariff. Elliot, a botanist and the first president of
the Charleston Literary and Philosophical Society, was also co-author, with
Robert Hayne, of the 1820 pamphlet *Remonstrance against an Increase of Duties on Imports*.[31] Elliot wrote to Carey that South Carolinians could accept
limited protection of a few necessary articles, but would always oppose "a great
combination to carry . . . a general system into effect." Surely it made more
sense, Elliot insisted to Carey, if "we . . . left to time and our rapidly progress-
ing population . . . we should at least have acquired a much better and more
natural position." Pursuing manufacturing as part of a "general system" pro-
mulgated by the national government allowed "a mode of legislation certainly
capable of great misapplication."[32] Elliot insisted that many southerners would
not support precisely the systematic approach to political economy that Carey
believed was vital for the Republic's survival. At around the same time, Carey
received a letter from Josiah Parks, also of Charleston. Parks explained that
"there could be neither happiness nor security in any medium between slavery and freedom—both blacks and whites would be sufferers—the danger lies
in the transition from one to the other." Parks insisted that it was essential to
"tak[e] the southern states as they are" and to allow them to determine the
future of slavery.[33]

During the crisis years of 1819 and 1820, Carey was also regularly receiving letters from northern allies in the struggle for the American System. These
letters reinforced his belief that those who shared his vision of political economy were no better able than southerners to comprehend the prioritizing necessary to secure it. No correspondent during these months did more to reveal
the problems Carey feared most than the New Yorker Eleazar Lord. Lord, the
founder of the Manhattan Fire Insurance Company, had traveled to Washington to advocate for the tariff and found himself in the midst of the Missouri crisis.[34] Lord's experiences led to fury at southerners, and a thoughtful
analysis that must have led Carey to realize that his political economy could
come only after sustained political activism. Lord depicted a Congress in which
southerners were united around the question of Missouri and slavery, and

equally united around preventing the American System. Yet Lord wondered (rhetorically), "why have not the representatives from the middle and northern states been more *united* in questions relative to the manufactures and industry of their states? And why have the representatives from the southern states been uniformly opposed to the others on these questions?"[35]

The answer, Lord insisted, was political economy and the very different effect it had in the South than the North. "In the southern states," Lord argued, "there is but one great general interest. This interest is liable to no fluctuations and changes—the labor is done by slaves who can neither remove nor apply their industry to new objects. The representatives therefore are always united as to their great interest and have taken ample care to protect it by law." Yet in the northern states,

> every man goes and comes as he pleases, changes the object of his pursuit whenever he is disposed. Representatives are chosen who are partisans to their several interests, and being assured that they cannot consist together, their representatives are never united on questions which concern any one of them. Hence such a tariff as we have and such a want of almost everything we ought to have.

The situation was truly alarming, Lord concluded, because "Nobody knows when the Missouri question will be over, or what temper it will leave for other subjects."[36]

These letters confronted Carey with the prospect of a South united around slavery and opposed to the new political economy. In addition, correspondents such as Lord forced Carey to see that southern obstruction was provoking a furious reaction. One of Carey's correspondents compared slaveholders to speculators and described them as "drones in the hive." Observing the unfolding Missouri crisis, he concluded that "the interests of the manufacturers as well as others of the productive classes are nearly connected if not wholly identified with the national interest while those of the unproductive [are] often at variance with the national interest."[37]

Such suspicion from both regions was antithetical to every aspect of Carey's thinking. But it also revealed that many southern planters and northern advocates for the American System did not understand the conditions of the new epoch that Carey believed explained the nation's current difficulties. The nation would flourish only if Carey's northern allies understood the vital contribution made by slavery, and if planters understood that their interests lay with the new political economy. Yet during the difficult years of 1819 and 1820, Carey's correspondents described "a southern interest so headstrong and blind," and claimed that there existed an unyielding hostility between "the northern and middle states, who do not breed the *Black Cattle* (two legged ones) for market" and the southern states who had "created so much ill will towards the non slaveholding states (where by the way) we must look for the chief establishments for carrying forward manufactures."[38]

As Carey contemplated the conditions wrought by panic and crisis in the early months of 1820, he also heard that "The greatest advocates for slavery are to be found in the capitol of the nation." One correspondent registered his disgust that the Republic's citizens held "in one hand the Declaration of Independence and the Bill of Rights and with the other shake the chains of servitude." What did this gross contradiction mean?, asked William Lee, a Massachusetts Republican and second auditor in William Crawford's Treasury Department. It was a "disgraceful exhibition. In this land of liberty, of man's last hopes—away with such cant our depreciation is too apparent." It was clear, insisted Lee, that southerners' "great object now is to create a number of new slave states so as to give that interest the preponderance in our country." Once they succeeded there would be no hope for a protective tariff or the rest of the American System. After all, Lee asked Carey, "do you think the southern nabob will permit you to tax him? No he will enjoy his thousands a year and make you pay the piper."[39] Such sentiments made it clear to Carey that his closest allies were, among other things, rejecting long-held arguments about "diffusionism," the claim that spreading slavery west would attenuate and weaken it as prelude to its ultimate extinction.[40] As they rejected diffusionism, their charged and furious language was also developing into revulsion for slavery. The letters Carey received described the "taunts of the Virginians and Georgians," claimed that southerners "would not see or hear candor," and insisted that the "southern interest *will be charged*" with a crime against the national interest due to "the unalterable policy of the slave holding states, to which their representatives will *now* more than ever adhere, to prevent the protection so vitally essential."[41]

Such claims likely terrified Carey. Missouri was connected to deep southern anxieties about the future of slavery, and those anxieties were stoked, in part, in reaction to the political economy and the view of the national government that Carey believed were essential to preserve republican society. And yet it was all a terrible and tragic mistake. Slaveholders, Carey believed, had no reason to fear his political economy. On the contrary, like all agriculturalists they should rather have feared the world that came without it: the conditions of the Panic of 1819. Carey's insights, he now understood during the Missouri crisis, had proved doubly true. In his conception of political economy, a growing domestic market had always assumed (and depended on) a vast number of slaves as producers and consumers (though involuntary ones). But now, in the messy world of politics and policy, the dependence of his political economy on the commitment of slaveholders was true for a second reason. Unless southerners led by slaveholders could be convinced to think differently, they would thwart the new political economy, and so doom Jefferson's empire of liberty.

The Missouri crisis galvanized Carey to speak clearly about race and slavery in the Republic in a way that few achieved before the development of the "positive good" thesis. Carey seized the opportunity to explain why slavery should expand west, and why his northern friends and colleagues should stop worrying about the mounting evidence that slavery would continue to grow in size and importance. By 1820 Carey had lived through more than a year of ruinous economic disaster that he believed his economic policies could have prevented. As the Missouri crisis began to rage again in 1820, Carey published the sorts of ideas that could provide the intellectual justification for an enduring slaveholding republic. In *Considerations On The Impropriety And Inexpediency of Renewing the Missouri Question*, Carey, the good republican, began by almost reflexively describing slavery as a "pernicious evil." And yet for any who wanted to think about slavery as something else, the remainder of the pamphlet taught them how to do so. Missouri, Carey argued, involved the fate of a nation that needed union and the new political economy in order to establish the empire of liberty. Since the Missouri crisis threatened disunion, citizens had to decide "whether this great and admirable republic is to remain united and prosperous, a monument of the beauty and efficacy of free institutions, or to be violently resolved into its original elements, and to become the theatre and prey of a fierce intestine conflict."[42]

Carey insisted that "the freedom and comfort of the African race are . . . objects worth a strenuous effort to obtain; but if they are to be bought at the expense of the peace and happiness of the country, the price is too great." Sectional conflict over Missouri could destroy union and the new political economy, and so provide "the possible destruction of our happy republic, the source

of prosperity and comfort to millions of a better race."[43] Here Carey provided
new thinking for a new epoch. Whether slavery eventually disappeared or not,
the nation would remain a monument to free institutions as long as it created a strong national government that pursued a proper political economy.
If it did so, it would ensure the happiness of the "better race," and that was
the only measurement for judging free institutions worthy serious consideration.

Furthermore, those free institutions were meant exclusively for the
"better race." Since free blacks were "depraved in their morals, debased in
intellect, and unqualified to perform the duties of citizens," free, republican
institutions, such as those in Missouri, deserved no bad marks for excluding
them. The condition of free blacks suggested that blacks were fit only for
slavery. Missouri had every right to ban free blacks because "the only object
contemplated by the Constitution, was the placing of white citizens of each
state on the same footing." Addressing directly the charge that Missouri's ban
of free blacks violated the privileges and immunities clause (and echoing the
concerns of Josiah Parks), Carey explained that "with the knowledge we possess of the opinions and views of the southern members of the convention, it
is difficult to believe that it could have been their intention to include free
negroes among the number of citizens to which this clause of the Constitution refers." The reason was obvious. It was the sensible policy of slave owners

> to shut them out from their confines. Nothing could be more
> dangerous to their power over the slaves, than the residence
> among them of free negroes, with the privileges of citizens. The
> greater the privileges and immunities bestowed on this class by
> some of the "free states," the stronger reason would there be for
> the "slave states" to refuse them an equality of privilege. It would
> seem probable, therefore, that the only object contemplated by the
> Constitution, was the placing of white citizens of each state on the
> same footing.

Blacks when slaves were essential to the Republic; free blacks had no place in
it. Indeed, the nation and its free institutions were safest with free blacks absent. That did not change, suggested Carey, whether slavery was legal or illegal
in any given state. Even if Missouri's constitution violated the nation's, "this
may perhaps be deemed a case in which a contravention of one of its articles,
if ever allowable, might with some propriety be winked at."[44]

Americans could properly judge the effectiveness of republican institutions, suggested Carey, by measuring the extent to which "the better race" enjoyed the material conditions necessary for independence and citizenship. If the nation pursued the new political economy, citizens would enjoy their republican birthright. The enslavement of millions, lamentable though it might be, assisted citizens in living as they deserved. The Missouri crisis would help to clarify "that the peace and prosperity of eight millions of freemen and Christians, may [not] rightfully be sacrificed to promote the welfare of a million and a half slaves."[45]

That Carey was saying something distinct about the future of slavery in the Republic can be seen by comparing his discussion of Missouri to Jefferson's response to the crisis. Most famously, Jefferson called it "a fire bell in the night," and is often given credit for prescience. But more revealing was a letter he sent to Albert Gallatin nine months after the fire bell comment. Here Jefferson insisted that the Missouri crisis had nothing to do with the concern many felt about slavery spreading west. The true antislavery position was to support slavery's westward expansion. For, insisted Jefferson,

> the removal of slaves from one state to another, no more than the removal from one country to another, would never make a slave of one human being who would not be so without it. Indeed, if there were morality in the question it is on the other side; because by spreading them over a larger surface, their happiness would be increased, and the burthen of their future liberation lightened by bringing a greater number of shoulders under it.[46]

Despite Jefferson's diffusionism, the letters Carey was receiving showed him how unpersuasive diffusionism was becoming to northern advocates of restriction in Missouri. Carey himself was clearly rejecting diffusionism. By supporting slavery in Missouri he had chosen between the needs of slaves and free blacks and those of "the better race." Since he believed he had to make this choice, clearly choosing "the freedom and comfort of the African race" would have meant supporting restriction. By 1820 Carey did not think that spreading slavery west would have any effect other than to further entrench the institution in the Republic. Carey's complex belief in the interconnections between and among political economy, national power, the degradation of economic crisis, and the potential violence that came with arguing about slavery pushed him to write in open and honest ways, and using authentic language and achieving a clarity regarding motivations about race and slavery that Jefferson never equaled.

Conclusion

The simultaneous crises of 1819 brought together all the issues that had concerned Carey since the dawn of his new epoch. The crises confirmed for him that questions of economic development and the future of slavery, for some time enmeshed in his thinking about political economy, were also inseparable in the nation's politics. The new political economy needed an expanding slavery with secure slave owners, any way Carey looked at it. Carey's experience from writing *The Olive Branch* to *Considerations Of The Impropriety* convinced him that the empire of liberty must also be a republic of slavery. Carey was one of the earliest and most prolific Americans to think about the processes and developments that would help create the most powerful capitalist economy the world had ever seen. He could imagine American capitalism in large part because he taught himself how to stop worrying about the monstrous abuse of the enslaved, and how to clearly separate the growth of slavery from any judgments about the Republic and the quality of its institutions. That Carey came to think as he did by 1820 was not inevitable; it was not foreordained. It was connected to his understanding of the conditions that existed in what he believed was a new world order that yielded both tremendous dangers and exciting possibilities.

And yet there are two speculative observations left to make. First, while Carey's complex thought was contingent, he very quickly relied on longstanding race prejudice and hatred that had long poisoned the land and so many of its people. When Carey decided that he needed to deny blacks membership in his enlightened world of universal comfort, ease, safety, fellowship, fair dealing, equity, justice, and a transcendent common humanity, it was cruelly easy for him to do so. Indeed, Carey had shown contempt for free blacks as far back as the Philadelphia yellow fever outbreak of 1793. Perhaps we can see Carey as a significant contributor to the rise of "racial modernity."[47]

And second, economic ideas like Carey's helped build another great source of human inequality, greed, and exploitation: the world of largely unregulated, untrammeled, and only at times creative destruction that was nineteenth-century American capitalism. Nobody more than Carey hoped to avoid what so many Jeffersonian Republicans knew to call "the European condition of society."[48] Yet the concentration of economic power that came with development of the domestic economy produced social conditions that did so much violence to Carey's egalitarian dreams that these conditions were by their very nature exploitative.[49]

In the final years of his life, Carey glimpsed something of this harsh new world, and begged the wealthy to look charitably upon the poor.[50] Yet rarely does it pay to be charitable when so much is measured by what pays, and the Republic would, until this day, find an unendurable number of its citizens (and aspirants to citizenship) living in the conditions Carey hoped to vanquish. Could Carey have sensed between 1815 and 1820 what he had begun to perceive by the early 1830s? He certainly knew of the terrible conditions of the European poor. But did he feel confident that American citizens would never experience those conditions of powerlessness, despair, vulnerability, and fear because his faith in his intricate understanding of the nation's problems allowed him to think that he could cordon off and assign lives of savage and unending brutality solely to slaves, and so prevent those conditions once and for all for his "better race"? Did Carey believe that the tremendous human costs of wrenching economic change could be entirely visited upon those he could tell himself were depraved, debased, and unqualified to live in freedom? It didn't work. And in 1833 Carey pleaded for charity for the many of his "better race" who had not achieved "an independent grade in society," who had failed to become "men of moderate fortune." By the 1830s many white citizens needed the charity Carrey called for, and the millions of unfree Americans even more desperately needed an acknowledgment of the shared humanity Carey denied them. When theorizing American capitalism, Carey was so often at his best when he was also at his worst; he had become a vital, thoughtful, tragic, and culpable embodiment of the nation that continued (and continues) to fuse its best and worst versions of itself in fiery, passionate, and violent embrace, parts that make a troubled whole.

CHAPTER 13

The Market, Utility, and Slavery in Southern Legal Thought

ALFRED L. BROPHY

Pre–Civil War Americans turned to all sorts of technology, from canals, steam power, and the telegraph to more obscure forms such as the daguerreotype and mining lamps, to hasten the pace of economic and moral progress. Law was another key technology they used. The law worked in favor of economic growth in several ways. First, judicial decisions self-consciously molded the law to promote economic efficiency. Second, legislatures used statutes to streamline credit markets, market transactions, and the formation of corporations. For the last several decades, scholars have often invoked Morton J. Horwitz's apt insight that there was an "instrumental conception" of law that it could and should be used to promote economic growth in the pre–Civil War era. Law was a transformative technology of capitalist development in the United States.[1]

Recently there has been an increased recognition of what one might call "proslavery instrumentalism," a utility-oriented application of law that forces scholarly attention southward in search of the nineteenth century's legal innovations. Certainly the economic analysis of slave law has been part of southern legal history, as Jenny Wahl's work on the common law of slavery, Ariela Gross's work on the slave market, and Calvin Schermerhorn's and Bonnie Martin's work on mortgages of humans reveal, but proslavery instrumentalism has not figured in recent accounts of southern modernity or in national accounts of the so-called market revolution. The law was designed (or modified) to sustain slavery across a broad spectrum of areas, including criminal law, contracts, trusts, and tort liability. Utility figured in the organization of slave law, just as it did in the more often touted decisions of northern and federal courts regarding bridge monopolies and riparian rights.[2] This chapter focuses attention on two emblematic southern jurists, Thomas Ruffin and Joseph Lumpkin, to suggest a reconsideration of slavery's formative importance to American capitalism. It then places Ruffin and Lumpkin in the context of other proslavery literature, and antislavery literature too, to demonstrate that the argument about the utility of slavery was widespread among southern jurists, lawyers, and legislators.

To grasp the centrality of utility in southern legal reasoning requires overcoming a venerable scholarly tradition of seeing sentiment—in the guise of paternalism—as the organizing principle of a slaveholding society. Eugene Genovese and Elizabeth Fox-Genovese are among the leading exponents of the view that proslavery southerners developed a critique of the market and saw slavery as offering an alternative to the free market. Many people at the time viewed slavery in such paternalistic terms, it is true. Thomas Cobb's *An Inquiry into the Law of Negro Slavery*, for instance, drew on the common trope that slaves were treated better than white workers who were subject to the vicissitudes of the free market. Likewise, Georgia Supreme Court justice Joseph H. Lumpkin spoke in 1850 to the South Carolina Institute about the virtues slavery brought to enslaved people: "The universal view of the South now is, that the spectacle of three hundred thousand barbarians, emerging, under the mild and humane treatment of their owners, into near four millions of civilized Christians, is not only without parallel in the history of the African race, but of the whole world." On July 24, 1850, David S. Kaufman, who then represented Texas in the U.S. House of Representatives, delivered an address to the joint Whig and Cliosophic literary societies at Princeton that was similar to Lumpkin's in its talk of the virtues of slavery. "In no country on earth is the African as happy," Kauffman said, "as useful to himself or to the country he inhabits, as the southern slave. Our inestimable slavery . . . confers unnumbered blessings upon the black man as well as the white." In the 1850s, much of the public discussion of slavery in the South was about the virtues of it for the slaves rather than the benefits to the enslavers.[3]

Behind such rhetorical posturing, however, was a legal system that organized slavery to the great benefit of slaveholders. The Constitution and federal statute law supported property rights in slaves, as southerners repeatedly said during debates over secession. Courts vigorously prosecuted slaves who sought to undermine the institution through rebellion. The common law provided a well-functioning market with a robust and sophisticated contract law that protected the rights of sellers and buyers, as well as providing a well-functioning credit market with mortgages on human beings. Moreover, it enforced trusts that facilitated the management of enslaved people and provided for insurance to spread the risk of slave ownership. The common law's considerations of utility were routinely used to justify laws to protect owners at the expense of slaves and nonslaveholding whites. Decisions protected the interests of slave owners by limiting their liability for harm caused by slaves while also limiting the liability of hirers of slaves for their treatment of slaves and for injuries that slaves received during the hire, for instance.[4]

Proslavery instrumentalism draws particular strength from recent efforts to understand slavery as a property regime as well as a labor regime. Such scholars as Gavin Wright, Robin Einhorn, and James Huston have drawn our attention to this, as did numerous southern jurists. With this frame, it is hardly surprising that proslavery jurists placed utility at the center of their jurisprudence as much as their northern counterparts did in this key era of capitalist transformation. Indeed, a national synthesis becomes vivid when one moves from the realm of judicial writing to a broader array of cultural production gesturing toward "rule of law," "protection of property," and social stability. Ultimately, then, we need to remember that, in contrast to the simultaneous rise in humanitarian, antislavery sentiments with capitalism that the intellectual historians David Brion Davis and Thomas Haskell have identified, there was also a proslavery law of the market. The intensification of market relations was not always a solvent upon the chains of slavery. Just as easily, the legal regime of the market could fasten those binds tighter. For, as Ralph Waldo Emerson recognized in the wake of the Fugitive Slave Act, law was among the many forces aligned against the enslaved. "The learning of the Universities, the culture of the eloquent society, the acumen of lawyers, the majesty of the Bench, the eloquence of the Christian pulpit, the stoutness of Democracy, the respectability of the Whig party are all combined," Emerson said, in the mission of kidnapping a fugitive slave. The legal system proved particularly effective in supporting slavery and the market.[5]

When legislators in the South discussed the future of slavery, they often focused on the right to property. When the Virginia House of Delegates debated a gradual abolition proposal in the spring of 1832 in the wake of the Nat Turner Rebellion, those who opposed the vague proposals warned of the dire consequences to disturbing any property rights. Property "is the very ligament which binds society together," said Representative James Gholson. "Without this principle, there is no civilization—no government." This was a common theme espoused by proslavery thinkers. Attacks on slaves as property were only the beginning. All social relations and property rights were vulnerable. Representative Kaufman warned his Princeton audience that reform threatened institutions other than slavery: "the present framework of society will be totally disorganized, property declared theft, and Agrarianism, Communism, Fourierism, and Socialism will supplant the present order of things; anarchy, and bloodshed close the horrific picture!" That is, property and slavery were closely allied in southern legal thought, and southern lawyers mobilized to protect each. Slavery's detractors realized this as well. For Emerson wrote in his journal in 1846 that "Slavery and anti-slavery is the question of property and no property . . . and anti-slavery dare not yet say that every man must do his own work. . . . Yet that is at last the upshot."[6]

One stark example of the law's support for slavery is North Carolina Supreme Court justice Thomas Ruffin's 1830 opinion in *State v. Mann*. Ruffin released John Mann, the renter of a female slave, from criminal liability for abusing and then shooting her. Though Ruffin began by lamenting "the struggle . . . in the Judge's own breast between the feelings of the man, and the duty of the magistrate," he advanced a series of rationales for why there could be no criminal liability for abuse of a slave in a white person's custody. Slaves will almost certainly perceive their situation as unjust. "What moral considerations," Ruffin asked rhetorically, "would be addressed to such a being, to convince him what, it is impossible but that the most stupid must feel and know can never be true"? To expect a slave "thus to labor upon a principle of natural duty, or for the sake of his own personal happiness," was unrealistic. Here Ruffin adopted a rule because he believed that slaves would not accept their position in southern society unless they were compelled to by force: "such services can only be expected from one who has no will of his own; who surrenders his will in implicit obedience to that of another." Such obedience only arises when the master has "uncontrolled authority over the body."[7] Ruffin's candid statement was extraordinary for its honesty and for its understanding that slaves would not abide by the southerners' moral philosophy, which taught that slaves should be content with their low place. *Mann* revealed the brutality of slavery and recognized that the authority of law came through violence rather than reason.

Ruffin advocated rules that subjected slaves to extraordinary control, for the good of southern society. Moreover, Ruffin followed a rule laid down by the community, which gained further strength because it was dictated by the needs of the community. Even though he claimed discomfort with the decision, Ruffin upheld the possessor's power, for no other rule could "operate to produce" submission of slaves to masters.[8] The opinion was thus part of the belief that antebellum judges were constrained by duty to uphold the society that surrounded them and that they could not change those rules.

The centrality of the utilitarian and instrumentalist impulses appeared again in the conclusion. "This we do upon the ground that this dominion is essential to the value of slaves as property, to the security of the master, and the public tranquility." In short, uncontrolled authority over the body of the slave was necessary to preserve slavery and southern society. The opinion thus represents the triumph of a proslavery instrumentalism, a cold calculation of the benefits from the rule Ruffin adopted and the costs involved in choosing another path. It was the fruit of the utilitarian calculus that governed American judges.[9]

Judges frequently engaged in utilitarian (economic) analysis in their opinions. In *Heathcock v. Pennington*, for instance, Justice Ruffin wrote of the low level of care required of those who rented slaves: "a slave, being a moral and intelligent being, is usually as capable of self preservation as other persons. Hence, the same constant oversight and control are not requisite for his preservation, as for that of a lifeless thing, or of an irrational animal." Ruffin, then, absolved an operator of a mine shaft of liability to his owner for the death of a young slave who was employed there and had, late at night, fallen into the shaft and died. *Heathcock* was part of the emergence of a modern tort law, which left the owner of a slave with a limited remedy and facilitated the operation of the mine at a low cost. The mine had to keep operating twenty-four hours a day, and "some one had necessarily to perform at those times":

No one could suppose that the boy, knowing the place and its dangers, would incur the risk of stumbling into the shaft by not keeping wide awake. It was his misfortune to resemble the soldier sleeping at his post, who pays the penalty by being surprised and put to death.[10]

Similarly, in *Parham v. Blackwelder*, Ruffin further explored the nature of slaves' personality and the law's need to decouple an owner's liability from torts committed by her slaves. *Parham* arose when a slave owned by Amelia Parham cut wood and carried it away from Elizabeth Blackwelder's property. There was no precedent supporting an owner's liability for the intentional torts of their slaves. Ruffin found that there was no liability, given the nature and extent of slavery:

> We believe the law does not hold one person answerable for the wrongs of another person. It would be most dangerous and unreasonable, if it did, as it is impossible for society to subsist without some persons being in the service of others, and it would put employers entirely in the power of those who have often, no good will to them, to ruin them.[11]

This kind of utilitarian reasoning pervaded Ruffin's opinions. Ruffin's 1832 opinion in *Scroggins v. Scroggins*, for instance, tracked his reasoning in *State v. Mann* as he denied a husband's request for a divorce. *Scroggins*—in which a husband sought divorce when he learned that his wife's child was part African American—presents an important parallel to *Mann* in that it takes the world as it is and expects individuals to bear a burden so that *overall* a better result emerges. For in *Scroggins*, Ruffin denies a divorce on the grounds that if divorces become too easy to obtain, that will undermine marriage and affect society more generally. For Ruffin reasoned that if couples knew they could not get out of marriage, they would accept it, and he thought that preferable to ending marriages.[12]

One unusual set of cases involving what was known as quasi-slavery (or sometimes quasi-freedom or nominal slavery) further reveals the centrality of economics and brutality to slave law. In quasi-slavery cases, humans were held in a state between slavery and freedom; their owners allowed them to work for their own account or otherwise have substantial control over their lives. Legislatures routinely prohibited such behavior by statute. For instance, South Carolina prohibited gifts of slaves that contained a promise "that such . . . slaves shall be held in nominal servitude." When someone violated that statute, the slaves were taken from the person who had received them and given to the donor's heirs. A North Carolina statute was broader. It prohibited owners from allowing slaves to work for themselves or to go about without supervision and thus tried to stop owners from engaging in quasi-slavery at any time, rather than just at the time they were giving away slaves. Judges filled in the gaps left by statutes and developed a sophisticated law to identify and stop owners from holding slaves in quasi-slavery. For instance, in 1822 the North Carolina Supreme Court held that a gift of slaves to the trustees of a Methodist church "to keep or dispose of as they shall judge most for the glory of God, and good of said slaves," was illegal. The court gave the slaves to the donor's heirs.[13]

That is where North Carolina precedent stood when Ruffin, who was then only a trial judge, heard the case of William Dickenson's gift of slaves to a Quaker meeting. After Dickenson's death his son had possession of the slaves and refused to hand them over to the Quaker Society. The Quakers lost before Judge Ruffin because they apparently planned to allow the slaves to work for their own account and did not seem to be otherwise interested in controlling the slaves. On appeal, William Gaston, who later served on the North Carolina Supreme Court and made mildly antislavery comments at a graduation address at the University of North Carolina in 1832, represented the Quakers. Gaston argued that it did not matter how the Quakers were treating the slaves. "No man is obliged to make a profit of his slaves," Gaston argued. But the North Carolina Supreme Court concluded that owners *were* obliged to make money out of slaves, or at least not allow them to have essentially their freedom. "If that law could be eluded by transferring slaves to this Society, there is no foreseeing to what extent the mischief might be carried," Justice Leonard Henderson wrote. "Numerous collections of slaves, having nothing but the name, and working for their own benefit, in the view and under the continual observation of others who are compelled to labour for their owners, would naturally excite in the latter, discontent with their condition, encourage idleness and disobedience, and lead possibly in the course of human events to the most calamitous of all contests, a bellum servile." A dissenting justice saw it differently. He thought that owners had broad discretion to govern their slaves. That dissent shows just how much the majority saw the state's interest in control over slaves and how much the majority was willing to impose control on owners.[14]

On the North Carolina Supreme Court Ruffin dealt with a number of cases of quasi-slavery. In 1849 he invalidated a gift of slaves from one neighbor to another. The neighbor had agreed to let the slaves manage their own time, which Ruffin saw as allowing them quasi-freedom. The donor's heirs ended up with title to the slaves. Ruffin began by noting the fundamental right of countries to protect themselves from dangers to health or morals. Ruffin's opinion revealed a stark contrast between the rights of slave owners to use their property as they liked and the community's interest in policing the boundaries of slavery. The community's interest won in this case, as it did in many others.[15] The cases on quasi-servitude have received little attention, but they penetrate to the heart of the issue for slave law. As the Florida Supreme Court concisely stated during the Civil War, "Our law recognizes no other status than that of absolute freedom or absolute slavery." Those who failed to keep the chains fastened tightly on enslaved people put the system of slavery at risk.[16]

Perhaps the most vocal support for the pro-market rules among southern jurists came from Joseph Henry Lumpkin of Georgia. Lumpkin embraced the market and an economic analysis of common law rules to limit liabilities of corporations, limit workers' rights of recovery against employers, and limit also what many saw as monopoly privileges. In his 1850 address to the South Carolina Institute, for instance, he summarized the ways to bring progress to the region. His advice stretched from better popular education to further development of manufacturing. He suggested, for instance, that South Carolina "look to her own laws, in order that labor, capital and population may be invited within her borders." He praised corporations in particular for their work at internal improvement: "associated wealth is, in no small degree, the cause of modern civilization."[17] Corporations, then, like slavery, were pillars of modern civilization.

The next year, Lumpkin's decision in *Shorter v. Smith* illustrated his attitudes toward respectful but careful treatment of corporations by narrowly construing the rights given by a charter. In *Shorter* a ferry operator requested an injunction to stop the building of a nearby bridge. The ferry operator had a charter from the state. The question then became how to interpret that charter. Did it grant an exclusive license? And if so, did that license prohibit competing bridges or only other ferries? Lumpkin distinguished English precedent, which suggested that ferry franchises were construed as excluding competition, by reference to American values of the free market. "In England, and other countries, which are governed by force, the performance of public duties by inn-keepers, owners of bridges and ferries, &c., can be coerced by the enforcement of legal penalties. Not so here; we have, and in the very nature of things can have, no other protection, but that which results from free and unrestricted competition."[18] Without an explicit grant of a monopoly, Lumpkin found it inappropriate to read one into the grant.

That narrow construction of grants owed much to Chief Justice Roger Taney's 1837 decision in *Charles River Bridge*, which Lumpkin quoted extensively. Lumpkin agreed completely with Taney's conclusion that "the grant of a public road, bridge, or ferry, confers the right to construct the improvements only, and to receive certain rates of tolls; but does not carry with it exclusive privileges, where none such are expressly given." Lumpkin presented the case as an easy one, established not just by logic but by an unbroken line of precedent as well. For there was a "uniform understanding of our people, that if the grantee intended to secure himself from competition, he must obtain a provision to that effect in his grant." Recent legislation showed, moreover, a hostility to monopolies; all persons were permitted to establish ferries and erect bridges on their own land.[19] Lumpkin framed his opinion in the language of competition; it was part of the accommodation of private rights with the growing economy.

In another charter interpretation case, *McLeod v. Savannah, Albany and Gulf Railroad*, Lumpkin again recalled that change was an element of life. "Old things must give place to new. The forest must yield to the waving harvest and golden fruit; the red man of the woods to the sturdy and stalwart Saxon; the turnpike to the canal, and both to the railway." The charter that had granted exclusive right to a toll bridge decades ago did not extend to prohibit a nearby railroad bridge. If the company's "profits have been impaired by this new mode of travel and transportation across rivers and morasses, they stand in no worse situation, and are no more entitled to compensation, than are thousands of individuals throughout the land, who are daily subjected to losses and ruin by new inventions and improvements," Lumpkin concluded.[20]

Similarly, *Haywood v. Mayor and Aldermen of Savannah* struck down a restriction on the amount of fish that could be purchased in the Savannah market. The restriction was a restriction on trade, which Lumpkin thought inappropriate. The market should prevail: "let the race and the battle be to the swift and the strong!"[21] Such cases, decided outside the context of slavery, illustrate the unified American jurisprudence, which facilitated the market by protecting expectations and contracts and subjected individuals and corporations to competition.

One other place to observe the consistency in attitudes toward the market and labor between northern and southern judges is the "fellow-servant rule," first introduced in the 1830s in the United Kingdom and quickly adopted throughout almost all of the United States. The idea was that employees did not have a right to sue their employers for injuries caused by fellow workers. The rationales behind this were that workers were in as good a position to protect against those injuries as employers, that employers should only be liable for their actions, not those of others, and that employees who did not like this could leave. The "fellow-servant rule" absolved corporations of much of their liability in hazardous industrial settings; it also left workers with little protection. This was the world of free contract that southerners so frequently criticized in their proslavery literature—the cruelties of the market leaving little protection against employers, corporations, and industrialization. In 1854, Lumpkin followed other courts in concluding that a worker who suffered injury through the fault of a coworker had no claim against their common employer. In that case a railroad worker's son, who was riding on the train with him, died in a train wreck that was caused by another worker's negligence. Lumpkin followed prior precedents, including Massachusetts chief justice Lemuel Shaw's opinion in *Farwell v. Boston and Worcester Railroad*.[22] That Lumpkin saw the issues in similar terms to Shaw illustrates how unified American jurisprudence was when it came to workers' rights against employers. It also illustrates the dominant ethos that injuries should be borne by the workers who suffered them rather than by the employer, who might have had at least an equal opportunity to protect workers against them.

The fellow-servant rule is a prime example of the way that American jurisprudence, North and South, was concerned with the promotion of economic development. One might also recall here that though Lemuel Shaw in 1836 wrote the *Commonwealth v. Aves* opinion that freed a slave who traveled with her owners to Massachusetts, in 1851 he refused a habeas corpus request for Thomas Sims, a fugitive slave. Thus, Lumpkin and Shaw were bound in many ways—by adherence to the economic reasoning that protected employers over employees and by adherence to a federal law of slavery. It is worth recalling here that dominant ideas in the United States were of classical liberalism and the strong protection of property rights, which promoted a vigorous market, and adherence to the rule of law, which lent further stability to that market. This also fits with Drew Faust's observation that northerners and southerners agreed on a great deal of moral philosophy.[23]

Yet slaves occupied a different position from that of free workers. In the 1846 case of *Scudder v. Woodbridge*, Lumpkin decided that the fellow-servant rule did not apply to slaves. Lumpkin turned to a basic economic analysis: liability had to be imposed on the employer of the slave in order to give an incentive to protect the slaves from danger. If the employer were not liable, there would be no incentive to protect slaves from harm. If there were no liability, Lumpkin feared, "the life of no hired slave would be safe."[24]

Lumpkin's general interest in the promotion of economic development and in efficiency appears also in cases where owners attempted to free their enslaved human property. His opinions reveal the interplay of legislation, precedent, and the influence of public policy, with a particular emphasis on the good of the community. For the Georgia legislature established the broad framework for owners who wanted to emancipate enslaved human property in 1818. That statute prohibited the freeing of people inside the state, but left open the right of owners to take enslaved people outside the state and free them. A series of decisions then had to interpret how that legislation affected the right of owners to dispose of their human property, as well as the state's general policy that was in favor of restricting emancipation, restricting the number of free black people, and maintaining control over Georgia's population of both free and enslaved African Americans.

Lumpkin's first major opinion on this matter came in 1848 in *Vance v. Crawford*. He upheld a will that allowed three slaves to choose to migrate to Liberia and be free. Lumpkin found this consistent with Georgia's policy, but he went on to observe it not permissible to free slaves within the state. State policy prohibited emancipation in the state. Freed slaves would pose a danger to the white community. "They are incapable of taking part with ourselves, in the exercise of self-government," Lumpkin wrote. He invoked the divine sanction for the Georgia government and again wrote about the virtues of slavery to the enslaved. Lumpkin believed the United States was "a model empire for the world," where "God in His wisdom planted on this virgin soil, the best blood of the human family." In the United States slaves would have a better life than elsewhere; they would even have a better life than many white workers. For Lumpkin believed that "the condition of our slaves . . . is infinitely better than it would have been, but for this very system of bondage, better than the lower orders in Europe, and better far than it would be, if they were emancipated here." Over the next dozen years Lumpkin revisited several times wills that freed slaves, and while he regularly upheld the wills, he increasingly criticized emancipation. He also increasingly praised the virtues of slavery.[25]

In other areas as well, such as the enforcement of contracts regarding slave sales, American jurisprudence was unified in its protection for property, particularly slave property. Moreover, one might recall that it was the law's enforcement of debt claims that set *Uncle Tom's Cabin* in motion. The sale of Uncle Tom and the threatened sale of little Harry were only the first places in Stowe's novel where the law was responsible for the harshness of slavery and where it protected the slave system; at other times the law prevented Tom's emancipation by St. Claire and turned Senator Byrd into a lawbreaker when he helped Eliza and Harry escape. The centrality of slaveholders' considerations of utility appeared, for instance, in Simon Legree's statement to Tom that he had "made up" his "mind and counted the costs" of punishing, indeed killing, Tom. Such considerations of efficiency should come as no surprise. For instance, Professor George A. Baxter of Hampden Sydney College published in 1836 a criticism of abolitionists. It focused on Brown University's President Francis Wayland's antislavery textbook, *Elements of Moral Philosophy*. Baxter explained quite simply that "when clearly ascertained," utility was the "guide of moral actions."[26]

Turning from the vantage of judges' opinions and their extrajudicial writings to the writings of lawyers and legislators reveals that utilitarian considerations were pervasive in antebellum thought. Thomas R. Dew, a professor at the College of William and Mary, wrote about how the interests of white Virginians were related to slave property and the money slaves generated for the state in his 1832 book, *Review of the Debates in the Virginia Legislature*. Dew's work quickly drew praise, including from South Carolina chancellor William Harper, who focused on the presumed benefits of slavery to the enslaved. "President Dew," Chancellor Harper wrote at the beginning of his 1838 *Memoir on Slavery*, "has shown that the institution of Slavery is a principal cause of civilization." Harper's next sentence then extended Dew: "Perhaps nothing can more evident than that it is the sole cause."[27]

The majority of northerners thought in similar utilitarian terms, if not in the same amplitude, about the contributions that slavery made to the enslaved. Daniel Webster's March 7, 1850, address during debate over the Compromise of 1850 criticized abolitionists for their unyielding moral positions, which did more harm than good for the cause of the enslaved. Abolitionists, Webster said, "are disposed to mount upon some particular duty, as upon a war-horse, and to drive furiously on and upon and over all other duties that may stand in the way." Their narrow reasoning admitted of few opportunities for compromise. Webster, by contrast, considered the entire spectrum of issues and balanced the costs of affection for the enslaved against the cost to the Union. That utilitarian calculus came out poorly for the enslaved.

Similarly, Senator John Bell of Tennessee used utilitarian calculations in debate over the Compromise of 1850. He spoke in even more proslavery terms than Webster as he weighed the factors used in his calculations. Abolitionists' conclusion that slavery was immoral, Bell thought, could not be proved. For the moral condemnation of slavery "is not arrived at in accordance with the Baconian method of reasoning, by which . . . we may safely deduce a general law of physical nature; and so of morality and government." Instead, Bell thought that slavery was "still contributing to advance the cause of civilization."[28]

One other vantage reveals the centrality of utilitarian considerations to proslavery legal thought: the perspective of the abolitionists who critiqued what proslavery judges were doing. In the wake of *Uncle Tom's Cabin*, Harriet

Beecher Stowe published a short volume titled *A Key to Uncle Tom's Cabin* to provide nonfiction details to back up her novel. She used Thomas Ruffin's opinion in *State v. Mann* in her discussion of slave law. Stowe detected "the conflict between the feelings of the humane judge and the logical necessity of a strict interpreter of slave-law."[29] Stowe now realized that the utilitarian calculations made by the legal system led to acceptance of slavery, and she criticized the cold, logical reasoning of the southern judges generally. "It is often and evidently not because judges are inhuman or partial but because they are logical and truthful that they announce from the bench in the calmest manner, decisions which one would think might make the earth shudder and the sun turn pale."[30] Men like Ruffin could be aware of the inhumanity of slave law, but they recognized that if slavery were to survive, the laws must be severely enforced. Because slavery was "a seething, boiling tide, never wholly repressed, which rolls its volcanic stream underneath the whole frame-work of society," it had to be met with "severity of law and inflexibility of execution."[31]

Abolitionists such as Harriet Beecher Stowe and the Unitarian minister William Ellery Channing are helpful in putting into relief the key points of antebellum legal thought. Channing's 1835 book *Slavery* advanced a sophisticated moral philosophy of sentiment with direct application to the legal treatment of slaves. Channing distinguished what was correct from what was expedient. To determine what was correct, he looked to "the great interests of humanity." Channing sought principles of action based on humanity.[32] Channing also engaged the proslavery arguments about property rights. He opposed legal arguments drawn from property with ideas about the inherent equality of humans. *Slavery* presented a sentiment-based critique of law; it suggested the proper response of the heart to cold law. Channing both understood the nature of the dominant modes of legal reasoning based on considerations of expediency and offered an alternative. "Is the General Good, then, the supreme law to which every thing must bow? . . . Must the Public Good prevail over purity and our holiest affections?," he asked.[33]

But it is important to remember that the abolitionist attacks on slavery and property as well were not the dominant ideas in the North. Stowe began her career with a short story titled "Love versus Law," which criticized a man for suing his neighbor to protect his property rights. But such attacks on property were unusual. Much more common was the support for property and the rule of law. In the months following passage of the Fugitive Slave Act of 1850, speakers to the Phi Beta Kappa societies at Harvard, Yale, and Brown all urged support for the rule of law, of which property rights were a central tenet. At Harvard, Professor Timothy Walker of the Cincinnati Law School worried that abolitionists and other reformers were fanatics who sought to tear up civilization. At Yale, the New York lawyer Daniel Lord found in lawyers and ministers a solution for the problem that Timothy Walker had identified. Lord told the Phi Beta Kappa Society that lawyers and ministers were a stabilizing force in society because they abided settled forms and through their professions served as bulwarks against change. Lord was quite sure that lawyers and ministers would stop the calls for changes in law and religion. For law in particular had a preference for ancient and settled ideas and for property rights. At Brown, often a place of antislavery advocacy in the 1840s and 1850s, William Greene spoke about the need for Americans to abide the Fugitive Slave Act because it had been passed through proper, democratic means.[34]

In summary, then, American judges embraced values of what we call economic efficiency and turned to empirical investigation to understand what path would produce the greatest utility. Those values of utility and empiricism led judges to seek a well-functioning market. It was a world of property, of releasing masters from control from the law, of rules that promoted a well-functioning slave system.

This connection between the market and slavery points up the relationship between capitalism and proslavery sentiments. We hear much from David Brion Davis's *Problem of Slavery in the Age of Revolution* on the relationship between capitalism and antislavery sentiments. Davis notes the correlation between the rise of antislavery sentiments and the rise of capitalism. Perhaps this is the result of a confluence between the interests of capitalism that promoted free labor over slavery and a widening of moral sensibilities made possible by the market, or perhaps it is partly the result of economic interests that the emerging industrial workers and investors had while they competed with enslaved labor. There is more than a little to the idea that capitalism—or trade and commerce, to use the language of the antebellum era—helped bring down slavery. In the "Young American," Emerson drew on common beliefs about the history of the market. Americans in the 1840s believed that trade allowed British merchants to purchase freedom from the Crown over the course of centuries. Trade and economic development had a positive image at the time, as the landscape art that celebrated Americans' industry revealed: "the historian will see that trade," Emerson wrote, "makes peace and keeps peace, and it will abolish slavery."[35]

Certainly, the power of economic interest and of trade that facilitated the enormous growth in the first sixty years of the nineteenth century was a powerful engine for change. Thus, while Davis has shown the important connections between the market and antislavery sentiments, there was also an important relationship between capitalism and proslavery thought. The engine of the market did not always point in one direction, toward antislavery. Slavery bound together the interests of the people of North and South, as well as Europeans and Americans. And southerners knew it. Justice Lumpkin recalled at the South Carolina Agricultural Fair in 1850 that England, "without raising one pound of cotton at home . . . has a population there of four millions directly or indirectly dependent on this trade."[36]

What, then, to make of the relationship between the market and slavery? Eric Williams's *Capitalism and Slavery* demonstrates the economic incentives that lay on the side of antislavery action in Great Britain. It is important that we recall and study the multiple and important economic impulses that lay behind the proslavery ideas and actions in the United States. The market, as we are daily reminded, is an incredibly powerful force, and the interests it supports are difficult, if not impossible, to resist. Law as a technology of the market reflects its values.

For a number of reasons, including the provincialism of northern courts (and thus their reluctance to cite southern opinions), the tradition of southern judges not to write as expansive opinions as northern judges, and the conservatism of southern judges with respect to departing from precedent, it is hard to locate areas of law where southern law advanced ahead of northern law. However, in areas like the spendthrift trust, which helped keep property within families, southern lawyers seem to have turned to that technology with vigor before northern lawyers did.[37] That is, the U.S. legal system was pro-market throughout, but the presence of slavery added a particularly strong impetus toward protection of property and of the market.

Considerations of utility were central to proslavery thought. For instance, much of the proslavery literature focuses on the economic catastrophe that attended the end of slavery in the Caribbean and that would attend the end of slavery in the United States. Similarly, proslavery legal decisions, like decisions involving corporations and property rights outside the context of slavery, turned on their effects on economic development.[38] In the minds of many southerners, the market and slavery were leading causes of civilization. We should take seriously southerners' understanding of the ways in which their world depended on slavery and the market and the role of legal technology in promoting both.

CHAPTER 14

Why Did Northerners Oppose
the Expansion of Slavery?

Economic Development and Education
in the Limestone South

JOHN MAJEWSKI

The recent literature on slavery has unexpectedly brought to light a new historical problem: why did the Republican Party oppose the expansion of slavery? Historians have commonly understood that most mainstream Republicans, whatever their moral objections to slavery, opposed the institution's expansion because of economic reasons. Slavery, in the minds of many Republicans, was incompatible with a flourishing free-labor economy. As the historian John Ashworth has put it, "It is no exaggeration to say that Republicans fought the Civil War primarily because they deplored the economic effects of slavery."[1] If slavery were allowed to expand, Republicans believed, lazy and indolent planters would monopolize the best lands, undermine the work ethic, and subvert economic progress. The Republican critique had a political component as well. The great wealth of southern planters—accumulated through the exploitation of their slaves—would allow slaveholders to manipulate the national government and become privileged aristocrats. Fear of the "slave power" became a rallying cry of Republicans.[2]

Within the past decade, though, a remarkably strong scholarly consensus has emerged that challenges the Republican economic critique of slavery. Recent scholarship emphasizes that the South's slaveholding society embraced a wide array of technological innovations: southern artisans worked steadily to improve cotton gins; southern cultivators successfully introduced new varieties of cotton seed; southern entrepreneurs built highly sophisticated flour mills and sugar refineries; and southern governments subsidized a growing and vibrant railroad network. Southern economic development created a far more complex society than one comprising only aristocratic planters, exploited slaves, and poor whites. The South developed its own urban middle class, which, Jonathan Daniel Wells argues, "easily and seamlessly incorporated vigorous support for slavery within a broader modernizing vision of the region's future."[3] The modernizing vision extended to planters, who supported scientific agriculture, transportation improvements, and urban growth. One recent synthesis concludes that slavery was not "an archaic institution that prevented the South from achieving the higher level of modernization obtained by the North."[4] With so much evidence suggesting that slavery was compatible with economic modernization, why did Republicans believe that slavery was antithetical to economic progress?

What makes the Republican position especially problematic is that slavery seemed to benefit the northern economy. Slavery, historians now argue, stood at the center of the world's capitalist economy. As many of the chapters in this volume make clear, northern industry, northern finance, and northern commerce benefited from slave labor. Southern slaveholders celebrated their central importance to the world economy, and they confidently believed that northerners would never endanger access to cotton and the lucrative southern markets. Why would Yankees, they asked, make war against slavery and kill the goose that laid the golden eggs? Historians are left with the same paradox that southerners could not explain: the northern economy benefited from the profits of slave labor, yet the majority of northerners willingly risked civil war to halt slavery's westward expansion. Capitalism, it seems, went to war against itself.

To explain this paradox, I focus on core strengths of the northern political economy that the recent literature has tended to neglect: the democratization of education and innovation. Northerners created the world's most successful educational system, one that provided widespread access to inexpensive common schools. In the 1849–1850 school year, 63 percent of children in the rural North between the ages of five and nineteen years attended school for at least part of the year, a percentage far higher than in the South and in most European nations.[5] The relatively high levels of learning, combined with the expansion of markets through transportation and communication improvements, facilitated the development of networks of inventors and innovators. Patents are one way of measuring the progress of northern innovation. Antebellum Americans patented tens of thousands of inventions before the Civil War, and per capita rates were well ahead of those of Great Britain, the nineteenth century's great industrial power. Northerners accounted for nearly 95 percent of the national total; the South, with nearly 33 percent of the nation's population, produced only 5.1 percent of the nation's patents.[6] Many Republicans believed that slavery, whatever its immediate economic benefits in providing cheap commodities for northern industry, was fundamentally hostile to the creative core of the northern economy. Antislavery activists in Louisville, Kentucky, summarized the critique in 1849: "Slavery and education are by their very nature at war with each other."[7]

This chapter analyzes one of the most economically successful regions of the South, a region I call the Limestone South, to show in greater detail the incompatibility of slavery and a northern economy focused on education and innovation. The Limestone South consisted of three distinct regions that shared rich limestone soils: Virginia's Shenandoah Valley, Kentucky's Bluegrass Region, and Tennessee's Nashville Basin. Taken as a whole, the Limestone South contained just over 22,000 square miles (approximately the size of current-day West Virginia) and just over one million residents, including 275,000 slaves. In many respects, the Limestone South confirms the current literature's emphasis on the flexible, modern nature of antebellum slavery. The region's fertile soils and moderate climate supported dense, prosperous agricultural populations with their accompanying commerce, industry, and cities. Nearly 16 percent of the population of the Limestone South lived in a census-defined urban area, which put it significantly ahead of midwestern states such as Indiana and Illinois. Manufacturing output in the Limestone South was also comparable to that of midwestern states. In contrast to the predictions of free- labor ideology, the history of the Limestone South suggests that slavery, in the right environmental conditions, could indeed support a thriving, diversified economy.

In other respects, though, the Limestone South shows how slavery created a political economy antithetical to long-term development. Residents of the Limestone South steadfastly refused to invest in an extensive system of public education. Despite its relatively advanced economy, far fewer white children in the Limestone South attended school than children in the Midwest. The lack of basic education, in turn, discouraged the formation of clusters of artisans, mechanics, and inventors who could improve production techniques and develop new technologies. In both rural and urban areas, inventive activity in the Limestone South was well behind that of the Midwest. In 1860 the artisans, mechanics, and inventors in Cleveland, for example, filed for many more patents than did residents of Louisville, even though Louisville had a far larger white population. Even though the Limestone South supported a diverse economy, the lack of innovation and invention posed a barrier to growth. Population growth in the Limestone Region slowed significantly in the 1840s and 1850s, while the free-labor Midwest continued its rapid ascent.

Viewed through the prism of the Limestone South, the Republican economic critique of slavery becomes compelling. The Limestone South shows that slavery flourished in a region with soils and climate similar to those of the North. Slavery's seeming compatibility with selected elements of economic modernity made the institution all the more insidious to northerners. Without some legal restriction, slavery could easily embed itself in the cities, towns, and farms of the Midwest and West. Once entrenched, slavery would have short-circuited the investment in education and technology so essential to long-term economic progress. Even though the northern economy profited from commodities produced by slave labor, Republicans nevertheless feverishly worked to stop slavery's expansion (and risked civil war) to protect their own vision of political economy.

Continuous Cultivation Versus Shifting Cultivation

One of the great ironies of the nineteenth-century economy is that the nation's most agrarian region also had the nation's worst soils. Suffering from frequent leaching, southern soils often lack calcium, phosphorus, and other key nutrients. Southern soils are often acidic, which inhibits the ability of many plants to take in whatever nutrients are available. To make matters worse, clover and other legumes—which return nitrogen to the soil and provide excellent fodder for cattle and livestock—failed to thrive in the South's warm and humid climate.[8] In response to poor soils and an inhospitable climate, southern farmers and planters used shifting cultivation. In shifting cultivation, farmers burned forest growth (typically pines, which are well adapted to acidic soils), which in turn produced large amounts of ash. The ash provided an excellent source of calcium, thus neutralizing the soil's natural acidity. After the ash had been leached out of the cropped land, farmers burned another plot, leaving the original land to long-term fallow for up to thirty years. While shifting cultivation is often associated with subsistence agriculture, nineteenth-century southerners successfully used it to grow cotton and other staple crops.[9]

Limestone soils, on the other hand, are rich in calcium and other nutrients. Kentucky's Bluegrass Region, Virginia's Shenandoah Valley and surrounding areas, and Tennessee's Nashville Basin all possess an abundance of limestone soils. The relatively moderate climate of these three areas allowed fodder crops to grow, which in turn made large-scale livestock operations possible. The cattle and other livestock efficiently recycled the rich nutrients back into the soil by way of manure, thus allowing agriculturalists to engage in continuous cultivation. In continuous cultivation, land rotated among crops such as wheat, corn, and hay, and then "rested" as clover, bluegrass, and other legumes replenished the soil while providing pasturage for livestock. Scientists classify limestone lands as alfisols. Most prevalent in the Midwest and in parts of the Northeast (such as New York's Mohawk River Valley), alfisols are usually highly productive. Scientists classify the acidic soils that characterized most of the South as ultisols, which are often associated with tropical and semitropical climates and shifting cultivation.[10]

Census statistics show the relationship among soils, climate, and agricultural regimes. Beginning in 1850, the Census Bureau began collecting data on the number of improved and unimproved acres on farms, with improved acreage defined as cropped fields or fenced pastures. Since the vast majority of cultivators using shifting cultivation did not bother to fence land in long-term fallow, their farms and plantations contained a high proportion of unimproved land. Table 14.1, based on the 1860 census, compares the percentage of improved land in the South, the North, and the Limestone South. In the South as a whole, only 33 percent of the land was improved; in cotton states such as South Carolina, the figure was 25 percent. In the Limestone South, nearly 62 percent of the land was improved, a figure broadly similar to that of the Northeast (63.8 percent improved) and actually ahead of most midwestern states (53.3 percent improved). The northern state that most resembled the Limestone South was Ohio. Ohio was settled at the same time as the Kentucky Bluegrass Region and the Nashville Basin, and most of its soils were alfisols. The percentage of improved land in Ohio (61 percent) was almost exactly the same as the percentage of improved land in the Limestone South.

The continuous-cultivation regimen of the Limestone South gave its landscape a more settled and ordered ambiance than the rest of the South. Antislavery critics often focused on the slovenly nature of the South's plantations and

Table 14.1. Percentage of Improved Land in Farms, 1860

Area	Improved land (%)
Northeast	**63.8**
Midwest	**53.3**
Border South	**39.0**
Maryland	62.1
Delaware	63.4
Kentucky	39.9
Missouri	31.3
Upper South	**32.76**
Virginia	36.8
North Carolina	28.2
Tennessee	32.9
Cotton South	**30.8**
South Carolina	28.2
Georgia	30.3
Mississippi	32.0
Alabama	33.4
Louisiana	29.1
Limestone South	**62.2**
Bluegrass Region	69.8
Nashville Region	51.5
Limestone Virginia	60.4
Overall North	**57.7**
Overall South	**33.3**

Source: Census statistics at Geostat Center, University of
Virginia Library, http://fisher.lib.virginia.edu/collections/stats
/histcensus/.

farms, pointing to their unfenced fields and acre after acre of scrubby pines. Yet
northerners visiting the Limestone South noted with delight the well-kept
fields, the substantial farm buildings, the well-maintained farmhouses, and the
ubiquitous stonewalls. Travelers visiting the Shenandoah Valley, according to
historian Warren Hofstra, came to see "a prosperous countryside, thriving market towns, a vibrant grain economy, and a town and country landscape" that
symbolized the promise of America's republican experiment.[11] Visitors to the
Bluegrass rhapsodized about the bucolic landscape. "A short visit to Kentucky,"
wrote a correspondent of Baltimore's *American Farmer*, was "more like a pleasant dream, than a reality. It was like flying over and looking down upon a
beautiful garden of lovely flowers and various fruits, without having time to

alight and exhale the odor of the one, or taste the sweets of the other."[12] Visitors took particular delight in seeing the improved livestock that roamed the finely manicured pastures. The Limestone South became particularly well known for its flourishing equestrian culture, which thrived in a region with excellent soils and a moderate climate to support a variety of nutritious grasses. For stock breeders and agricultural writers, prize-winning bulls and horses became celebrities of sorts. One correspondent of the *Spirit of the Times,* a periodical devoted to horse racing and livestock breeding, wrote that in visiting stock farms near Nashville, he saw "the celebrated bull Frederick. He is very large, and is indeed among the first bulls in America."[13]

Another characteristic of the Limestone South was its diverse array of crops. The Bluegrass Region was well suited for growing hemp, which was used to produce rope, canvas, and bagging. Indeed, when the earliest white settlers arrived in Kentucky, they found huge canebrakes (thickets of a local species of bamboo) that indicated particularly fertile soils suitable for hemp production. Farmers and planters in the Nashville Basin increasingly focused on cotton, especially as cotton prices exploded in the 1850s. The farmers and planters of the Shenandoah Valley concentrated on wheat and livestock; the region would become known as the "breadbasket of the Confederacy" during the Civil War. Because of the diversity of crops grown in the Limestone South and the differing levels of improved land in the various subregions, it might be possible that crop choice (as opposed to environmental conditions) influenced the adoption of continuous cultivation. Such claims, however, cannot account for why tobacco farmers in the Bluegrass Region utilized continuous cultivation, while tobacco farmers on the ultisols of eastern Virginia adopted shifting cultivation. Similarly, it is not clear why cotton growers in the Nashville Region were more likely to use continuous cultivation than cotton growers in South Carolina, Mississippi, and Alabama. The sheer diversity of agricultural production in the Limestone South indicates that environmental factors (and not crop choice) largely determined the choice of cultivation regimes.

Cultivation Regimes, Population Growth, and Economic Development

Shifting cultivation and continuous cultivation constituted rational responses to differing environmental conditions, and both could be profitable. In terms of general economic development, however, continuous cultivation had a crucial advantage: it utilized far more land for productive economic activity. Shifting cultivation meant that most land remained unused; cropped acreage was like an island surrounded by an ocean of pine forests and scrublands. In continuous cultivation, agriculturalists farmed a far higher proportion of their land, resulting in a densely populated landscape that could support a larger rural population. In contrast, areas with shifting cultivation (consisting of mostly unimproved land) had low population densities. Shifting cultivation, however rational from the standpoint of an individual farmer or planter, came at the cost of limiting rural population and suppressing the development of markets for goods and services.

The Limestone South had a much different demographic trajectory than the rest of the South. Let us suppose that the Limestone Region had been consolidated into a single state, with the appropriate adjustments made to the populations of Kentucky, Virginia, and Tennessee. As Table 14.2 summarizes, the Limestone South would have been the smallest southern state in terms of square mileage, yet the second largest in terms of overall population. Only Virginia—with an area some four times greater than that of the Limestone South—would have had more people. The Limestone South would have easily surpassed any southern state in population per square mile. One might suppose that the Limestone South's substantial lead resulted from its higher urbanization rates (documented below), but even if we isolate *rural* population per square mile, the Limestone South was still ahead of other southern states. When compared to regions outside the South, the Limestone South's population density lagged well behind that of the New England and Mid-Atlantic states but was slightly ahead of that of the Midwest. Taken together, Ohio, Indiana, and Illinois had a population of forty persons per square mile, somewhat behind the Limestone South's forty-seven persons per square mile. Ohio's population density (fifty-seven persons per square mile) was higher than the Limestone South's, but the Buckeye State's population density was only marginally ahead of the Bluegrass Region's (fifty-two persons per square mile).

The big difference between the Midwest and the Limestone South, of course, was slavery. Since the Limestone South's dynamic economy generated substantial opportunities for a large and growing white population, slavery appeared somewhat less significant in percentage terms (26 percent of the region's population). While this percentage was somewhat lower than that of

Table 14.2. Population Statistics for the Limestone South and Selected States, 1860

State/Region	Total population (N)	Proportion slave (%)	Population per square mile (N)	Slaves per square mile (N)
Limestone South	**1,050,218**	**26.1**	**47.6**	**12.4**
Bluegrass	537,161	23.0	52.9	12.2
Nashville	268,406	36.1	48.8	17.6
Virginia	244,651	22.2	38.0	8.4
Midwest	**5,401,890**	——	**40.4**	——
Ohio	2,339,511	——	56.6	——
Indiana	1,350,428	——	37.3	——
Illinois	1,711,951	——	30.4	——
South	**10,259,016**	**36.2**	**12.8**	**4.6**
Kentucky	618,523	16.4	20.4	3.4
North Carolina	992,622	33.4	18.8	6.3
Tennessee	841,395	21.3	22.9	4.9
Virginia	1,351,667	36.3	20.8	30.9
Alabama	964,201	45.1	18.6	8.4
Georgia	1,057,286	43.7	17.9	7.8
Louisiana	708,002	46.8	14.8	6.9
Mississippi	791,305	55.3	16.6	9.2
South Carolina	703,708	57.2	22.6	12.9
Texas	604,215	30.2	2.3	0.68

Source: Census statistics from Geostat Center, University of Virginia Library, http://fisher.lib .virginia.edu/collections/stats/histcensus/.

the overall average of the South (37 percent), it was nevertheless higher than that of Confederate states such as Tennessee and Arkansas. If we examine the density of slaves per square mile, however, the Limestone South was a close second to South Carolina and substantially ahead of most of the Cotton South. In this respect, the Limestone South complicates Ira Berlin's well-known distinction between a society with slaves and a slave society. In Berlin's analysis, many societies have had some form of slavery, but only some of these have developed into full-blown slave societies complete with a powerful planting class and a legal and political system devoted to protecting slavery.[14] The Limestone South falls into its own ambiguous category. Slavery in the Limestone South generated a powerful planter elite (especially in the Bluegrass Region and the Nashville Region), but slaveholding planters coexisted with large numbers of yeoman farmers, artisans, merchants, and manufacturers. The

Limestone South, in other words, integrated a vibrant free-labor economy with a significant number of slaves.

The significant free-labor component of the Limestone South did little to undermine slavery. Demographically, slavery's importance fell slightly relative to that of the free population. As the demand for slaves in the cotton South increased in the 1840s and 1850s, more planters in Kentucky and Virginia sold "surplus" slaves in the domestic slave trade. By the 1850s, Louisville and Lexington had become major slave-trading centers, leading one historian to sardonically note that "Traders increased in Kentucky to such an extent that by 1860 there were as many slave dealers as there were mule traders."[15] Despite the growth of the slave trade, between 1840 and 1860, the overall slave population of the Limestone South increased by nearly 38,000 (Table 14.3). Most of that increase took place in the Nashville Basin, where demand for slave labor remained strong because of higher cotton prices. Even in the limestone areas of Kentucky and Virginia, the absolute number of slaves increased slightly. While the proportion of slaves declined from 29 percent of the population in 1840 to 27 percent of the population in 1860, this small drop hardly challenged the survival of the institution. By way of contrast, slavery in Maryland (where the institution was indeed on the verge of extinction) fell from 19 percent of the population in 1840 to 12 percent in 1860.

The continuing importance of slavery did not hinder the development of a substantial manufacturing sector devoted to processing the region's diverse array of crops. Hemp cultivation, which required the rich soils of the Bluegrass Region to be grown on a commercial basis, gave rise to a significant rope, cordage, and bagging industry. By 1860 the Bluegrass Region contained 157 such manufacturers, employing more than 2,000 workers.[16] Whisky distilling—a by-product of the plentiful corn and rye crops and the clear, pure water from limestone streams and wells—flourished throughout the Limestone South, most especially in the Bluegrass Region and Nashville Basin. In the limestone regions of Virginia, wheat production created a vibrant milling industry. As early as 1800, some 400 mills served the farmers and planters of the Shenandoah Valley.[17] The area's thriving agricultural economy also created a demand for more blacksmiths, more carpenters, more wheelwrights, more teamsters, and a variety of skilled and semiskilled workers. Data from the 1860 census confirm this point. In terms of value added—a measure of manufacturing output that subtracts the initial raw materials from the final value of the manufactured goods—

Table 14.3. Changes in Slave Population for the Limestone South, 1840–1860

Region	No. of slaves, 1840 (% of population)	No. of slaves, 1860 (% of population)
Total, Limestone South	**236,897 (29)**	**274,639 (26)**
Bluegrass Region	113,401 (28)	123,812 (23)
Nashville Basin	73,288 (30)	96,880 (36)
Limestone Virginia	50,208 (27)	53,947 (22)

Source: Census statistics at Geostat Center, University of Virginia Library, http://fisher.lib
.virginia.edu/collections/stats/histcensus/.

the Limestone South produced more than two times value added per person ($16.72 versus $7.72) than did the rest of the South. If one isolates the value of goods and services that depended on local demand, the gap becomes even wider. In terms of per capita value added in the building and construction trades, for example, the Limestone South produced five times more than the rest of the South ($2.81 versus forty-two cents); for consumer goods (such as boots and shoes, hats, books, and furniture), the Limestone South produced nearly four times as much as the rest of the South ($3.36 versus ninety cents).

This manufacturing base of the Limestone South was a far cry from the industrial economy of the Northeast, which produced a vast profusion of manufactured goods, including textiles, railroad equipment, and steam engines. The experience of the Limestone South does not necessarily demonstrate that slavery was compatible with the most advanced forms of nineteenth-century industrial capitalism. The experience of the Limestone South suggests, however, that slavery was not a barrier to the initial stages of industrialization that characterized much of the Midwest. The per capita value added for all manufacturing in the Midwest was just under $17, or about the same at that of the Limestone South.[18] The Limestone South and the Midwest also had similar rates of urbanization. Despite its relatively small geographic area, the Limestone South had thirteen census-defined urban areas (towns and cities with a population of at least 2,500) in 1860, which was more than any other slave state. Four of these cities—Louisville (population 68,033), Nashville (16,988), Covington (16,471), and Alexandria (12,654)—ranked among the nation's 100 largest.[19] The overall urbanization rate of 16 percent was far greater than any state in the Confederacy. The Bluegrass Region generated especially robust urban growth. Containing seven census-defined cities, the Bluegrass Region exceeded the national urbanization rate and was ahead of all midwestern states, including Ohio.

The Limestone South and Public Education

The economic success of the Limestone South presents historians with a fascinating case study. On the one hand, the region had all of the elements that northerners associated with the anti-enlightenment impulses of the South: a large population of slaves, politically powerful plantation owners, and a culture that valorized traditional masculine pursuits such as horse racing, drinking, and dueling.[20] Yet on the other, the planter culture that flourished in the Limestone South coexisted with more middle-class cultural norms revolving around improvement and progress. Historians have noted the limestone regions—like many urbanized areas in the South—developed along distinctly Whig lines as both planters and nonplanters embraced improved agriculture, town building, and internal improvements. Especially in towns and cities, civic associations of all types sprang into existence. Even in the smallish town of Winchester, Virginia, schools and libraries, churches, and theater flourished by the early nineteenth century.[21] One historian of the Bluegrass Region has even argued that by 1830, the "rise of the middle class" had eclipsed the earlier influence of the plantation gentry.[22] Given the presence of these progressive economic and cultural values, it seems possible that the Limestone South might have developed vigorous educational institutions despite the presence of slavery.

Despite high levels of economic development, the Limestone South fell behind the Midwest in developing a public school system. The Kentucky Bluegrass Region, the most developed of the Limestone South's three main areas, suggests that economic inequality tied to slavery discouraged investment in education. Kentucky's first "public" school system consisted of a system of land grant academies. The 1798 law established a series of academies throughout the state (one academy for each county) and provided each with a 6,000-acre land grant. The academy's trustees surveyed and then sold the land, which usually provided just enough money to construct a modest building. Tuition provided revenue for operating expenses (mostly the salaries of the teachers), but was well beyond the means of most ordinary families. Such a system, in the words of historian William E. Ellis, reflected the view of the planter elite that "the commonwealth needed trained ministers, businessmen, lawyers, and other public servants and not an educated general population. The prevailing slavocracy set the tone for Kentucky society and dominated state government until the end of the Civil War."[23]

A state-supported system of common schools eventually replaced the land grant academies, but for decades, public investment remained limited. Schools in the Bluegrass, like schools elsewhere in antebellum America, could potentially tap three sources of revenues: the state government, local property taxes, and student tuition.[24] In the North, state support and local property taxes usually kept tuition at local common schools (often called a "rate bill") to less than a dollar per term, which allowed many ordinary families to send their children to school.[25] Common schools in the Bluegrass Region, in contrast, could rely only on intermittent state support, with little or no revenue from local property taxes. To fund common schools, Kentuckians established a literary fund, which consisted of stock in state-charted banks. In 1830 the fund held securities amounting to $140,000, generating a paltry income of less than $8,500. As an 1830 legislative report noted, the endowment generated an income so small as to be "a useless expenditure of money."[26] Families were expected to provide the bulk of the school's operating expenses. With common schools charging high tuition rates, attendance for white children lagged far behind their northern counterparts. Not surprisingly, only 11,000 students attended common schools throughout the state.[27]

In 1838, the state established a more substantial school fund that consisted of $850,000 of "Bonus Funds" from the federal government. Instead of simply giving the money to the school fund, though, the state spent the money on other projects and then gave state bonds to the school fund. The state paid the interest on the bonds to the school fund, which theoretically generated $40,000 in revenue for common schools. The financially strapped state government, though, sometimes refused to pay the money, reasoning that obligations to other creditors took precedence. As the interest owed by the state government to the school fund accumulated to unsustainable levels, the General Assembly in 1845 authorized the governor to literally burn the state bonds in the school fund. With little in the way of state money, and rampant disorganization at every level, attendance at common schools lagged. As late as 1847, only 2,733 children in the Bluegrass Region (about 2 percent of the children ages five to nineteen years) attended common schools. As one Kentucky newspaper put it, "The Common School System of Kentucky is a mockery."[28]

A series of reforms beginning in 1848 helped transform Kentucky's common schools. Embarrassed by the financial shenanigans surrounding the school fund, the General Assembly restored the old bonds and added new ones, so that by 1851, the school fund held $1.2 million in assets. More important, the General Assembly authorized a statewide referendum on a property tax that would exclusively benefit common schools. In 1848, voters overwhelmingly approved the tax (which collected two cents for every $100 in property) by a margin of more than two to one. By 1851 the school fund had more than $133,000 in revenue to spend, and enrollments increased accordingly. Census records indicate that 43 percent of white children ages five to nineteen attended schools in Kentucky. Returns compiled from the Kentucky Office of Superintendent of Public Instruction, which required all school districts receiving state aid to report student attendance in common schools, indicated similar results. The 1851 report showed that in 967 rural school districts in the Bluegrass Region, 39 percent of children between five and sixteen years of age attended common schools.[29] That was better than in most southern states, but still well behind the rate for the rural North, where more than 63 percent of children ages five to nineteen years attended school in 1850. If the age range is adjusted to five to fourteen years, then the northern figures rises to 90 percent.[30]

A closer look at the data from the Superintendent's report suggests how slavery hindered a greater democratization of education. To receive state aid, every school district was required to send information on the number of children, the number of students attending school, the tuition the school charged for each term, and the length of the school year. In rural counties, Bluegrass common schools charged tuition averaging $2.78 per term (the median figure was $3.00), while non-Bluegrass schools charged $2.12 per term (with a median of $2.00). These tuition charges were significantly higher than those of northern schools, where tuition for common schools averaged $1.00 per term in places such as upstate New York. In the Inner Bluegrass—the particularly fertile counties in which plantation slavery was especially strong—common school tuitions could be particularly high. Fifty school districts in the Inner Bluegrass charged students $4.00 or more per term, which was the equivalent of the price of a private academy in the North.

Regression analysis confirms that counties with the most slaves tended to charge the most for common schools. The regression in Table 14.4 uses the average tuition for each county in 1851 as the dependent variable, while the independent variables include the percentage of slaves in a county's population and several dummy variables indicating the geographic location of each county. A one percentage point increase in slavery was associated with an increase of nearly two cents in tuition. Common schools in a county with

Table 14.4. Slavery, Geography, and School Tuition

Independent variable: Tuition for common schools in
Kentucky, 1851

Regression statistics		
Multiple R	0.68096627	
R^2	0.46371506	
Adjusted R^2	0.44064904	
Standard error	0.50370818	
No. of observations	98	

Dependent variables	Coefficients	t-Statistic
Intercept	2.01815474	14.01605
Percent enslaved	0.01789615	2.944732
Outer Bluegrass	0.29080652	2.313542
Appalachia	−0.317263	−2.28995
Inner Bluegrass	0.55806839	2.333242

Source: Compiled from the county returns published in *Report of
the Superintendent of Public Instruction to the General Assembly of
Kentucky* (Frankfort, Ky.: A. G. Hodges and Co., 1851).

40 percent of its population enslaved, the regression implies, charged nearly
eighty cents more per term than a county with no slaves. Even after the impact of slavery is held constant, residents in the Bluegrass paid a significantly
higher tuition than residents in other parts of the state. Schools in Appalachia—
serving a less wealthy and more dispersed population—charged significantly
less, as most families could not afford to pay high tuitions.[31] The lower tuition, however, meant that most Appalachian schools offered students a single
three-month term of instruction every academic year. Schools in the Bluegrass
Region, on the other hand, offered an average 5.3 months of instruction. Rather
than use state funds to help fully democratize education, Bluegrass residents
instead used state money to subsidize common schools that resembled private
academies.

The way state funding was structured helps account for why Bluegrass
residents used state funds to support expensive common schools. The Kentucky General Assembly specified that each district was to receive funding according to the total number of children in each district, not the number of
students in each district. This created the incentive for elites in each district
to charge high tuition so that each student attending school (presumably
from wealthy families who could afford to pay) reaped higher levels of state

support. To take one of the extreme examples, District One in Clark County (which was located in the particularly wealthy Inner Bluegrass) charged its students $8 for each three-month term, which was astoundingly high even by Kentucky standards. The district received sixty cents for each of fifty-three children residing in the district, which came to a total of $31.80. Only sixteen students attended the school, however, which meant that the state subsidized each student to the tune of $2.00. This Kentucky "common" school, in essence, was often an elite institution that received state support. Educational reformers noted the inequities of the state's funding model—the fewer students in each school, the greater the subsidy for each individual student. Distributing educational funds on a per-child basis, the state superintendent of instruction declared in 1851, is "evil and wrong," as it essentially gave school districts "a bounty for their indifference and neglect."[32]

The absence of local property taxes made the inequities in state funding particularly glaring. Northern localities commonly used a property tax to complement state subsidies to make schooling more available. The counties in the Bluegrass, blessed with high land values, could have easily done the same. According to the 1850 census, rural counties in the Bluegrass instituted local property taxes that raised nearly $16,000, which came to about twenty-five cents per student. Local property taxes varied widely—some rural counties had no tax and others raised fairly significant sums. Bourbon County, for instance, raised $1,800 via its property tax, which came to $1.66 per child in the county. Such a sum, in conjunction with state aid and more modest tuition costs, might have helped significantly expand common school enrollments. The high tuition costs in Bourbon schools ($3.26 per student), though, meant that this money would instead subsidize a small fraction of families that could afford the expensive tuition. Students who could already afford high tuition costs received an additional subsidy of $3.43 through local property taxes.

The lack of a more democratic enlightenment in the Limestone South had pernicious economic consequences. Economists have long held that investment in human and social capital is vital for long-run economic development. The increased investment in schooling in the North helped spur the "democratization of invention." Patenting rates were especially high in the industrial cities of the Northeast, where networks of inventors could find financing and markets for their work.[33] The same Northeastern states, of course, also provided many of their citizens with an inexpensive education, which provided a strong foundation for a culture of inventiveness. By the 1850s, networks of inventors began to appear in the Midwest. In 1860 alone, Ohioans filed 329 patents, or about 141 per million residents. Despite having a similar economic structure as Ohio, the residents of the Limestone South filed for fifty-two patents in 1860, or about 50 per million residents. Residents of Ohio's Cuyahoga County—which includes the city of Cleveland—filed forty-nine patents in 1860, a number almost equal to the total filed in the Limestone South.[34] Cleveland (population 43,417) was significantly smaller than Louisville (population 68,417) in 1860, yet its residents produced far more patents.

The relative dearth of patenting pointed to a long-term weakness of the Limestone South. For all of its flourishing cities, towns, and manufacturing, the Limestone South experienced significantly less population growth. Whereas the Midwest was attracting significant numbers of immigrants, the Limestone South fared less well. Between 1840 and 1860 the population of the Limestone South increased 24.7 percent, certainly a respectable number that was far better than that for tidewater Virginia, low-country South Carolina, and other more settled areas of the South. The Limestone South, however, lagged significantly behind Ohio, where the population increased 54 percent over the same period. No wonder that a number of residents in the Limestone South (especially in the Bluegrass Region and the limestone regions of Virginia) feared that slavery was undermining the region's long-term economic vitality! According to one historian, "it was almost a cliché in antebellum Kentucky to call slavery a drain on the state's economy and argue that Kentucky's overall economic condition could be improved by an exclusive reliance on free white labor."[35]

Education, Democracy, and the Republican Critique of Slavery

Bluegrass residents had every opportunity to dramatically increase common school attendance along northern lines but instead supported policies that restricted educational opportunity. The slaveholders who dominated Kentucky educational policy believed that "reforming" education meant subsidizing elite institutions so that a relatively narrow group of men could provide the state with enlightened leadership. An 1830 legislative report, for example, advocated using the limited resources of the state's Literary Fund to subsidize colleges and academies. Giving academies money to buy the latest scientific instruments, for example, would allow academies to train teachers so as to "render essential aid in the establishment of common schools."[36] The flourishing academies would then set an example for the rest of a county, so that "public attention at least will be aroused," and eventually voters would support a local property tax. In similar fashion, subsidizing colleges was important to keep the rich ("who will at any expense, give their children a liberal education") from sending their sons out of state. These young men, in turn, would become "teachers of common schools, and diffuse through society the blessings of popular education."[37] So long as the elite were properly educated, schooling for the masses would take care of itself.

Kentuckians viewed common schools that lacked guidance from elites with considerable skepticism. As part of the 1830 report, the legislature commissioned Benjamin Peers to examine northern common schools to find a suitable model for Kentucky. While extolling state support for common schools, Peers nevertheless emphasized the importance of local enthusiasm. That support, Peers asserted, could come about only through the efforts of respectable gentlemen. He explained that the success of the common schools in Worcester and Springfield, Massachusetts, for example, resulted from gentlemen patrons "who spared no pains to awaken the interest of the people to the education of their children, enforced with considerable rigor the statute requiring the examination of instructors, assisted and encouraged the teachers by advice and frequent visits, and paid particular attention to procuring the composition and distribution of the best school books." Universal education in the North, Peers argued, began at the top. Indeed, Peers worried that northerners had built too many schools without sufficient thought to the quality of their schools. Northern states had succeeded in providing nearly universal education, but only through "the multiplication of *bad* schools."[38] Teachers needed to be better paid, Peers claimed, so that more respectable young men would make it a career.

Instead of generating calls for greater public support for common schools so that teachers could receive more pay, these arguments reinforced calls to subsidize elite institutions. Peers himself recommended a scheme in which each county in Kentucky selected "one young man" to receive state support "for a course of study and practice for the business of teaching," thus setting an example for others to follow.[39] Without more respectable gentlemen in education, common schools teachers would be unworthy of state support. Arguing against a provision that would mandate state support for education in the 1850 Kentucky state constitution, Ben Hardin of Nelson County (in the Outer Bluegrass) argued that "The worse taught child in the world, is he who is taught by a miserable country school master." Rather than fund common schools, Hardin recommended that tax revenue "should be appropriated to the endowment of colleges and academies, for the education of young men capable of teaching, than to be thrown away, as here proposed."[40] The class bias in Hardin's argument is obvious, but it reflected the lived reality of many Bluegrass planters, whose children often attended academies or expensive public schools.[41] Bluegrass residents seemed to have embraced a slaveholder's vision of enlightenment that explicitly started at the top before trickling its way down to the general population.

Such a vision was heresy to antislavery northerners. While northerners celebrated how their region democratized learning and education, they lambasted the lack of education in the South. "Ignorant" was a favorite epithet of Republicans describing nonslaveholding whites. They attributed the lack of educational opportunities to the domineering spirit of large slaveholders, who allegedly denied educational opportunities to protect their own political power. According to the New York lawyer William Jay, slaveholders depended "on the acquiescence of the major part of the white inhabitants to their domination," so slaveholders had no interest "to promote the intellectual improvement of the inferior class."[42] Similarly, an anonymous 1853 contributor to the antislavery periodical *The Independent* equated nonslaveholding white southerners with "the serfs of Russia. A large part of them are unable to read and write." Slaveholders did "their political thinking and reading for them."[43] The situation for slaves, antislavery northerners made clear, was even worse. In one of the subplots of Harriet Beecher Stowe's *Uncle Tom's Cabin*, George Harris, a Kentucky slave, is hired out by his master to work in a rope and cordage factory. George invents a machine for cleaning hemp, which "displayed quite as much mechanical genius as Whitney's cotton-gin." Despite the desperate entreaties of the factory owner, the enraged master, whose own status has been threatened by George's invention, takes George home to the plantation and forces him to work "the meanest drudgery of the farm."[44] George's eventual escape highlighted Stowe's point that slavery, education, and opportunity could not coexist.

Northerners celebrated how widespread access to educational institutions helped create a sense of economic opportunity and upward mobility that was a hallmark of free-labor ideology. Abraham Lincoln was a case in point. The poverty of Lincoln's childhood—as well as the aloofness of his father to educational pursuits—meant that Lincoln had a rather rudimentary formal education. Perhaps with his own experience in mind, he consistently advocated higher funding for public schools. In his very first political address, Lincoln told the voters of Sangamon County, Illinois, that "I desire to see the time

when education, and by its means, morality, sobriety, enterprise and industry, shall become much more general than at present, and should be gratified
to have it in my power to contribute something to the advancement of any
measure which might have a tendency to accelerate the happy period."[45] Much
later in his political career, Lincoln saw education as a central pillar of the
North's free-labor economy. "The old general rule was that *educated* people did
not perform manual labor," Lincoln argued in 1859 in an address before the
Wisconsin State Agricultural Society. Proslavery theorists "assumed that labor
and education are impossible"—they believed, in fact, that education for workers was "pernicious and dangerous." The North's free-labor system, on the
other hand, sought to unite the work of the hands with the work of the mind.
"Free Labor insists on universal education," Lincoln concluded.[46]

Lincoln linked education to the North's inventive and industrial economy. Innovation, he told audiences in an 1859 speech entitled "Discoveries and
Inventions," came about through "*observation, reflection,* and *trial*" that had
become ingrained as "a *habit*."[47] Theses habits in turn depended on reading,
writing, and education to end the "slavery of the mind." Lincoln was the
living embodiment of a mind-set that valued creativity and curiosity. He
delighted in mechanical innovation; as a lawyer riding with the Illinois circuit court, he visited farmers to witness demonstrations of the latest farm
implements. Such curiosity led to practical results. In 1849 Lincoln patented
a "Manner of Buoying Vessels," which he hoped would allow steamships to
navigate shallow water.[48] Although Lincoln's invention never saw practical
use, the experience reinforced his believe that all workers could become innovators through education. Farmers, for example, could use "book-learning"
to cultivate not only crops but "a relish, and facility" for discovering and
pursuing unsolved problems. Farmers, he told the Wisconsin Agricultural
Society, should study botany, chemistry, and "the mechanical branches of
Natural Philosophy" to turn their occupation into an intellectual pursuit. A
farmer trained "in the country school, or higher school" could find an "ex-
haustless source of profitable enjoyment. Every blade of grass is a study; and
to produce two, where there was but one, is both a profit and a pleasure."[49]

The Limestone South and the Spread of Slavery

In many respects, the Limestone South's vibrant economy undermined Republican arguments that slavery *invariably* led to destructive farming prac-

tices, that slavery *invariably* limited population growth, and that slavery *invariably* deterred the growth of cities and manufacturing. The Limestone South's history certainly indicates that there was a definite ceiling on how far a slave economy could advance, but that ceiling was far higher than what many critics of slavery imagined.[50] With both a substantial population of slaves and a prosperous, free-labor economy, the Limestone South defied the conventional categories of the antebellum period. The Limestone South was surely exceptional. It was exceptional, however, because of its unique geography, and not in the degree of its commitment to slavery. If other areas of the South had had the same rich soils and moderate climate of the Limestone Region, they would have likely experienced much higher levels of economic development despite the presence of slavery.

On a deeper level, the Limestone South suggests that antislavery northerners had good reason to fear that slavery could spread throughout the Midwest and West. There were no immutable economic factors or geographic barriers that would have made slavery unworkable in Ohio and elsewhere in the Midwest. Slavery as an institution could spread far beyond the plantations of the southern periphery; the evidence suggests that it could very well have become integrated into the midwestern economy. Contemporaries often assumed that northerners abolished slavery in their own states because the institution was not economically viable in an economy of smaller farms and more cities, industry, and commerce. The experience of the Limestone South suggests that a free-labor economy could coexist in areas where slavery was still significant. Long-term developmental problems aside, the economy of the Limestone South reinforces Gavin Wright's argument that slavery, as an expropriation of labor from slaves to masters, could benefit slaveholders in a wide variety of contexts.[51] If slaveholders in the Bluegrass Region could expropriate the labor of tens of thousands of slaves, there was no climatic, geographic, or environmental reason why Ohioans could not. Slavery was very much a political choice.

That slavery was a political choice brings us back to Lincoln and the Republicans. Lincoln was well aware that slavery flourished in the Kentucky Bluegrass Region, with soils and a climate similar to Ohio's. Speaking in Cincinnati, Lincoln asked why Ohio was free of slavery while Kentucky was "entirely covered" with it. Was it climate? "No!" Lincoln emphatically answered. "A portion of Kentucky was further north than this portion of Ohio." How about soils? "No! There is nothing in the soil of one more favorable to slave labor than the other."[52] Lincoln credited the Northwest Ordinance with

keeping slavery out of Ohio. The Northwest Ordinance was a conscious political decision—one of many, according to Lincoln, made by the founding
fathers to limit the spread of slavery and set the stage for its ultimate extinction. Indeed, even after the Northwest Ordinance had been passed, it took a
substantial antislavery movement in Illinois (Lincoln's own state) to prevent
the institution from taking root. And if slavery could have taken root and
spread throughout the Midwest, it could have defined the economic and political mainstream of the nation. "A house divided against itself cannot stand,"
Lincoln famously declared in 1858. Speaking in the aftermath of the *Dred Scott*
decision, which invalidated the Missouri Compromise, Lincoln raised the possibility that slavery might spread throughout the nation. "Either the *opponents* of slavery, will arrest the further spread of it, and place it where the public
mind shall rest in the belief that it is in the course of ultimate extinction; or
its *advocates* will push it forward, till it shall become alike lawful in *all* the
States, *old* as well as *new*—*North* as well as *South*."[53]

If slavery had indeed become "lawful in *all* states," the experience of the
Limestone South indicates that it might have stunted the growth of educational institutions and technological networks that were at the heart of the
northern economy. It should be kept in mind that wealthy slaveholding
planters were a distinct minority in the Limestone South, yet they nevertheless exerted profound political power. Even the presence of a small number of
planters might have influenced the development of school systems. Social
mobility—the hallmark of the Republican economic vision—might have become significantly more limited for ordinary white families. Perhaps this is
the answer to the paradox of why a political party representing the interests
of capitalism so ardently opposed slavery, even though slavery was in many
ways foundational to the nineteenth-century economy. Most northern bankers and merchants were perfectly content to make profits from the cotton
trade; most northern farmers had no qualms about supplying southern markets with corn, beef, and pork; and most northern manufacturers cared little
if they sold their products to slaveholders. It was one thing to depend on
southern markets but quite another to live in a nation, state, or locality where
slaveholders sets the rules governing access to education and opportunity.
Northern farmers, artisans, and laborers instinctively feared that the inequality inherent in slavery would spell the end to the creative core of the
northern economy. The educational system of the Limestone South suggests
that they were right.

NOTES

INTRODUCTION

1. The label comes from Don E. Fehrenbacher, *The Slaveholding Republic: An Account of the United States Government's Relations to Slavery*, ed. Ward M. McAfee (New York: Oxford University Press, 2001), but builds on such foundations as Nathan I. Huggins, "The Deforming Mirror of Truth: Slavery and the Master Narrative of American History," *Radical History Review* 49 (1991): 25–48; Edmund Morgan, *American Slavery–American Freedom: The Ordeal of Colonial Virginia* (New York: W. W. Norton, 1975); Peter H. Wood, "Slave Labor Camps in Early America: Overcoming Denial and Discovering the Gulag," in *Inequality in Early America*, ed. Carla G. Pestana and Sharon V. Salinger (Hanover, N.H.: University Press of New England, 1999), 222–38; Barbara J. Fields, "Slavery, Race, and Ideology in the U.S.A.," *New Left Review* 181 (May/June 1990): 95–118; David Roediger, *Wages of Whiteness: Race and the Making of the American Working Class* (New York: Verso, 1991); and Evelyn Nakano Glenn, *Unequal Freedom: How Race and Gender Shaped American Citizenship and Labor* (Cambridge, Mass.: Harvard University Press, 2002). This overall reevaluation of American history is nicely assessed in Russell R. Menard, "'Capitalism and Slavery': Personal Reflections on Eric Williams and Reconstruction of Early American History," in *The World Turned Upside-Down: The State of Eighteenth-Century American Studies at the Beginning of the Twenty-First Century*, ed. Michael V. Kennedy and William G. Shade (Bethlehem, Pa.: Lehigh University Press, 2001), 321–33.

2. The most ambitious books on this front are Walter Johnson, *River of Dark Dreams: Slavery and Empire in the Cotton Kingdom* (Cambridge, Mass.: Harvard University Press, 2013); Greg Grandin, *The Empire of Necessity: Slavery, Freedom, and Deception in the New World* (New York: Metropolitan Books, 2014); Edward E. Baptist, *The Half Has Never Been Told: Slavery and the Making of American Capitalism* (New York: Basic Books, 2014); and Sven Beckert, *Empire of Cotton: A Global History* (New York: Knopf, 2014). The larger move in the scholarship is reviewed by Julia Ott, "Slaves: The Capital That Made Capitalism," *Public Seminar* 1 (Summer 2014), online; Timothy Shenk, "Apostles of Growth," *Nation*, November 24, 2014; Scott Reynolds Nelson, "Who Put Their Capitalism in My Slavery?," *Journal of the Civil War Era* 5 (June 2015): 289–310; Matthew Pratt Guterl, "Slavery and Capitalism: A Review Essay," *Journal of Southern History* 81 (May 2015): 405–20; and John J. Clegg, "Capitalism and Slavery," *Critical Historical Studies* 2 (Fall 2015): 281–304.

3. *General Convention, of Agriculturalists and Manufacturers, and Others Friendly to the Encouragement and Support of the Domestic Industry of the United States* (Baltimore, 1827), 15; *Proceedings of the Fourth New-England Anti-Slavery Convention, Held in Boston, May 30, 31, and*

June 1 and 2, 1837 (Boston: Isaac Knapp, 1837), 45; Alexander McCaine, *Slavery Defended from Scripture, Against the Attacks of the Abolitionists, in a Speech Delivered Before the General Conference of the Methodist Protestant Church, in Baltimore, 1842* (Baltimore: William Woody, 1842), 8–9; *Statistics of the Woollen Manufactories in the United States* (New York: W. H. Graham, 1845), 33–39; William Gregg, *Essays on Domestic Industry: or, An Enquiry into the Expediency of Establishing Cotton Manufactures in South Carolina* (Charleston: Burges and James, 1845), 50; John Forsyth, "The North and the South," *De Bow's Review* 17 (October 1854): 365.

4. Orpheus T. Lanphear, *A Discourse Delivered at the United Service of the Congregational Churches, Fast Day, April 10th, 1856* (Lowell, Mass.: Brown and Morey, 1856), 31–32; Thomas Prentice Kettell, *Southern Wealth and Northern Profits . . .* (New York: G. W. and J. A. Wood, 1860); Samuel Powell, *Notes on "Southern Wealth and Northern Profits"* (Philadelphia: C. Sherman and Son, 1861), 9; George McHenry, *The Cotton Trade: Its Bearing upon the Prosperity of Great Britain and Commerce of the American Republics, considered in connection with the system of Negro Slavery in the Confederate States* (London: Saunders, Otley, and Co., 1863), 109.

5. From the vantage of the lower Mississippi Valley in the wake of the Louisiana Purchase, Walter Johnson urges an analysis that "begins from the premise that in actual historical fact there was no nineteenth-century capitalism without slavery. However else industrial capitalism *might* have developed in the absence of slave-produced cotton and Southern capital markets, it did not develop that way." See Johnson, *River of Dark Dreams*, 254.

6. Eric Williams, *Capitalism and Slavery* (Chapel Hill: University of North Carolina Press, 1944); Barbara L. Solow and Stanley L. Engerman, eds., *British Capitalism and Caribbean Slavery: The Legacy of Eric Williams* (New York: Cambridge University Press, 1987); Cedric J. Robinson, "Capitalism, Slavery, and Bourgeois Historiography," *History Workshop Journal* 23 (Spring 1987): 122–40; Heather Cateau and S. H. H. Carrington, eds., *Capitalism and Slavery Fifty Years Later: Eric Eustace Williams—a Reassessment of the Man and His Work* (New York: Peter Lang, 2000); Christopher Leslie Brown, *Moral Capital: Foundations of British Abolitionism* (Chapel Hill: University of North Carolina Press for the Omohundro Institute of Early American History and Culture, 2006); David Ryden, *West Indian Slavery and British Abolition, 1783–1807* (New York: Cambridge University Press, 2009); Seymour Drescher, *Econocide: British Slavery in the Era of Abolition*, 2nd ed. (Chapel Hill: University of North Carolina Press, 2010); Barbara L. Solow, reply by David Brion Davis, "The British and the Slave Trade," *New York Review of Books*, January 12, 2012. See also William Darity, Jr., "British Industry and the West Indies Plantations," *Social Science History* 14 (Spring 1990): 117–49; Darity, "From the Dissertation to *Capitalism and Slavery*: Did Williams' Abolition Thesis Change?," in Eric Williams, *The Economic Aspect of the Abolition of the West Indian Slave Trade and Slavery*, ed. Dale Tomich (Lanham, Md.: Rowman and Littlefield, 2014), xi–xxiv.

7. Sidney Mintz, *Sweetness and Power: The Place of Sugar in Modern History* (New York: Viking, 1985); Joseph E. Inikori, *Africans and the Industrial Revolution in England: A Study in International Trade and Economic Development* (New York: Cambridge University Press, 2002); Nicholas Draper, *The Price of Emancipation: Slave-Ownership, Compensation and British Society at the End of Slavery* (New York: Cambridge University Press, 2010); Catherine Hall, Nicholas Draper, Keith McClelland, Katie Donington, and Rachel Lang, *Legacies of British Slave-Ownership: Colonial Slavery and the Formation of Victorian Britain* (New York: Cambridge University Press, 2014). One recent if little noticed effort to tell the broadest story of American economic development through slavery is Gene Dattel, *Cotton and Race in the Making of America: The Human Costs of Economic Power* (Chicago: Ivan R. Dee, 2009).

8. Philip S. Foner, *Business & Slavery: The New York Merchants and the Irrepressible Conflict* (Chapel Hill: University of North Carolina Press, 1941); Douglass C. North, *The Economic Growth of the United States, 1790–1860* (Englewood Cliffs, N.J.: Prentice-Hall, 1961); Barrington Moore, *Social Origins of Dictatorship and Democracy: Lord and Peasant in the Making of the Modern World* (Boston: Beacon Press, 1966), 116; James Oakes, *The Ruling Race: A History of American Slaveholders* (New York: Knopf, 1982); John Ashworth, *Slavery, Capitalism, and Politics in the Antebellum Republic*, vol. 1 (New York: Cambridge University Press, 1995); Adrienne Davis, " 'Don't Let Nobody Bother Yo' Principle': The Sexual Economy of American Slavery," in *Sister Circle: Black Women and Work*, ed. Sharon Harley and the Black Women and Work Collective (New Brunswick, N.J.: Rutgers University Press, 2002), 103–27; Robin L. Einhorn, *American Taxation, American Slavery* (Chicago: University of Chicago Press, 2006); Ronald Bailey, "The Slave(ry) Trade and the Development of Capitalism in the United States: The Textile Industry in New England," *Social Science History* 14 (Fall 1990): 373–414; David Waldstreicher, *Runaway America: Benjamin Franklin, Slavery, and the American Revolution* (New York: Hill and Wang, 2004). The most recent addition is Calvin Schermerhorn, *The Business of Slavery and the Rise of American Capitalism, 1815–1860* (New Haven, Conn.: Yale University Press, 2015). For a historiographical overview, see Seth Rockman, "The Unfree Origins of American Capitalism," in *The Economy of Early America: Historical Perspectives and New Directions*, ed. Cathy Matson (University Park: Pennsylvania State University Press, 2006), 335–61.

9. The intense cyberspace reaction to the *Economist*'s dismissive review of Baptist's book in the fall of 2014 brought slavery's importance to capitalism before readers of *Salon*, *Politico*, *Jacobin*, and the *New York Times*: "Blood Cotton," *Economist*, September 6, 2014; Baptist, "What the *Economist* doesn't get about Slavery—and My Book," *Politico*, September 7, 2014, http://www.politico.com/magazine/story/2014/09/economist-review-slavery-110687_full.html; Ellora Derenoncourt, "The Slaver's Objectivity," *Jacobin*, September 10, 2014, https://www.jacobinmag.com/2014/09/the-slavers-objectivity/; Felicia R. Lee, "Harvesting Cotton-Field Capitalism," *New York Times*, October 4, 2014; Michael Schulson, " 'It's Symbolic Annihilation of History, and It's Done for a Purpose. It Really Enforces White Supremacy': Edward Baptist on the Lies We Tell about Slavery," *Salon*, November 9, 2014, http://www.salon.com/2014/11/09/it's_symbolic_annihilation_of_history_and_it's_done_for_a_purpose_it_really_enforces_white_supremacy_edward_baptist_on_the_lies_we_tell_about_slavery/; Beckert, "How Cotton Remade the World," *Politico*, January 30, 2015, http://www.politico.com/magazine/story/2015/01/civil-war-cotton-capitalism-114776.html#.VcDlSIuCiwI; Beckert, "Slavery and Capitalism," *Chronicle of Higher Education*, December 12, 2014; Beckert, "America's First Big Business? Not the Railroads, But Slavery," *PBS Newshour*, February 12, 2015, http://www.pbs.org/newshour/making-sense/americas-first-big-business-railroads-slavery/; Beckert, "How the West Got Rich and Modern Capitalism Was Born," *PBS Newshour*, February 13, 2015, http://www.pbs.org/newshour/making-sense/west-got-rich-modern-capitalism-born/; Greg Grandin, "Capitalism and Slavery," *Nation*, May 1, 2015, http://www.thenation.com/article/capitalism-and-slavery/.

10. Robin L. Einhorn, "Slavery," *Enterprise & Society* 9 (September 2008): 491. Scholars in other social sciences are also in the process of centering slavery in institutional development. See Graziella Bertocchi and Arcangelo Dimico, "Slavery, Education, and Inequality," *European Economic Review* 70 (October 2014): 197–209; Suresh Naidu, "Suffrage, Schooling, and Sorting in the Post-Bellum U.S. South," NBER Working Paper 18129 (Cambridge, Mass.: National Bureau of Economic Research, June 2012); Kenneth Chay and Kaivan Munshi, "Black

Networks After Emancipation: Evidence from Reconstruction and the Great Migration," draft paper (December 2013), http://www.histecon.magd.cam.ac.uk/km/greatmigrationdec2013text .pdf (accessed 20 July 2015); Avidit Acharya, Matthew Blackwell, and Maya Sen, "Southern Slavery and Its Political Legacy: How America's Peculiar Institution Continues to Affect American Politics Today," unpublished manuscript; and Jean-François Mouhot, "Past Connections and Present Similarities in Slave Ownership and Fossil Fuel Usage," *Climate Change* 105 (March 2011): 329–55.

11. Randall Robinson, *The Debt: What America Owes to Blacks* (New York: Dutton, 2000); Eric Foner, "Slavery's Fellow Travelers," *New York Times*, July 13, 2000; Brent Staples, "How Slavery Fueled Business in the North," *New York Times*, July 24, 2000; "Forum: Making the Case for Racial Reparations," *Harper's Magazine*, November 2000, 37–51; "Slavery Era Insurance Registry," California Department of Insurance, http://www.insurance.ca.gov/01 -consumers/150-other-prog/10-seir/ (accessed December 11, 2015); Tamar Lewin, "Calls for Slavery Restitution Getting Louder," *New York Times*, June 4, 2001; Raymond A. Winbush, ed., *Should America Pay? Slavery and the Raging Debate on Reparations* (New York: Amistad, 2003); "An Update on Corporate Slavery," *New York Times*, January 31, 2005; Robin Sidel, "A Historian's Quest Links J.P. Morgan to Slave Ownership," *Wall Street Journal*, May 10, 2005; Darryl Fears, "Seeking More than Apologies for Slavery," *Washington Post*, June 20, 2005; J.P. Morgan Chase Press Release, January 20, 2005 (in authors' possession); Wachovia press release, June 1, 2005 (in authors' possession); *Slavery & Justice: Report of the Brown University Steering Committee on Slavery and Justice* (Providence, R.I.: Brown University, 2006), http://www.brown .edu/Research/Slavery_Justice/documents/SlaveryAndJustice.pdf. For historical perspective, see Martha Biondi, "The Rise of the Reparations Movement," *Radical History Review* 87 (Fall 2003): 5–18. For a compendium of primary documents, see Alfred L. Brophy, *Reparations: Pro and Con* (New York: Oxford University Press, 2006).

12. Ta-Nehisi Coates, "The Case for Reparations," *Atlantic*, June 2014; "Room for Debate: Are Reparations Due African-Americans?," *New York Times*, June 9, 2014, http://www .nytimes.com/roomfordebate/2014/06/08/are-reparations-due-to-african-americans; Hilary McD. Beckles, *Britain's Black Debt: Reparations for Slavery and Native Genocide* (Mona: University of West Indies Press, 2013); Jonathan Holloway, "Caribbean Payback," *Foreign Affairs*, April 2, 2014, http://www.foreignaffairs.com/articles/141090/jonathan-holloway/caribbean -payback; Don Rojas, "Will the Caribbean Reparations Initiative Inspire a Revitalization of the US Movement?," *Nation*, May 23, 2014, http://www.thenation.com/article/179990/will -caribbean-reparations-initiative-inspire-revitalization-us-movement#.

13. Charles Blow, "Escaping Slavery," *New York Times*, January 5, 2013; Larry Wilmore, "Denunciation Proclamation," *The Daily Show with Jon Stewart*, video (6:05), February 24, 2014, http://thedailyshow.cc.com/videos/fr7m1i/denunciation-proclamation; Christopher Suellentrop, "Slavery as New Focus for a Game: *Assassin's Creed: Liberation* Examines Colonial Blacks," *New York Times*, January 28, 2014; Brooks Barnes and Michael Cieply, "'12 Years' Enjoys a Seemingly Narrow Victory," *New York Times*, March 4, 2014; N. D. B. Connolly, "Black Culture Is Not the Problem," *New York Times*, May 1, 2015; Jelani Cobb, "Last Battles," *New Yorker*, July 6, 2015; Nshira Turkson, "The Necessary Recklessness of Campus Protests," *Atlantic*, December 10, 2015, http://www.theatlantic.com/politics/archive/2015/12/campus -protests/419505/.

14. "Complicity: How Connecticut Chained Itself to Slavery," *Hartford Courant*, September 29, 2002; expanded as Anne Farrow, Joel Lang, and Jennifer Frank, *Complicity: How the North Promoted, Prolonged, and Profited from Slavery* (New York: Ballantine Books, 2005).

Paul Davis, "The Unrighteous Traffick: Rhode Island's Slave History," seven-article series, *Providence Journal*, March 12–19, 2006. For the New-York Historical Society's 2005 exhibition, see http://www.slaveryinnewyork.org; for *Traces of the Trade* and its screenings, see http://www.tracingcenter.org/general-programs/screenings-and-events/ (accessed June 8, 2014). On historical home museums, exhibitions, and historical societies, see Linda Matchan, "One House, Two Histories in Medford," *Boston Globe*, September 3, 2013; Edward Rothstein, "When Slavery and Its Foes Thrived in Brooklyn," *New York Times*, January 17, 2014; Roberta Smith, "Sugar? Sure, But Salted with Meaning," *New York Times*, May 12, 2014; "History and Human Rights Perspectives on Connecticut: Sagas, Scandals, Spirits, and Slavery," Haddam (Conn.) Historical Society Lecture Series, April–October 2014. The scholarly literature on slavery in the North is now well developed: Joanne Pope Melish, *Disowning Slavery: Gradual Emancipation and "Race" in New England, 1780–1860* (Ithaca, N.Y.: Cornell University Press, 1998); Martin H. Blatt and David Roediger, eds., *The Meaning of Slavery in the North* (New York: Garland Publishing, 1998); Ira Berlin and Leslie Harris, eds., *Slavery in New York* (New York: New Press, 2005); C. S. Manegold, *Ten Hills Farm: The Forgotten History of Slavery in the North* (Princeton, N.J.: Princeton University Press, 2010); James J. Gigantino II, *The Ragged Road to Abolition: Slavery and Freedom in New Jersey, 1775–1865* (Philadelphia: University of Pennsylvania Press, 2014).

15. W. E. B. DuBois, *The Suppression of the African Slave-Trade to the United States of America, 1638–1870* (New York: Longmans, Green, and Co., 1896), 194; Stuart Hall, "Race, Articulation and Societies Structured in Dominance," in *Sociological Theories: Race and Colonialism* (Paris: UNESCO Publishing, 1980); Eric Wolf, *Europe and the People Without History* (Berkeley: University of California Press, 1982); Robin Blackburn, *The Making of New World Slavery: From the Baroque to the Modern, 1492–1800* (New York: Verso, 1997); Cedric J. Robinson, *Black Marxism: The Making of the Black Radical Tradition* (1983; reprint Chapel Hill: University of North Carolina Press, 2000).

16. Kenneth Pomeranz, *The Great Divergence: China, Europe, and the Making of the Modern World Economy* (Princeton, N.J.: Princeton University Press, 2000). See also Andre Gunder Frank, *ReOrient: Global Economy in the Asian Age* (Berkeley: University of California Press, 1998); Robert Marks, *Origins of the Modern World: A Global and Ecological Narrative* (Lanham, Md.: Rowman and Littlefield, 2002).

17. For example, Julie Greene, *The Canal Builders: Making America's Empire at the Panama Canal* (New York: Penguin, 2009); Greg Grandin, *Fordlandia: The Rise and Fall of Henry Ford's Forgotten Jungle City* (New York: Metropolitan Books, 2009); Daniel E. Bender and Jana K. Lipman, eds., *Making the Empire Work: Labor and United States Imperialism* (New York: NYU Press, 2015).

18. For overviews of the new history of capitalism, see Sven Beckert, "History of American Capitalism," in *American History Now*, ed. Eric Foner and Lisa McGirr (Philadelphia: Temple University Press for the American Historical Association, 2011), 314–35; Jeffrey Sklansky, "The Elusive Sovereign: New Intellectual and Social Histories of Capitalism," *Modern Intellectual History* 9 (2012): 233–48; and Seth Rockman, "What Makes the History of Capitalism Newsworthy?," *Journal of the Early Republic* 34 (Fall 2014): 439–66.

19. As Walter Johnson has argued, the tendency to generalize about capitalism from its most exceptional manifestation, the factory landscape of nineteenth-century England, places too much attention on wage labor as the system's distinguishing characteristic and obscures capitalism's reliance on a spectrum of exploitative labor relations. See Johnson, "The Pedestal and the Veil: Rethinking the Capitalism/Slavery Question," *Journal of the Early Republic* 24

(Summer 2004): 299–308, and idem, *River of Dark Dreams*, 252–54; John Tutino, *Making a New World: Founding Capitalism in the Bajío and Spanish North America* (Durham, N.C.: Duke University Press, 2011); Peter Linebaugh and Marcus Rediker, *The Many-Headed Hydra: Sailors, Slaves, Commoners, and the Hidden History of the Revolutionary Atlantic* (Boston: Beacon Press, 2000); and Marcel van der Linden, "Re-constructing the Origins of Modern Labor Management," *Labor History* 51 (November 2010): 509–22.

20. Ian Baucom, *Specters of the Atlantic: Finance Capital, Slavery, and the Philosophy of History* (Durham, N.C.: Duke University Press, 2005); Jonathan Levy, *Freaks of Fortune: The Emerging World of Capitalism and Risk in America* (Cambridge, Mass.: Harvard University Press, 2012), 21–59; Sharon Ann Murphy, "Securing Human Property: Slavery, Life Insurance, and Industrialization in the Upper South," *Journal of the Early Republic* 25 (Winter 2005): 615–52; Michael Ralph, "'Life . . . in the Midst of Death': Notes on the Relationship between Slave Insurance, Life Insurance, and Disability," *Disability Studies Quarterly* 32, no. 3 (2012): online journal; Anita Rupprecht, "Excessive Memories: Slavery, Insurance, and Resistance," *History Workshop Journal* 64 (Autumn 2007): 6–28; Carl Wennerlind, *Casualties of Credit: The English Financial Revolution, 1620–1720* (Cambridge Mass.: Harvard University Press, 2011), 161–234; Scott Reynolds Nelson, *A Nation of Deadbeats: An Uncommon History of America's Financial Disasters* (New York: Alfred A. Knopf, 2012), 126–48; Jessica M. Lepler, *The Many Panics of 1837: People, Politics, and the Creation of a Transatlantic Financial Crisis* (New York: Cambridge University Press, 2013); Edward E. Baptist, "Toxic Debt, Liar Loans, Collateralized Human Beings, and the Panic of 1837," in *Capitalism Takes Command: The Social Transformation of Nineteenth-Century America*, ed. Michael Zakim and Gary J. Kornblith (Chicago: University of Chicago Press, 2012), 69–92.

21. The reinforcing relationship of capitalism and antislavery found its most persuasive articulation in Thomas L. Haskell, "Capitalism and the Origins of the Humanitarian Sensibility, Part I," *American Historical Review* 90 (April 1985): 339–61, reprinted alongside contributions from David Brion Davis and John Ashworth in *The Antislavery Debate: Capitalism and Abolitionism as a Problem in Historical Interpretation*, ed. Thomas Bender (Berkeley: University of California Press, 1992).

22. Robert William Fogel and Stanley L. Engerman, *Time on the Cross: The Economics of American Negro Slavery* (Boston: Little, Brown, 1974); Robert William Fogel, *Without Consent or Contract: The Rise and Fall of American Slavery* (New York: W. W. Norton, 1989).

23. David Eltis and Martin Halbert, *Voyages: The Transatlantic Slave Trade Database*, www.slavevoyages.org; David Eltis and David Richardson, eds., *Extending the Frontiers: Essays on the New Transatlantic Slave Trade Database* (New Haven, Conn.: Yale University Press, 2008); Stephen Behrendt, "Markets, Transaction Cycles, and Profits: Merchant Decision Making in the British Slave Trade," *William and Mary Quarterly* 58 (January 2001): 171–204; William A. Pettigrew, *Freedom's Debt: The Royal African Company and the Politics of the Atlantic Slave Trade, 1672–1752* (Chapel Hill: University of North Carolina Press, 2013); Sheryllyne Haggerty, "Risk and Risk Management in the Liverpool Slave Trade," *Business History* 51 (2009): 817–34; Rachel Chernos Lin, "The Rhode Island Slave-Traders: Butchers, Bakers, and Candlestick-Makers," *Slavery & Abolition: A Journal of Slave and Post-Slave Studies* 23 (December 2002): 21–38; Paul E. Lovejoy and David Richardson, "Trust, Pawnship, and Atlantic History: The Institutional Foundations of the Old Calabar Slave Trade," *American Historical Review* 104 (1999): 333–55; Leonardo Marques, "Slave Trading in a New World: The Strategies of North American Slave Traders in the Age of Abolition," *Journal of*

the Early Republic 32 (Summer 2012): 233–60; Jeremy Krikler, "A Chain of Murder in the Slave Trade: A Wider Context of the *Zong* Massacre," *International Review of Social History* 57 (December 2012): 393–415; Sowande' Mustakeem, " 'She must go overboard & shall go overboard': Diseased Bodies and the Spectacle of a Murder at Sea," *Atlantic Studies* 8 (2011): 301–16; Kenneth Morgan, "Remittance Procedures in the Eighteenth-Century British Slave Trade," *Business History Review* 79 (Winter 2005): 715–49; Bertie Mandelblatt, "A Transatlantic Commodity: Irish Salt Beef in the French Atlantic World," *History Workshop Journal* 63 (2007): 18–47; Justin Roberts, "Uncertain Business: A Case Study of Barbadian Plantation Management, 1770–93," *Slavery & Abolition: A Journal of Slave and Post-Slave Studies* 32 (2011): 247–68. The most comprehensive account of the numerous transactions of a single voyage is Robert Harms, *The Diligent: A Voyage Through the World of the Slave Trade* (New York: Basic Books, 2002).

24. Stephanie Smallwood, *Saltwater Slavery: A Middle Passage from Africa to American Diaspora* (Cambridge, Mass.: Harvard University Press, 2007); Marcus Rediker, *The Slave Ship: A Human History* (New York: Viking, 2007); Jennifer Morgan, *Laboring Women: Reproduction and Gender in New World Slavery* (Philadelphia: University of Pennsylvania Press, 2004); Amy Dru Stanley, "Slave Breeding and Free Love: An Antebellum Argument over Slavery, Capitalism, and Personhood," in Zakim and Kornblith, *Capitalism Takes Command*, 119–44; Ned and Constance Sublette, *The American Slave Coast: A History of the Slave-Breeding Industry* (Chicago: Lawrence Hill Books, 2016).

25. Dale W. Tomich, *Through the Prism of Slavery: Labor, Capital, and World Economy* (Lanham, Md.: Rowman and Littlefield, 2004); "The Second Slavery: Mass Slavery, World-Economy, and Comparative Microhistories, Parts I and II," special issues of *Review (Fernand Braudel Center)* 31 (2008); Anthony Kaye, "The Second Slavery: Modernity in the Nineteenth-Century and the Atlantic World," *Journal of Southern History* 75 (August 2009): 627–50; Roquinaldo Ferreira, "The Suppression of the Slave Trade and Slave Departures from Angola, 1830s–1860s," in Eltis and Richardson, eds., *Extending the Frontiers*, 313–34. The "Second Slavery" model finds a place for the United States in this history, in contrast to the very compelling model put forward in Philip D. Curtin, *The Rise and Fall of the Plantation Complex: Essays in Atlantic History* (New York: Cambridge University Press, 1990).

26. Beckert, *Empire of Cotton*, esp. chaps. 2, 5, 6.

27. Brian Schoen, *The Fragile Fabric of Union: Cotton, Federal Politics, and the Global Origins of the Civil War* (Baltimore: Johns Hopkins University Press, 2009), 45–47. Hendrik Hertzberg, "Over There," *New Yorker*, August 1, 2011 ("the South was the Saudi Arabia of cotton"). See also Adam Rothman, *Slave Country: American Expansion and the Origins of the Deep South* (Cambridge, Mass.: Harvard University Press, 2005); and Stuart Bruchey, *Cotton and the Growth of the American Economy, 1790–1860* (New York: Harcourt, Brace, and World, 1967). Benjamin Parker to Lewis Hill, July 8, 1835, Correspondence of Lewis Hill, 1834–1860, MssBR, box 92, folder 5, Henry E. Huntington Library, San Marino, Calif.

28. Michael Tadman, *Speculators and Slaves: Masters, Traders, and Slaves in the Old South* (Madison: University of Wisconsin Press, 1989); Walter Johnson, ed., *The Chattel Principle: Internal Slave Trades in the Americas* (New Haven, Conn.: Yale University Press, 2004); idem, *Soul by Soul: Inside the Antebellum Slave Market* (Cambridge, Mass.: Harvard University Press, 1999); Steven Deyle, *Carry Me Back: The Domestic Slave Trade in American Life* (New York: Oxford University Press, 2005). Gavin Wright, *Slavery and American Economic Development* (Baton Rouge: Louisiana State University Press, 2006), stresses the importance of slavery as a property

regime but ultimately contends "it was not slavery, but the post-Revolutionary War abolitions and the exclusion of slavery from the Northwest Territory that launched the American economy on its modern trajectory" (123).

29. Recent scholarship on the antebellum South has stressed the region's modernity. See Jonathan Daniel Wells, *Origins of the Southern Middle Class, 1800–1861* (Chapel Hill: University of North Carolina Press, 2004); Tom Downey, *Planting a Capitalist South: Masters, Merchants, and Manufacturers in the Southern Interior, 1790–1860* (Baton Rouge: Louisiana State University Press, 2006); Frank J. Byrne, *Becoming Bourgeois: Merchant Culture in the South, 1820–1865* (Lexington: University Press of Kentucky, 2006); Aaron W. Marrs, *Railroads in the Old South: Pursuing Progress in a Slave Society* (Baltimore: Johns Hopkins University Press, 2009); John Majewski, *Modernizing a Slave Economy: The Economic Vision of the Confederate Nation* (Chapel Hill: University of North Carolina Press, 2009); Michele Gillespie, "Building Networks of Knowledge: Henry Merrell and Textile Manufacturing in the Antebellum South," in *Technology, Innovation, and Southern Industrialization: From the Antebellum Era to the Computer Age,* ed. Susanna Delfino and Michele Gillespie (Columbia: University of Missouri Press, 2009), 97–124; and L. Diane Barnes, Brian Schoen, and Frank Towers, eds., *The Old South's Modern Worlds: Slavery, Region, and Nation in the Age of Progress* (New York: Oxford University Press, 2011).

30. Richard Follett, *The Sugar Masters: Planters and Slaves in Louisiana's Cane World, 1820–1860* (Baton Rouge: Louisiana State University Press, 2005), 24, 31; David R. Roediger and Elizabeth D. Esch, *The Production of Difference: Race and Management of Labor in U.S. History* (New York: Oxford University Press, 2012), 19–39; Mark M. Smith, *Mastered by the Clock: Time, Slavery, and Freedom in the American South* (Chapel Hill: University of North Carolina Press, 1997); Martha Jane Brazy, *An American Planter: Stephen Duncan of Antebellum Natchez and New York* (Baton Rouge: Louisiana State University Press, 2006); R. Keith Aufhauser, "Slavery and Scientific Management," *Journal of Economic History* 33 (December 1973): 811–24; Jacob Metzer, "Rational Management, Modern Business Practices, and Economies of Scale in the Ante-Bellum Southern Plantations," *Explorations in Economic History* 12 (1975): 123–50; and Paul W. Gates, *The Farmer's Age: Agriculture, 1815–1860* (1960; reprint New York: Harper and Row, 1968), 291.

31. Bill Cooke, "The Denial of Slavery in Management Studies," *Journal of Management Studies* 40 (December 2003): 1895–1918; Lorena S. Walsh, *Motives of Honor, Pleasure, and Profit: Plantation Management in the Colonial Chesapeake, 1607–1763* (Chapel Hill: University of North Carolina Press for the Omohundro Institute of Early American History and Culture, 2010); Louis J. Stewart, "A Contingency Theory Perspective on Management Control System Design Among U.S. Ante-Bellum Slave Plantations," *Accounting Historians Journal* 37 (June 2010): 91–120; Richard K. Fleischman, David Oldroyd, and Thomas N. Tyson, "Monetising Human Life: Slave Valuations on US and British West Indian Plantations," *Accounting History* 9 (2004): 35–62; idem, "Plantation Accounting and Management Practices in the US and the British West Indies at the End of Their Slavery Eras," *Economic History Review* 64 (2011): 765–97; Jan Richard Heier, "Accounting for the Business of Suffering: A Study of the Antebellum Richmond, Virginia, Slave Trade," *Abacus: A Journal of Accounting, Finance and Business Studies* 46 (2010): 60–83.

32. Angela Lakwete, *Inventing the Cotton Gin: Machine and Myth in Antebellum America* (Baltimore: Johns Hopkins University Press, 2003); Darla Thompson, "Circuits of Containment: Iron Collars, Incarceration, and the Infrastructure of Slavery" (PhD diss., Cornell University, 2014).

33. Richard Holcombe Kilbourne, *Slave Agriculture and Financial Markets in Antebellum America: The Bank of the United States in Mississippi, 1831–1852* (London: Pickering and Chatto, 2006); Elbra David, " 'In Pursuit of their Livelihood': Credit and Debt Relations Among Natchez Planters in the 1820s," in *Southern Society and Its Transformations, 1790–1860*, ed. Susanna Delfino, Michele Gillespie, and Louis M. Kyriakoudes (Columbia: University of Missouri Press, 2011), 217–46; John R. Killick, "The Cotton Operations of Alexander Brown and Sons in the Deep South, 1820–1860," *Journal of Southern History* 43 (1977): 169–94. The history of financial intermediation in the southern economy owes greatly to Harold D. Woodman, *King Cotton and His Retainers: Financing and Marketing the Cotton Crop of the South, 1800–1925* (Lexington: University Press of Kentucky, 1968). On the extent to which southern merchants are not easily assimilated into the history of capitalism, see Scott P. Marler, *The Merchants' Capital: New Orleans and the Political Economy of the Nineteenth Century* (New York: Cambridge University Press, 2013).

34. Daniel Lord, *The Effect of Secession upon the Commercial Relations Between North and South, and upon Each Section* (London: Henry Stevens, 1861), 61.

35. Steven Hahn, *The Political Worlds of Slavery and Freedom* (Cambridge, Mass.: Harvard University Press, 2009), 14–17; David Christy, "Cotton Is King," in *Cotton Is King, and Pro-Slavery Arguments . . .* , ed. E. N. Elliott (Augusta, Me.: Pritchard, Abbott and Loomis, 1860), 55; John Denis Haeger, *The Investment Frontier: New York Businessmen and the Economic Development of the Old Northwest* (Albany: SUNY Press, 1981), 37; Charles C. Bolton, *Poor Whites of the Antebellum South: Tenants and Laborers in Central North Carolina and Northeast Mississippi* (Durham, N.C.: Duke University Press, 1994), 75–77; C. Peter Magrath, *Yazoo Law and Politics in the New Republic: The Case of* Fletcher v. Peck (Providence, R.I.: Brown University Press, 1966). On the concept of remote communities of interest, see Ted Maris-Wolf, " 'Of Blood and Treasure': Recaptive Africans and the Politics of Slave Trade Suppression," *Journal of the Civil War Era* 4 (March 2014): 53–83. Comparable work on these networks includes Chris P. Evans, *Slave Wales: The Welsh and Atlantic Slavery, 1660–1850* (Cardiff: University of Wales Press, 2010); Bertie R. Mandelblatt, " 'Beans from Rochel and Manioc from Prince's Island': West Africa, French Atlantic Commodity Circuits, and the Provisioning of the French Middle Passage," *History of European Ideas* 34 (2008): 411–23; idem, "A Transatlantic Commodity"; and Jeremy Prestholdt, "On the Global Repercussions of East African Consumerism," *American Historical Review* 109 (June 2004): 755–81. Although significant debates in economic history were not framed in these terms, the focus on interregional trade attested to the relationship of northern and western producers to plantation economies. See Albert Fishlow, "Antebellum Interregional Trade Reconsidered," in *New Views on American Economic Development: A Selective Anthology of Recent Work*, ed. Ralph L. Andreano (Cambridge, Mass.: Schenkman Publishing Co., 1965), 187–200.

36. Amy Dru Stanley, *From Bondage to Contract: Wage Labor, Marriage, and the Market in the Age of Slave Emancipation* (New York: Cambridge University Press, 1998); Christopher Tomlins, *Freedom Bound: Law, Labor, and Civic Identity in Colonizing English America, 1580–1865* (New York: Cambridge University Press, 2010); David Waldstreicher, *Slavery's Constitution: From Revolution to Ratification* (New York: Hill and Wang, 2009); George William Van Cleve, *A Slaveholders' Union: Slavery, Politics, and the Constitution in the Early American Republic* (Chicago: University of Chicago Press, 2010); David F. Ericson, *Slavery in the American Republic: Developing the Federal Government, 1791–1861* (Lawrence: University Press of Kansas, 2011); idem, *The Debate over Slavery: Antislavery and Proslavery Liberalism in Antebellum America* (New York: NYU Press, 2000); Jonathan A. Glickstein, *American Exceptionalism, American Anxiety:*

Wages, Competition, and Degraded Labor in the Antebellum United States (Charlottesville: University of Virginia Press, 2002); Gautham Rao, "The Federal *Posse Comitatus* Doctrine: Slavery, Compulsion, and Statecraft in Mid-Nineteenth Century America," *Law and History Review* 26 (January 2008): 1–56.

CHAPTER 1. TOWARD A POLITICAL ECONOMY OF SLAVE LABOR

The author would like to thank Tinenenji Banda, Rudi Batzell, Kathryn Boodry, Vincent Brown, Holly Case, Derek Chang, Joyce Chaplin, Mycah Conner, Christine Desan, Norberto Ferreras, Lara Heimert, Walter Johnson, Rafael Marquese, Suresh Naidu, Jon Parmenter, Caitlin Rosenthal, Joshua Rothman, Aaron Sachs, Suman Seth, Eric Tagliacozzo, Dale Tomich, and Jeremy Williams for comments and other help with this text in its various stages and incarnations.

1. John Blassingame argues that Ball's owner was probably the entrepreneur, politician, and part-time general Wade Hampton I, who by the early 1800s had pushed his way to becoming one of the wealthiest men in the United States: John W. Blassingame, ed., *Slave Testimony: Two Centuries of Letters, Speeches, Interviews, and Autobiographies* (Baton Rouge: Louisiana State University Press, 1977), xxiii–xxvi.

2. Frederick Engels, *The Condition of the Working Class in England*, ed. Victor Kiernan (New York: Penguin Books, 1987). It would require too massive a footnote to summarize the historiography of British industrialization. While it is widely agreed that the textile industry was the leading sector, not all scholars concede the significance of leading sectors in the transformation of agricultural economies into industrial ones. Many of these debates are summarized in Joel Mokyr, *The Enlightened Economy: An Economic History of Britain, 1700–1850* (New Haven, Conn.: Yale University Press, 2009), and Gregory Clark, *A Farewell to Alms: A Brief Economic History of the World* (Princeton, N.J.: Princeton University Press, 2007). For the dynamic, causal role of the New England cotton textile industry in the wider development of U.S. industry, see David R. Meyer, *The Roots of American Industrialization* (Baltimore: Johns Hopkins University Press, 2003).

3. Virtually none of the canonical works by historians of U.S. slavery discusses cotton labor in anything but the most abstract of terms. A good example is Eugene D. Genovese, *Roll, Jordan, Roll: The World the Slaves Made* (New York: Pantheon Books, 1974), which acknowledges that cotton had to be picked, and picked by somebody, on only two of its 800-odd pages (pp. 321–22). There, as in almost all other works on cotton slavery, the author manages not to describe how picking took place, how it was experienced, or what its implications might have been. One very recent and welcome exception is Sean M. Kelley, *Los Brazos de Dios: A Plantation Society in the Texas Borderlands, 1821–1865* (Baton Rouge: Louisiana State University Press, 2011), 106–14; another is Walter Johnson, *River of Dark Dreams: Slavery and Empire in the Cotton Kingdom* (Cambridge, Mass.: Harvard University Press, 2013), esp. 244–49; and I try to do the same in Edward E. Baptist, *The Half Has Never Been Told: Slavery and the Making of American Capitalism* (New York: Basic Books, 2014), esp. 111–44.

4. See these excellent histories of how that empire was built and how those slave trades were created: Adam Rothman, *Slave Country: American Expansion and the Origins of the Deep South* (Cambridge, Mass.: Harvard University Press, 2005); Joshua Rothman, *Flush Times and Fever Dreams: A Story of Capitalism and Slavery in the Age of Jackson* (Athens: University of

Georgia Press, 2012); and Walter Johnson, *Soul by Soul: Life inside the Antebellum Slave Market* (Cambridge, Mass.: Harvard University Press, 1999), and his *River of Dark Dreams*.

5. Charles Ball, *Slavery in the United States: A Narrative of the Life and Adventures of Charles Ball* . . . (New York: John Taylor, 1837), 47–48, 128–30; see also Theodore D. Weld, ed., *American Slavery As It Is: Testimony of a Thousand Witnesses* (New York: American Anti-Slavery Society, 1839), 101, a text filled with reports of travelers and others who saw scantily clad or unclad slaves working in the southwestern fields in the 1810s and 1820s.

6. *"From the Ohio Atlas.* Slavery in Florida. No. 1," reproduced in Paul Finkelman, ed., *Slave Rebels, Abolitionists, and Southern Courts: The Pamphlet Literature* (New York: Garland Press, 1988), 285–86. A Natchez cotton entrepreneur-enslaver referred to this season of planting and cultivation as "the most pushing time of the crop": John Knight to William Beall, May 7, 1845, John Knight Papers, William P. Perkins Library, Duke University, Durham, N.C. (hereafter Duke); see also Johnson, *River of Dark Dreams*, 220; Steven F. Miller, "Plantation Labor Organization and Slave Life on the Cotton Frontier: The Alabama-Mississippi Black Belt, 1815–1840," in *Cultivation and Culture: Labor and the Shaping of Slave Life in the Americas*, ed. Ira Berlin and Philip Morgan (Charlottesville: University of Virginia Press, 1993), 155–69.

7. Ball, *Slavery in the United States*, 117–19; William Anderson, *Life and Narrative of William Anderson* . . . (Chicago: Daily Tribune Book and Job Printing Office, 1857), 19 ("Carry the fore row"); Thomas Spalding, "Cotton—Its Introduction, and Progress of its Culture, in the United States," *Farmers' Register: A Monthly Publication* 6 (November 1834): 353–63.

8. Israel Campbell, *An Autobiography: Bond and Free* (Philadelphia: The author, 1861); Henry Bibb, *Narrative of the Life and Adventures of Henry Bibb, an American Slave, Written By Himself* (New York: The author, 1849), 115–17; Ball, *Slavery in the United States*, 148–51; Kate Pickard, *The Kidnapped and the Ransomed* (Syracuse, N.Y.: William T. Hamilton, 1856), 155; Thomas Wallace Knox, *Camp-Fire and Cotton-Field: Southern Adventure in Time of War, Life with the Union Armies, and Residence on a Louisiana Plantation* (New York: Blelock and Co., 1865), 356. For testimony from former slaves, see George Rawick, ed., *The American Slave: A Composite Autobiography*, 3rd ser., 41 vols. (Westport, Conn., 1971–1979), hereafter cited as *AS*, followed by supplemental series designation (if any), volume number, page, and state abbreviation: John Walton, *AS*, 5.2, 125–30, s2, 10, 3946–51 (Tex.); Lee Pierce, *AS*, s2, 8.1, 3092–3109 (Tex.); Litt Young, *AS*, 5.2, 227–336 (Tex.); John Glover, *AS*, 2.2, 138–47 (S.C.). On workday regimentation, see Jacob Metzer, "Rational Management, Modern Business Practices, and Economies of Scale in Antebellum Southern Plantations," in *Without Consent or Contract: The Rise and Fall of American Slavery*, vol. 1, *Technical Papers: Markets and Production*, ed. Robert William Fogel, Stanley L. Engerman, et al. (New York: W. W. Norton, 1992), 191–215; and Mark M. Smith, *Mastered by the Clock: Time, Slavery, and Freedom in the American South* (Chapel Hill: University of North Carolina Press, 1997), although Smith's timepiece revolution is almost entirely post-1830. Robert William Fogel, meanwhile, argues that slaves' workdays typically included longer breaks than on northern free farms in *Without Consent or Contract: The Rise and Fall of American Slavery* (New York: W.W. Norton, 1989), 79. This is not borne out by ex-slaves' accounts, like that of Sarah Wells, *AS*, 11.1, 89 (Ark.); Charlie Aarons, *AS*, 6.1, 1 (Ala.); or Angie Garrett, *AS*, 6.1, 133 (Ala.).

9. Israel Campbell uses "plantation system" to draw an explicit contrast between Mississippi and Kentucky in *Autobiography*, 33; for what people enslaved in the Chesapeake and Kentucky might have experienced, see Benjamin Henry Latrobe, Sketchbook 3, no. 33, Maryland Historical Society, Baltimore, available at http://hitchcock.itc.virginia.edu/SlaveTrade/collection

/large/NW0048.JPG (accessed November 27, 2015). On Lowcountry cultivation practices and Sea Island cotton, see Joyce Chaplin, *An Anxious Pursuit: Agricultural Innovation and Modernity in the Lower South, 1730–1815* (Chapel Hill: University of North Carolina Press for the Omohundro Institute of Early American History and Culture, Williamsburg, Virginia [OIEAHC], 1993); and Philip D. Morgan, "Work and Culture: The Task System and the World of Lowcountry Blacks, 1700 to 1880," *William and Mary Quarterly* 39, no. 3 (1982): 563–99. Sea Island cotton was a specialized strain that was made into a luxury cloth for a boutique market. It was, it should be clear, distinct from the short-staple (short-fibered) cotton that was grown in the southern interior, including at the place where Charles Ball was enslaved in South Carolina. This "upland" or short-staple cotton was the cotton of the Industrial Revolution, the kind that Eli Whitney's gin was designed to process and the kind that became the most widely traded global commodity of the nineteenth century.

10. "Some of our rows": [John] Neal to Dear Mother and Brother, August 6, 1829, Neal Family Papers, Southern Historical Collection, Louis Round Wilson Library, University of North Carolina at Chapel Hill (hereafter SHC); Allen Sidney, interview in Blassingame, ed., *Slave Testimony*, 521–29. Enslavers also tried other experiments. Sidney identified efforts to enforce silence in the fields. This requirement would not be universally followed, and perhaps would be abandoned, but despite historians' various and contradictory claims about the role of singing in production, the rhythms of traditional work songs hardly provided a brake on the pace of work in the nineteenth-century cotton field or increased its efficiency: Paul David and Peter Temin, "Slavery: The Progressive Institution?," in *Reckoning with Slavery: A Critical Study in the Quantitative History of American Negro Slavery*, ed. Paul A. David, Herbert G. Gutman, Richard Sutch, Peter Temin, and Gavin Wright (New York: Oxford University Press, 1976), 165–230, esp. 206–7n46, which suggests that the "rhythm" of enslaved labor produced considerable efficiencies. David and Temin argue that this can be found in Haitian *coumbite* and in West African forms of collective labor. I suggest here that the whip might have had something to do with the efficiencies of slave labor camps.

11. Ball, *Slavery in the United States*, 67, 160–62; Okah Tubbee, *A Sketch of the Life of Okah Tubbee* (Toronto: H. Stephens, 1852), 23; John Warren testimony in Benjamin Drew, *A North-Side View of Slavery: The Refugee; or, The Narratives of Fugitive Slaves in Canada* (Boston: John P. Jewett, 1856), 184; for those who prefer testimony from white observers (as opposed to black targets and survivors), there are many like these: "Testimony of Philemon Bliss," in Weld, ed., *American Slavery As It Is*, 104; William N. Blane, *An Excursion Through the United States and Canada During the Years 1822–1823, By an English Gentleman* (London: Baldwin, 1824), 150–51. In addition to frequent references to subregional differences, see the typical descriptions of whips in the Chesapeake: cat-o'-nine tails, short rawhide whips, as opposed to long single-lashed whips: Charles Crawley, *AS*, 16.5, 8–9 (Va.); Willie Vester to Benjamin H. Vester, March 19, 1837, Benjamin H. Vester Papers, Duke; I. Campbell, *Autobiography*, 33; Bibb, *Narrative*, 116–17; A. K. Bartow to J. J. Phillips, April 23, 1849, folder 1, Ivan P. Battle Papers, SHC.

12. Sven Beckert, *Empire of Cotton: A Global History* (New York: Knopf, 2014).

13. James L. Huston, *Calculating the Value of Union: Slavery, Property Rights, and the Economic Origins of the Civil War* (Chapel Hill: University of North Carolina Press, 2003); Fogel, *Without Consent or Contract*, 87.

14. Michel Foucault, *Discipline and Punish: The Birth of the Prison* (New York: Pantheon, 1977); idem, *The Order of Things: An Archaeology of the Human Sciences* (New York: Pantheon, 1971); idem, *The History of Sexuality*, vol. 1 (New York: Pantheon, 1978). For masters

of suspicion, see Paul Ricouer, *Freud and Philosophy: An Essay on Interpretation* (New Haven, Conn.: Yale University Press, 1970).

15. Michel Foucault, *Power/Knowledge: Selected Interviews and Other Writings, 1972–1977* (New York: Pantheon, 1980).

16. Robert Farrar Capon, *Parables of Grace* (Grand Rapids, Mich.: W. B. Eerdmans, 1988), is the best discussion thereof. See also James C. Scott, *Domination and the Arts of Resistance: Hidden Transcripts* (New Haven, Conn.: Yale University Press, 1990).

17. Scott, *Domination and the Arts of Resistance.* At the same time, processes of production that required particular skill, like the ones Charles Ball had mastered in the wheat fields of Maryland, gave to the dominated psychological and real independence. Enslavers who profited from uncommonly skilled slaves were both enriched and rendered slightly dependent by the restricted good of those skills.

18. A good example of this is James Henry Hammond, who was unable to force the enslaved people on a slave labor camp at the edge of the Lowcountry to shift from task-based to gang-based methods of cotton cultivation in the 1830s. See Drew Gilpin Faust, *James Henry Hammond and the Old South: A Design for Mastery* (Baton Rouge: Louisiana State University Press, 1985), 69–104; Chaplin, *An Anxious Pursuit,* 326–27; Charles Joyner, *Down by the Riverside: A South Carolina Slave Community* (Urbana: University of Illinois Press, 1984), 43–46; Peter Coclanis, "How the Low Country Was Taken to Task: Slave-Labor Organization in Coastal South Carolina and Georgia," in *Slavery, Secession, and Southern History*, ed. Robert L. Paquette and Louis Ferleger (Charlottesville: University of Virginia Press, 2000), 59–78; Philip D. Morgan, "Task and Gang Systems: The Organization of Labor on New World Plantations," in *Work and Labor in Early America*, ed. Stephen Innes (Chapel Hill: University of North Carolina Press for the OIEAHC, 1988), 189–220; and idem, *Slave Counterpoint: Black Culture in the Eighteenth-Century Chesapeake and Lowcountry* (Chapel Hill: University of North Carolina Press for the OIEAHC, 1998), 179–94. The task system did nothing, of course, to protect slaves or their children from the essential unhealthiness of the swampy Lowcountry environment, and they suffered and died in vast numbers from malaria throughout the years of slavery. See William Dusinberre, *Them Dark Days: Slavery in the American Rice Swamps* (New York: Oxford University Press, 1996).

19. M. Tournillon to Nicholas Trist, February 28, 1821, folder 22, Nicholas Trist Papers, SHC.

20. Slaves "on hand": J. Garner to A. Cuningham, February 1, 1830, Alexander Cuningham Papers, Duke; slave sale money "in hand": Brown and Armistead to E. B. Hicks, August 1, 1821, Alexander Cuningham Papers, Duke; Kenner & Co. to J. Minor, January 26, 1826, folder 31, Minor Papers, SHC; "cotton": David Ker to Mary Ker, May 7, 1812, folder 2, Ker Family Papers, SHC; letter "come to hand": E. Fraser to M. White, August 28, 1806, Maunsel White Papers, SHC; passim in folders 1834–35, Jarratt-Puryear Papers, Duke. Slaves also "came to hand": Tyre Glen to Isaac Jarratt, December 23, 1833, Jarratt-Puryear Papers, Duke; J. Richards to Cashier of Bank of United States, March 14, 1815, box 2E949, Bank of State of Mississippi Records, Natchez Trace Collection, ser. G, part 3, reel 1, RASP (*Records of Ante-Bellum Southern Plantations*, microfilm series, University Publications of America, Fredericksburg, Md.). "Notes of hand" are everywhere, even lost: Abijah Hunt to R. Sparks, June 14, 1809, folder 1, Ker Family Papers, SHC.

21. Geoffrey Parker, *The Military Revolution, 1500–1800: Military Innovation and the Rise of the West*, 2nd ed. (New York: Cambridge University Press, 1996); William McNeill, *The Pursuit of Power: Technology, Armed Force, and Society Since AD 1000* (Chicago: University of Chicago

Press, 1982); Charles Tilly, *Coercion, Capital, and European States, AD 990–1992* (Cambridge, Mass.: Basil Blackwell, 1990); Rafael de Bivar Marquese, *Feitores do corpo, missionários da mente: Senhores, letrados e o controle dos escravos nas Américas, 1660–1860* (São Paulo: Companhia das Letras, 2004); Justin Roberts, *Slavery and Enlightenment in the British Atlantic, 1750–1807* (New York: Cambridge University Press, 2013); Lorena S. Walsh, *Motives of Honor, Pleasure, and Profit: Plantation Management in the Colonial Chesapeake, 1607–1763* (Chapel Hill: University of North Carolina Press for the OIEAHC, 2010).

22. There is a significant historiography on the dominance of U.S. cotton in the worldwide cotton trade during the nineteenth century. For the purposes of the present text I refer readers to the notes in Sven Beckert, "Emancipation and Empire: Reconstructing the Worldwide Web of Cotton Production in the Age of the American Civil War," *American Historical Review* 109 (December 2004): 1405–38, which contains citations to most of the relevant nineteenth- and twentieth-century works, or, again, to Beckert, *Empire of Cotton*.

23. Key elements of the rise of the West had become evident by 1800—the growth of state capacity (military and otherwise), the emergence of coherent financial sectors, the growth of long-distance trading capacity, the contribution of colonies to metropolitan growth, the emergence of consumer demands and commodity fetishes around the pole of sugar. The role of slavery in these is perhaps most effectively understood through three seminal works: Sidney W. Mintz, *Sweetness and Power: The Place of Sugar in Modern History* (New York: Viking Penguin, 1985); Robin Blackburn, *The Making of New World Slavery: From the Baroque to the Modern, 1492–1800* (New York: Verso, 1997); and Stuart B. Schwartz, *Sugar Plantations in the Formation of Brazilian Society: Bahia, 1550–1835* (New York: Cambridge University Press, 1985).

24. Kenneth Pomeranz, *The Great Divergence: China, Europe, and the Making of the Modern World Economy* (Princeton, N.J.: Princeton University Press, 2000). There's a rich irony in those economic historians who on the one hand defend Pomeranz from what they see as bullying from cultural historians while on the other hand ignoring his powerful argument for the centrality of sugar and cotton to the development of Western industrial capitalism. Pomeranz echoes, in his own very different way, the rich historiography on modernization and industrialization by such anticolonial Caribbean scholars as Eric Williams, *Capitalism and Slavery* (Chapel Hill: University of North Carolina Press, 1944); C. L. R. James, *The Black Jacobins: Toussaint L'Ouverture and the San Domingo Revolution*, 2nd ed. (New York: Vintage Books, 1963); Walter Rodney, *How Europe Underdeveloped Africa* (London: Bogle-L'Ouverture Publications, 1972); and Horace Campbell, *Rasta and Resistance: From Marcus Garvey to Walter Rodney* (Trenton, N.J.: Africa World Press, 1987). See also African critiques such as Joseph Inikori, *The Atlantic Slave Trade: Effects on Economies, Societies, and Peoples in Africa, the Americas, and Europe* (Durham, N.C.: Duke University Press, 1992). For African American critiques of Western exceptionalist models of the Great Divergence, see W. E. B. DuBois, *Black Reconstruction: An Essay Toward a History of the Part Which Black Folk Played in the Attempt to Reconstruct Democracy in America, 1860–1880* (New York: Simon and Schuster, 1935); David Levering Lewis, *W. E. B. DuBois: Biography of a Race, 1868–1919* (New York: Henry Holt, 1993), and idem, *W. E. B. DuBois: The Fight For Equality and the American Century, 1919–1963* (New York: Henry Holt, 2000), for passages describing DuBois's social science research on the ground in the cotton South and his account of the history thereof in both his *Souls of Black Folk* (1903) and *Black Reconstruction*; and, later, Angela Y. Davis, *Women, Race, and Class* (New York: Random House, 1981); Manning Marable, *How Capitalism Underdeveloped Black America: Problems in Race, Political Economy, and Society* (Boston: South End Press, 1983). Much of the historiography is unfolded in Cedric Robinson, *Black Marxism: The Making*

of the Black Radical Tradition, 2nd ed. (Chapel Hill: University of North Carolina Press, 2000), and Robin D. G. Kelley, *Freedom Dreams: The Black Radical Imagination* (Boston: Beacon Press, 2002).

25. The statistics come from Lewis Cecil Gray, *History of Agriculture in the Southern U.S. to 1860*, 2 vols. (Washington, D.C.: Carnegie Institution of Washington, 1933), 2:692–93. The dominance of southern cotton—accounting for 88 to 99 percent of the British market—was even more complete over the continental ones. See Baptist, *The Half Has Never Been Told*, 114.

26. Mokyr, *The Enlightened Economy*; Pomeranz, *Great Divergence*.

27. Ball, *Slavery in the United States*, 184–87; Solomon Northup, *Twelve Years a Slave*, as told to and edited by David Wilson (Auburn, N.Y.: Derby and Miller, 1852), 134, 142–43; William Walker, *Buried Alive (Behind Prison Walls) for a Quarter of a Century* (Saginaw, Mich.: Friedman and Hynan, 1892), 17; Anderson, *Life and Narrative*, 18; J. W. C. Pennington, *Narrative of the Events of the Life of J. H. Banks* (Liverpool: M. Rourke, 1861), 68; Mary Younger testimony in Drew, *A North-Side View of Slavery*, 258. We should note this on the profitability of women versus men in cotton fields: enslavers still considered men more profitable than women, in part because men picked more cotton. But the ratio of male/female productivity was closer to one in cotton picking than in the key operations of other crops. At the same time, it was greater than one (men were more productive), and enslavers were regularly enraged about the frequency with which women missed cotton picking time because of menstruation, pregnancy, childbirth, and recovery—hence the lower price for women in the New Orleans and other markets (about 70 percent of male prices). "To make money men are required[,] or boys large enough": John Haywood to George W. Haywood, February 5, 1842; see also John Haywood to George W. Haywood, March 17, 1839, Haywood Family Papers, SHC; "[because] We have not a pregnant woman on the plantation[,] the females are the better pickers and have saved much the larger portion of the crop": Paul Cameron to Duncan Cameron, December 2, 1845, folder 973, Cameron Papers, SHC.

28. Ball, *Slavery in the United States*, 217; see also Mary Ker to Isaac Baker, November 19, 1820, Ker Family Papers, SHC; J. S. Haywood to Dear Sister, May 3, 1839, folder 156, Haywood Family Papers, SHC; A. K. Barlow to J.J. Phillips, April 23, 1849, folder 1, Ivan P. Battle Papers, SHC; James Harriss to Thomas Harriss, September 14, 1845, Thomas W. Harriss Papers, Duke; John Knight to William Beall, February 7, 1844, and April 14, 1844, John Knight Papers, Duke; Robert B. Beverley to Robert Beverley, September 3, 1833, sec. 13, Beverley Family Papers, Virginia Historical Society (hereafter VHS).

29. Alan Olmstead and Paul Rhode, "Biological Innovation and Productivity Growth in the Antebellum Cotton Economy," NBER Working Paper 14142 (Cambridge, Mass.: National Bureau of Economic Research, 2008), 22; James Magruder Account Book and Plantation Journal, 1796–1818, Magruder Papers, RASP, ser. N, reel 12; R. & M. Timberlake to Dear Mother and Brother, December 26, 1829, Neal Family Papers, SHC; Wm. R. Arick to Joseph S. Copes, October 22, 1846, folder 82, Joseph Slemmons Copes Papers, Special Collections, Howard-Tilton Library, Tulane University; see also Elley Plantation Book, 1855–1856, RASP, ser. N, reel 10; early daily totals from Charles Rowand, "Cotton," *American Farmer* 3, no. 38 (December 14, 1821): 298; Ball, *Slavery in the United States*, 186–87; Magnolia Plantation Journal, August 31, 1838, folder 429, Ballard Papers, SHC; 1835 numbers from Burrell Fox to Eliza Neal, September 25, 1835; 100–30 pounds per day in 1829 from R. and M. Timberlake to Dear Mother and Brother, December 26, 1829, both Neal Family Papers, SHC; see Phanor Prudhomme Cotton Book, 1836, folder 267, and Phanor Prudhomme Cotton Book, 1852, folder 271, both Prudhomme Family Papers, SHC; D. W. McKenzie to Duncan McLaurin, September 26, 1840,

folder 1838–1840; John Ford Thompson Diary, July 6, 1841, [51], Benson-Thompson Papers, Duke.

30. Olmstead and Rhode, "Biological Innovation and Productivity Growth," 1–2.

31. D. A. Farnie, *The English Cotton Industry and the World Market, 1815–1896* (Oxford: Oxford University Press, 1979), 199.

32. Fogel et al., eds., *Without Consent or Contract*, vol. 1, *Technical Papers*, 72–80; John Olson, "Clock Time Versus Real Time: A Comparison of the Lengths of the Northern and Southern Agricultural Work Years," ibid., 216–40; Metzer, "Rational Management," ibid., 191–215; Robert W. Fogel and Stanley L. Engerman, "Explaining the Relative Efficiency of Slave Agriculture in the Antebellum South," *American Economic Review* 67 (1977): 275–96.

33. Olmstead and Rhode, "Biological Innovation and Productivity Growth." They retell the argument in a series of articles, but the essence of it is contained in the paper cited here. J. A. Turner, *The Cotton Planter's Manual: Being a Compilation of Facts From the Best Authorities on the Culture of Cotton; Its Natural History, Chemical Analysis, Trade, and Consumption; And Embracing a History of Cotton and the Cotton Gin* (New York: O. Judd and Co., 1857), 36, 99–102; John Hebron Moore, *Agriculture in Ante-Bellum Mississippi* (New York: Bookman Associates, 1958), 27–36, 145–60.

34. Planters wrote obsessively in their agricultural publications about the quest for new cotton varieties, which some selected and marketed to peers under iconic brand names such as "Mastodon," "100 Seed," "Sugar Loaf," and "Prolific." Turner, *The Cotton Planter's Manual*, 99–102. A later (1865) edition of Turner's book reproduces an 1848 claim about a new seed "with extraordinary picking qualities. . . . There are many planters who put the gain at fifty, seventy-five, and even one hundred per cent." Not four hundred percent, he's trying to sell it—and he hedges even further: "I do not promise that much." Turner, *The Cotton Planter's Manual* (New York: O. Judd and Co., 1865), 105.

35. Historians have studied the language of "improving" and "scientific" planters as an anxious rhetoric of modernity and control. In this discourse, planters credited themselves with experiments and decisions about techniques of cultivation, as well as the bio-engineering of plants, while completely obscuring the reality that forced labor performed the work. The columns of agricultural improvement journals hide the fact that in real life, enslavers were measuring not the output of seeds but the output of enslaved human beings laboring under threat of violence. Johnson, *River of Dark Dreams*, is particularly perceptive on this point, but see also Chaplin, *An Anxious Pursuit*; and Drew Gilpin Faust, "The Rhetoric and Ritual of Agricultural Reform in Antebellum South Carolina," *Journal of Southern History* 45, no. 3 (1979): 541–68. In their uncritical reproduction of planters' claims, Olmstead and Rhode, in the essay cited here and in succeeding articles, paint a picture of planters as continually and consciously adapting and innovating the cotton seeds. Their story swallows planter rhetoric, and also reproduces the general story-line of books and articles written by traditionalist agricultural historians who wanted to find the sources of agricultural progress for the rest of the United States in improved seeds, methods of fertilizing, and machinery—exactly the kinds of things that the state universities that sponsored them promised legislatures they were creating in their departments of agriculture and agronomy.

36. For instance, the economists compare the picking rates in the new cotton districts, which grew and harvested short-staple cotton (the kind used by most textile mills), with the picking rates of a handful of Sea Island cotton plantations in the Carolina Lowcountry. The picking rates in the first group rose over time, while the latter stayed flat. They assume the same organization of labor in both sites, and thus attribute the increase to a difference in

seeds. But the labor systems in the two locations were demonstrably different, as the numerous historians of the Lowcountry already cited in this essay have definitively shown. In the interior, on the short-staple cotton frontier, people were forced to work to dark and punished if they did not meet a particular, individual quota. When they did, picking quotas were raised. In the Lowcountry, on Sea Island cotton operations, people worked until they picked enough to complete a task that was generalized for most adult hands and that did not change over decades. See Morgan, "Work and Culture." Indeed, the case of James Henry Hammond, cited earlier in these notes, can be drawn to its conclusion to show the error. Hammond gave up his attempt to impose the upcountry pushing system and its associated dawn-to-dusk, heavily invigilated labor because of persistent resistance to it by the enslaved people at his Silver Bluff "plantation," which made the short-staple cotton found in the upcountry and interior and not the Sea Island cotton usually used with the task system. Yet because of this passive and active resistance, he reverted to the Lowcountry task system in which enslaved people there had worked before he acquired the property through marriage to his wife. Hammond then complained for years afterward about the low productivity of cotton operations there in general and the inefficiency of cotton picking in particular. Given that Hammond deployed the Lowcountry task system for short-staple/upland cotton planted by seeds "bio-engineered" for "pickability" and got little to no increase in cotton productivity over time (and the data that Faust offers support Hammond's own analysis of that), readers can draw their own conclusions about the role of seeds versus labor systems in driving efficiency increases. See Faust, *James Henry Hammond and the Old South*, 69–104.

37. Beckert, *Empire of Cotton*, esp. 122–30; J. Talboys Wheeler, *Handbook to the Cotton-Cultivation in the Madras Presidency* (London: Virtue Brothers, 1863), 228, 231; W. Nassau Lees, *Tea Cultivation, Cotton, and Other Agricultural Experiments in India: A Review* (London: W. H. Allan, 1863), 97–100, 141–42.

38. Trevon Logan, "A Time (Not) Apart: A Lesson in Economic History from Cotton Picking Books," *Review of Black Political Economy* 42, no. 4 (2015): 301–22, shows, albeit with a small sample, that on one Mississippi farm in the 1960s, African American children picked about 8 percent less than enslaved children a little over a century before. In general, individual picking records are almost completely absent from the post-emancipation archive—not an accident, since picking records were used to answer the question of whether an enslaved person would be whipped or not. And after emancipation, free adults were no longer whipped for short picking—they were simply paid less, or fired. One should note that, with the exception of Logan, who shows a lower picking rate than that in slavery, those who argue that the picking rate rose typically cite planter testimony or a Department of Agriculture source, such as the 125 pounds per worker per day figure for the Mississippi Delta in the 1920s cited on the last page of Warren C. Whatley, "Southern Labor Contracts as Impediments to Cotton Mechanization," *Journal of Economic History* 47, no. 1 (1987): 45–70. Even this represents no real change from apparent average picking rates across the cotton South in the 1850s. For the dangers of accepting planter claims about twentieth-century picking rates, especially in the context of their attempts to use the Department of Agriculture for their own ends during the New Deal and World War II, see Nan E. Woodruff, "Pick or Fight: The Emergency Farm Labor Program in the Arkansas and Mississippi Deltas during World War II," *Agricultural History* 64 (Spring 1990): 81.

39. From the available data, no population of free cotton pickers appears to have equaled in total productivity (with remotely similar machine, chemical, and seed technology) the enslaved cotton picker circa 1860. See Fogel, *Without Consent or Contract*, 98–102, for a roughly

35 percent post-emancipation productivity decline in southern cotton production as of 1880. Fogel attributes the decline to the end of the ability of enslavers to coerce regimented labor in what he calls "the gang system." On the other hand, Roger Ransom and Richard Sutch, in *One Kind of Freedom: The Economic Consequences of Emancipation* (Cambridge: Cambridge University Press, 1977), argue that post-emancipation labor productivity actually increased. But Ransom and Sutch admit to putting their thumb on the scale, intervening in the data on the presumption that freedpeople "with[drew] female labor" from the fields and thus collectively devoted fewer total hours to cotton cultivation. Fogel faults Ransom and Sutch's analytical decision, as do I for an additional reason: women and children most certainly continued to work for picking wages during the rush of the cotton harvest, as photographs, contemporary accounts, memoirs, and school schedules in cotton areas continued to reveal well into the mid-twentieth century. Picking remained the bottleneck of cotton production until the mechanical picker replaced hand labor in the twenty years between the end of World War II and the passage of the Voting Rights Act. Picking continued to set the overall level of production, but without the whip and the rest of the pushing system we encounter in the accounts of survivors, picking meant something different.

40. Levi Woodbury, "Cotton: Cultivation, Manufacture, and Foreign Trade of," *House Executive Documents,* 24th Cong., 1st Sess., vol. 4, no. 146 (Washington, D.C., 1836). Stuart Schwartz and Richard Follett both make the case for sugar production as modernizing, semi-industrial processes, but this case has not been made for cotton growing and harvesting. See Richard Follett, *The Sugar Masters: Planters and Slaves in Louisiana's Cane World, 1820–1860* (Baton Rouge: Louisiana State University Press, 2005); Schwartz, *Sugar Plantations.* Northern critics of slavery such as Frederick Law Olmsted, in the late antebellum period, made the case (as had Adam Smith and Karl Marx) that slave production was not only premodern but anti-modern. That the nineteenth century's revolutions of production also continued to depend on skill and tradition makes them both like and unlike the labor of the cotton revolution in still more interesting ways. See, e.g., David Montgomery, *Fall of the House of Labor: The Workplace, the State, and American Labor Activism, 1865–1925* (New York: Cambridge University Press, 1987); and Harry Braverman, *Labor and Monopoly Capital: The Degradation of Work in the Twentieth Century* (New York: Monthly Review Press, 1974). For the cultural image of cotton in the twentieth century, see D. Clayton Brown, *King Cotton in Modern America: A Cultural, Political, and Economic History Since 1945* (Jackson: University Press of Mississippi, 2011).

41. Adam Smith, *An Inquiry into the Nature and Cause of the Wealth of Nations* (London: Methuen and Co., 1904), book 1, chap. 8.

42. Even some antebellum southern observers saw "the tedious operation of manual cotton-picking" as premodern, comparing it to the sickle, while the cotton gin (a machine) was the more efficient scythe, shaped by modernity's application of knowledge to the ancient tasks of agriculture: "The Profession of a Planter or Farmer," *American Farmer* 2, no. 7 (May 12, 1820): 52; Frederick Law Olmsted, *The Cotton Kingdom: A Traveller's Observations on Cotton and Slavery in the American Slave States, 1853–1861,* edited and with an introduction by Arthur M. Schlesinger (New York: Modern Library, 1984), 811.

43. Thomas Holt, *The Problem of Freedom: Race, Labor, and Politics in Jamaica and Britain, 1832–1938* (Baltimore: Johns Hopkins University Press, 1992); Joshua Leavitt, *The Financial Power of Slavery: The Substance of an Address Delivered in Ohio, in September, 1840* (n.p., 1841); Olmsted, *Cotton Kingdom*; Vermont Investors to Sec'y of the Treasury, February 3, 1862, in *The Wartime Genesis of Free Labor: The Lower South,* ed. Ira Berlin, Thavolia Glymph, Steven F. Miller, Joseph P. Reidy, Leslie S. Rowland, and Julie Saville (New York:

Cambridge University Press, 1990), 124–51; E. S. Philbrick to a Massachusetts Businessman, April 12, 1862, ibid., 182–87; HQ 2 Brigade SC Expeditionary Corps to Supt. Contrabands at Beaufort, SC, April 4, 1862, ibid., 180–81.

44. Evsey Domar, "The Causes of Slavery: A Hypothesis," *Journal of Economic History* 30, no. 1 (1970): 18–32.

45. See the works of Barrington Moore, Eugene Genovese, and Elizabeth Fox-Genovese; and see the road testing of the model in Shearer Davis Bowman, *Masters and Lords: Mid-19th Century U.S. Planters and Prussian Junkers* (New York: Oxford University Press, 1993).

46. Daron Acemoglu and James Robinson, *Why Nations Fail: The Origins of Power, Prosperity, and Poverty* (New York: Crown, 2012). One might ask whether or not military-industrial sectors or financial capital sectors can achieve similar kinds of destructive hegemony.

47. Ball, *Slavery in the United States,* 212, 216; see William Russell from John Knight to William Beall, August 12, 1844, box 2, John Knight Papers, Duke.

48. I. Campbell, *Autobiography*, 33–35.

49. John Brown, *Slave Life in Georgia: A Narrative of the Life, Sufferings, and Escape of John Brown,* ed. Louis Chamerovzow (London, 1855), 128–32; Anderson, *Life and Narrative,* 18–19; Henry Watson, *Narrative of Henry Watson, a Fugitive Slave* (Boston: Bela Marsh, 1848), 19–20; I. Campbell, *Autobiography,* 33–39; Charles Thompson, *Biography of a Slave* (Dayton, Ohio: United Brethren Publishing House, 1875), 37–38; Ball, *Slavery in the United States,* 216–18; Drew, *A North-Side View of Slavery,* 249; Bibb, *Narrative,* 117; Pennington, *Narrative . . . J. H. Banks,* 68; Northup, *Twelve Years a Slave,* 166–68, 178–79; John Andrew Jackson, *The Experience of a Slave in South Carolina* (London: Passmore and Alabaster, 1862), 10, 12, 23; Eliza Suggs, *Shadow and Sunshine* (Omaha, Neb.: n.p., 1906), 72–73; Pickard, *The Kidnapped and the Ransomed,* 274. For references in 1930s WPA interviews, see Blassingame, ed., *Slave Testimony,* 434; Clifton H. Johnson, ed., *God Struck Me Dead: Religious Conversion Experiences and Autobiographies of Negro Ex-Slaves* (Nashville, Tenn.: Social Science Institute, Fisk University, 1945), 199; Gus Askew, *AS,* 6.1, 15 (Ala.); Sarah Wells, *AS,* s2, 2.1, 89 (Ark.); Sarah Ashley, *AS,* 16.1, 34–35 (Tex.).

50. For thoughtful assessments of the possibilities and problems opened by sources generated by the formerly enslaved, see Blassingame, ed., *Slave Testimony,* xvii–lxv; and Charles T. Davis and Henry Louis Gates, Jr., eds., *The Slave's Narrative* (New York: Oxford University Press, 1985). Recent attempts to dismiss these sources have often come from scholars who are not students of the African experience in New World slavery, and they often expose utter unfamiliarity with the half century of discussion about these sources among scholars who study the experience and culture of the enslaved.

51. C. Vann Woodward, "History from Slave Sources," *American Historical Review* 79, no. 2 (1974): 470–81; Heather Andrea Williams, *Help Me to Find My People: The African American Search for Family Lost in Slavery* (Chapel Hill: University of North Carolina Press, 2012); Joyner, *Down by the Riverside,* among many others.

52. Marion Starling, *The Slave Narrative: Its Place in History,* 2nd ed. (Washington, D.C.: Howard University Press, 1988), 234.

53. Edward E. Baptist, "'Stol' An' Fetched Here': Enslaved Migration, Ex-Slave Narratives, and Vernacular History," in *New Studies in the History of American Slavery,* ed. Edward E. Baptist and Stephanie M. H. Camp (Athens: University of Georgia Press, 2006), 243–74. In general, on the usefulness of the 1930s narratives, see Mia Bay, *The White Image in the Black Mind: African-American Ideas about White People, 1830–1925* (New York: Oxford University Press, 2000), esp. 113–16, and George Rawick, "General Introduction" to *AS,* s1.11, xxxix. For

links between the nineteenth-century and 1930s narratives, links that likely trace back to older traditions of vernacular discussion and thought, see William L. Andrews, *To Tell a Free Story: The First Century of Afro-American Autobiography, 1760–1865* (Urbana: University of Illinois Press, 1985), 274; Marion W. Starling, *The Slave Narrative: Its Place in American History* (1946; repr., Boston: G. K. Hall, 1981); Davis and Gates, eds., *The Slave's Narrative*; Henry Louis Gates, Jr., *The Signifying Monkey: A Theory of Afro-American Literary Criticism* (New York: Oxford University Press, 1988). For the argument that critics have the causality backward—that nineteenth-century survivors' narratives (or "freedom narratives," as we might properly call them) are a major source of, rather than derivative of, abolitionist ideology, see Baptist, *The Half Has Never Been Told*, 187–98, and the references therein to a rich literature on the history of abolitionism.

54. See Paul D. Escott, *Remembering Slavery: A Record of Twentieth-Century Narratives* (Chapel Hill: University of North Carolina Press, 1979); Charles L. Perdue, Jr., Thomas E. Barden, and Robert K. Phillips, eds., *Weevils in the Wheat: Interviews with Virginia Ex-Slaves* (Charlottesville: University of Virginia Press, 1976). The historian Wilma Dunaway, a leading expert on slavery in the mountain South, checked hundreds of the 1930s interviews against other available sources and reported, "I have come away from this effort with a deep respect for the quality and the reliability of these indigenous narratives. When I tested ex-slave claims against the public records, I found them to be more accurate than most of the slaveholder manuscripts that I scrutinized, and quite *often they were much less ideologically blinded than many of the scholarly works I have consulted*"(emphasis added). Wilma Dunaway, *Slavery in the American Mountain South* (Cambridge: Cambridge University Press, 2003), 12.

55. At least thirty-two WPA interviewees give specific information about the methods of labor extraction in cotton picking, and twenty-eight of them specifically describe it as being driven by measurement and violent coercion. Meanwhile, of approximately twenty-five sources collected in the *Documenting the American South* online collection of nineteenth-century published memoirs and autobiographies that describe the experiences of enslaved people who lived in the cotton South before 1861, at least twenty individuals testify directly to the existence of this system: Israel Campbell, Charles Thompson, William Walker, Charles Ball, Henry Bibb, John Brown, William Webb, Henry Watson, J. H. Banks, William Anderson, Louis Hughes, Solomon Northup, John Andrew Jackson, Eliza Suggs, and the multiple individuals interviewed by Kate Pickard and by Benjamin Drew (see http://docsouth.unc.edu/neh/ [accessed July 16, 2015]). The five who did not testify to this system were, like Louisa Picquet or William Hayden, not field slaves when they were in the cotton South, or, like Okah Tubbee, do not specifically describe cotton picking. There is, in short, overwhelming and virtually unanimous evidence on this point from those who survived cotton field labor and reported their experiences.

56. Nor were these survivors atypical, as some will surely claim. Fifty is a very large number in the history of slavery-survivor testimony about anything. And they were distributed widely across the South's cotton belt. If we map the geographic locations where these survivors report they endured the pushing system and cotton picking, we find that their distribution nearly mirrors the map of cotton growing in the 1860 South, covering virtually every geographic region. See map at http://blogs.cornell.edu/edbaptist/2015/11/26/mapping-sites-where-testifying -survivors-of-slavery-encountered-the-whipping-machine/ (accessed November 29, 2015).

57. See Michel-Rolph Trouillot, *Silencing the Past: Power and the Production of History* (Boston: Beacon Press, 1997). Some individuals might read in this paragraph the inference I am calling them "racists"—which name-calling of course, is a terrible crime, to judge from the rage such naming generates. But I am comforted by understanding that their reaction is

what America's greatest historian predicted—or so I infer from John Hope Franklin's description of his own historical process in writing *From Slavery to Freedom*. In the Jim Crow–corrupted libraries and archives of the 1940s, he tracked (at immeasurable personal cost) America's past through the holds of slave ships, fields of cotton that ran up to the whipping post, and auction houses that destroyed families. At the end of his research, "I had seen it all, and in the seeing I had become bewildered, and yet in the process I had lost my own innocence." John Hope Franklin, *Mirror to America: The Autobiography of John Hope Franklin* (New York: Farrar, Straus, & Giroux, 2007), 128. We wait in hope for the day when some scholars no longer demand to be treated as presumptively *innocent* of racism even as they replicate four hundred years of categorical rejection of black testimony about black life and death. Until that day comes, scholars who do not or cannot make such demands must continue to identify not only the crime but the cover-up. In short, in 2015, we should not be arguing about whether or not people who were forced by threat of violence to pick cotton actually have anything useful to say about how coerced cotton picking worked.

58. Robert B. Beverley to Robert Beverley, September 3, 1833, and August 28, 1842, Beverley Family Papers, VHS; J. Monett, appendix C, in J. W. Ingraham, *The South-West, By a Yankee* (New York: Harper and Brothers, 1835), 2:285–86; Knox, *Camp-Fire and Cotton-Field*, 348; Weld, ed., *American Slavery As It Is*, 96, 98 ("So many pounds").

59. For the perspective of an enslaved driver who was required to keep track of the numbers in his head, and wanted to use the overseer's slate, "which hung in his cabin," but was afraid to reveal that he could read, write, and figure, see C. Thompson, *Biography of a Slave*, 41–42; I. Campbell, *Autobiography*, 33–35. See also Ball, *Slavery in the United States*, 212, 216 (quotation). For more evidence of rising quotas, see Robert B. Beverley to Robert Beverley, September 3, 1833 and August 28, 1842, Beverley Family Papers, VHS. By 1860, Paul Cameron expected 200 pounds per day from hands on his Mississippi Delta plantation in Tunica County: W. T. Lamb to Paul Cameron, September 16, 1860, folder 1210, Cameron Family Papers, SHC. For increased overall extraction of labor in the southwest, see L. A. Finley to Caroline Gordon, February 17, 1853, folder 10, Gordon and Hackett Family Papers, SHC; T. J. Brownrigg to Richard Brownrigg, January 29, 1836, folder 4, Brownrigg Family Papers, SHC; A. K. Barlow to J. J. Philips, April 23, 1849, folder 1, Ivan P. Battle Papers, SHC; J. S. Haywood to G. W. Haywood, April 4, 1835, folder 144, Haywood Family Papers, SHC. See also J. S. Haywood to Dear Sister, May 3, 1839, folder 156, Haywood Family Papers, SHC; Paul Cameron to Duncan Cameron, December 13, 1845, folder 974; W. T. Lamb to Paul Cameron, December 1, 1860, folder 1213, Cameron Family Papers, SHC. In Edwin Epps's slave labor camp near the Red River in Louisiana, Solomon Northup saw Epps whip one person or another on the evening of almost every day of the cotton-picking season. Northup, new to such work, was often the victim. Northup also reported the daily minimum for many enslaved people to be 200 pounds in the late 1840s (Northup, *Twelve Years a Slave*, 125, 135).

60. Faster pickers were not safe, as numerous sources attest that they too had to meet their quotas or be whipped: I. Campbell, *Autobiography*, 39; Walker, *Buried Alive*, 17; Brown, *Slave Life in Georgia*, 129; Bibb, *Narrative*, 117; Northup, *Twelve Years a Slave*, 166; Suggs, *Shadow and Sunshine*, 72–73; Salena Taswell, *AS*, 17, 303–7, 372–76 (Fla.). But again, if one doesn't believe formerly enslaved people's own testimony about the realities of their enslavement, one can also look at the records of enslavers. Particularly telling are the records kept by Bennet Barrow, an enslaver of East Feliciana Parish, who kept a "Record of Punishments" for much of 1840–1841. See Edwin A. Davis, ed., *Plantation Life in the Florida Parishes of Louisiana, 1836–1846* (New York: Columbia University Press, 1943), esp. 419–22, 431–40. Among the

seventy-three people who definitely picked cotton in the records of 1840–1842, at least forty-one were whipped for poor picking. They were whipped for poor or short picking a total of eighty-five times in those two years, which included about thirty total weeks or 210 days of picking. For those who think that survivors' narratives exaggerate the frequency of whippings, this means almost three whippings a week for cotton picking—or one every two and a half days. In addition, in these records, there is a positive relationship between the average amount of cotton picked and the number of times one was whipped. See chart at http://blogs.cornell.edu/edbaptist/2015/11/18/19/ (accessed November 29, 2015). More to the point, there is not a negative relationship between the two: Ben, the second fastest picker, was whipped twice for poor cotton picking. Dave Bartley, the third faster, was whipped three times for poor cotton picking. Wash, who averaged almost 350 pounds in the records, was whipped six times for that "offense," while Wade (386 pounds) was whipped four times for poor picking. And so on. Although Barrow's documentary impulses were unusually strong, as we know of no other enslaver who kept a systematic record of whippings and other "punishments," there is no reason to think that he was unusually harsh, especially since what he recorded is pretty much what one might have predicted from reading the testimony of slavery's survivors. Herbert Gutman makes a compelling argument for the representativeness of Barrow in *Slavery and the Numbers Game: A Critique of Time on the Cross* (Urbana: University of Illinois Press, 1975), 31–33.

61. See my visualization of quotas over time, as reported in nineteenth-century and 1930s survivors' accounts of cotton picking: http://blogs.cornell.edu/edbaptist/2015/11/17/survivors-of-slavery-remember-how-much-cotton-they-were-required-to-pick-to-escape-a-whipping/ (accessed November 29, 2015).

62. Northup, *Twelve Years a Slave*, 168; Knox, *Camp-Fire and Cotton-Field*, 348, 356.

63. Bibb, *Narrative*, 117; Louis Hughes, *Thirty Years a Slave: From Bondage to Freedom* (Milwaukee, Wis.: South Side Printing, 1897); Pickard, *The Kidnapped and the Ransomed*, 77; Andy Brice, *AS*, 2.1, 75 (S.C.); Mary Kincheon Edwards, *AS*, s2, 4.1, 1278–82; J. T. Trowbridge, *A Picture of the Desolated States, and the Work of Restoration, 1865–1868* (Hartford, Conn.: L. Stebbins, 1868), 386, shows a former slave overseer trying to use this tactic in postslavery wage labor. Ball, *Slavery in the United States*, 271–73, reports a system of Sunday picking and overplus pay, but much of this seems to have disappeared over the next half century.

64. Brown, *Slave Life in Georgia*, 194. This was a full half century before Frederick Winslow Taylor supposedly timed "Schmidt," the pig-iron carrier, at the Bethlehem Steel Mill, which Taylor then presented as the origin point of the theory of "scientific management." Robert Kanigel, *The One Best Way: Frederick Winslow Taylor and the Enigma of Efficiency* (New York: Viking Adult, 1997); Jill Lepore, "Not So Fast," *New Yorker*, October 12, 2009.

65. Brown, *Slave Life in Georgia*, 128–29, 172; Jackson, *The Experience of a Slave*, 9–10; Northup, *Twelve Years a Slave*, 165 ("whipped up smartly"), 179; Watson, *Narrative of Henry Watson*, 20; Drew, *A North-Side View of Slavery*, 140–41; Anderson, *Life and Narrative*, 19.

66. Irella Battle Walker, *AS*, 5.2, 122–33, s2, 10, 3931–40 (Tex.).

67. The survivors' accounts that talk about cotton picking are virtually universal in insisting not only that tasks or stints were individual (or varied by age, gender, and/or experience) but that weighing took place at the end of the day. Usually this was after dark, and the sources concur that whipping (or, in a few cases, being placed in the stocks) followed for those who were not "up to the task": Mingo White, *AS*, 6.1, 413–20 (Ala.); Martin Ruffin, *AS*, 5.1, 265–67 (Tex.); Addie Vinson, *AS*, 13.2, 97–101 (Ga.); George Womble, *AS*, 13.2, 179–90 (Ga.); Benjamin Henderson, *AS*, 12.2, 173–82 (Ga.); Marshal Butler, *AS*, 12.1, 160–70 (Ga.); Sarah Wells, *AS*, 11.1, 89–96 (Ark.); Fannie Dorum, *AS*, 8.2, 180–82 (Ark.); Cyrus Bellus, *AS*, 8.1,

141–44 (Ark.); Lee Pierce, *AS*, s2, 8.1, 3092–3109 (Tex.); Austin Grant, *AS*, 4.2, 81–92 (Tex.); Monroe Brackins, *AS*, 4, 124–29 (Miss.); John Glover, *AS*, 2.2, 138–47 (S.C.); Lettie Nelson, *AS*, 10, 209–18 (Ark.); Lewis Brown, *AS*, 8, 286–89 (Ark.); Bert Strong, *AS*, S2, 9, 3755–60 (Tex.); Adeline Hodges *AS*, 6, 181–84 (Ala.); Litt Young, *AS*, 5.2, 227–336 (Tex.); Pickard, *The Kidnapped and the Ransomed*, 274; Jackson, *The Experience of a Slave*, 12; Suggs, *Shadow and Sunshine*, 72–73; Northup, *Twelve Years a Slave*, 165–68, 178–79; Pennington, *Narrative . . . J. H. Banks*, 67–68; Bibb, *Narrative*, 117; Watson, *Narrative of Henry Watson*, 19–20; Drew, *A North-Side View of Slavery*, 249; Ball, *Slavery in the United States*, 212–13; Brown, *Slave Life in Georgia*, 129, 172; C. Thompson, *Biography of a Slave*, 37; I. Campbell, *Autobiography*, 34–39.

68. Williamson Pease, as quoted in Drew, *A North-Side View of Slavery*, 132; I. Campbell, *Autobiography*, 34–35; Jackson, *The Experience of a Slave*, 12; John Glover, *AS*, 2.2, 138–47 (S.C.); Sarah Wells, *AS*, 11.1, 89–96 (Ark.). Aside from the abundant evidence that whippings were quite common, those who postulate (in a variant of the *Homo economicus* fallacy) that slave owners would not be "irrational" enough to beat productive workers into temporary or extended unproductivity should consider the effect of exemplary punishment. Certainly enslaved people had plenty of opportunity to consider that effect.

69. Jeremy Prestholdt, "On the Global Repercussions of East African Consumerism," *American Historical Review* 109, no. 3 (2004): 755–81; Beckert, *Empire of Cotton*. For the argument that consumers are primary beneficiaries of slavery, see http://delong.typepad.com/113_F07/20070910_cuibono.pdf (accessed December 11, 2015). DeLong argues that they are *the* primary beneficiaries; I would place them *among* the primary beneficiaries.

70. Dale Tomich, "Slavery in Historical Capitalism: Toward a Theoretical History of the Second Slavery," in *Escravidão e capitalismo histórico: História e historiografia: Brasil, Cuba, Estados Unidos, século XIX*, ed. Ricardo Salles and Rafael de Bivar Marquese (São Paulo: Civilizacão Brasileira, forthcoming).

71. *Trans-Atlantic Slave Trade Database* (http://www.slavevoyages.org/ [accessed July 16, 2015]). We could say that the forced migration of human beings continued, and even accelerated in the nineteenth century, for the same reasons that free immigration to the New World accelerated after 1800. Rapid acceleration of economic growth after 1800—what we call the Industrial Revolution, the beginning of a modern capitalist economic world—created (massively increased) demand for labor. But of course, free immigrants were free, and they wanted to be subsistence farmers, in many cases. Enslaved migrants could not choose, and they were sent to the zones where the most profitable commodities could be made.

72. John Komlos, "Shrinking in a Growing Economy? The Mystery of Physical Stature during the Industrial Revolution," *Journal of Economic History* 58 (September 1998): 779–802; Mintz, *Sweetness and Power*; and the arguments and literature on environmental capacity and calorie production collected in Pomeranz, *Great Divergence*.

73. William J. Rorabaugh, *The Alcoholic Republic: An American Tradition* (New York: Oxford University Press, 1979).

74. Dale W. Tomich, *Through the Prism of Slavery: Labor, Capital, and World Economy* (Lanham, Md.: Rowman and Littlefield, 2004).

75. Rafael de Bivar Marquese, "African Diaspora, Slavery, and the Paraíba Valley Coffee Landscape: Nineteenth-century Brazil," *Review (Fernand Braudel Center)* 31 (2008): 195.

76. A point of interpretation explained most effectively by Johnson, *River of Dark Dreams*, 151–73; see also Baptist, *The Half Has Never Been Told*, 127.

77. Henry Clay from *AS*, s1, 12, 111–12 (Okla.); Martin Heidegger, *The Question Concerning Technology and Other Essays*, trans. William Lewin (New York: Harper, 1977).

78. This is the definition adopted by many historians of torture. On the other hand, the international law is a bit different. Page DuBois, *Torture and Truth* (New York: Routledge, 1991); John Langbein, *Torture and the Law of Proof: Europe and England in the Ancien Régime* (Chicago: University of Chicago Press, 1977); Edward Peters, *Torture*, 2nd ed. (Philadelphia: University of Pennsylvania Press, 1996); Foucault, *Discipline and Punish*. By the UN Convention Against Torture, deliberate violence against an imprisoned or otherwise bound individual becomes torture when it is designed to extract information or a confession, to serve as a punishment, or to inflict intimidation, or when it is based on discrimination. When, more recently, the U.S. government has denied that acts of extreme cruelty carried out by its agents fall under the definition of torture, the denials have elicited so much outrage in no small part because most people accept part or all of the UN's definition of what constitutes torture. See William F. Schulz, ed., *The Phenomenon of Torture: Readings and Commentary* (Philadelphia: University of Pennsylvania Press, 2007).

79. I. Campbell, *Autobiography*, 37–38; George Womble, *AS*, 13.2, 179–90 (Ga.).

80. Northup, *Twelve Years a Slave*, 159; John Haywood to G. W. Haywood, February 5, 1842, Haywood Family Papers, SHC; Monett in Ingraham, *The South-West*, 2:286; Watson, *Narrative of Henry Watson*, 20–21; Jackson, *The Experience of a Slave*, 23; George Womble, *AS*, 13.2, 179–90 (Ga.). For enslavers' objection to help, see I. Campbell, *Autobiography*, 36–39; Austin Grant, *AS*, 4.2, 81–92 (Tex.); Thomas Cole, *AS*, s2, 3, 783–90 (Tex.). After emancipation, cotton planters complained that African American elders no longer pushed young people to work as hard at cotton picking: Francis W. Loring and Charles F. Atkinson, *Cotton Culture and the South Considered with Reference to Emigration* (Boston: A. Williams, 1869), 4.

81. Northup, *Twelve Years a Slave*, 134, 142–43.

82. For most humans, the left side of the brain is the side most heavily involved in analytical, detailed, specific processes and thoughts. These processes include language production and processing and skilled work with the hands. The right side of the brain is more responsible for "global" processes such as a general perception of the world, and many believe it to be more artistic, more emotional. This right-left brain division should not be overstated, for both sides of the brain work together, and the nature of the asymmetry is not the same in all people. In a minority of left-handers, for example, language faculties are primarily based in the right side of the brain rather than the left. See I. C. McManus, *Right Hand, Left Hand: The Origins of Asymmetry in Brains, Bodies, Atoms, and Cultures* (Cambridge, Mass.: Harvard University Press, 2002).

83. Salena Taswell, *AS*, 17, 303–7, 372–76 (Fla.).

84. Weld, ed., *American Slavery As It Is*, 69; Ball, *Slavery in the United States*, 215. Here was the rest of the story of the woman who did not get the sleight of it: "I whipped her, and if I did it once I did it five hundred times, but I found she *could* not; so I put her to carrying rails with the men. After a few days I found her shoulders were so *raw* that every rail was *bloody* as she laid it down. I asked her if she would not rather pick cotton than carry rails. 'No,' said she, 'I don't get whipped now.'"

85. Adeline Hodges *AS*, 6.1, 181 (Ala.); Brown, *Slave Life in Georgia*, 176 ("irksome"); Ball, *Slavery in the United States*, 218 ("fatiguing" and "never thoroughly").

86. In addition to the history of scientific management and time-and-motion studies, we could look to the stretch-out—the speedup of machines in the textile factories of the U.S. South in the 1920s—which found an echo in the Lordstown, Ohio, auto factories of the 1960s and 1970s. In more recent decades, the increasing use of quotas and other pressures placed on manufacturing workers and even skilled professionals has been part of the story of increasing

productivity and flat or decreasing real wages. Management has a history; it develops and changes over time. It changed in the course of slavery, and those changes are, some argue, part of the history of management: Bill Cooke, "The Denial of Slavery in Management Studies," *Journal of Management Studies* 40, no. 8 (2003): 1895–1918. And then there are the Amazon fulfillment warehouses, which use a huge array of techniques pioneered in the cotton fields to extract intense and continuous labor from employees. These employees are not enslaved. But they are powerfully disadvantaged in the contemporary economy, for various reasons. And they are ultimately expected to figure out the efficiencies of movement for themselves, even as their quotas are raised. See Mac McClelland, "I Was a Warehouse Wage Slave," *Mother Jones*, March/April, 2012; Simon Head, "Worse than Walmart: Amazon's Sick Brutality and Secret History of Ruthlessly Intimidating Workers," *Salon*, February 23, 2014, http://www.salon.com/2014/02/23/worse_than_wal_mart_amazons_sick_brutality_and_secret_history_of_ruthlessly_intimidating_workers/; Jamie Grierson, "Amazon 'Regime' Making British Staff Physically and Mentally Ill, Says Union," *Guardian*, August 18, 2015, http://www.theguardian.com/technology/2015/aug/18/amazon-regime-making-british-staff-physically-and-mentally-ill-says-union.

CHAPTER 2. SLAVERY'S SCIENTIFIC MANAGEMENT

1. The next day, when the cotton was "not so good" and the morning was "quite cold," the hands brought in only 2,202 pounds. Eli J. Capell, Plantation diary for 1842, vol. 8, Capell Family Papers, MSS 56, 257, 1751, 2501, 2597, Louisiana and Lower Mississippi Valley Collections, Louisiana State University Libraries, Baton Rouge.

2. Alfred D. Chandler, Jr., *The Visible Hand: The Managerial Revolution in American Business* (Cambridge, Mass.: Harvard University Press, 1977), 63–64. Interestingly, feudal management may not have been as primitive as Chandler's remark intended: see T. K. Dennison, *The Institutional Framework of Russian Serfdom* (New York: Cambridge University Press, 2011).

3. Bill Cooke, "The Denial of Slavery in Management Studies," *Journal of Management Studies* 40 (December 2003): 1895–1918; see also Marcel van der Linden, "Re-constructing the origins of Modern Labor Management," *Labor History* 51, no. 4 (2010): 509. And for an earlier precedent, see R. Keith Aufhauser, "Slavery and Scientific Management," *Journal of Economic History* 33 (December 1973): 811–24.

4. This landscape has shifted radically since the text of this chapter was first circulated in 2011. On the role of race in the development of northern management practices, see David R. Roediger and Elizabeth D. Esch, *The Production of Difference* (New York: Oxford University Press, 2012). On slavery and capitalism more generally, see most recently, among many others, Walter Johnson, *River of Dark Dreams: Slavery and Empire in the Cotton Kingdom* (Cambridge, Mass.: Harvard University Press, 2013); Edward E. Baptist, *The Half Has Never Been Told: Slavery and the Making of American Capitalism* (New York: Basic Books, 2014); Calvin Schermerhorn, *The Business of Slavery and the Rise of American Capitalism, 1815–1860* (New Haven, Conn.: Yale University Press, 2015); and Sven Beckert, *Empire of Cotton: A Global History* (New York: Alfred A. Knopf, 2014). Many of these recent arguments also have long-standing precedents in research on the semi-industrial nature of Caribbean sugar production. For examples, see Sidney Wilfred Mintz's classic *Sweetness and Power: The Place of Sugar in Modern History* (New York: Viking, 1985), and more recently B. W Higman, *Plantation Jamaica, 1750–1850: Capital*

and Control in a Colonial Economy (Kingston, Jamaica: University of the West Indies Press, 2008), and Justin Roberts, *Slavery and the Enlightenment in the British Atlantic, 1750–1807* (New York: Cambridge University Press, 2013). There has also been an increase in research on slavery among historians of accounting. For further discussion, see the "Human Capital" section of this chapter and note 85.

5. Capell, Plantation diaries for 1842–1867, vols. 8–30, Capell Family Papers. See also Wendell Holmes Stephenson, "A Quarter-Century of a Mississippi Plantation: Eli J. Capell of 'Pleasant Hill,'" *Mississippi Valley Historical Review* 23 (December 1936): 358.

6. Capell, Plantation diaries for 1843–1845, vols. 8–10, Capell Family Papers.

7. Capell, Plantation diaries for 1840–1862, vol. 15, Capell Family Papers. See also vols. 16–27 for additional Affleck books, by far the most common method used by Capell during this period.

8. Thomas Affleck to James Henry Hammond, January 3, 1855, 262–66, box 32, folder 10, Thomas Affleck Papers, MSS 3, 4, 1110, 1263, 1264, Louisiana and Lower Mississippi Valley Collections, Louisiana State University Libraries, Baton Rouge.

9. Ibid.

10. Ibid. On Affleck's life and varied interests, see also Robert W. Williams, "Thomas Affleck: Missionary to the Planter, the Farmer, and the Gardener," *Agricultural History* 31 (July 1957): 40–48. On Affleck from a different perspective, see Jan R. Heier, "A Content Comparison of Antebellum Plantation Records and Thomas Affleck's Accounting Principles," *Accounting Historians Journal* 15 (Fall 1988): 131–50.

11. Farmer's Record and Account Book advertisement, *Subscription Books* (n.p.: Fairbanks, Palmer and Co., 1850), 531.

12. G. R. Clark, Eustatia Plantation Account Book (1861), vol. 649, Ohio History Center Archives Library, Columbus, http://dbs.ohiohistory.org/africanam/html/det2b9e.html?ID=13902.

13. Thomas Affleck, "Explanation of Records and Accounts," in any edition of the Cotton Plantation Record and Account Book. For example, Capell, Plantation diaries for 1840–1862, vol. 15, Capell Family Papers.

14. Advertisement, *Affleck's Southern Rural Almanac*, 1860, 1–6.

15. Thomas Affleck to James Henry Hammond, January 3, 1855, 262–66, Thomas Affleck Papers.

16. Thomas Affleck, "Instructions to Overseers," Plantation Record and Account Book.

17. Advertisement, *Affleck's Southern Rural Almanac*, 1854, p. 2.

18. Capell, Plantation diary for 1857, vol. 23, Capell Family Papers.

19. Thomas Affleck, "Advertisement for the Third Edition of the Cotton-Plantation Record and Account Book," in *Southern Rural Almanac, and Plantation and Garden Calendar* (Washington, Miss.: Thomas Affleck, 1854), 2.

20. "The Farmer's Record and Account Book" was advertised by I. D. Affleck as "revised and improved" from the eighth edition of the "Plantation Record and Account Book" published by his father. "The Farmer's Record and Account Book," *Select readings for public and private entertainment* (Detroit: Fairbanks, Palmer and Co., 1886), 531, available at http://hdl.handle.net/2027/mdp.39015059899321.

21. Thomas Affleck to B. M. Norman, January 6, 1851, box 32, folder 6, Thomas Affleck Papers.

22. Ibid.

23. On Affleck's relationship with J. M. Weld, see various letters in box 32, folder 7, Thomas Affleck Papers.

24. Thomas Affleck to B. M. Norman, February 14, 1854, box 32, folder 9, Thomas Affleck Papers.

25. Affleck to Hammond, January 3, 1855, box 32, folder 10, Thomas Affleck Papers. In addition to books mentioned by Affleck, see, e.g., the 1857 books of the Natchez planter Robert Stewart, who used a very similar Statement of Cotton Book, printed by W. H. Fox. Robert H. Stewart Family Account Books, Louisiana and Lower Mississippi Valley Collections, Louisiana State University Libraries, Baton Rouge.

26. On southern efforts at improvement and modernization, see John Majewski, *Modernizing a Slave Economy: The Economic Vision of the Confederate Nation* (Chapel Hill: University of North Carolina Press, 2009); and Steven G. Collins, "System, Organization, and Agricultural Reform in the Antebellum South, 1840–1860," *Agricultural History* 75 (Winter 2001): 1–27.

27. Plantations with more than ten slaves were approximately one quarter of all cotton growers, but they produced more then three quarters of all cotton. Plantations with more than thirty slaves were less than ten percent of all cotton growers, but they produced half of all cotton. Calculations are based on William N. Parker and Robert E. Gallman, Southern Farms Study, 1860, ICPSR07419-VI (Ann Arbor, Mich.: Inter-university Consortium for Political and Social Research, 1991), doi:10.3886/ICPSR07419.VI.

28. Thomas Affleck to Norman, January 6, 1851, box 32, folder 11, Thomas Affleck Papers.

29. Andrew Flynn, Plantation Book, M-1057, Southern Historical Collection, Louis Round Wilson Library, University of North Carolina, Chapel Hill.

30. Farquhar Macrae, "Forms for an Overseer's Journal and Monthly Reports, Suited to a Southern Plantation," in *The Farmers' Register*, ed. Edmund Ruffin, vol. 3 (Richmond, Va.: Edmund Ruffin, 1836), 163–65.

31. See books printed by Leapidge & Bailey in London and used on Prospect Estate in Jamaica. Plantation journals for Prospect Estate, January 1, 1787–December 31, 1793, Barclays Group Archives, Dallimore Road, Wythenshawe, Manchester.

32. *The Workman's Account Book on an Easy and Economical Plan* (Boston: Theodore Abbot, 1828); *The Workman's Account Book on an Easy and Economical Plan* (Boston: Theodore Abbot 1849).

33. David Young of Perth, *The Farmers Account-Book of Expenditure and Produce for Each Day, Month, and Year* (Edinburgh: David Young, 1788).

34. Another area in which North and South "faced off" in accounts was Civil War finance, and in this theater, the South ultimately came up short. However, while the financial policy of the South did weaken its position in the Civil War, this was not for lack of numerical sophistication. Rather, as Richard Lester writes, the South's strategic decision to withhold sales of cotton in order "to coerce Great Britain and France to support its cause" left it cripplingly short on cash when the war extended longer than expected. Richard I. Lester, *Confederate Finance and Purchasing in Great Britain* (Charlottesville: University of Virginia Press, 1975), 5. On balance, classic works on Confederate finance show the complexity of southern efforts despite this strategic error. See also Richard Cecil Todd, *Confederate Finance* (Athens: University of Georgia Press, 1954).

35. Pleasant Suit, *The Farmer's Accountant and, Instructions for Overseers* (Richmond, Va.: J. MacFarlan, 1828), xiv.

36. Clark, Eustatia Plantation Account Book.

37. For Affleck's instructions to add additional space for a running total, see his letter to Damrell and Moore, June 26, 1854, box 32, folder 9, Thomas Affleck Papers.

38. Charles Thompson, *Biography of a Slave* (Dayton, Ohio: United Bretheren Publishing House, 1875), 37–41.

39. Henry Bibb, *Narrative of the Life and Adventures of Henry Bibb, an American Slave, Written by Himself* (New York: Author, 1849), 116–17.

40. James O. Breeden, *Advice Among Masters: The Ideal in Slave Management in the Old South* (Westport, Conn.: Greenwood Press, 1980), 258–59.

41. Henry Watson, *Narrative of Henry Watson, a Fugitive Slave* (Boston: Bela Marsh, 1848), 19–20.

42. John Brown, *Slave Life in Georgia*, ed. Louis Alexis Chamerovzow (London: W. M. Watts, 1855), 129.

43. Solomon Northup, *Twelve Years a Slave* (Auburn, N.Y.: Miller, Orton and Mulligan, 1855), 167–68.

44. Brown, *Slave Life in Georgia*, 128–29. Baptist, *The Half Has Never Been Told*, 116–43, describes the structure of violence in what he calls the "pushing system" in more extensive detail.

45. Cooke, "The Denial of Slavery in Management Studies," 1905; Frederick Law Olmsted, *The Cotton Kingdom: A Traveller's Observations on Cotton and Slavery in the American Slave States, 1853–1861*, vol. 1 *(Civil War)* (New York: Mason Brothers, 1861), 128; idem, *Walks and Talks of an American Farmer in England* (New York: G. P. Putnam, 1852), 38. As early as the 1940s, Bauer and Bauer described the slowing of labor as a strategy of resistance. Raymond A. Bauer and Alice H. Bauer, "Day to Day Resistance to Slavery," *Journal of Negro History* 27 (October 1942): 388–419. On the perils of overemphasizing resistance, see Walter Johnson, "On Agency," *Journal of Social History* 37 (2003): 113–24.

46. Israel Campbell, *An Autobiography, Bond and Free . . .* (Philadelphia: C. E. P. Brinckloe, 1861), 33–35.

47. Breeden, *Advice Among Masters*, 257–58.

48. On fidelity funds, see Robert Bruce Davies, *Peacefully Working to Conquer the World: Singer Sewing Machines in Foreign Markets, 1854–1920* (New York: Arno Press, 1976), 65.

49. Capell, Plantation diary for 1852–53, vol. 18, Capell Family Papers.

50. See Thompson, *Biography of a Slave*, 41: "The overseer used a slate on which to set down the weights of cotton, which was hanging in his cabin." See also Campbell, *Autobiography*, 33–35: "He kept a slate with each hand's name on it, and would put each draft of cotton down as they brought it in."

51. Alan L. Olmstead and Paul W. Rhode, "Biological Innovation and Productivity Growth in the Antebellum Cotton Economy," *Journal of Economic History* 68 (2008): 1123–71. See also *Creating Abundance: Biological Innovation and American Agricultural Development* (New York: Cambridge University Press, 2008). See Johnson, *River of Dark Dreams*, 152–54, on Petite Gulf cotton, and Baptist, *The Half Has Never Been Told*, 126–30, 445–46n31. For previous discussions of plantation productivity (using total factor productivity instead of cotton picking), see the debate surrounding Robert William Fogel and Stanley L. Engerman, *Time on the Cross: The Economics of American Negro Slavery* (Boston: Little, Brown, 1974), and Robert William Fogel, *Without Consent or Contract: The Rise and Fall of American Slavery* (New York: W. W. Norton, 1989). Although Fogel and Engerman do not adequately emphasize violence, their explanation for high rates of productivity is a kind of "speedup" in the pace of labor,

a mechanism more compatible with Baptist's "whipping-machine" than with Rhode and Olmsted's account.

52. In a sense, I am suggesting that accounting was what economists call a "general purpose technology." It helped planters reap the benefits of all kinds of innovations and communicate their findings through the southern agricultural press. On these technologies, see, for example, Paul A. David, "The Dynamo and the Computer: An Historical Perspective on the Modern Productivity Paradox," *American Economic Review* 80, no. 2 (1990): 355–61; Nicholas Crafts, "Steam as a General Purpose Technology: A Growth Accounting Perspective," *Economic Journal* 114, no. 495 (2004): 338–51; Nathan Rosenberg and Manuel Trajtenberg, "A General-Purpose Technology at Work: The Corliss Steam Engine in the Late-Nineteenth-Century United States," *Journal of Economic History* 64, no. 1 (2004): 61–99.

53. On the southern press, see, e.g., John F. Kvach, *De Bow's Review* (Lexington: University Press of Kentucky, 2013); On the longer history of agricultural innovation, see Joyce E. Chaplin, *An Anxious Pursuit: Agricultural Innovation and Modernity in the Lower South, 1730–1815* (Chapel Hill: IEAHC/University of North Carolina Press, 1993); and Lorena Seebach Walsh, *Motives of Honor, Pleasure, and Profit: Plantation Management in the Colonial Chesapeake, 1607–1763* (Chapel Hill: OIEAHC/University of North Carolina Press, 2010).

54. Thomas Affleck to Hammond, January 3, 1855, box 32, folder 10, 262–66, Thomas Affleck Papers.

55. Chandler, *The Visible Hand*, 119.

56. Edward Frost and Horry Estate Slave List, 1841, ser. C, pt. 2, roll 1, 0134, RASP (*Records of Ante-Bellum Southern Plantations*, microfilm series, University Publications of America, Fredericksburg, Md.).

57. Frederick Law Olmsted, *Journeys and Explorations in the Cotton Kingdom: A Traveller's Observations on Cotton and Slavery in the American Slave States*, vol. 2 (London: Sampson Low, Son and Co., 1861), 177.

58. "Practice of Agriculture," in *Southern Cultivator*, vol. 4 (Augusta, Ga., 1846), 11.

59. Frederick Law Olmsted, *A Journey in the Seaboard Slave States: With Remarks on Their Economy* (New York: Dix and Edwards, 1856), 420.

60. Ibid., 57.

61. Clark, Eustatia Plantation Account Book.

62. "Practice of Agriculture," *Southern Cultivator*, vol. 4 (1846), 11.

63. "Sea Island Cotton Planting," *Southern Cultivator*, vol. 6 (1848), 135.

64. Lewis Cecil Gray, *History of Southern Agriculture in the United States to 1860*, 2 vols. (Washington, D.C.: Carnegie Institution of Washington, 1933), 1:552–53. The "task-acre" should not be confused with what Walter Johnson has evocatively called a "trinomial algebra of bales per hand per acre" (and elsewhere bales per acre per hand). While Johnson's language is evocative and gestures toward the overall outlook of planters, these exact calculations would have been unusual. As Johnson acknowledges, labor was the limiting factor in production, and calculations about acreage generally focused on how much land to plant per slave in order to maximize labor output. The task-acre was a way of determining the optimal amount of land for one enslaved hand to farm, not a way of getting the most out of land production. On the trinomial, see Johnson, *River of Dark Dreams*, 153, 197, 246.

65. Stephenson, "A Quarter-Century of a Mississippi Plantation," 361.

66. Capell, Plantation diary for 1850, vol. 15, Capell Family Papers.

67. James D. B. De Bow, *De Bow's Review* 23 (1857): 126; Frederick Law Olmsted, *A Journey Through Texas, or, A Saddle-Trip on the Southwestern Frontier* (New York: Dix, Edwards and Co., 1857), 208. On De Bow, see Kvach, *De Bow's Review*.

68. Frederick Winslow Taylor, *The Principles of Scientific Management* (New York: Harper and Brothers, 1911), 55.

69. Plowden C. J. Weston, *Rules for the Government and Management of Plantation* (Charleston, S.C.: A. J. Burke), 8.

70. Taylor, *Principles of Scientific Management*, 59.

71. Ibid, 55.

72. "A Day's Work," in *The Soil of the South*, vol. 6 (Columbus, Ga.: W. H. Chambers, 1848), 85–86.

73. "Reply to 'A Day's Work,'" in *The Soil of the South*, vol. 6 (Columbus, Ga.: W. H. Chambers, 1848), 103.

74. Jacob Metzer, "Rational Management, Modern Business Practices, and Economies of Scale in the Ante-bellum Southern Plantations," *Explorations in Economic History* 12 (April 1975): 123–50.

75. July 15, 1769, as quoted in Gray, *History of Southern Agriculture in the United States*, 1:550. George Washington kept meticulous accounts, and Affleck cites Washington as a source (see Capell, Plantation diary, 1858, vol. 24, Capell Family Papers).

76. Richard Follett, *The Sugar Masters: Planters and Slaves in Louisiana's Cane World, 1820–1860* (Baton Rouge: Louisiana State University Press, 2007), 112–13.

77. Breeden, *Advice Among Masters*, 197.

78. "Drinks for Harvest," in *The Merchants' & Planters' Almanac, for the Year of Our Lord and Saviour 1855* (New Orleans: Converse and Co., 1854).

79. Affleck, as quoted in Follett, *The Sugar Masters*, 71–72.

80. These details can be found in the instructions found in the opening pages of any volume of Thomas Affleck's Plantation Record and Account Book.

81. Malvern Hill Plantation, Account Book, 1860–61, copy obtained from the personal collection of Stanley L. Engerman. Original archive could not be located.

82. Capell, Plantation diary for 1851, vols. 14,16, MSS 56, Capell Family Papers.

83. Henry Wiencek, *Master of the Mountain: Thomas Jefferson and His Slaves* (New York: Farrar, Straus and Giroux, 2012), 8–9.

84. Capell's practices vary across Plantation diaries, vols. 14–20, Capell Family Papers.

85. For an overview of this literature, see Thomas Tyson and Richard Fleischman, "The History of Management Accounting in the U.S.," *Handbooks of Management Accounting Research* 2 (2006): 1071–89; and Gary John Previts and Barbara Dubis Merino, *A History of Accountancy in the United States* (Columbus: Ohio State University Press, 1998), 98, 163, 218. On early examples of the use of depreciation outside the United States, see Lee Parker and Richard Fleischman, *What Is Past Is Prologue: Cost Accounting in the British Industrial Revolution, 1760–1850* (New York: Garland Press, 1997).

86. The last decade has seen an explosion of research by accounting historians. Affleck's discussion of depreciation is noted in Richard K. Fleischman and Thomas N. Tyson, "Accounting in Service to Racism: Monetizing Slave Property in the Antebellum South," *Critical Perspectives on Accounting* 15 (April 2004): 376–99. The best treatment of the implications of valuing slaves can be found in Richard K. Fleischman, David Oldroyd, and Thomas N. Tyson, "Monetising Human Life," *Accounting History* 9 (July 2004): 35–62. See also Richard K. Fleischman, David Oldroyd, and Thomas N. Tyson, "Plantation Accounting and Management Practices

in the U.S. and the British West Indies at the End of Their Slavery Eras," *Economic History Review* 64 (March 2011): 765–97; and Cheryl S. McWatters and Yannick Lemarchand, "Accounting Representation and the Slave Trade," *Accounting Historians Journal* 33 (December 2006): 1–37.

87. Several economic historians have explored the theoretical implications of thinking about slaves as capital assets, but these discussions generally pay less attention to actual accounting practices. See, e.g., Roger L. Ransom, *Conflict and Compromise* (Cambridge: Cambridge University Press, 1989), 42–44; and Ralph V. Anderson and Robert E. Gallman, "Slaves as Fixed Capital: Slave Labor and Southern Economic Development," *Journal of American History* 64 (June 1977): 24–46.

88. Duncan Clinch Slave List, 1859, RASP, ser. C, pt. 2, roll 1, 0134.

89. Stephenson, "A Quarter-Century of a Mississippi Plantation," 373.

90. Thomas Chase to Thomas Affleck, August 19, 1865, box 31, folder 52, Thomas Affleck Papers. On the project, see also box 31, folders 52–63.

CHAPTER 3. AN INTERNATIONAL HARVEST

1. Emory Johnson, T. W. Van Metre, G. G. Huebner, and D. S. Hanchett, *History of Domestic and Foreign Commerce of the United States*, 2 vols. (Washington, D.C.: Carnegie Institution of Washington, 1915), 2:48–49; Paul Gates, *The Farmer's Age: Agriculture, 1815–1860* (New York: Holt, Rinehart, and Winston, 1960), 167.

2. The total bushels for both New York and Pennsylvania had fallen in the antebellum years, but significantly only for New York (which grew 13 million bushels in 1850 but only 8.7 million bushels in 1860). The New England states had mostly abandoned the crop by 1860. Percy Bidwell and John Falconer, *History of Agriculture in the Northern United States, 1620–1860* (Washington, D.C.: Carnegie Institution of Washington, 1925), 323. Recent work emphasizes the pan-American ties among slaveholders in the antebellum period, which appear to have helped Virginia remain in the top five wheat producers nationwide at a time when states such as Illinois and Wisconsin were sending unheard-of quantities of small grains to urban markets in the Northeast. Matthew Pratt Guterl, *American Mediterranean: Southern Slaveholders in the Age of Emancipation* (Cambridge, Mass.: Harvard University Press, 2008); Gerald Horne, *The Deepest South: The United States, Brazil, and the African Slave Trade* (New York: NYU Press, 2007).

3. William Carter Hughes, *The American Miller and Millwright's Assistant* (Philadelphia: Henry Carey Baird, 1855), 152–65. See also John C. Brush, *A small tract entitled, A candid and impartial exposition of the various opinions on the subject of the comparative quality of the wheat and flour in the northern and southern sections of the United States, with a view to develope the true cause of the difference* (Washington, D.C.: Jacob Gideon, Jr., 1820).

4. The U.S. Navy commissary, for example, specified that flour, "when required for shipment abroad, shall be fully equal to the best description of Richmond flour, in all the qualities essential to its preservation in tropical climates." *New-Hampshire Patriot and State Gazette*, March 27, 1845.

5. James Irwin, "Exploring the Affinity of Wheat and Slavery in the Virginia Piedmont," *Explorations in Economic History* 25 (July 1988): 295–322.

6. For an explanation of the early to mid-nineteenth-century agricultural improvement doctrines through which some planters tried to revitalize Old South farmlands, see Steven Stoll,

Larding the Lean Earth: Soil and Society in Nineteenth-Century America (New York: Hill and Wang, 2002), esp. 13–67.

7. Guano, wheat, and railroads were tightly linked, further highlighting the back-and-forth dynamic with South America characteristic of the antebellum wheat boom. Allan Comp, "Grain and Flour in Eastern Virginia: 1800–1860" (PhD diss., University of Delaware, 1978), 116–22, 197.

8. For one book-length interpretation of Ruffin's agricultural philosophies, see William M. Mathew, *Edmund Ruffin and the Crisis of Slavery in the Old South: The Failure of Agricultural Reform* (Athens: University of Georgia Press, 1988).

9. Augusta and Rockbridge Counties (the McCormick farm lay on the border between the two) were top-ranked iron producers in the Valley, and in the top handful of counties at the state level. U.S. Department of Interior, Census Office, *Manufactures of the United States in 1860; Compiled from the Original Returns of the Eighth Census, under the Direction of the Secretary of the Interior* (Washington, D.C., 1865), 604–37.

10. For useful accounts of how race and gender have shaped cultural understandings of who can practice science or technology, see Nina Lerman, "Categories of Difference, Categories of Power: Bringing Gender and Race to the History of Technology," *Technology and Culture* 51 (October 2010): 893–918; Zorina Khan, *The Democratization of Invention: Patents and Copyrights in American Economic Development, 1790–1920* (New York: Cambridge University Press, 2005); Harold Cook, "Global Economies and Local Knowledge in the East Indies: Jacobus Bontius Learns the Facts of Nature," in *Colonial Botany: Science, Commerce, and Politics in the Early Modern World*, ed. Londa Schiebinger and Claudia Swan (Philadelphia: University of Pennsylvania Press, 2005), 100–118; Susan Scott Parrish, "Diasporic African Sources of Enlightenment Knowledge," in *Science and Empire in the Atlantic World*, ed. James Delbourgo and Nicholas Dew (New York: Routledge, 2008), 281–310; Neil Safier, "Global Knowledge on the Move: Itineraries, Amerindian Narratives, and Deep Histories of Science," *Isis* 101 (March 2010): 133–45; Helen Tilley, "Global Histories, Vernacular Science, and African Genealogies; or, Is the History of Science Ready for the World?," *Isis* 101 (March 2010): 110–19; and Kathleen Murphy, "Translating the Vernacular: Indigenous and African Knowledge in the Eighteenth-Century British Atlantic," *Atlantic Studies* 8 (March 2011): 29–48.

11. William Hutchinson, *Cyrus Hall McCormick: Seed-Time, 1809–1856* (New York: Century Co., 1930), 27.

12. Ibid., 165.

13. Ibid., 188.

14. The McCormick reaper's place of origin has often been ignored by scholars. One eminent historian of the Industrial Revolution, for example, describes the reaper as "invented by the American Cyrus McCormick in 1832 for the flat, wide-open midwestern fields." Joel Mokyr, *The Lever of Riches: Technological Creativity and Economic Progress* (New York: Oxford University Press, 1990), 138.

15. However, the Upper South has been posited as one of the zones of decline left behind by the Second Slavery. The idea of a moribund system of slavery in the Upper South has been restated most recently in Edward E. Baptist, *The Half Has Never Been Told: Slavery and the Making of American Capitalism* (New York: Basic Books, 2014). Despite proclamations of a "slow death for slavery" in the Upper South, the state of Virginia still had more slaves than any other state in the Union in 1860; it was so enmeshed in the institution that despite being a slave exporter of major importance for the rise of the cotton southwest, the state still increased its own enslaved population by 42 percent between 1800 and 1860. Half a million enslaved Virginians

remained in the Old Dominion, allowing the state's planters to put more tobacco on the market than any other state in the Union in 1860. Virginia also held its spot in the top five wheat producers nationwide, despite rapid growth in both sectors at the national level. In 1860, Virginia made 13 million bushels. Ohio made 15 million. Indiana made 16.8 million, Wisconsin 15.6 million, and Illinois an impressive 23.8 million bushels. Bidwell and Falconer, *History of Agriculture*, 323.

16. Cotton alone accounted for 51.5 percent of U.S. export totals in 1860, while breadstuffs constituted 15 percent. Johnson et al., *History of Domestic and Foreign Commerce*, 48.

17. Knowledge, experiment, and even science have been centered in a few accounts of economic change. Perhaps slavery scholars could follow suit. Joel Mokyr, "The Intellectual Origins of Modern Economic Growth," *Journal of Economic History* 65 (June 2005): 285–351; Margaret Jacob, *Scientific Culture and the Making of the Industrial West* (New York: Oxford University Press, 2005). These scholars have also begun to explore the technological contributions made by nonelite actors. Joel Mokyr has uncovered a world of "micro-inventions" developed by artisan "tinkerers," who may not have shaken the world with utterly novel inventions but who performed the arguably more pivotal work of incrementally improving big, unworkable ideas. Mokyr, *Lever of Riches*. See also Robert Gordon, "Who Turned the Mechanical Ideal into Mechanical Reality?," *Technology and Culture* 29 (October 1988): 744–78. For analyses of collective, incremental technological change in the context of antebellum U.S. slavery, see Merrit Roe Smith, *Harpers Ferry Armory and the New Technology: The Challenge of Change* (Ithaca, N.Y.: Cornell University Press, 1977); and Angela Lakwete, *Inventing the Cotton Gin: Machine and Myth in Antebellum America* (Baltimore: Johns Hopkins University Press, 2003).

18. The McCormick plantation, ironically, has been refurbished as part of the Agricultural Experiment Station of Virginia Tech.

19. Hutchinson, *Cyrus Hall McCormick: Seed-Time*, 26.

20. Lynn Nelson, *Pharsalia: An Environmental Biography of a Southern Plantation, 1780–1880* (Athens: University of Georgia Press, 2007).

21. William Weaver, for example, a well-known ironmaster of Rockbridge County, managed a highly productive 800-acre wheat farm using six McCormick plows. He also had two mills on his property: a gristmill, which ground corn into meal to feed his enslaved workforce, and a merchant mill, which manufactured flour bound for Richmond. "Farming of Mr. William Weaver, Rockbridge County, Virginia," *Farmer's Register* 10 (1843): 411–12. For a book-length analysis of Weaver's slave-centered agro-industrial complex, see Charles Dew, *Bond of Iron: Master and Slave at Buffalo Forge* (New York: W. W. Norton, 1994).

22. By the 1830s there were hundreds of different kinds of affordable threshers available on the market nationwide. Peter McClelland, *Sowing Modernity: America's First Agricultural Revolution* (Ithaca, N.Y.: Cornell University Press, 1997), 167–70, 177, 129.

23. Alan Olmstead and Paul Rhode, *Creating Abundance: Biological Innovation and American Agricultural Development* (Cambridge: Cambridge University Press, 2008), 43–45.

24. Edmund Ruffin, "Experiments to Show the Proper State of Wheat for Reaping," *Farmer's Register* 9 (1841): 470.

25. William Carmichael, "The Adaptation of Particular Wheats to Particular Localities.— Patent Machines," *Farmer's Register* 10 (1843): 89.

26. Agricola [pseud.], "For the Enquirer. The Wheat Market of Richmond," *Richmond Enquirer*, August 4, 1837. Emphasis added.

27. Paul Clemens, *The Atlantic Economy and Colonial Maryland's Eastern Shore: From Tobacco to Grain* (Ithaca, N.Y.: Cornell University Press, 1980), 184–86. Many wheat farms also

grew tobacco for market. Tobacco was mostly grown in small patches, and its seasonal labor requirements lined up conveniently with those of wheat. New philosophies of crop rotation advocated the cultivation of tobacco-wheat-corn-fallow crops in consecutive seasons on particular fields. Stephen Tripp, *Yankee Town, Southern City: Race and Class Relations in Civil War Lynchburg* (New York: NYU Press, 1997); Robert Joseph, *The Tobacco Kingdom: Plantation, Market and Factory in Virginia and North Carolina, 1800–1860* (Durham, N.C.: Duke University Press, 1938).

28. For more explanation of the idea of the plantation laboratory, see Daniel Rood, "Plantation Technocrats: A Social History of Knowledge in the Slaveholding Atlantic World, 1830–1865" (PhD diss., University of California, 2010), esp. 21–72.

29. McClelland, *Sowing Modernity*, 62.

30. Hutchinson, *Cyrus Hall McCormick: Seed-Time*, 90–91.

31. "Hussey's Grain Cutter. Report of the Board of Trustees of the Maryland Agricultural Society for the Eastern Shore of Maryland," *Farmer's Register* 4 (1836): 413.

32. The many experiments provided Virginia's rural public with a practical form of education that cannot be captured by counting numbers of schools in particular regions of the country.

33. Gerald Judd of Virginia Tech's Agricultural Experiment Station writes that McCormick "had an excellent blacksmith, a slave named Joe. . . . His ingenuity, and the skills of the blacksmith, led to the reciprocal cutting bar demonstrated so successfully first in 1831." Janet Baugher Downs, Earl J. Downs, and Nancy T. Sorrells, eds., *Mills of Augusta County* (Staunton, Va.: Augusta County Historical Society, 2004), 155.

34. Diane Barnes, *Artisan Workers in the Upper South: Petersburg, Virginia, 1820–1865* (Baton Rouge: Louisiana State University Press, 2008); Melvin Ely, *Israel on the Appomattox: A Southern Experiment in Black Freedom from the 1790s Through the Civil War* (New York: Alfred A. Knopf, 2004); Dew, *Bond of Iron*; John Bezis-Selfa, *Forging America: Ironworkers, Adventurers, and the Industrious Revolution* (Ithaca, N.Y.: Cornell University Press, 2004); James Sidbury, "Slave Artisans in Richmond, Virginia, 1780–1810," in *American Artisans: Crafting Social Identity*, ed. Howard Rock, Paul Gilje, and Robert Asher (Baltimore: Johns Hopkins University Press, 1995), 48–62.

35. The shift to a more diversified crop mix by tobacco-only planters of pre-1750 Virginia created a new gendered division of labor. Wheat cultivation and its ancillary tasks offered opportunities for slaves to wield limited but meaningful authority and autonomy, but almost all of these new tasks—such as flour milling, plowing, harrowing, cradling, and carting—were given primarily to men. Lorena Walsh, *Motives of Honor, Pleasure, and Profit: Plantation Management in the Colonial Chesapeake, 1607–1763* (Chapel Hill: OIEAHC/University of North Carolina Press, 2010), 622. This particular gendered division of labor explains the predominant role of (black and white) men in the invention of the reaper. For numerous other instances in which women developed new technologies and were at times able to claim credit for them, see Khan, *Democratization of Invention*, esp. 128–81; Judith McGaw, "Women and the History of American Technology," *Signs* 7 (Summer 1982): 799–828; Rebecca Herzig, "Gender and Technology," in *A Companion to American Technology*, ed. Caroline Pursell (Oxford: Oxford University Press, 2004); and Autumn Stanley, *Mothers and Daughters of Invention: Notes for a Revised History of Technology* (New Brunswick, N.J.: Rutgers University Press, 1995).

36. Obed Hussey, "Proposal to Try Hussey's Reaping Machine," *Farmer's Register* 9 (1841): 302.

37. Hutchinson, *Cyrus Hall McCormick: Seed-Time*, 89.

38. Ibid., 185.

39. Ibid., 225; Corbin Braxton, "Account of the Operation of M'Cormick's Virginia Reaper," *Farmer's Register* 10 (1843): 503–4.

40. Hutchinson, *Cyrus Hall McCormick: Seed-Time*, 157. The laborers mentioned by Hutchinson were probably skilled cradlers, slaves or free workers who were well paid by wheat farmers in the rush time of harvest to apply their rare manual skill to the fields of the Valley. The cradle was an improvement over the scythe because it could mow the wheat and drop it into sheaves, instead of spraying the stalks in a haphazard manner. Arthur G. Peterson, "Flour and Grist Milling in Virginia: A Brief History," *Virginia Magazine of History and Biography* 43 (April 1935): 103.

41. Hussey, "Proposal to Try Hussey's Reaping Machine," 302.

42. Earlier cultural historians have explored everyday Americans' relationship to new industrial technologies in the nineteenth century. John Kasson, *Civilizing the Machine: Technology And Republican Values in America, 1776–1900* (New York: Hill and Wang, 1976); Carole Sheriff, *The Artificial River: The Erie Canal and the Paradox of Progress, 1817–1862* (New York: Hill and Wang, 1996).

43. Hutchinson, *Cyrus Hall McCormick: Seed-Time*, 216.

44. For more on skilled labor in southern cities, see Barnes, *Artisan Workers*, and Emma Hart, "Charleston and the British Industrial Revolution, 1750–1790," in *Global Perspectives on Industrial Transformation in the American South*, ed. Susanna Delfino and Michele Gillespie (Columbia: University of Missouri Press, 2005), 26–49. For a study of the widespread community of cotton gin manufacturers dispersed throughout the Cotton Belt, whose existence challenges the myth of Eli Whitney's lightning-from-the-sky inspiration and places the technology squarely within a broad context of similar predecessors, competitors, and collaborators, see Lakwete, *Inventing the Cotton Gin*.

45. Comp, "Grain and Flour," 112, 116.

46. Hutchinson, *Cyrus Hall McCormick: Seed-Time*, 83.

47. Ibid., 87–88. Harvesting labor on antebellum wheat plantations took on a fast-paced, industrial cast similar to that much more famously described by sugar-mill scholars such as Sidney Mintz, *Sweetness and Power: The Place of Sugar in Modern History* (New York: Penguin, 1985), and C. L. R. James, *Black Jacobins: Toussaint L'Ouverture and the San Domingo Revolution* (New York: Random House, 1963). However, while sugar had to be pushed through the entire milling and crystallization process quite hastily, once wheat was reaped and protected from the rain, it "could be threshed when time permitted." Marketing factors more than chemical necessity pushed planters to gather wheat faster. Gates, *Farmer's Age*, 35.

48. Hussey, "Proposal to Try Hussey's Reaping Machine," 302.

49. "Hussey's Grain Cutter," 413–14.

50. William B. Harrison, "Hussey's Reaper," *Farmer's Register* 9 (1841): 434.

51. Standard accounts of antebellum American science emphasize its Baconian, empirical bent. In this view, nineteenth-century practitioners compiled data and reproduced experiments with great gusto while largely ignoring broader frameworks. George Daniels, *American Science in the Age of Jackson* (Tuscaloosa: University of Alabama Press, 1968); Hugh Richard Slotten, *Patronage, Practice, and the Culture of American Science: Alexander Dallas Bache and the U.S. Coast Survey* (New York: Cambridge University Press, 1994). For more recent insight into how a focus on firsthand observation in the field could short-circuit the authority of European men of science and open a space for colonial or postcolonial contributors, see James Delbourgo, *A Most Amazing Scene of Wonders: Electricity and Enlightenment in Early America*

(Cambridge, Mass.: Harvard University Press, 2006); Andrew Lewis, "A Democracy of Facts, an Empire of Reason: Swallow Submersion and Natural History in the Early American Republic," *William and Mary Quarterly* 62 (October 2005): 663–96; Jorge Cañizares-Esguerra, *Nature, Empire, and Nation: Explorations in the History of Science in the Iberian World* (Stanford, Calif.: Stanford University Press, 2006); and Antonio Barrera-Osorio, *Experiencing Nature: The Spanish American Empire and the Early Scientific Revolution* (Austin: University of Texas Press, 2006).

52. For an analogous system of land-labor-time management, see Mart Stewart's incisive analysis of low-country Georgia rice plantations, which highlights how the "hydraulic system" particular to rice cultivation shaped the organization of workers' everyday tasks. Mart Stewart, *"What Nature Suffers to Groe": Life, Labor, and Landscape on the Georgia Coast, 1680–1920* (Athens: University of Georgia Press, 1996), 127–29.

53. A. Nicol, "Notes on Sandy Point Estate, No. IV," *Farmer's Register* 9 (1841): 586.

54. Ibid., 586.

55. Ibid., 586. Emphasis added.

56. Ibid., 586.

57. Ibid., 588.

58. For the classic statement of this influential view, see H. J. Habbakuk, *American and British Technology in the Nineteenth Century: The Search for Labour-Saving Inventions* (New York: Cambridge University Press, 1962). For a recent criticism of the "induced innovation hypothesis" (the idea that the high cost of labor spurred the development of machines that would reduce work hours), see Olmstead and Rhode, *Creating Abundance*.

59. For an exploration of time consciousness and time discipline in a slave society, see Mark M. Smith, *Mastered by the Clock: Time, Slavery, and Freedom in the American South* (Chapel Hill: University of North Carolina Press, 1997).

60. Harrison, "Hussey's Reaper," 434.

61. See Harry Braverman, *Labor and Monopoly Capital: The Degradation of Work in the Twentieth Century* (New York: Monthly Review Press, 1975), for this aspect of Taylor's reform of the labor process.

62. Harrison, "Hussey's Reaper," 434.

63. Ibid., 434.

64. Ibid., 434.

65. Wilma Dunaway, *The First American Frontier: Transition to Capitalism in Southern Appalachia, 1700–1860* (Chapel Hill: University of North Carolina Press, 1996), 115–16. For evocative accounts of Maryland's polyglot crews of wandering cradlers, a characterization that differs in emphasis from my own, see Max Grivno, *Gleanings of Freedom: Free and Slave Labor along the Mason-Dixon Line, 1790–1860* (Urbana: University of Illinois Press, 2011).

CHAPTER 4. NEIGHBOR-TO-NEIGHBOR CAPITALISM

1. The sale from Duplantier to Massi can be found in Clerk of Court, East Baton Rouge Parish, West Florida Records, vol. 6, p. 655, Baton Rouge, La.

2. On the reluctance of historians to delve into the history of financial markets and their connections to slavery and capitalism, see Edward E. Baptist, "Toxic Debt, Liar Loans, Collateralized and Securitized Human Beings, and the Panic of 1837," in *Capitalism Takes Com-*

mand: The Social Transformation of Nineteenth-Century America, ed. Michael Zakim and Gary J. Kornblith (Chicago: University of Chicago Press, 2012), 72, 89.

3. On the funding of slave economies, see Baptist, "Toxic Debt," 81 and generally; on the liquidity of slaves, 79, 90–91.

4. Data on the 10,000-plus mortgages are compiled from information gathered in several regional studies. The sampling methods in the studies were as follows: The first study analyzed more than 6,000 equity mortgages of land, slaves, and personal property filed in more than 60,000 pages of public records in Virginia and South Carolina. The Virginia samples were from both colonial and national eras: twenty-two years in the colonial period (1745 through 1755, and 1765 through 1775) and fifteen years in the national period (1817 through 1821, 1835 through 1839, and 1855 through 1859). Specifically, the nineteenth-century samples were centered on the years of the panics before the Civil War, which were framed by the two years before and the two years following. Data were collected from all the equity mortgages recorded in the deed books of six counties selected in three geographic regions: in Northern Virginia, Culpeper and Fauquier Counties; in the Piedmont, Albemarle and Goochland Counties; and in Southside, Halifax and Lunenburg Counties. Albemarle County (AC), Land Records, Deed Books (LRDB), vols. 1, 4, 5, 6, 20, 21, 22, 32, 33, 34, 35, 36, 37, 53, 54, 55, 56, 57, 58; Culpeper County (CC), LRDB, vols. A, B, D, E, F, G, HH, II, KK, LL, MM, NN, 2, 3, 4, 12, 13, 14; Fauquier County (FC), LRDB, vols. 2, 3, 4, 5, 6, 21, 22, 23, 24, 25, 26, 34, 35, 36, 37, 38, 39, 54, 5, 56, 57, 58; Goochland County (GC), LRDB, vols. 4, 5, 6, 7, 8, 9, 10, 11, 22, 23, 24, 30, 31, 32, 37, 38, 39; Halifax County (HC), LRDB, vols. 1, 2, 3, 4, 5, 6, 7, 8, 9, 10, 12, 13, 26, 27, 28, 29, 30, 42, 43, 44, 45, 46, 55, 56, 57, 58; Lunenburg County (LC), LRDB, vols. 1, 2, 3, 4, 10, 11, 12, 13, 14, 15, 24, 25, 30, 31, 35, 36 (all Library of Virginia, Richmond). The South Carolina data also represent three geographic zones: Edgefield County, Fairfield County, and the Lowcountry. Sampling was complicated by the South Carolina recording system. Early colonial legislation required that only documents formally recorded in Charleston be enforced by the courts. This practice continued into the nineteenth century. In addition, many of the county conveyance books are not extant. For South Carolina, the data were collected from the following nineteenth-century records: Edgefield County (EC), Conveyance Books (CB), vols. 33, 34, 35, 36, 37, 38, 47, 48, AAA, HHH, III, JJJ, KKK; Fairfield County (FC), CB, vols. Y, Z, AA, BB, CC, LL, MM, NN, UU, VV; Records of the Secretary of State (RSS), Charleston Series (CS), Bills of Sales, vol. M; RSS, Charleston Mortgage Series (CMS), vols. O-8, P-8, 3P, 3Q, 3S, 3W, 3X, 3Y, 3Z, 4I, 4H, 4 K, 4L, 4M, 4N, 5H; RSS, Columbia Mortgage Series (CoMS), vols. 1, 2, C, I pts. 1 and 2, K pts. 1 and 2, X, Y, Z, AA pts. 1 and 2 (South Carolina Archives and History Center, Columbia). Fortunately, studies by Russell Menard and David Hancock give us invaluable insights into the debt instruments recorded in Charleston from 1706 to 1775 (see note 9 below). The South Carolina study begins with the nineteenth-century mortgage records and covers the same fifteen-year sample years as in the Virginia sample. Data on the use of human collateral in Louisiana are drawn from purchase money mortgages as well as from equity mortgages. In the colonial period, the completed samples include the Opelousas territory and the West Florida parishes of Louisiana, with the Orleans district sample in process. In the national period, the sample for St. Landry Parish is complete and for East Baton Rouge Parish it is nearing completion, while data collection from Orleans Parish records has begun. The national-era sample for Louisiana covers the same fifteen years as in the Virginia and South Carolina samples. Beginning in the 1830s, the legislature required that abstracts of all mortgages were to be recorded in Mortgage Books. The expanded Louisiana sample draws data from

all of the recorded purchase money and equity mortgages, whether of land, slaves, or personal property, with the following exceptions: Data from sheriffs' sales or those ordered by civil courts, including probate courts, are not included, but the sample does cover private probate sales. The sample also excludes mortgages in marriage contracts or given as a bond required for holding public office or a position of trust, such as those given by executors, trustees, or tutors. The reasons to exclude sheriff's sales and include private probate sales were, first, to keep the sample focused on the mortgage market created by private parties in the ordinary course of business, and second, to limit the three-region sample to a reasonable size. For Louisiana, the sources were housed with the Clerk of Court, St. Landry Parish (CCSLP), Colonial Documents and Extracts (CDE), 1764–1781, 1781–1783, 1783–1784, 1785–1786, 1786–1788, 1788–1789, 1789, Miscellaneous–1793; Clerk of Court, East Baton Rouge Parish (CCEBR), Spanish West Florida (SWF), vols. 1–19. For the nineteenth century, the following records were examined: in CCSLP, all the surviving unbound documents from the year 1817, plus Notarial Books (NB), vols. A, B; Conveyance Books (CB), vols. C-1, D-1, E-1, F-1; Judge George King, Civil, no. 1; Civil Mortgage Books (MB), vols. 2, 7, 8, 9. To date, in CCEBR, data have been collected from: Judge's Books (JB), vols. A, C, D, E, G, H; MB R; Conventional Mortgage Books (CMB), vols. E, J–L. New Orleans Notarial Archives, French Colonial Records box 2 (1730s), box 3 (1730s, 1740s); Cristoval DeArmas, vol. 1 (1818); Carlile Pollock, vols. 1, 3, 31, 58 (1818); Felix DeArmas, vols. 44, 45, 46 (1835); William Boswell, vols. 31, 32, 33, 34, 35, 36, 37 (1835); Edward Barnett, vols. 56, 57, 58 (1855); Octave DeArmas, vols. 60, 61, 62 (1855); Edward Barnett, vols. 68, 69, 70, 71, 72 (1859); Octave DeArmas, vols. 72, 73, 74 (1859).

5. See especially the new study by Edward E. Baptist, *The Half Has Never Been Told: Slavery and the Making of American Capitalism* (New York: Basic Books, 2014).

6. Bonnie Martin, "Slavery's Invisible Engine: Mortgaging Human Property," *Journal of Southern History* 76 (November 2010): 817–66.

7. See New Orleans Notarial Archives, Colonial Records, box 2, folder 8.

8. *Chamberlayne v. Maynard*, 1734. Goochland County, Va., Colonial Chancery Court Cases, box 1, Library of Virginia, Richmond.

9. For instance, Russell Menard and David Hancock found that much of the credit needed for economic expansion in colonial South Carolina came from local lenders and that slaves were the dominant collateral used. See Russell R. Menard, "Financing the Lowcountry Export Boom: Capital and Growth in Early South Carolina," *William and Mary Quarterly*, 3rd ser., 51 (October 1994): 659–78; idem, *Sweet Negotiations: Sugar, Slavery, and Plantation Agriculture in Early Barbados* (Charlottesville: University of Virginia Press, 2006), 61–66; and David Hancock, "'Capital and Credit with Approved Security': Financial Markets in Montserrat and South Carolina, 1748–1775," *Business and Economic History* 23 (Winter 1994): 61–84.

10. The four mortgages on Jacques can be found in the records of the Clerk of Court, St. Landry Parish, Mortgage Book 1, vol. 1, pp. 262–63, 348, 373; vol. 2, p. 952.

11. New Orleans Notarial Archives, Edward Barnett, vol. 3, p. 558.

12. Bonnie Martin, "The Color of Credit: A Lending Network of Free People of Color in Early Louisiana," paper presented at the conference, "Charting New Courses in the History of Slavery and Emancipation," Center for the Study of the Gulf South at the University of Southern Mississippi and the Department of History at the University of South Alabama, Long Beach, Miss., March 2010; Martin, "Slavery's Invisible Engine," 850–53.

13. For more on the possible explanations, see Martin, "Slavery's Invisible Engine," 836–49.

14. For examples of connections of local banks to international financiers, see Baptist, "Toxic Loans," 80–83.

15. The dollars are in 2015-U.S. dollar equivalents because the data are drawn from the larger study, which must compare various currencies across the eighteenth and nineteenth centuries.

16. On August 24, 1821, the Union Bank of South Carolina lent Benjamin Montgomery of Fairfield County $3,400, secured by ten slaves. Six of the slaves were male, including Peter, a coachman, Will, a carpenter, and one boy, Peter. Four women completed the human collateral. Records of the Secretary of State, South Carolina, Columbia Series, book C, p. 346. For a loan of $9,700 made by the Mechanics Bank, City of Augusta, see Columbia Series, book K, p. 255. For a loan by the State Bank of Charleston, see Charleston Series, book 4I, p. 441. For the Commercial Bank of Columbia, see Charleston Series, book 3Z, p. 278. South Carolina banks were more conservative in the amount of credit allowed per slave. See Bonnie Martin, "Banks, Building Societies, and Speculators: Profiting from Human Collateral in 19th-Century South Carolina," paper presented at the Annual Meeting of the American Historical Association, New York, January 2009.

17. Joshua D. Rothman, *Flush Times & Fever Dreams: A Story of Capitalism and Slavery in the Age of Jackson* (Athens: University of Georgia Press, 2012), 7–8.

18. For more on the international, national, and regional financial tactics and crosscurrents churning in the cotton economy and the panics, see the following sources. Each pulls us into the exciting vortex of big money streams and regional cotton production. Calvin Schermerhorn, *The Business of Slavery and the Rise of American Capitalism, 1815–1860* (New Haven, Conn.: Yale University Press, 2015); Baptist, *The Half Has Never Been Told*; Kathryn Boodry, "The Common Thread: Slavery, Cotton and Atlantic Finance from the Louisiana Purchase to Reconstruction" (PhD diss., Harvard University, 2014); Jessica M. Lepler, *The Many Panics of 1837: People, Politics, and the Creation of a Transatlantic Financial Crisis* (New York: Cambridge University Press, 2013); Rothman, *Flush Times & Fever Dreams*.

19. Boodry, "The Common Thread." See also John Killick, "Risk, Specialization and Profit in the Mercantile Sector of the Nineteenth Century Cotton Trade: Alexander Brown and Sons, 1820–1880," *Business History* 16 (January 1979): 1–16; and Edwin J. Perkins, *Financing Anglo-American Trade: The House of Brown, 1800–1880* (Cambridge: Cambridge University Press, 1975).

20. *Manufactures of the United States in 1860 compiled from the Original Returns of the Eighth Census* (Washington, D.C.: Government Printing Office, 1865), 196,199, 202, 203. Table 4.3 also shows the same comparisons using projections of equity *plus* purchase money mortgages. While no data from purchase money mortgages in Virginia and South Carolina were entered into the database, observations during the course of the Virginia and South Carolina research suggest the number of purchase money mortgages outnumbered equity mortgages by three or four to one. In Louisiana, the number of purchase money mortgages outnumbered the number of equity mortgages by more than two to one. If we focus on the records sampled in St. Landry, since our comparisons are to similar locales in Virginia and South Carolina, the number of purchase money mortgages exceeded the equity mortgages by more than two to one for the national period sampled, more than three to one in the 1855–1859 period, and more than four to one in the year 1859, which is the year that set the 1860 census crop values used in Table 4.3. Similarly, if we look at the amount of capital raised in St. Landry, the amounts raised by purchase money mortgages exceeded those raised by equity mortgages by just under three to one for the national period, by more than three to one in the 1855–1859 period, and by seven to one in 1859. Based on these ranges, the decision to use the two to one ratio is probably quite conservative.

21. Baton Rouge and its environs could not compare to New Orleans in the number of manufacturing businesses—there were thirteen in Orleans Parish—but the census shows that East Baton Rouge Parish did have two of the state's "machinery establishments, steam engines, etc." In addition, Orleans Parish and East Baton Rouge Parish each had two printing businesses. In comparison, St. Landry posted no entries on the Manufacturing schedule.

22. Examples of works on the lack of sophistication in the southern economy include Eugene D. Genovese, *The Political Economy of Slavery: Studies in the Economy & Society of the Slave South* (New York: Pantheon Books, 1965); Douglass C. North, *The Economic Growth of the United States, 1790–1860* (New York: W. W. Norton, 1966); Gavin Wright, *The Political Economy of the Cotton South: Households, Markets, and Wealth in the Nineteenth Century* (New York: W. W. Norton, 1978); idem, *Old South, New South: Revolutions in the Southern Economy since the Civil War* (New York: Basic Books, 1986); idem, *Slavery and American Economic Development* (Baton Rouge: Louisiana State University Press, 2006); and John Majewski, *Modernizing a Slave Economy: The Economic Vision of the Confederate Nation* (Chapel Hill: University of North Carolina Press, 2009), 16–17.

23. On the mortgaging of serfs in mid-nineteenth-century Russia, see Steven L. Hoch, "The Banking Crisis, Peasant Reform, and Economic Development in Russia, 1857–1861," *American Historical Review* 96 (June 1991): 795–820.

24. David Hancock, "Self-Organized Complexity and the Emergence of an Atlantic Market Economy, 1651–1815," in *Atlantic Economy during the Seventeenth and Eighteenth Centuries: Organization, Operation, Practice, and Personnel*, ed. Peter A. Coclanis (Columbia: University of South Carolina Press, 2005), 30–71, quotation at 30–31. Laura Croghan Kamoie's chapter, "Planters' Exchange Patterns in the Colonial Chesapeake: Toward Defining a Regional Domestic Economy," in Coclanis, ed., *Atlantic Economy*, 323–43, also redirects attention from the export trade and toward the "diversification and development" of "local markets and domestic economies," and to credit networks based on kinship and other local connections; see esp. 323, 326, 331.

25. See discussion above, and see Martin, "Slavery's Invisible Engine." See Baptist, "Toxic Debt," 80, for a nineteenth-century variation. There is a fundamental difference in the networking patterns that we have found, however. While David Hancock and Edward Baptist document the power of the local as it stretched out to international markets, my data show that many of the local nineteenth-century credit markets remained just that—local. Moreover, nineteenth-century borrowers and lenders did not faithfully mimic the eighteenth-century credit patterns. In a number of places, the mortgage profiles changed dramatically in collateral preference and contract format—at least at first glance. What seem to be reversals are better understood as shifts in collateral emphasis. Perhaps the best way to think about what happened is as a diversification. Collateral use patterns changed when land values increased, when regions became slave-exporting zones, and when the institutions that accepted slave-related credit multiplied.

CHAPTER 5. THE CONTOURS OF COTTON CAPITALISM

1. *Seventh Census of the United States*, Population Schedules, Mississippi, Madison County, 312; *Third Census of the United States*, Population Schedules, South Carolina, Union County, 133; *Fifth Census of the United States*, Population Schedules, South Carolina, Spartanburg County, 322; *Fifth Census of the United States*, Population Schedules, Mississippi, Wilkinson County, 277 (all Washington, D.C., U.S. Census Bureau).

2. Wilkinson County Deed Book G (1830–1832), 317–18, 660–62; Wilkinson County Deed Book K (1836–1838), 255–56, Mississippi Department of Archives and History, Jackson (hereafter MDAH).

3. Wilkinson County Deed Book H (1833–1835), 6–8, 483–86; Wilkinson County Deed Book J (1835–1836), 148; Wilkinson County Deed Book K (1836–1838), 255–56; *Woodville (Miss.) Republican*, November 23, 1833; Wilkinson County Combination Tax Rolls, 1833–1835, Auditor of Public Accounts, RG29, MDAH.

4. *Woodville (Miss.) Republican,* January 24, 1835; Madison County Deed Book C (1835–1836), 56–58, 64–65, MDAH.

5. Useful syntheses describing the broad context for the bubble economy of the 1830s include John Lauritz Larson, *The Market Revolution in America: Liberty, Ambition, and the Eclipse of the Common Good* (New York: Cambridge University Press, 2009); Daniel Walker Howe, *What Hath God Wrought: The Transformation of America, 1815–1848* (New York: Oxford University Press, 2007); and Charles Sellers, *The Market Revolution: Jacksonian America, 1815–1846* (New York: Oxford University Press, 1991). For a short introduction to the subject, see Sean Wilentz, "Society, Politics, and the Market Revolution, 1815–1848," in *The New American History,* ed. Eric Foner, revised and expanded ed. (Philadelphia: Temple University Press, 1997), 61–84. On the development of the American banking sector, the "war" over the rechartering of the Second Bank of the United States, and the liberalization of credit after its defunding, see Howard Bodenhorn, *A History of Banking in Antebellum America: Financial Markets and Economic Development in an Era of Nation-Building* (Cambridge: Cambridge University Press, 2000); Ralph C. H. Catterall, *The Second Bank of the United States* (Chicago: University of Chicago Press, 1902); J. Van Fenstermaker, *The Development of American Commercial Banking, 1782–1837* (Kent, Ohio: Kent State University Bureau of Economic and Business Research, 1965); Bray Hammond, *Banks and Politics in America* (Princeton, N.J.: Princeton University Press, 1957), chaps. 10–15; John M. McFaul, *The Politics of Jacksonian Finance* (Ithaca, N.Y.: Cornell University Press, 1971); Reginald Charles McGrane, *The Panic of 1837: Some Financial Problems of the Jacksonian Era* (Chicago: University of Chicago Press, 1924); Robert V. Remini, *Andrew Jackson and the Bank War* (New York: W. W. Norton, 1967); Larry Schweikart, *Banking in the American South from the Age of Jackson to Reconstruction* (Baton Rouge: Louisiana State University Press, 1987); William G. Shade, *Banks or No Banks: The Money Issue in Western Politics, 1832–1865* (Detroit: Wayne State University Press, 1972); Walter Buckingham Smith, *Economic Aspects of the Second Bank of the United States* (Cambridge, Mass.: Harvard University Press, 1953); Peter Temin, *The Jacksonian Economy* (New York: W. W. Norton, 1969); and Jean Alexander Wilburn; *Biddle's Bank: The Crucial Years* (New York: Columbia University Press, 1967).

6. Important works on post-Revolutionary settlement and economic development in the southwest include Joan E. Cashin, *A Family Venture: Men and Women on the Southern Frontier* (Baltimore: Johns Hopkins University Press, 1991); Thomas C. Clark and John D. W. Guice, *Frontiers in Conflict: The Old Southwest, 1795–1830* (Albuquerque: University of New Mexico Press, 1989); William C. Davis, *A Way Through the Wilderness: The Natchez Trace and the Civilization of the Southern Frontier* (New York: HarperCollins, 1995); Don H. Doyle, *Faulkner's County: The Historical Roots of Yoknapatawpha* (Chapel Hill: University of North Carolina Press, 2001), esp. 23–156; Daniel S. DuPre, *Transforming the Cotton Frontier: Madison County, Alabama, 1800–1840* (Baton Rouge: Louisiana State University Press, 1997); Walter Johnson, *River of Dark Dreams: Slavery and Empire in the Cotton Kingdom* (Cambridge, Mass.: Harvard University Press, 2013); David J. Libby, *Slavery and Frontier Mississippi, 1720–1835* (Jackson: University Press of Mississippi, 2004); James David Miller, *South by Southwest: Planter Emigration*

and Identity in the Slave South (Charlottesville: University of Virginia Press, 2002); John Hebron Moore, *The Emergence of the Cotton Kingdom in the Old Southwest: Mississippi, 1770–1860*
(Baton Rouge: Louisiana State University Press, 1988); Christopher Morris, *Becoming Southern: The Evolution of a Way of Life, Warren County and Vicksburg, Mississippi, 1770–1860* (New
York: Oxford University Press, 1995); James Oakes, *The Ruling Race: A History of American Slaveholders* (New York: Vintage, 1982); and Adam Rothman, *Slave Country: American Expansion
and the Origins of the Deep South* (Cambridge, Mass.: Harvard University Press, 2005). See also
Edward E. Baptist, *The Half Has Never Been Told: Slavery and the Making of American Capitalism* (New York: Basic Books, 2014), which situates the antebellum southwest at the center of
its argument for the predication of capitalism broadly on slavery.

7. James Roger Sharp, *The Jacksonians Versus the Banks: Politics in the States after the Panic
of 1837* (New York: Columbia University Press, 1970), 27; A. Barton Hepburn, *History of Currency in the United States* (New York: Macmillan, 1915), 127.

8. *Boston Daily Courier*, July 11, 1835; *Chicago American*, July 25, 1835; *Scioto Gazette* (Chill-
icothe, Ohio), August 19, 1835; *New York Evening Post*, November 10, 1835; *New York Courier
and Enquirer*, September 8, 1835 (quotation).

9. Joseph G. Baldwin, *The Flush Times of Alabama and Mississippi: A Series of Sketches* (New
York: D. Appleton and Co., 1853), 50, 83–84, 87, 88, 89, 263.

10. William F. Gray, *From Virginia to Texas, 1835* (Houston: Gray, Dillaye, and Co., 1909),
26, 28, 41–42, 52–53, quotations at 28, 52.

11. Lewis Cecil Gray, *History of Agriculture in the Southern United States to 1860*, 2 vols.
(Washington, D.C.: Carnegie Institution of Washington, 1933), 2:1027. Sven Beckert details
the global significance of cotton and the role played by the United States in its development
as a commodity in *Empire of Cotton: A Global History* (New York: Alfred A. Knopf, 2014), esp.
chaps. 5 and 9.

12. Stuart Bruchey, ed., *Cotton and the Growth of the American Economy: 1790–1860: Sources
and Readings* (New York: Harcourt Brace, 1967), 7, 9–10, 16–17, 19, 21, 23.

13. Sharp, *Jacksonians Versus the Banks*, 54.

14. Malcolm Rohrbough, *The Land Office Business: The Settlement and Administration of
American Public Lands, 1789–1837* (New York: Oxford University Press, 1968), 226–32; Edwin
Arthur Miles, *Jacksonian Democracy in Mississippi* (Chapel Hill: University of North Carolina
Press, 1960), 117–20. On Choctaw and Chickasaw removal, also see Mary Elizabeth Young,
Redskins, Ruffleshirts, and Rednecks: Indian Allotments in Alabama and Mississippi, 1830–1860
(Norman: University of Oklahoma Press, 1961); Clark and Guice, *Frontiers in Conflict*, chap. 12;
Arthur H. DeRosier, Jr., *The Removal of the Choctaw Indians* (Knoxville: University of Ten-
nessee Press, 1970); and Samuel J. Wells, "Federal Indian Policy: From Accommodation to
Removal," in *The Choctaw before Removal*, ed. Carolyn Keller Reeves (Oxford: University
Press of Mississippi, 1985), 181–213.

15. Marvin Bentley, "Incorporated Banks and the Economic Development of Mississippi,
1829–1837," *Journal of Mississippi History* 35, no. 4 (1973): 381–401; John Hebron Moore,
Agriculture in Ante-Bellum Mississippi (New York: Bookman Associates, 1958), 69; Bruchey, ed.,
Cotton and the Growth of the American Economy, 18–19; Miles, *Jacksonian Democracy in Mississippi*, 143–44. On banks and banking in early Mississippi, also see Bentley, "The State Bank
of Mississippi: Monopoly Bank on the Frontier (1809–1830)," *Journal of Mississippi History* 40,
no. 4 (1978): 297–318; Charles Hillman Brough, "The History of Banking in Mississippi," in
Publications of the Mississippi Historical Society, ed. Franklin L. Riley (Oxford: Mississippi
Historical Society, 1901), 3:317–40; Richard Holcombe Kilbourne, Jr., *Slave Agriculture and*

Financial Markets in Antebellum America: The Bank of the United States in Mississippi, 1831–1852 (London: Pickering and Chatto, 2006); Dunbar Rowland, "Banking," in *Encyclopedia of Mississippi History: Comprising Sketches of Counties, Towns, Events, Institutions and Persons*, ed. Dunbar Rowland, 2 vols. (Madison, Wis.: Selwyn A. Brant, 1907), 1:181–97; Sharp, *Jacksonians Versus the Banks*, 55–88; Robert C. Weems, Jr., "Mississippi's First Banking System," *Journal of Mississippi History* 29, no. 4 (1967): 386–408.

16. Herbert A. Kellar, "A Journey Through the South in 1836: Diary of James D. Davidson," *Journal of Southern History* 1, no. 3 (1935): 355; William Henry Sparks, *The Memories of Fifty Years* (Philadelphia, 1870), 364; Joseph Holt Ingraham, *The South-West by a Yankee*, 2 vols. (New York: Harper and Brothers, 1835), 2:86, 95; Burrell Fox to Aaron Neal, November 12, 1835, Neal Family Papers, box 1, folder 8, Southern Historical Collection, Louis Round Wilson Library, University of North Carolina at Chapel Hill.

17. Bentley, "Incorporated Banks and the Development of Mississippi," 387, 389, 390; Miles, *Jacksonian Democracy in Mississippi*, 73–74; Dennis East, "New York and Mississippi Land Company and the Panic of 1837," *Journal of Mississippi History* 33, no. 4 (1971): 299–331; Richard Bolton to Lewis Curtis, September 8, 1835, New York and Mississippi Land Company: Records, 1835–1889, box 1 (Correspondence, 1835–1837), folder 1, Wisconsin Historical Society, Madison.

18. Baldwin, *Flush Times*, 87; Miles, *Jacksonian Democracy in Mississippi*, 130–31, 143–44; Fenstermaker, *Development of American Commercial Banking*, 152–53; Brough, "History of Banking in Mississippi," 324–27; McGrane, *Panic of 1837*, 24–27; Miles, *Jacksonian Democracy*, 130–31.

19. By way of comparison, the enslaved population of Mississippi grew by around 32,000 during the 1820s. That effected a doubling of the slave population in the state over the course of the decade, but numerically the average number of slaves imported annually during the 1820s was only about a quarter of the average number imported annually during the 1830s (Moore, *Emergence of the Cotton Kingdom*, 118; Moore, *Agriculture in Ante-Bellum Mississippi*, 69).

20. Michel Chevalier, *Society, Manners, and Politics in the United States* (Boston: Weeks, Jordan, and Co., 1839), 400; Ingraham, *South-West by a Yankee*, 2:91.

21. Edward E. Baptist, "Toxic Debt, Liar Loans, Collaterized and Securitized Human Beings, and the Panic of 1837," in *Capitalism Takes Command: The Social Transformation of Nineteenth-Century America*, ed. Michael Zakim and Gary J. Kornblith (Chicago: University of Chicago Press, 2012), 69–92; Ulrich B. Phillips, *American Negro Slavery* (New York: D. Appleton and Co., 1918), chart opposite 370.

22. On the speculative nature of the domestic slave trade, see Steven Deyle, *Carry Me Back: The Domestic Slave Trade in American Life* (New York: Oxford University Press, 2005), esp. chap. 4; Robert H. Gudmestad, *A Troublesome Commerce: The Transformation of the Interstate Slave Trade* (Baton Rouge: Louisiana State University Press, 2003); Walter Johnson, *Soul by Soul: Life Inside the Antebellum Slave Market* (Cambridge, Mass.: Harvard University Press, 1999); and Michael Tadman, *Speculators and Slaves: Masters, Traders, and Slaves in the Old South* (Madison: University of Wisconsin Press, 1989). For considerations of the percentages of enslaved people brought by traders to the Lower South generally and Mississippi specifically, see Deyle, *Carry Me Back*, 289; Johnson, *Soul by Soul*, 5–6; Tadman, *Speculators and Slaves*, 44; Libby, *Slavery and Frontier Mississippi*, 61; and Charles Sackett Sydnor, *Slavery in Mississippi* (New York: D. Appleton and Co., 1933), 144–57.

23. Baldwin, *Flush Times*, 237; Chevalier, *Society, Manners, and Politics*, 400. On the financing of the cotton plantation economy, see Harold D. Woodman, *King Cotton and His*

Retainers: Financing and Marketing of the Cotton Crop of the South, 1800–1925 (Lexington: University Press of Kentucky, 1968), chaps. 1–16. As demonstrated by Jesse Mabry and detailed by the recent work of Bonnie Martin, also vital to local credit systems in the slave South were mortgages backed by slaves, as slaves already in an owner's possession could be leveraged to buy still more slaves in what Martin has termed the "invisible engine" driving the expansion of slave-based capitalism. See Bonnie Martin, "Slavery's Invisible Engine: Mortgaging Human Property," *Journal of Southern History* 76, no. 4 (2010): 817–66.

24. *United States Gazette,* in the *New York Observer and Chronicle*, February 22, 1840.

25. Ibid.; *Groves v. Slaughter,* 40 U.S. 449 (1841), 481; *Natchez Courier,* in *Christian Secretary,* May 20, 1837.

26. Sydnor, *Slavery in Mississippi,* 157–62.

27. Ibid., 162–63; *Groves v. Slaughter,* 452–54.

28. *Green v. Robinson,* 6 Miss. 80 (December 1840), 102; *Groves v. Slaughter,* 453–54. Also see *Glidewell et al. v. Hite et al.,* 6 Miss. 110 (December 1840), 111–12.

29. On southwestern states' efforts to ban the interstate slave trade in the years after the Southampton insurrection, see Lacy K. Ford, *Deliver Us from Evil: The Slavery Question in the Old South* (New York: Oxford University Press, 2009), 449–60.

30. *Groves v. Slaughter,* 452; Sydnor, *Slavery in Mississippi,* 163–65, 168–69; Ford, *Deliver Us from Evil,* 455–57. The ban's unpopularity was immediately evident, and in 1833 the legislature submitted a constitutional amendment to a popular vote that would repeal it. Mississippi voters approved the repeal by a margin of more than four to one, but Mississippi law required that constitutional amendments receive at least 50 percent of the total number of votes cast for the legislature in the year they were proposed in order to pass. The amendment to repeal the ban on the interstate trade failed to achieve that standard, and the trade thus remained technically unconstitutional.

31. The most recent work on the slave insurrection scare of 1835 includes Johnson, *River of Dark Dreams*, chap. 2, and Joshua D. Rothman, *Flush Times and Fever Dreams: A Story of Capitalism and Slavery in the Age of Jackson* (Athens: University of Georgia Press, 2012). Also see Laurence Shore, "Making Mississippi Safe for Slavery: The Insurrection Panic of 1835," in *Class, Consensus, and Conflict: Antebellum Southern Community Studies*, ed. Orville Vernon Burton and Robert C. McMath, Jr. (Westport, Conn.: Greenwood Press, 1982), 96–127; Christopher Morris, "An Event in Community Organization: The Mississippi Slave Insurrection Scare of 1835," *Journal of Social History* 22, no. 1 (1988): 93–111; David Grimsted, *American Mobbing, 1828–1861: Toward Civil War* (New York: Oxford University Press, 1998), 144–56; James Lal Penick, Jr., *The Great Western Land Pirate: John A. Murrell in Legend and History* (Columbia: University of Missouri Press, 1981), esp. chap. 5; Libby, *Slavery and Frontier Mississippi,* chap. 6; Kenneth S. Greenberg, *Honor and Slavery* (Princeton, N.J.: Princeton University Press, 1997), 143–45; William W. Freehling, *The Road to Disunion: Secessionists at Bay, 1776–1854* (New York: Oxford University Press, 1990), 110–13; Clement Eaton, *The Freedom-of-Thought Struggle in the Old South* (New York: Harper and Row, 1964), 95–99; and Edwin A. Miles, "The Mississippi Slave Insurrection Scare of 1835," *Journal of Negro History* 32 (January 1957): 48–60.

32. Thomas Shackelford, *Proceedings of the Citizens of Madison County, Mississippi, at Livingston, in July, 1835, in Relation to the Trial and Punishment of Several Individuals Implicated in a Contemplated Insurrection in this State* (Jackson, Miss., 1836), 8–11, 14.

33. *Jackson Mississippian,* July 17, 1835.

34. Kellar, "A Journey Through the South," 355; *Jackson Mississippian,* March 24, 1837.

35. Historians have long debated the causes of the Panic of 1837, arguing particularly over whether the crisis resulted from foreign or domestic causes and over the role played by Andrew Jackson's banking policies. Varying perspectives on these arguments can be found in many of the works on banking and finance cited above. The admittedly oversimplified summary here attempts to place the major contributors scholars have identified in some kind of balance and draws most heavily on the work of Jessica Lepler, Peter Rousseau, and Peter Temin. See Jessica M. Lepler, *The Many Panics of 1837: People, Politics, and the Creation of a Transatlantic Financial Crisis* (Cambridge: Cambridge University Press, 2013); Peter L. Rousseau, "Jacksonian Monetary Policy, Specie Flows, and the Panic of 1837," *Journal of Economic History* 62, no. 2 (2002): 457–88; and Temin, *Jacksonian Economy,* esp. chap. 4.

36. *Niles' Weekly Register* (Baltimore), June 3, 1837.

37. Moore, *Agriculture in Ante-Bellum Mississippi,* 70–71; Young, *Redskins, Ruffleshirts, and Rednecks,* 177–78; J. A. Orr, "A Trip from Houston to Jackson, Miss., in 1845," *Publications of the Mississippi Historical Society* 9 (1906): 175; McGrane, *Panic of 1837,* 118.

38. William H. Wills, "A Southern Traveler's Diary, 1840," *Publications of the Southern History Association* 8 (1904): 35–36; Franklin L. Riley, "Diary of a Mississippi Planter, January 1, 1840, to April, 1863," *Mississippi Historical Society Publications* 10 (1909): 318.

39. McGrane, *Panic of 1837,* 117; Moore, *Agriculture in Ante-Bellum Mississippi,* 72–73; Orr, "A Trip from Houston to Jackson," 175–76; Wills, "A Southern Traveler's Diary," 35; Riley, "Diary of a Mississippi Planter," 317–18.

40. Kilbourne, *Slave Agriculture and Financial Markets,* 138–39; Moore, *Agriculture in Ante-Bellum Mississippi,* 72; Phillips, *American Negro Slavery,* chart opposite 370; *Jackson Mississippian,* May 5, 1837.

41. Bradley G. Bond, *Political Culture in the Nineteenth-Century South: Mississippi, 1830–1900* (Baton Rouge: Louisiana State University Press, 1995), 83–84; Miles, *Jacksonian Democracy in Mississippi,* 142–43; Sharp, *Jacksonians Versus the Banks,* 63–64; Brough, "History of Banking in Mississippi," 327–29.

42. *Jackson Mississippian,* April 21, 1837.

43. *Jackson Mississippian,* April 21 and May 19, 1837.

44. Ibid. For examples of Mississippi Supreme Court cases ruling against slave traders attempting to recover debts from resident Mississippians, see *Green v. Robinson,* 6 Miss. 80 (December 1840); *Glidewell et al. v. Hite et al.,* 6 Miss. 110 (December 1840); *Brien v. Williamson,* 8 Miss. 14 (1843); and *Thomas et al. v. Phillips,* 12 Miss. 358 (1845).

45. *Groves v. Slaughter,* 449–52, 482.

46. Ibid., 496–503, quotation at 502. On the significance of *Groves v. Slaughter,* also see David L. Lightner, "The Supreme Court and the Interstate Slave Trade: A Study in Evasion, Anarchy, and Extremism," *Journal of Supreme Court History* 29 (November 2004): 236–42; and Paul Finkelman, *An Imperfect Union: Slavery, Federalism, and Comity* (Chapel Hill: University of North Carolina Press, 1981), 266–71.

47. *Groves v. Slaughter,* 503–10, quotation at 503.

48. Ibid., 510–17, quotations at 516.

49. Ibid., 515–17, quotation at 517.

50. *Fourth Annual Report of the American Anti-Slavery Society* (New York: American Anti-Slavery Society, 1837), 50–52.

51. Joshua Leavitt, "The Financial Power of Slavery," *Emancipator and Free American,* October 22, 1840. On abolitionists' use of the panic to draw attention to economic distortions

wrought by slavery, and on the significance of Leavitt's tract, see Julian P. Bretz, "The Economic Background of the Liberty Party," *American Historical Review* 34, no. 2 (1929): 252–56.

52. *Fourth Annual Report of the American Anti-Slavery Society*, 55; Bretz, "Economic Background of the Liberty Party," 253.

53. *Fourth Annual Report of the American Anti-Slavery Society*, 57, 56, 52.

54. Ibid., 51; Leavitt, "The Financial Power of Slavery"; Kilbourne, *Slave Agriculture and Financial Markets*, 108–9, 127–40, quotation at 127.

55. Gray, *History of Agriculture*, 1027; Sharp, *Jacksonians Versus the Banks*, 60–88; Miles, *Jacksonian Democracy in Mississippi*, 146–59; Bond, *Political Culture in the Nineteenth-Century South*, 82–89; Schweikart, *Banking in the American South*, 26–27, 180–82.

56. Madison County Deed Book G (1839–1840), 330–32, MDAH.

57. Madison County Deed Book G (1839–1840), 361, and Madison County Deed Book I (1841–1843), 322–23, MDAH; Seventh Census of the United States, Slave Schedule, Mississippi, Madison County; Moore, *Emergence of the Cotton Kingdom*, 118.

CHAPTER 6. "BROAD IS DE ROAD DAT LEADS TER DEATH"

1. *Petition of William Wilson to the Virginia General Assembly*, December 23, 1800, Legislative Petitions, State Archives Collections, Library of Virginia, Richmond (original provided by Sandra Treadway via email on February 12, 2011). I thank Loren Schweninger, James Sidbury, Elizabeth Dunn, Nedra Lee, and Sandra Treadway for their assistance in locating and transcribing this petition. For more on the Prosser Conspiracy, see Douglas Egerton, *Gabriel's Rebellion: The Virginia Slave Conspiracies of 1800 and 1802* (Chapel Hill: University of North Carolina Press, 1993); Michael Nicholls, *Whispers of Rebellion: Narrating Gabriel's Conspiracy* (Charlottesville: University of Virginia Press, 2011); Philip J. Schwarz, ed., *Gabriel's Conspiracy: A Documentary History* (Charlottesville: University of Virginia Press, 2012); and James Sidbury, *Ploughshares into Swords: Race, Rebellion and Identity in Gabriel's Virginia 1790–1810* (Cambridge: Cambridge University Press, 1997).

2. See Vincent Brown, *The Reaper's Garden: Death and Power in the World of Atlantic Slavery* (Cambridge, Mass.: Harvard University Press, 2008); James M. Davidson, "Keeping the Devil at Bay: The Shoe on the Coffin Lid and Other Grave Charms in Nineteenth- and Early Twentieth-Century America," *International Journal of Historical Archaeology* 14 (2010): 614–49; Erik R. Seeman, *Death in the New World Cross-Cultural Encounters, 1492–1800* (Philadelphia: University of Pennsylvania Press, 2010); Douglas Egerton, "A Peculiar Mark of Infamy: Dismemberment, Burial, and Rebelliousness in Slave Societies," in *Mortal Remains: Death in Early America*, ed. Nancy Isenberg and Andrew Burstein (Philadelphia: University of Pennsylvania Press, 2003), 148–60; and Drew Gilpin Faust, *The Republic of Suffering: Death and the American Civil War* (New York: Alfred A. Knopf, 2008).

3. I expand on this in my forthcoming book, *The Price for Their Pound of Flesh: The Value of Human Property from Preconception to Postmortem* (Boston: Beacon Press, 2017).

4. Jennifer L. Morgan, "Partus Sequitur Ventrem," paper delivered at the "Sexuality and Slavery" conference, Institute for Historical Studies, University of Texas, Austin; Berry, *The Price for Their Pound of Flesh*, chap. 1; and Christopher Curtis, "*Partus Sequitur Ventrem*: Slavery, Property Rights, and the Language of Republicanism in Virginia's House of Delegates, 1831–1832," *Australian Journal of Legal History* 6 (2000): 93–114.

5. See Alfred Brophy, *Reparations: Pro and Con* (New York: Oxford University Press, 2008); Ariela Gross, "'When Is The Time of Slavery?' The History of Slavery in Contemporary Legal and Political Argument," *California Law Review* 96 (2008): 283–321; and Adrienne D. Davis with A. A. Aiyetoro, "Historic and Modern Social Movements for Reparations: The National Coalition of Blacks for Reparations in America (N'COBRA) and Its Antecedents," *Texas Wesleyan Law Review* 16 (2010): 687.

6. *Petition of William Wilson to the Virginia General Assembly.*

7. Frances Kemble, *Journal of a Residence on a Georgian Plantation in 1838–1839* (1863; reprint Cambridge: Cambridge University Press, 2009).

8. See, e.g., Daina Ramey Berry, "'In Pressing Need of Cash': Gender, Skill, and Family Persistence in the Domestic Slave Trade," *Journal of African American History* 92 (Winter 2007): 22–36, and idem, "We'um Fus Rate Bargain: Value, Labor, and Price in a Georgia Slave Community," in *The Chattel Principal: Internal Slave Trades in the Americas*, ed. Walter Johnson (New Haven, Conn.: Yale University Press, 2004): 55–171; David Eltis and David Richardson, "Prices of African Slaves Newly Arrived in the Americas, 1673–1865: New Evidence on Long-Run Trends and Regional Differentials," and Laird W. Bergad, "American Slave Markets During the 1850s: Slave Price Rises in the United States, Cuba, and Brazil in Comparative Perspective," both in *Slavery in the Development of the Americas*, ed. David Eltis, Frank D. Lewis, and Kenneth L. Sokoloff (Cambridge: Cambridge University Press, 2004); Robert William Fogel and Stanley L. Engerman, *Time on the Cross: The Economics of American Negro Slavery* (Boston: Little, Brown, 1974), 59–126; Lawrence J. Kotlikoff, "The Structure of Slave Prices in New Orleans, 1804–1862," *Economics Inquiry* 17 (October 1979): 496–518; Peter C. Mancall, Joshua L. Rosenbloom, and Thomas Joseph Weiss, "Slave Prices in the Lower South, 1722–1815," NBER Working Paper 120 (Cambridge, Mass.: National Bureau of Economic Research, 2000); and Peter Passell and Gavin Wright, "The Effects of Pre–Civil War Territorial Expansion on the Price of Slaves," *Journal of Political Economy* 80 (November–December 1972): 1188–1202.

9. See, e.g., Berry, *Pound of Flesh*; Josiah C. Nott, "Statistics of Southern Slave Population: With Special Reference to Life Insurance," *De Bow's Review* 4 (November 1847): 275–89; Todd L. Savitt, "Slave Life Insurance in Virginia and North Carolina," *Journal of Southern History* 43 (November 1977): 583–600; Eugene D. Genovese, "The Medical and Insurance Costs of Slaveholding in the Cotton Belt," *Journal of Negro History* 45 (July 1960): 146–55; and Sharon Anne Murphy, "Securing Human Property: Slavery, Life Insurance, and Industrialization in the Upper South," *Journal of the Early Republic* 25 (Winter 2005): 615–52.

10. Walter Johnson, *Soul by Soul: Life Inside the Antebellum Slave Market* (Cambridge, Mass.: Harvard University Press, 1999).

11. Terri Snyder, *The Power to Die: Slavery and Suicide in British North America* (Chicago: University of Chicago Press, 2015); Richard Bell, *We Shall Be No More: Suicide and Self-Government in the Newly United States* (Cambridge, Mass.: Harvard University Press, 2012).

12. *Andrew Bunch v. William Smith*, 1851 WL 2545 (S.C. App. L.), in J. S. G. Richardson, *Reports of Cases at Law, Argued and Determined in the Court of Appeals and Court of Errors of South Carolina* (Columbia, S.C.: A. S. Johnston, 1851), 4:581–85.

13. Ibid.

14. Theodore Dwight Weld, ed., *American Slavery As It Is: Testimony of a Thousand Witnesses* (New York: American Anti-Slavery Society, 1839), 90.

15. Ibid., 89–90. Coroner's inquests varied by state and county and it is difficult to determine the fiscal impact of such hearings. The archives of the Monmouth County, New Jersey,

County Clerk's Office contain coroner inquests from 1786 to 1915, which is an unusually complete set of records. See http://www.visitmonmouth.com/page.aspx?Id=1695 (accessed January 15, 2013).

16. Unfortunately, the historical record does not indicate the outcome of this inquest, but the fact that it occurred addresses the link between capitalism and slavery. I maintain that explorations of postmortem financial values add to our understanding of appraisals and sales prior to death. We cannot discuss enslaved persons' prices without looking at the full spectrum of their valuation.

17. Samuel Williams to Dear Son, December 14, 1836, Samuel Williams Papers, 1836–1850, Special Collections, University of Kentucky, Lexington. I thank Eliza Robinson of the National Humanities Center, Durham, N.C., for locating this source.

18. Samuel Williams to Dear Son, December 25, 1836, Samuel Williams Papers. See also Bonnie Martin, "Slavery's Invisible Engine: Mortgaging Human Property," *Journal of Southern History* 76 (November 2010): 817–66.

19. My contribution to the suicide ecology is to explore self-destruction at the moment of separation and sale. Doing so embraces the "historical cost accounting" Nell Painter challenges scholars to accomplish in "Soul Murder and Slavery: Toward a Fully Loaded Cost Accounting," in *U.S. History as Women's History: New Feminist Essays*, ed. Linda Kerber, Alice Kessler-Harris, and Kathryn Kish Sklar (Chapel Hill: University of North Carolina Press, 1995), 125–46. See also Bell, *We Shall Be No More*; Brown, *The Reaper's Garden*; Michael A. Gomez, *Exchanging Our Country Marks: The Transformation of African Identities in the Colonial and Antebellum South* (Chapel Hill: University of North Carolina Press, 1998); Louis A. Pérez, *To Die in Cuba: Suicide and Society* (Chapel Hill: University of North Carolina Press, 2005); William D. Pierson, "White Cannibals, Black Martyrs: Fear, Depression, and Religious Faith as Causes of Suicide Among New Slaves," *Journal of Negro History* 62 (April 1977): 147–59; Terri L. Snyder, "Suicide, Slavery, and Memory in North America," *Journal of American History* 97 (June 2010): 39–62, and idem, *The Power to Die*; and Daniel E. Walker, "Suicidal Tendencies: African Transmigration in the History and Folklore of the Americas," *Griot* 18 (Spring 1999): 10–18.

20. Works Progress Administration (WPA), *Slave Narratives: A Folk History of Slavery in the United States from Interviews with Former Slaves*, "Annie Tate," North Carolina Narratives, vol. 2, pt. 2 (Washington, D.C.: Library of Congress, 1941), 332–34, http://www.memory.loc.gov (accessed December 9, 2009).

21. *The Liberator* (Boston), June 6, 1835.

22. WPA, *Slave Narratives*, Texas Narratives, pt. 1, 88, www.gutenberg.net (accessed December 9, 2009). For evidence of reunification, see Heather Williams, *Help Me to Find My People: The African American Search for Family Lost in Slavery* (Chapel Hill: University of North Carolina Press, 2012).

23. Charles Ball, *Slavery in the United States* (New York: John Taylor, 1837), 69–70.

24. The literature on life insurance and slavery contains scattered information on compensation for deceased bondpeople. See, e.g., Josiah C. Nott, "Statistics of Southern Slave Population: With Special Reference to Life Insurance," *De Bow's Review* 4 (November 1847): 275–89; Todd L. Savitt, "Slave Life Insurance in Virginia and North Carolina," *Journal of Southern History* 43 (November 1977): 583–600; and Genovese, "Medical and Insurance Costs." More recent work in this field includes Sharon Anne Murphy, *Investing in Life: Insurance in Antebellum America* (Baltimore: Johns Hopkins University Press, 2013); Karen Ryder, "'Permanent Property': Slave Life Insurance in the Antebellum Southern United States, 1820—1866"

(PhD diss., University of Delaware, 2012); and Michael Ralph, "'Life . . . in the midst of Death': Notes on the Relationship Between Slave Insurance, Life Insurance and Disability," *Disability Studies Quarterly* 32 (2012), http://dsq-sds.org/article/view/3267/3100 (accessed July 26, 2015).

25. Ian Baucom, *Specters of the Atlantic: Finance Capital, Slavery, and the Philosophy of History* (Durham, N.C.: Duke University Press, 2005); James Walvin, *The Zong: A Massacre, the Law and the End of Slavery* (New Haven, Conn.: Yale University Press, 2011); Hugh Thomas, *The Slave Trade: The Story of the Atlantic Slave Trade: 1440–1870* (New York: Simon and Schuster, 1999).

26. George Hendrick and Willene Hendrick, *The Creole Mutiny: A Tale of Revolt Aboard a Slave Ship* (Chicago: Ivan R. Dee, 2003); Jonathan Levy, *Freaks of Fortune: The Emerging World of Capitalism and Risk in America* (Cambridge, Mass.: Harvard University Press, 2012).

27. T. Stephen Whitman, *The Price of Freedom: Slavery and Freedom in Baltimore and Early National Maryland* (Louisville: University Press of Kentucky, 1997).

28. Ralph, "Life . . . in the midst of Death."

29. Broadside, *Planters' Life Insurance Company*, Rare Book, Manuscript, and Special Collections Library, Duke University, Durham, N.C.

30. Haxall Family Papers, 1835–1920, Virginia Historical Society, Richmond (hereafter VHS).

31. Berry, *The Price for Their Pound of Flesh*; Calvin Shermerhorn, *The Business of Slavery and the Rise of American Capitalism 1815–1860* (New Haven, Conn.: Yale University Press, 2015).

32. According to Murphy and Savitt, four-year policies were not common as most companies agreed to one to two year policies that required renewal at the end of the term. Additionally, "few slaveowners took out policies on valuable or favorite servants not hired out." Savitt, "Slave Life Insurance in Virginia and North Carolina," 583; Murphy, "Securing Human Property."

33. Haxall Family Papers, 1835–1920, VHS. The American Life Insurance and Trust Company also contained language to nullify policies in cases of an enslaved person's suicide.

34. Alan Taylor, *The Internal Enemy: Slavery and War in Virginia, 1772–1832* (New York: W. W. Norton, 2013). For an extensive discussion of executions and compensation see David Barry Gaspar, "'To Bring Their Offending Slaves to Justice': Compensation and Slave Resistance in Antigua 1669–1763," *Caribbean Quarterly* 30 (September–December 1984): 45–60; Vincent Brown, "Spiritual Terror and Sacred Authority in Jamaican Slave Society," *Slavery & Abolition* 24 (2003): 24–53; and Berry, *Pound of Flesh*.

35. Alfred, Charles, and Stephen were hired out to work at the Beaver and Raccoon pits of the Clover Hill Coal Company, which involved dangerous work in underground mines. See *Virginia Life Insurance Company*, VHS; and Ralph, "Life . . . in the midst of Death."

36. See Nancy C. Frantel, *Chesterfield County Virginia Uncovered: The Records of Death and Slave Insurance for the Coal Mining Industry, 1810–1895* (Westminster, Md.: Heritage Books, 2008).

37. Frantel, *Chesterfield County Virginia Uncovered*, 68–91.

38. Samuel Williams to Dear Son, December 25, 1836, Samuel Williams Papers.

39. Leslie M. Harris and Daina Ramey Berry, eds., *Slavery and Freedom in Savannah* (Athens: University of Georgia Press, 2014); Seth Rockman, *Scraping By: Wage Labor, Slavery, and Survival in Early Baltimore* (Baltimore: Johns Hopkins University Press, 2009), 262; Amy Dru Stanley, *From Bondage to Contract: Wage Labor, Marriage and the Market in the Age of Slave Emancipation* (Cambridge: Cambridge University Press, 1998).

40. *Texas State Gazette*, December 6, 1851.

41. *Race and Slavery Petitions Project*, Series I, Legislative Petitions, Record Group 100, Records of the Legislature, Memorials and Petitions, Texas State Library-Archives, Austin. This is a direct reference to Fifth Amendment due process claims, determined in 32 U.S. (7 Pet.) 243 (1833).

42. Ibid.

43. For the Gabriel Prosser Conspiracy, see note 1. For the John Brown executions, see Franny Nudelman, *John Brown's Body: Slavery, Violence & the Culture of War* (Chapel Hill: University of North Carolina Press, 2004); Paul Finkelman, ed., *His Soul Goes Marching On: Responses to John Brown and the Harpers Ferry Raid* (Charlottesville: University of Virginia Press, 1995); and Richard J. Hinton, *John Brown and His Men; with Some Account of the Roads They Traveled to Reach Harper's Ferry* (New York: Funk and Wagnalls, 1894).

44. Schwarz, ed., *Gabriel's Conspiracy*, xxv.

45. "Sentence of David, 1802," James Davidson Papers, South Caroliniana Library, University of South Carolina, Columbia.

46. Weld, ed., *American Slavery As It Is*, 90.

47. Ibid., 90.

48. Albert Raboteau, *Slave Religion: The "Invisible Institution" in the Antebellum South* (New York: Oxford University Press, 1978); Eugene D. Genovese, *Roll Jordan Roll: The World the Slaves Made* (New York: Oxford University Press,1976); Brown, *The Reaper's Garden*; Walter Rucker, *The Rivers Flows On: Black Resistance, Culture and Identity Formation in Early America* (Baton Rouge: Louisiana State University Press, 2007); Stephanie Smallwood, *Saltwater Slavery: A Middle Passage from Africa to American Diaspora* (Cambridge, Mass.: Harvard University Press, 2007).

49. Davidson, "Keeping the Devil at Bay"; Seeman, *Death in the New World*. See also the classic work such as Raboteau, *Slave Religion*, and Lawrence Levine, *Black Culture and Black Consciousness: Afro-American Folk Thought from Slavery to Freedom* (New York: Oxford University Press, 1977).

50. John S. Mbiti, *Africans Religions & Philosophy* (Portsmouth, N.H.: Heinemann, 1990); Raboteau, *Slave Religion;* Rucker, *The Rivers Flows On*; Jason Young, *Rituals of Resistance: African Atlantic Religion in Kongo and the Lowcountry South in the Era of Slavery* (Baton Rouge: Louisiana State University Press, 2011).

51. Much of the work on enslaved burials evolved from the New York African Burial Ground Project. See, e.g., Ira Berlin and Leslie Harris, eds., *Slavery in New York* (New York: New Press, 2005); Allison Blakely, "Putting Flesh on the Bones: History-Anthropology Collaboration on the New York City African Burial Ground Project," in *African Re-Genesis: Confronting Social Issues in the Diaspora*, ed. Jay B. Haviser and Kevin C. MacDonald (London: University College of London Press, 2006), 62–69; Thomas J. Davis, *A Rumor of Revolt: The 'Great Negro Plot,' in Colonial New York* (Amherst: University of Massachusetts Press, 1900); Andrea E. Frohne, "Reclaiming Space: The African Burial Ground in New York City," in *'We Shall Independent Be': African American Place Making and the Struggle to Claim Space in the United States*, ed. Angel David Nieves and Leslie M. Alexander (Boulder: University Press of Colorado, 2008), 489–510; and Joyce Hansen and Gary McGowan, *Breaking Ground, Breaking Silence: The Story of New York's African Burial Ground* (New York: Henry Holt, 1988). For other studies on death and burial, see Egerton, "A Peculiar Mark of Infamy"; Faust, *Republic of Suffering*; Brown, *The Reaper's Garden*, and idem, "Spiritual Terror and Sacred Authority in a Jamaican Slave Society," *Slavery & Abolition* 24 (2003): 24–53; João José Reis, *Death Is a Festival: Funeral Rites and Rebellion in Nineteenth-Century Brazil* (Chapel Hill: University of

North Carolina Press, 2003); and Karla F. C. Holloway, *Passed On: African American Mourning Stories* (Durham, N.C.: Duke University Press, 2002).

52. WPA, *Slave Narratives,* Georgia Narratives, 251.

53. Ibid., 251

54. Ibid., 251.

55. Ibid., 252.

56. Charles Wesley, *Hymns for Children*, 1763, or *The Southern Harmony* (1835), http://www.hymnary.org/text/and_am_i_born_to_die (accessed July 22, 2013). Several former slaves recalled this hymn in their narratives when interviewed by WPA fieldworkers in the 1930s.

57. WPA, *Slave Narratives,* Texas Narratives, pt. 1, 279, www.gutenberg.net (accessed December 2009).

58. Ibid., 53.

59. WPA, *Slave Narratives*, Georgia Narratives.

60. New International Version of the Bible, Matthew 7:13–14.

61. Wesley, *Hymns for Children*, 1763.

CHAPTER 7. AUGUST BELMONT AND THE WORLD THE SLAVES MADE

1. See Edward E. Baptist, *The Half Has Never Been Told: Slavery and the Making of American Capitalism* (New York: Basic Books, 2014); Richard Kilbourne, Jr., *Slave Agriculture and Financial Markets in Antebellum America: The Bank of the United States in Mississippi, 1831–1852* (London: Pickering and Chatto, 2006).

2. See Douglass C. North, *The Economic Growth of the United States 1790–1860* (New York: W. W. Norton, 1966), 10; Sven Beckert, *The Empire of Cotton: A Global History* (New York: Alfred A. Knopf, 2014); Kathryn Boodry "The Common Thread: Slavery, Cotton and Atlantic Finance from the Louisiana Purchase to Reconstruction" (PhD diss., Harvard University, 2014); Harold Woodman, *King Cotton and His Retainers: Financing and Marketing the Cotton Crop of the South* (Columbia: University of South Carolina Press, 1969). Friedrich Engels's "iron cable" observation entered American political discourse as an illustrative quote within an 1858 Department of the Interior report to Congress: John C. Claiborne, *Report of the Secretary of the Interior*, 35th Congress, 1st Sess., Executive Document no. 35, read and ordered tabled March 22, 1858, 93. For additional context, see Brian Schoen, *The Fragile Fabric of Union: Cotton, Federal Politics and the Global Origins of the Civil War* (Baltimore: Johns Hopkins University Press, 2009), 225.

3. See Peter E. Austin, *Baring Brothers and the Birth of Modern Finance* (London: Pickering and Chatto, 2007); Howard Bodenhorn, *A History of Banking in Antebellum America: Financial Markets and Economic Development in an Era of Nation-Building* (Cambridge: Cambridge University Press, 2000); John Crosby Brown, *A Hundred Years of Merchant Banking: A History of Brown Brothers and Company, Brown Shipley & Company and the Allied Firms, Alexander Brown and Sons, Baltimore; William and James Brown and Company, Liverpool; John A. Brown and Company, Browns and Bowen, Brown Brothers and Company, Philadelphia; Brown Brothers and Company, Boston* (New York: n.p., 1909); Niall Ferguson, "The Rise of the Rothschilds: The Family Firm as a Multinational," in *The World of Private Banking*, ed. Youssef Cassis (Farnham: Ashgate, 2009); Niall Ferguson, *The House of Rothschild*, vol. 1, *Money's Prophets* (New York: Viking, 1998); George D. Green, *Finance and Economic Development in the Old South: Louisiana Banking, 1804–1861* (Stanford, Calif.: Stanford University Press, 1972); David

Kynaston, *The City of London: A World of Its Own, 1815–1890* (London: Chatto and Windus, 1994); Ralph Hidy, *The House of Baring in American Trade and Finance: English Merchant Bankers at Work, 1763–1861* (Cambridge, Mass.: Harvard University Press, 1949); Edwin Perkins, *Financing Anglo-American Trade: The House of Brown, 1800–1880* (Cambridge, Mass.: Harvard University Press, 1975).

4. The firm of McConnel & Kennedy had extensive involvement in the trade in cotton, especially Sea Island cotton, in the early nineteenth century and made numerous purchases for shipment to Glasgow and Paisley. See Papers of McConnel & Kennedy and McConnel & Co., 1715–1888, John Rylands University Library, Manchester, UK, GB133 MCK; Norman Buck, *The Development of the Organization of Anglo-American Trade, 1800–1850* (New York: Greenwood Press, 1968).

5. Leland H. Jenks, *The Migration of British Capital to 1875* (New York: Alfred A. Knopf, 1927).

6. Charles Kindleberger, *A Financial History of Western Europe* (New York: Oxford University Press, 1993), 216; Ferguson, *The House of Rothschild*, 164; Hidy, *The House of Baring*; Austin, *Baring Brothers*, 28; Perkins, *Financing Anglo-American Trade*, 19, Appendix A.

7. On the raising of the loan for the Abolition Act, see Nicholas Draper, *The Price of Emancipation: Slave Ownership, Compensation and British Society at the End of Slavery* (Cambridge: Cambridge University Press 2010), 107–14. The most salient example of Rothschild avoidance of entanglement with slave ownership involves the firm's extensive involvement with John Forsyth. Forsyth, the U.S. secretary of state from 1834 to 1841, was also a slave planter and obtained numerous unsecured advances from the Rothschild Paris house. When he died, his son attempted to settle the debt with an offer of slaves and land, an offer that was refused outright by the Paris and London houses. John Forsyth to August Belmont, New York, May 31, 1842, Rothschild Archive, London (hereafter RAL), XI/62/2A. August Belmont, New York, to N. M. Rothschild & Sons, London, April 27, 1842, RAL XI/62/2A. See also Boodry, "The Common Thread."

8. See Austin, *Baring Brothers*, 38–40.

9. John Killick, "The Cotton Operations of Alexander Brown and Sons in the Deep South, 1820–1860," *Journal of Southern History* 43 (May 1977): 187.

10. Larry Schweikart, *Banking in the American South from the Age of Jackson to Reconstruction* (Baton Rouge: Louisiana State University Press, 1987), 48–49.

11. Irene D. Neu, "J. B. Moussier and the Property Banks of Louisiana," *Business History Review* 35 (Winter 1961): 550–57; Ralph Hidy, "The Union Bank of Louisiana Loan, 1832: A Case Study in Marketing," *Journal of Political Economy* 47 (April 1939): 232–53; Schweikart, *Banking in the American South*, chaps. 1–2; Austin, *Baring Brothers*, 32–36; Kilbourne, *Slavery Agriculture and Financial Markets*, 35–48. It is worth noting that Barings offered the bonds issued by the Union Bank of Louisiana on the markets in London and in cooperation with Hope & Co. on markets in Amsterdam. Additionally, for a period in the 1840s, N. M. Rothschild held the majority of the bonds in the Morris Canal Bank of Louisiana.

12. On the evolution of the factorage system, see Alfred Holt Stone, "The Cotton Factorage System of the Southern States," *American Historical Review* 20 (April 1915): 557–65; Stuart Bruchey, *The Colonial Merchant: Sources and Readings* (New York: Harcourt, 1966); Stuart Bruchey, ed., *Cotton and the Growth of the American Economy, 1790–1860: Sources and Readings* (New York: Harcourt, 1967); and Woodman, *King Cotton and His Retainers*.

13. Bruchey, ed., *Cotton and the Growth of the American Economy*, 176.

14. On advances on cotton, see Perkins, *Financing Anglo-American Trade*, 94–96. See also Woodman, *King Cotton and His Retainers*, 34–35.

15. William Bowen to Joseph Shipley, November 25, 1845, Brown Brothers Harriman Records, MS 78, New-York Historical Society.

16. N. M. Rothschild & Sons to Alphonse de Rothschild, December 27, 1848, RAL /224.

17. Thomas Wren Ward to Joshua Bates, October 10, 1835, Baring Papers, National Archives of Canada, Ottawa, ON.

18. The explosion in the sale of shares in the Mississippi Company was funded by the printing of paper money with which to buy them. The notes were printed by the Banque Royale, which also happened to own the Mississippi Company and was, coincidentally, run by John Law in his position as the controller of finance. Since Law did not have access to British wealth, he resorted to simply printing his own currency. On John Law, see Rebecca Spang, "The Ghost of Law: Speculating on Money, Memory and Mississippi in the French Constituent Assembly," *Historical Reflections/Réflexions Historiques* 31 (Spring 2005): 3–25. Other examples include the tulip mania in Holland and the South Sea Bubble in England in the eighteenth century.

19. Cited in Perkins, *Financing Anglo-American Trade*, 99.

20. For cotton prices, see Bruchey, ed., *Cotton and the Growth of the American Economy*, Table 3-P.

21. See Peter Temin, *The Jacksonian Economy* (New York: W. W. Norton, 1969); Killick, "Cotton Operations of Alexander Brown and Sons"; and Jessica Lepler, *The Many Panics of 1837: People, Politics and The Creation of a Transatlantic Financial Crisis* (New York: Cambridge University Press, 2013).

22. N. M. Rothschild & Sons to August Belmont, May 1837, American Letter Copy Books, RAL II/10/1.

23. James de Rothschild to his nephews, London, May 25, 1837, RAL XI/101/0/8/13.

24. David Black, *The King of Fifth Avenue: The Fortunes of August Belmont* (New York: Dial Press, 1981), 5, 22, 39.

25. August Belmont to N. M. Rothschild & Sons, September 12, 1839, RAL XI/62/0C/2/35.

26. James de Rothschild to his nephews, London, September 15, 1839, RAL XI/101/2/4/63.

27. N. M. Rothschild & Sons to C. G. Allhussen Esq, New Orleans, October 3, 1837, RAL II/10/1.

28. August Belmont, New York, to N. M. Rothschild & Sons, London, November 30, 1847, RAL XI/62/3B; August Belmont, New York, to N. M. Rothschild & Sons, London, October 26, 1848, RAL XI/62/3B.

29. August Belmont, New York, to N. M. Rothschild & Sons, London, October 12, 1852, RAL XI/62/5.

30. Betty de Rothschild, Paris, to Alphonse de Rothschild, March 7, 1849, RAL 000/930 58/1/222.

31. August Belmont's letter to N. M. Rothschild & Sons, May 6, 1851, RAL XI/62/6, is one example: "There has been some news in our cotton market and prices have gone up about 3/8 ct from the lowest point, in consequence of advices from the south of a killing frost in some parts of Alabama & Tennessee in which I have not much belief. . . . [T]here has been so much cotton planted that we have every prospect for a large crop & this with the now established fact that the present crop cannot fall short of 2300m bales must keep prices down."

32. August Belmont to N. M. Rothschild & Sons, November 30, 1847, RAL XI/62/3B.

33. August Belmont to N. M. Rothschild & Sons, October 26, 1848, RAL XI/62/3B.

34. Ibid.

35. Perkins, *Financing Anglo-American Trade*, 245–47.

36. August Belmont to N. M. Rothschild & Sons, April 29, 1843, RAL XI/62/2a/2/44.

37. August Belmont to N. M. Rothschild & Sons, November 29, 1845, RAL XI/62/3A.

38. August Belmont to N. M. Rothschild & Sons, April 19, 1859, RAL XI/62/8.

39. Killick, "The Cotton Operations of Alexander Brown and Sons," 71.

40. See Ferguson, *The House of Rothschild*.

41. Benjamin Davidson to N. M. Rothschild & Sons, September 12, 1849, RAL XI/38/81B.

42. August Belmont to N. M. Rothschild & Sons, November 20, 1857, RAL XI/62/7A.

43. Betty de Rothschild to Alphonse de Rothschild, May 16, 1849, RAL 000/930 58/1/222.

44. Betty de Rothschild to Alphonse de Rothschild, March 7, 1849, RAL 000/930 58/1/222.

45. See Black, *The King of Fifth Avenue*, 52–57.

46. Betty de Rothschild to Alphonse de Rothschild, March 7, 1849, RAL 000/930 58/1/222.

47. On the lease of the Royal Mint Refinery, see Ferguson, *The House of* Rothschild, 70; and RAL XI/09 and RAL XI/24. This move toward vertical integration was also employed by Rothschild in the firm's purchase of an ironworks in Vítkovice in 1843 to produce tracks for the Chemin de Fer du Nord. On vertical integration, see Alfred Chandler, *The Visible Hand: The Managerial Revolution in American Business* (Cambridge, Mass.: Harvard University Press, 1977), 287, 312.

48. See Heather Cox Richardson, *West from Appomattox: The Reconstruction of America after the Civil War* (New Haven, Conn.: Yale University Press, 2007); David Igler, *The Great Ocean: Pacific Worlds from Captain Cook to the Gold Rush* (New York: Oxford University Press, 2013); Richard White, *Railroaded: The Transcontinentals and the Making of Modern America* (New York: W. W. Norton, 2012); and Elliot West, *The Contested Plains: Indians, Goldseekers and the Rush to Colorado* (Lawrence: University Press of Kansas, 1998).

49. August Belmont to N. M. Rothschild & Sons, July 17, 1863, RAL XI/62/11.

CHAPTER 8. "WHAT HAVE WE TO DO WITH SLAVERY?"

1. Frederick Douglass, *Life and Times of Frederick Douglass: An Autobiography* (1892; reprint New York: Gramercy, 1993), 282. Douglass believed that among white northerners there was little interest in answering this important question until 1854.

2. Charles Sumner, "Union Among Men of all Parties Against the Slave Power and the Extension of Slavery, Speech Before A Mass Convention at Worcester, June 28, 1848," in *Charles Sumner, His Complete Works*, vol. 2 (Boston: Lee and Shepard, 1900), 233.

3. Of a total population in 1775 of approximately 678,749 people in New England, 16,153 were African American, so the precise percentage is 2.3 percent. These totals represent my calculations, based on the colonial census data.

4. Ira Berlin, *Many Thousands Gone: The First Two Centuries of Slavery in North America* (Cambridge, Mass.: Belknap Press of Harvard University Press, 1998), 369–71. For another usage of this paradigm about the "marginal" value of slavery in the "North" in yet another widely cited and now tenth anniversary edition, see Peter Kolchin, *American Slavery, 1619–1877* (New York: Hill and Wang, 1993, 2003), 29: "Unlike the North, where slavery was increasingly marginal, the South developed as a true slave society. . . ." In his updated and expanded approach, *Generations of Captivity: A History of African-American Slaves* (Cambridge, Mass.:

Belknap Press of Harvard University Press, 2003), Berlin restated this approach (8–9) and concluded that by the end of the 1760s, "the North remained a society with slaves" (88).

5. Berlin, *Generations of Captivity*, 9; Kolchin, *American Slavery*, 29–30. Keith Bradley noted that, based on this rubric, only five "true slave societies" have existed: Brazil, the Caribbean, the southern states of the United States, ancient Athens, and Roman Italy. Keith Bradley, *Slavery and Society at Rome* (New York: Cambridge University Press, 1994), 12–16.

6. David Brion Davis, *Inhuman Bondage: The Rise and Fall of Slavery in the New World* (New York: Oxford University Press, 2006), 41.

7. There are some disagreements over the precise definitions of this framework. See Orlando Patterson, *Freedom*, vol. 1, *Freedom in the Making of Western Culture* (New York: Basic Books, 1992), 31; Elsa V. Goveia, *Slave Society in the British Leeward Islands at the End of the Eighteenth Century* (New Haven, Conn.: Yale University Press, 1965), vii; Michael Craton, "Slavery and Slave Society in the British Caribbean," in *The Slavery Reader*, ed. Gad J. Heuman, and James Walvin (New York: Routledge, 2003), 104; Peter Garnsey, *Ideas of Slavery from Aristotle to Augustine* (New York: Cambridge University Press, 1996), 2.

8. Throughout the essay I use both "the West Indies," as contemporaries in the colonial era did, and the modern, postcolonial designation, "the Caribbean."

9. My approach in this chapter is inspired by Eric Williams, *Capitalism and Slavery* (1944; reprint New York: Capricorn Books, 1966).

10. Marcus Rediker, presentation at the International Labor Consortium, University of Pittsburgh, 2004. Ronald Bailey, "The Slave(ry) Trade and the Development of Capitalism in the United States: The Textile Industry in New England," *Social Science History* 14 (Fall 1990): 373; idem, "Africa, the Slave Trade, and the Rise of Industrial Capitalism in Europe and the United States: A Historiographic Review," *American History: A Bibliographic Review* 2 (1986): 1–91; Philip D. Curtin, *The Rise and Fall of the Plantation Complex: Essays in Atlantic History*, 2nd ed. (New York: Cambridge University Press, 1998).

11. Curtin, *The Rise and Fall of the Plantation Complex*, esp. xi–xii, sets out the framework.

12. Ibid., xiii.

13. June 2, 1641, in *Winthrop's Journal*, vol. 2, ed. James Kendall (New York: Charles Scribner's Sons, 1908), 31.

14. June 1647, ibid., 328.

15. Ibid.

16. Williams, *Capitalism and Slavery*, 110.

17. Sir Charles Whitworth, *State of the Trade of Great Britain in its Imports and Exports* (London, 1776), 63–64. See also John McCusker, "The Current Value of English Exports," in *Essays in Economic History of the Atlantic World* (New York: Routledge, 1997), 150–64.

18. The Customs Ledger of Imports and Exports, British North America, 1768–1772, CUST 16/1, PRO, TNA, London, lists a prodigious variety of goods, as do John J. McCusker and Russell R. Menard, *The Economy of British America, 1607–1789* (Chapel Hill: University of North Carolina Press, 1991), 283–87. See also T. H. Breen, "'Baubles of Britain': The American and Consumer Revolutions of the Eighteenth Century," *Past and Present* 119 (May 1988): 73–104.

19. Ralph Davis, "English Foreign Trade, 1700–1774," *Economic History Review* (December 1962): 285–303.

20. Gloria L. Main and Jackson T. Main, "Economic Growth and the Standard of Living in Southern New England, 1640–1774," *Journal of Economic History* 48 (March 1988): 29.

Other useful studies include Carole Shammas, "Consumer Behavior in Colonial America," *Social Science History* 6 (1982): 67–86, and idem, "How Self-Sufficient Was Early America?," *Journal of Interdisciplinary History* 13 (1982): 247–72.

21. This was often accomplished through the circulation and use of "bills of exchange." A useful operational overview is W. T. Baxter, *The House of Hancock, Business in Boston, 1724–1775* (Cambridge, Mass.: Harvard University Press, 1945), 11–38.

22. "Testimony of George Walker of Barbados," March 16, 1775, in *Proceedings and Debates of the British Parliament Respecting North America*, vol. 5, *1754–1783*, ed. R. C. Simmons and P. D. G. Thomas (White Plains, N.Y.: Kraus International Publications, 1986), 556.

23. Russell Menard has recently challenged the "sugar revolution" concept and proposed a "sugar boom" instead. Russell Menard, *Sweet Negotiations: Sugar, Slavery, and Plantation Agriculture in Early Barbados* (Charlottesville: University of Virginia Press, 2006). For details on the sugar expansion, see Richard Dunn, *Sugar and Slaves: The Rise of the Planter Class in the English West Indies, 1624–1713* (1972; reprint Chapel Hill: University of North Carolina Press, 2000); Robin Blackburn, *The Making of New World Slavery* (New York: Verso, 1997), 401–56; McCusker and Menard, *The Economy of British America, 1607–1789*, 144–68; and Richard Sheridan, *Sugar and Slavery: An Economic History of the British West Indies, 1623–1775* (Baltimore: Johns Hopkins University Press, 1973).

24. *Substance of the evidence of the Petition, Presented by the West-India Planters and Merchants to the House of Commons* (London, 1775), 4.

25. The quotation is from "Testimony of George Walker," in *Proceedings and Debates*, 556.

26. [Edward Littleton], *The Groans of the Plantations* (London, 1689), 17.

27. Report of Governor Ward to Board of Trade, Newport, January 9, 1740, in *Records of the Colony of Rhode Island*, vol. 5, ed. John Russell Bartlett (Providence, R.I.: Knowles, Anthony & Company, State Printers, 1860), 13.

28. Illegal slaving activity continued, and perhaps another 5,000 slaves were sold in the West Indies, principally Cuba, between 1808 and 1859, with varying degrees of involvement by New Englanders. Overall slaving activity is from www.slavevoyages.org and Jay Coughtry, *The Notorious Triangle: Rhode Island and the African Slave Trade, 1700–1807* (Philadelphia: Temple University Press, 1981), 233–37.

29. Rachel Chernos Lin, "The Rhode Island Slave-Traders: Butchers, Bakers, and Candlestick Makers," *Slavery and Abolition* 23 (December 2002): 21–38.

30. Gregory E. O'Malley, *Final Passages: The Intercolonial Slave Trade of British America, 1619–1807* (Chapel Hill: University of North Carolina Press, 2014), Table 12, 202–3, 212–13.

31. Coughtry, *The Notorious Triangle*, 165, 170–71.

32. Ibid., 80–90.

33. Ibid., 81.

34. Eric Kimball, "'An Essential Link in a Vast Chain': New England and the West Indies, 1700–1775" (PhD diss., University of Pittsburgh, 2009), 45–47.

35. Calculation based on the Customs Ledger of Imports and Exports, British North America, 1768–1772, CUST 16/1, PRO, TNA, London.

36. John McCusker, "The Rum Trade and the Balance of Payments of the Thirteen Continental Colonies, 1650–1775, Parts 1–2" (PhD diss., University of Pittsburgh, 1970), 438–41.

37. Testimony of George Walker, in Simmons and Thomas, eds., *Proceedings and Debates of the British Parliament Respecting North America*, vol. 5, 560.

38. Calculation based on the Customs Ledger of Imports and Exports, British North America, 1768–1772, CUST 16/1, PRO, TNA, London.

39. Testimony of Seth Jenkins, in Simmons and Thomas, eds., *Proceedings and Debates of the British Parliament Respecting North America*, vol. 5, 495.

40. James Hedges, *The Browns of Providence Plantation*, vol. 1, *The Colonial Years* (Providence, R.I.: Brown University Press, 1952), 86–122; Alexander Starbuck, *History of the American Whale Fishery from its Earliest Inception to the Year 1876* (Waltham, Mass., 1878), 152–53.

41. Kimball, "An Essential Link," 58.

42. Samuel Martin, *An Essay on Plantership* (Antigua: T. Smith, 1750), 29–30.

43. Dunn, *Sugar and Slaves*, 195.

44. Ibid., 195.

45. Testimony of George Walker, in Simmons and Thomas, eds., *Proceedings and Debates of the British Parliament Respecting North America*, vol. 5, 557.

46. Edward Long, *History of Jamaica*, vol. 3 (London, 1774), sec. 310, "Sea-Fish," p. 867, lists thirty-nine different, locally available fish.

47. Captain Leake's Answer to the Board of Trade, October, 1699, in *Calendar of State Papers Colonial, America and West Indies*, vol. 17, edited by Cecil Headlam (London: Mackie and Co., 1908), 319–21.

48. For the herring trade, see John Knox, *A View of the British Empire, More Especially Scotland* (London, 1785), 313; and John M. Mitchell, *The Herring: Its Natural History and National Importance* (Edinburgh, 1864), 211–12.

49. My estimate based on Jamaica NOSL, CO 142/14, London, PRO, TNA, London.

50. My calculations are based on Appendix 9 in *Proceedings of the Hon. House of Assembly of Jamaica, on the Sugar and Slave-Trade* (London, 1793), 26.

51. Calculation based on the Customs Ledger of Imports and Exports, British North America, 1768–1772, CUST 16/1, PRO, TNA, London.

52. *Connecticut Colonial Records*, vol. 14 (Hartford: 1887), 498. All the quotations in this paragraph are from this source. Trumbull noted a few rare exceptions to this pattern: "now and then a vessel to Ireland with Flaxseed, and to England with Lumber and Potashes, and a few to Gibraltar and Barbary."

53. Ibid.

54. Ibid.

55. Ibid.

56. Joseph Avitable, "The Atlantic World Economy and Colonial Connecticut" (PhD diss., University of Rochester, 2009).

57. Kimball, "An Essential Link," 184.

58. My thanks to Karwan Fatah-Black, who graciously shared his data set on horse imports into Surinam, on which my calculation is based.

59. My calculations are based on the Customs Ledger of Imports and Exports, British North America, 1768–1772, CUST 16/1, PRO, TNA, London.

60. Richard Sheridan, *Sugar and Slavery*, 208–33.

61. Ibid., 124–207.

62. My calculations are based on the Customs Ledger of Imports and Exports, British North America, 1768–1772, CUST 16/1, PRO, TNA, London.

63. Kimball, "An Essential Link," 444–46.

64. My calculation is derived from Andres Poey, "A Chronological Table, comprising 400 Cyclonic Hurricanes which have occurred in the West Indies and in the North Atlantic within 362 Years, from 1493 to 1855," *Journal of the Royal Geographic Society* 25 (1853): 291–328. See also

Matthew Mulcahy, *Hurricanes and Society in the British West Indies* (Baltimore: Johns Hopkins University Press 2006).

65. For a useful overview of how some of these wars impacted the Caribbean, see Richard Pares, *War and Trade in the West Indies, 1739–1763* (Oxford: Clarendon Press, 1936).

66. Ship's cargo listing for the *Rising Sun*, cleared on January 23, 1771, which contained an entry for "Twelve wood frames for the negro huts." Miscellaneous Records, Portsmouth Athenaeum, Portsmouth, N.H.

67. McCusker, "The Rum Trade and the Balance of Payments of the Thirteen Colonies, 1650–1775," 773.

68. Ibid., 772.

69. David Eltis, "The Slave Economies of the Caribbean: Structure, Performance, Evolution and Significance," in *General History of the Caribbean*, vol. 3, *The Slave Societies of the Caribbean*, ed. Franklin W. Knight (London: UNESCO Publishing, 1997), 117.

70. Estimates based on the Customs Ledger of Imports and Exports, British North America, 1768–1772, CUST 16/1, PRO, TNA, London. Direct exports from the middle colonies accounted for 35 percent and from the southern colonies for about 33 percent.

71. Maine at this time was technically part of Massachusetts and was often referred to as a "province."

72. Kimball, "An Essential Link," 238.

73. Wells and York were very important shipbuilding port towns. Ibid., 446.

74. William Douglass, *A Summary, History and Political, of the First Planting, Progressive Improvements, and Present State of the British Settlements in North America*, vol. 1 (London, 1760), 539.

75. Bernard Bailyn and Lotte Bailyn, *Massachusetts Shipping 1697–1714: A Statistical Study* (Cambridge, Mass.: Belknap Press of Harvard University Press, 1959), 20–22, concluded that by 1702, Boston was already "one of the major maritime centers of the Atlantic world" and "second only to London."

76. For the impact of the American Revolution, see Selwyn H. H. Carrington, "The American Revolution and the British West Indies' Economy," *Journal of Interdisciplinary History* 17 (Spring 1987): 823–50.

77. John Adams to Secretary Livingston, Paris, June 23, 1783, in *The Works of John Adams*, ed. Charles Francis Adams, 10 vols. (Boston: Little, Brown, , 1853), 8:74.

78. John Adams to Secretary Livingston, Paris, July 3, 1783, in *The Works of John Adams*, 8:79. Adams stressed in this same letter how "The West India commerce now gives us most anxiety" since it was so vital, and likely to be prohibited.

79. Charles W. Toth, "Anglo-American Diplomacy and the British West Indies (1783–1789)," *Americas* 32 (1976): 418–36. Even during this supposed "closing," exceptions were made for "emergency" supplies, which had the effect of nullifying the very intent of the law.

80. Herbert C. Bell, "British Commercial Policy in the West Indies, 1783–93," *English Historical Review* 31 (July 1916): 429–41; Alice B. Keith, "Relaxations in the British Restrictions on the American Trade with the British West Indies, 1783–1802," *Journal of Modern History* 20 (March 1948): 1–18; Selwyn H. H. Carrington, "The American Revolution, British Policy and the West Indian Economy, 1775–1808," *Revista/Review Interamericana* 22 (Autumn/Winter 1992): 72–108, esp. 94–102.

81. John H. Coatsworth, "American Trade with European Colonies in the Caribbean and South America, 1790–1812," *William and Mary Quarterly* 24 (April 1967): 243–66. Regrettably, because of the absence of customs records before 1790, "for the most part there is a lack of

sufficient statistical evidence with which to obtain a reasonably sound overall view of overseas trade and shipping from 1775–1790," thus making the sort of colony or port-specific type of analysis provided here extremely difficult. See James F. Shepherd and Gary M. Walton, "Economic Change after the American Revolution: Pre- and Post-War Comparisons of Maritime Shipping and Trade," *Explorations in Economic History* 13 (1976): 397–422, quotation at 397.

82. Although there are some scholarly disagreements about the level of per capita growth in the pre-1840 era, there is consensus that "from 1793 to 1807, the period of American neutrality . . . favorable trade conditions produced by the Napoleonic Wars greatly benefited American shipping," especially between 1793 and 1807. Claudia D. Goldin and Frank D. Lewis, "The Role of Exports in American Economic Growth During the Napoleonic Wars, 1793–1807," *Explorations in Economic History* 17 (1980): 7–8.

83. Joseph Inikori, *Africans and the Industrial Revolution in England, A Study in International Trade and Economic Development* (New York: Cambridge University Press, 2002), esp. 156–214.

84. Seymour Drescher, *Econocide: British Slavery in the Era of Abolition*, 2nd ed. (Chapel Hill: University of North Carolina Press, 2010), 17. He identifies these years as 1788–1807 on p. 16, but see his entire discussion through pp. 19–25.

85. Ibid., 67.

86. David Brion Davis, foreword to the second edition of *Econocide*, xvi.

87. Douglass C. North, *The Economic Growth of the United States, 1790–1860* (New York: W. W. Norton, 1966), 36.

88. Ibid, 36–37, though North's discussion from pp. 36–58 is directly relevant to the growth and importance of these trading patterns in the years between 1790 and 1815. North's discussion on p. 37 quoted Samuel Elliot Morrison's *Maritime History of Massachusetts*, which related the importance of this trade without identifying the linkage to the plantation complex in the Caribbean—and especially the African slave laborers at the center of it.

89. Adam Seybert, in *Statistical Annals of the United States of America* (Philadelphia, 1818), 281.

90. Ibid., 281.

91. Ibid., 281.

92. Ibid., 281n88.

93. The Boston records were destroyed in a fire in 1894. See "The Remarks by Mr. Winslow Warren," in *The Proceedings of the Massachusetts Historical Society*, 2nd ser., vol. 12, *1897–1899* (Boston: Massachusetts Historical Society, 1899), 194.

94. I have chosen 1802 to start because this was the first year that customs reports separated domestic and foreign exports and ended with 1808 because the precipitous fall of this branch of commerce as a result of the 1807 Embargo Act is visible thereafter.

95. Regionally, however, the Mid-Atlantic states of New York and Pennsylvania consistently reexported even larger amounts, ranging from 45 to 49 percent.

CHAPTER 9. "NO COUNTRY BUT THEIR COUNTING-HOUSES"

1. Louis A. Pérez, ed., *Impressions of Cuba in the Nineteenth Century: The Travel Diary of Joseph J. Dimock* (Wilmington, Del.: Scholarly Resources, 1998), xii; Laird W. Bergad, *Cuban Rural Society in the Nineteenth Century: The Social and Economic History of Monoculture in Matanzas* (Princeton, N.J.: Princeton University Press, 1990), 322n28. See also Stephen M.

Chambers, *No God But Gain: The Untold Story of Cuban Slavery, the Monroe Doctrine, and the Making of the United States* (New York: Verso Books, 2015).

2. See Don E. Fehrenbacher, *The Slaveholding Republic: An Account of the United States Government's Relations to Slavery*, completed and edited by Ward M. McAfee (New York: Oxford University Press, 2001); and Steven Hahn, *The Political Worlds of Slavery and Freedom* (Cambridge, Mass.: Harvard University Press, 2009), 1–54.

3. See Manuel Moreno Fraginals, *The Sugarmill: The Socioeconomic Complex of Sugar in Cuba, 1760–1860*, trans. Cedric Belfrage (New York: Monthly Review Press, 1976); Robert L. Paquette, *Sugar Is Made with Blood: The Conspiracy of La Escalera and the Conflict Between Empires over Slavery in Cuba* (Middletown, Conn.: Wesleyan University Press, 1988); Bergad, *Cuban Rural Society in the Nineteenth Century*; and Laird W. Bergad, Fe. Iglesias García, and María del Carmen Barcia, *The Cuban Slave Market, 1790–1880*, Cambridge Latin American Studies 79 (Cambridge: Cambridge University Press, 1995).

4. See Linda Kerrigan Salvucci, "Development and Decline: The Port of Philadelphia and Spanish Imperial Markets, 1783–1823" (PhD diss., Princeton University, 1985), 94–95.

5. Javier Cuenca Esteban, "Trends and Cycles in U.S. Trade with Spain and the Spanish Empire, 1790–1819," *Journal of Economic History* 44 (June 1984): 540–41. See also Linda K. Salvucci, "Atlantic Intersections: Early American Commerce and the Rise of the Spanish West Indies (Cuba)," *Business History Review* 79 (Winter 2005): 781–809, 806.

6. James R. Fichter, *So Great a Profit: How the East Indies Trade Transformed Anglo-American Capitalism* (Cambridge, Mass.: Harvard University Press, 2010), 112–13.

7. Dale W. Tomich, *Through the Prism of Slavery: Labor, Capital, and World Economy* (Lanham, Md.: Rowman and Littlefield, 2004), 63–64.

8. Christopher Kingston, "Marine Insurance in Britain and America, 1720–1844: A Comparative Institutional Analysis," *Journal of Economic History* 67 (June 2007): 379–409; Glenn Crothers, "Commercial Risk and Capital Formation in Early America: Virginia Merchants and the Rise of American Marine Insurance, 1750–1815," *Business History Review* 78 (Winter 2004): 629–30.

9. See Herman E. Kross and Martin R. Blyn, *A History of Financial Intermediaries* (New York: Random House, 1971); Holger Engberg, "Capital Formation and Economic Development: The Role of Financial Institutions and Markets," in *The Insurance Industry in Economic Development*, ed. Bernard Wasow and Raymond D. Hill (New York: NYU Press, 1986); Howard Bodenhorn, *A History of Banking in Antebellum America: Financial Markets and Economic Development in an Era of Nation-Building* (Cambridge: Cambridge University Press, 2000); Robert E. Wright, *Origins of Commercial Banking in America, 1750–1800* (Lanham, Md.: Rowman and Littlefield, 2001).

10. Fichter, *So Great a Profit*, 112–13, 263.

11. Robert Dalzell, *Enterprising Elite: The Boston Associates and the World They Made* (Cambridge, Mass.: Harvard University Press, 1987), 4.

12. See Louis A. Pérez, Jr., *Cuba and the United States: Ties of Singular Intimacy* (Athens: University of Georgia Press, 1990); idem, *The War of 1898: The United States and Cuba in History and Historiography* (Chapel Hill: University of North Carolina Press, 1998); Richard Gott, *Cuba: A New History* (New Haven, Conn.: Yale University Press, 2004); and Louis A. Pérez, Jr., *Cuba in the American Imagination: Metaphor and the Imperial Ethos* (Chapel Hill: University of North Carolina Press, 2008).

13. Quoted in Pérez, *Cuba in the American Imagination*, 30.

14. John Quincy Adams, *The Russian Memoirs of John Quincy Adams, His Diary from 1809 to 1814* (New York: Arno Press and The New York Times, 1970), 83; John Quincy Adams, St. Petersburg, to Robert Smith, Washington, D.C., January 7, 1810, in *The Writings of John Quincy Adams*, vol. 3, ed. Worthington Chauncy Ford (New York: Macmillan, 1914), 375–76.

15. Alexander Everett, St. Petersburg, to Oliver Everett, Boston, December 13, 1809, Alexander Hill Everett Diaries, 1809–1841, Everett-Noble Papers, Massachusetts Historical Society, Boston.

16. See Adams, *Russian Memoirs*, 175, 181–82, 263.

17. See Levett Harris, "Exported from St. Petersburg in American Vessels Ao. 1805," roll 1, Despatches from U.S. Consul at St. Petersburg, National Archives, Washington, D.C. (hereafter cited as Despatches from St. Petersburg); Levett Harris, "Particulars of the Goods passed the Sound for the Baltic Markets in American Vessels from the 1st January to the 1st December 1811," roll 2, Despatches from St. Petersburg; Levett Harris, "Statements as to the Baltick trade & Sound dues in the year 1811," roll 2, Despatches from St. Petersburg; "List of American Vessels at Archangel, 1810," Joseph V. Bacon Memorandum Book, Ship MSS 42, Phillips Library, Peabody-Essex Museum, Salem, Mass.

18. This material is taken from a complete survey of 4,428 ship entrances and 3,771 ship clearances published in 210 issues of the *Boston Gazette* from January 1, 1810, to January 2, 1812.

19. This material is taken from the Portsmouth, New Hampshire, Impost Books, 1810–1811; Salem, Massachusetts, Impost Books, 1810–1811; Newport, Rhode Island, Impost Books, 1810–1811; and Bristol-Warren, Rhode Island, Impost Books, 1810–1811, National Archives and Records Administration, Waltham, Mass.

20. *New York Commercial Advertiser*, February 6, 1810; John Quincy Adams, St. Petersburg, to Thomas Bolyston Adams, October 11, 1810, in *Writings of John Quincy Adams*, 3:521.

21. At the height of the U.S.-Russia trade, from 1809 to 1811, American ships exported 13,763,088 pounds of cotton to Russia; in the same period, they exported 28,198,580 pounds of sugar (including brown and white) and 10,445,900 pounds of coffee. Timothy Pitkin, *A Statistical View of the Commerce of the United States* (Hartford, Conn.: Charles Hosmer, 1816), 234.

22. See, e.g., *Diario de la Habana* (Havana, Cuba), September 6, 1811, Despatches from the U.S. Consul at Havana, roll 2, National Archives, Washington, D.C. (hereafter cited as Despatches from Havana).

23. Alfred W. Crosby, Jr., *America, Russia, Hemp, and Napoleon: American Trade with Russia and the Baltic, 1783–1812* (Columbus: Ohio State University Press, 1965), 74.

24. Douglas A. Irwin, "New Estimates of the Average Tariff of the United States, 1790–1820," *Journal of Economic History* 63 (June 2003): 510.

25. James Duncan Phillips, *Salem and the Indies* (Cambridge, Mass.: Riverside Press, 1947), 40; Mary Caroline Crawford, *The Famous Families of Massachusetts* (Boston: Little, Brown, 1930), 163n3.

26. See John D'Wolf, *Voyage in the North Pacific and a Journey Through Siberia* (Cambridge, 1861), Gansevoort-Lansing Collection, Manuscripts and Archives Division, New York Public Library.

27. Peter T. Dalleo, "McKean Rodney: U.S. Consul in Cuba: The Havana Years, 1825–1829," *Delaware History* 22, no. 3 (1987): 204–5. See also William Barnes and John Morgan, *The Foreign Service of the United States* (Washington, D.C.: Historical Office, Bureau of Public Affairs, Department of State, 1961); Thomas Bailey, *A Diplomatic History of the American People* (New York: Appleton-Century-Crofts, 1964).

28. Geo. C. Morton ["acting American Consul at the Havana"], November 18, 1795, roll 1, Despatches from Havana.

29. William Bentley, September 11, 1798, in William Bentley, *The Diary of William Bentley, 1793–1802* (Salem, Mass.: Essex Institute, 1907), 282; Edward Gray, *William Gray, of Salem, Merchant; A Biographical Sketch* (Boston: Houghton Mifflin, 1914), 23.

30. "Signed by Messrs Sta Maria & Cuesta of the City of Havana," February 14, 1798, box 1, folder 3, William Gray Papers, Phillips Library, Peabody-Essex Museum, Salem, Mass.

31. The "embargo" here refers to one stage (December 1807–March 1809) in a series of complex national trade restrictions from 1807 to 1812. Thomas Andrew Bailey, *A Diplomatic History of the American People*, 7th ed. (New York: Meredith Publishing Co., 1964), 134.

32. September 10, 1797, September 8, 1799, in Bentley, *The Diary of William Bentley*, 282, 317; E. Gray, *William Gray*, 24; *Washington Federalist*, September 10, 1808; *North Star* (Danville, Vt.), September 3, 1808.

33. In 1808, Adams borrowed this reference from the U.S. senator from Massachusetts, Timothy Pickering. John Quincy Adams (Washington, D.C.) to Harrison Gray Otis, March 31, 1808, *Writings of John Quincy Adams*, 3:203; E. Gray, *William Gray*, 25–26.

34. See *Boston Columbian Centinel*, April 3, 1813.

35. E. Gray, *William Gray*, 20.

36. *Salem Gazette*, December 19, 1809.

37. For a sense of the extensive, sympathetic historiography related to Adams and U.S. foreign policy see Samuel Flagg Bemis, *John Quincy Adams and the Foundations of American Foreign Policy* (New York: Knopf, 1949); William E. Weeks, *John Quincy Adams and American Global Empire* (Lexington: University Press of Kentucky, 1992); James E. Lewis, Jr., *John Quincy Adams: Policymaker for the Union* (Wilmington, Del.: Scholarly Resources, 2001).

38. William Gray, Boston, to John Quincy Adams, St. Petersburg, April 25, 1810, quoted in E. Gray, *William Gray*, 52; John Quincy Adams, St. Petersburg, to William Gray, Boston, August 3, 1810, in *Writings of John Quincy Adams*, 3:465–66.

39. Crosby, *America, Russia, Hemp, and Napoleon*, 172–73; John Quincy Adams, St. Petersburg, to William Gray, October 20, 1810, in *Writings of John Quincy Adams*, 3:519–20; David W. McFadden, "John Quincy Adams, American Commercial Diplomacy, and Russia, 1809–1825," *New England Quarterly* 66, no. 4 (1993): 617–18; Greg G. Williams, *The French Assault on American Shipping, 1793–1813: A History and Comprehensive Record of Merchant Marine Losses* (Jefferson, N.C.: McFarland and Co., 2009), 228, 70.

40. Francis Gregory, *Nathaniel Appleton: Merchant and Entrepreneur, 1779–1861* (Charlottesville: University of Virginia Press, 1975), 50; Crosby, *America, Russia, Hemp, and Napoleon*, 172–73.

41. Levett Harris, St. Petersburg, to Robert Smith, Washington, December 12/24, 1810, roll 2, Despatches from St. Petersburg.

42. Kingston, "Marine Insurance in Britain and America," 19; *Boston Gazette*, June 3, 1811.

43. Alexander Everett, February 5, 1810, p. 110, folder "A.H. Everett Journal Narrative, Aug. 1809–Sep. 1811," Everett-Noble Papers.

44. John Quincy Adams, February 4, 1814, *Russia Diary*, 575; Crosby, *America, Russia, Hemp, and Napoleon*, 176.

45. Alexander Hill Everett Diaries, February 24–May 31, 1840, Everett-Noble Papers; John Spear Smith Diary, roll 5, Samuel Smith Family Papers, National Archives, Washington, D.C. (hereafter cited as SSFP); Stephen Cullen Carpenter, *Memoirs of the Honorable Thomas Jefferson* (Printed for the Purchasers, 1809), 213–23.

46. John Spear Smith, St. Petersburg, to Samuel Smith, Baltimore, May 1, 1810, roll 3, SSFP.

47. See John Quincy Adams, *Russian Memoirs*, 263; Brothers Cramer (St. Petersburg) to George and John D'Wolf (Bristol), July 13, 1815, D'Wolf Papers, Papers of the American Slave Trade, pt. 2, roll 9, Rhode Island Historical Society, Providence; John Spear Smith, St. Petersburg, to Samuel Smith, Baltimore, April 2, 1810, roll 3, SSFP.

48. Thomas Hazard, New Bedford, Mass., to Samuel Hazard, Archangel, Russia, March 31, 1812; April 9, 1812; Thomas Hazard, Jr., Letter Book, 1811–1816, Miscellaneous Manuscripts Collection, Manuscripts and Archives, Sterling Memorial Library, Yale University, New Haven, Conn.

49. Crosby, *America, Russia, Hemp, and Napoleon*, 225; N. N. Bolkhovitinov, *The Beginnings of Russian-American Relations, 1775–1815* (Cambridge, Mass.: Harvard University Press, 1975), 222.

50. Moreno Fraginals, *The Sugarmill*, 30. See also Francisco Arango y Parreño, *Discurso sobre la Agricultura de La Habana y Medios de Fomentaria*, vol. 1, *1792*, 65–72; Dale Tomich, "The Wealth of Empire: Francisco Arango y Parreño, Political Economy, and the Second Slavery in Cuba," *Comparative Studies in Society and History* 45, no. 1 (2003): 5.

51. Pérez, *Cuba and the United States*, 5–13.

52. Depending on how it is calculated, Linda Salvucci estimates, based on U.S. exports, that the peak years of U.S.-Cuba trade in this period were 1806–1814 or 1799–1801 and 1806–1807: Salvucci, "Development and Decline," 90; see also Crosby, *America, Russia, Hemp, and Napoleon*, 116–17; Herminio Portell Vilá, *Historia de Cuba en sus Relaciones con los Estados Unidos y España*, vol. 1 (1938; reprint Miami: Mnemosyne Publishing, 1969), 157; Pitkin, *A Statistical View of the Commerce of the United States*, 167; Roland T. Ely, *La Economía Cubana entre las dos Isabeles, 1492–1832*, 3rd ed. (Bogotá: Aedita Editores, 1962), 58; and Francisco Pérez de la Riva, *El Café: Historia de su cultivo y explotación en Cuba* (Havana: Jesús Montero, editor, 1944), 28, 50.

53. George A. Cushing, Havana, to Nathl Jones, April 10, 1800, George A. Cushing Letterbook, Baker Library, Harvard Business School, Boston.

54. James Anderson, Havana, to James Madison (Washington, D.C.), January 11, 1808, roll 2, Despatches from Havana.

55. "Exp sobre la construccion de un muelle . . . de D. Juan Latin y D. Antonio Gleau," 1810, Real Consulado y Junta de Fomento, legajo 3285, Archivo Nacional de Cuba, Havana.

56. James D'Wolf, New York, to Edward Spalding, March 15, 1825, box 1, folder 8, Cuban Heritage Collection, University of Miami.

57. See H. Toler, Boston, to Edward Spalding, Bristol, October 6, 1823, box 1, folder 6, Edward Spalding Papers, Cuban Heritage Collection, University of Miami.

58. On Vincent Gray's lineage, see William S. Coker, "Indian Traders of the Southeastern Spanish Borderlands," in *The Hispanic Experience in North America*, ed. Lawrence Clayton (Columbus: Ohio State University Press, 1992), 113; idem, "How General Andrew Jackson . . . ," *Gulf Coast Historical Review* 3, no. 1 (1987): 87.

59. John Morton, Havana, to Vincent Gray, July 15, 1802, roll 1, Despatches from Havana.

60. See Charles D'Wolf, Vancluse, to Edward Spalding, Matanzas, January 20, 1824, Edward Spalding Papers, box 1, folder 7, Cuban Heritage Collection, University of Miami; George D'Wolf to Edward Spalding, January 10, 1825, box 1, folder 2, Edward Spalding Papers, Rhode Island Historical Society, Providence.

61. Under U.S. law (of March 22, 1794, and May 10, 1800), no ship could legally be built or outfitted in a U.S. port for the slave trade, and U.S. citizens were banned from serving as crew members or owning property on similar ships. Elizabeth Donnan, ed., *Documents Illustrative of the Slave Trade to America*, 4 vols. (Washington, D.C.: Carnegie Institution, 1932), 3:257–59, 337, 379.

62. Salvucci, "Development and Decline," 96–98, 124.

63. Vincent Gray, Havana, to James Madison, March 2, 1803, roll 1, Despatches from Havana.

64. Vincent Gray, Havana, to Alexander Hamilton, New York, April 26, 1803, Harold Coffin Syrett, ed., *The Papers of Alexander Hamilton* (New York: Columbia University Press, 1961–87).

65. Vincent Gray, Havana, to James Madison, January 14, 1805; Vincent Gray, Havana, to James Madison, January 14, 1805, roll 1, Despatches from Havana.

66. Vincent Gray, Havana, to James Madison, April 28, 1804, and May 8, 1804, roll 1, Despatches from Havana.

67. *New York Commercial Advertiser*, May 17, 1805.

68. Henry Hill, Havana, to James Madison, August 30, 1805, roll 1, Despatches from Havana.

69. Geoffrey Gilbert, "Maritime Enterprise in the New Republic: Investment in Baltimore Shipping, 1789–1793," *Business History Review* 58 (Spring 1984): 20; Roy Nichols, "Trade Relations and the Establishment of the U.S. Consulates in Spanish America, 1779–1809," *Hispanic American Historical Review* 13, no. 3 (Aug. 1933): 310.

70. James Anderson, Havana, to James Madison, March 27, 1807, roll 1, Despatches from Havana.

71. James Anderson, Havana, to James Madison, May 13, 1807, roll 1, Despatches from Havana.

72. *Alexandria (Va.) Daily Advertiser*, March 13, 1807.

73. Miscellaneous Treasury Accounts of the General Accounting Office, account no. 27,893, RG 217, National Archives, Washington, D.C.; Bemis, *John Quincy Adams and the Foundations of American Foreign Policy*, 164.

74. William Shaler, New York, to John Graham, June 19, 1810, and Nath Ingraham, New York, to Robert Smith, June 29, 1810, roll 2, Despatches from Havana; Alf Andrew Heggoy, *Through Foreign Eyes: Western Attitudes Toward North Africa* (Washington, D.C.: University Press of America, 1982), 8–9.

75. Nathaniel Ingraham, New York, to James Madison, February 18, 1811, *The Papers of James Madison Digital Edition*, ed. J. C. A. Stagg (Charlottesville: University of Virginia Press, Rotunda, 2010).

76. See J. C. A. Stagg, *Borderlines in Borderlands* (New Haven, Conn.: Yale University Press, 2009), 136–42.

77. William Shaler, "Sketches," roll 2, Despatches from Havana.

78. William Shaler, Havana, to Secretary of State, June 14, 1811, July 8, 1811, roll 2, Despatches from Havana.

79. William Shaler, Havana, to James Monroe, Washington, D.C., December 6, 1811, roll 2, Despatches from Havana.

80. "Nota. Las Cortes Espanoles convocadas en la Isla de Leon . . . ," December 1, 1811, roll 2, Despatches from Havana.

81. Richard Hackley to James Monroe, September 10 and 27, 1811, in *The Papers of James Madison Digital Edition*; William Shaler to James Monroe, September 17, 1811, roll 2, Despatches from Havana.

82. William Shaler, October 21, 1811, roll 2, Despatches from Havana; Richard Hackley to Monroe, September 10, 1811, in *The Papers of James Madison Digital Edition*.

83. "Nota. Las Cortes Espanoles convocadas en la Isla de Leon . . . ," December 1, 1811, Despatches from Havana.

84. William Shaler, Fundador Estate, to James Monroe, Washington, D.C., October 21, 1811, William Shaler, Havana, to James Monroe, Washington, D.C., November 13, 1811, roll 2, Despatches from Havana.

85. *Independent Chronicle* (Boston), July 31, 1806; "Expediente seguido por Nataniel Fellowes," 1807, Legajo 379, Expediente 16, Archivo Nacional de Cuba, Havana; See also *Proceedings of the Massachusetts Historical Society*, February 1906, 54.

86. Nathaniel Fellowes, Havana. to Harrison Gray Otis, December 1, 1818, roll 4, Harrison Gray Otis Papers, Massachusetts Historical Society; "Expediente seguido por Nataniel Fellowes," 1807, Legajo 379, Expediente 16, Archivo Nacional de Cuba, Havana.

87. William Shaler, Havana, to James Monroe, Washington, D.C., November 13, 1811, and "Shaler's Sketches," 1811, roll 2, Despatches from Havana.

88. Matt Childs, *The 1812 Aponte Rebellion in Cuba and the Struggle against Atlantic Slavery* (Chapel Hill: University of North Carolina Press, 2006), 160–62.

89. John Quincy Adams, *Diary* 28, May 15, 1812, 376, Adams Family Papers, Massachusetts Historical Society, Boston.

90. "When [Alexander I of Russia] was attacked by Napoleon in 1812, it was because he would not exclude American shipping from his ports." George Dangerfield, *The Era of Good Feelings* (1952; reprint Chicago: Ivan R. Dee, 1980), 55; N. N. Bolkhovitinov, *The Beginnings of Russian-American Relations*, 235–36.

CHAPTER 10. THE COASTWISE SLAVE TRADE AND A MERCANTILE
COMMUNITY OF INTEREST

1. Joseph C. Miller, *Way of Death: Merchant Capitalism and the Angolan Slave Trade* (Madison: University of Wisconsin Press, 1988), 657 (first quotation); Marcus Rediker, *The Slave Ship: A Human History* (New York: Viking, 2007), 140 (second quotation); Robert Gudmestad, *Steamboats and the Rise of the Cotton Kingdom* (Baton Rouge: Louisiana State University Press, 2011), 155 (third quotation); James Walvin, *The Zong: A Massacre, the Law and the End of Slavery* (New Haven, Conn.: Yale University Press, 2011); Stephanie Smallwood, *Saltwater Slavery: A Middle Passage from Africa to American Diaspora* (Cambridge, Mass.: Harvard University Press, 2007); Robert Harms, *The Diligent: A Voyage through the Worlds of the Slave Trade* (New York: Basic Books, 2002).

2. Edward E. Baptist, *The Half Has Never Been Told: Slavery and the Making of American Capitalism* (New York: Basic Books, 2014); Michael Tadman, *Speculators and Slaves: Masters, Traders, and Slaves in the Old South* (Madison: University of Wisconsin Press, 1996); J. B. Pritchett and H. Freudenberger, "A Peculiar Sample: The Selection of Slaves for the New Orleans Market," *Journal of Economic History* 52 (March 1992): 109–28; Steven Deyle, "Rethinking the Slave Trade: Slave Traders and the Market Revolution in the South," in *The Old South's*

Modern Worlds, ed. L. Diane Barnes, Brian Schoen, and Frank Towers (New York: Oxford University Press, 2011), 104–19; Steven Deyle, *Carry Me Back: The Domestic Slave Trade in American Life* (New York: Oxford University Press, 2005); Robert H. Gudmestad, *A Troublesome Commerce: The Transformation of the Interstate Slave Trade* (Baton Rouge: Louisiana State University Press, 2003); Tomoko Yagyu, "Slave Traders and Planters in the Expanding South: Entrepreneurial Strategies, Business Networks, and Western Migration in the Atlantic World, 1787–1859" (PhD diss., University of North Carolina, Chapel Hill, 2006), chaps. 2–3; Phillip Davis Troutman, "Slave Trade and Sentiment in Antebellum Virginia" (PhD diss., University of Virginia, 2000). The 1830s saw the peak of the interstate and interregional movement of enslaved people. Roughly 15 to 20 percent were carried on ships (Charles H. Wesley, "Manifests of Slave Shipments along the Waterways, 1808–1864," *Journal of Negro History* 27 [April 1942]: 155–74). Michael Tadman contends that about a third of New Orleans inward slave manifests are missing from archives, based on independent evidence, which indicates that estimates of shipboard transport of the enslaved, based on surviving inward slave manifests to New Orleans, are probably low by a third (Michael Tadman, "The Demographic Cost of Sugar: Debates on Slave Societies and Natural Increase in the Americas," *American Historical Review* 105 [2000], Appendix 2).

3. Déborah Oropeza Keresey, "La esclavitud Asiática en el virreinato de la Nueva España, 1565–1673," *Historia Mexicana* 61 (July–September 2011): 5–57; Eric Scott Doescher, "First Family of Fortune: The Rise of Nicholas Brown and Company, 1750–1770" (master's thesis, Brown University, 2006); Walter E. Minchinton, "The Seaboard Slave Trade of North Carolina," *North Carolina Historical Review* 71 (January 1994): 1–61; Donald M. Sweig, "The Importation of African Slaves to the Potomac River, 1732–1772," *William and Mary Quarterly* 42 (1985): 507–24; Pieter C. Emmer, "The History of the Dutch Slave Trade: A Bibliographical Survey," *Journal of Economic History* 32 (September 1972): 728–29.

4. K. K. Ahonen, "From Sugar Triangle to Cotton Triangle: Trade and Shipping between America and Baltic Russia, 1783–1860" (PhD diss., University of Jyväskylän, 2005), 246 (quotation); Sven Beckert, *Empire of Cotton: A Global History* (New York: Knopf, 2014); Klas Rönnbäck, "Consumers and Slavery: Diversified Markets for Plantation Produce and the Survival of Slavery in the Nineteenth Century," *Review (Fernand Braudel Center)* 33 (2010): 69–88.

5. Website of the Frederick Douglass–Isaac Myers Maritime Park, http://www.douglassmyers.org (accessed March 8, 2014); Report of October 25, 1820, U.S. Customs Service, Port of Baltimore, Md., Office of the Surveyor of Customs, Orders and Reports Concerning Slaves on Ships, February–December 1820, folder February–December 1820, National Archives and Records Administration, Mid-Atlantic Branch, Philadelphia (NARA-MA); Scott Reynolds Nelson, *A Nation of Deadbeats: An Uncommon History of America's Financial Disasters* (New York: Alfred A. Knopf, 2012), chap. 5; Seth Rockman, *Scraping By: Wage Labor, Slavery, and Survival in Early Baltimore* (Baltimore: Johns Hopkins University Press, 2009), chap. 2.

6. Report of October 25, 1820, U.S. Customs Service, Port of Baltimore, Md., Office of the Surveyor of Customs, Orders and Reports Concerning Slaves on Ships, February–December 1820, folder February–December 1820, NARA-MA (quotation); Inward Slave Manifest, New Orleans, October 23, 1820 (*Unicorn*), National Archives and Records Administration, Washington, D.C. (NARA), M1895, roll 1, images 590–97; Charles Keenan, *C. Keenan's Baltimore Directory for 1822 and 1823* (Baltimore: J. R. Matchett, 1822), 66; *Mississippi State Gazette*, March 4, 1820, 1; June 2, 1821, 4.

7. Troutman, "Slave Trade and Sentiment," 415–29; Gudmestad, *A Troublesome Commerce*, 17–20; Michael Tadman, *Speculators and Slaves: Masters, Traders, and Slaves in the Old South* (Madison: University of Wisconsin Press, 1996).

8. Inward Slave Manifest, New Orleans, October 23, 1820 (*Unicorn*), NARA M1895, roll 1, images 590–96.

9. Keenan, *C. Keenan's Baltimore Directory for 1822 and 1823*, 20, 40, 66, 67, 92, 94, 100, 101, 118, 130, 135, 168, 181, 199, 204, 205, 217, 228, 242, 249, 252, 273, 277, 283, 289, 304, 308.

10. Inward Manifest, New Orleans, October 14, 1820 (*Unicorn*), NO-151, box 35, folder November 1820, National Archives and Records Administration, Southwest Branch, Fort Worth (NARA-SW); Inward Slave Manifest, New Orleans, October 23, 1820 (*Unicorn*), NARA M1895, roll 1, images 590–97.

11. Douglas A. Irwin, "New Estimates of the Average Tariff of the United States, 1790–1820," *Journal of Economic History* 63 (June 2003): 506–13; Charles E. McFarland and Nevin E. Neal, "The Nascence of Protectionism: American Tariff Policies, 1816–1824," *Land Economics* 45 (February 1969): 22–30.

12. That calculation takes eighteen cents a pound, the going rate for New Orleans cotton in New York at the time, multiplied by 300 (each bale weighted about 300 pounds at the time), to get $54 per bale (New York *Patron of Industry*, December 27, 1820, 4; Ulrich Bonnell Phillips, *Life and Labor in the Old South* [1930; reprint Columbia: University of South Carolina Press, 2007], 177 [quotation]); *Louisiana Advertiser*, December 8, 1820, 3; *Liverpool Mercury*, February 9, 1821, 263; February 23, 1821, 270; Philippe Pedesclaux, vol. 15, Act 1308, July 15, 1820; Works Progress Administration (WPA), Survey of Federal Archives in Louisiana, *Ship Registers and Enrollments of New Orleans, Louisiana*, vol. 1, *1804–1820* (Baton Rouge: Louisiana State University Library, 1942), 93.

13. Jessica M. Lepler, *The Many Panics of 1837: People, Politics, and the Creation of a Transatlantic Financial Crisis* (New York: Cambridge University Press, 2013), chap. 1; Walter Johnson, *River of Dark Dreams: Slavery and Empire in the Cotton Kingdom* (Cambridge, Mass.: Harvard University Press, 2013), chap. 9; Robert M. Grant, "The Knowledge-Based View of the Firm," in *The Strategic Management of Intellectual Capital and Organizational Knowledge*, eds., Chun Wei Choo and Nick Bontis (New York: Oxford University Press, 2002), 133–48; Alan Burton-Jones, *Knowledge Capitalism: Business, Work, and Learning in the New Economy* (New York: Oxford University Press, 1999); John R. Killick, "The Cotton Operations of Alexander Brown and Sons in the Deep South, 1820–1860," *Journal of Southern History* 43 (May 1977): 169–94; Edwin J. Perkins, *Anglo-American Trade: The House of Brown, 1800–1880* (Cambridge, Mass.: Harvard University Press, 1975); Robert Greenhalgh Albion, *Square-Riggers on Schedule: The New York Sailing Packets to England, France, and the Cotton Ports* (Princeton, N.J.: Princeton University Press, 1938).

14. *Baltimore Patriot*, April 26, 1822, 2 (quotation); *Boston Commercial Gazette*, September 26, 1822, 1; *Massachusetts Repertory*, October 22, 1822, 2; March 13, 1823, 2; *New-York Daily Advertiser*, November 3, 1823, 2; *Courrier de la Louisiane*, April 16, 1821, 6; *Baltimore Patriot* March 29, 1821, 2; May 3, 1821, 2; August 30, 1821, 3; *Liverpool Mercury* July 13, 1821, 15; Chris Evans, "The Plantation Hoe: The Rise and Fall of an Atlantic Commodity," *William and Mary Quarterly* 69 (January 2012): 71–100; Joseph C. Miller, "The Dynamics of History in Africa and the Atlantic 'Age of Revolutions,'" in *The Age of Revolutions in Global Context c. 1760–1840*, ed. David Armitage and Sanjay Subrahmanyam (New York: Palgrave Macmillan, 2010), 101–24; Stephen Behrendt, "Markets, Transaction Cycles, and Profits: Merchant Decision Making in the British Slave Trade," *William and Mary Quarterly* 58 (January 2001): 171–204; Paul

Butel, *The Atlantic* (London: Routledge, 1999), 221–40; Albion, *Square-Riggers on Schedule*; Frank R. Kent, *The Story of Alexander Brown & Sons* (Baltimore: Alexander Brown and Sons, 1925), 109.

15. Providence *Rhode-Island American*, March 9, 1819, 3 (quotation); *New-York Gazette*, April 10, 1819, 6; *New York Mercantile Advertiser*, April 24, 1819, 1; *New York National Advocate* April 28, 1819, 2; WPA, *Ship Registers and Enrollments of New Orleans, Louisiana*, vol. 1, 5.

16. *Baltimore American and Commercial Daily Advertiser*, September 20, 1819, 2 (quotation); Inward Slave Manifest, New Orleans, June 9, 1819 (*Almy*), NARA M1895, roll 1, image 283.

17. Inward Manifest, New Orleans, July 23, 1819, box 32, folder July 1819, NARA-SW; Irene D. Neu, "J. B. Moussier and the Property Banks of Louisiana," *Business History Review* 35 (Winter 1961): 555; Betsy Swanson, *Historic Jefferson Parish: From Shore to Shore* (Gretna, La.: Pelican, 2003), 152–53.

18. *Norfolk Gazette and Publick Ledger*, January 14, 1816, 3; *Richmond Commercial Compiler*, July 3, 1818, 1; Inward Slave Manifest, New Orleans, June 9, 1819 (*Almy*), NARA M1895, roll 1, image 283; Inward Manifest, New Orleans, July 23, 1819, box 32, folder July 1819, NARA-SW; *New-York Daily Advertiser*, January 4, 1831, 2 (freight rates); Ralph Clayton, *Cash for Blood: The Baltimore to New Orleans Domestic Slave Trade* (Bowie, Md.: Heritage Books, 2007), 625–39; Herman Freudenberger and Jonathan B. Pritchett, "The Domestic United States Slave Trade: New Evidence," *Journal of Interdisciplinary History* 21 (1991): 447–77.

19. Hugues Lavergne, vol. 1, Act 4, July 27, 1819, NONA; *Rhode-Island American*, October 5, 1819, 3; March 4, 1820, 3; *Boston Columbian Centinel*, November 27, 1819, 2; *New-Bedford Mercury*, January 7, 1820, 3; *Philadelphia Franklin Gazette* January 17, 1820, 3; *Providence Patriot*, January 29, 1820, 3; *New-Bedford Mercury*, March 2, 1821, 3.

20. Inward Manifest, New Orleans, November 10, 1820 (*Margaret Wright*), NO-151, box 35, folder November 1820, NARA-SW; Inward Slave Manifests, New Orleans, October 14–20, 1820 (*Margaret Wright*), NARA M1895, roll 1, images 524–29, 584–88; Norfolk, Va., *American Beacon*, November 7, 1820, 1; September 30, 1820, 3; October 10, 1820, 3; *Liverpool Mercury*, May 3, 1822, 351; November 1, 1822, 3.

21. WPA, Survey of Federal Archives in Louisiana, *Ship Registers and Enrollments of New Orleans, Louisiana*, vol. 2, *1821–1830* (Baton Rouge: Louisiana State University Library, 1942), 19; Paul F. Lachance, "The Foreign French," in *Creole New Orleans: Race and Americanization*, ed. Arnold R. Hirsch and Joseph Logsdon (Baton Rouge: Louisiana State University Press, 1992), 120n38.

22. Hugues Lavergne, vol. 9, Act 1644, January 15, 1823; vol. 9, Act 1662, January, 1823, NONA; Inward Slave Manifest, New Orleans, November 21, 1822 (*Brazillian*), NARA M1895, roll 2, images 460–65.

23. Inward Slave Manifest, New Orleans, December 9, 1824 (*Factor*), NARA M1895, roll 3, image 861 (quotation); Inward Slave Manifest, New Orleans, October 21, 1822 (*Brazillian*), NARA M1895, roll 2, images 460–63; Hugues Lavergne, vol. 8, Act 1605, December 14, 1822, NONA; *Louisiana Bank v. Kenner's Succession*, 1 La. 384 (1830); Grant, "The Knowledge-Based View of the Firm"; WPA, *Ship Registers and Enrollments of New Orleans, Louisiana*, vol. 2, 19; Alcée Fortier, *Louisiana, Comprising Sketches of Parishes, Towns, Events, Institutions, and Persons, Arranged in Cyclopedic Form*, vol. 3 (Madison, Wis.: Century Historical Association, 1914), 298; Joseph A. Scoville, *The Old Merchants of New York City*, vol. 1 (New York: Thomas R. Knox and Co., 1885), 46–48.

24. *Baltimore Patriot*, March 11, 1818, 2; March 26, 1819, 2; May 19, 1819, 2; October 28, 1819, 3; February 27, 1822, 2; March 4, 1822, 2; *New York Evening Post*, July 26, 1821, 2; *New-*

buryport (Mass.) Herald, June 18, 1819, 3; *New Orleans Gazette and Commercial Advertiser,* March 22, 1819, 1; *Boston Gazette,* June 21, 1819, 4; *New-York Daily Advertiser,* December 25, 1820, 2; Toni Ahrens, *Design Makes a Difference: Shipbuilding in Baltimore, 1795–1835* (Bowie, Md.: Heritage Books, 1998), 134.

25. Inward Slave Manifests, New Orleans, March 19–23, 1822 (*Lapwing*), NARA M1895, roll 2, images 637–47; 645 (quotation); Keenan, *C. Keenan's Baltimore Directory for 1822 and 1823,* 160; Inward Slave Manifests, New Orleans, March 19–23, 1822 (*Lapwing*), NARA M1895, roll 2, images 637–47; *Baltimore Patriot,* March 18, 1822, 2; April 3, 1822, 2; June 4, 1822, 2; June 6, 1822, 3; July 8, 1822, 3; July 9, 1822, 3; August 30, 1822, 3; September 24, 1822, 3; November 16, 1822, 2; February 21, 1823, 2; March 18, 1823, 2; March 20, 1823, 2; June 21, 1823; 2, September 5, 1823, 2; September 16, 1823, 2; November 21, 1823, 2; January 16, 1824, 2; *City Gazette* (Charleston, S.C.), July 15, 1822, 3; July 21, 1823.

26. *Baltimore Gazette and Daily Advertiser,* February 12, 1827, 2, February 13, 1827, 2; February 15, 1827, 3; February 24, 1827, 3; May 23, 1827; June 4, 1827, 3; June 15, 1827, 3; July 30, 1827, 3, November 14, 1827, 3; *New-York Commercial Advertiser* April 11, 1827, 3; *City Gazette* (Charleston, S.C.), May 17, 1827, 2; *Louisiana Advertiser* March 19, 1827, 3; *New-York Daily Advertiser* July 17, 1827, 1; Inward Slave Manifests, New Orleans, February 15, 1827 (*Lapwing*), NARA M1895, roll 4, images 597–600.

27. Ralph Clayton, *Cash For Blood,* 633; Inward Manifests, New Orleans, December 6, 1827 (*Lapwing*), NARA M1895, roll 4, images 558–63; Edward Alpers, "The Other Middle Passage: The African Slave Trade in the Indian Ocean," in *Many Middle Passages: Forced Migration and the Making of the Modern World,* ed. Marcus Rediker, Cassandra Pybus, and Emma Christopher (Berkeley: University of California Press, 2007), 20–38; Rediker, *The Slave Ship,* chaps. 4–5.

28. Jonathan Levy, *Freaks of Fortune: The Emerging World of Capitalism and Risk in America* (Cambridge, Mass.: Harvard University Press, 2012), chap 2; Walter Johnson, "White Lies: Human Property and Domestic Slavery Aboard the Slave Ship *Creole,*" *Atlantic Studies* 5 (August 2008): 237–63; Eric Robert Taylor, *If We Must Die: Shipboard Insurrections in the Era of the Atlantic Slave Trade* (Baton Rouge: Louisiana State University Press, 2006), 147–51; Phillip D. Troutman, "Grapevine in the Slave Market: African American Geopolitical Literacy and the 1841 *Creole* Revolt," in *The Chattel Principle: Internal Slave Trade in the Americas,* ed. Walter Johnson (New Haven, Conn.: Yale University Press, 2004), 203–33.

29. Inward Slave Manifests, New Orleans, November 13, 1829 (*Lafayette*), NARA M1895, roll 6, images 462–73; Inward Slave Manifests, New Orleans, October 30, 1830 (*Lafayette*), NARA M1895, roll 6, images 765–70; Inward Slave Manifests, New Orleans, April 26, 1831 (*Lafayette*), NARA M1895, roll 6, images 945–47; Inward Slave Manifest, New Orleans, November 6, 1831 (*Lafayette*), NARA M1895, roll 6, images 1114–18; vol. 2, ser. 5, folder 417, Ballard Papers, Southern Historical Collection, University of North Carolina, Chapel Hill; *Baltimore Patriot,* January 1, 1830, 2; *Phenix Gazette* (Alexandria, Va.), January 4, 1830, 2; Kari J. Winter, *The American Dreams of John B. Prentis, Slave Trader* (Athens: University of Georgia Press, 2011), 121–24; James A. McMillin, *The Final Victims: Foreign Slave Trade to North America, 1783–1810* (Columbia: University of South Carolina Press, 2004), Appendix B.

30. Robert E. Wright, *The Wealth of Nations Rediscovered: Integration and Expansion of American Financial Markets, 1780–1850* (New York: Cambridge University Press, 2002), chap. 8; Richard Sylla, "Financial Systems and Economic Modernization," *Journal of Economic History* 62 (June 2002): 277–92; Peter L. Rousseau and Richard Sylla, "Emerging Financial Markets and Early U.S. Growth," *Explorations in Economic History* 42 (January 2005): 1–26; Martijn

Konings, *The Development of American Finance* (New York: Cambridge University Press, 2011), chaps. 1–4.

31. Anthony E. Kaye, "The Second Slavery: Modernity in the Nineteenth-Century South and the Atlantic World," *Journal of Southern History* 75 (August 2009): 627–50; Calvin Schermerhorn, "Capitalism's Captives: The Maritime United States Slave Trade, 1807–1850," *Journal of Social History* 47 (Summer 2014): 897–921; Eric Williams, *Capitalism and Slavery*, ed. Colin A. Palmer (1944; reprint Chapel Hill: University of North Carolina Press, 2007), chaps. 7–10; Robin Blackburn, *The Making of New World Slavery: From the Baroque to the Modern, 1492–1800* (New York: Verso, 1997), chap. 12.

32. Calvin Schermerhorn, *The Business of Slavery and the Rise of American Capitalism, 1815–1860* (New Haven, Conn.: Yale University Press, 2015), chap. 4.

33. Follett, *The Sugar Masters*; John M. Sacher, *A Perfect War of Politics: Parties, Politicians, and Democracy in Louisiana, 1824–1861* (Baton Rouge: Louisiana State University Press, 2003), 51; Tadman, "The Demographic Cost of Sugar"; Green, *Finance and Economic Development in the Old South*, chaps. 1–2.

34. *Genius of Universal Emancipation*, Nov. 13, 1829, 75, cited in Francis Jackson Garrison, *William Lloyd Garrison, 1805–1879, The Story of his Life, Told by his Children*, vol. 1, *1805–1835* (New York: Century Co., 1885), 165 (quotations); *Baltimore Gazette and Daily Advertiser*, May 30, 1829, 2; Inward Manifest, New Orleans, November 10, 1820 (*Unicorn*), NO-151, box 35, folder November 1820, NARA-SW; Inward Slave Manifest, New Orleans, December 23, 1827 (*Lapwing*), NARA M1895, roll 4, images 560–61; Inward Slave Manifest, New Orleans, March 20, 1819, (*Commodore Patterson*) NARA M1895, roll 1, images 102–3; Inward Slave Manifest, New Orleans, January 5, 1819, (*Emilie*) NARA M1895, roll 1, images 186–87; Inward Slave Manifest, March 2, 1819, (*Missouri*) NARA M1895, roll 1, images 84–85; *Baltimore Patriot*, October 24, 1820, 3; Henry Mayer, *All on Fire: William Lloyd Garrison and the Abolition of Slavery* (New York: St. Martin's Press, 2000), chap. 5; Calvin Schermerhorn, "What Else You Should Know About Baltimore," *Time*, May 31, 2015, http://time.com/3901537/baltimore-slavery-history/.

35. Johnson, *River of Dark Dreams*, chap. 10; Adam Hochschild, *Bury the Chains: Prophets and Rebels in the Fight to Free an Empire's Slaves* (New York: Mariner Books, 2006), chap. 8.

CHAPTER 11. WAR AND PRIESTS

1. Yarrow Mamout was an African Muslim who eventually gained his freedom and became a landowner and businessman in Georgetown. Charles Wilson Peale and James Alexander Simpson painted portraits of Mamout, who, a biographer suggests, might be posing in both portraits in the blue uniform of a Georgetown student. One of Beall's sons attended the college, and Simpson taught art there. Georgetown was originally part of Montgomery County, Maryland. In 1814 Pius VII restored the Society of Jesus. Paul R. O'Neill and Paul K. Williams, *Georgetown University* (Charleston, S.C.: Arcadia, 2003), 9–16; John M. Daley, *Georgetown University: Origins and Early Years* (Washington, D.C.: Georgetown University Press, 1957), 94–96; Robert Emmett Curran, *The Bicentennial History of Georgetown University: From Academy to University, 1789–1889* (Washington, D.C.: Georgetown University Press, 1993), 1:46–48; Michael Pasquier, *Fathers on the Frontier: French Missionaries and the Roman Catholic Priesthood in the United States, 1789–1870* (New York: Oxford University Press, 2010), 25–31; Georgetown College, Expense Book, February 12, 1794–February 12, 1802, esp. the entries for April 22,

1795, December 14, 1796, December 21, 1796, October 24, 1796, January 3, 1797, and January 15, 1798; Georgetown College, Book of Expenses and Remittances, October 1796–December 1799, esp. 120; Georgetown College, Ledger A, Financial Ledgers, 3 vols., 1789–1799, esp. 1:78, 94, 99, 2:120, Special Collections Research Center, Georgetown University Library, Washington, D.C. Brooke Beall Ledger, 1790–1798, 112, MS 111, Furlong Baldwin Library, Maryland Historical Society, Baltimore (hereafter MHS); James H. Johnson, *From Slave Ship to Harvard: Yarrow Mamout and the History of an African American Family* (New York: Fordham University Press, 2012), esp. 98–99; Kathleen M. Lesko, Valerie Babb, and Carroll R. Gibbs, *Black Georgetown Remembered: A History of Its Black Community from the Founding of "The Town of George" in 1751 to the Present* (Washington, D.C.: Georgetown University Press, 1991), 1–11; Sylviane A. Diouf, *Servants of Allah: African Muslims Enslaved in the Americas* (1998; New York: New York University Press, 2013), 107, 119–20; see Peter Kenney, "Consultations" (1832), 7, box 126, folder 2, Maryland Province Archives of the Society of Jesus, Special Collections Research Center, Georgetown University Library, Washington, D.C. (hereafter GUSC).

2. William W. Warner, *At Peace with All Their Neighbors: Catholics and Catholicism in the National Capital, 1787–1860* (Washington, D.C.: Georgetown University Press, 1994), 7; Barbara Jeanne Fields, *Slavery and Freedom on the Middle Ground: Maryland during the Nineteenth Century* (New Haven, Conn.: Yale University Press, 1985), 13; John Carroll, "Last Will and Testament," November 22, 1815, in *The John Carroll Papers*, ed. Thomas O'Brien Hanley, 3 vols. (Notre Dame, IN: University of Notre Dame Press, 1976), 3:369–73; John Gilmary Shea, *Memorial of the First Centenary of Georgetown College, D.C., Comprising a History of Georgetown University* (Washington, D.C.: printed for the College, 1891), 9–10; *New-York Weekly Museum*, March 7, 1789; Georgetown College, College Catalogs, 1791–1850, box 1, vol. 1, GUSC; President and Professors of George Town College to George Washington, March 1, 1797, and March 15, 1797, and Louis Guillaume Valentin DuBourg to Mrs. Martha Custis Washington, July 20, 1798, George Washington Papers, ser. 4, General Correspondence, Library of Congress.

3. The college was chartered to grant degrees in 1815. Edward B. Bunn, *"Georgetown": First College Charter from the U. S. Congress (1789–1954)* (New York: Newcomen Society, 1954); Thomas E. V. Smith, *The City of New York in the Year of Washington's Inauguration, 1789* (New York: Anson D. F. Randolph, 1889); John Fenwick to Ignatius Fenwick, June 12, 1789, Capt. Ignatius Fenwick Papers, MS 1274, Furlong Baldwin Library, MHS.

4. "The Address from the Roman Catholics to Washington," 1790, and "Washington to the Roman Catholics of the United States of America," March 12, 1790, in Peter Guilday, *The Life and Times of John Carroll: Archbishop of Baltimore* (New York: Encyclopedia Press, 1922), 1:363–67; George Washington to the Synod of the Dutch Reformed Church in North America, October 1789, George Washington to the Society of Quakers, October 1789, George Washington to the Presbyterian Ministers of Massachusetts and New Hampshire, November 2, 1789, and George Washington to the Hebrew Congregation at Newport, August 18, 1790, in *The Papers of George Washington*, ed. W. W. Abbot and Dorothy Twohig (Charlottesville: University of Virginia Press, 1987–), 4:263–77, 6:284–86; see also Fritz Hirschfeld, *George Washington and the Jews* (Newark: University of Delaware Press, 2005).

5. Thomas Hughes, *History of the Society of Jesus in North America: Colonial and Federal* (London: Longmans, Green, 1917), 1:247–93, 344–46; Andrew White, *A Relation of the Colony of the Lord Baron of Baltimore, in Maryland, Near Virginia; A Narrative of the First Voyage to Maryland* (Baltimore: Maryland Historical Society, 1847); Nelson Waite Rightmyer, *Maryland's*

Established Church (Baltimore: Diocese of Maryland, 1956), 5; Margaret C. DePalma, *Dialogue on the Frontier: Catholic and Protestant Relations, 1793–1883* (Kent, Ohio: Kent State University Press, 2004), 5–6.

6. The Catholic community closed St. Mary's Chapel after that assault and reused the bricks for a manor house on the safer ground of St. Inigoes. Hughes, *History of the Society of Jesus in North America*, 1:562–64, 2:13–45, 155, 480; Rightmyer, *Maryland's Established Church*, 5–7; Joseph A. Agonito, "St. Inigoes Manor: Portrait of a Nineteenth Century Jesuit Plantation," 2–5, Dr. Lois Green Carr Research Collection, SC 5906-10-83, Maryland State Archives, Annapolis; Nelson Waite Rightmyer, *Parishes of the Diocese of Maryland* (Reisterstown, Md.: Educational Research Associates, 1960), 1–2; John D. Krugler, *English and Catholic: The Lords Baltimore in the Seventeenth Century* (Baltimore: Johns Hopkins University Press, 2004), 242–43; Thomas Murphy, "Jesuit Slaveholding in Maryland, 1717–1838: Real Poverty and Apparent Wealth on the Jesuit Farms," in *Studies in African American History and Culture*, ed. Graham Russell Hodges (New York: Routledge, 2001), esp. 37–39.

7. Arthur J. Riley, "Catholicism in New England to 1788" (PhD diss., Catholic University of America, 1936), esp. 180–93, in Catholic University of America, *Studies in American Church History*, vol. 24; DePalma, *Dialogue on the Frontier*, 6–11; Mary Peter Carthy, *English Influences on Early American Catholicism* (Washington, D.C.: Catholic University of America Press, 1959), 12–19.

8. Dongan received the Castleton estate on Staten Island. Although he returned to Ireland in 1688 to succeed his brother as Earl of Limerick, the Castleton grant lived into the next century as the largest single slaveholding on the island. Robert Emmett Curran, *Papist Devils: Catholics in British America, 1574–1783* (Washington, D.C.: Catholic University of America Press, 2014), 124–25; David S. Lovejoy, *The Glorious Revolution in America* (1972; Hanover, N.H.: University Press of New England, 1987), 282–84; William J. McGucken, *The Jesuits and Education: The Society's Teaching Principles and Practice, Especially in Secondary Education in the United States* (1932; reprint Eugene, Ore.: Wipf and Stock, 2008), 55–56; D. P. O'Neill, "Liberation of Spanish and Indian Slaves by Governor Dongan," United States Catholic Historical Society, *Historical Records and Studies*, vol. 3, pt. 1 (January 1903), 213–16. John Fiske, *The Dutch and Quaker Colonies in America*, 2 vols. (Boston: Houghton, Mifflin, 1899), 2:289; DePalma, *Dialogue on the Frontier*, 7–8. Jacob Leisler's holdings were valued at 15,000 guilders in a 1674 tax assessment. See "Valuation of Property in New York in 1674," in *Ecclesiastical Records, State of New York* (Albany, N.Y.: James B. Lyon, 1901), 1:641–42. Also see Francina Staats, "Last Will and Testament," August 19, 1728, "Abstracts of Unrecorded Wills Prior to 1790," vol. 11, *Collections of the New–York Historical Society for the Year 1902* (New York: printed for the society, 1903), 186–88.

9. Kenneth Scott, "The Slave Insurrection in New York in 1712," *New-York Historical Society Quarterly* (January 1961), 47–67; New York Colony, *Census of Slaves, 1755* (New York, 1755); "An Act for Preventing Suppressing and Punishing the Conspiracy and Insurrection of Negroes and Other Slaves," December 10, 1712, "An Act for the More Effectual Preventing and Punishing the Conspiracy and Insurrection of Negro and Other Slaves; for the Better Regulating Them and for Repealing the Acts Herein Mentioned Relating Thereto," October 29, 1730, *Colonial Laws of New York, From the Years 1664 to the Revolution* (Albany, N.Y.: James B. Lyon, 1894), 1:761–67, 2:679–88; Elizabeth Donnan, ed., *Documents Illustrative of the History of the Slave Trade to America* (New York: Octagon, 1965), 3:462–508; New York Colony Treasurer's Office, Reports of Goods Imported (Manifest Books) to New York, esp. boxes 1–4, New York State Archives, Albany. See also Isaac Levy and merchant trade in Philadelphia. Darold D.

Wax, "Negro Imports into Pennsylvania, 1720–1766," *Pennsylvania History* 32 (July 1965), 261–87.

10. Mordecai Gomez's slave, Cajoe (alias Africa), was also arrested. Colonists routinely searched for fugitive Spanish Indians and Spanish Negroes, and their advertisements betray the expansive geography of slavery. Spanish Indians had also participated in 1712 revolt. Oath of Allegiance to George II by Jews in American Colonies, April 27, 1741, Papers of Jacques Judah Lyons, box 14, folder 35, American Jewish Historical Society Archives, New York; Daniel Horsmanden, *The New York Conspiracy*, edited and with an introduction by Thomas J. Davis (Boston: Beacon Press, 1971), esp.178–87, 249–51, 260–62, and appendices; *American Weekly Mercury*, July 23, 1741. Scott, "The Slave Insurrection in New York in 1712"; *Boston Evening-Post*, April 9, 1739.

11. Craig Steven Wilder, *Ebony & Ivy: Race, Slavery, and the Troubled History of America's Universities* (New York: Bloomsbury, 2013); Donald G. Tewksbury, *The Founding of American Colleges and Universities Before the Civil War with Particular Reference to the Religious Influences Bearing upon the College Movement* (New York: Teachers College, 1932), 16–33, 55–60.

12. Catholic families in the British colonies routinely bypassed the colleges in New Spain and New France. Moses Lindo to Sampson and Solomon Simson, April 17, 1770, and corporation of the College of Rhode Island to Moses Lindo, January 1, 1771, Rhode Island College Miscellaneous Papers, 1763–1804, box 1, folder 1, Brown University. Jacob R. Marcus, *The Colonial American Jew, 1492–1776* (Detroit: Wayne State University Press, 1970), 3:1198–1211; Jacob Rader Marcus, *Early American Jewry: The Jews of New York, New England, and Canada, 1649–1794* (Philadelphia: Jewish Publication Society of America, 1951), 1:64–68, 79, 164; Oscar Reiss, *The Jews in Colonial America* (New York: McFarland, 2004), 175–77; Edwin Wolf and Maxwell Whiteman, *The History of the Jews of Philadelphia from Colonial Times to the Age of Jackson* (1956; reprint Philadelphia: Jewish Publication Society of America, 1975), 14–27.

13. J. Fairfax McLaughlin, *College Days at Georgetown* (Philadelphia: J. B. Lippincott, 1899), 17–20; Maura Jane Farrelly, *Papist Patriots: The Making of an Early Catholic Identity* (New York: Oxford, 2012), 181–85; Bernard Ward, *History of St. Edmund's College, Old Hall* (London: Kegan Paul, Trench, Trübner, 1893), 50–95; Peter Guilday, *The English Catholic Refugees on the Continent, 1558–1795* (New York: Longmans, Green, 1914), esp. 1:63–120, 141–45; Ronald Hoffman, *Princes of Ireland, Planters of Maryland: A Carroll Saga, 1500–1782* (Chapel Hill: University of North Carolina Press, 2000), 99–101; Annabelle M. Melville, *John Carroll of Baltimore: Founder of the American Catholic Hierarchy* (New York: Charles Scribner's Sons, 1955), 8–12; Lewis Leonard, *Life of Charles Carroll of Carrollton* (New York: Moffat, Yard, 1918), 241–49; Thomas Murphy, *Jesuit Slaveholding in Maryland, 1717–1838* (New York: Routledge, 2001), 3–32; John Gilmary Shea, *The Catholic Church in Colonial Days* (New York: John G. Shea, 1886), 40–50; James Hennesey, "Neither the Bourbons nor the Revolution: Georgetown's Jesuit Founders," in *Images of America in Revolutionary France*, ed. Michèle R. Morris (Washington, D.C.: Georgetown University Press, 1990), 1; Cornelius Michael Buckley, *Stephen Larigaudelle Dubuisson, S.J. (1786–1864) and the Reform of the American Jesuits* (Lanham, Md.: University Press of America, 2013); Shea, *Memorial History of the First Century of Georgetown College*, 23, 69; Charles Carroll (son) to Charles Carroll (father), July 23, 1761, *Maryland Historical Magazine*, 11:177–78.

14. In 1776 the estate of the first Johns Hopkins, grandfather of the philanthropist, included six black men, twelve black women, and twenty-five black children in Anne Arundel County. Charles Carroll (father) to Charles Carroll (son), April 16, 1759, in *Unpublished Letters of Charles Carroll of Carrollton, and of His Father Charles Carroll of Doughoregan*, ed. Thomas

Meagher Field (New York: United States Catholic Historical Society, 1902), 20, 29–32; Robert W. Hall, *Early Landowners of Maryland*, vol. 1, *Anne Arundel County, 1650–1704* (Lewes, Del.: Colonial Roots, 2003), 32–33; Betty Stirling Carothers, comp., *1776 Census of Maryland*, 12, Furlong Baldwin Library, MHS; Charles Carroll (father) to Charles Carroll (son), September 1, 1762, *Maryland Historical Magazine*, 11:272–74.

15. John Fenwick to Ignatius Fenwick, March 14, 1784, Capt. Ignatius Fenwick Papers; *The American Missions: Maryland Jesuits from Andrew White to John Carroll*, An Exhibit in the Special Collections Division, Georgetown University Library, Washington, D.C., September 27–November 29, 1976, entry 10; see Jesuit and non-Jesuit wills, Maryland Province Archives, box 25, folders 6–12; Hughes, *History of the Society of Jesus in North America*, 1:281–82.

16. *American Missions*, entry 9; Agonito, "St. Inigoes Manor," 2–3; lists of lands and acreage held by the Jesuits in Maryland and Pennsylvania, Maryland Province Archives, box 23, folder 9; James Walter Thomas, *Chronicles of Colonial Maryland* (Cumberland, Md.: Eddy, 1913), 218–19.

17. Patrick Smyth, "*The Present State of the Catholic Missions Conducted by the Ex-Jesuits in North America*" (Dublin: P. Byrne, 1788), 17–19; *American Catholic Historical Researches* (July 1905), 193–206. Joseph Mobberly, *Diary*, pt. 1, 20–21, Brother Joseph P. Mobberly, S.J., Papers, 1805–27, folder 1, GUSC; Agonito, "St. Inigoes Manor," 11–16. The births are recorded on the front inside cover of "Old Records," pigskin account book from St. Thomas Manor, Maryland Province Archives, box 3, folder 8. See also John Carroll to Cardinal Leonardo Antonelli, March 1, 1785, and John Carroll to John Thayer, July 15, 1794, in Hanley, ed., *John Carroll Papers*, 1:179–82, 2:122–23.

18. Thomas O'Brien Hanley, *Charles Carroll of Carrollton: The Making of a Revolutionary Gentleman* (Washington, D.C.: Catholic University of America Press, 1970), 175–82; Whitman H. Ridgway, *Community Leadership in Maryland, 1790–1840: A Comparative Analysis of Power in Society* (Chapel Hill: University of North Carolina Press, 1979), 327; Charles Carroll (son) to Charles Carroll (father), November 5, 1769, *Maryland Historical Magazine*, 12:285–86.

19. Farrelly, *Papist Patriots*, 220–57; *A Declaration of Rights, and the Constitution and Form of Government, Agreed to by the Delegates of Maryland, in Free and Full Convention Assembled* (Annapolis, Md.: Frederick Green, 1776), 11–14; Peter Wiernik, *History of the Jews in America, from the Period of the Discovery of the New World to the Present Time* (New York: Jewish Press, 1912), 125–27; H. M. Brackenridge, *Speeches on the Jew Bill, in the House of Delegates of Maryland* (Philadelphia: J. Dobson, 1829). The Carrollses advertised regularly in the *Maryland Gazette*, including an appeal on September 5, 1754, for the capture of the "New Negro," Caesar, and three indentured servants, Robert Cox, George Dale, and John Oulton.

20. David Noel Doyle, *Ireland, Irishmen and Revolutionary America, 1760–1820* (Dublin: Mercier, 1981), 167; James Breck Perkins, *France in the American Revolution* (Boston: Houghton Mifflin, 1911), 241–25; Martin I. J. Griffin, *Catholics and the American Revolution* (Philadelphia: privately printed, 1911), 233–52; *Connecticut Courant and Weekly Intelligencer*, 4 May 1779; David W. Robson, *Educating Republicans: The College in the Era of the American Revolution, 1750–1800* (Westport, Conn.: Greenwood, 1985), 110.

21. General Washington's personal secretary was an Irish Catholic. Thomas P. Phelan, "Colonel John Fitzgerald: Aide-de-Camp and Secretary to General George Washington," *Journal of the American Irish Historical Society* 18 (1919): 233–44.

22. Hennesey, "Neither the Bourbons nor the Revolution," 5; Griffin, *Catholics and the American Revolution*, 250; Thomas, *Chronicles of Colonial Maryland*, 218–20, 269–71; Doyle, *Ireland, Irishmen and Revolutionary America*, 51–76; David Lee Russell, *The American Revolu-*

tion in the Southern Colonies (Jefferson, N.C.: McFarland, 2000), 14–16; David T. Gleeson, ed., *The Irish in the Atlantic World* (Columbia: University of South Carolina Press, 2010); Maurice J. Bric, *Ireland, Philadelphia and the Re-invention of America, 1760–1800* (Dublin: Four Courts, 2008), 1–45; Thomas D'Arcy McGee, *A History of the Irish Settlers in North America, from the Earliest Period to the Census of 1850* (Boston: Office of the American Celt, 1851), 23–32; Chris Beneke, "The 'Catholic Spirit Prevailing in Our County': America's Moderate Religious Revolution," in *The First Prejudice: Religious Tolerance and Intolerance in Early America*, ed. Chris Beneke and Christopher S. Grenda (Philadelphia: University of Pennsylvania Press, 2011), 279; Thomas J. Fleming, *Beat the Last Drum: The Siege of Yorktown, 1781* (New York: St. Martin's Press, 1963), 102; Abbé Claude C. Robin, *New Travels through North-America: In a Series of Letters; Exhibiting, the History of the Victorious Campaign of the Allied Armies, under His Excellency General Washington, and the Count de Rochambeau, in the Year 1781 . . .* (Philadelphia: Robert Bell, 1783), 44–47.

23. Robert Arthur, *The End of a Revolution* (New York: Vantage, 1965); Thomas E. Chávez, *Spain and the Independence of the United States: An Intrinsic Gift* (Albuquerque: University of New Mexico Press, 2002), 8–13; Lee Kennett, *The French Forces in America, 1780–1783* (Westport, Conn.: Greenwood, 1977), 7–36; Stephen Bonsal, *When the French Were Here: A Narrative of the Sojourn of the French Forces in America, and Their Contribution to the Yorktown Campaign Drawn from Unpublished Reports and Letters of Participants in the National Archives of France and the MS. Division of the Library Congress* (Garden City, N.Y.: Doubleday, Doran, 1945), 3–7.

24. Agonito, "St. Inigoes Manor," 7–9; Griffin, *Catholics and the American Revolution*, 252; Benjamin Quarles, *The Negro in the American Revolution* (Chapel Hill: University of North Carolina Press, 1961), 116–18; Warner, *At Peace with All Their Neighbors*, 3–5; Philip A. Crowl, *Maryland During and After the Revolution: A Political and Economic Study* (Baltimore: 1943); Ronald Hoffman, *A Spirit of Dissension: Economics, Politics and Revolution in Maryland* (Baltimore: Johns Hopkins University Press, 1973).

25. Carroll was installed in office on August 15, 1790, while in England. Frances Sergeant Childs, *French Refugee Life in the United States, 1790–1800: An American Chapter of the French Revolution* (Baltimore: Johns Hopkins University Press, 1940), 9–19.

26. Patrick Henry arranged for the small Catholic community to meet in the Virginia capitol. Joseph Fenwick, Bordeaux, to Captain Ignatius Fenwick, Maryland, March 21, 1787, May 31, 1787, October 11, 1788, December 8, 1790, Capt. Ignatius Fenwick Papers; "Return of the Consuls and Vice-Consuls of the United States of America," *New-York Magazine; or, Literary Repository*, August 1791, 487; John R. G. Hassard, *John Hughes, First Archbishop of New York* (New York: D. Appleton, 1866), 26; James Haltigan, *The Irish in the American Revolution and Their Early Influence in the Colonies* (Washington, D.C.: Patrick J. Haltigan, 1908), 270; *Maryland Gazette*, October 6, 1791–December 15, 1791; James V. Crotty, "Baltimore Immigration, 1790–1830: With Special Reference to Its German, Irish, and French Phases" (PhD diss., Catholic University of America, 1951), 22–23.

27. Charles G. Herbermann, *The Sulpicians in the United States* (New York: Encyclopedia Press, 1916), 16–23; John B. Boles, *Religion in Antebellum Kentucky* (1976; Lexington: University of Kentucky Press, 1995), 54–56; Alphonsus Lesousky, "Centenary of St. Mary's College, St. Mary, Kentucky," *Catholic Historical Review* (October 1921), 154n–157n; François D'Ivernois to Thomas Jefferson, September 5, 1794, in *The Papers of Thomas Jefferson*, ed. John Catanzariti (Princeton, NJ: Princeton University Press, 1950–), 28:123–33; Thomas Jefferson to George Washington, February 23, 1795, in *The Writings of George Washington: Being His Correspondence,*

Addresses, Messages, and Other Papers, Official and Private, Selected and Published from the Original Manuscripts; with a Life of the Author, Notes, and Illustrations, ed. Jared Sparks (Boston: Ferdinand Andrews, 1838), 11:473–76.

28. Georgetown College, College Catalogs, 1791–1850, box 1, vol. 1; *Georgetown University Alumni Directory* (Washington, D.C.: Georgetown University Alumni Association, 1957); *American Missions*, entries 69–70; Shea, *Memorial History of the First Century of Georgetown College*, 24; "An Account of the Foundation and Progress of the College of St. Mary's, Baltimore," *Companion and Weekly Miscellany*, August 16, 1806; Curran, *Bicentennial History of Georgetown University*, 1:54–56. On the chartering of St. Mary's College, see *Maryland Gazette*, January 3–24, 1805.

29. The rescues were dramatic. About 3 P.M. on July 9, 1793, several ships carrying hundreds of refugees had landed in Baltimore. Dozens of vessels followed with approximately a thousand white people and hundreds of enslaved black people. A relief committee of prominent Marylanders greeted the white passengers, and the state appropriated funds to aid their relocation. *Maryland Gazette*, July 11, 1793, January 18, 1809; Crotty, "Baltimore Immigration, 1790–1830," 22–25; DeWitt Clinton, "Address Before the Free School Society in the City of New York" (1809), in *The Life and Writings of DeWitt Clinton*, ed. William W. Campbell (New York: Baker and Scribner, 1849), 323.

30. The corporation retained the profits from any sale of enslaved people or increase of other capital stock at Bohemia. "Proceedings of the Corporation of Roman Catholic Clergy," August 25, 1795, March 29, 1797, August 22. 1799, October 9, 1799, Maryland Province Archives, box 23, folders 9–10.

31. Proceedings of the Corporation of Roman Catholic Clergy, October 9, 1799, May 24. 1803, April 25, 1804, and February 3, 1806, Maryland Province Archives, box 23, folders 10, 13; Georgetown College, Minutes of the Board of Directors of Georgetown College from 1797–1815, entry for March 29–31, 1808, in Minutes of the Board of Directors, 1 September 1, 1797, through July 11, 1815, box 1, GUSC; Murphy, "Jesuit Slaveholding in Maryland, 1717–1838," 38. Father Joseph Moseley noted, "David arrived from ye White Marsh to St. Joseph's, ye 10th of January 1767, formerly Mr. Neale's Negroe at Deer-Creek in Baltimore." Joseph Moseley, St. Joseph's Church Account Book, 1764–1767, Maryland Province Archives, box 49, folder 2. See also Father Neale's agreements for the training of women servants and his Register, 1827–1832, which records the births and baptisms of enslaved children, Maryland Province Archives, box 15, folders 17, 18; Curran, *Bicentennial History of Georgetown University*, 32; Newtown Ledger, 1817–1823, 80–81, Maryland Province Archives, box 46, folder 1.

32. Robert Emmett Curran, *Shaping American Catholicism: Maryland and New York, 1805–1915* (Washington, D.C.: Catholic University Press of America, 2012), 35; Mobberly, *Diary*, pt. 1, 14; Agonito, "St. Inigoes Manor," 11–13. See Mobberly's comments on the overseers: St. Inigoes Receipt Book, 1804–1832, 55–58, Maryland Province Archives, box 44, folder 1.

33. Peter Kenney, "Temporalities, 1820," 11, Maryland Province Archives, box 126, folder 7.

34. Gilbert J. Garraghan, "The Beginnings of St. Louis University," *St. Louis Catholic Historical Review*, October 1918, 85–101; Kenneth J. Zanca, ed., *American Catholics and Slavery: 1789–1866* (Lanham, Md.: University Press of America, 1994), 153–56; Joseph Aloysius Griffin, *The Contribution of Belgium to the Catholic Church in America, 1523–1857* (Washington, D.C.: Catholic University of America, 1932); Obituary for the Reverend Charles Felix Van Quickenborne *Catholic Telegraph*, August 31, 1837.

35. "Reasons for giving a preference to the Indian Mission before any other. Given by F. Chas. C. Vanquickenborne," ca. 1831, in Peter Kenney, "Missouri Mission, 1831–32, Consultors Diary," and Peter Verhaegen to William McSherry, July 10, 1837, July 19, 1837, January 4, 1838, November 27, 1839, Maryland Province Archives, box 128, folders 2–4.

36. Brown added that Verhaegen's other slaves were treated far better. A year earlier, Verhaegen had presided at the opening of a church for people of color. Wilder, *Ebony & Ivy*, prologue; Curran, *Shaping American Catholicism*, 34–42; Thomas Brown, St. Louis University (probably to William McSherry, Georgetown), October 21, 1833, Maryland Province Archives, box 40, folder 5; Rev. Father Peter Kenney, "Extraordinary Consultation," August 20, 1832, and "Memorial, 1832," Maryland Province Archives, box 126, folders 2, 6; *Catholic Telegraph*, June 2, 1832.

37. Murphy, *Jesuit Slaveholding in Maryland*, 76–77, 203–4; Kenney, "Temporalities, 1820," 11, and Kenney, "Extraordinary Consultation," August 20, 1832, 20, Maryland Province Archives, box 126, folders 2, 7; Peter Verhaegen to William McSherry, February 9, 1837, Maryland Province Archives, box 128, folder 4; see the correspondence, mortgage certificates, 1838, and articles of agreement between Thomas Mulledy, S.J., and Henry Johnson and Jesse Baley, June 19, 1838, Maryland Province Archives, box 40, folders 9, 10.

38. Hassard, *John Hughes*, 23–24; George P. Schmidt, *The Old Time College President* (New York: Columbia University Press, 1930), esp. 32–33.

CHAPTER 12. CAPITALISM, SLAVERY, AND THE NEW EPOCH

1. Mathew Carey in the *Philadelphia Democratic Press*, April 24, 1819. Henry Clay (whom Carey eagerly supported) used the term "new epoch," a notion that Carey fully endorsed. *The Life and Speeches of Henry Clay*, ed. James B. Swain, 2 vols. (New York: Greeley and McElrath, 1843), 1:140; Andrew Shankman, "Neither Infinite Wretchedness Nor Positive Good: Mathew Carey and Henry Clay on Political Economy and Slavery During the Long 1820s," in *Contesting Slavery: The Politics of Bondage and Freedom in the New American Nation*, ed. John Craig Hammond and Matthew Mason (Charlottesville: University of Virginia Press, 2011), 247–66.

2. John R. Van Atta, "Western Lands and the Political Economy of Henry Clay's American System, 1819–1832," *Journal of the Early Republic* 21 (2001): 633–65, esp. 635. John L. Larson has recently proclaimed Carey's central importance to understanding the early American republic and pleaded for further research on him: John Lauritz Larson, "An Inquiry into the Nature and Causes of the Wealth of Nations," *Journal of the Early Republic* 35 (2015): 1–23, 14–15.

3. These remarks dissent from a central argument of Daniel Walker Howe, *What Hath God Wrought: The Transformation of America, 1815–1848* (New York: Oxford University Press, 2007). See Andrew Shankman, "John Quincy Adams and National Republicanism," in *A Companion to John Adams and John Quincy Adams*, ed. David Waldstreicher (Malden, Mass.: Wiley-Blackwell, 2013), 263–80.

4. The full title was *The Olive Branch, Or Faults On Both Sides, Federal and Democratic. A Serious Appeal On The Necessity Of Mutual Forgiveness And Harmony* (Philadelphia: M. Carey, 1814). See also Edward C. Carter II, "Mathew Carey and the 'Olive Branch,' 1814–1818," *Pennsylvania Magazine of History and Biography* 89 (1965): 399–415.

5. Carey, *The Olive Branch*, 2nd ed., 1815, 6, 62–63, 253.

6. Ibid., 253.

7. Ibid., 253.

8. Ibid., 281–84.

9. The pamphlet's full title was *A Calm Address To The Eastern States, On The Subject Of Slave Representation In the Senate; And The Hostility To Commerce Ascribed To The Southern States. By The Author Of* The Olive Branch (Boston: Rowe and Hooper, 1814).

10. Ibid., 18, 45–47.

11. Mathew Carey, *Essays On Political Economy, Or The Most Certain Means Of Promoting The Wealth, Resources, And Happiness of Nations: Applied Particularly to the United States* (Philadelphia, 1822), 69, 200. The 1822 collection brought together many of the pamphlets Carey had published between 1816 and 1821. For Clay's similar concerns, see *Life and Speeches of Henry Clay*, 1:140, 149–50, 222. For Madison, see Drew R. McCoy, *The Last of the Fathers: James Madison and the Republican Legacy* (Cambridge, Mass.: Harvard University Press, 1989).

12. Carey, *Essays On Political Economy*, 96.

13. Ibid., 198–99.

14. Ibid., 62–63, 184.

15. Mathew Carey, *Reflections On The Subject Of Emigration From Europe With A View To Settlement In The United States* (Philadelphia, 1826), v, 13.

16. Edward C. Carter II, "The Birth of a Political Economist: Mathew Carey and the Recharter Fight of 1810–1811," *Pennsylvania History* 33 (1966): 274–88.

17. Mathew Carey, *Reflections On The Present System Of Banking In The City Of Philadelphia, With A Plan To Revive Confidence, Trade, And Commerce, And Facilitate The Resumption Of Specie Payments* (Philadelphia, 1817), 7.

18. Carey, *Essays On Political Economy*, 67.

19. McCoy, *Last of the Fathers*.

20. *Life and Speeches of Henry Clay*, 1:170.

21. Richard E. Ellis, *Aggressive Nationalism: McCulloch v. Maryland and the Foundation of Federal Authority in the Young Republic* (New York: Oxford University Press, 2007).

22. For Hammond, see Ellis, *Aggressive Nationalism*; for Niles, see Robert E. Shalhope, *The Baltimore Bank Riot: Political Upheaval in Antebellum Maryland* (Champaign: University of Illinois Press, 2009).

23. Duncan MacLeod, "The Triple Crisis," in *The Growth of Federal Power in American History*, ed. Rhodri Jeffreys-Jones and Bruce Collins (De Kalb: Northern Illinois University Press, 1983), 13–24; Brian Schoen, *The Fragile Fabric of Union: Cotton, Federal Politics, and the Global Origins of the Civil War* (Baltimore: Johns Hopkins University Press, 2009); Matthew Mason, *Slavery and Politics in the Early American Republic* (Chapel Hill: University of North Carolina Press, 2006), 75–86, 158–212.

24. *Papers of Henry Clay*, 10 vols., ed. James F. Hopkins (Lexington: University Press of Kentucky, 1959–91), 1:530–31.

25. Ibid., 1:532–33.

26. Steven Hahn, *The Political Worlds of Slavery and Freedom* (Cambridge, Mass.: Harvard University Press, 2009).

27. Douglas Egerton, *Charles Fenton Mercer and the Trial of National Conservatism* (Jackson: University Press of Mississippi, 1989); Robin Einhorn, *American Taxation, American Slavery* (Chicago: University of Chicago Press, 2006).

28. Macon, quoted in Mason, *Slavery and Politics*, 162–63.

29. Mathew Carey, *Addresses Of The Philadelphia Society For The Promotion Of National Industry* (Philadelphia: M. Carey, 1819); Andrew Shankman, " 'A New Thing on Earth': Alexander Hamilton, Pro-Manufacturing Republicans, and the Democratization of American Political Economy," *Journal of the Early Republic* 23 (2003): 323–52, 347.

30. Carey, *Essays On Political Economy*, 200.

31. Schoen, *The Fragile Fabric of Union*, 112.

32. Stephen Elliot to Mathew Carey, April 25, 1820, Edward Carey Gardiner Collection (ECG), Mathew Carey Papers (MCP), box 23, folder 3, no. 70, Historical Society of Pennsylvania (HSP), Philadelphia.

33. Josiah Parks to Mathew Carey, March 27, 1820, ECG, MCP, box 23, folder 7, no. 253, HSP.

34. *Dictionary of American Biography*, ed. Allen Johnson and Dumas Malone, 20 vols. (New York: Charles Scribner's Sons, 1921–36), 11:405–6.

35. Eleazar Lord to Mathew Carey, February 18, 1820, ECG, MCP, box 23, folder 4, no. 136, HSP. Emphasis in original.

36. Ibid.

37. Jonathan Leonard to Mathew Carey, June 16, 1820, ECG, MCP, box 23 folder 3, no. 106, HSP.

38. William Lee to Mathew Carey, September 25, 1819, ECG, MCP, box 23, folder 4, no. 114; ? to Mathew Carey, April 21, 1820, ECG, MCP, box 23, folder 3, no. 59, HSP. Emphasis in original.

39. William Lee to Mathew Carey, January 28, 1820, ECG, MCP, box 23, folder 4, no. 118, HSP. For more on Lee, see Mary Lee Mann, ed., *A Yankee Jeffersonian: Selections from the Diary of William Lee of Massachusetts Written from 1796 to 1840* (Cambridge, Mass.: Harvard University Press, 1958).

40. Lacy K. Ford, *Deliver Us from Evil: The Slavery Question in the Old South* (New York: Oxford University Press, 2009), 54–76.

41. Eleazar Lord to Mathew Carey, February 3, March 3, March 18, April 21, April 27, 1820, ECG, MCP, box 23, folder 5, nos. 137, 139, 143, 164, HSP. Emphasis in original.

42. "A Pennsylvanian," *Considerations On The Impropriety And Inexpediency Of Renewing The Missouri Question* (Philadelphia: Mathew Carey, 1820), 3–4.

43. Ibid., 5–7.

44. Ibid., 52, 54–55.

45. Ibid., 52–55.

46. Thomas Jefferson, *Writings*, ed. Merrill D. Peterson (New York: Library of America, 1984), 1449; Merrill D. Peterson, ed., *The Portable Thomas Jefferson* (New York: Penguin, 1975), 567–69.

47. Mathew Carey, *A Short Account Of The Malignant Fever, Lately Prevalent In Philadelphia: With A Statement of the Proceedings That Took Place On The Subject In Different Parts Of The United States* (Philadelphia, 1793), 76–78; James Brewer Stewart, "The Emergence of Racial Modernity and the Rise of the White North, 1790–1840," *Journal of the Early Republic* 18 (1998): 181–217.

48. Andrew Shankman, *Crucible of American Democracy: The Struggle to Fuse Egalitarianism and Capitalism in Jeffersonian Pennsylvania* (Lawrence: University Press of Kansas, 2004), 74–95.

49. Robert J. Steinfeld, *Coercion, Contract, and Free Labor in the Nineteenth Century* (Cambridge: Cambridge University Press, 2001).

50. Mathew Carey, *Appeal To The Wealthy Of The Land Ladies As Well As Gentlemen, On The Character, Conduct, Situation, And Prospects Of Those Whose Sole Dependence For Subsistence Is On The Labour Of Their Hands* (Philadelphia: M. Carey, 1833).

CHAPTER 13. THE MARKET, UTILITY, AND SLAVERY IN SOUTHERN LEGAL THOUGHT

1. Alfred L. Brophy, "The Republics of Liberty and Letters: Progress, Union, and Constitutionalism in Graduation Addresses at the Antebellum University of North Carolina," *North Carolina Law Review* 89 (September 2011): 1879, 1916–21 (discussing images of technological progress in addresses); Daniel Lord, *On the Extra-Professional Influence of Lawyers and Ministers* (New York: S. S. Chatterton, 1851), 15 (noting that discussing technological advances, such as "the inventions of the electrical telegraph and daguerreotype, the new developments of steam navigation, the discoveries in geology, the disinterment of long buried cities, the interpretation of languages for centuries unknown," was unsettling well-seated ideas); Morton J. Horwitz, *The Transformation of American Law, 1780–1860* (Cambridge, Mass.: Harvard University Press, 1977), 1–16 (speaking of an "instrumental conception" of law, which promoted economic growth).

2. L. Diane Barnes, ed., *The Old South's Modern Worlds: Slavery, Region, and Nation in the Age of Progress* (New York: Oxford University Press, 2011); Charles Sellers, *The Market Revolution: Jacksonian America, 1815–1846* (New York: Oxford University Press, 1991), 34–69 (discussing the market revolution's relation to law in northern states); Jenny Wahl, *The Bondsman's Burden: An Economic Analysis of the Common Law of Southern Slavery* (Cambridge: Cambridge University Press, 2002); Ariela J. Gross, *Double Character: Slavery and Mastery in the Antebellum Southern Courtroom* (Princeton, N.J.: Princeton University Press, 2002); Calvin Schermerhorn, *The Business of Slavery and the Rise of American Capitalism, 1815–1860* (New Haven, Conn.: Yale University Press, 2015); Bonnie Martin, "Slavery's Invisible Engine: Mortgaging Human Property," *Journal of Southern History* 76 (November 2010): 1–50. This fits with the picture that has emerged of the pre–Civil War era as one in which judges cared deeply about efficiency: e.g., Horwitz, *Transformation of American Law*, 1–16. It is also consistent with the extensive literature on the economic health of slavery. See, e.g., Robert Fogel, *Without Consent or Contract: The Rise and Fall of American Slavery* (New York: W. W. Norton, 1989).

3. See, e.g., Eugene Genovese and Elizabeth Fox-Genovese, "Slavery, Economic Development, and the Law: The Dilemma of the Southern Political Economists, 1800–1860," *Washington & Lee Law Review* 41 (Winter 1984): 1; Gregory Alexander, *Commodity and Propriety: Competing Visions of Property in American Legal Thought, 1776–1970* (Chicago: University of Chicago Press, 1997), 211–40; Thomas R. R. Cobb, *An Inquiry into the Law of Negro Slavery* . . . (Philadelphia: T. W. and J. Johnson, 1858), 1:cxxxiii; Joseph Henry Lumpkin, *An Address Delivered Before the South-Carolina Institute, at its Second Annual Fair, on the 19th November, 1850* (Charleston, S.C.: Walker and James, 1851), 15; David S. Kaufman, *Address . . . Before the American Whig and Cliosophic Societies of the College of New Jersey, June 25th, 1850* (Princeton, N.J.: J. T. Robinson, 1850), 17–18.

4. See, e.g., James Henley Thornwell, *The State of the Country* (Columbia, S.C.: Southern Guardian, 1861), 20, 24–25 (discussing the Constitution's protection of slavery and arguing that Lincoln's election was a violation of the Constitution); Willoughby Newton, *Virginia and the Union: An Address, Delivered Before the Literary Societies of the Virginia Military Institute* (Rich-

mond, Va.: Macfarlane and Fergusson, 1858), 26 (discussing the North's violation of the South's constitutional rights regarding slavery); Alfred L. Brophy, "The Nat Turner Trials," *North Carolina Law Review* 91 (May 2013): 1817–80 (prosecution of enslaved people who rebelled); Gross, *Double Character* (sophisticated contract law to support slave market); Stephen D. Davis and Alfred L. Brophy, "'The most solemn Act of my life': Family, Property, Will and Trust in the Antebellum South," *Alabama Law Review* 62 (2011): 757, 786 (use of trusts to manage enslaved people and to provide income to beneficiaries); Karen Kotzuk Ryder, "'Permanent Property': Slave Life Insurance in the Antebellum Southern United States, 1820–1866" (PhD diss., University of Delaware, 2012) (insurance to spread risk and make slavery more stable economically); Wahl, *Bondsman's Burden*, 1–26, 142–73 (discussing tort cases that limited liability); Thomas D. Morris, *Southern Slavery and the Law, 1619–1860* (Chapel Hill: University of North Carolina Press, 1996); and Walter Johnson, "Inconsistency, Contradiction, and Complete Confusion: The Everyday Life of the Law of Slavery," *Law and Social Inquiry* 22 (1997): 405–33 (summary of slave law's uses and inconsistencies). In short, the increasingly sophisticated technology of law that promoted the market also promoted slavery. See Christopher Tomlins, *Freedom Bound: Law, Labor, and Civic Identity in Colonizing English America, 1580–1865* (Cambridge: Cambridge University Press, 2010), 5, 68–69, 506 (viewing "law" as a technology used for colonization).

5. Gavin Wright, *Slavery and American Economic Development* (Baton Rouge: Louisiana State University Press, 2006); Robin L. Einhorn, "Slavery," *Enterprise & Society* 9 (2008): 491–506; James L. Huston, *Calculating the Value of the Union: Slavery, Property Rights, and the Economic Origins of the Civil War* (Chapel Hill: University of North Carolina Press, 2003). See also Harry N. Scheiber, "Private Rights and Public Power: American Law, Capitalism, and the Republican Polity in NineteenthCentury America," *Yale Law Journal* 107 (1997): 823–61 (arguing that depiction of a strong pro-regulatory policy toward property rights in early America was subordinate to the protection of property); contrast William Novak, *The People's Welfare: Law and Regulation in Nineteenth-Century America* (Chapel Hill: University of North Carolina Press, 1996) (depicting the pervasive ethic of support for regulation of property); and Ralph Waldo Emerson, "The Fugitive Slave Law: Address to the Citizens of Concord, 3 May, 1851," in *The Complete Works of Ralph Waldo Emerson*, vol. 11, *Miscellanies*, ed. Edward Waldo Emerson (Boston: Houghton, Mifflin,, 1904), 177.

6. "House of Delegates," *Richmond Enquirer*, January 21, 1832, 2; Kaufman, *Whig and Cliosophic Societies*, 28; Ralph Waldo Emerson, *Journals of Ralph Waldo Emerson: With Annotations* (Boston: Houghton, Mifflin, 1912), 205; see generally Alfred L. Brophy, "Property and Slavery in Southern Legal Thought: From Missouri Compromise Through Civil War" (PhD diss., Harvard University, 2001).

7. *State v. Mann*, 13 N.C. (2 Dev.) 263, 264, 266 (1830). There is now an extensive literature on *Mann*, including Sally Greene, "State v. Mann Exhumed," *North Carolina Law Review* 87 (2009): 701–56; Eric L. Muller, "Judging Thomas Ruffin and the Hindsight Defense," *North Carolina Law Review* 87 (2009): 757–98; Mark Tushnet, *State v. Mann in History and Literature* (Lawrence: University Press of Kansas, 2003); and Timothy Huebner, *The Southern Judicial Tradition: State Judges and Sectional Distinctiveness, 1790–1890* (Athens: University of Georgia Press, 1999), 146–52.

8. *State v. Mann*, 13 N.C. at 266.

9. *State v. Mann*, 13 N.C. at 263, 268. See, e.g., Horwitz, *Transformation of American Law*, 1–16 (discussing judges' turn to utility as a guide); and Alfred L. Brophy, "Reason and Sentiment: The Moral Worlds and Modes of Reasoning of Antebellum Jurists," *Boston University*

Law Review 79 (1999): 1161, 1207–13 (discussing economic analysis among pre–Civil War judges). There was a broad condemnation of Jeremy Bentham and utilitarian reasoning for its focus on the greatest happiness of the community. See, e.g., James Henley Thornwell, "An Address Delivered Before the Literary Societies of Davidson College . . . 1838," 10 (typescript, Wilson Library, University of North Carolina) (explicitly criticizing Bentham).

10. *Heathcock v. Pennington*, 33 N.C. (11 Ired.) 640 (1850).

11. *Parham v. Blackwelder*, 30 N.C. 446 (1848).

12. *Scroggins v. Scroggins*, 14 N.C. (3 Dev.) 535, 537 (1832).

13. "Act to Prevent Emancipation of Slaves," *South Carolina Statutes at Large* 11 (Act of December 1841), 168–69; "An Act Concerning Slaves and Free Persons of Color," *North Carolina Revised Statutes* (Raleigh, Turner, and Hughes, 1837), 579–80, chap. 111, secs. 31, 32; *Huckaby v. Jones*, 9 N.C. (2 Hawks) 120 (1822) (slaves given to the Methodist Church). See also *Hunter v. Green*, 22 Ala. 329 (1858).

14. *Trustees of Quaker Society of Contentnea v. Dickenson*, 12 N.C. (1 Dev.) 189 (1827).

15. *Lemmond v. Peoples*, 41 N.C. (6 Ired. Eq.) 137 (1849). See also *Lea v. Brown*, 56 N.C. 141 (1857).

16. *Miller v. Gaskins*, 11 Fla. 73 (1864).

17. Lumpkin, *Address Before the South-Carolina Institute*, 33–34. For more on Lumpkin, see Huebner, *Southern Judicial Tradition*, 70–98.

18. *Shorter v. Smith*, 9 Ga. 517, 527 (1851).

19. *Shorter v. Smith*, 9 Ga. at 526, 529. Lumpkin also spoke about the importance of railroads in his agricultural society address. See Lumpkin, *Address Before the South-Carolina Institute*, 33–34.

20. *McLeod v. Savannah, Albany and Gulf Railroad*, 25 Ga. 445, 459–60 (1858).

21. *Haywood v. Mayor and Aldermen of Savannah*, 12 Ga. 404, 412 (1853).

22. See, e.g., *Farwell v. Boston & Worcester R.R. Corp.*, 45 Mass. 49, 57 (1842) (advancing the fellow-servant rule and concluding that "we are not aware of any principle which should except the perils arising from the carelessness and negligence of those who are in the same employment, these are the perils which the servant is as likely to know, and against which he can as effectually guard"); *Illinois C.R. Co. v. Cox*, 21 Ill. 20, 26 (1858) ("one servant should not recover against the common master for the carelessness of his fellow-servant . . . it must be understood that each servant, when he engages in a particular service, calculates the hazards incident to it, and contracts accordingly"); *Shields v. Yonge*, 15 Ga. 349, 357–58 (1854) (finding that because the decedent's father was an employee of the railroad, any claim filed by his father was barred by the fellow-servant rule).

23. *Commonwealth v. Aves*, 35 Mass. 193 (1836); Robert S. Cover, *Justice Accused: The Anti-Slavery Judge and the Judicial Process* (New Haven, Conn.: Yale University Press, 1975), 176–77. Leonard W. Levy's *The Law of the Commonwealth and Chief Justice Shaw* (Oxford: Oxford University Press, 1957) portrays in detail Shaw's respect for property rights and for promotion of economic growth. Some question how much the law really was proslavery. See, e.g., Jeffrey M. Schmitt, "The Antislavery Judge Reconsidered," *Law and History Review* 29 (2011): 797–834. Drew Faust, *A Sacred Circle: The Dilemma of the Intellectual in the Old South, 1840–1860* (Baltimore: Johns Hopkins University Press, 1977), 130.

24. *Scudder v. Woodbridge*, 1 Ga. 195, 200 (1846). See also *Gorman v. Campbell*, 14 Ga. 137, 143 (1853) (rejecting the fellow-servant rule in cases involving slaves, because "humanity to the slave, as well as proper regard for the interest of the owner" requires that slaves be given special protection).

25. *Vance v. Crawford*, 4 Ga. 445, 459 (1848). See also *Cleland v. Waters*, 19 Ga. 35 (1855) (upholding a will allowing slaves to choose whether they would remain in slavery or be taken outside the state, freed, and sent to Liberia). But see *Adams v. Bass*, 18 Ga. 130 (1855) (refusing to follow a will that ordered slaves to be taken to Indiana and freed because Indiana no longer allowed this); *American Colonization Society v. Gartrell*, 23 Ga. 448 (1857) (refusing to allow slaves to be given to American Colonization Society).

26. Harriet Beecher Stowe, *Uncle Tom's Cabin* (Boston: J. P. Jewett and Co., 1852), 2:273; George A. Baxter, *An Essay on the Abolition of Slavery* (Richmond, Va.: Thomas Whyte, 1836), 6.

27. "Professor Dew on Slavery," in *The Pro-slavery Argument . . .* (Charleston: Walker, Richards and Co., 1852), 287, 391; William Harper, "Memoir on Slavery," ibid., quotation at 3.

28. "Speech of Mr. Webster," *Congressional Globe*, 31st Cong., 1st Sess., Appendix, 269, 271; "Saturday, July 6, 1850," *Congressional Globe*, 31st Cong., 1st Sess., Appendix, 1102, 1105, 1106 (Bell's speech).

29. Harriet Beecher Stowe, *A Key to Uncle Tom's Cabin* (Boston: John P. Jewett and Co., 1853), 77.

30. Ibid., 82.

31. Ibid.

32. William E. Channing, *Slavery* (Boston: James Munroe and Co., 1835), 1 ("The first question to be proposed by a rational being is, not what is profitable, but what is right"), 4.

33. Ibid., 16. See also idem ("The consciousness of our humanity involves the persuasion, that we cannot be owned as a tree or a brute").

34. Stowe, *Uncle Tom's Cabin*, 1:113–20; Harriet Beecher Stowe, "Love versus Law," in *The Mayflower; Or, Sketches of Scenes and Characters Among the Descendants of the Pilgrims* (New York: Harper and Brothers, 1846), 19–79; Timothy Walker, *The Reform Spirit of the Day: An Oration Before the Phi Beta Kappa Society of Harvard University, July 15, 1850* (Boston: James Munroe and Co., 1850); Lord, *On the Extra-Professional Influence of Lawyers and Ministers*, 15; William Greene, *Some of the Difficulties in the Administration of a Free Government: A Discourse, Pronounced Before The Rhode Island Alpha Of The Phi Beta Kappa Society, July 8, 1851* (Providence: John F. Moore, 1851), 35.

35. See, e.g., Thomas Bender, ed., *The Anti-Slavery Debate: Capitalism and Abolitionism As a Problem in Historical Interpretation* (Berkeley: University of California Press, 1992) (summarizing Davis's perspective that capitalism supported free labor in opposition to slavery and Haskell's perspective that capitalism led to a widening moral sense); Ralph Waldo Emerson, "Lecture on the Times," in *Ralph Waldo Emerson: Essays and Lectures*, ed. Joel Porte (New York: Library of America, 1983), 211, 221. On the image of trade, see, e.g., Henry Hallam, *View of the State of Europe in the Middle Ages* (New York: Harper and Brothers, 1837); Thomas R. Dew, *The Laws, Customs, Manners, and Institutions of Ancient and Modern Nations* (New York: Appleton, 1852); and Alfred L. Brophy, "Property and Progress: Landscape Art and Property Law in Antebellum America," *McGeorge Law Review* 40 (2009): 603–59.

36. Lumpkin, *Address to the South-Carolina Institute*, 17.

37. See Davis and Brophy, "Family, Property, Will and Trust in the Antebellum South," 786–91 (discussing the incidence of spendthrift trusts in the pre–Civil War South).

38. This interpretation fits with recent histories of the old South, which have found a robust embrace of ideas of progress and market alongside proslavery thought. See, e.g., Peter S. Carmichael, *The Last Generation: Young Virginians in Peace, War, and Reunion* (Chapel Hill:

University of North Carolina Press, 2005); and John Majewski, *Modernizing a Slave Economy: The Economic Vision of the Confederate Nation* (Chapel Hill: University of North Carolina Press, 2009).

CHAPTER 14. WHY DID NORTHERNERS OPPOSE THE EXPANSION OF SLAVERY?

The author is grateful for the comments of participants at the economic history workshops at Harvard and Yale, as well as the participants of the "Slavery's Capitalism" conference. Lisa Jacobson and Peter Lindert also provided excellent advice, and Masha Fedorova and Grant Stanton provided excellent research assistance.

1. John Ashworth, *Slavery, Capitalism, and Politics in the Antebellum Republic,* vol. 1, *Commerce and Compromise, 1820–1850* (New York: Cambridge University Press, 1995), 80.

2. On the Republican critique of the southern economy, see Eric Foner, *Free Soil, Free Labor, Free Men: The Ideology of the Republican Party Before the Civil War* (New York: Oxford University Press, 1970), 40–72.

3. Jonathan Daniel Wells, "The Southern Middle Class," *Journal of Southern History* 75 (August 2009): 75.

4. L. Diane Barnes, Brian Schoen, and Frank Towers, "Introduction," in *The Old South's Modern Worlds: Slavery, Region, and Nation in the Age of Progress* (New York: Oxford University Press, 2011), 14.

5. Sun Go and Peter Lindert, "The Uneven Rise of American Public Schools in 1850," *Journal of American History* 70 (March 2010): 4. See also Claudia Goldin and Lawrence F. Katz, *The Race Between Education and Technology* (New York: Cambridge University Press, 2008), 129–62; and see Michelle Connolly, "Human Capital and Growth in the Postbellum South: A Separate But Unequal Story," *Journal of Economic History* 64 (June 2004): 363–99.

6. Zorina B. Khan, *The Democratization of Invention: Patents and Copyrights in American Economic Development, 1790–1920* (New York: Cambridge University Press, 2005), 189. Khan argues that "The South, the least democratic region in the United States, might paradoxically provide the strongest evidence for the favorable effects of individual liberty and opportunity for incentives for contributions at the technological frontier in the nineteenth century" (125).

7. *Address to the Non-Slaveholders of Kentucky* (Louisville, Ky., 1849), 6.

8. Julius Rubin, "The Limits of Agricultural Progress in the Nineteenth-Century South," *Agricultural History* 49 (1975): 362–73; Douglas Helms, "Soils and Southern History," *Agricultural History* 74 (2000): 736–43.

9. On shifting cultivation, see John Majewski, *Modernizing a Slave: The Economic Vision of the Confederate Nation* (Chapel Hill: University of North Carolina Press, 2011), 22–52; Jack Temple Kirby, *Poquosin: A Study in Rural Landscape and Society* (Chapel Hill: University of North Carolina Press, 1995); Stanley Wayne Trimble, *Man-Induced Soil Erosion on the Southern Piedmont, 1700–1970* (Ankeny, Ia.: Soil Conservation Society of America, 1974), 43–51; and Lois Green Carr and Russell R. Menard, "Land, Labor, and Economies of Scale in Early Maryland: Some Limits to Growth in the Chesapeake System of Husbandry," *Journal of Economic History* 49 (June 1982): 407–18.

10. Helms, "Soil and Southern History"; S. W. Buol, F. D. Hole, R. J. McCracken, and R. J. Southard, *Soil Genesis and Classification*, 4th ed. (Ames: Iowa State University Press, 1997); Henry D. Foth and John W. Schaffer, *Soil Geography and Land Use* (New York: John Wiley and Sons, 1980), 177–98.

11. Warren R. Hofstra, *The Planting of New Virginia: Settlement and Landscape in the Shenandoah Valley* (Baltimore: Johns Hopkins University Press, 2005), 334.

12. "On the Husbandry of Kentucky," *American Farmer* 1 (January 15, 1840): 1.

13. "Tennessee Stock" 10 (July 11, 1840); *Spirit of the Times*, 1840, 223.

14. Ira Berlin, *Many Thousands Gone: The First Two Centuries of Slavery in North America* (Cambridge, Mass.: Harvard University Press, 1998), 95–108.

15. T. D. Clark, "The Slave Trade Between Kentucky and the Cotton Kingdom," *Mississippi Valley Historical Review* 21 (December 1934): 337.

16. James F. Hopkins, *A History of the Hemp Industry in Kentucky* (Lexington: University Press of Kentucky, 1951), 147.

17. Hofstra, *Planting of New Virginia*, 292.

18. Viken Tchakerian, "Productivity, Extent of Markets, and Manufacturing in the Late Antebellum South and Midwest," *Journal of Economic History* 54 (1994): 500.

19. For a ranking of the top 100 cities in 1860, see Stewart Blumin, *The Urban Threshold: Growth and Change in a Nineteenth-Century American Community* (Chicago: University of Chicago Press, 1976), 223–26.

20. Dueling, while not widespread, was nevertheless accepted as part of masculine culture, especially among wealthy planters. It is not surprising that Andrew Jackson—Indian fighter, military hero, and wealthy Nashville planter—engaged in numerous duels over his career. Yet even Henry Clay, who considered himself a refined Bluegrass planter and an opponent of dueling, could not resist challenging several of his political opponents after heated arguments. R. Gerald Alvey, *Kentucky Bluegrass Country* (Jackson: University Press of Kentucky, 1992), 216–21.

21. Hofstra, *Planting of New Virginia*, 316–17.

22. Craig Thompson Friend, *Along the Maysville Road: The Early American Republican in the Trans-Appalachian West* (Knoxville: University of Tennessee Press, 2005), 217–67.

23. William E. Ellis, *A History of Education in Kentucky* (Lexington: University Press of Kentucky, 2011), 8–9, quotation at 8.

24. In northern localities, tuition was often called the "rate bill." The educational reports from Kentucky use the term "tuition," which I use here.

25. Nancy Beadie, "Tuition Funding for Common Schools: Education, Markets, and Market Regulation in Rural New York, 1815–1850," *Social Science History* 32 (Spring 2008): 121–22.

26. *Report of the Committee of Education of the House of Representatives of Kentucky*, 2nd ed. (Lexington, Ky.: Joseph G. Norwood, 1830), 4.

27. Ibid, 3.

28. Quoted in Ellis, *A History of Education in Kentucky*, 25.

29. Go and Lindert, "The Uneven Rise of American Public Schools," 4.

30. Scholars have noted that the published statistical compilations are filled with errors, and thus should be treated with caution. The patterns evident in the data, however, are consistent with results elsewhere.

31. Residents of Appalachia, it should be emphasized, still paid higher tuition than northern children. Nor did a significantly higher percentage of children in Appalachia attend common schools than in the Bluegrass Region—in both areas only 40 percent of children attended common schools.

32. *Report of the Superintendent of Public Instruction to the General Assembly of Kentucky* (Frankfort, Ky.: A. G. Hodges and Co., 1851), 22.

33. Kenneth L. Sokoloff, "Inventive Activity in Early Industrial America: Evidence from Patent Records, 1790–1846," *Journal of Economic History* (December 1988): 813–50; idem, "Invention, Innovation, and Manufacturing Productivity Growth in the Antebellum Northeast," in *American Economic Growth and Standards of Living before the Civil War*, ed. Robert E. Gallman and John Joseph Wallis (Chicago: University of Chicago Press, 1992), 345–78; Zorina Khan and Kenneth L. Sokoloff, "'Schemes of Practical Utility': Entrepreneurship and Innovation Among 'Great Inventors' in the United States, 1790–1865," *Journal of Economic History* 48 (1993): 289–307.

34. Calculated from *Report of the Commissioner of Patents for the Year 1860*, vol. 1 (Washington, D.C.: George W. Bowman, 1861).

35. Harold D. Tallant, *Evil Necessity: Slavery and Political Culture in Antebellum Kentucky* (Lexington: University Press of Kentucky, 2003), 10.

36. *Report of the Committee on Education of the House of Representatives of Kentucky* (1830), 7.

37. Ibid., 8.

38. Ibid., 27, 38.

39. Ibid., 38.

40. *Report of the Debate and Proceedings of the Convention for the Revision of the Constitution of the State of Kentucky* (Frankfort, Ky.: A. G. Hodges), 891.

41. Calculated from the published returns of the 1850 census.

42. William Jay, "Address to the Inhabitants of New Mexico and California . . . On the Social and Political Evils of Slavery," in *Miscellaneous Writings on Slavery* (Boston: John P. Jewett, 1853), 501.

43. W.S.P., "White Slavery," *The Independent* 5 (March 17, 1853): 44. For the more general antislavery critique of the unrefined South, see Richard L. Bushman, *The Refinement of America: Persons, Houses, and Cities* (reprint, New York: Vintage Books, 1993), 390–98.

44. Harriet Beecher Stowe, *Uncle Tom's Cabin* (Boston: John P. Jewett, 1852), 28, 30.

45. Roy P. Basler, ed., *The Collected Works of Abraham Lincoln*, 9 vols. (New Brunswick, N.J.: Rutgers University Press, 1953), 1:8.

46. Ibid., 3:480.

47. Lincoln's speech is reprinted in Jason Emerson, *Lincoln the Inventor* (Carbondale: Southern Illinois University Press, 2009), 70.

48. Emerson, *Lincoln the Inventor*, 10–18.

49. Basler, ed., *Collected Works of Abraham Lincoln*, 3:480.

50. Even Lincoln admitted that it might take at least a century for slavery to disappear after its expansion was blocked in the western territories, suggesting that the institution had far more economic flexibility than was commonly assumed among Republicans. See Stanley L. Engerman, *Slavery, Emancipation, & Freedom: Comparative Perspectives* (Baton Rouge: Louisiana State University Press, 2007), 11.

51. Gavin Wright, *Slavery and American Economic Development* (Baton Rouge: Louisiana State University Press, 2006), 113–21.

52. Basler, ed., *Collected Works of Abraham Lincoln*, 3:456.

53. Ibid., 2:462. Lincoln feared that another Supreme Court decision similar to *Dred Scott* "is all that slavery now lacks of being alike lawful in all the states. Welcome or unwelcome, such decision is probably coming, and will soon be upon you, unless the power of the present political dynasty shall be met and overthrown" (467).

Edward E. Baptist is Professor of History at Cornell University and author of *The Half Has Never Been Told: Slavery and the Making of American Capitalism* (2014), which won the 2015 Hillman Prize for Book Journalism.

Sven Beckert is Laird Bell Professor of History at Harvard University and currently a Visiting Professor of Business Administration at Harvard Business School. He is the author of *The Monied Metropolis: New York City and the Consolidation of the American Bourgeoisie* (2001) and *Empire of Cotton: A Global History* (2014), which won the Bancroft Prize and was a finalist for the Pulitzer Prize in History.

Daina Ramey Berry is Associate Professor of History and African and African Diaspora Studies at the University of Texas, Austin. She is the author of *Swing the Sickle for the Harvest Is Ripe: Gender and Slavery in Antebellum Georgia* (2007) and *The Price for Their Pound of Flesh* (2017).

Kathryn Boodry is Visiting Assistant Professor of History at the University of Oregon. She was a Schwartz Postdoctoral Fellow at the New York Historical Society in 2014 and served as Director of The American Project at the Rothschild Archive, London.

Alfred L. Brophy is the Judge John Parker Distinguished Professor of Law at the University of North Carolina, Chapel Hill. His books include *Reconstructing the Dreamland* (2002) and *Reparations Pro and Con* (2006).

Stephen Chambers received his Ph.D. in history from Brown University. He is the author of *No God But Gain: The Untold Story of Cuban Slavery, the Monroe Doctrine, and the Making of the United States* (2015).

Eric Kimball is Assistant Professor of History at the University of Pittsburgh at Greensburg. His current book project examines trade between New Englanders and the wider Atlantic slave economies of the eighteenth-century Caribbean.

John Majewski is Professor of History at the University of California, Santa Barbara. He is the author of *Modernizing a Slave Economy: The Economic Vision of the Confederate Nation* (2009) and *A House Dividing: Economic Development in Virginia and Pennsylvania Before the Civil War* (2000).

Bonnie Martin is an independent scholar and coeditor of *Linking the Histories of Slavery in North America and Its Borderlands* (2015), a collection of essays on slavery in North America from prehistoric time to the present.

Seth Rockman is Associate Professor of History at Brown University, where he has taught since 2004. His 2009 book, *Scraping By: Wage Labor, Slavery, and Survival in Early Baltimore*, won the Merle Curti Prize from the Organization of American Historians, the Philip Taft Labor History Book Prize, and the H. L. Mitchell Prize from the Southern Historical Association.

Daniel B. Rood is Assistant Professor of History at the University of Georgia. He was given the Agricultural History Society's Wayne D. Rasmussen Award for "Bogs of Death: Slavery, the Brazilian Flour Trade, and the Mystery of the Vanishing Millpond in Antebellum Virginia," published in the *Journal of American History*. He is also author of the forthcoming book, "The Reinvention of Atlantic Slavery: Circuits of Techno-Science in the Greater Caribbean, 1830–1860."

Caitlin Rosenthal is Assistant Professor of History at the University of California, Berkeley. Her current book project explores the relationship between slavery, calculation, and American capitalism.

Joshua D. Rothman is Professor of History and Director of the Frances S. Summersell Center for the Study of the South at the University of Alabama. He is the author of *Flush Times and Fever Dreams: A Story of Capitalism and Slavery in the Age of Jackson* (2012), which won the Frank L. and Harriet C. Owsley Award from the Southern Historical Association.

Calvin Schermerhorn is Associate Professor of History at Arizona State University. He is the author of *Money over Mastery, Family over Freedom: Slavery in the Antebellum Upper South* (2011) and *The Business of Slavery and the Rise of American Capitalism, 1815–1860* (2015).

Andrew Shankman is Associate Professor of History at Rutgers University, Camden. He is the author of *Crucible of American Democracy: The Struggle to Fuse Egalitarianism and Capitalism in Jeffersonian Pennsylvania* (2003) and the editor of *The World of the Revolutionary American Republic: Land, Labor, and the Conflict for a Continent* (2014) and *Anglicizing America: Empire, Revolution, Republic* (2015).

Craig Steven Wilder is Professor of History at the Massachusetts Institute of Technology. His most recent book is *Ebony & Ivy: Race, Slavery, and the Troubled History of America's Universities* (2013).

INDEX

An f or t following a page number indicates a figure or table, respectively.

ACKNOWLEDGMENTS

We are grateful to the volume's contributors, who have worked diligently to provide empirically rich scholarship that explicates the relationship of American slavery to American capitalism. A project such as this takes significant energy, resources, and the generous contributions of a wider community, and we want to thank Ronald Bailey, Deborah Baum, Ian Beamish, Elizabeth Blackmar, Julian Bonder, James Campbell, Betsy Cazden, Joyce Chaplin, Stanley Engerman, Walter Johnson, Sarah Kidwell, Sara Ladds, Kaivan Munshi, Shaun Nichols, Marisa Quinn, Richard Rabinowitz, Ian Russell, Jody Soares, Amy Dru Stanley, John Stauffer, Scott Turner, Cécile Vidal, Michael Vorenberg, Lorena Walsh, Ted Widmer, and Ken Zirkel. A special thank you also to David Kertzer in his capacity as provost of Brown University, to the Center for American Political Studies at Harvard University, and to Harvard's Program on the Study of Capitalism for providing the much-needed resources that made work on this project possible.

From the beginning, the University of Pennsylvania Press has taken an interest in this project and helped us in many ways big and small to shepherd it to publication. We want to thank, in particular, Robert Lockhart, who has been the most patient of editors, as well as David Waldstreicher and Gary Kornblith, who provided a thoughtful and thorough critique of the essays. Thank you to Marjorie Pannell, Brian Ostrander, and Noreen O'Connor-Abel for their production work. Nancy C. Gerth compiled the index. Last but not least, we appreciate the support of Harvard's History Department, which made the production of this volume possible.

*   *   *

We dedicate this volume to Ruth J. Simmons, the eighteenth president of Brown University. Ruth Simmons provided crucial leadership in directing scholarly and public attention to slavery and its institutional legacies at a time when universities, insurance companies, banks, and other institutions had almost entirely ignored this important part of their history. The self-study she commissioned at Brown University served as an inspiration to our project, as it has to many others across the United States and across the world. President Simmons's belief that our ability to capture the future rests on our willingness to come to terms with the past, however difficult that task may be, has motivated our work on this volume as well. As important, we appreciate her belief in substantive academic research as essential to redressing the most urgent political, social, and moral questions of our time.